CORRELATED FILMS

Five 16 mm sound motion pictures have been especially prepared for this book by the McGraw-Hill Text-Film Department.

Planning for Personal and Professional Growth

Shows four schoolteachers who have made certain adjustments and achieved success in their teaching to various degrees (19 min).

Effective Learning in the Elementary School

Shows a fifth-grade teacher and her class as they plan their daily work for the study of a unit on pioneer life (20 min).

Guiding the Growth of Children

Shows how a teacher may work to understand each child and to guide him in his growth and development (18 min).

Promoting Pupil Adjustment

Shows that a teacher must be alert and sensitive to student problems if classroom learning is to be effective, and illustrates ways by which teachers can facilitate pupil adjustment (20 min).

Broader Concepts of Curriculum

Points out the great increase which is taking place in enrollments in secondary schools and some of the causes for this growth (21 min).

McGRAW-HILL SERIES IN EDUCATION

Harold Benjamin, Consulting Editor-in-Chief

ARNO A. BELLACK   Teachers College, Columbia University
CONSULTING EDITOR, CURRICULUM AND METHODS
IN EDUCATION

HAROLD BENJAMIN   Emeritus Professor of Education
George Peabody College for Teachers
CONSULTING EDITOR, FOUNDATIONS IN EDUCATION

HARLAN HAGMAN   Wayne State University
CONSULTING EDITOR, ADMINISTRATION IN EDUCATION

NICHOLAS HOBBS   George Peabody College for Teachers
CONSULTING EDITOR, PSYCHOLOGY AND
HUMAN DEVELOPMENT IN EDUCATION

WALTER F. JOHNSON   Michigan State University
CONSULTING EDITOR, GUIDANCE, COUNSELING,
AND STUDENT PERSONNEL IN EDUCATION

FOUNDATIONS IN EDUCATION

Harold Benjamin, Consulting Editor

BRUBACHER   Modern Philosophies of Education

COOK–COOK   A Sociological Approach to Education

COX–MERCER   Education in Democracy

DE YOUNG–WYNN   Introduction to
American Public Education

GOOD   Dictionary of Education

RICHEY   Planning for Teaching

THUT   The Story of Education

WIGGIN   Education and Nationalism

WYNN   Careers in Education

planning for teaching

AN INTRODUCTION TO EDUCATION

THIRD EDITION

ROBERT W. RICHEY
Professor of Education
Indiana University
Bloomington, Indiana

McGRAW-HILL BOOK COMPANY, INC.
New York   London   Toronto

PLANNING FOR TEACHING

EDITOR'S FOREWORD

In the half century 1913–1963, professional education in the United States passed through two chief stages and entered into a third stage.

The first of these stages was definitely under way in 1913. It may be called the technical-instrumental era. Various achievement and mental tests, some of which had been in the process of development for decades before 1913, now attained substantial prestige. The best methods, the most satisfactory curricula, the correct motivations, and the least subjective evaluation devices were thought to be the inevitable outcomes of the new scientific study of education. An educational psychology of bonds and synapses, complete with laws and cases to fit the new educational concepts, was available and was widely employed. Human nature, infinitely varied, was also conceived to be as infinitely variable, as were the possible neural combinations.

This was a powerful approach to teacher education. It held almost undisputed sway for twenty years. It ended with a crash in 1930–1934 as economic depression, among other factors, lowered the boom on it.

Obviously the teacher-education institutions of the United States now have more and better instruments and techniques for the scientific study of education than were ever available in the 1913–1933 period. The great difference between the technical-instrumental era and the two which have followed is that the teacher-educators of the later periods lost much of their all-encompassing faith in the so-called scientific instruments. Fifty years ago those instruments were symbols of new and spectacularly efficient patterns of education. Since 1933 they have increasingly become merely tests, devices, and methods which are regarded as being useful tools in the hands of teachers of skill and dedication.

The second stage was marked by new orientations to groups. Educational institutions and operators were now looked upon as defenders of a new and better social order, if not indeed builders of one. New general and educational psychologies were at hand to support this concept. The human nature so lately regarded as infinitely perfectible was now looked upon as infinitely adjustable. There was, furthermore, a considerable gap between these two objectives. The teacher who in the technical-instrumental era had been taught to think of himself as a response-conditioner now learned that he was really a group engineer. If he did not know exactly how to be such a technician, he could at least learn to act like one.

This second era, which we may call the social-adjustment era, lasted about fifteen to twenty years. Since 1945–1950 its main concepts, while still prevalent, have become relatively less important in teacher education. The world's new time of troubles, which seemed to be ending with the close of World War II, came more and more to be regarded as just beginning when the mushroom-shaped clouds above Hiroshima and Nagasaki drifted lazily eastward over the Pacific. The revolts of colonial masses, the establishment of new nations, the development of nuclear-armed powers, the flaring of brush wars here and there, and the shifting alliances and antagonisms of societies jockeying for positions in the possible coming of a real fire storm—these are quite different from J. M. Rice's studies of economy of time in spelling, from Courtis' handwriting scales, and even from the humanitarian concerns of schools in the 1933–1945 era.

This time of global troubles has influenced the teacher-education concepts and institutions of the United States much more than the members of the profession are commonly aware. Like most people actually living on a shore pounded by great historical events, they see the breakers dash against the headlands and roll along the beaches; they hear the thunder of the surf; they feel the biting spray on their faces; but they find it difficult to judge the strength and bearings of the chief current of the affairs of their times.

That current is deep. It moves steadily in one main direction. It is swinging into a new period of progress and the wider freedom which is always necessary to progress. This period is one in which teachers of the United States and teachers of many other countries, some of them not now regarded as particularly friendly to the United States, will be the key leaders unless they themselves deliberately abdicate that role.

The signal mark of this third era is a new understanding of the place of education and the role of the teacher in our society. This is the period, beginning so recently but stretching certainly into the next century, when very great achievements will be made by teachers. Every golden age has of necessity its shock brigades. If this first global golden age occurs, it will be because the teachers have led those brigades with brilliance.

The first edition of *Planning for Teaching* was a pioneer adventure that was oriented to educating teachers for this third period. It reached this difficult goal in brilliant fashion. Its clear exposition, detailed illustrations, and memorable development of principles combined to make it one of the most widely used texts in its field. The second edition extended and enhanced the sound reputation gained by its predecessor.

In this third edition the author again draws upon his long experience in helping prospective teachers understand the rapidly changing society which they are planning to serve, his clear and consistent breadth of vision in presenting the details of a teaching career, and his own contagious enthusiasm for the future.

Professor Richey is well qualified for his task. He has had a distinguished record as the chief of a teacher-education program in Thailand, and as a consultant to teacher-educators in many other countries. His background both abroad and here fits him uniquely for helping to initiate young people into the company of those teachers who are prepared to practice their profession creatively and precisely.

Professor Emeritus,   *Harold Benjamin*
George Peabody College
for Teachers

PREFACE

The contents of the book represent the results of fifteen years of intensive experimentation with an introductory course in education in which over 15,000 students have been enrolled at Indiana University and its branches. The book also reflects the results of a nationwide survey conducted by the McGraw-Hill Book Company for suggestions for the revision of the book. It is a real pleasure to express appreciation to students and colleagues at Indiana University and to the educators throughout the nation for their generous efforts and thoughtful suggestions, out of which have come many modifications and improvements in the book.

Although this edition is a major revision, every effort has been exerted to maintain the same clearly defined purposes as were used in the first and second editions—to help a student in gaining a valid and comprehensive knowledge of what is involved in teaching and in a teaching career to the extent that: 1) he acquires a broad background of information about teaching and engages in a variety of activities that will provide greater meaning to subsequent course-work, 2) he sees clearly the tasks which lie ahead in developing into an effective teacher, 3) he gains a reasoned dedication to the profession, and 4) he plans with care and insight his preparation for, as well as his professional growth after, entering the profession.

In the revision, Chapters 9 and 13 of the second edition have been brought together to form Part IV, "Our Educational Heritage." Chapter 14 has been divided into two chapters to form Part VI, "Nature of Our School System." Chapter 1 and a portion of Chapter 5, and Chapters 3 and 4 in the second edition have been combined. The chapter on "Opportunities in Education" has been moved to Part I of the new edition. Chapters 16 and 17 have been combined. Three new chapters, "Looking Ahead: Why Teach?" "Professional Organizations and Publications," and "Financing Our Schools," have been added. Chapter 6 of the second edition has been deleted. The present arrangement of the chapters according to parts now provides for greater flexibility and a variety of approaches that may be used in an introductory course. Resource sections containing checklists, selected readings, audio-visual materials, and other relevant materials, are located at the end of each Part.

All of the content has been checked and, when necessary, rewritten in terms of the increased maturity or sophistication level of college students today. All data have been brought up to date as nearly as possible in order to reflect recent changes, developments, and trends. Information from the 1960 census has been incorporated and some educational implications have been noted. Projections on such matters as school and college enrollments, teacher-demand needs, school finance, occupational needs, gross national products, teacher preparation, salaries, etc., are presented. National and world populations are projected to the year A.D. 2000. Recent technological advances, such as airborne and closed circuit television instruction, teaching machines, and language laboratories are discussed and some implications for teacher preparation are included. A special effort has been made to include recent research findings on teachers and teaching. The "self-concept" has been treated more adequately. The material has been personalized to a greater extent in order to assist students in identifying themselves with the content. Topics are approached to a greater degree from the point of view of encouraging students to explore the topics further and to expand their understandings of the teaching profession. More attention is given to the international aspects of education, to the role of private and parochial schools in America, to issues and problems, to recent critics of American education, and to contributions made by outstanding educators such as James B. Conant. Efforts have been made to help students become skilled observers of pupil behavior and teaching-learning situations. The needs of both elementary and secondary teachers are taken into consideration, and greater emphasis is given to teaching on the college level.

The greatly increased number of charts, graphs, and diagrams appearing in this edition are designed to assist students in visualizing important concepts and information. The photographs have been increased in number, decidedly improved, and selected with great care. A highly selective annotated list of 16 mm films, filmstrips, and recordings has been included at the ends of Chapters 1 and 18 and in the resource section for each Part, with the hope that their use will assist the student in grasping the concepts and principles involved. Five 16 mm sound motion films have been especially prepared for this book by the Text-Film Department of the McGraw-Hill Book Company in order to demonstrate the ideas dealt with in certain chapters.

Other major changes have been made in the end-of-chapter materials. "Questions for Your Consideration" have been added in order to stimulate thoughtful concern and discussion on basic ideas, concepts, and plans for teaching. The "Activities for You to Pursue" frequently have been improved. These activities, which emphasize the *doing*, encourage the student to work independently or in groups along lines of special interest, with stress placed upon the study of pupils, schools, teachers, and communities. The lists of suggested readings at the end of Chapters 1 and 18 and in the resource section for each Part have been radically updated and annotated with the hope that the student will be encouraged to read beyond the confines of this book, to pursue special interests, and to become acquainted with many other books and periodicals in the field of education.

Education, like every other profession, has technical terms and specialized meanings attached to certain words. Since it has been necessary to use some of these terms in this book, a glossary has been included in which the frequently used terms not always defined in the context of the book are explained.

It is impossible to give adequate recognition to all of the individuals who have participated in the revision of this book. Attention already has been directed to the many students, colleagues, and educators throughout the nation who have contributed generously through their suggestions and critical appraisals. Some contributions, however, are of such magnitude that they require special attention.

Miss Kathleen Dugdale critically read all of the manuscript and gave valuable suggestions. Dr. Nancy Davis helped revise Chapter 7. Dr. Maurice McGlasson helped revise Chapter 6 and write Chapter 8. Dr. Robert Garvue helped rewrite Chapter 16 and write Chapter 17. Dr. Fred Bentley and Mr. Joseph D'Ambrosio gave valuable assistance in the preparation of the manuscript. Dr. Carolyn Guss and Miss Helen Dzur helped prepare the lists of audio-visual materials. Without the help of these individuals the deadline for the manuscript would not have been met.

I wish to extend appreciation to the many publishers, and especially to departments of the National Education Association and to the U.S. Office of Education for their willingness to grant permission to use various materials. Mrs. Beatrice Clump Lee of the Research Division, National Education Association was most helpful in locating and in forwarding current relevant publications. Miss Katherine Peterson of the Bureau of the Census supplied 1960 census statistics as soon as they were available. Carl Purcell of the National Education Association contributed generously from his photograph files.

In a more personal sense, I wish to express my deep gratitude to my wife, Eloise, who typed the manuscript and shared many of the problems in revising the book, and to my son Bob who helped in every way possible. Without their solid support and encouragement there would have been no revision. Finally, I wish to remember my father who, until his death, showed great interest and gave much encouragement in the development of this book.

Robert W. Richey

TO THE STUDENT

Students in education today are vitally interested in being both successful and happy in life. One of the best ways for you to accomplish this is to engage in comprehensive planning during the initial stages of preparing for your life work. An introductory course in education, therefore, should provide many opportunities for you to gain a thorough understanding of what is involved in a teaching career—to the extent that you see clearly the tasks ahead in developing into an effective teacher. An introductory education course should also test further the wisdom of your decision to become a teacher, so that you may be able to develop a reasoned dedication to the profession. It should help you plan with care and insight your preparation for teaching as well as your professional growth after·entering the field. As a result of this type of course, subsequent studies and other professional activity should have greater meaning and purpose to you.

Planning for Teaching is designed to assist you in accomplishing these purposes of an introductory course in education. The book is divided into six integral parts. Each part is preceded by an overview designed to assist you in sensing clearly the relations of the chapters involved to the central purpose of the book. Part I attempts to increase your understanding of and skill in planning a career in teaching. The arrangement of the four chapters should assist you in grasping the logical sequence of some fundamental steps involved in career planning: i.e., you clarify the values and goals you desire in life; you study the teaching profession to see whether its potential values are consistent with your life values; you carefully examine the personal and professional requirements for success in the field; you evaluate yourself in terms of these requirements and then develop detailed plans for meeting them. Emphasis is placed upon both individual and group aspects of planning. You also will examine certification requirements and explore the wide range of opportunities that a career in education provides, so that your interests and abilities may best be utilized and your success and happiness in the profession proportionately increased. The needs for both elementary and secondary prospective teachers are taken into consideration.

Part II is concerned with such vital questions as: What relationships do teachers have with community members, pupils, parents, and other members of the profession? How does a teacher guide the educational growth of boys and girls? What are some of the philosophical and psychological bases of modern educational practices? What is the status of teaching as a profession and how does it differ from other professions? What obligations and responsibilities will you have as a member of the teaching profession?

In Part III you consider such realistic matters as salary, sick leave, tenure, and retirement benefits. In Part IV, you explore some of the historical forces that have shaped our educational system as well as theories of education.

Part V is designed to help you view the broad aspects of education and the professional challenge with which teachers today are faced. Special attention is given to the interrelationship of the school and the community and the resulting effect upon the role of the teacher. Some of the persistent problems and issues which you will face in teaching are pointed out. You are encouraged to plan ways in which you may aid in the solution of these problems and contribute effectively to the fuller realization of the school's function in a democratic society.

In Chapter 18 you are encouraged to assess some of the gains you have made in the course and to formulate further plans for moving effectively and happily into the teaching profession.

With the possible exception of Part I and Chapter 18, the organization of the book is flexible, and a variety of approaches may be used. For example, you may wish to consider Part III, "Economic Aspects of Teaching," before Part II, "Teachers and Their Work." On the other hand, you may prefer to give early consideration to Part IV, "Our Educational Heritage" or to Part V, "Broader Concepts of Education." The order in which the various parts of the book are considered is a matter for the instructor and you to decide.

CONTENTS

1
LOOKING AHEAD: WHY TEACH?

Congratulations upon your interest in becoming a teacher. Assuming that you are well suited for such a career, you may look forward to an exciting and challenging life.

The importance of education to the welfare of our country is sensed by the general public more clearly than ever before. Good teachers are a vital necessity to the progress as well as the safety of our nation. Never before have greater responsibilities rested upon the teaching profession.

The increased importance that teachers and teaching have acquired in our society becomes apparent as you read various articles and books, or listen to radio and television programs that are concerned with the welfare of our country. Such titles as "Pursuit of Excellence," "Developing Our Human Resources," "Our Man-power Shortages," "Are Our Schools Good Enough?" "What's Wrong with Our Schools?" and "Needed—More and Better Teachers" are indicative of the burst of concern for the quality of education in this country.

Specialists in many professions are sharing their talents in the education of our young people. For example, educators work with engineers in developing a variety of electronic instructional devices that may facilitate the learning process. Scientists and mathematicians are contributing technical assistance in developing programs in science and mathematics in keeping with the ever-increasing demands that result from our technological advancements. Architects are assisting educators in designing school plant facilities that will provide for greater flexibility of programs

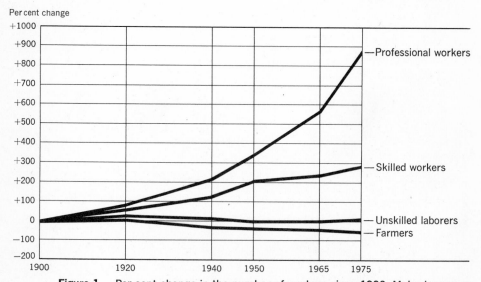

Figure 1. Per cent change in the number of workers since 1900. Major increases will occur in occupations requiring the most education and training. (*Source:* National Education Association.)

as well as for the use of a wide variety of instructional materials. Scholars in the various academic disciplines are assisting educators in developing programs that will adequately meet the needs of youth as they face a demanding and rapidly changing world. Read Bruner's book *The Process of Education* [19] and Silberman's article "The Remaking of American Education" in *Fortune Magazine* [144] if you wish to learn of some very exciting educational changes being made through such efforts.

The successful orbiting of Sputnik No. 1 in 1957 perhaps did more than any other single recent event to focus the attention of the general public upon the need for good schools. This spectacular success of the Russians shook the American public out of a relatively complacent, self-satisfied status with respect to world position and attitude toward education. Immediately following this event a clamor for better schools arose. There also was a shift in thinking from education for peace to education for survival. Subsequent advances, especially those made by the Russians, have tended to stimulate further research concerning better ways of educating youth.

IMPORTANCE OF EDUCATION

This burst of concern for education in America has paralleled the upsurge of demands for independence and economic advancement among hundreds of millions of people abroad who have little of either. In their own awakening they see education as indispensable to their quest for growth and dignity [31:1].

At the center of these new educational demands stands the teaching profession, which is being challenged to meet the needs of our own people for a far better knowledge and understanding of others. It is being challenged at the same time to help emerging nations in the creation and rapid improvement of their educational systems. Will the rapid technological, economic, and social development which these developing countries demand take place through totalitarian regimentation or under conditions of growing individual freedom and responsibility? This is a crucial educational as well as social, economic, and political question.

With considerable concern, we note the tremendous importance which the Russians in recent years have placed upon education in such areas as the sciences, mathematics, and the various vocations. We also note the phenomenal technological progress that has paralleled the Russians' emphasis upon education. We realize, however, that education in a totalitarian or dictatorial form of government is highly controlled and is designed to serve only highly selected ends. Individual initiative and freedom are denied, and students are told by those in authority what to believe and what to do. Likewise, the noted historian, Toynbee, cautions that "any state or people that succumbs to this temptation (high specialization of technology and scientific knowledge) seems likely to defeat its own purpose, for even the disinterested pursuit of science becomes sterile if it runs in narrow ruts. Specialization in particular branches of natural science soon runs dry if it is cut off from its source in comprehensive and philosophical scientific thinking" [173:9]. What precautions should our schools and colleges take in view of Toynbee's statement?

Education and the Dignity of Man.   Education has a much broader and deeper meaning for our way of life. In our society we value highly the dignity and worth of the individual and are committed to the development of free, rational, and responsible citizens. We want each individual to achieve the promise that is in him. We want him to be worthy of a free society and capable of strengthening it.

The authors of the excellent pamphlet *The Pursuit of Excellence: Education and the Future of America* emphasize very effectively the deep concern of our society for the dignity and worth of the individual [121:1]:

The greatness of a nation may be manifested in many ways—in its purposes, its courage, its moral responsibility, its cultural and scientific eminence, the tenor of its daily life. But ultimately the source of its greatness is in the individuals who constitute the living substance of the nation.

A concern for the realization of individual potentialities is deeply rooted in our moral heritage, our political philosophy, and the texture of our daily customs. It is at the root of our efforts to eliminate poverty and slums at home and to combat disease and disaster throughout the world. The enthusiasm with which Americans plunge into projects for human betterment has been considered by some critics to be foolishly optimistic. But though we may have gone to extremes in a naive belief that we could cure all of mankind's ills, we need not be ashamed of the impulse. It springs from our deepest values. We do not believe that men were meant to live in degradation and we are foes of the poverty and ignorance which produces that result. We deplore the destruction of human potentialities through disease, and we are prepared to fight such destruction wherever we meet it. We believe that man—by virtue of his humanity—should live in the light of reason, exercise moral responsibility, and be free to develop to the full the talents that are in him.

Our devotion to a free society can only be understood in terms of these values. It is the only form of society that puts at the very top of its agenda the opportunity of the individual to develop his potentialities. It is the declared enemy of every condition that stunts the intellect, moral and spiritual growth of the individual. No society has ever fully succeeded in living up to the stern ideals that a free people set themselves. But only a free society can even address itself to that demanding task.

The above statement quite clearly expresses our concept of what constitutes a good life, and our ultimate values. The increasingly greater implementation of this concept is of crucial importance, not only for us but for people throughout the free nations of the world.

All over the world peoples are striving for a new and fuller meaning of life. No challenge is more important than to give meaning to the idea of human dignity. This task is all the more complex because the answer will be found less in what we say than in what we do. It will be found partly in the scale of our achievement, but even more importantly in the quality of our lives [121:2].

Billions

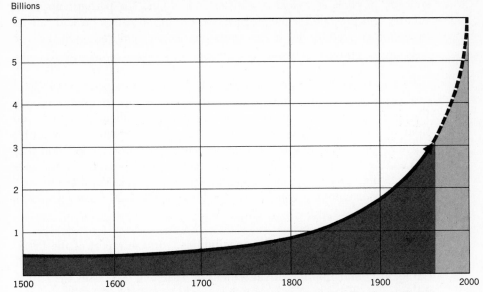

Figure 2. Past and projected population of the world. What educational problems arise if the population of the world approximately doubles between 1960 and the year 2000? (*Source: Saturday Review.*)

As a teacher, you have a unique opportunity to help individuals both here and abroad to achieve this new and fuller meaning of life. Is there a better or more satisfying basic reason for teaching?

The concept of the dignity and worth of the individual is not relatively new. Mankind has been working toward its fuller realization for a long time.

You will recall that the Declaration of Independence refers to "the inalienable rights—Life, Liberty and the pursuit of Happiness." Our forefathers, in order to be more specific about the matter, formulated the Bill of Rights. A similar statement is to be found in the French Declaration of the Rights of Man (1789). Free nations throughout the world have embodied the concept in such documents as the Atlantic Charter (1941), the Charter of the United Nations (1945), and the Universal Declaration of Human Rights (1948) adopted by the General Assembly of the United Nations. Reread this Universal Declaration of Human Rights and note the strong emphasis placed upon the dignity of the individual.

Our free public school system reflects our deep desire that each student have the opportunity to develop the talents within him so that he may live a constructive and effective democratic life. No other country in the world provides opportunities of this kind that are equal to those in the United States.

Our nation's free public schools have unlocked the door of opportunity for millions. Despite great diversification of race, religion, national origin, and social and economic family background, our schools have contributed to the development of great inventors, scientists, statesmen, businessmen, lawyers, physicians, teachers, artists, and others. "In perhaps no other country is it possible for people of modest origin to rise so far and so fast. In no other country have the common people achieved such a large measure of political power, social status, and economic prosperity. The success of America is the story of faith in the common man" [40:3–4].

As a further effort to get each child to develop his capacities for effective democratic living, each state requires children to attend school. These compulsory education laws place a moral obligation upon each child to develop his abilities to the fullest extent possible. As a future teacher, you will be responsible for devising programs of education that will enable American children to reach their highest potentials for democratic living. The future of our nation rests to a considerable measure upon the extent to which all teachers fulfill this basic responsibility [122:1].

Education and Democratic Responsibilities. In the report of the President's Commission on National Goals, John W. Gardner, President of Carnegie Foundation for Advancement of Teaching, expresses the strong feeling that "Education is essential not only to individual fulfillment but to the vitality of our national life. The vigor of our free institutions depends upon educated men and women at every level of the society. At this moment in history, free institutions are on trial."[1]

You will recall that, throughout the history of our country, national leaders have emphasized that education was fundamental to the preservation of freedom and self-government. George Washington, in his Farewell Address of 1796, strongly encouraged the spread of knowledge: "Promote then, as an object of primary importance, institutions for the general diffusion of knowledge. In proportion as the structure of a government gives force to public opinion, it is essential that public opinion is enlightened." Thomas Jefferson warned that "if a nation expects to be ignorant and free in a state of civilization it expects what never was and never will be." He felt that "if the condition of man is to be progressively ameliorated . . . education is the chief instrument for effecting it." Abraham Lincoln stated that, "upon the subject of education, not presuming to dictate any plan or system respecting it, I can only say that I view it as the most important subject which we as a people can be engaged in."

You also may recall statements being made by more recent presidents regarding the fundamental role our schools play in the preservation and improvement of our way of life. Franklin D. Roosevelt, for example, stated that "our ultimate security, to a large extent, is based upon the individual's character, information, and attitude, and the responsibility rests squarely upon those who direct education in America." Dwight D. Eisenhower maintained that "because our schools help shape the mind and character of our youth, the strength or weakness of our educational sys-

---

[1] The President's Commission on National Goals, *Goals for Americans*, © 1960 by The American Assembly, Columbia University, New York. Reprinted by permission of Prentice-Hall, Inc., Englewood Cliffs, N.J., p. 81.

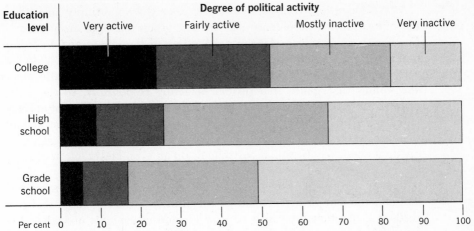

Figure 3. The relationship of education and political activity of American citizens, as indicated by a representative sample of 8,000 adults. What educational problems are related especially to the very inactive political groups of people? (*Source:* U.S. Chamber of Commerce.)

tem will go far to determine the strength or weakness of our national wisdom and our national morality tomorrow. That is why it is essential to our nation that we have good schools. And their quality depends upon all of us." In a message to Congress, delivered February 6, 1962, John F. Kennedy stated that: "No task before our nation is more important than expanding and improving the educational opportunities of all our people. The concept that every American deserves the opportunity to attain the highest level of education of which he is capable is not new to this Administration—it is a traditional ideal of democracy. But it is time that we moved toward the fulfillment of this ideal with more vigor and less delay.

"For education is both the foundation and the unifying force of our democratic way of life—it is the mainspring of our economic and social progress—it is the highest expression of achievement in our society ennobling and enriching human life. In short, it is at the same time the most profitable investment society can make and the richest reward it can confer."

Responsible citizens in all segments of American life express their faith in education in many ways. As will be indicated in a later chapter, they pay much money in the form of taxes to support free public schools and colleges. They donate both time and money for educational purposes. Approximately one-quarter million people serve on school boards. More than 11 million people are members of the National Congress of Parents and Teachers. Mothers and fathers frequently make great sacrifices in order that their children may stay in school. Citizens in all walks of life continue to expect the schools to accept more responsibility for the education of youth and adults which reflects the persistent faith that both the individual and our American way of life can be improved through education. You as a future teacher will play a key role in this endeavor.

As we move into the future you will have the opportunity, as well as the obligation, to perpetuate and to strengthen our democratic way of life. Youth must gain a clear understanding of the values and traditions that have emerged from mankind's search for desirable ways of living. They must have an operational understanding of the democratic ideals and values that guide free people in acting responsibly, so that, ultimately, the welfare of society is seen as the combined welfare of all individuals. Factual knowledge alone does not ensure wise decision making since decisions are made largely in terms of the ideals and goals an individual cherishes. How can our schools do an even better job in meeting this basic need in a free world?

The increasing technological complexity which characterizes modern life, and the complexity of modern social organization demand that succeeding generations of youth acquire increasing amounts of knowledge. As an educator, you face the challenge of discovering new ways in which the learning of increasingly greater amounts of knowledge may be compressed into shorter periods of time. Through your creative efforts you may be able to make valuable contributions to the profession. Without increasingly greater depth and breadth of knowledge, young men and women will be unable to cope adequately with the complexity of problems and preserve the freedoms for which we have striven.

John W. Gardner, in his book titled *Excellence* [59:159–160], sounds a warning which all teachers should heed as they work with boys and girls:

> The importance of competence as a condition of freedom has been widely ignored (as some newly independent nations are finding to their sorrow). An amiable fondness for the graces of a free society is not enough. Keeping a free society free—and vital and strong—is no job for the half-educated and the slovenly. Free men must be competent men. In a society of free men, competence is an elementary duty. Men and women doing competently whatever job is theirs to do tone up the whole society. And a man who does a slovenly job—whether he is a janitor or a judge, a surgeon or a technician—lowers the tone of the society. So do the chiselers of high and low degree, the sleight-of-hand artists who always know how to gain an advantage without honest work. They are the regrettable burdens of a free society.

Individual competence, however, is not enough to ensure a strong, vibrant, creative, and productive society. Teachers must help boys and girls to value the dignity of work and the establishment of high standards of performance in all phases of life. Youth must learn to accept the responsibility for setting their own high standards of performance, for serving as their own hard disciplinarians, and for demanding quality performance upon the part of their fellow men. They must feel that satisfaction at the level of mediocrity will result in the decay of the ideals that have made this country great. They must feel a sense of pride in and dedication to their work and to the basic ideals of our society.

Of course, pride and dedication are qualities that must be drawn from rather than taught to individuals. But you as a teacher can do much to stimulate and encourage the development of such qualities in girls and

The increasing technological complexity which characterizes modern life demands that succeeding generations of youth acquire increasing amounts of knowledge. We can scarcely afford anything less than the best education possible for youth. *(Photograph from Standard Oil Company of New Jersey.)*

boys. Your feeling of pride and devotion to your work as a teacher may do much to inspire this type of reaction in youth as they later move into their various fields of work. You may also encourage pupils to take dedicated approaches to their various school responsibilities, to study the lives of others who reflect these qualities, to discover occupations that are best suited to their interests and abilities, and the like. Do everything possible to help boys and girls to thirst for knowledge rather than belittle its value, to desire constructive work rather than shirk responsibility, to appreciate rather than criticize the work of others, to admire rather than scorn the success of others, to be optimistic rather than pessimistic about their future, to strive for the best rather than be satisfied with mediocrity, and to feel the thrill of success rather than the hopeless acceptance of failure.

Education and Equality of Opportunity. From your reading of such important documents as the Declaration of Independence and the Universal Declaration of Human Rights, you have noted the dominant belief which free nations have in the equality of men. Education is the medium through which this belief can best be recognized.

If we are to respect the dignity of man, however, we must provide educational opportunities for each individual to develop his talents to the fullest. In other words, we are committed to the proposition that we must provide equal educational opportunities for all of the children in our society. This is a distinctive ideal of the American school system.

This proposition has a number of far-reaching implications for you as a teacher. How will you provide programs of education that meet the great diversification of abilities, interests, and needs of boys and girls? How will you further remove such barriers as poverty, prejudice, and ignorance that interfere with equal educational opportunities? How will you stimulate, encourage, and enhance the development of each individual's potentialities for effective democratic living?

Education and Economic Growth and Welfare.   The economic growth of the United States is without parallel in the world. Although we comprise only about 6 per cent of the world's population and occupy less than 7 per cent of the world's land area, we produce over 40 per cent and consume nearly one-third of the world's goods and services. The results of our scientific and industrial knowledge have provided us with more of the material things than ever before. Our standards of living are the highest in the world.

The production potential of our nation is so great that it is possible for us to provide aid to other countries who seek to improve their standards of living. Throughout Asia, Africa, and Latin America, new nations are attempting to improve their economics. It is important for us to help them develop the vitality of a free economy and reduce the economic inequalities that exist around the world, since one of the best guarantees of a free world is a strong and growing economy.

Walter W. Heller, a nationally recognized economist, interestingly points out how education plays an extremely important role in the growth and welfare of our economy, as well as in the security of our nation [71:9]:

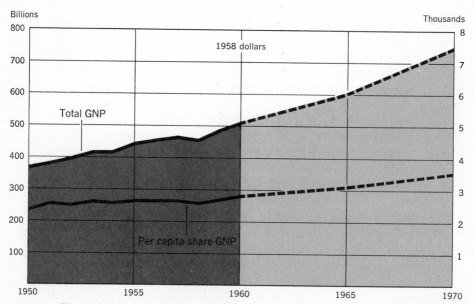

Figure 4.   Gross national product of the United States, 1950–1970. The United States has the manpower resources for a much higher standard of living during the 1960s. How should the schools continue to help in raising our standard of living? (*Source:* U.S. Department of Labor.)

Policies designed primarily to stimulate economic growth often turn out to have a desirable dual purpose because the roots of economic growth lie deep in the economic and social strata. Education is a beautiful example. America has valued education for its own sake and has led the world in provision of free public education at all levels of society. Now it is apparent that education has improved the quality of the labor force, and that this investment in humans has been one of the major factors in the economic growth of the last half century. . . .

The relationship between education and our military strength and national survival is equally direct. Higher and higher levels of education are required to supply a literate and well-trained source of military manpower in an age of electronic and nuclear weapons; to match and overcome the gains of the Soviet Union in missiles and space exploration; and, most important, to provide the understanding and wisdom required to outdo the Soviets in the competition for the minds of men. In this broad sense, education is a powerful weapon of great importance to our national defense. It spells the difference between being the world's first-rate and the world's second-rate power, scientifically and militarily.

If we are to maintain world leadership, we must show that a free democratic society can solve its home problems—poverty, insecurity, unemployment, and inequalities of opportunity. Achievement of faster rates of economic progress and full use of our growing physical and human capacity is the surest way to demonstrate the resilience and vitality of our free economy.

Our economic welfare will be further strengthened through increased development of our human resources. In the future, more scientists, doctors, teachers, statesmen, engineers, and the like will be needed. Technological advancements will require more highly skilled technicians. A strong and growing economy will require increasingly greater amounts

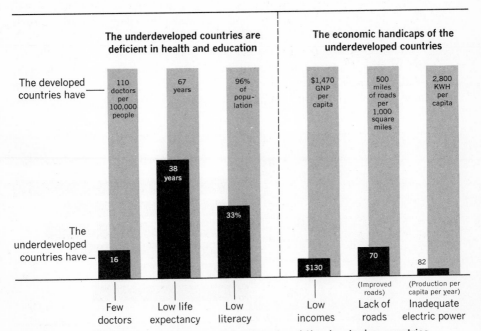

Figure 5.   The gap between the underdeveloped and the developing countries. To what extent are good schools and competent teachers directly related to the development of any country? (*Source:* Bureau of Public Affairs.)

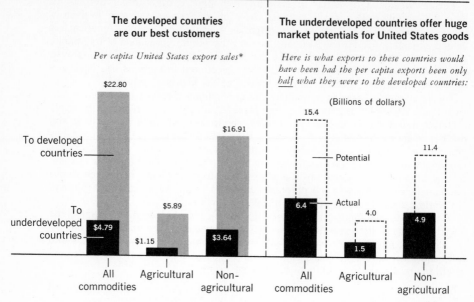

The developed countries are our best customers

Per capita United States export sales*

$22.80

$16.91

To developed countries ———

$5.89

To underdeveloped countries ———

$4.79

$1.15

$3.64

| All commodities | Agricultural | Non-agricultural |

The underdeveloped countries offer huge market potentials for United States goods

Here is what exports to these countries would have been had the per capita exports been only half what they were to the developed countries:

(Billions of dollars)

15.4

Potential

11.4

6.4

Actual

4.0

1.5

4.9

| All commodities | Agricultural | Non-agricultural |

* Based on population of the developed and the underdeveloped areas and United States exports in 1959, United States commercial exports excluding military hardware.

Figure 6. What the gap in the development of countries means to the economy of the United States. (*Source:* Bureau of Public Affairs.)

of education for all. Basically, the attitude and quality of teachers will affect the extent to which boys and girls make the effort to continue their education and develop their abilities.

The strength of our future economy will also be affected by the extent to which future citizens will make wise use of our natural resources —soil, minerals, forests, and water. As a teacher, you have the opportunity to help youth understand how the use of these resources have been

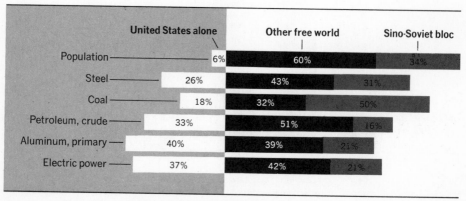

	United States alone	Other free world	Sino-Soviet bloc
Population	6%	60%	34%
Steel	26%	43%	31%
Coal	18%	32%	50%
Petroleum, crude	33%	51%	16%
Aluminum, primary	40%	39%	21%
Electric power	37%	42%	21%

Figure 7. Where the balance of world resources lies. Our continued economic growth is dependent upon the wise use of our resources and upon trade with other parts of the free world. (*Source:* Bureau of Public Affairs.)

Lifetime income (earnings), thousands of dollars

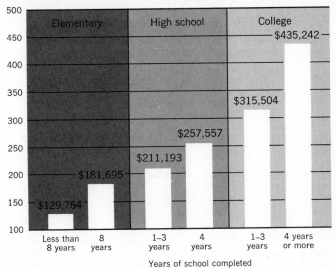

Years of school completed

Figure 8. Life-time income (earnings) from age 18 to death, based on arithmetic means for males, according to years of school completed. (*Source:* National Education Association.)

abused and how they can conservatively use and develop them in the future so that quality of living may be enhanced.

In Figure 8 you note that, in general, there is a direct relationship between the level of education and the economic advancement of individuals. Business and industry are demanding more and more education as a requirement for employment. For this reason, an even higher correlation between education and the economic success of future citizens may be expected. As a teacher, therefore, you will be helping others raise the level of their economic potentialities.

You find a striking relationship between education and economic growth if you compare educational development, natural resources, and per capita income in various nations throughout the world [43:46]. Note in Table 1 that Denmark and Mexico present an interesting contrast.

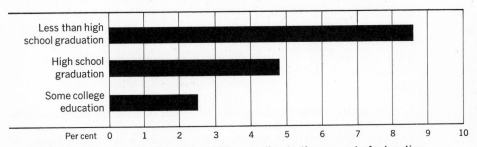

Figure 9. Per cent unemployed in 1959 according to the amount of education. There is a direct relationship between employment and amount of education. (*Source:* U.S. Department of Labor.)

Mexico has abundant natural resources. Until recently, it had neglected education. Its per capita income in 1958 was the equivalent of $266. A century ago Denmark had a very low per capita income and its soil was not rich. It had few minerals and the growing season was short. But the people decided to place much emphasis upon developing good schools for their children. The per capita income in 1958, in contrast with Mexico's, was $910. Likewise, Colombia, very rich in natural resources but low in education, produced only $154 per capita. On the other hand,

TABLE 1   RELATIONSHIP OF NATURAL RESOURCES, EDUCATION, AND INCOME IN SELECTED COUNTRIES

Nation	Natural resources	Educational development	Per capita income, 1958
Brazil	High	Low	$ 918
United States	High	High	2,069
Denmark	Low	High	910
Mexico	High	Low	266
New Zealand	High	High	1,224
Colombia	High	Low	154
Switzerland	Low	High	1,312

Source: Adapted from "Education and Economic Growth," *National Education Association Journal,* vol. 51, no. 2, pp. 46-47, National Education Association, Washington, February, 1962.

Switzerland, with limited resources but a well-developed educational program, ranked first in Europe in per capita income in 1958. These examples can be duplicated in many other countries. They show clearly that, regardless of natural resources, the development of educational potential increases per capita income. For this reason, it is so very important for us to build increasingly greater strength into our educational system and to help other countries to do likewise.

Democracy and Quality Teachers.   In the history of our country we have never faced a period in which the demand for education has been greater. It seems obvious that, barring world catastrophe, the demands for educated intelligence will become increasingly greater.

In order to add strength to our nation and survive the strong threats to our way of life, increasing numbers of our most able young people must become teachers. Our future welfare rests so heavily upon the quality and quantity of education received by the young that only the best should teach. To them will fall the task of aiding our schools in their attempt to:

1. Have pupils master the knowledge and skills essential to happy and productive living.

2. Identify and develop to the fullest extent possible the special talents or abilities of each pupil.

3. Foster creative approaches, upon the part of youth, to the problems of daily living and to the improvement of society.

4. Help boys and girls develop effective skills for living and working together in an increasingly interdependent world.

5. Assist youth in gaining increasing skill in self-direction and in fulfilling their responsibilities to society.

6. Help youth gain a reasoned conviction to the concepts of freedom, justice, and dignity of man.

These are tasks that call for the best to enter the teaching profession. We, as a nation, can afford no less since our most important resources are the capacities, the energy, and the character of our people.

Alvin C. Eurich, of the Ford Foundation, in addressing the Chamber of Commerce of the United States, very effectively summarized the importance of education and the challenge with which we are faced [50].

America still means promise; it is still a land of opportunity. At this juncture of our history perhaps our greatest opportunity is in the education of our children. If we fail in this, we fail all succeeding generations. But there can be no bright future—as there never has been in any field—if we maintain the status quo. We cannot stand still. Every nation in the history of mankind has been defeated totally and miserably when it strove merely to protect what it had. New nations, including our own, have risen to the top through hardship and struggle, through ingenuity and the courage to create new patterns. Innovation has been basic to our economic well-being and growth. It is also basic to education, for creative imagination in education will determine our future and the future of our children.

Can you think of any better reason for being a teacher?

SATISFACTIONS IN TEACHING

The fact that education plays such a fundamental role in the welfare of our lives does not mean that everyone would be happy if he were to be a teacher. You probably know of teachers who seem to be discontented, unhappy, and insecure. Some of them appear to look upon teaching as a job for which the pay check is the only reward. They leave the school building as soon as the last bell rings and hate to return in the morning. Some teachers are disillusioned, cynical, and bitter over inadequacies and inconsistencies in the present school system. Frequently, and perhaps in an attempt to gain pity, they discourage able students from entering the teaching profession.

On the other hand, you doubtless know of other teachers who seem to regard teaching as a challenge from which decided satisfactions are gained. They seem to feel an obligation to each boy and girl in helping him realize his maximum capacity to learn and to live constructively. They sense the dignity and worth of the profession in which they work. They possess a contagious enthusiasm for their work. Each day seems to hold new opportunities and challenges. Certainly, they can and do become angry, annoyed, and irritated. They may worry and lose sleep over some students or over problems involving parents. But the satisfactions of guiding youth and seeing them perform and grow and develop far outweigh these deterrents.

If you do not take into account the time that a person sleeps, approximately one-half of his time is spent on the job. What he does to earn a living has some effect upon his outlook upon life, his leisure-time activities, his socioeconomic status, his family relationships, his citizenship responsibilities, the kind of people with whom he associates, his stimulation for self-improvement, and his attitude toward himself and others.

In the first part of this chapter you sensed one of the very important satisfactions or values to be gained from being a teacher. Perhaps there are others that may especially appeal to you. Many people fail to gain maximum happiness and personal satisfaction from their work simply because they do not fully sense the values inherent in their careers. What then are some of the other values to be gained from being a teacher?

Part of a Huge Enterprise.   As a teacher you will be a part of one of the largest enterprises in the United States. Approximately one-fourth of the population of our nation is enrolled in public and private schools and colleges. In later chapters of this book you will learn the breakdown of this tremendous population as well as the billions of dollars spent for education.

Membership in a Large Profession.   Teaching is the largest single profession in the world, with over 2 million members in the United States alone. In 1961, the breakdown was as follows [86:5]:

1,400,000	Teachers in public elementary and secondary schools
220,000	Teachers in private elementary and secondary schools
130,000	School administrators, supervisors, consultants, researchers, and other specialists in elementary and secondary schools
350,000	Professional personnel in higher education institutions
25,000	Professional staff members in professional organizations, in government offices of education, and in private agencies with educational programs
2,125,000	Total

During the next few years the number of teachers will increase considerably, owing to the increase in the number of children, the tendency for boys and girls to remain in school for a greater number of years, and the upward as well as downward extension of our school system. Kindergartens and, to some extent, nursery schools are being increasingly recognized as a part of public school experiences. Rather rapid strides are being made in the field of adult education. More and more, the general public is recognizing the fact that some educational facilities must be made available to adults in order to develop and maintain well-informed, intelligent, happy citizens. Because of amazing technological advancements in recent years, there has been a decrease in the number of working hours required of men and an increase in the amount of leisure time. The services of the educator are again needed to help adults develop ways of profitably using their leisure time.

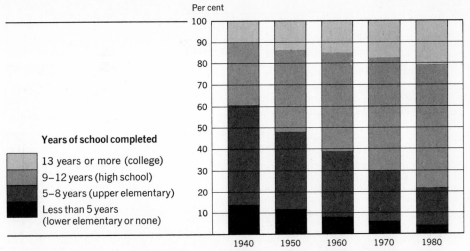

Per cent

Years of school completed

- 13 years or more (college)
- 9–12 years (high school)
- 5–8 years (upper elementary)
- Less than 5 years (lower elementary or none)

1940   1950   1960   1970   1980

Figure 10. Years of school completed by those in the United States who are 25 or more years old. The educational attainment of adults will continue to rise. What effect will this condition have upon the educational needs of youth and of adults? (*Source:* Bureau of the Census.)

Regardless of where you go in the world, it is relatively simple to find other teachers. You should find it easy to become acquainted with them through these common interests. Thus you can expand your circle of friends and your professional understanding.

As a teacher you will be expected to attend a number of professional meetings. You will be a member of your local teacher organization. You will have your state as well as your national meetings to attend. In these meetings you will have many opportunities to work and become acquainted with a large group of people, from many areas, who are dedicated to a common and basic cause in a democratic society.

Variety of Opportunities. The field of education includes many kinds of work other than classroom teaching. Although the classroom teacher is the center of the process of educating the young, different professions are necessary in order that he may accomplish his purpose. There are administrators, personnel officers, nurses, attendance officers, test and research experts, business officers, counselors, supervisors, department heads, special teachers, teacher-education professors, and many others who enter into the scene. In a later chapter of this book you will explore in detail the wide variety of opportunities within the school system alone.

A teaching background also often proves beneficial for various non-professional types of work. For example, personnel officers in industry frequently seek prospective employees who have had teaching experience for various types of work, such as selling, guidance, placement, research, on-the-job training, and public relations. There are many types of work closely associated with teaching, such as camp counselor, sponsor of a 4-H club, boy or girl scout administrator, public health worker, home

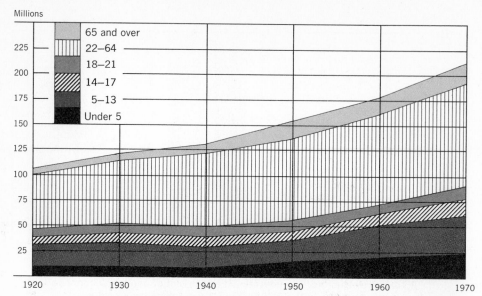

Figure 11. Fifty years of population growth in the United States. Decided increases have taken place in the younger and older age populations. How do these changes affect the teaching profession? (*Source:* National Education Association.)

demonstrator, agricultural agent, book salesman, and educational consultant.

As you prepare for a career in education, you owe to yourself a very careful study of the great variety of opportunities that are available. Do the very best job possible in planning for the type of work in which you are most interested and for which you are best suited. Furthermore, your plans may change as you gain new information and experience and meet new conditions. You have the satisfaction of knowing that there is much room in which to utilize your specific interests and abilities.

Economic Security. Economic security should be mentioned as one value inherent in a career in education. Though it is true that educators do not receive pay commensurate with salaries in some other occupations, and the amount of work and time they contribute is great, it nonetheless should be remembered that a career in education is normally a very stable one, extending over many years. There are no frequent strikes or general layoffs which provoke feelings of uncertainty and upset long-range budget planning. As compared with workers in some occupations, a teacher has much less chance of being dismissed unfairly. Many states have enacted laws to protect the tenure of teachers whose services are satisfactory, so that they may be free from the worry of losing their jobs.

In contrast to most doctors or lawyers, a teacher has his clientele established as soon as he accepts a position. This makes it possible for him to move from place to place without suffering the great initial loss experienced in some of the other professions.

As long as there are homes and children, there will be a need for teachers. If the foundation of our society should topple, our schools would be one of the last agencies to disappear. There are, then, a number of desirable economic factors inherent in a career in education.

Prestige. Occupations differ in regard to the respect or prestige generally assigned to them by members of a community. In earlier days the prestige of the teacher was not very high. A number of reasons account for the low esteem placed upon teaching as an occupation: at that time salaries were exceedingly poor, the profession often was considered a side line or a stepping stone to some other occupation, the standards were minimal, and the function of the school was limited.

There is considerable evidence that the prestige of teachers is increasing. For example, in the Roper poll conducted by *Life Magazine*, a large sampling of people throughout the United States were asked to rank five occupations in the order of their importance to the community [130:14]. The results were as follows: teachers, 31.3 per cent; clergymen, 27.1 per cent; public officials, 19.1 per cent; merchants, 12.8 per cent; lawyers, 9.7 per cent. Thus, almost a third of the people polled believed that of these five occupational groups, teachers are the most important contributors to the life and well-being of the community.

In 1962, George Gallup, director of the American Institute of Public Opinion, found that the prestige of the teaching profession definitely had increased. In a nationwide survey, which was identical to one conducted in 1953, a representative sample of adults was handed a card listing a number of major professions and was then asked: "Suppose a young man came to you and asked your opinion about taking up a profession. Assume that he was qualified to enter any of these professions, which one would you first recommend to him?" The following listing shows the difference in the public's rating of occupations:

	1953	1962
1. Doctor	29%	23%
2. Engineer—builder	20	18
3. Professor—teacher	5	12
4. Clergyman	7	8
5. Government career	3	7
6. Lawyer	6	6
7. Business executive	7	5
8. Dentist	6	4
9. Banker	2	2
Other	7	4
None, don't know	8	11

Gallup found that twice as many women as men—16 per cent to 8 per cent—selected teaching as the one they would recommend. He concluded that evidently women give less weight to financial considerations than do men.

The trend of future thinking on careers, in the opinion of Gallup, is probably revealed best by the youngest group interviewed—persons in the 21–29 age group. Teaching came second among the choices of people in this age group. Their recommendations were as follows:

1.	Doctor	26%
2.	Professor—teacher	18
3.	Engineer—builder	17
4.	Lawyer	8
5.	Government career	7
6.	Dentist	5
7.	Clergy	4
8.	Business executive	3
9.	Banker	2
	Other	4
	None, don't know	6

Perhaps a number of factors have contributed to this change. As previously indicated, the complexity of our technological and social world has placed an increasingly higher premium upon the need for education. Teachers are the chief instruments for obtaining this education. Research studies indicate that members of professions requiring extended and rigorous preparation tend to have greater prestige than those for which little training is required. As will be emphasized later, the number of years required to become a teacher has increased significantly. There is considerable evidence to support the fact that the holding power of a profession increases as the standards for entrance increase. T. M. Stinnett, of the National Commission on Teacher Education and Professional Standards, indicates that [85:45]: "the better and more intensive a man's training, the more likely he is to stay with the profession he's trained for. If a young man has invested a lot of time and effort to get a highly prized and respected certificate, he's not likely to chuck it all and go into another line of work." You may feel certain that the amount of respect and prestige accorded teachers will continue to rise as professional standards, salaries, and the quality of members within the profession continue to rise.

Contacts with Others.   You will contact many people in addition to the pupils and teachers with whom you work. Parents and community members come from various walks of life and usually represent different classes, creeds, nationalities, and races. You will mix with doctors, lawyers, ministers, nurses, merchants, carpenters, bricklayers, and many others and discuss the problems of their children as well as of the community. Here is a vast reservoir of life which you can explore and from which a broadening of interests, knowledge, abilities, and satisfactions may be gained. Here also is the opportunity for you to assume a role of leadership that goes beyond the innocuous public relations responsibilities expected of teachers in the past. If you are effective in your work, both school and community are likely to become better places in which to live.

Helping Others to Live More Fully.   The teacher occupies a unique position, that of helping others achieve happiness and a rich and full life. The school's primary function in society is to transmit and progressively refine our cultural heritage to the young. The effectiveness of this process rests especially in the hands of the teacher. It is the teacher's obligation to weigh, evaluate, and separate the finer aspects of our culture that should be transmitted to the oncoming generation. It is his obligation to develop in youth those behavior patterns that hold promise for increasing the effectiveness of living in a democratic society. It is his obligation to help raise in every way possible the level of civilization, to the end that life may be more abundant for every individual.

The teacher has the rich opportunity of developing in the mind and heart of each boy and girl the ideals and standards of behavior that will give direction to life. He has the advantage of working with a child during his most formative years. Next to parents, the teacher in most cases plays the most important role in shaping the behavior of boys and girls.

The teacher also has the opportunity to guide and inspire boys and girls in such ways that they may make significant contributions to their fellow men. Henry Aelanas once said, "A teacher affects eternity. He can never tell where his influence stops." In Visher's study of all the people listed in an issue of *Who's Who in America* [179:23], most of these leaders reported that a teacher had had a great deal of influence upon their development and subsequent achievement. Very often someone who has distinguished himself feels this indebtedness. A large measure of his success was due to the help and inspiration he received from some teacher, to whom he openly pays tribute. For example, Bernard Baruch [9:415], who has distinguished himself internationally in recent years and has served as adviser to Presidents and national leaders from the time of Woodrow Wilson, has paid tribute to someone who was a teacher and

A teacher has many opportunities for developing in the mind and heart of each pupil the ideals and standards of behavior that will give direction to the pupil's life.
(Photograph by Carl Purcell, National Education Association.)

principal in New York City schools for more than half a century. Since his tribute alludes to a number of the values in teaching, the passage is quoted at length:

Some 70 years ago, my father brought us from a town in rural South Carolina to live in New York City. A few days after our arrival, my mother took my three brothers and me—aged 6, 8, 10, and 12—to Grammar School 69 on West 54th Street. There the kind superintendent, Matthew J. Elgas, after questioning, placed us in suitable grades.

When I, the 10-year-old, was taken into a classroom, I clung closely to my mother's skirt. I saw what seemed like innumerable faces swimming in a fog before my frightened eyes.

Then, I heard a voice, a gentle, kind voice. Someone approached me and said, while she placed her hand upon my shoulder, "Now, Bernard, I am so happy to have you. I am sure the other boys are also pleased. Will you sit in this seat?" I sat behind a little desk, and the class went on without paying any attention to me.

As the class was about to be dismissed, the teacher said, "Will some boy volunteer to take Bernard home and call for him in the morning until he knows his way to and from school?" The whole class volunteered. She picked a kind, generous boy, Clarence Housman, who acted as my guide, and who, 20 years later, became my partner.

As the days wore on, all the fears engendered by a great city, which had horse cars and rumbling elevated trains and great noises, disappeared.

I did not realize then that this teacher, Katherine Devereux Blake, was smoothing my way, encouraging me in my studies, and holding up to me the precepts which I should follow. She stimulated her pupils to do their best work and showed them the joy of striving and the joy of recognized personal accomplishment.

It is not given to every teacher to carry her work into so-called high places. But all teachers have the opportunity to formulate character, stimulate ambitions and hopes, and help the next generation to come closer to their own best selves.

Miss Blake always told us, "Do the best you can. When you have done that, you have equaled the efforts or results accomplished by any other boy."

It is the teachers, and especially those who deal with the very young, who have made the character and conscience of America what it is today. It is they who will continue to implant ethics, decency, character, and a determination to do the very best. They have made America what it is and must continue to be.

Teachers and nurses are the ones who do most for society and are least recognized for what they contribute. "A teacher affects eternity; he can never tell where his influence stops."

I have in my hand a book. It has been a kind of bible to me. It is a book given to me 70 years ago by my beloved teacher, Katherine Devereux Blake. In it, she inscribed these words, "Awarded to Bernard Baruch for gentlemanly deportment and general excellence."

That was the first prize I ever received. Never have I received another so dear to me.

How could anyone put in so few words what would give to the one who received it more inspiration and courage than "For gentlemanly deportment and general excellence"? If one would strive to deserve that award, he would lead a useful life that would end in happiness to him and to all.

Many, many times have I taken that book, which I have treasured all these 70 years, and read that inscription. It is a volume containing *Oliver Twist* and *Great Expectations* by Charles Dickens.

I did not see as much of my beloved teacher as I would have liked, or should have done. We never enjoy sufficiently or show proper devotion to those who influence our lives the most. We seem to take them for granted and know that no matter what we do or do not do, their loving care and loyalty will persist thru all the years.

Every now and then when I would visit Miss Blake, she would always say, "And now, Bernard, I know you have been a good boy." That meant that she expected me to carry on with "gentlemanly deportment and general excellence." I couldn't disappoint her.

I wish I could adequately express my thanks and appreciation to that beautiful character. I know what she has done for me and the countless thousands whose lives she touched. And if those of us who have benefited by this close contact with her have helped our fellow men in any way it is due to a large extent to our great teacher, Katherine Devereux Blake.

When we go to the Great Beyond, I hope it will be my good fortune to go where Miss Blake will meet me and lead me to my seat, as she did so many years ago.

Louise Sharp [142] has done a masterful job of assembling statements made by 120 outstanding contemporary men and women in which they describe how teachers influence the lives of others. Take a few minutes and read what they have to say.

A frail young teacher from England, named Anna, influenced the future of Thailand [84]. As a result of having lived in Thailand for a period of three years, the author can testify that the contributions of Anna to that country were quite real. In ways sometimes unknown to them, teachers, through the lives of those they teach, do much to determine the course of civilization.

The teacher has a definite opportunity to be of help to parents. Educators increasingly realize that the education of children is a joint responsibility, to be shared by both the home and the school. Most parents are anxious to receive information, helpful suggestions, and assistance from teachers concerning the effective education of their children. It is the professional obligation of the teacher to give parents this service. There will be some parents, however, who will show more interest in the yield of certain grain crops, or the social life of the country club, or the latest style of clothes and models of cars than in the education of their children. At this point the teacher is challenged to broaden the values held by such parents.

The school occupies a unique position—to lead the way in improving life in a community. It is the teacher's business to see that the school does exert constructive influences in the community, and to become an active agent in fulfilling this function. The teacher has an excellent opportunity to extend his interests and efforts beyond the classroom; many types of organizations seek his services. Some of these organizations will have as their primary function the improvement of life in the community, whereas others will be seeking to promote certain vested selfish interests. The teacher has the responsibility of deciding upon the groups with which he will align his efforts and abilities. As you continue to read about the function of the school in a democratic society, you will sense almost limitless opportunities for a teacher to be of service. The extent to which you realize these opportunities depends largely upon your desire, insight, ability, and wise use of energies in the time that is available.

Molding Behavior. You perhaps have watched a potter artistically molding raw clay into a beautiful object. As a teacher, you are a potential artist, but you will deal with animate objects. You may have the opportunity of molding some of the greatest masterpieces of mankind. As you endeavor to shape the behavior patterns of boys and girls, you may feel that some of your time and effort is ineffective and wasted. Michelangelo, when he was criticized for wasting so much marble as he carved a statue, gave the following reply: "Yes, the marble is wasted, but the statue grows." Your statue, in the life of every child, is growing as you mold those behavior patterns that will produce happy, effective, democratic citizens.

Aristotle stated that, "No man goes about a more godly business than he who is concerned with the right upbringing of his own and other people's children." Daniel Webster once wrote these lines: "If we work upon marble, it will perish. If we work upon brass, time will efface it. If we rear temples, they will crumble to dust. But if we work upon men's immortal minds, if we imbue them with principles—we engrave on these tablets something which no time can efface, and which will brighten and heighten to all eternity."

As you face the responsibility that will rest in your hands, think and plan what you will teach your pupils as well as the manner in which you will teach them. Remember always that you are building future behavior patterns, and that you need a clear concept of the patterns desired in our society. If the foundation of good habits is well established, the structure should withstand the storms and stresses of the future. As one Biblical proverb reads: "Train a child in the way he should go, and when he is old he will not depart from it."

Most people wish that they could retain to some degree the wholesome, sparkling, buoyant spirit of youth. With due respect to other professions, the doctor, lawyer, and nurse deal primarily with individuals who are ill, older, depressed, and burdened with problems and difficulties. Of course, youth has some problems and illnesses with which the teacher is concerned; but there is a decided difference between youth and older people in terms of mental outlook upon life. Young people are so full of pep and vigor that they challenge you in every field of human emotions. You laugh with them, study with them, and play with them day after day and year after year. They seek to fill your life so full of their trust, joy, and respect that it is difficult for a teacher to become mentally old.

Intellectual Stimulation. Teaching places a high premium upon intellectual stimulation. With few exceptions, it is the teacher's fault if he finds his work to be dull, drab, and monotonous. The curiosity of his pupils is a constant prod to further intellectual activity. As a youngster's interests develop, his questions and problems are so varied that a teacher is challenged to explore many new areas of learning and relationships. The study of human nature, child growth and development, and the learning process never cease to be an intellectual growing edge for the effective teacher. New findings and insights, reported in education research periodicals, provide further sources of stimulation to the teacher.

The teacher is not expected to be a walking encyclopedia of knowledge, but a guide who leads the pupils into wider areas of learning. A guide must have a broad background which continues to be enriched, and from which new and creative responses arise to the needs of pupils.

State and local boards of education continue to demand higher levels of preparation for teachers. No longer is it possible in many states to rest upon the laurels of a bachelor's degree. It is reasonable to believe that five years of initial preparation will be, in the not too distant future, a common requirement for teaching. The salary schedules of many school systems give definite recognition of, and incentive for, further intellectual pursuit by teachers.

Many school administrators feel that a program of in-service education of their teachers is a most essential part of the total school program. These programs are designed to keep teachers intellectually alive and alert, so that the instruction of students will be continuously improved. The nature of in-service education will be discussed in greater detail later.

A premium also is placed upon understanding human nature, as mentioned previously. This is an open field of activity. It has no limitations,

The enthusiasm and vigor of youth is a constant challenge and source of stimulation for a teacher. *(Photograph from Standard Oil Company of New Jersey.)*

for as soon as you have reached one plateau of understanding, another appears before you. Each child, each parent, and each community member has a unique personality and must be dealt with as an individual. To meet the interests and needs of these various individuals is a never-ending source of excitement.

Home and Family. Many of you are looking forward to the establishment of a home and the rearing of children. You will want this home to be a happy and wholesome one, and you will try to do the best job possible in helping your children grow into healthy, effective citizens. These factors are to be considered in planning a career.

The preparation for teaching should increase greatly your chances of realizing fully the above goals. Teaching places a high premium upon effective human relations. If one is skilled in understanding and working with others, his chances of realizing a healthy, happy home life will be good. Not only should the husband-and-wife relationship be of a more wholesome nature because of teaching experience but also their circle of friends should be greater.

The teacher is in a position to study the significance of good home life, through the behavior of children. Through his continuous association with boys and girls, the teacher can develop insight into their interests, needs, wants, and problems. He sees the influence of various types of home conditions on the growth and development of children. He senses the importance of good home-school relationships. Through these

In what ways may preparation for teaching increase your chances for a happy and wholesome family life?
(*Photograph by Carl Purcell, National Education Association.*)

understandings, insights, and experiences, the teacher should be an exemplary parent.

A woman teacher's many community contacts tend to increase her opportunities for marriage. In spite of the stereotyped and erroneous notion that a young lady who enters the teaching profession is doomed to become an old maid, Dr. James F. Bender, director of the National Institute of Human Relations, states that school teachers are the top candidates for wives, and lists the following 10 reasons to justify the statement [14:430]:

1. They are above average in health, beauty, and intelligence.
2. They have a deep affection for children.
3. They are eager to marry and wish to bear two or more children.
4. They have well-protected jobs, safe during a recession.
5. They have nice voices and don't talk too much.
6. Their regular hours and frequent vacations permit them to be good housewives.
7. Their studious habits and common sense are invaluable to young men starting in business or a profession.
8. Their high ideals make them lovable, tender, sympathetic, and understanding beyond the average.
9. They are established in jobs and ready for marriage at the golden age for it—22 to 25 years.
10. Divorce is rare among teachers.

Endicott, Director of Placement at Northwestern University, studied the alumni data at Northwestern and found that the school of education graduates were out-marrying graduates of the liberal arts school. Al-

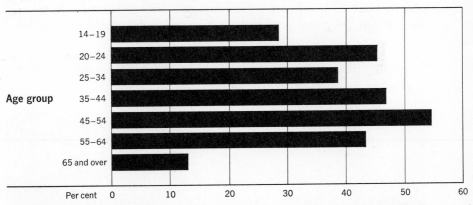

Figure 12. Per cent of women in each age group who will be in the labor force in 1970. What modifications should be made in the public school education of girls? What obligations do public schools have to adult women? (*Source:* U.S. Department of Labor.)

though the combining of two careers means added responsibilities, it is possible, by careful planning, to be a very successful teacher as well as wife.

There are a number of other reasons why a career in teaching combines with marriage more satisfactorily than with most careers. (1) The wife can follow her husband to whatever community his work takes him—a small town or a large city, near to home or far away—and usually she can secure a teaching position. (2) It is possible to keep abreast of current thought and happenings in the profession during the time the children are small, when the wife may not care to hold a position. (3) A teacher can reenter the profession readily. She may choose to do so on only a half-day basis. In view of the current teacher shortage, it is probable that the number of half-day positions will increase. (4) The profession is valuable in bringing up one's own family. For example, the training received in child or adolescent psychology certainly should help a teacher in guiding children through various stages of their development.

Opportunities During Vacation Periods.   In contrast with people in other full-time occupations, teachers have a considerable amount of free time over which they exercise control. During the school year, the fairly liberal Christmas and Easter vacations provide opportunity for rest and recreational activities.

The teaching profession is also unique among careers in the amount of vacation provided during the summer months. Although there are some trends toward extending the length of the teacher's work year, you may look forward to having from two to three months of free time each year. You may see this long period of time as an opportunity to broaden yourself culturally through extended travel, reading, research, or advanced study. You may wish to supplement your teaching salary and at the same time improve your effectiveness as a teacher. The science teacher may secure work in a research laboratory; the art teacher may do interior decorating; the commercial teacher may seek employment in some busi-

A breadth of experience and a greater depth of understanding are the rewards for many teachers who travel during the summer months for their personal and professional enrichment. (*Photograph from the Division of Travel Service, National Education Association.*)

ness office; the elementary teacher may wish to be a camp counselor or a playground supervisor. The variety of activities that will prove profitable and professionally beneficial is great.

Teachers frequently find that their jobs provide opportunities to engage in creative work, especially during the long summer vacations. Many teachers have written short stories, poems, novels, and plays; painted pictures; composed symphonies; or made other artistic contributions of value. Probably many chose teaching as a career because it stimulated creative imagination and offered long vacations in which to indulge this imagination.

SUMMARY

In the first part of this chapter you doubtless sensed the basic role that education has played in the growth and development of our nation. More than ever before in the history of mankind, progress in the welfare as well as the security of our nation is, to a great extent, dependent upon how well our schools fulfill their role. Stated differently, the need for quality education has never been greater, and, in the years to come, the need will increase still more. This, therefore, constitutes one of the important reasons for becoming a teacher.

In the second part of the chapter several other reasons for teaching were indicated. Perhaps one of the most important of these is the satisfaction gained from being of service to others; seeing youth change, grow, develop, and become successful. Their success, in a sense, is an extension of the teacher's success. Through helping students live fuller and more satisfying lives, the teacher gains a value that is not always present in some of the other professions.

All of the values inherent in a teaching career are related. The extent to which these values are gained is dependent largely upon the attitude and the planned vigor with which you approach the task.

Obviously the educator's life is no Utopia. There are headaches, disappointments, and problems, as in any occupation. It is impossible to deal with the realities of life, the development and growth of youth, and the adjustment problems of mankind and have all of life be "sweetness and light."

A career in education offers a maximum challenge to anyone who finds in it a life work. In the educator's hands rests the primary responsibility for assisting each individual to develop to his maximum capacity for democratic living. The teacher is a molder of American minds; he is a builder of a better tomorrow.

QUESTIONS FOR YOUR CONSIDERATION

1. What features of the American school system have especially contributed to the phenomenal growth and success of America?

2. How will you as a teacher seek to contribute to the security of our nation?

3. Did you ever experience any school practices and procedures that showed a lack of respect for the dignity and worth of the individual? If so, how will you attempt to avoid the use of such practices and procedures?

4. Are there any evidences that we are losing some of the ideals that have made this country great? If so, what are they, and how will you attempt to inculcate these ideals into the minds of your pupils?

5. Does the concept of equal educational opportunity mean that all pupils receive the same kind and amount of education?

6. What basic differences in the aims of education exist between Russia and the United States? How does the work of teachers in these two countries differ?

7. You are aware of the need for more money for schools and colleges in the United States. Should the United States continue to give financial aid for educational purposes to other nations?

8. What did John W. Gardner mean by his statement that: "At this moment in history, free institutions are on trial?" What evidences would support (or not support) such a statement?

9. In an age of advancing technology, upon what bases can you defend a program of general education as a part of your college education?

10. Is it the duty of the teacher to tell boys and girls what they should believe? How will you attempt to mold the minds of Americans?

11. Can you justify free public education in a democracy? Is it a luxury or a necessity?

12. How can we justify spending so much effort and money in trying to educate all children when future progress will depend so much upon the contributions of academically talented pupils?

ACTIVITIES FOR YOU TO PURSUE

1. Read Louise Sharp's book, *Why Teach?* and analyze the influences that teachers exert upon the lives of others.

2. If you are undecided as to your career, list all possible values inherent in each occupation you are considering. Compare and contrast the listing with your life values.

3. Talk with teachers whom you admire regarding the values they see in teaching.

4. Read one or more of the many fictional and biographical books related to teachers or teaching. Discuss with your classmates the values of teaching revealed in each book you read.

5. Consider some of the teachers for whom you have the least admiration. No doubt they will be cross, narrow-minded, and unsympathetic. Attempt to analyze and list the things they seem to value in life as well as the values they see in teaching.

6. List what you consider to be the major challenges that teaching holds for you. Discuss these challenges with some of your former public school teachers, with your college teachers, or with other students who plan to teach, to see whether they share your challenges.

7. Discuss with your friends and fellow classmates the prestige of the typical teacher today in comparison with the prestige of the typical member of other professions. How do you account for any differences that exist?

8. List what you consider to be the chief disadvantages of teaching as a career. Formulate plans for avoiding these difficulties.

OTHER SOURCES OF IDEAS AND INFORMATION FOR CHAPTER 1

● **SUGGESTED READINGS**

Bruner, Jerome S.: *The Process of Education,* Harvard University Press, Cambridge, Mass., 1961. Presents some very interesting and challenging views on education resulting from a conference attended by leading scholars and educators.

Callahan, Raymond E.: *An Introduction to Education in American Society,* 2d ed., Alfred A. Knopf, Inc., New York, 1960. Chapters 1 and 2 discuss the challenge which teachers face and the potential of education.

Education for Freedom and World Understanding, U.S. Office of Education Bulletin OE 10016, 1962. A report of the working committees of the conference on Ideals of American Freedom and the International Dimensions of Education which was held in Washington, March 26–28, 1962.

Fischer, John H.: "Why Teach?" *National Education Association Journal,* vol. 51, no. 4, p. 31, National Education Association, Washington, April, 1962. Discusses the needs, demands, and rewards of teaching.

Fletcher, C. Scott (ed.): *Education: The Challenge Ahead,* W. W. Norton Company, Inc., New York, 1962. Emphasizes the leadership role which especially institutions of higher learning should play in our society and the free world.

Invitation to Teaching, National Education Association, Washington, 1960. A very brief statement of challenges and opportunities in the teaching profession.

Neff, Kenneth L.: *Education and the Development of Human Technology,* Bulletin 1962, no. 20, U.S. Office of Education, 1962. Discusses the use of planned educational growth to promote economic development.

The President's Commission on National Goals: *Goals for Americans,* Prentice-Hall, Inc., Englewood Cliffs, N.J., 1961. Chapters 1, 2, and 3 deal with American fundamentals and national goals in education.

The Pursuit of Excellence: Education and the Future of America, Panel Report V of the Special Studies Project, America at Mid-Century Series, Doubleday & Company, Inc., Garden City, N.Y., 1958. Indicates the role of education in furthering the democratic values of freedom and dignity of the individual.

Ragan, William B.: *Teaching America's Children,* Holt, Rinehart and Winston, Inc., New York, 1961. Chapter 1 indicates what teaching is like, and points out some challenging aspects of teaching.

Schultz, Theodore W.: "Education and Economic Growth," in Nelson B. Henry (ed.), *Social Forces Influencing American Education,* The Sixtieth Yearbook of the National Society for the Study of Education, Part II, University of Chicago Press, Chicago, Ill., 1961, pp. 46–88. Presents an excellent discussion on the relationship of education to economic growth.

Sharp, D. Louise (ed.): *Why Teach?,* Holt, Rinehart and Winston, Inc., New York, 1957. Presents many statements of prominent people concerning teachers.

Silberman, Charles E.: "The Remaking of American Education," *Fortune,* April, 1961, pp. 125–130, 197, 198, 201. Indicates a number of very interesting new developments in schools throughout the nation.

• SUGGESTED FILMS, FILMSTRIPS, AND RECORDINGS

Films (16 mm)

And Gladly Teach (National Education Association, 28 min, color). Discusses teachers and "the company they keep." It points out the satisfactions and opportunities in teaching.

Appointment with Youth (McGraw-Hill, 27 min). Presents a high school teacher recalling college days and earlier experiences as a teacher as he seeks answers to the question, "Is teaching a good profession?" Concludes that teaching gives deep personal satisfaction of doing a good job and that it is a good profession which needs good teachers.

Assignment: Tomorrow (National Education Association, 32 min). Deals with the vital role of the schoolteacher in the life of our country. Stresses the importance of the teacher's work in the classroom, the place of teachers as citizens in the community, and their contributions as members of professional organizations.

Born Equal (Australian Instructional Films, 11 min). Uses specific examples to interpret the Declaration of Human Rights as it emerges out of the United Nations Charter. Stresses the acceptance of individual responsibilities as well as rights, and emphasizes the necessity of nations' supporting the provisions of the Declaration.

Education Is Good Business (State University of Iowa, 11 min, color). Emphasizes the direct relationship between a town's prosperity and the quality of its educational system by contrasting communities and quoting statistics from the U.S. Chamber of Commerce. Also compares income levels and educational standards of various countries.

Our Teacher, Mary Dean (Firth Films, 22 min, color). Depicts the satisfactions a teacher finds in her work and in her life outside the school.

Secure the Blessings (National Education Association, 25 min). Discusses the role of education in the United States as it prepares people to use the democratic method of solving problems. Shows five adults who are trying to solve their various problems in human relations objectively, and says that it was in school that these individuals learned to make decisions.

Teaching (Carl F. Mahnke Productions, 10 min). Begins by discussing such attractive features of teaching as contact with young people, long summer vacations, relative economic security through tenure laws and contract, a pension, and stimulus to continual self-improvement; outlines personal and professional qualifications. Concludes with suggestions on getting into the field and a discussion of the responsibilities and opportunities of teaching.

Filmstrips

Challenge to American Education (New York Times, 57 fr.). Evaluates the educational process in the United States after the explosive effects of the sputniks; compares United States and Soviet systems; presents new vistas in shaping youth training and careers.

Directions for the Future   (National Education Association, 115 fr., color). Presents backgrounds in such fields as technological development, urbanization, population growth, which should be considered in planning instructional programs in the elementary school.

Education in a Democracy   (Curriculum Films Inc., 26 fr., color). The meaning of democratic education—its importance in maintaining an enlightened citizenry, availability to all, and opportunities it affords for an unhampered pursuit of knowledge.

Let's Take a Look at Teaching   (Wayne University, 50 fr.). Gives an overview of the teaching profession and what it has to offer in terms of salary, tenure, working conditions, opportunities for travel, and individual interests. Pictures a typical school day showing the varied demands on the teacher, and her responsibilities.

Recordings

Education, the Foundation of Business   (Educational Recording Service, 33⅓ rpm). Willis A. Sutton, former superintendent of schools of Atlanta, Georgia, and past president of the NEA, indicates how education affects the economic life of a community.

A Forward Look for the Teaching Profession   (Educational Recording Service, 33⅓ rpm). W. S. Elsbree, professor of education, Teachers College, Columbia University, presents a challenge to anyone planning to teach.

• FIGURE CREDITS

Figure 1.   (*Source:* "Schools and Scholarship in Demand," *Research Bulletin,* vol. 37, no. 3, p. 76, National Education Association, Research Division, Washington, October, 1959.)

Figure 2.   (*Source:* Harrison Brown and E. K. Fedorov, "Too Many People in the World?" *Saturday Review* Feb. 17, 1962, p. 18.)

Figure 3.   (*Source: Education: An Investment in People,* U.S. Chamber of Commerce, Education Department, 1955, p. 11. From: Elmo Roper, *Political Activity of American Citizens.*)

Figure 4.   (*Source: Manpower: Challenge of the 1960's,* U.S. Department of Labor, 1961, p. 3.)

Figure 5.   (*Source: An Act for International Development: A Program for the Decade of Development,* Department of State Publication 7205, General Foreign Policy Series 169, Office of Public Services, Bureau of Public Affairs, Washington, 1961, p. 46.)

Figure 6.   (*Source: An Act for International Development: A Program for the Decade of Development,* Department of State Publication 7205, General Foreign Policy Series 169, Office of Public Services, Bureau of Public Affairs, Washington, 1961, p. 174.)

Figure 7.   (*Source: An Act for International Development: A Program for the Decade of Development,* Department of State Publication 7205, General Foreign Policy Series 169, Office of Public Services, Bureau of Public Affairs, Washington, 1961, p. 6.)

Figure 8.   (*Source:* Data from "Education and Lifetime Earnings," *Research Bulletin,* vol. 39 no. 2, p. 59, National Education Association, Research Division, Washington, May, 1961.)

Figure 9.   (*Source: Manpower: Challenge of the 1960's,* U.S. Department of Labor, 1961, p. 17.)

Figure 10.   (*Source:* "Projections of Educational Attainment in the United States: 1960 to 1980," *Current Population Reports, Series* P-20, no. 91, p. 2, U.S. Department of Commerce, Bureau of the Census, Jan. 12, 1959.)

Figure 11.   (*Source:* "More Responsibility for Workers in the 1960's," *Research Bulletin,* vol. 39, no. 3, p. 91, National Education Association, Research Division, Washington, October, 1961.)

Figure 12.   (*Source: Manpower: Challenge of the 1960's,* U.S. Department of Labor, 1961, p. 7.)

I

ASPECTS OF PLANNING

Part I of this book is concerned with the nature and process of life planning in an increasingly complex and interdependent society, not only as it relates to you personally but also as it pertains to the lives of those whom you may teach. While emphasis is placed upon planning a career in teaching, it is to be recognized that this aspect of planning is only a phase of the total process of life planning.

The material in Part I is organized to assist you in understanding the process of planning your career and in going through the basic steps that are involved. As a background for this process, you noted in the preceding chapter the crucial importance of education in the transmission, preservation, and progressive improvement of our American society. Since the teacher occupies a most strategic position in this process, the careful and comprehensive planning of a career in teaching is of the utmost urgency. Other values in teaching also were discussed briefly.

In Chapter 2 you will note a number of techniques and procedures that should help you in planning your career in the teaching profession. Chapter 3 suggests ways in which you may identify and build up your strengths and overcome your personal and professional weaknesses as you attempt to fulfill the many essentials for a happy and successful career. Chapter 4 is concerned with certification requirements for entering the profession and with resources and procedures for continuing your professional growth after graduation. In Chapter 5 you will note the wide range of opportunities that a career in education provides.

The remaining parts, and their respective chapters, in this book are designed to build added meaning into the content of Part I. As you proceed through the book, refer to Part I from time to time in order to maximize the effectiveness of formulating your plans.

2
PLANNING YOUR CAREER IN TEACHING

The amount of success and happiness you experience in teaching will depend to a great extent upon how dedicated you become and how thoroughly you prepare for the job. Through careful planning while you are in college, you can lay the cornerstone that will lead to a meaningful and satisfying professional career.

Unfortunately, many students do not give careful consideration to their decision to become teachers, or to the basic attributes required for successful teaching, or to the means by which they can develop into the most competent teachers possible, or to the specific type of position for which they wish to prepare. When they become juniors or seniors, they often wish to modify their plans for teaching. Usually these students find that they must take extra courses, postpone the date of their graduation, and plan courses in terms of what they have already taken rather than of what they *should* have taken.

Many students feel that once they have decided upon a teaching career, there is little need for further planning. Planning to them is confined largely to such problems as passing the required number of courses for certification, earning enough money to stay in college, and getting a job upon graduation. They fail to see that planning a career in education is a phase of life planning, that fundamental values in life are involved, that career plans are integrally related to home life and citizenship, that the completion of collegiate professional training is only an initial phase

As with any major objective in life, comprehensive planning is essential in order to realize it. How effective are you in your personal planning? (*Photograph Courtesy of Post-Dispatch Pictures, from Black Star.*)

in the professional life of an educator, that the successful completion of professional courses does not ensure professional success regardless of the quality of the courses, or that the full realization of values inherent in a teaching career depends largely upon the extent to which the individual attempts to realize those values. After graduation some of these students find that they are ill-suited for teaching and are miserable in their work. Society, likewise, suffers from their dissatisfactions and inadequacies.

The Nature of Career Planning. Planning is essentially a continuous life process in which action is directed by an individual's critically reasoned values and goals. It involves the constant weighing of these values and goals. The planner identifies courses of action as well as possible alternative courses of action for reaching these goals, and selects those that seem most promising. He searches for all possible help, both in himself and in the environment, and selects those which seem to be most desirable. He uses these resources as he proceeds step by step toward his goal. He carefully appraises the progress he makes and prepares to meet difficulties which are likely to occur in the course of pursuing his planned objective. In brief, he has a clear idea of *what* he wants, *why* he wants it, and *how* he is to achieve it.

All plans obviously are tentative in nature. In fact, the very essence of planning is one of continuous change, modification, and adaptation. You can, therefore, expect many of the details of your master plan or blueprint to change as the years pass. But your master plan gives direction to your professional growth. The details enable you to expend energy efficiently and to gain greater realization of your goals in life.

Some Group Aspects of Planning. Practically all personal problems in a complex society are related to other people. Furthermore, in planning for teaching you face the need for developing a high degree of skill in group planning, since a major concern of the school today is to assist boys and girls in gaining proficiency in the solution of group as well as individual problems. Group planning and action, with its consequent outcome, is the epitome of a democratic society.

Much value is to be gained from the group aspects of career planning. Through this procedure you will find what kinds of ideas other prospective teachers hold. You will be able to make better use of resources as a result of the sharing that takes place in a group. The quality of thinking probably will be higher than when you plan alone. The exchange of ideas is unlike the exchange of money, for each idea presented tends to set off a chain of other ideas for each group member. If you give your friend an idea and he gives you an idea, both of you have two ideas; but if you give your friend a dollar and he gives you a dollar, each has only one dollar. Furthermore, group planning brings about a feeling of

The exchange of facts, opinions, and plans with others should add breadth and depth to your plans for teaching.
(*From Black Star, photograph by Dick Greening.*)

closeness and an interest in and concern for the other members of the group, by means of which human relationships are improved. Skill in the democratic process is gained, and competence in guiding the growth of others toward more effective democratic living is enhanced.

SUGGESTED STEPS IN PLANNING YOUR CAREER IN EDUCATION

The broad outline of steps to be followed in planning your career in education is no different from that to be followed in planning for any career. Consequently, not all of your efforts will be lost if, after thoroughly exploring teaching as a profession, you come to the thoughtful conclusion that this is not the life work for which you are best suited. Your efforts will make it easier for you to plan in terms of another occupational objective.

The suggested steps in planning are not infallible, but they will at least allow you to marshal your resources in orderly fashion and to avoid undue or worthless labor. At the same time, you may wish to deviate to some extent from the steps suggested, as you work out the details of your procedure. What seems logical to one may not seem logical to another, and you should expect to revise and modify these steps as you see fit.

Importance of Values and Goals in Career Planning. An individual normally seeks to do the things that seem important to him. In other words, the things he values provide the foundation for his goals. It is important, therefore, that an individual's vocational goals be consistent with what he desires, strives for, and approves in life. For example, an outdoor career is advisable for the person who values nature above the man-made city environment; a financially fruitful life work for the person who values most the things which money will buy; a working environment productive in social welfare for the one man-made city environment; a financially fruitful life work for the person who values service to humanity above other things in life. On the other hand, if a person's attention is directed toward goals not of his own choosing, or goals embodying values which may be in conflict with other values that rank higher in his thinking, then his effort to reach them probably will not persist in the face of the more significant values.

Values are the intangible bases for behavior. They constitute the foundation for the things we cherish in life. They may be expressed in such terms as freedom, equality, individualism, dignity of man, self-respect, democracy, cooperativeness, service to mankind, the golden rule, prestige, trustworthiness, dependability, thrift, and open-mindedness. If a man values honor, for example, he establishes goals of conduct which allow expression of that value. His personal goals become manifestations of the ideals he holds to be important.

Values are acquired. They are cultural—learned through experience [138:71].

Man's behavior is governed by the values he has come to accept during the years of cumulative experiences that make up his lifetime. What he thinks, what he looks upon as "good," and what he does are controlled and restricted by the chains forged by his values: uplifting or debasing, humane or bestial—whatever his experience has made them.

Since the life experiences of no two individuals are the same, it is understandable that one man's values are not the same as another's in every detail. On the other hand, every society has certain values which characterize it, and the individuals who have grown up in that society tend to hold those values in common. In America, respect for the uniqueness and worth of the individual, freedom, and equality are examples of common basic values.

Since the school is concerned with the development, strengthening, and transmission of values considered to be desirable in this society, it is important for you, as a future teacher, to have a clear and functional understanding of them.

Since each person develops his own values, some of his values will be more important to him than others. In fact, they will range from mild preferences to intense convictions. You can determine what an individual values most in life by observing the decisions or choices he makes. As you study others, you sense that many people never consciously examine their basic values or test the internal consistency of them. When you see this, you recognize that in planning your career you need first to think seriously about what seems to be of most importance to you in life. You then test these values for internal consistency. Since the teacher as a person is the most important single factor in the classroom, it is extremely important for him to have a clearly reasoned and consistent set of values which are in harmony with the tenets of a democratic society.

It is relatively easy for you to identify a few of your outstanding values, such as service to mankind, and to use them as criteria for testing your career choice. It is more difficult to analyze all of your values in great

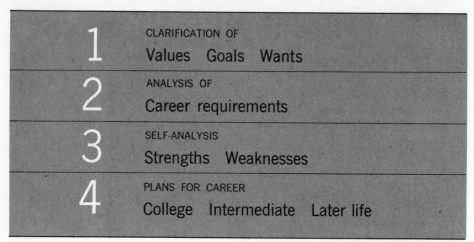

Figure 13. Major steps involved in planning a career.

detail and to derive a whole pattern of criteria for testing teaching as a career. But if you construct this pattern as completely as you can, you will be much more certain of your decision.

Each occupation has its unique pattern of inherent values that may be pursued by an individual who engages in that occupation. In the latter half of Chapter 1, you examined some of these values. If you discover that teaching fails to meet a significant number of the tests you have set up, you have your warnings that conflict between your life work and your personal values is likely and that hopes of achieving your real goals through this career are weak.

In summarizing the steps in planning that have been indicated thus far, emphasis is placed upon the desirability of your thinking long and hard about the following questions:

1. What do I value in life?
2. Why are these my values?
3. Are these values desirable?
4. Are these values internally consistent?
5. What life goals emerge from my values?
6. Can I best realize my life goals through a career in education?

As soon as you have answered the above questions to your satisfaction, you are ready to move to the second major step in career planning.

Influence of Requirements upon Planning for Teaching. In the previous discussion, relatively little attention was given to teaching, except to point out that a career in education should be consistent with your values and goals. Any career has certain requirements that must be met regardless of your values and goals. Each career carries its own peculiar set of requirements for success. For example, a career in professional baseball requires physical fitness and skill. A career in the medical or the legal profession requires preparation in the things which make it a profession.

A career in religion requires faith. A career as a winetaster requires a discriminating palate. We should not conclude, however, that physical fitness and skill are all the requirements for a career in professional baseball, or that a discriminating palate is the sole requisite of winetasting.

Perhaps no career imposes more varied requirements on the successful worker than does teaching. Although general competency as a citizen seems to include most of the requirements for success in many careers, it is only the first requisite in teaching. Above and beyond this requirement lie the many aspects of special expertness demanded of the teacher. The basic concern at this point is to emphasize the need for you to make an analysis of the requirements which a career as a teacher imposes. Your analysis should consist of something more than a mere stocktaking of your present qualifications. However, as has been indicated, this stocktaking is a necessary step. If the analysis of all your qualifications reveals certain deficiencies which you cannot or do not wish to remove, you again have warning of trouble ahead. Likewise, revelation of unusual strengths in this analysis should bear strong implication for your future, and your plans in the field of education should involve use of these special strengths.

Your understanding of the competencies for teaching should be increased and broadened through the reading of subsequent sections of this book, especially Chapter 3. Certification requirements prescribed by the respective states are discussed in Chapter 4. In Chapter 6 you will receive a rather clear indication of what will be required of you in order to perform adequately the many duties expected of teachers. Chapters 7, 12, 13, and 14 will also provide a rather comprehensive listing of unique skills, information, and artistry that a teacher needs in order to fulfill the broad functions of education in a democratic society.

Influence of Other Factors upon Planning for Teaching. Many other factors need to be taken into consideration in order to plan a career in education wisely. Various sections of this book are designed to help you in this regard. For example, you owe yourself a searching analysis of the various economic aspects that may be involved, such as salary, sick leave, retirement, tenure (Chapters 9 and 10). Furthermore, a career in education will give a wider range to your interests and abilities than will many other occupations. Should you be a nursery or kindergarten teacher? Would you like teaching in the elementary school? Would you enjoy teaching in the junior high school? Would you be interested in high school teaching? Could you teach on the college level? Should you do specialized teaching, i.e., teaching the gifted, the physically handicapped, the mentally retarded, or the emotionally disturbed? For what advancement opportunities should you plan? Explore this vast range of opportunities so that your abilities and interests may best be utilized and your success and happiness in the profession may be proportionately increased (Chapter 5).

To plan your career competently, learn about the system in which you will be working—how the schools developed (Chapter 11), how they are organized (Chapter 16) and financed (Chapter 17), what changes may be expected during the time you will be associated actively with them, what crucial problems schools are faced with today (Chapter 15), and how and to what extent you may contribute to the solution of these problems. As you continue your reading and planning, you will discover other factors which should be investigated and evaluated.

Importance of Removing Deficiencies and Capitalizing on Strengths.

Career planning really becomes alive when you actively formulate steps for overcoming deficiencies and building up strengths. Your strengths are likely to persist and increase if you make intelligent use of them; your deficiencies may be due only to your present lack of preparation and experience. Therefore, extend your self-analysis to considering action which will make use of strengths and remedy weaknesses. Your academic preparation in subject fields, for example, is something which you may not yet have completed. Make a reasonably accurate estimate of both the time and the effort needed to eliminate this deficiency. In the same manner, estimate your success in removing other academic deficiencies or in appraising your chances of capitalizing on your strengths.

As you continue to plan you may discover certain personal weaknesses which you are unable to remove through course work. Since teaching is so highly a job of "human engineering," it is extremely important that you formulate plans for removing any deficiencies you may discover.

Importance of Self-appraisal in Planning for Teaching.

Cervantes advised, "Make it thy business to know thyself, which is the most difficult lesson in the world." His advice is certainly appropriate for anyone engaged in the process of planning a career. Understanding yourself is essential for understanding others. Two psychologists report the following about the relationship of self-understanding to understanding of others [77:6]:

> What the teacher sees in the student, the way he feels about him, and what he derives from his dealings with him will be influenced not only by the kind of person the student is but also the kind of person the teacher is and by the kind of situation that is created when the two are together. To the extent that the student's behavior, as seen by the instructor, reflects the instructor's own perceptions and attitudes, he will be unable to understand the student unless he understands himself. Similarly, the way in which the instructor interprets or evaluates a student's attitudes or conduct will be influenced by his own values, likes, and dislikes. The greater this influence is, the more the instructor's perception of his student will be a reflection of himself rather than an objective, or unbiased, reaction. Therefore, it is essential for the instructor to take stock of his own involvement and, as far as possible, make allowance for it.

You may recall teachers who readily took offense to well-meant suggestions; teachers who were highly authoritarian in behavior and assumed that students were disobedient if they voiced any disagreements; teachers who were defensive in their opinions and interpreted questions as forms of attack. Perhaps you will be able to recall other teachers and friends whose judgments reflected more the kinds of persons they were than the persons being judged.

Jersild and Associates feel that understanding oneself and others involves more than an intellectual process [77:9]:

> One can master the facts, principles, and laws contained in a hundred books on psychology and still understand neither oneself nor others. Self-understanding requires integrity rather than mere cleverness. It involves emotion. To know oneself, one must be able to feel as well as think. One must be able to recognize feelings, face them, and deal with them in constructive ways; and this is something quite different from reading or talking about them with detachment.

You may conclude, therefore, that how you view yourself—your self-image or self-concept—will have an important bearing upon your success as a teacher. It is extremely important for you, as a prospective teacher, to study yourself frankly and honestly in an attempt to discover any weaknesses that might greatly handicap your future success and happiness. When these weaknesses have been identified, positive plans may be formulated in order to overcome them.

Further Suggested Procedures for Planning Your Career. In order to do a really effective job in planning for teaching, you will need to answer to your own satisfaction a number of questions and engage in certain activities. The following five major courses of action should help you in rounding out your plans in a concrete, workable manner.

Putting your plans on paper. Many people have found that the act of writing out their plans is in itself of great help to them. The necessary labor involved in selecting and weaving in the various ideas causes planners to be more critical and objective. This procedure—often called "writing the planning paper"—has been used in colleges and universities for a number of years with considerable evidence of worthwhile results.

Many students experience difficulty in getting started in the writing of their plans. This is understandable in view of the fact that planning is, or at least should be, the most highly individual task that you will undertake. By virtue of differences in backgrounds, values absorbed, and goals desired, you differ from every other student. Unfortunately, our school system and our social setting are such that the average student has had little encouragement to come to grips with himself. Furthermore, most students seem to experience difficulty in putting down in black and white the things which they have always thought about.

There is no specific method of approach to prescribe for *all* students faced with the planning of a life career. Begin your planning in any manner which will bring the greatest benefit. Some students, for example, start by listing their strong points; others list their weaknesses, e.g., the things over which they worry. Some choose to list the major decisions with which they are or will be faced, and to indicate the many aspects of their present and future life that may be affected by these decisions. Other students choose to study critically those previous experiences that have caused them to be the way they are today. In the latter approach, the student does not attempt to write an autobiography, but rather to isolate those aspects of his background that he believes have a bearing upon his problem of deciding and/or planning a life work.

In the light of a previous discussion it would seem that you should first indicate all the things that you value in life, i.e., those things which are central to your beliefs and behavior. Directly or indirectly, values are involved in every decision you make, now and in the future; consequently, give thoughtful consideration to values. You may find it helpful to group them under major headings such as the following, which are merely suggestive. You may also use an objective instrument such as the Allport-Vernon Scale of Values to help clarify your beliefs further.

Intellectual values—such as scholarship, truth, knowledge, opportunities for self-expression, high standards of morals and ethics, clear and logical thinking.

Physical and personal values—such as health and vitality, attractiveness, pleasing personality, and successful marriage and family life.

Occupational values—such as service to mankind, intellectual stimulation, prestige, contacts with others, favorable working conditions, a reasonable degree of financial security, industriousness, self-sufficiency, opportunities for advancement, opportunities for creativeness, and opportunities for combining your occupation harmoniously with family life.

Adjustment values—such as sense of personal worth, respect for human personality, tolerance, self-respect, independence, friendship, sense of humor, happiness, cooperativeness, and opportunities for choice and self-direction.

Social values—such as social approval, stability, honesty, generosity, loyalty, kindness, fairness, justice, and impartiality.

Aesthetic values—such as beauty, attractiveness of surroundings, and appreciation of cultural influences.

Recreational values—such as ample time to devote to recreational activities, freedom to participate in a wide variety of activities, and stimulation to develop interests.

In addition to listing these values, check to see whether they are consistent with each other, and analyze each critically to determine why you hold it, as well as whether it is desirable to continue to hold it. In order to gain an adequate understanding of the origin of these values, dip critically into your background. Early childhood experiences are much more important than one is inclined to suspect, so far as the formation of his values is concerned.

Any analysis of your values will automatically necessitate a consideration of goals. The balance sheet that you construct of your values and goals should assist you greatly in being objective and facile in the other aspects of your planning.

Talking to others about your background, values, and goals. You doubtless have discussed your life plans at length with your parents, your public school teachers, your school friends, and various older adults in your home community; and you will probably want to consult these people again, especially your parents, as you continue with your planning.

In view of the fact that college provides a superb opportunity for you to extend greatly your contacts, avail yourself of this resource for planning. In your beginning course in education you will contact many other students interested in the same career possibilities that you are. Both in and out of class you will have the opportunity to share your values, goals, and plans, and to think them through critically. Activities such as participation in the Student National Education Association organization provide additional opportunities for engaging in intelligent, meaningful, and fruitful discussions. Seek out your college instructors as well as specialists in other fields, from whom you may receive valuable aid. In short, avail yourself of every possible opportunity to analyze and appraise your background, values, and goals. It is primarily through this process that your thinking is deepened and clarified, your horizons are extended, and your planning is directed. Furthermore, the act of engaging in these experiences should enable you to gain facility for helping the pupils whom you may teach to do likewise.

Some students experience difficulty in initiating the type of activities suggested above. If you are one of these, you may find it helpful to submit a list of your values and goals, or a self-rating, to someone for his opinion of it. Usually these activities produce fruitful discussions if they are approached in a sincere, honest, positive manner. Through this technique you extend the number of eyes through which you see yourself.

Appraising your general abilities as a prospective teacher. In order to use your time and energy most effectively in college as well as in later life, study how you compare now with what you want to be in the future. This kind of comparison gives direction to your efforts.

You will be able to appraise many of your abilities in terms of the requirements for success in teaching. For example, you can appraise your ability to master subject matter. Although the teacher must possess much more, information is still a very important element in his success. Obviously, you must succeed academically in completing the college requirements. Your college academic record will bear some positive relation to success in teaching; i.e., the very poorly prepared teacher will probably not experience the success of one who has an excellent academic preparation. Colleges recognize this probability by requiring students to have specified minimum grade point averages before they recommend a graduating student for teacher certification.

Perhaps one of the most effective ways of analyzing your abilities for teaching is to use various check lists or self-rating scales that have been prepared. One of these scales is located in the Resource Section for Part I of this book. As you check yourself on it, keep in mind that no rating of this kind should be considered final, and that the rating represents only your present abilities. You should be able to do much to improve your ratings for teaching fitness through carefully planned future experiences.

After you have rated yourself, ask your adviser or some other competent person who knows you well to rate you on this same scale. Compare your ratings and discuss especially those ratings that differ greatly. Ask your adviser or friend to help formulate plans whereby you may remove the weaknesses and increase the strengths that you have for teaching.

Obtaining objective data on your specific abilities.   In using the preceding check list you perhaps felt the need for objective data to support some of the relatively subjective judgments you made, especially if the appraisal of someone else differed appreciably from your own rating. You should be able to locate considerable objective data to help you appraise yourself and plan your future.

Data on your physical health may be obtained from your college health clinic or your family physician. Your speech department or clinic can give you objective data concerning your speech and hearing. A good personality test administered and interpreted by a clinician can supply emotional stability and personal adjustment data.

Practically every college and university today requires entering students to take a battery of tests. You may never have learned the result of these tests. For the purposes of planning a career, go to the proper agency in your school and ask for a copy of the results. Ordinarily the registrar's office, the guidance department, or some other agency administering the entrance tests will be glad to help you get these results. You are almost certain to find results on intelligence and English-ability tests. Intelligence tests generally sample skill in the use of language symbols, nonlanguage abilities, apperceptive processes, spatial relationships, and logical and mathematical aspects of reasoning. The English tests usually cover at least three aspects of reading: vocabulary, speed of reading, and level of comprehension. If, for example, your English scores are appreciably lower than your intelligence-test scores, you may conclude that you are not reading at your maximum capacity. In this case seek assistance and, if possible, plan to visit a reading clinic for consultation and advice.

More and more colleges are requiring students to take some type of occupational-preference or interest test. Such tests attempt to indicate fields in which a particular person would be likely to experience happiness and success. Although the results of these tests are not conclusive, they do indicate data worthy of consideration.

Many students pursuing a specialized course in college tend to neglect their personal development along broad cultural lines. Educators generally agree that a teacher should have a well-rounded background in addition to the other requirements for teaching. Therefore, avail yourself of some kind of test that will indicate your achievement in each of the broad fields of knowledge. Plan to strengthen, either through course work or on your own, your understanding of areas in which you appear especially weak. Furthermore, gain evidence of the extent to which you are keeping abreast of the current happenings in each of these areas.

Teachers should be especially skilled in human relationships. Therefore, make good use of any instrument that may provide data for you in

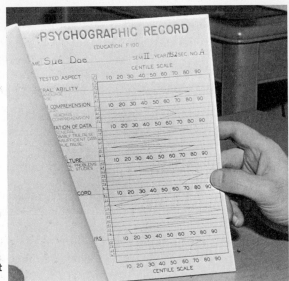

Secure as much objective test data upon yourself as possible. Use a convenient scale for plotting these data. What kind of a profile do you have? What appear to be your strengths and weaknesses? What factors need most attention?

this regard. Your success in planning will be determined to a large degree by the extent to which you are able to draw logical conclusions from information at your disposal.

You may think of other kinds of test data that you will need in developing your plans. If your college does not provide the various tests for which you find a need, you can apply at the nearest testing agency. The cost is comparatively low, and the service usually includes a profile as well as an interpretation of the scores.

Remember that objective test data have limitations, and these limitations are to be kept in mind at all times. In order to ensure profitable use of the information, a careful evaluation by a qualified person of the purpose and the results of each test is an essential part of any testing program.

You may wish to develop a graphic picture of the information obtained in order to gain more value from it. Construct a profile chart or psychograph of all your test results. The psychograph would also help your adviser gain a better picture of you.

In the specific types of activities listed, you have by no means exhausted the possibilities through which you might approach your self-appraisal and over-all problem of planning. You probably will discover additional activities which will be of equal or greater benefit to you in your planning.

Formulating your plans for the future. Planning for the future involves preparing for three rather clearly defined periods: the years in which you are still in college, the first five or ten years after graduation, during which time you are becoming adjusted to your life's work, and your later life, which extends into old age.

If you are a senior or graduate student, it is obvious that the amount of planning which you can do while still in college is fairly limited. You are faced more immediately with the need for detailed plans for the second period, the first five or ten years after graduation.

The material that follows is roughly divided into these three periods, and a few suggestions are given that may be of help to you.

Years in which you are in college.   College is an unusual environment in which you are able to take advantage of many learning situations that may not present themselves in your local surroundings. For this reason your plans during the college years may differ significantly from other plans you may make.

If you feel, for example, that you need to improve your ability to work cooperatively and harmoniously with others, become an active member in some campus activities. You may be interested in opportunities to assume positions of leadership and responsibility; develop certain traits such as sincerity, politeness, and understanding; subscribe to professional magazines; and participate in various discussion groups to develop the characteristics of a mature thinker. There are also many opportunities on campus and in the community that you can utilize to acquire a broad cultural education.

Other plans may include attempts to develop skills and insights for working with children. These include observing and participating in as many teaching situations as possible, taking part in camp and club activities with children, and acting as playground director or camp counselor during the summer.

Years immediately after college.   You will want to consider the problem of finding a position where you are most likely to be successful. A number of changes may be necessary before you find the environment and the job in education where you want to spend the rest of your life. As you will note in the latter part of this chapter as well as in Chapter 4, certification requirements are increasing so rapidly that you should plan on getting a master's degree in the relatively near future.

Give detailed consideration to plans for marriage, for locating and financing a home, for purchasing a car, for raising a family, and for securing the necessities of life. Since increasing numbers of married women are working, consider this possibility in your plans. Under such circumstances the life of both the husband and the wife are affected—the wife, particularly, after the arrival of children. Such factors should be included in your planning.

Your social position in your community is another important aspect of your life. Consider becoming a member of civic and professional organizations as well as participating in other kinds of services within your community.

Prospective periods of summer employment provide many opportunities for systematic and constructive planning. Capitalize on the opportunities to promote continuous intellectual growth. Your recreational interests tend to change as you become older; hence, you will be less able to take part in activities that necessitate much physical energy. This should be considered in your planning for now and for later life.

Make plans whereby you can provide for your future financial security and for that of your dependents, through insurance, retirement benefits, etc. You cannot foretell when misfortune will come to your family.

Years in later life.   There is much merit in looking far into the future and doing some "intelligent dreaming." Many people find added enjoyment, happiness, and security during their later years of life as a result of long-range planning.

It is largely during this later period that your family begins to leave home and seek employment elsewhere, and that you often face much loneliness. A wide variety of cultural and recreational interests, a concern with civic and professional activities, a wise use of the increased time at your disposal, and an enlarged circle of friends can do much to promote wholesome adjustment at this time. It is important that you plan for this now.

If your plans are comprehensive and carefully constructed, you will derive much satisfaction from a job well done. In addition, your outline should serve as a useful guide in the future, and should result in the elimination of much frustration which results from lack of foresight.

PROGRAMS OF TEACHER EDUCATION

Since more people are engaged in teaching than in any other profession in the world, it is to be expected that institutions of higher education are engaged in the preparation of more teachers than of members of any other profession. Of more than 2,000 institutions of higher education in the United States, approximately 1,150 are specifically approved by state departments of education for the preparation of teachers. One thousand and eleven of these institutions are accredited by regional associations, and three hundred and seventy-four were accredited by the National Council for Accreditation of Teacher Education in June 1962. The list of approved teacher-education institutions include 105 public and 139 private universities, 190 public and 572 private general or liberal arts colleges, 44 public and 11 private teachers colleges, 32 technical schools, 51 junior colleges, and 6 unclassified schools [6:151].

It is significant to note the steady change being made in the institutions preparing teachers. One hundred and four teachers colleges and normal schools have become state colleges or universities since 1951. This is a continuation of a trend away from single-purpose teacher-education institutions. Many interpretations have been given to these shifts, especially the shift from teachers colleges to state colleges. Armstrong and Stinnett feel that the real explanation appears to hinge upon two factors [6:22]:

(1) The trend toward professionalization of teaching which has resulted in the adoption in most states of college degrees and the completion of prescribed curricula for beginning teachers (which practice obtains in all recognized professions), and thus in the growing acceptance of teacher education as an integral

part of higher education and as an accepted professional discipline. (2) In recent years, the pressures of increased enrollments have forced state legislatures to consider two alternatives: (a) to authorize the building of new colleges, or (b) to utilize existing ones by converting single-purpose teachers colleges into general or multiple-purpose colleges. Choice of the latter alternative as being more economical and feasible obviously helps to explain the widespread conversions described above.

Another significant trend is the decline in the number of junior colleges approved for teacher education. This trend may be attributed to the tendency to establish the degree as a minimum requirement for teacher certification. Undoubtedly this trend will continue.

Importance of Teacher Education.   The growing importance of teacher education is reflected in the trends indicated above. In general, universities have shown little or no interest in the preparation of teachers until the last few decades.

That recognition of the crucial importance of teacher education has been particularly slow in universities is due in part to the feeling that "anyone who knew his subject would be able to teach it." Strange as it may seem, there are some professors on college campuses, especially those in subject-matter areas, who voice this same feeling and express grave doubts about the value of professional education courses. In fact, they may vociferously condemn such courses, and the student preparing to teach often is either confused or inclined to develop negative attitudes toward the importance of professional education courses. Often the violence of the controversy between the relative importance of subject-matter courses and professional courses is directly proportional to the lack of understanding of the field being condemned.

Some critics point to the fact that, on the college level and in private schools, you find good teachers who have not taken any courses in education. The fallacy of the argument lies in the fact that they are excellent in spite of their deficiencies. One may ask the question, "How much better might they have been?" Arthur Bestor, in "How Should America's Teachers Be Educated?" [15:16–19] discusses this situation, and in this same periodical [16:20–24] Karl Bigelow takes issue with Bestor's point of view. Individuals who are well informed in both areas seldom enter into any such controversy. The issue is well summarized in the following passage [91:261–262]:

Certainly, one unable to read cannot teach another to read. Yet it seems quite possible that while all of us can read with greater or less ease, we might still experience difficulty in teaching first graders how to decipher the printed page. The need for skill in teaching is rather obvious in the primary grades. It is less obvious, though hardly less necessary, in the high school. In stressing the importance of "method," even with advanced students, the advocate of professional training for teachers is not attempting to depreciate the value of a knowledge of subject matter. He regards such knowledge as not only important, but essential, to acceptable teaching. He would readily admit that the greater the mastery a teacher has of his subject matter field, the better able he should be to teach it. But he contends that knowledge of subject matter alone is not sufficient for the greatest success in teaching.

It is hard to believe that prior to the establishment of this first public normal school in Lexington, Massachusetts in 1839, no specific institutions were concerned with the preparation of teachers.

The attitude of professional school people is that the end of education is not merely a mastery of subjects, any more than the purpose of surgery is to remove bodily organs from sick patients. If one's condition is not improved by the removal of a diseased appendix, it would be rather difficult to demonstrate the value of the operation. To the modern teacher, the purpose of teaching languages, history, physics, etc., is not merely that the pupil should have a greater fund of information in these fields. It is of more moment that, as a result of broader experiences along these lines, the learner's life may be made richer, more joyous, and more useful to himself and to society. As unskilled medical treatment might aggravate the patient's condition rather than improve it, so a bungling teacher, in his well-meant effort to secure achievement in subject matter, may destroy the larger values that schools and education are designed to create and foster.

The fallacy of the belief that an effective teacher needs only a thorough knowledge of subject matter may be illustrated in another way. As Chandler [26:5] points out, a passenger who has traveled extensively by air may feel that his experience qualifies him to pilot a plane. He may know much about aerodynamics, theory of flight, engines, flight patterns, regulations, schedules, etc. If he should attempt to take charge of a flight, without having gone through the necessary long and intensive program of training, he immediately would discover the difference between being a pilot and flying as a passenger. Chandler feels that "the difference between lay teaching and professional teaching is comparable to the contrast between the recommendations of home remedies given by a layman for the sick and injured and the professional medical prescription and advice given by a doctor" [26:5].

There are other reasons why some prospective teachers may feel that a thorough knowledge of subject matter is about the only requirement for successful teaching. Unfortunately most of these students have attended schools in which attention has been given to little more than the sheer mastery of assigned subject matter. Furthermore, there is an element of security to be found by some students in assuming that the function of the teacher is to teach subject matter per se. These students, more than any others, have need for professional education.

Educational researchists, such as Smith at the University of Illinois and Turner and Fattu at Indiana University, have been conducting some sophisticated research that sheds light upon the controversy. Turner and Fattu, for example, have been working upon the assumption that any profession, to be worthy of the name, possesses an extensive and growing body of systematic, organized, and abstract knowledge which can be mastered only over an extended period of time by individuals selected for their aptitude, and which is used to perform an essential public service better than any other group can perform such service. As a case in point, medical men ultimately justify their claim to professional status by being better able to solve problems within their domain because they are more competent than any other group in medical diagnosis and treatment. Similarly, teachers should be more competent than any other group in solving problems within their domain of competence. Their research [176:1–29] clearly indicates that: (1) teachers who have had a methods course perform better than those who have had none; (2) bachelor's degree graduates from teacher-education programs perform significantly better than graduates in other areas including liberal arts; (3) teachers who have had teaching experience perform significantly better than those without such experiences; (4) teachers with one year of experience perform significantly better than those with no experience; (5) teachers with three to five years experience perform significantly better than those with one year of experience; and (6) teachers in large school districts where in-service teacher education is supported perform significantly better than those in small districts. This research should support you if you become involved in a discussion of the issue regarding the value of professional education.

General Pattern of Teacher Education.   It is perfectly understandable, in the light of American education's brief and rapid development, that considerable variation exists in the specific nature of programs to be found in teacher-education institutions today. Even if it were desired, no standardized pattern of preparation is to be found. There are, however, some characteristics that are common to most teacher-education programs for the elementary and secondary levels. These programs may be studied in terms of three major areas: general education, subject-matter specialization, and professional education. In general, approximately one-half of your college work will fall in the area of general education if you plan to teach on the secondary school level, and definitely more than one-half will fall in that area if you plan to become an elementary school teacher. If you plan to become a secondary teacher, approximately one-third of your work will involve subject-matter specialization, and not more than one-sixth will be in professional education. As an elementary teacher, approximately one-eighth of your work may involve specialization and one-fourth will be classified as professional education. Since elementary teachers generally teach all of the subjects offered in the elementary school, they need to take more courses in each of the major subject fields, which leaves less opportunity for specialization. Likewise, they must be concerned with methodology for all subject fields rather than with one or more subject areas of specialization, as is required for secondary school teachers.

There has been considerable controversy, especially during recent years, over the proportionate distribution of general and specialized course work and of professional education course work. Some of the critics seem to feel that a four-year teacher-education program consists almost entirely of methodology or professional education. They bitterly condemn the "educationalist" for most of the weaknesses in the American school system upon the grounds that almost all of a prospective teacher's education involves "learning how to teach." The facts of the case are these: approximately three-fourths of a prospective elementary teacher's preparation for teaching and approximately five-sixths of a prospective

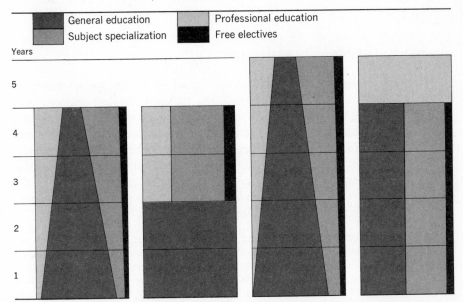

Figure 14.   Four prevailing program patterns of teacher education in the United States. What are the advantages and disadvantages of each pattern?

secondary school teacher's preparation involves study in the various subject areas. It would not seem excessive to devote from one-sixth to one-fourth of a student's time in college to a consideration of what education is for, of what young children and adolescents are like, and of how effective learning can best be promoted; and to gain some experience under expert guidance. Educationalists, in their feverish efforts to keep the amount of professional education to a minimum, realize that anything short of this proportionate amount does violence to any program designed to produce effective teachers.

You should view general education, specialization in one or more teaching fields, and professional education as interrelated parts of a total program. The Committee on the National Commission on Teacher Education Association, who prepared the report *New Horizons for the Teaching Profession,* feel that [100:59]:

General education, specialization in a teaching field, and professional education can and should make an important contribution to helping the student to develop intellectual curiosity, a positive attitude toward learning, and a disposition to examine, inquire, and analyze; to build skills of logical analysis and of reasoned and orderly consideration of ideas; to gain understanding of and competence in using the different forms of reasoning employed in various fields; and to deepen respect for all areas of knowledge.

Further, a student should have opportunity in all parts of his program to become acquainted with resources for continuing inquiry and to build facility in their use. No part of a teacher education program is complete if it fails to give direct attention to helping the student derive principles and generalizations and to examine his actions on the basis of them. Important skills basic to effective interpersonal relationships must be a deliberate focus, not in one aspect of a program but throughout the total of planned experiences of every student.

Any discussion of the parts should be viewed in terms of the above desired outcomes of the total program.

General education. General education refers to the broad fields of knowledge, such as the humanities, the life and physical sciences, and the social and behavioral science, that are designed to help you in solving personal problems and those of the society in which you live. General education is focused upon the needs and responsibilities which men have in common. It is designed to help you in becoming a more alert, cultivated, and responsible individual and citizen [86:39]. According to the report on *New Horizons for the Teaching Profession,* a program of general education should help the individual [adapted, 86:39–40]:

1. To develop understanding and use of major ideas and principles of the various divisions of knowledge as they bear on the range of common human concerns. The achievement of this goal involves: developing intellectual curiosity; becoming acquainted with resources for continuing inquiry and study in a field, and how to use them; gaining an appreciation and respect for all areas of knowledge; acquiring experience with synthesizing and integrative properties of knowledge.

2. To cultivate those skills and habits of thought which constitute intellectual competence; for example, the ability to think logically and clearly, to gather relevant data, to draw conclusions from established facts. The student should gain understanding of and competence in using the different forms of reasoning employed in the various fields. Becoming a disciplined and independent thinker calls for: having a disposition to examine, inquire, analyze; being willing to admit one's convictions and having ability to defend them; acting on principle and daring to be different in supporting convictions.

3. To develop skills of communication and effective interaction with others. Each individual needs sufficient command of communication skills (lingual, numerical, and graphic) to be able to express his ideas clearly and to understand and intelligently utilize the rapidly developing mass media. He also needs to possess the skills that relate to a wholesome quality of interaction with others— the skills basic to effective interpersonal relationships.

4. To help the individual to examine intellectually his value system. The stu-

dent may have essential knowledge, the skills of intellectual workmanship, and intellectual curiosity. Yet these rational processes may be of little worth unless they are tempered by moral responsibility and guided by values which derive from and fit into a reasoned view of existence.

5. To help the individual gain perspective regarding the relation of an area of specialization to all other fields.

Members of the teaching profession as persons need the same general education important for all thoughtful people. For the educator as a professional, however, general education has unusual urgency. *The teacher stands before his pupils in a special way, as a symbol and example of the educated person in the best sense of that term.* If he is a rounded and informed person, with lively curiosity in many fields, he will stimulate students to join him in these interests. Further, his broad educational background will make him sensitive to pupil interests. Then, too, the teacher's central and critical role in the twentieth century, that of helping learners to intellectualize their experiences, gain new insights and develop the motivation to continue to learn and the ability to cope with the unknown, requires a new dimension in his own general education.

As you analyze the program which your institution requires of students preparing to teach, you doubtless will find certain required courses in oral and written communication, literature and the arts, social sciences, and life and physical sciences which constitutes the program of general education. By virtue of your public school experience, you already have gained considerable understanding and skill in each of these areas, although you may feel that you are weak in one or more of these areas. Regardless of what the situation may be, analyze your background critically in each of these broad areas. Your performance on standardized tests or inventories as well as your understanding of current affairs should assist in an analysis of your present status. There is much that you can do before graduation and after you begin teaching to develop the rich general background which you owe to yourself and to the pupils you will teach.

Subject-matter specialization. An elementary teacher is responsible for teaching virtually all subject fields. Although some schools do have special teachers in such areas as art, music, and physical education, there is a trend for the elementary teacher to assume increasing responsibility for these special subjects. As a result, he needs a more thorough grounding in many areas of learning than does the secondary teacher. In addition to breadth of background, the elementary teacher must develop enough depth of understanding in each of the areas to guide children into increasingly rich and challenging learning experiences.

A secondary teacher is certified in one or more subject areas. He is responsible for bringing to his pupils a large store of knowledge in the courses he teaches. For this reason he takes a greater amount of advanced work in one or more subject areas than does the elementary teacher.

In advanced academic courses, you are likely to find students who are preparing for many occupations. You may discover that these courses have been designed to meet the needs of all the students rather than of prospective teachers only. The student who plans to do nuclear research will have a somewhat different approach to the content of a physics course than you will. He will be concerned with the knowledge and skills that the course has to offer in terms of research in nuclear physics. But you, as a teacher, will be concerned with the implications of the course for guiding the intellectual growth of boys and girls.

Most secondary teachers begin teaching in small schools where it usually is necessary to teach in at least two subject fields. Only larger schools have sufficient classes in English, for example, to occupy a teacher's full time. For this reason, it is highly desirable to be certified in more than one subject, unless you wish to become a special teacher in such fields as fine arts, music, vocational home economics, or agriculture. You may be able, by very careful planning, to complete the certification requirements for a third or a fourth subject area. For example, some of your course work may be used to meet general education requirements, and some of the work needed for your major or minor may be applicable toward the requirements of a third or fourth certification area. Often only a small amount of additional work is needed to increase your number of areas. Effort spent in exploring such possibilities may prove very profitable, especially in securing the first teaching position.

The information contained in Chapter 5 should help you in making an intelligent and firm decision with regard to your field or fields of specialization. You also may wish to consult the education placement office to determine the probable future supply and demand for teachers having the same specializations in which you are interested.

As soon as you have decided upon the combination of subjects desired, you are ready to plan the course work. Institutions vary considerably in regard to the amount required for majors and minors. Also, within an institution the work demanded for a major or minor varies in different subject areas. Study carefully the respective requirements established by your teacher-education institution and plan accordingly. If you anticipate teaching in another state, consult the specific state requirements for certification in the subject areas you elect in order that you may meet these requirements, if possible, upon graduation.

Professional education. During the past two or three decades rapid strides have been made in the professional education of teachers. This progress has been fostered especially by far-reaching research in the field of psychology. Techniques similar to those of the social psychologist, sociologist, and anthropologist have assisted educators in expanding the areas of investigation to include the more intangible aspects of education. Hundreds of studies have been made on such problems as the learning process, individual differences in pupils, methods of evaluating pupil progress, curriculum organization, child growth and development, utilization of community resources, and audio-visual materials. Educational philosophers have provided clarification of the function of the school in society. The cooperative efforts of public school and teacher-education personnel have helped to clarify the professional needs of the teacher.

All these factors, and many others, have aided in establishing the professional education of teachers as a unique and scientific function.

The various statements of competencies listed in Chapter 3 indicate many qualities required of a successful teacher. It is this body of specialized knowledge, skills, and techniques that distinguishes teaching as a profession. Professional education courses are designed to assist students to develop the essential requirements for membership in the profession.

Teacher-education institutions differ considerably in the specific ways in which they attempt to develop the professional competencies of teachers. This variation results from such factors as differences in state certification requirements, continued experimentation in the preparation of teachers, and rapid developments in teacher education. Any student who anticipates transferring to another institution during the time of his preparation for teaching should exercise great care in selecting his courses. Difference in requirements are so great among institutions that credits awarded at one college may not meet the specific demands of another. Whenever a transfer is anticipated, a student should check on the acceptability of the course work to be taken prior to the transfer. Careful planning along these lines often saves disappointment and delays in accepting desired teaching positions.

In spite of variations in the details of professional programs for teachers, there is a fairly common pattern in evidence. The programs generally can be divided into the following major areas, although the emphasis on each varies among institutions as well as within institutions according to the area or level of specialization:

1. Introduction to education
2. General and educational psychology
3. General methods
4. Special methods
5. Student teaching

From your reading, you doubtless have sensed the general content of each of the above-mentioned areas. Much of the remaining portion of this book will help you in seeing more clearly the rationale of these areas. The values, insights, understandings, and skills you gain in the sequence of professional courses required for certification will be affected greatly by the extent to which you recognize the crucial need for each.

Students in elementary education generally are required to take more professional course work, mostly in special methods, than are students in secondary education. As indicated previously, elementary teachers are responsible for the child's education in all areas of knowledge, while secondary teachers specialize in one or more areas. Furthermore, elementary teachers tend to be more concerned with a child's total development, which requires many and deep professional understandings; whereas secondary teachers are more concerned with the teaching of their areas of specialization.

The type of professional preparation for elementary and secondary teachers is often similar in the initial stages. There is an increasing tendency to explore the problems common to all teachers and to provide an integrated program for them. Differentiation designed for specialization usually occurs when prospective teachers take special methods courses.

Institutions differ considerably with respect to the length of time during which a student will take his professional education. Some institutions will concentrate the program into the last year of college work. It is more common, however, to reserve professional education courses for the last two years of a four-year program. Currently there is a trend to spread a prospective teacher's professional learning throughout his entire college career. This trend is based upon the assumption that for a rich development of professional insights and techniques an extended period of time is required. Creative teaching does not consist of a "bag of tricks" and "cookbook recipes." Nor is it a "hot-house" product. Only time can provide the experiences from which prospective teachers may gain deep insights into human beings, the nature of the learning process, and creative ways of guiding boys and girls into expanding areas of effective living.

The authors of *New Horizons for the Teaching Profession* feel that all professional education should not be postponed to the fourth year of teacher preparation for the following reasons [86:65]: "(1) there is need for ideas about teaching to mature and to be tested before the student undertakes responsibility for the trusteeship of the teacher, and (2) when

Education courses are of much greater value to students who have had many and varied contacts with boys and girls in a teaching-learning situation since these students bring to their courses greater understanding of the behavior, interests, abilities, individual differences, and general characteristics of boys and girls. (*Photograph by Carl Purcell, National Education Association.*)

the student has selected teaching as his profession, the motivation that comes from exploring what is involved in teaching enhances rather than detracts from the values gained from work in general education."

Another reason why many prospective teachers fail to gain maximum benefit from professional education courses results partly from their limited experience in a leadership capacity and in their understanding of children and adults. When you, as a teacher-to-be, are responsible for guiding experiences of boys and girls, the experiences have greater meaning.

A number of institutions are requiring students to observe many teaching-learning situations, beginning with the first year of college. Case studies of children and participation in classroom stiuations are part of other professional education courses and are studied prior to a period of supervised student teaching.

There is much that you can do in gaining a greater understanding of the behavior, interests, abilities, individual differences, and general characteristics of boys and girls. Many students participate in such valuable activities as teaching Sunday-school classes, serving as a camp counselor, working in a youth center or a settlement house, serving as a life guard or playground supervisor, or doing some baby sitting. Your college courses will have much greater meaning when you can relate the concepts and principles discussed to rich and varied experiences which you have with boys and girls.

The college campus should serve as your laboratory, in which you can study and gain greater skill in working with people—another important competence in successful teaching. Leadership experiences can be gained from participation in such activities as student government, sports, school publications, dramatics, musical activities, social and religious clubs, and Student National Education Association activities. School employment officials usually express much interest in the extent of participation in such activities since they tend to indicate competence in working effectively with others.

The college campus may offer many opportunities for you to expand your cultural background, such as concerts, lectures, plays, art exhibits, etc. There also is the library with a wealth of books, periodicals, magazines, and newspapers from which you may gain breadth of understanding of the past as well as the present. During the time that you are in college you will want to establish the habits that will enable you to be a well-rounded, cultured person who is sensitive to the events in the world and to enriching opportunities in life.

These are only a few of the many kinds of profitable experiences through which you may gain greater competence as a teacher. You owe yourself and your pupils the finest background possible for building the professional learnings, skills, and techniques of successful teaching.

Five-Year Programs in Teacher Education. In considering educational growth and change during the 1960s, Sam M. Lambert, Director of the

Research Division of the National Education Association, maintains that the bachelor's degree in the relatively near future will be "outmoded as a basic requirement for teaching because it is becoming more difficult for a person to learn enough in four years to teach all the knowledge that should be acquired by today's children in youth" [47:47]. The President's Commission on National Goals advocated that by 1970 every state should require one year beyond the bachelor's degree as a requirement for secondary school teaching [114:82]. In 1960, almost half of the nation's high school teachers possessed a master's degree, and an increasing number of elementary teachers were earning the degree.

In view of this decided trend, a few teacher-education institutions already have experimented with programs of five consecutive years of preparation for teaching. In studying five-year programs, Henry Harap of the Division of Higher Education in the United States Office of Education, found that there is no predominant curriculum pattern [67:19]. In spite of considerable difference in the sequence of courses in general education, the curriculum falls into the following patterns:

1. Two years of general education followed by a three-year program of professional education, including subject-matter specialization
2. General education, subject-matter specialization, and professional education integrated in each year of the program
3. A year of professional education added to a four-year liberal arts program
4. Two years of subject matter and general education plus three years of subject matter and professional education

Although this is a trend in teacher education with which you should be familiar, no mass shift away from the four-year bachelor's degree program followed by a master's degree program is probable within the next decade. Harap indicates that advocates of the five-year program are not optimistic about its adoption for the following reasons [67:21]:

It is clear that the four-year sequence will remain as the dominant pattern of training for teaching for many years to come. Arguments for the four-year liberal arts—professional education sequence are powerful; it is unhurried and proceeds as a planned, step-by-step sequence; it permits the college graduate to begin contributing to society sooner; a four-year program, followed by several years of experience in teaching, is an assurance of more profitable graduate study both in the individual's teaching field and in education; the financial investment of the fifth year is an unreasonable expectation for great numbers of prospective teachers, particularly women whose teaching careers may be short; not all prospective teachers are able to profit from graduate study.

SUMMARY

As you think about yourself as a part of society, you recognize the role which planning plays in this increasingly complex and interdependent culture. You then begin to realize that an intelligent application of the process necessitates your becoming skilled not only in planning your own life, but also in helping those whom you teach to do likewise. Furthermore, you and your pupils need to develop your planning and working together in the solution of common problems.

Several steps have been suggested for use in outlining the details of your plans for teaching. One of your first responsibilities is to determine the things in life that really seem important to you—your values. These values largely determine the things you seek to accomplish. You then look at a career in education to see whether it holds promise of fulfilling these needs. You must meet certain requirements to qualify for a teaching position. You face the responsibility of critically and comprehensively appraising yourself in terms of these requirements. You then develop detailed schemes for moving from where you are to where you want to go, keeping in mind that plans are always tentative, and that modifications are made as unforeseen factors develop.

Later, when you have acquired better understanding of the work of the teacher, the requirements for preparation, the competencies needed, the purposes of education, and so forth; you will need to do some re-evaluating of your thinking.

By far the larger proportion of prospective teachers now receive their preparation in institutions of college rank. Virtually all teacher-education institutions have been greatly concerned with improving the quality of teaching as well as with increasing the amount of preparation for the profession.

Although considerable variation exists in the programs provided by different institutions, the preparation of teachers can be considered in terms of the following three major aspects: general education, subject-matter specialization, professional education. Educational programs for elementary teachers tend to provide for relatively large amounts of general and professional education, whereas secondary teachers tend to specialize in one or more subject areas and to take correspondingly less general and professional education. Professional education courses embody the specialized professional knowledge, skills, and techniques essential for successful teaching.

QUESTIONS FOR YOUR CONSIDERATION

1. Why is it more important for you to carefully plan your career in teaching than it would have been if you had started 30 years ago?

2. How does society suffer if an individual makes an unwise selection of a career?

3. In your opinion, what values should a person have in life if he plans to teach?

4. "Values are acquired parts of an individual's life." What are some of the implications of this statement for the experiences you will plan for your pupils, and the personal influence you will attempt to exert upon your pupils?

5. In what ways do the values held in common by people in America differ from those that characterize people in an autocratic society?

6. In what ways might long-range planning have improved the lives of some of your friends?

7. Some people feel that group planning and work reduces everyone to the level of mediocrity. Is this necessarily true? If not, how can group work contribute to the development of the unique talents of an individual?

8. In addition to a thorough grounding in subject matter, what specific understandings, skills, and techniques are, in your opinion, essential to success in the teaching profession?

9. What leadership experiences with boys and girls have been of most value to you as a prospective teacher? Why? What other types of experiences should you have before you begin teaching?

10. In your opinion, what percentage of time should be devoted to general education, to specialized subject matter, and to professional education in a four-year teacher-education program? What are the reasons for this distribution?

11. What student teaching and other professional laboratory experiences must you complete in order to graduate?

12. What are your reactions to the current trends in teacher-education programs, as discussed in this chapter?

13. What are the advantages and disadvantages of a teacher taking graduate work without having had some full-time teaching experience?

ACTIVITIES FOR YOU TO PURSUE

1. Make a list of the things you really value in life. After careful study, try to arrange them in descending order according to their importance to you. Reflect upon your past experiences and try to determine why you attach importance to each of your values. Examine them carefully to see whether they are compatible with each other. Opposite this list indicate all the values you see in education as a career. Compare and contrast these two listings to determine the extent to which they seem compatible.

2. Question seriously some of your close friends regarding what they value most in life. In what ways do the values they hold differ from yours? How do you account for these differences? In what ways are their career plans being affected by their values?

3. Talk to some people who have been very successful in their careers. Question them regarding long-range plans they have followed in order to gain success. Study also the careers of some people who have not been very successful. What differences do you

find between the career planning done by successful and unsuccessful people?

4. Talk with people who have retired. You will find some who are happy and well adjusted in their retirement, whereas others are not. Attempt to determine whether long-range planning, or the lack of it, accounts to some extent for the differences.

5. Assume that you as a teacher should be skilled in helping your pupils plan together in the effective solution of common problems. Consider some college activities in which you might engage for purposes of increasing your skill in this regard.

6. As suggested previously, collect as many objective data as possible on your special abilities for teaching. Study these data carefully, seeking help from your college instructors if needed; formulate plans for overcoming your weaknesses and building up your strengths.

7. Write a paper called "What I Value in Life," "What Life Means to Me," "My Philosophy of Life," or on a similar topic suggested in this chapter.

8. An increased number of educators feel that there are many common elements in the preparation of elementary and secondary teachers. Discuss with your colleagues the proposition that competency for teaching is the same, regardless of level. At what point, if any, should the preparation of elementary and secondary teachers be differentiated?

9. Some colleges and universities have developed programs in which all professional work for teachers is concentrated in the fifth year of college. Discuss with your colleagues the advantages and disadvantages of such a plan.

10. Read the articles written by Bestor and Bigelow that were indicated previously in this chapter. Try to identify any weakness in the arguments of each writer.

3
COMPETENCIES AND PERSONAL GROWTH FOR TEACHING

What is needed to be a good teacher? Some people feel that all you need is a firm grasp of subject matter. Others maintain that you must be a good disciplinarian primarily. Still others think that you must be a born teacher. Indeed the range of opinions is great.

Perhaps people feel more qualified to judge the competencies for teaching than for any other profession. This feeling is understandable when you consider the fact that people generally have had greater contact with teachers than with other occupational groups. It is estimated that the average person has had close contact with approximately 60 teachers by the time he leaves high school. Furthermore people are interested in the characteristics of a good teacher. Their success in school was directly related to the capabilities of their instructors. If they are parents, they are interested in their children's scholastic advancement. If they are in business or industry, they are concerned that teachers help youth gain knowledge and develop effective skills for earning a living.

What teacher competencies will be required in order to fully develop this child's abilities for living effectively and constructively in our society? (*Photograph by Carl Purcell, National Education Association.*)

As a prospective teacher you are very much concerned with the competencies essential to success in teaching. Having identified these competencies, you also are concerned with ways in which you can become the most competent teacher possible. This chapter, therefore, is designed to give you some help in regard to these two central factors: to assist you in your attempts to recall the many teachers you have had, and to analyze carefully those who stand out as having been especially good. As you study each of them, write down the reason or reasons why you consider them outstanding. Have your friends engage in the same kind of activity. Compare and contrast your list with theirs.

In making this analysis you will probably note considerable difference in the personalities of the teachers. Some may have been quiet, gentle, and warm. Others may have been outgoing and aggressive. Whatever their differences, you may safely conclude that there is no *one* personality which teachers must have in order to be successful. Further study also may reveal that there is no *one* method of teaching that will ensure success. Each of your outstanding teachers probably had a distinct personality as well as style of teaching.

The differences that you find in the characteristics of good teachers should not alarm you too much. Nor should you be discouraged if educators tell you frankly that they are not absolutely certain of the competencies that will ensure anyone's success in teaching. It is true that they know something about the abilities required, but they hesitate to say with complete conviction that a particular individual will be a very successful teacher and that another will be unsuccessful.

One reason why it is difficult to predict teaching success is that a teacher deals with the most complex thing in the world—the human being. A successful teacher must be able to affect people in such ways that desirable changes occur in behavior. He must be able to encourage the individual to think and to make intelligent decisions; he must guide his behavior with increasing effectiveness toward constructive, democratic ends. The complexity of the interaction of the teacher with his pupils is so great that superior teaching assumes the characteristics of an art which cannot be fully analyzed. Horace Mann, long ago, recognized this fact when he wrote in 1853, in his *First Annual Report,* the following: "Teaching is the most difficult of all arts and the profoundest of all sciences. In its absolute perfection it would involve a complete knowledge of the whole being to be taught, and of the precise manner in which every possible application would affect it."

In planning a career in education, your next major step is to examine searchingly the competencies which generally are conducive to success in teaching. As you examine each one, bear in mind that it is integrally

65

related to all the others. The analysis you make should serve as a background from which you will be able to formulate specific and long-range plans for meeting these requirements to the highest degree possible. Obviously the thoroughness of the plans you make will be dependent upon the comprehensiveness and discernment with which you study these requirements.

Determining the Requirements for Teaching.   Hundreds of studies have been made of the personal and professional characteristics of teachers in an attempt to establish which traits are the most desirable for teachers to possess and which are definite handicaps. We shall examine the results of some of these studies. It may also be profitable for you to understand several techniques that have been used to collect the information. With this knowledge you may be able to conduct similar investigations on your own. Study these results carefully, analyze yourself in terms of them, and then establish specific and detailed plans for meeting as many of these requirements as possible while you are in college. You will be unable to meet all of them, since some require a lifetime of experience, study, and effort.

Studying what teachers do.   From an historical standpoint, especially, you should be familiar with the very exhaustive and comprehensive study conducted by Charters and Waples in 1929 [27:18] in an effort to determine desirable qualifications for teaching. They approached the problem by studying what teachers did. After tabulating the duties performed by teachers, they carefully studied the skills, abilities, and knowledges required in order to perform these duties successfully. They listed the following 25 traits needed by teachers: adaptability, attractive personal appearance, breadth of interest, carefulness, considerativeness, cooperation, dependability, enthusiasm, fluency, forcefulness, good judgment, health, honesty, industry, leadership, magnetism, neatness, open-mindedness, originality, progressiveness, promptness, refinement, scholarship, self-control, and thrift. The meaning of each of these traits was carefully defined by the authors.

Studying the critical behavior of teachers.   In 1960, Ryans published the results of an extensive and rigorous scientific analysis of teacher characteristics. This study was sponsored by the American Council on Education [133:1–416]. As an initial step in the study, teacher supervisors, college teachers, school principals, teachers, student teachers, and students in education methods courses were asked to make analytical reports upon teacher behavior in specific situations which might make a difference between success or failure in teaching. These reports served as a basis for the construction of a "critical incidence" blank upon which significant behavior relative to teaching might be recorded. The more than 500 critical incidents submitted by the participants in the study were reduced to the following list of generalized behaviors [133:82]:

GENERALIZED DESCRIPTIONS OF CRITICAL BEHAVIORS OF TEACHERS

Effective behaviors	Ineffective behaviors
1. Alert, appears enthusiastic.	1. Is apathetic, dull, appears bored.
2. Appears interested in pupils and classroom activities.	2. Appears uninterested in pupils and classroom activities.
3. Cheerful, optimistic.	3. Is depressed, pessimistic; appears unhappy.
4. Self-controlled, not easily upset.	4. Loses temper, is easily upset.
5. Likes fun, has a sense of humor.	5. Is overly serious, too occupied for humor.
6. Recognizes and admits own mistakes.	6. Is unaware of, or fails to admit, own mistakes.
7. Is fair, impartial, and objective in treatment of pupils.	7. Is unfair or partial in dealing with pupils.
8. Is patient.	8. Is impatient.
9. Shows understanding and sympathy in working with pupils.	9. Is short with pupils, uses sarcastic remarks, or in other ways shows lack of sympathy with pupils.
10. Is friendly and courteous in relations with pupils.	10. Is aloof and removed in relations with pupils.
11. Helps pupils with personal as well as educational problems.	11. Seems unaware of pupils' personal needs and problems.
12. Commends effort and gives praise for work well done.	12. Does not commend pupils, is disapproving, hypercritical.
13. Accepts pupils' efforts as sincere.	13. Is suspicious of pupil motives.
14. Anticipates reactions of others in social situations.	14. Does not anticipate reactions of others in social situations.
15. Encourages pupils to try to do their best.	15. Makes no effort to encourage pupils to try to do their best.
16. Classroom procedure is planned and well organized.	16. Procedure is without plan, disorganized.
17. Classroom procedure is flexible within over-all plan.	17. Shows extreme rigidity of procedure, inability to depart from plan.
18. Anticipates individual needs.	18. Fails to provide for individual differences and needs of pupils.
19. Stimulates pupils through interesting and original materials and techniques.	19. Uninteresting materials and teaching techniques used.
20. Conducts clear, practical demonstrations and explanations.	20. Demonstrations and explanations are not clear and are poorly conducted.
21. Is clear and thorough in giving directions.	21. Directions are incomplete, vague.
22. Encourages pupils to work through their own problems and evaluate their accomplishments.	22. Fails to give pupils opportunity to work out own problems or evaluate their own work.
23. Disciplines in quiet, dignified, and positive manner.	23. Reprimands at length, ridicules, resorts to cruel or meaningless forms of correction.
24. Gives help willingly.	24. Fails to give help or gives it grudgingly.
25. Foresees and attempts to resolve potential difficulties.	25. Is unable to foresee and resolve potential difficulties.

Admittedly some value or subjective judgments were involved in the formulation of these descriptive statements, the list does tend to objectify the types of behavior that make a difference in the success or failure of teachers.

Questioning pupils.   Another technique that has been used extensively is that of questioning pupils regarding the qualities of teachers they admire. It has been found that boys and girls who have spent considerable time with a teacher are able to pass rather valid judgments regarding his competence. Talk with some boys and girls after the first week of a school term and see how well they have the teacher "sized up."

Witty [186:386] analyzed approximately 12,000 letters on "The Teacher Who Has Helped Me Most" that were submitted by pupils from grades 2 to 12 all over the nation. The teacher traits mentioned most frequently by the pupils, in the order of their frequency, were the following: (1) cooperativeness, democratic attitude, (2) and (3) kindliness and consideration for the individual, patience, (4) wide variety of interests, (5) general appearance and pleasing manner, (6) fairness and impartiality, (7) sense of humor, (8) good disposition and consistent behavior, (9) interest in pupil's problems, (10) flexibility, (11) use of recognition and praise, (12) unusually proficient in teaching a particular subject.

Effectively developing the creative abilities of youth requires a high degree of skill and insight upon the part of the teacher. (*Photograph by Carl Purcell, National Education Association.*)

Witty summarized his findings by stating that "these boys and girls appear to be grateful to the school in proportion to the degree that it offers security, individual success, shared experience, and opportunities for personal and social adjustments. And these are precisely the factors which promote good learning."

Witty conducted three additional nationwide contests in an attempt to verify and expand the findings gained from the first contest. He found that the 12 traits mentioned previously were cited consistently, although their order varied from year to year [185:312].

In another study conducted by Richey and Fox [128:45], over 3,905 representative high school pupils in Indiana were asked to check the characteristics of the teacher they liked best. Ninety per cent or more of them checked the following characteristics: ability to explain lessons clearly, fairness in grading, willingness to give extra help when needed, a good sense of humor, and ability to get along well with other teachers. Next in order were such attributes as knowledge of subject matter, a pleasant disposition, a happy disposition with a tendency to smile a lot, and a pleasant speaking voice. From 63 to 78 per cent marked the following characteristics: possessing an understanding of student problems, having no favorites, dressing attractively, being a real pal both in and out of school, displaying a personal interest in the pupil, being businesslike in the classroom and insisting on punctuality, not griping about things, and insisting upon hard work. Fifty-four per cent or less of the pupils checked the following items: helped me out when I was in trouble, said nice things about my work, was nice looking, didn't bawl us out in front of other pupils, never got angry with me, and did not make me work hard. Only 17 per cent of the pupils checked the last-mentioned item.

Analyzing biographies of outstanding teachers.   Another method of gaining understanding of competencies for teaching is to read carefully some of the many biographies as well as fiction books that have been written on outstanding teachers. You may remember, for instance, the heart-warming story of Hilton's *Goodbye, Mr. Chips.* You may find biographies to be especially helpful in gaining an understanding of the artistic qualities that characterize outstanding teaching as well as the human factors that have rich meaning in the lives of boys and girls. Discussion of these and other books may prove profitable. What seemed to be the life values of the teachers mentioned? What did they consider the job of the teacher to be? How were they able to stimulate the interest of boys and girls and to guide their growth toward desirable ends?

Studying the functions of education.   One method of stating the competencies necessary for teaching is to formulate the objectives of American education. The Educational Policies Commission [120:50,72,90,108] developed a statement of objectives, which is expressed in terms of pupil behavior. It goes almost without saying that any teacher should exemplify these objectives and be effective in realizing them in others. Thus, in addition to appraising yourself as a prospective teacher, become familiar with this statement of purposes, which is to be found in Chapter 14. Furthermore, evaluate your own public school experiences to determine the extent to which you yourself have accomplished these objectives.

Educators' statements of competencies.   Educators singly and in groups have developed lists of competencies for teaching, based upon their experiences as teachers and their observations of, and work with, other teachers. These lists often take the form of rating scales used in evaluating the work of a teacher on the job and of students engaged in their student teaching. You may wish to see the scale on which your success in student teaching will be appraised, and study carefully the competencies involved. By having a clear understanding of these competencies you will be able to plan specific experiences that you should gain prior to your student teaching.

The California Council on Teacher Education published a statement [51:6–11] of teaching competencies in order to elaborate the function of student teaching and to give direction to the evaluation of student teachers. The council believes that ". . . a statement of behavior, what the teacher actually does, is more helpful than vague references to qualities such as personality, intelligence, appearance, and character. Such qualities are important to the extent that they reflect themselves in the behavior of successful teachers." The statement of these competencies is included in the Resource Section of Part I. As you read the statement, ponder your present status concerning each of them, your probable status at the end of your college preparation, and your potential after graduation.

There are many other statements of teacher competencies that have been formulated by individual educators as well as by groups of educators. These may be found in various books and periodicals. You are encouraged to use them to assist you in planning thoroughly for teaching.

Some Implications for Your Planning.   As you study various lists of competencies, you may be amazed at the number of requirements for teaching. The school of today requires far more of teachers than the school of yesterday. This fact is understandable when you consider the expanding function of the school in American life. In earlier days the school in this country was limited primarily to teaching boys and girls the fundamental skills of reading, writing, and arithmetic. The home, the church, and the community provided most of the other learnings essential for effective citizenship. Life was relatively simple. Today, however, life is much more complex. This is due especially to the tremendous technological advancements that have been made. Great changes have also taken place in our social, economic, and political life. The function of the school must change and expand in order to meet the needs of youth today and tomorrow. These changes give rise to new and broader requirements for teachers.

The teacher of today understands the cultural context in which all education takes place. He sees clearly the significance of industrialization, urbanization, corporativeness, economic planning, cultural lag, cultural fragmentation, the growth of a scientific attitude toward problems, and other outstanding characteristics of the contemporary American scene as they affect the lives of the people. He has the ability to understand modern problems in terms of historical conditions, to recognize the recurrent nature of many educational concerns, to use the resources of the past when faced with the problems of the present, and thus to discriminate between worthy traditional solutions and those solutions which are no longer pertinent. He understands the process whereby values are inculcated for the guidance of our conduct and judgments. He demonstrates, through his attitudes, skills, and habits, a basic understanding of democracy as a way of perpetuating the values of our culture, as a process by which each may develop his best self, as a method for solving problems, and as a process of disciplining himself for the betterment of our common lives. He possesses a critical understanding of the function of communities as agencies directing human growth and of the school as one agency by which society seeks to provide for its continued expansion as well as for the development of the individual. He sees the school as an institution which is charged with a major responsibility in determining the direction and character of this growth. He recognizes that the manner in which he goes about the teaching of boys and girls is determined by what he conceives to be the real function of education.

Educational research, during the past several years, has revealed new

In order to provide adequately for differing abilities and interests of pupils, teachers must be able to plan for and guide the work of the individual, as well as of the group within their classrooms. (*Photograph from Perrysburg Public School, Perrysburg, Ohio.*)

insights regarding human behavior and the learning process. The teacher of today needs an extensive understanding of the nature of individual development in all its various aspects so that he may recognize and anticipate the increasing needs of the student and provide the conditions which will promote his maximum growth. He is aware of the ways in which people are alike and of the ways in which they differ. He understands how the individual may become more like others and yet unique as he attains maturity. He comprehends thoroughly the nature of human learning, both in terms of the learner's habits, attitudes, skills, and abilities, and in terms of his own role as an effective guide in the learning process. It is essential, furthermore, for him to possess expert skill in guiding the education of others toward desirable ends.

Some Teacher-competency Self-appraisal Forms. You may find some forms, specifically designed for self-appraisal, to be helpful to you. For your convenience, one of these forms, which is concerned with the teacher's personality, has been included in the Resource Section for Part I. Obtain other forms from your teacher-placement office to use in self-appraisal.

As you can detect from your study of competencies thus far, it is important for you to make a careful study of your personality in order to discover your strengths for teaching as well as any qualities that may be a handicap to success. Frequently, one undesirable personality trait may overshadow many desirable ones. Use other students, especially those preparing for teaching, as a basis for comparison in rating yourself on the various items in the teacher's personality check list.

If, after you have finished rating yourself on the check list, you find that you rank high on some items, do not assume that room for growth is impossible. Everyone can improve himself with respect to any item listed. For example, regardless of how beautiful a woman is, she usually seeks to improve her personal appearance. Because of this feminine trait, hairdressers and cosmetics manufacturers flourish. The schools would be fortunate, indeed, if teachers would attempt to improve themselves professionally to the same degree that women seek to enhance their personal appearance.

It is very important for you to cultivate a personality pattern that will exert a healthy and desirable effect upon your pupils. Remember that what you are as a person is by far the most potent subject matter that will be in your classroom. To paraphrase Emerson, "I cannot hear what you *say*, when what you are thunders so loud!" Furthermore, children are highly imitative, and it is through imitation especially that behavior patterns are established.

There has been some recent significant research completed on types of teacher personalities and their effect upon various groups of children [70:1–82]. Heil and his associates developed and applied what is called a "Manifold Interest Schedule" to over 50 public school teachers of grades 4, 5, and 6, and measured the progress of their children against the personality types of teachers identified by the schedule. It was found that children with a teacher having one type of personality made 50 per cent more academic progress than did children with a teacher having a decidedly different personality.

Another instrument, called the "Children's Feeling Test," developed by Professor Heil and his associates, made it possible to identify four categories of children's personality. One type of teacher appeared to have a deleterious effect upon children of the least well-adjusted category, whereas another type had a definitely beneficial effect upon such children.

As a result of this study, Heil and his associates concluded that the type of the teacher's personality appears to have much effect on the progress of his pupils. Furthermore, it appears that the clear overriding factor in determining children's academic achievement is a positive and definite personality [70:66–68].

PERSONAL GROWTH TOWARD TEACHING

Much of your personal growth toward effective teaching is concerned with intangibles that are not learned in formal ways. In fact, you may get little direct help in this regard from all of the formal courses you take in your preparation for teaching. You do have available in your college environment, however, many resources that you may use. The amount of growth you make will depend largely upon you. Of course, your professors, counselors, and close friends may be able to help you identify some of your strengths and weaknesses for teaching, and to suggest appropriate resources.

Professional Maturity. A good teacher is, first of all, a happy person who approaches problems with a positive attitude. He analyzes mistakes and failures in terms of positive values that may be gained. He has developed effective techniques for meeting the common personal and professional problems of life and he attempts to think through objectively to an effective solution of any unusual problems that occur. He is able to contribute constructively to discussions and activities. He is responsive to the ideas and needs of others. He normally conceals impatience, anger, chagrin, and other evidences of inner disturbance that might upset the work of a group. He is a solid, stable kind of person, upon whom you can depend.

The professional mature person is truly interested in other people. He shows his interest by being a good listener and attending with real enthusiasm to the problems, accomplishments, and experiences of others. He cooperates in their activities and invites them to share his. He tries to help others, both friends and strangers. He observes others whenever there is opportunity, and this improves his understanding of human beings and of himself.

In order to exert positive influences in the classroom, a teacher must be well adjusted, cheerful, and able to approach life constructively.
(*Photograph from the* Planning for Teaching *series of motion pictures.*)

A professionally mature person knows himself. The man with self-understanding recognizes that people are driven by both good and bad motives, and that people must learn to identify the motives under which they operate. He knows that sound emotional expression is to be encouraged, and that there are many frustrations in life.

Because he knows himself well, he is able to understand others. Although he holds an ideal personality as his objective, he does not expect people—or even himself—to be perfect. Because he sees the behavior of people in terms of their motivations and background of experience, he can accept them as individuals traveling the road with him, sometimes successfully, sometimes not.

The professionally mature person substitutes adult goals for those of childhood. Whereas the child simply wants, the adult considers his wants in relation to others and to the future as well as the present. The truly mature people look for intrinsic qualities in their activities, for the real worth. They often work long and hard for distant ends, goals that sometimes seem almost unattainable. But they know the difference between the difficult and the impossible. The immature person is quick to say "Oh, what's the use?"

The professionally mature person knows what he values. It is essential that you determine the things that mean most to you, the ideals for which you stand, and the extent to which you will compromise character for gain. You must act alone in accordance with your beliefs and ideas; you are called upon to be critical and independent in your thinking; you must take the responsibility for your actions. To attempt to excuse yourselves for adolescent deeds is to deny being mature.

The professionally mature person has self-control over his actions.   Getting mad, telling people off, bawling people out, or pounding tables normally is evidence of lack of self-control rather than of mature behavior. True, every individual is expected to stand up for his rights, his ideas, and his ideals. People who see their goals clearly and can speak cogently in their defense are needed more today than in any other period of civilization.

A professionally mature person appraises his behavior in terms of its effect upon others.   No person is free and unhampered; each is bound by ties to other people. Your words and deeds may be a pattern for someone, and your actions set off a chain reaction of untold importance. You need to think through any proposed behavior and try to anticipate its implications for yourself and others.

Growth in professional maturity means systematically removing weaknesses and building strengths.   Remember that your image of yourself often is reflected in how others see you.

A careful analysis of your own personality traits is most desirable in planning for teaching. Someone you know may be of invaluable help to you in this respect. Ask him to speak frankly and to the point, to help determine why you may alienate others—even though what he says may hurt. Above all, try to avoid the tendency to interrupt by trying to explain and justify each criticism. As soon as he has finished his appraisal, discuss ways in which you may improve, and try to carry into action any suggestion your critic makes. Also, it may prove helpful if you think carefully about the persons you know who do not seem to have many friends. What kinds of people are they? Do they talk too much? Are they insincere? Do they pry into business not their own? Are they thoughtless and rude? Do they ask too much and give too little? Do they expect everything to be worked out in their favor? Are they jealous? Is any one of these people *you?*

It is normal for all people to be self-critical when they think thoughts that are unworthy of their better selves, when they are angry and behave rudely, or when they strike out in self-defense. They must recognize these defects because the road to improvement lies through objective self-criticism.

Every man has known failure at some time or another unless he has never attempted anything. Fortunately, the human mind can often turn failure into success. Ability to face failure with constructive attitudes has been given to each individual. To the inquiring mind failure often teaches more than success.

One factor which helps in the understanding and accepting of self is the honest determination of motives. Motives are a spur to action and exert a great influence over behavior. Positive motives—desire for the simple physical comforts, a need to belong, a longing for friendship—are wholesale drives to improve living. Negative motives—feelings of boredom, guilt, and inferiority, a fear of suffering—develop into personality problems.

The mature person has motives that are, on the whole, positive. They push him to make satisfactory adjustments to problems that he must face. He accepts certain motives wisely, with the good of himself and others in mind.

The immature person may experience motives that are in conflict with the more acceptable motives of his group, or in conflict with his own acquired sense of right and wrong. When such a conflict arises, he fails to meet his difficulties squarely. He may avoid facing the issue in one fashion or another. He may rationalize his behavior or project his faults to others. He may deny participation. He may just run away. In more serious cases he may become intoxicated, hysterical, or extremely aggressive.

Motives are closely associated with emotions. Many people have come to look upon emotionality as something to be frowned upon and to be repressed. To experience and to show emotion is human. Many of the finest things of our society, such as music and art, are emotional expressions. Ordinary people respond to the warm smile of the dirty-faced little boy at the curb.

Emotions are normal. Let your enthusiasm show forth; put your heart into your activities; be the real *you*. Emotion guided by temperance and sincerity opens the door to friendship; coldness and high-handed reserve lock it securely.

Your understanding of yourself will be revealed by the extent to which you can recognize your weaknesses, capitalize upon your strengths, focus a clear eye upon your motives, and permit healthy emotional expression. To refuse to look at yourself objectively is to fail to tap the most important resource for self-improvement.

Growth in Poise and Security.　Often personal poise and security are greatly influenced by factors which are more easily controlled than some of the inner feelings previously discussed. Those who are at ease in dress and manner, whose voice and speech are pleasing to others, develop into mature successful individuals. Being confident of personal appearance is a great asset. Almost all of us can recall at least one instance in which we felt ill at ease because of inappropriate dress or because of some lack of fastidiousness. An inventory of personal appearance, like the one in the Resource Section for Part I, may assist you in appraising habits that affect your appearance. If you should find yourself to be quite negligent in regard to any of the items in the check list, now is the time to start doing something about it so that the habit of being careful of your personal appearance will be part of you when you begin teaching.

Superintendents frequently remark that young people often lose the jobs they seek, almost before they speak a word, because of their untidy or inappropriate dress. Personnel managers in business and industry report a high incidence of people failing to be employed because of careless habits affecting personal appearance.

In times past, teachers often wore drab, unattractive clothes because they were forced by the profession to look austere, and by poverty to be penurious. Navy, black, brown, and other dark colors were considered serviceable and not distracting to the children.

Today teachers command salaries which allow them to dress moderately well. Teachers dress in good taste like other professional people. They express something of their individuality in their choices.

Your students will be greatly interested in what you wear and how well you wear it. Young children especially will be interested even in the jewelry you wear. They will enjoy bright color and variety in your daily attire. Remember how deadly some of your teachers were if they continued to wear the same suits or dresses every day; if their shirts, suits, or dresses seemed never to have been pressed; and if their shoes were in a bad state of repair. And you were forced to look at these teachers at least one period each day throughout the school year. Untidiness is related more to slovenly habits rather than to intellectual excellence. Undoubtedly the classes of such teachers would have been more stimulating if you could also have looked to them for clues to good dress habits. How will you treat your students in this regard?

New teachers are often tempted to wear out their leftover campus clothes during their first year of work. This may be desirable if your clothes are those that give you a sense of well-being and appropriateness. On the whole, however, campus fashions are not the most appropriate. You may need the aid of more mature dress to help you take your place as a person responsible for boys and girls. If you watch the purchases

What the teacher wears will be of much interest to the pupils. Through the way you dress, you will be able to provide pupils with clues to good dress habits. (*Photograph by Carl Purcell, National Education Association.*)

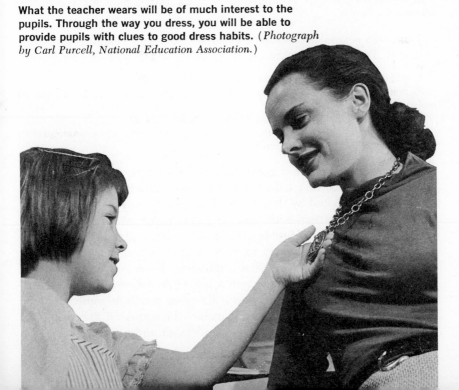

you make as you prepare for the professional responsibilities of student teaching, the transition to dressing for your first job will be easy.

In spite of all that has been said here about dress, what you actually do will depend ultimately upon the situation in which you find yourself. The community you choose for your first teaching position will have certain customs in dress which you as a wise beginner will want to follow. Do not be unduly impressed by the more staid members of the group, but adopt the style which seems applicable to those of your age in your work. You have a right to be an individual, but you also have a responsibility to the group you have chosen to work with.

A faultless appearance is not all that is required to give poise and self-confidence before friends and professional associates. You must know how to act as well as how to look.

Good manners are especially important to teachers. They smooth the way for pleasant relationships with others and provide examples for children to follow. To have good manners you must constantly think of yourself in the other person's place, and act accordingly. High on the list of professional courtesies are these:

1. Be considerate of students and of those with whom you work.
2. Make students feel at ease with you, and give them your complete attention.
3. Learn to be a good listener.
4. Avoid talking about yourself too much.
5. Keep confidential information to yourself.
6. Generally avoid controversial issues in professional discussions which may become bitter and personal.
7. Do your best to pour oil on troubled waters.
8. Never criticize your associates; such action creates problems and seldom solves a single one.

There are several questions which may help you evaluate your own behavior. Try them on some recent situation which was disturbing.

1. Did your action show thoughtfulness for all concerned?
2. Were your manners the kind which you could recommend for others to imitate?
3. Did you feel that you were handling the situation well?
4. If you were uncertain of the proper action, have you since attempted to think through what you should have done?

Everyone should have a good reference source of information about what constitutes correct behavior in various situations. Individuals who are liked and accepted by their professional groups may serve as patterns. Discussing such matters with your friends is thoroughly respectable.

First impressions are very important. Although a pleasing appearance and genteel manners may help to create a good impression, your manner of speaking may utterly ruin that impression. Have you ever been surprised by the high feminine voice of a big, husky fellow, or by the harsh voice of a pretty girl? How do you react when you hear someone speak in a distinctive accent or with mannerisms which make it impossible for you to understand? Is your own voice pleasant and attractive?

Teachers normally speak several thousands of words each day. How pleasant and attractive will they be? Is your speech a good index of the kind of person you are? Have you ever listened carefully to your voice and speech patterns? Is there any room for improvement? (*Photograph by Carl Purcell, National Education Association.*)

Voices and speech sometimes are an excellent index of an individual's personality. Speech may reveal a bright, sunny nature or a gloomy, complaining one. Speech may show strength or weakness of personality. Speech may show intelligence or ignorance.

Although most people have acceptable speech, almost everyone can improve his speech if he knows his own special needs. There is the true story of a young first-grade teacher who complained to her principal, "I can't underthtand why tho many of my children lithp." Children are great and often unconscious imitators. It is doubly important, then, for adults to perfect their speech—not only to improve themselves, but to serve as an adequate model for children.

As a prospective teacher you should make arrangements with a speech therapist for a voice and speech test. With the expert's help, you can make a careful study of the results. A trained worker will be able to help you with suggestions about pronunciation, tone quality, pitch, speed, and enunciation. There are prescribed remedial measures to assist you in each of these areas.

If professional help is not available, try making a voice record. You will hear your voice approximately as others hear it. Certain problems may be obvious at once. How do you like your voice? Is your voice too high or too low to be pleasant? Are your words monotonous? Are there nervous pauses and repetitions? Do you speak too fast or too slowly to be distinctly understood? Do you hesitate on the pronunciation of words? Do you speak with expression appropriate to the speech? Are you sure of the correctness of your grammar? The check list on voice and speech that appears in the Resource Section for Part I may help you appraise yourself systematically.

Building Personal Resources.   Dress, manners, and speech are not all that are required, however, in order to be a really interesting person. Many people, though perfectly groomed, still stand on the outside looking in. What personal resources do you have that will command interest and admiration of others and, at the same time, contribute to your well-rounded development?

Almost everyone has one or more hobbies or special interests he pursues during his leisure time—music, sports, collecting, hiking, boating, photography, etc. The list of such activities is almost endless. All those that give pleasure to the individual and are worthy of being shared with others help to build personal resources.

Reading is another resource for the maturing individual. The reading of books stimulates the imagination, challenges thought, and relaxes the mind from the strains of the day. Of course, different people read for different reasons. Many persons do little to vary their reading diet; others flit from book to book and gain little from any of them. To be wholly profitable, read both for pleasure and for gain. Most young professional people tend to forget the latter.

While you are in college you are likely to feel that lessons give ample reading of the instructive type. Sometimes there seems to be so much that has to be read that there is no time to read freely for fun. For the

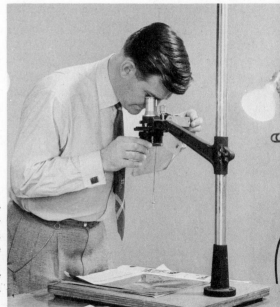

Photography is a popular hobby and through it many teachers have found a means of preparing effective instructional materials.
(*Photograph from the National Education Association.*)

sake of your well-rounded development, however, attempt to vary your daily diet of college books. The relaxed reader who has enjoyed reading something is normally in a good state of mind.

There are also resources to be found in travel. New faces and new scenes often provide the challenge needed when the routine of daily living seems to weigh heavily upon you. There are many agencies supplying information on where and how to go. Through travel many teachers take pictures and collect other materials that provide excellent instructional resources for their classes. Your next trip will not be too early for you to start collecting such materials.

For those who must plan finances more carefully, there are also many travel possibilities. Summer job opportunities are available at the national park hotels; forest ranger work has appeal for many young men; service on Great Lakes' steamers combines sailing fun and financial return; working in a department store in a large city is a stimulating change and a good chance to gain skill in working with adults; camp counseling combines outdoor living and opportunities to know children.

Several colleges and universities offer inexpensive tours for their students, permitting them to earn college credit while traveling. The National Education Association conducts tours to many spots in the United States, Canada, and Mexico. All these travel excursions cost a minimum of money and are expertly conducted.

Making Choices.   In all your resource-building activities you must make many choices. You cannot do everything. There are numerous pleasures to be had in life, but life may become so crowded with their pursuit that there is no energy left with which to enjoy them. A friend once remarked, "Saying that you are too busy isn't an original excuse. It merely means that you are not adult enough to make wise choices."

Many choices are simply a matter of picking the things which are of greatest interest and importance at the moment. Other choices involve the making of value judgments, the careful selection of activities in the light of their real worth. How do you choose the movies you attend? Do you select on the basis of reviews, previews, type of picture, actors, or some other factor? How do you determine your radio or television fare? What are the merits of detective fiction and soap operas? Do you read the kinds of novels that measure up to your standards? Do you engage in leisure-time activities that you would be proud to be seen doing?

Value judgments and choice making are simplified for those whose ideals and standards point the direction that should be taken. For most people such standards spring from a belief in the goodness and power of God, a belief which they have verified in their experience with one another. Some young people have grown up firmly grounded in religious conviction, equipped to solve problems and to stand for the good. Their choices are made in the light of principles of worthy behavior.

Decisions are easier, too, for the person who has selected his specific goals. If you do not want to be carried hither and yon by every fancy, if you do not want to be wholly directed by other persons, it is important to know where you are going and what kind of person you want to be.

Some students refuse to believe that there are basic laws for good that must be obeyed. Their choices are made in the light of their own desires, and they are constantly puzzled by the need to make decisions. They rationalize their own undesirable behavior and excuse their own shortcomings. To be thus without resources to make wise choices can be frightening in today's disturbed world.

Learning to Solve Problems.   Rich personal resources are a wonderful insurance for future happiness and an ever-present help in meeting the many problems that confront us in daily living. The person of resources does not waste time or energy in refusing to face his difficulties. He faces them and he solves them. Any avoidance of so doing is an indication of lack of maturity.

Carrying out resolute action involves several types of activities. The first is to recognize and isolate the problem. In one text-film[1] Ada Adams, a forlorn young high school student, came to her English class the first day, the target of all eyes because of her unattractive dress, her habit of dropping things, and her refusal to talk. Many teachers had known Ada. They had ignored her; they had excused themselves from helping her because they were too busy. They had left the job to someone else. Ada's sympathetic teacher saw almost at once that here was a child who needed help, and after careful observation the teacher faced the problem. Ada was not accepted by others; it was obvious why she was not accepted. How could Ada be helped to find security in her social group?

The teacher began to marshal the facts she needed to solve the problem —the second step. Information and data had to be secured. The teacher had a conference with Ada; she studied her test scores; she talked to the other teachers; she visited Ada at home.

Then the teacher tried various approaches to a solution. She did not expect that all attempts would be successful. She was sure she would fail on some. She decided to put Ada's talent for art to work and enlisted the help of certain teachers to utilize the girl's ability. She gave Ada a responsible job in a committee that needed some sketches drawn. She encouraged the girls to include Ada in their plans. Thus she had taken the third step—she had formulated various solutions and had given them trials.

When Ada successfully designed the costumes for a play, her classmates were enthusiastic. Encouraged by the girls to untie her long hair and wear a sweater and skirt, Ada actually looked like one of the group. Her schoolwork improved because her teachers were helping to capitalize upon her talents.

In the story of Ada Adams, the results were not perfect. The teacher's last task—the evaluation of results—was the hardest, but she was able to

[1] *Learning to Understand Children*, McGraw-Hill Text-Films, New York, black and white, sound, 47 min, parts I and II.

see which techniques were most successful and which had failed. And she had learned much that would help her with other students.

Whether the problems you meet are more trivial, or less, than Ada Adam's, they require a similar process of thinking and planning. The problem must be identified, information gathered, tentative solutions formulated and tried, and results evaluated. Then generalizations may be made which apply to other situations.

Many problem-solving tasks involve the element of critical thinking. This is extremely important these days when everyone is bombarded with the ideas and persuasions of others and is urged to accept ready-made answers to pressing problems. Independent thinking well supported by reliable evidence is the responsibility of the effective citizen and professional person.

Working with People.   In most of the pursuits of life, whether they are problem-solving adventures or hobby fun, people sooner or later must learn to work with others. Those who are continually at odds with their associates may be like the ten-year-old who said to her one friend, "Oh, I do wish you and I were the only ones in the world; then we could do as we please and run a hotel!"

Perhaps the first prerequisite in learning to get along with others is to understand them. The more you know about yourself, of course, the more you can know about others. Your fears, successes, and motives are probably shared by the vast majority of people.

The teacher knows that his pupils cannot learn respect for the worth and contributions of others merely by studying about them. They must put their beliefs into action. The teacher is alert to the many opportunities to guide children in the direction of understanding, and acceptance of differences among people.

The teacher himself sets an example in his attitude toward his own pupils. He learns to think of each as an individual. He does not reject a single one for any reason. He accepts the adults whom he meets in the school scene—parents, superintendents, supervisors, and custodians—in very much the same way.

Real acceptance goes deep. It involves appreciating the motives of others and minimizing secondary considerations. It calls upon a person to encourage his friends and to help them capitalize on their abilities and find a place in the group. One thing more is necessary: the acceptance of others' success and the willingness to assist them to it. This is perhaps the hardest task for those who work and share the honor of a job together. But the welfare of the group demands that each should have an opportunity to succeed, and that the chance for success should be promoted whenever possible.

Probably success in understanding and accepting others rests on interest in them. Those who are interesting to you are seldom your enemies. Some young people show pseudo concern with others, merely to reflect their own personalities. This is all too obvious to everyone. Real interest

Teaching requires a high degree of skill in working with others—colleagues, pupils, parents, and other community members. While in college are you taking advantage of the many opportunities afforded to develop this skill? *(Photograph from the National Education Association.)*

manifests itself in other ways—in sincere attempts to help, in recognition of merit, in willingness to listen, and in a desire to be with and to work with others.

Participating in Group Work. While in college you have many opportunities to work with both adults and children. Membership in clubs, fraternities, church and welfare organizations, sports groups, and professional societies offers a chance to learn the skills of cooperation that lead to habits of good group membership and leadership.

A good group member has several outstanding characteristics: First, he is a cooperating individual, freely contributing his ideas for group consideration and genuinely evaluating the ideas of others. He treats all suggestions put forth as worthy of attention. He does not monopolize the conversation. He tries to make his special experience count for as much as possible. He gives supporting data when he can. He thinks in terms of group purposes and plans, placing the collective welfare above his personal gains and satisfactions. He tends to avoid "either-or" situations or arguments. He selects what seem to be the good ideas advanced by others and helps incorporate them into the general thinking. He thoroughly and promptly fulfills the responsibilities delegated to him. He does not become discouraged in the initial stages. He realizes that group discussion progresses slowly at first but is often productive in the long run. He trusts group thinking and action, realizing that each individual is superior to the rest in some respects, and that the thinking of the collective body is usually clearer and more productive than that of a single member.

In order to increase your effectiveness as a group participant you may find it helpful to check yourself in regard to some questions titled "Am

I a Good Group Participant?" which appear in the Resource Section for Part I.

One application of the principles of group participation can be a class discussion of some of the topics or problems found at the end of each chapter in this book. In order to get started, your instructor may temporarily assume leadership in helping your group select its subjects. After this initial step, he may wish to turn over his role to members of the group as quickly as possible, so that they may gain leadership experience.

All members of the group should help decide how the group will attack the topic. Such projects as reading in the library, interviewing, bringing resource people to the classroom, writing reports, viewing films, having panel discussions, and the like may be involved. It may seem desirable for small groups to work on certain aspects of the problem and to report their findings to the entire group. The techniques of approaching problems are many, and you, as a prospective teacher, will want to become skilled in all of them.

In developing a plan of action, it is important for the group to understand clearly the topic to be discussed or the problem to be solved, to explore the sources of information available, to decide how to obtain the necessary data, and to determine how to organize and use them. As soon as these steps have been completed the group is ready to carry the plans into action. It should then evaluate the over-all success with which it has worked.

Serving as a Group Leader.   There is a significant difference between being a group participant and serving as discussion group leader. Since the latter more nearly approximates the role you will play as a teacher, gain as much leadership skill as possible while in college in your course work and extracurricular activities. As a group leader keep in mind the following:

1. Help the group define the problem clearly—its nature and scope or delimitations.
2. Encourage all participants to share their thinking, information, and experience.
3. Provide opportunity for all points of view to be expressed.
4. Keep the discussion directed to the problem.
5. Help group members to clarify their thinking and to summarize their progress.
6. Utilize all resources represented in the experience of group members.
7. Strive to develop a cohesive and productive group.
8. Avoid trying to save time by telling the group the right answer.

Keep in mind that the leader is not a group instructor; he is a guide trying to arrange conditions so that each member will do creative thinking. Group discussion is not a debating society. While disagreements are to be expected, the task of the group is to find more truth than each member brings to any group meeting. Help the group, therefore, to view the task as a cooperative quest in which thinking is creative rather than combative.

Using Time Most Effectively.   Your development as a good teacher will be affected by the extent to which you become increasingly skilled in the wise use of your time. As Shakespeare advised, "Let every man be master of his time. . . ."

On an average, you have about eight hours each day which you spend in other ways than in going to classes, studying, sleeping, eating, and attending to personal grooming. The kinds of things you can do with this portion of time are numerous, and your opportunities for promoting your personal growth toward teaching are great.

As a college student you undoubtedly recognize the wisdom of planning your personal time, and you understand desirable procedures that may be used. For this reason the only points to be made are that the problem of using time effectively is ever present, that you need to check periodically to see whether or not you are using your time most profitably, that skill in the wise use of time may be gained as you work intelligently upon the problem and plan accordingly, that provision should be made for a well-balanced program of activities which takes into consideration all aspects of your personal growth, and that skill gained in the effective use of your time while in college will pay high dividends in your work as a teacher and as a citizen.

SUMMARY

In this chapter you have been concerned with competencies for teaching and with personal growth toward teaching. The results of several studies on teacher competencies have been presented so that you could compare them, note similarities, and evaluate yourself in regard to them.

Keep in mind that any statement of competencies for teaching must be considered as a whole. Specific competencies are listed for purposes of study and clarification.

No one can expect to meet all the competencies for teaching to the highest degree, either at the time of graduation or at the end of a lifetime teaching career. But with each year of experience, it is a teacher's professional obligation to move to a fuller realization of his potential. Weaknesses can be made strong, and strengths can be made stronger; hence there is always the horizon of greater fulfillment.

Your personal growth toward teaching is not to be achieved by merely following a recipe, even such a one as has been given in this chapter. Each individual is different in needs and abilities. Study yourself in the light of those qualities that seem characteristic of desirable professional people and then plan to acquire the ones you now appear to lack. The suggestions given here will point the way to many other possibilities. Call upon friends and teachers to assist you in your program of self-improvement. Explore the hundreds of opportunities that your college campus offers. Don't miss a single one that will be helpful to you.

Careful planning and conscientious execution of those plans will assist you in becoming a worthwhile citizen, a well-adjusted person, and an individual who understands himself; one who is poised and secure, who can solve problems, and who knows how to work with others. Such a person can become important in his own right and can justify the investment of time and energy needed to help him take his place in his chosen profession. His values and ideals will be clearly recognized by all who know him. His personality will mark him as the kind of individual the modern world needs.

QUESTIONS FOR YOUR CONSIDERATION

1. From your observations what are the most common weaknesses of beginning teachers? How can you avoid such weaknesses when you begin teaching?

2. How can you gain greater understanding of the emotional and social needs of children?

3. Do you feel that your image of yourself often is reflected in how others see you? Can you present any evidence to support this point, and what are the implications for your success as a future teacher?

4. In what ways does a teacher's personality affect the progress of his pupils? Can you recall incidents that support your point of view?

5. What particular interests or hobbies did your high school teachers have? Did these interests or hobbies contribute to their effectiveness as teachers? Explain.

6. Does a school administrator or supervisor have the right to criticize a teacher for being untidy or inappropriately dressed? If so, why?

7. What instances can you recall in which poor manners upon the part of teachers had detrimental effects upon the learning of pupils?

8. What qualities of voice and speech in teachers are conducive to good discipline in the classroom?

9. How did you spend your time during the past week? Was your time distributed in such a manner that you would experience a maximum amount of growth toward teaching?

10. Should a married woman teacher ever be forbidden to teach? If so, when?

ACTIVITIES FOR YOU TO PURSUE

1. Interview informally a number of boys and girls about the qualities that they think teachers should have. Have them also indicate the qualities which they dislike the most in teachers. Check your findings against those of Witty.

2. Draw a line vertically through the center of a piece of paper. On the left-hand side, list the factors that characterize the teacher whom you most disliked while in school. On the right-hand side, list the factors that characterize the teacher you like best. At the bottom of the page, list the characteristics of the teacher who was of most value to you. Compare and contrast the characteristics listed for all three in an effort to determine common elements. Check your results against the findings listed in this chapter.

3. Review the various statements of competencies indicated in the Resource Section for Part I, and evaluate your present status with respect to each of them. You may wish to use a scale, ranging from "very little" to "greatly," for checking yourself on each of the items.

4. Check yourself on the "Check List of Important Factors in the Teacher's Personality" which appears in the Resource Section of Part I, and underline the qualities or traits in which you need to improve. Try to formulate some first steps to take in overcoming your weaknesses.

5. Consult your director of student teaching regarding competencies against which you will be evaluated in your student teaching. Secure copies of any forms that may be used, and study them carefully. Formulate specific plans for overcoming any weaknesses that may be revealed from a study of these forms.

6. Consult your local school superintendent regarding any rating forms he may use in evaluating the work of his teachers. Secure copies of these forms if possible and study them carefully.

7. Discuss with an experienced school superintendent the qualities he looks for when he is employing teachers. Also ask him to list the main weaknesses of beginning teachers.

8. Ask several of your close friends to use the check lists presented in this chapter to appraise your appearance and your speech. Compare their ratings of you with your own. Consider ways to work on the problems revealed by their comments.

9. Consult with the counseling services on your college campus to locate the various agencies which may be of service to you in your program of self-improvement.

10. Explore the catalogue of courses offered in your school to find those that you may utilize to broaden your interests or help overcome a personality problem. Consider such courses as mental hygiene, philosophy and ethics, science fields that are new to you, arts and crafts, camp counseling, folk dancing, sports, speech improvement, writing, or dramatics. There are sure to be many helpful possibilities.

11. Investigate the possibilities of working with a group of children or young people in your community. Explore opportunities in scouting groups, community centers, recreation programs, church schools, and the like.

12. In your future group activities carefully appraise the extent to which you fulfill the characteristics of a good group member. Formulate ways to strengthen any characteristics in which you find yourself to be weak.

13. Keep an accurate record of how you spend your time during a fairly normal week of school. At the end of the week analyze the distribution of your time to see whether you are making the best use of it. You may wish to discuss the results with your friends and instructors and to plan ways of gaining more value from the free time you have available.

4

CERTIFICATION AND FUTURE PROFESSIONAL GROWTH

If you feel that you have a good chance of acquiring the professional skills, attitudes, and abilities required for teaching, what more do you need to do in order to become a member of the profession?

You have to be licensed to teach, just as you have to be licensed to practice medicine, dentistry, or law. In other words, the state, territory, or other educational authority must attest to your competence before you are permitted to practice your profession.

How do you get this license, credential, or certificate? You get it by completing successfully a prescribed curriculum as discussed in the previous chapter. You also will need to engage in various professional activities and complete certain requirements after you have been certified.

CERTIFICATION OF EDUCATORS

A number of the older teachers whom you know may not have a bachelor's degree; in fact, some have had very little college credit. You may wonder why they are permitted to teach, while you are required to take so much more college work. A brief historical sketch of teacher certification may help you in understanding this situation, and may indicate the tremendous amount of progress that has been made in the professionalization of teaching.

Progress in Certification of Teachers. Not many years ago, about the only qualification required for becoming a teacher was willingness to "keep school." Local employing officials usually considered "a bit of larnin'" desirable but not always essential. Samuel R. Hall, in his *Lectures on School Keeping*, published in 1829, quoted a writer who was criticizing the low standards for teachers at that time [124:495–496].

> Every stripling who has passed four years within the walls of a college, every dissatisfied clerk who has not ability enough to manage the trifling concerns of a retail shop, every young farmer who obtains in the winter a short vacation from the toils of the summer—in short, every person who is conscious of his imbecility in other business, esteems himself fully competent to train the ignorance and weakness of infancy into all the virtue and power and wisdom of maturer years—to form a creature, the frailest and feeblest that heaven has made, into the intelligent and fearless sovereign of the whole animated creation, the interpreter and adorer, and almost the representative of divinity.

Prior to the turn of the century a typical elementary teacher had less than the equivalent of a high school education. In these early days a few ambitious and professionally serious individuals attended what were commonly called normal schools to prepare themselves for teaching. These normal schools existed for the express purpose of serving the personal interests and needs of prospective teachers. They served essentially the same function as do the business schools today. In spite of their services, it is reported that as late as World War I approximately half of the 600,000 teachers in the country had no more than four years of education beyond the eighth grade [155:57].

In earlier days the common method of ascertaining a person's fitness for teaching was an examination. This examination frequently amounted to an interview in which the candidate was asked a few questions by the employing official, who often was very poorly qualified to judge the answers he received. Later, prospective candidates were given a written examination that was usually constructed, administered, and scored by the local school board, superintendent, or county superintendent. Far too often these examinations were most inadequate and amounted to little more than mere formalities.

Eventually a number of objections were raised, primarily by teachers, to the system of certifying teachers through local examinations. In the first place the examinations were not standardized for more than a small area of the state, and therefore the successful candidate was qualified to teach only in the district in which the examination was taken. Furthermore, there often was little evidence that merit, as revealed by the examination results, constituted the basis upon which appointments were made.

Improvements in the examination system of certifying teachers were gained by granting to some state agency, such as the state department of public instruction, the authority to supervise and coordinate certification procedures. As a result of this change, the responsibility for constructing and scoring examinations for teacher certification became a state function. Certificates for teaching thus became valid throughout the state.

It is important to note that local communities and school officials usually were very reluctant to release to the state the authority for certifying teachers. Many communities felt that they were losing certain rights and that no means remained for reserving teaching position for local talent. This factor accounts largely for the slow progress that has been made in teacher certification.

Since 1922, certification requirements for beginning teachers definitely have improved. Increasing emphasis has been placed upon college preparation for teaching, with less emphasis upon examinations as a means of certification. Two-year normal schools have given way to four-year teachers colleges. State departments of instruction have established certain standards of training for the various institutions engaged in the preparation of teachers. The state department normally accepts for certification the graduates recommended by the teacher-education institutions within its domain. This procedure gives control over teacher education to the state and standardizes the minimum certification requirements.

Progress in teacher certification has resulted in a number of benefits: It has contributed much to the establishment of teaching as a profession. Pupils today are protected from incompetent teachers who gained the right to teach through unethical means. Competent teachers are pro-

This competent teacher knows that special collections often provide a basis for important classroom learnings. State teacher certification laws are designed to protect the educational welfare of youth. (*Photograph from the Indiana State Teachers Association.*)

tected from competition with unqualified teachers. Teachers are encouraged to improve their competence for teaching. Since the control for teacher certification is vested in the state, it is possible to have a continuous inventory of teachers and their qualifications.

Present Status of Certification Standards.   All the states and territories now have laws governing the certification of teachers in their respective areas. These laws in general indicate that certification is based on an applicant having completed an approved program of teacher education, including student teaching or its equivalent, in an accredited college or university. It is not possible to describe accurately the more detailed provisions governing certification without discussing the laws of each state separately. Since certification is a state function, each state has developed its own certification requirements, resulting in considerable difference among the states in regard to the amount of training required and the types of certificates granted.

Each year Robert C. Woellmer and M. Aurilla Wood publish a booklet titled *Requirement for Certification of Teachers, Counselors, Librarians, Administrators for Elementary Schools, Secondary Schools, Junior Colleges,* that lists the certification requirements in each state. Every two years W. Earl Armstrong and T. M. Stinnett publish a report, titled *A*

Manual on Certification Requirements for School Personnel in the United States, which details trends and specific data concerning certification qualifications, plus the addresses of the chief state certifying officers. The state department of education, in the state in which you wish to teach, will also send you, without charge, information about local requirements.

You will find these reports helpful in planning your work, especially if you are attending college outside your home state or are considering the possibilities of teaching in various other areas. You can save time and disappointment if, early in your training, you consult the specific certification requirements for the states in which you plan to teach.

A *general* idea of minimum certification requirements in states and territories in 1961 may be gained from Table 2. But if you plan to teach in a state other than the one in which you are taking your college work, do not depend upon a listing such as Table 2, since the requirements may have been raised. For example, Arizona is to require a bachelor's degree in 1963 for an elementary teacher's certificate. Also the total hours required in professional education may include certain specific courses,

TABLE 2   MINIMUM REQUIREMENTS FOR LOWEST REGULAR TEACHING CERTIFICATES BY STATES AND TERRITORIES*

State	Elementary school			High school		
	Degree or no. of semester hours required	Professional education required, semester hours	Directed teaching required, semester hours	Degree or no. of semester hours required	Professional education required, semester hours	Directed teaching required, semester hours
Alabama	B	30	3	B	24	3
Alaska	B	24	C	B	18	C
Arizona	B	18	6	5	18	6
Arkansas	60	12	3	60	12	3
California	B	24	8	5	22	6
Colorado	B	AC	AC	B	AC	AC
Connecticut	B	30	6	B	18	6
Delaware	B	30	6	B	18	6
District	B	24	6	5	18	6
Florida	B	20	6	B	20	6
Georgia	B	18	6	B	18	6
Hawaii	B	18	AC	B	18	AC
Idaho	B	20	6	B	20	6
Illinois	B	16	5	B	16	5
Indiana	B	30	6	B	18	5
Iowa	B	20	5	B	20	5
Kansas	B	24	5	B	20	5
Kentucky	B	28	8	B	17	8
Louisiana	B	24	4	B	18	4
Maine	96	AC	AC	B	12	0

* AC means approved curriculum; B means bachelor's degree of specified preparation; 5 means bachelor's degree plus a fifth year of appropriate preparation, not necessarily completion of master's degree; C means a course.

Source: W. Earl Armstrong and T. M. Stinnett, *A Manual on Certification Requirements for School Personnel in the United States,* National Commission on Teacher Education and Professional Standards, National Education Association, Washington, 1961, p. 24.

TABLE 2 *(continued)*

State	Elementary school			High school		
	Degree or no. of semester hours required	Professional education required, semester hours	Directed teaching required, semester hours	Degree or no. of semester hours required	Professional education required, semester hours	Directed teaching required, semester hours
Maryland	B	26	8	B	18	6
Massachusetts	B	18	2	B	12	2
Michigan	B	20	5	B	20	5
Minnesota	B	30	6	B	18	4
Mississippi	B	36	6	B	18	6
Missouri	B	20	5	B	20	5
Montana	64	AC	AC	B	AC	AC
Nebraska	40	8	3	B	18	3
Nevada	B	18	4	B	18	4
New Hampshire	B	AC	6	B	21	6
New Jersey	B	36	6	B	24	6
New Mexico	B	24	6	B	18	6
New York	B	36	12	B	18	6
North Carolina	B	18	3	B	18	3
North Dakota	64	16	3	B	16	3
Ohio	B	28	6	B	17	6
Oklahoma	B	21	6	B	21	6
Oregon	B	20	4	B	24	6
Pennsylvania	B	36	6	B	18	6
Puerto Rico	68	53	6	B	29	5
Rhode Island	B	30	6	B	18	6
South Carolina	B	21	6	B	18	6
South Dakota	60	15	3	B	20	5
Tennessee	B	24	4	B	24	4
Texas	B	24	6	B	24	6
Utah	B	30	8	B	22	8
Vermont	B	18	6	B	18	6
Virginia	B	18	6	B	15	4–6
Washington	B	AC	AC	B	AC	AC
West Virginia	B	20	5	B	20	5
Wisconsin	64	26	8	B	18	5
Wyoming	B	20	C	B	20	C

such as philosophy of education, or tests and measurements. Even the general categories vary considerably in semester hours demanded. In 1961 the range of necessary professional education courses ran from 8 to 53 semester hours, with a median of 18. Semester hours in student teaching ranged from 2 to 12, with a median of 6. In the past, these differences have made it difficult for teachers to move freely from one state to another.

Most states have requirements for teacher certification in addition to those indicated in Table 2. In 1961, for instance [6:33], thirty-two states and territories required that applicants be citizens of the United States. Twenty-six, a decrease of three since 1955, required the signing of an oath of allegiance or loyalty to the United States and the state. Eleven required as a prerequisite evidence of having been hired to teach. Forty-one required a recommendation from the college in which the student did his work or from the employing office if he is an experienced teacher. General health certificates were required in twenty-three states and territories, and chest X rays were required in fourteen. Fifteen states specified special courses, such as American history. American government, health education, or a history of that particular state as a requirement for certification. Eighteen states specified no minimum age; two specified age 17; twenty-eight indicated age 18; three required age 19; and one state specified age 20 [6:15]. Specific state requirements may be found in the manual by Armstrong and Stinnett, indicated above. Your college library or placement office will probably have a copy of this publication.

Trends in the Certification Standards for Elementary Teachers.   Table 2 indicates that an amazing amount of progress has been made in raising the certification standards for elementary teachers. As of September, 1961, a total of 43 states and territories were enforcing the bachelor's degree as the minimum requirement for the lowest regular certificate for beginning elementary school teachers [6:24]. All but 1 (Nebraska) of the remaining 7 states and Puerto Rico were enforcing the requirement for prospective elementary school teachers to have at least two years of college work. Two of these states (Arkansas, Sept. 1, 1963; South Dakota, Sept. 1, 1968) specified future dates when the bachelor's degree would be a requirement. Ten years prior to 1961, by way of contrast, only 17 states required the bachelor's degree, 3 required at least three years, 17 two years, 9 one year, and 2 states less than one year.

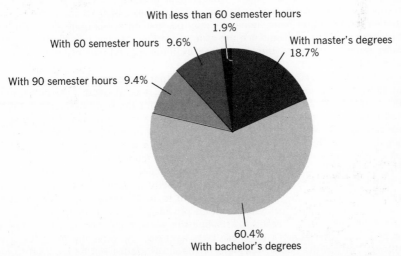

Figure 15.   Preparation of elementary school teachers in 1961–1962. In recent years, dramatic improvement has been made in the preparation of elementary school teachers. Why can further improvements be anticipated? (*Source:* National Education Association.)

A number of factors have contributed to the radical rise of the certification requirements. Undoubtedly, the rapid adoption of the single-salary schedule has played a significant role in the increase in these requirements. Also there has been a growing understanding of the significance and plan of elementary education in our society. The thinking of educators, as reflected in the following statement written in 1941, doubtless helped others to see the wisdom of raising the certification standards for elementary school teachers [91:269–270].

Today, it would be regarded as quite absurd if we should propose that doctors might treat small children after two years of medical training but must complete the full course to qualify for practice on adults. Educators are beginning to question whether it is any more logical to permit teachers of the very young to begin the practice of their profession with but half the training demanded of teachers of more advanced students. The doctor who aspires to be a "baby specialist" expects to take more, and not less, than average training. Since modern psychology is beginning to suggest that the whole scale of one's life is largely fixed by early experience, we are coming to appreciate as never before the vital need of high-type teaching in the elementary school.

Shortly after 1941, a well-known authority in the field of school administration was criticizing the policy of assigning the superior teachers to the upper grades and of giving the lower grades to the mediocre teachers [124:498–499].

School officials and the general public are coming to realize more and more that teachers of the lower grades need as much preparation as teachers of the upper grades; in fact, they are gradually coming to realize that there are valid reasons for requiring an even larger amount of preparation for teachers of the lower grades. They are coming to realize that the pupils in the lower grades need much more personal guidance from their teachers than the pupils in the upper grades. The pupils in the lower grades must acquire the tools of learning, and those tools cannot be acquired without the tutelage of a teacher. In the upper grades, on the other hand, pupils already possess an acquaintance with the tools of learning and in consequence are able to work somewhat independently. Those older pupils learn much through their own initiative, and they often learn in spite of poor teaching.

It may be properly contended, therefore, that the elementary school, and especially the first part of the elementary school, is of greatest importance among the school levels because it lays the foundation for the pupil's educational career and for life. It should have "prior rating" so far as the resources of the public are concerned; it is democracy's school *par excellence*. In those early years the pupils acquire the tools of knowledge and form habits and ideals which will remain with them throughout life. Unless the proper foundation is laid in the lower grades, the best superstructure for future educational accomplishment cannot be erected. Moreover, because they must start early to earn their living, or because secondary schools are not readily available to them, many pupils are unable to secure more formal education than that provided by the elementary school, and this is another potent reason for making the elementary school as thorough and as practical as possible. When these facts have become generally known by school officials and by the public, teachers in the lower grades will be required to have as much education as (if not more education than) teachers in the upper grades. And let not the teachers of the secondary schools and colleges forget the same facts, because where importance and difficulty of work are concerned they must humbly bow before the teachers of elementary schools.

It is not uncommon to find people, including some educators, expressing concern over the rising standards for elementary teachers. They feel that this trend will tend to increase the alarming shortage. There is considerable evidence, however, to indicate that the supply of elementary teachers generally *increases* as standards are raised. This increasing supply-standards ratio is paralleled in other professions, e.g., law and medicine. The reasons are largely that higher standards are usually accompanied by higher salaries; both standards and salary operate to enhance the prestige of a profession. When all three factors—standards, salary, and prestige—are strengthened, the supply of potential candidates attracted to the field increases.

In regard to the preschool level, 14 states in 1961 required public nursery school teachers and 40 states required public kindergarten teachers to hold certificates [6:12]. Normally, all states maintaining nursery and kindergarten schools at public expense require certification.

Trends in the Certification Standards for Secondary Teachers.   For a number of years a bachelor's degree from a recognized college has been the standard requirement for high school teaching. In 1961 all states except one were enforcing at least the bachelor's degree for beginning high school teachers. Arkansas is to require the bachelor's degree for certification beginning in September, 1963.

Nine states in 1961 were requiring the completion of the fifth year of training for high school teachers by the end of a specified number of years of teaching. Many educators feels that five years of college training will become a common standard for the preparation of secondary teachers in the relatively near future. A number of teacher-education institutions already include a fifth year of training as a regular part of the program. An increasing number of areas provide higher salaries for the beginning teacher who has had five years of preparation.

Since secondary teacher-education programs generally do not require a great number of professional courses, the range in 1961 (12 to 29 semester hours, a median of 18) was not so great as in the case of the elementary teacher-education program. In student teaching the semester hours required ranged from 0 to 8, with 6 as the median.

Trends in Certification Standards of Administrators, Supervisors, and Other School Personnel.   An increasing number of states are requiring school personnel such as administrators, principals, supervisors, speech and hearing therapists, audio-visual directors, librarians, psychologists, and guidance officers to hold special certificates appropriate for their respective positions. These certificates usually require some successful teaching experience in addition to college course work applicable to the specific position.

As you may see from Table 3, in 1961 a master's degree or more was required for an elementary school principal certificate in 67 per cent of the states and territories; for a secondary school principal certificate in

79 per cent; and for a superintendent of schools certificate in 88 per cent of the states and territories [6:9–30]. In 1955 the certification requirement of five or more years of training was specified in 19 states for elementary school principals, in 30 states for secondary principals, and in 36 states

TABLE 3   SUMMARY OF MINIMUM PREPARATION REQUIRED BY STATES FOR ADMINISTRATIVE CERTIFICATES, JULY 1, 1961

Number of college years of preparation or degrees required	Number of states requiring		
	Elementary school principal	Secondary school principal	Superintendent of schools
7 years or doctor's degree	0	0	1
6 years plus, but less than doctor's degree	0	0	0
6 years	0	0	7
Master's degree plus, but less than 6 years	3	6	4
Master's degree	32	35	34
Bachelor's degree plus, but less than 5 years	10	7	3
Bachelor's degree	6	3	1
Less than bachelor's degree	0	0	0
No certificate issued	1	1	2
Total	52	52	52

Source: W. Earl Armstrong and T. M. Stinnett, *A Manual On Certification Requirements for School Personnel in the United States,* National Commission on Teacher Education and Professional Standards, National Education Association, Washington, 1961, p. 9.

for superintendents of schools. Compare these numbers with those in Table 3 and you will note the strong trend, during this six-year period of time, toward increasing the requirements for administrative certificates.

There is considerable evidence to support the feeling that states will move rapidly toward the six-year requirement for administrative certificates. In 1961 eight states already required that much training. Undoubtedly other states will follow, especially since, beginning in 1964, the American Association of School Administrators will require new members to have six or more years of appropriate training.

Some states require that in order to qualify for a principal's or supervisor's position, a candidate must hold a valid teacher's certificate for the level he wishes to administrate. For example, a state may specify that a person must hold an elementary teacher's certificate and complete the prescribed graduate work to be eligible for an elementary principals' or supervisor's certificate. Requirements such as these indicate healthy trends in the certification of administrators and supervisors. Unfortunately there still are far too many elementary principals who receive appointments solely on their merits as high school athletic coaches or teachers, and who know little about the administration and organization of a good elementary school.

Trends in the certification of other school personnel, such as supervisors, counselors, psychologists, speech and hearing therapists, and guidance directors, are not as pronounced as are those for school administrators. It is inevitable that the requirements for certifying such school personnel will be raised even more. Many educators visualize a sixth year of training as necessary for competence to perform such technical tasks.

Certification Standards Prescribed by School Systems. Certification laws constitute minimum requirements established by a particular state for teachers. However, each school system within the state is free to establish requirements that exceed these minimums to whatever degree it desires. This means that you may be able to meet the state certification standards without being able to teach in a particular system. Therefore, try to familiarize yourself with the requirements of specific school systems in which you may desire to teach. Bear in mind that successful people seldom are content to meet bare minimums; usually superior preparation pays dividends.

The practice in school systems of requiring higher standards than the state minimums tends to raise the educational level of teachers. Unfortunately the practice is limited primarily to school systems which have an economic advantage over others. Most rural areas are able to demand only the state requirements. The school systems of especially larger cities may also require an applicant for a position to take a series of tests. These tests may cover language expression, reasoning ability, general culture, and professional information. A number of school systems require applicants to take the National Teacher Examination. This test is given each year in approximately 150 centers throughout the United States. Information about the test may be secured by writing to National Teacher Examination, Educational Testing Service, Princeton, New Jersey.

Trends in the Certification Standards for College Teachers. In 1961, there were 13 states that required teachers in public-supported junior colleges to hold certificates [6:12]. In general, these were states in which the junior colleges were a part of the public-supported system and in which they were usually maintained by the local school districts as an extension of secondary education. Four states required teachers in the state teachers colleges to hold certificates.

Normally each institution of higher learning establishes its own requirements for teachers, but the requirements may vary, within any one institution, according to subject field. In order to secure a full-time appointment on the college level, a person normally must have at least a master's and usually a doctor's degree. Successful public school teaching experience is almost a universal requirement for teaching professional education courses.

A number of questions have been raised regarding the desirability of developing some form of licensure for those teaching in college and graduate school. The report, *New Horizons for the Teaching Profession,* prepared by a committee of the National Commission on Teacher Education and Professional Standards of the National Education Association, indicates several differences that bear on the question that are worthy of note [86:153–154]:

The freedom of the student at these levels to choose his school and to choose whether to go to school at all has bearing only insofar as the protection of the individual is concerned; it has no bearing on the state's obligation to the rest of the society.

A second, more important difference is that college and graduate students should be expected to study on their own initiative, to depend relatively little on the teacher to show them how to learn what he has to offer. Yet adults still learn more rapidly and more thoroughly from a wise and skillful teacher. And as added knowledge and techniques have to be mastered by modern specialists, the efficiency with which they learn has become vitally important for their lives and the lives entrusted to them. It may be necessary to waive the requirement of teaching qualifications for various temporary functions as lecturer, consultant, clinical demonstrator, and so on, in order to get a person with other qualifications essential for the position. Such positions, however, are the exception, and they are used to best advantage in an institution whose policy-making staff has the full range of qualifications.

Third, the candidates for full-time college and university positions can usually be chosen from a world-wide roster of experts. But this is no reason to condone the choice of a person who is below standard in any qualification requisite for the responsibility offered to him.

Fourth, the choice of personnel can be made in first-rate colleges and universities by expert judges since they are the source of the best available judgment in their fields of specialization. Yet the expertness that can be counted on is limited to one field. It does not necessarily encompass all the essential elements of competence as a teacher.

Fifth, college and university departments have a responsibility, which is far less marked in the schools, to advance human knowledge beyond what may be believed or appreciated in the surrounding society. The institution of higher education needs all the freedom necessary for this peculiar and sometimes unpopular service. But the necessary freedom does not include the freedom for inept and unskilled teaching.

Consequently, an increasing number of college and university teachers and administrators are of the opinion that somehow a minimum level of professional teaching competence should be assured throughout higher education.

In view of these differences the committee makes the following recommendation [86:155]:

The qualifications essential for college and university teaching may not be subject to as general agreement as are those for high school teaching, or for university teaching in other countries where a candidate may be judged largely on his delivery of a lecture in his field. Before a standard can be adopted which will win assent, the elements of it will have to be hammered out by groups of specialists who have the respect of university teachers and administrators. A basic recommendation, therefore, is that such groups be brought together to define and propose the qualifications which they believe ought to be required. Only on the basis of such a proposal can there be useful talk of a license requirement in higher education.

Influence of Professional Organizations on Certification Standards.
Significant progress in the raising of standards has, as in other professions, come primarily from the efforts of members rather than from the general public. Teachers are probably in the best position to judge the standards essential for accomplishing their function. Unfortunately, in some communities selfish motives and an unwillingness to pay for teachers with high qualifications have retarded greatly the improvement of certification standards.

The National Education Association has been outstanding in its efforts to raise the certification standards for teachers. Since the turn of the century it has advocated five years of college training for high school teachers. It now stresses the importance of all public school teachers having at least five years of college preparation.

Mention should be made of the influence of certain accrediting agencies, such as the Association of Secondary Schools and Colleges. In order for a secondary school to become a member, which is a high honor, it must meet many relatively high standards established by the association. The association checks annually upon its members to make certain that these standards are being maintained.

Influence of Teacher-education Institutions upon Certification Standards.   Mention has been made of the positive effect that teacher-education institutions have had upon the improvement of certification standards. Provisions for college training in each state have almost invariably exceeded the minimum certification requirements. For instance, today it is possible to secure a doctor's degree in elementary education in institutions where the state certification requirement for elementary teachers is two college years or less.

Teacher-education institutions have been concerned with more than an increase in the number of years of training for teachers. Intensive efforts are being made continuously to improve the *quality* of training. It should always be borne in mind that the quality of teachers produced is far more important in the lives of children than is the number of years of teacher education prescribed for certification.

Types of Teacher Certificates.   In earlier days it was the practice to grant "blanket" certificates to teachers whereby they were permitted to teach virtually all subjects in all grades. One of the positive trends in certification has been the differentiation of licenses granted for specialized grade levels and/or subject areas of instruction. Today a definite distinction is common for certificates granted to elementary and secondary school teachers. The laws in some states even make distinctions in the grade levels of elementary schools, such as lower, intermediate, and upper elementary.

Secondary school certificates usually are granted on the basis of subject area or areas which the student has studied. Forty-one states in 1961 issued endorsed certificates, that is, certificates on which are endorsed the one or more teaching fields or subjects in which the holder meets the specified requirements of the state [6:16]. There is a trend to grant licenses in terms of *major fields of knowledge* rather than of specific subject areas. For instance, a teacher may be licensed to teach social studies and science rather than only history and chemistry. In time this major-area trend will decrease the odd combination of subjects that many beginning teachers often are asked to teach.

Upon meeting your state and college certification requirements, you normally will be recommended by your college to members of the state education department for the type of certificate for which you have prepared. Most states grant to beginning teachers some form of provisional license which specifies a limited period of validity. After this time has expired it may be renewed, provided certain conditions have been met; or it may be exchanged for a higher type of certificate. Many states provide for the granting of some form of permanent certificate, usually upon evidence of a specified number of years of successful teaching and additional professional work. A permanent certificate, normally different from a life certificate, remains valid only so long as the holder teaches continuously or is not out of teaching beyond a specified number of years.

There is a trend away from the granting of life certificates to teachers. Many educators feel that standards change rapidly and long-term certificates tend to stifle professional growth. They feel that the state should maintain some control over the training qualifications of its teachers. So much progress in teacher education is being made that a high standard today may easily become a low one within a decade. Unless some control is retained, the injurious effects of life certificates exist long after the practice has been abolished—until the last holder of a life certificate has retired.

Some certificates expire through nonuse. Policies for renewal vary from state to state. The candidate is generally required to take some additional college work to reinstate the license.

The laws governing certification in the various states usually specify the conditions under which it may be revoked. If it can be proved that a teacher is immoral, incompetent, intemperate, or guilty of unprofessional conduct, he stands a chance of losing his certificate.

Emergency Certificates.   You may meet teachers who hold only emergency, substandard, or temporary permits. These names are used to define certificates issued to persons who do not meet the prescribed course requirements. The issuance of these certificates has been a serious problem since World War II. In 1946, one in seven employed teachers was on an emergency certificate [6:22–23]. During the next seven years, however, the ratio dropped to approximately one in fourteen. For the school year 1961–62 the ratio was one in fifteen [49:12]. Approximately 70 per cent of the emergency certificates involve elementary teachers.

Several things should be remembered with respect to this group: First, many of them are actually close to meeting all requirements for certification and are good teachers. Second, the number of teachers required to care for the mounting throngs of boys and girls has exceeded the number of available qualified teachers. Third, relatively low salaries prevented many desirable teachers from remaining in the profession. Fourth, while some of these people should be weeded out, many should be encouraged to stay for the significant contributions they can make and are making. Ways and means should be provided whereby those in the latter group can bolster their training, gain their professional certificates, and continue their teaching.

Certification of Teachers in Private Schools.   Only fifteen states, either by law or regulation, require teachers in private or parochial schools, at some school level or under certain conditions, to hold certificates [6:12]. Twelve of these states require elementary school teachers in private schools to hold certificates. Nine states require high school teachers in private schools to hold certificates. The predominant practice in privately supported and controlled schools is to require certification only in case the school seeks accreditation by the state, or to issue certificates upon the voluntary requests of teachers in the private schools. Twenty-nine states in 1961 followed these practices at one or more school levels [6:12].

A number of conflicting principles are involved when one considers whether or not private and church-related school teachers should meet certification requirements. For church-related schools you have the principle of separation between church and state. Should the state impose *its* definition of competence upon such a school or does the church-related school have a right to insist upon its concept of competence? Private schools have fought for freedom of decision in selecting teachers in order to maintain the excellence of their institutional programs. They feel that any attempt to curtail this freedom would violate the principle of free enterprise and would handicap the development of outstandingly good educational programs. On the other hand, the state, in fulfilling its educational responsibility, has an obligation to protect all boys and girls from persons of substandard qualifications. The authors of *New Horizons for the Teaching Profession,* in viewing the problem, express the following point of view [86:153]:

> Once the license represents a valid standard of competence, and once the granting of licenses is based on demonstrated competence there remains no valid argument against its application to both public and private schools—church-related, independent, and proprietary. Indeed it then becomes the moral obligation of the state to apply the standard throughout its jurisdiction.

In the years ahead the question of certification of teachers in private and church-related schools may develop into an interesting issue. As a member of the profession you will want to give further thought to it.

Reciprocity in Teacher Certification.   Differences in the certification requirements of the individual states have handicapped the free movement of teachers throughout the United States. For example, a teacher certified to teach in New York might not meet the specific requirement for teaching in Texas. A number of factors have accentuated this problem: rapid transportation and communication; fluctuation in teacher supply and demand; and differences in salaries, tenure, retirement benefits, etc. Thus the problem of reciprocity in teacher certification has become a national problem.

Such organizations as the Council of Co-operation in Teacher Education of the American Council on Education, and the National Commission on Teacher Education and Professional Standards of the National Education Association have been quite concerned with this problem and have brought together a variety of groups who have had a logical concern for its solution. Particularly noteworthy in searching for a solution to the problem has been the National Association of State Directors of Teacher Education and Certification. Members of the Association long ago agreed with leaders in the profession that the growing migration of teachers ought to be encouraged. They agreed upon the following advantages of the free movement of teachers [18:14].

1. It tends to bring about balance between teacher supply and demand; which is essential, not only to teacher welfare and prestige, but to improved educational opportunities for children.
2. It promotes national unity.
3. It tends to destroy provincialism and the inbreeding of ideas and practices in local school systems.
4. It provides a means whereby states having low standards of preparation may raise those standards to a desirable minimum.
5. It promotes teacher growth in service.

The members of the Association also agreed that the following points should form the basis upon which progress in the reciprocity of teacher certification could take place [18:14]:

1. The certification of teachers is a function of the state and should never be delegated to other agencies.
2. Certification laws should grant broad general authority and not include detail which prevents flexibility in administration.
3. The baccalaureate degree should be the minimum level of preparation at which reciprocity becomes operative.
4. Only those who are graduates of teacher-education institutions approved by state departments of education and accredited by regional or national accrediting agencies should be accepted for certification by another state.
5. The definition of a good teacher should be the same throughout the nation.
6. The initial certificate should be issued only upon the recommendation of the head of the department of education of the teacher-preparing institution.

Reciprocity agreements have been established, with varying degrees of success, among states within the New England, Southern, and Central regions of the United States. In 1961, a total of 18 states reported that they are members of reciprocity compacts [6:17].

The National Association of State Directors of Teacher Education and Certification adopted a recommendation in 1958 that National Council for Accreditation of Teacher Education (NCATE) accreditation should be made the basis of reciprocity among the states. In other words, graduation from an institution accredited by NCATE should be sufficient grounds for reciprocity in teacher certification. The regulation adopted by the state of Iowa appears to be typical [6:18]:

Graduates with bachelor's degrees of colleges and universities outside Iowa which at the time of the applicant's graduation are fully accredited by the National Council for Accreditation of Teacher Education shall be eligible for a regular teacher's certificate covering the area or level of teaching for which the candidate is recommended by his preparing institution. This policy applies only to the applicants who have graduated from the regularly approved teacher education program that is specifically accredited by NCATE. This policy relates also to the certification of school service personnel such as superintendents, principals, supervisors, and school psychologists, provided the minimum level of graduate work specified in Iowa's standards is attained.

Since 1958, rapid progress has been made by states in using NCATE accreditation as a basis of reciprocity. For example, 19 states had adopted such a base in September, 1961, and by the end of the year the number had increased to 26—Alabama, Colorado, Delaware, Florida, Georgia, Illinois, Indiana, Iowa, Kentucky, Louisiana, Maine, Maryland, Mississippi, Missouri, Nebraska, North Dakota, Oregon, Pennsylvania, Rhode Island, Tennessee, Texas, Utah, Vermont, Washington, West Virginia,

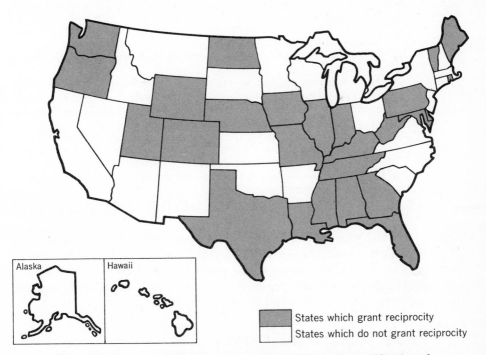

Figure 16.   States which grant reciprocity privileges in the certification of teachers to graduates of institutions accredited by the National Council for Accreditation of Teacher Education, June, 1962. How many more states have since been added to the list? (*Source:* National Council for Accreditation of Teacher Education.)

and Wyoming. It appears that NCATE accreditation will be the chief basis of reciprocity and that future graduates of institutions holding such accreditation (374 in 1962 which graduate over 70 per cent of all students prepared to teach) will not experience as much difficulty in moving from one state to another as have teachers in the past. Graduates of non-NCATE-accredited institutions are expected to meet the specific regulations of the states in which they seek certification, as has been the case in the past.

Some Recommendations on Certification. Previous mention has been made to the publication *New Horizons for the Teaching Profession,* prepared by a committee of the National Commission on Teacher Education and Professional Standards. The Committee expressed the feeling that certification of professional personnel will be effective [86:240]:

1. When the state maintains its authority to administer the issuance of licenses to teachers, but delegates to the profession responsibility for determining standards to be employed in licensure.
2. When the only purpose of legal licensure is to provide visible evidence that the candidate is competent as a beginning teacher.
3. When other purposes, now too frequently applied to licensure are achieved:
   a. By accreditation of institutions and programs ensuring that candidates have been carefully selected and well prepared and are competent as beginning teachers.
   b. By institutional accountability for their recommendations of candidates for licensure.
   c. By wisdom of school and college officials in assignment of functions to personnel.
   d. By professional conduct by individuals in assuming only those assignments for which they are prepared and competent.
4. When the state issues only one license, the initial entrance license for teachers, based:
   a. Upon completion of an NCATE-accredited program of preparation.
   b. Upon recommendation by the preparing institution on the basis of demonstrated competency as a beginning teacher.
   c. Upon recommendation of teaching competence by the appropriate organization of teachers.
5. When specialized licenses beyond the basic one are developed and administered by the profession itself through its various associations of specialists.

You and your colleagues may wish to explore the implications of these statements for the future. Perhaps you should read the publications to gain further understanding of the position taken by the committee. Undoubtedly, further changes in certification requirements will be made, and these changes may affect you and your future plans.

FUTURE PROFESSIONAL GROWTH

The general public expects members of any profession to continue their educational and technical growth after entering their respective professions. For example, a medical doctor, even though he was graduated 30 years ago, is expected to have an understanding of recent research in the field of medicine and to utilize the findings of that research. Further, it is expected that each year of his practice will contribute to his expertness in diagnosis and treatment. In a similar fashion, teachers have a moral obligation to the general public and to their students to be aware of the rapid progress being made in the field of education. Each additional year of teaching should result in increased expertness in guiding the educational growth of children; otherwise, the policy of providing salary increases for each additional year of experience is an unwise practice.

Teachers must be well acquainted with recent research findings in regard to effective learning procedures, child growth and development, and newer techniques in teaching. Our understanding of the field of human relations is growing rapidly. The great expansion of knowledge which we are experiencing outdates much of the information gained a decade or more ago. Rapid changes are being made in community life, and in social, economic, and political thinking which have far-reaching educational ramifications. If teachers are to fulfill their professional obligations, they must constantly be students of the world as it is today and as it may be tomorrow.

Educators recognize that the fundamental purpose of preservice professional education is to provide the prospective teacher with the knowledge, skills, techniques, and attitudes necessary for initial service. Perhaps one of the most important attitudes to develop during this period of time is the desire to learn and to improve.

It is an unfortunate commentary that many teachers do not maintain the spirit of the learner; they degenerate into teaching automatons. Many of them permit themselves to fall into a rut where they remain throughout their professional lives. In fact, many of them fall into the rut and proceed to dig the rut deeper; they regress rather than egress. Whereas education is potentially one of the most inspiring and intellectualizing professions, many employees neglect the opportunity to learn which is ever present; they forget that they are dealing with the most stimulating and precious, yet baffling, materials in the world, namely, the minds of pupils. School employees must constantly battle that most frequently found and devastating disease of all institutions, "institutional paralysis"; although the disease "creeps" and is painless, it will eventually kill its victim if it is not eliminated [124:536].

In formulating your plans for a career in education, make detailed provisions for your in-service growth. Frequently the concept of in-service growth is limited to professional education only. Actually anything that will promote your competence as a teacher may be classified as in-service growth. If you are familiar with the current developments in fields outside of education as well as within it, your effectiveness in the classroom and community should be increased. For practical purposes, formulate your plans so that they will be in harmony with the three major areas of your undergraduate preparation: general education, subject-matter specialization, and professional education.

Obviously, many of the things you will want to do will be highly individual and dependent upon your own needs, desires, and initiative. You may find that no definitely organized sources of assistance exist for meeting your particular needs. On the other hand, there are in-service educational needs common to all teachers for which sources of assistance generally are provided. Among these are supervision of teaching, reading, teacher education, conferences and workshops, and professional organizations.

Supervision.   Almost all schools provide for some form of supervision. In small schools the principal or superintendent usually assumes, along with his administrative duties, the responsibilities of staff supervision. An increasing number of large school systems have established special personnel who devote full time to the supervision of instruction. A few school systems have designated one or more supervisors to work primarily with beginning teachers in getting them off to a good start, whereas other supervisors work with the more experienced teachers in helping them to improve their teaching.

Theoretically, supervision is concerned with the improvement of teaching. Modern concepts picture the supervisor as a well-educated, tactful, sympathetic, and constructive person who seeks to help each teacher realize his full capacity for educating boys and girls. The teacher looks upon the supervisor as a coworker from whom guidance and valuable assistance may be gained.

Study carefully the kind of supervision provided in any school system in which you may plan to teach. Although increasing numbers of schools provide the constructive, cooperative help indicated above, there still remain some systems in which supervisors consider their main responsi-

Your principal or supervisor, can help you with problems, especially those you may have when you begin teaching. (*Photograph by Carl Purcell, National Education Association.*)

bility to be that of *inspection* rather than guidance. Begin teaching in a school system in which you will receive a maximum amount of friendly, constructive assistance in the solution of problems that inevitably will arise; a system in which you may develop into a happy, well-adjusted professional worker.

Many teacher-education institutions realize that follow-up assistance, to beginning teachers especially, is an important part of their programs. Obviously, a teacher's education is not completed upon receiving a diploma. A few institutions have extended their services by having staff members visit graduates on the job several times during the first year of teaching to help in every way possible. Some institutions invite recent graduates to return to the campus for one or more days to receive help on problems that have been encountered. Almost all institutions encourage their graduates to write or return to the campus for professional assistance.

A very large number of institutions automatically secure reports from employing officials on their graduates during the first year of teaching. These reports help an institution to locate graduates urgently in need of assistance, to evaluate the effectiveness of its teacher-education program, and to secure data that may be used in recommending people for better positions.

Teachers' Meetings.   You will be attending various kinds of teachers' meetings which may be of some help to you in your professional growth. Most of these meetings will involve the teachers in your school building, but some of them may involve all of the teachers in the school system.

Too frequently in the past teachers' meetings have been administration-dominated and have been run in a dictatorial fashion. They have been used too frequently as a "clearinghouse" for administrative detail and for the consideration of "housekeeping" problems. As a result, many teachers have felt that they received little or no professional help from these meetings and dreaded having to attend them.

Today teachers are taking more active roles in teachers' meetings. These meetings are planned in terms of purposes and are conducted in a spirit of helpfulness. Teachers participate in establishing the purposes of the meetings and in conducting them. A variety of problems experienced by the teachers may be discussed. School policies may be reviewed, formulated, and adopted. Improvement or formulation of new curricular programs, research projects, grading practices and policies, school community relationships and projects, and a host of other activities may constitute the concerns of teachers in these meetings. Here you have the opportunity to become an important member of a team and to gain professional assistance from your colleagues.

Conferences and Workshops.   Many teacher-education institutions and public school systems provide educational conferences of one or more days' duration to aid the in-service growth of teachers. These conferences

Workshops provide teachers excellent opportunities to improve their professional insights and skills. (*Photograph from the National Education Association.*)

are somewhat similar to institutes, as they were called in earlier days. Conferences that are limited to one day usually consist of meetings in which outstanding educators discuss educational problems with the teachers and administrators. Often these conferences are designed to provide inspiration and to encourage professional growth.

For the past 25 years the workshop idea has experienced phenomenal growth. Basically, an educational workshop consists of a group of educators working cooperatively and intensively for several days on problems of concern to the group.

Workshops have the following common characteristics:

1. Working sessions are planned around the interests and problems identified by the participants. As examples, the members of the group may wish to improve their techniques of appraising the progress of pupils, or the methods of teaching arithmetic. The problems selected by the group are delimited to such scope that successful progress can be made during the time available.

2. The organization of the workshop is flexible in order that group work may proceed in solving problems. There is no fixed program with lectures. Consultants are available for participation in group work and for individual conferences.

3. Although much of the work is done through small groups, general meetings serve such purposes as planning work sessions, sharing experiences, learning about new developments of interest to the entire group, or gaining specific assistance relating to the problems selected for study.

4. Various resources are available to facilitate progress in solving problems. The most significant resources are the members of the workshop group—participants and consultants.

Increasing numbers of teacher-education institutions are providing workshop opportunities, on the campus or in the field, for which college credit is given. Many school systems sponsor workshops in which various members work on major educational problems, such as discipline, science instruction, or reporting to parents.

The intellectual stimulation gained from participation in a well-conducted workshop is bound to add much to a teacher's professional growth. Furthermore, when the collective intelligence of a group of educators is focused upon problems of common concern, fundamental improvements in educational practice will take place.

Professional Organizations.   You will be concerned with at least three types of professional organizations—your local, state, and national teacher associations—and the effect of each upon your future professional growth. Since each of these associations will be discussed at length in a later chapter, the primary concern at this point is to see them as an integral part of an in-service educational program.

The amount of growth that you will gain through professional organizations will depend largely upon your initiative, your ability to work effectively with others, your desire to be an active member of the various organizations, and the adequacy of your plans for this type of growth. In addition to the many other values that may accrue, active participation should give you deep satisfaction and stimulation.

Additional College and University Work.   Almost all the larger teacher-education institutions and universities provide extensive summer sessions. In view of the fact that teachers normally constitute the major enrollment, the summer programs are designed specially to meet the needs of this group of students. Some prospective teachers use the summer session as a means of gaining additional credits or of speeding up their preparations for teaching. Experienced teachers often use the summer period for bring-

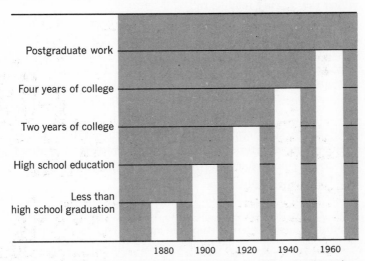

Figure 17.   Trend in the preparation of the typical public school teacher. Why must this trend continue? (*Source:* National Education Association.)

ing their qualifications up to standard, working for advanced degrees, and/or extending their professional or subject-matter background, independent of degree credit.

Summer-session programs usually attempt to serve the needs of these

Many teachers take college work during the summer months to work toward advanced degrees and/or improve their professional competence. (*Photograph by Carl Purcell, National Education Association.*)

groups of students. The summer sessions generally are staffed by regular faculty members, but some large institutions attempt to secure the services of one or more outstanding educators also. This practice enables teachers to study with various educational leaders of the nation.

Some teachers combine summer-school study with other types of experiences. For example, you can attend a college or university located near an ocean or high in the mountains where the weather is pleasant, or in some section of the country with which you are not well acquainted. A rapidly increasing number of colleges are granting credit during summer sessions for conducted tours to other countries. In fact, a special department has been established in the National Education Association which assists teacher-education institutions in planning and conducting these tours. In this manner the entire world becomes the classroom from which the teacher may learn.

Extension courses and correspondence courses often are available to teachers during the regular school year. Statistics indicate that many teachers avail themselves of these opportunities to extend their professional and/or subject-matter backgrounds. Extension courses are offered on Saturdays or during the week by institutions in specified centers, usually where the interests and needs of a relatively large number of teachers may be met. In planning for teaching, take into consideration these educational opportunities, keeping in mind, however, the possible strain upon your time and energy. It would be exceedingly unwise for you to sacrifice your effectiveness in the classroom for what might be purely personal gains.

Give serious consideration to additional college work as you plan for your future professional growth. As noted previously, the fifth year of training is fast becoming the rule rather than the exception. The growth of knowledge in all fields is so great that you cannot stand still—you either drop back or you move ahead in your competence in teaching. Professional courses almost invariably prove much more interesting, meaningful, and helpful to a teacher after he has had some experience. Additional work should broaden your understanding of and insights into educational problems and should make your work a fascinating challenge to you. Furthermore, the better positions generally come to those who are best prepared for them. Salary schedules and standards in different school systems place increasingly higher demands upon the preparation of school employees. It is important that you plan not only to meet these demands but to go beyond them.

Reading.   The printed word never ceases to be a source of intellectual stimulation and growth, regardless of a person's occupation. Teachers should be especially skilled in using books, periodicals, bulletins, and magazines as a source of professional growth.

Perhaps more printed material is available in the field of education than in any other profession. The material is so great that, regardless of how avid a reader you may be, it would be virtually impossible to find time to read all of the current material published. Hence, you will be faced with the problems of becoming familiar with the different kinds of material available, establishing some criteria of selection, and planning a reading program that will enable you to experience the optimum amount of growth.

During your preparation for teaching, become acquainted with outstanding educational literature which may prove helpful to you later.

During your preparation for teaching, become well acquainted with the kinds of educational literature that will be of the most help to you when you begin teaching. Books, bulletins, and periodicals are excellent resources for you to use in improving your professional competence. (*Photograph by Carl Purcell, National Education Association.*)

Start developing your professional library long before you begin teaching.

Many new professional books are published each year. In the *National Education Association Journal* a list of the best books in each of the major fields of education is published yearly. Almost all professional periodicals contain notices of new books being released. Often reviews are included. Since it is impossible to read all the books being published, you will find book reviews especially helpful in extending the scope of your literary contacts and in selecting materials for careful study.

Educational periodicals constitute the "newspaper of the teaching profession" [91:374]. They report the latest happenings of the school world, the controversial issues that are being debated, the latest theories that are being passionately advocated, and the most recent findings of educational research.

The majority of educational periodicals are published by national, state, and local professional organizations, although a few of them are private enterprises. There are so many that it is not possible to discuss them adequately in the space available here. Virtually every significant aspect of education is covered by some kind of periodical. The articles appearing in periodicals are classified and catalogued in *The Education Index*, which is valuable in locating current literature pertaining to any significant educational problem. During your preparation for teaching, spend some time browsing through as many different periodicals as possible in order to become acquainted with the problems considered and the value of each periodical to you. Any wide-awake teacher knows where to go to secure assistance in the solution of problems and to gain professional insights and stimulation.

Membership in your national and state education associations entitles you to receive their respective monthly periodicals, the contents of which are of general interest to all educators. Subscribe to some periodical that is directed to your specific area of interest and/or specialization. The extent of your subscription to professional periodicals beyond this point is a matter that only you will be able to determine. You owe to yourself the number of subscriptions that will enable you to experience maximum professional growth. In some schools, teachers plan and share their personal subscriptions so as to avoid duplications and gain extensive coverage of periodical literature. Many schools provide in the budget for limited subscriptions to periodicals and for purchase of professional books for the in-service growth of teachers.

Do not limit your plans for reading to professional literature only. You owe to your pupils and to yourself as a citizen a good understanding of local, state, national, and international current affairs. Be familiar with some of the best books that are being published. Your reading should be so planned that your general education and your knowledge in your areas of academic specialization continue to expand as long as you live.

Other Sources of Growth.   When well planned, your participation in community affairs can add much to your effectiveness as a citizen, your understanding of the needs of children and the community forces that play upon them, and the ability to develop harmonious working relationships between the school and the home. The teacher who fails to avail himself of the stimulation and growth that may come from active community participation is usually destined to become a cloistered, uninteresting person whose effectiveness in the classroom is limited.

It should be relatively easy for you to enter into the life of the community. Generally, the services of teachers are sought eagerly. It is important for you to remember, however, that your first obligation is to the boys and girls you teach, and that the community activities in which you engage must be planned in terms of the welfare of these children.

Travel provides a never-ending source of intellectual stimulation and enrichment to the teacher. It is limited primarily by one's financial means. The average teacher should be able to plan for at least one extensive trip within the United States each summer and for one or more trips abroad during his professional career. In addition to the personal and professional growth accrued, many teachers collect photographs, movies, specimens, and other items during their travels in order to enrich the classroom experiences of their pupils.

In recent years the practice of public school teachers exchanging positions, usually for one year, has received considerable attention. Much may be said for this plan, as it increases teachers' understanding of other areas and adds to their professional growth, especially when the exchange takes place on an international level.

It has been recognized for many years that teachers may profit from observing the work of others. A number of school systems are establishing policies that provide opportunities during the regular school year for teachers to visit outstanding schools and to observe other teaching methods. The practice permits comparing and contrasting to gain new ideas and insights that improve professional competencies.

SUMMARY

During the past 50 years the certification requirements for teaching have increased steadily. With higher certification requirements, teaching has become more widely recognized as a profession. The function of certifying teachers has been centralized in the state department of education.

The completion of approved teacher-education programs, rather than teacher examinations, now forms the basis for certification. Licenses have been differentiated according to the nature of the preparation. Life licenses have been gradually abolished. The level of preparation has been raised for all types of certificates. Specialized courses in education have been required in the preparatory programs of teachers.

These advancements have come primarily through the efforts of those within the profession. Teacher-education institutions, accrediting agencies, such as the National Council for the Accreditation of Teacher Education, and the National Education Association have provided outstanding leadership. Present-day graduates, especially those trained for the elementary level, generally enter the profession much better prepared than teachers already in service. Since this condition provides added incentive for experienced teachers to gain additional training, the average level of preparation possessed by all teachers is higher than it used to be. A positive relationship seems to exist between the increase in the requirements for teaching and the supply of those entering the profession.

Preservice preparation constitutes only the minimum amount required for entering the profession. As long as you remain in teaching, you have a moral obligation to yourself and your students to continue to improve your professional competence. Several sources of in-service growth have been noted to help you formulate long-range plans. You doubtless will find many other sources that will enable you to meet your specific needs. Basically, the extent of your growth will depend on your desire to fulfill adequately your function as an educator and on your concern with raising the level of the teaching profession.

QUESTIONS FOR YOUR CONSIDERATION

1. What are the procedures for securing a teacher's certificate in the state in which you plan to teach?

2. Why are temporary certificates usually granted to beginning teachers?

3. Upon what grounds can a teacher's certificate be revoked?

4. Do you feel that a teacher should be required to sign an oath of allegiance or loyalty to the United States? What are your reasons?

5. Should the requirements for elementary teachers be as high as, if not higher than, the requirements for secondary teachers? Why?

6. For what reasons should states require elementary and secondary school principals and superintendents to have six or more years of college work for certification?

7. What are the advantages and disadvantages of using the results of the National Teacher Examination in the screening of teacher applicants?

8. What are the advantages and disadvantages of granting life certificates to teachers?

9. How would you solve the problem of reciprocity in teacher certification?

10. What is your position with respect to requiring private and church-related school teachers to be certified? What are the reasons for your position?

11. Recall one or more teachers who, in your opinion, have ceased to grow professionally. What were the causes? In what ways have their pupils suffered?

12. Many school systems require teachers periodically to earn credit through additional college course work, travel, or research. What merits, if any, do you see in such requirements?

ACTIVITIES FOR YOU TO PURSUE

1. Examine a recent copy of Armstrong and Stinnett's *A Manual on Certification Requirements for School Personnel in the United States*. Compare the specific requirements for teaching in the state in which you have some interest. Have any changes taken place?

2. Compare the requirements for teaching prescribed by the following: your state, the institution in which you are preparing for teaching, a rural school system, and a very large school system, all of which are within the same state.

3. Examine a copy of *The Education Index* and become thoroughly familiar with its potential value to you. In order to gain skill in its use, list a number of current articles that deal with some educational problem in which you are interested.

4. Browse through as many professional periodicals as possible in your college library. Note on a sheet of paper for each periodical you examine such things as the following: name of the periodical, publisher, editor, frequency of publication, cost per year, summary of the kinds of problems considered, and potential value to you. You may wish to keep these sheets in a folder for future reference, especially when you plan your professional subscriptions and when you meet various educational problems.

5. Construct a list of professional books that you feel should be in your personal library when you begin teaching.

6. Consult a list of professional organizations, as that in *The Educational Directory*, published by the Office of Education, and note those with which you may wish to associate yourself as a teacher. It will be helpful to record pertinent data, i.e., purposes, cost of membership, and publications, regarding each for future reference.

7. Investigate the sources of in-service growth provided for teachers in school systems in which you may be interested in locating.

8. Make a list of some things you would like to do after you begin teaching to make your job more interesting and effective.

5
OPPORTUNITIES IN EDUCATION

You will probably find a good position more readily and enjoy greater success and happiness in your teaching if you review your plans in terms of the many opportunities in education. To do this, you will want to know what opportunities exist at the various levels and in all subject areas. There are greater demands at some levels and in some subject areas than in others. Furthermore, the law of supply and demand has some effect upon the salaries of teachers. Teachers prepared in specialties where the demand exceeds the supply tend to receive higher salaries than do those prepared in oversupplied specialties.

Obviously, you should not choose to teach a particular level or subject area solely because it holds the best promise of immediate employment. It would be exceedingly unwise to prepare for elementary teaching, for which there is great demand, if you are more skilled in working with older pupils and certain that you will be happier with them. A sound, intelligent decision in regard to age level and subject areas certainly will increase your chances of success and satisfaction from a career in education.

Unfortunately, many prospective teachers make decisions in terms of inadequate or erroneous data. Some decide to teach secondary school because, having been recently graduated, they are more familiar with this level. But if they investigate elementary schools they often find themselves much better qualified to work with young children. Other students decide to teach high school largely because of the prestige that secondary teachers have over elementary teachers. Still others find themselves preparing in English or social studies education because they do not know of opportunities in other areas, such as speech or hearing therapy or library science, in which they would have been interested and well qualified.

Your final decision in regard to the age level and subject area should depend on a number of factors: the nature of your personality, the experiences you have had—especially with children—your interests and aptitudes, and supply and demand in the teaching field.

As you read this chapter and other materials on opportunities in education, and as you observe in school situations, ask yourself such questions as the following: With what age level can I work most successfully? What academic areas interest me most? Do I prefer to work with individuals rather than groups? Have I explored all of the different kinds of work of teachers? Would college teaching interest me? What type of work do I eventually want to do?

Your first position probably will entail classroom teaching. Most educators, regardless of the type of work in which they now are engaged, have taught in a public school classroom for a period of time. In considering the opportunities related to public school teaching, you will be concerned with such matters as the number in the profession, the ratio of men and women, the opportunities available, and the chances of securing a position in the area and level of most interest to you.

Number in the Profession.   Your chances to realize your special abilities and interests are affected to some extent by the number of persons engaged in the profession. You may be interested in the distribution, ac-

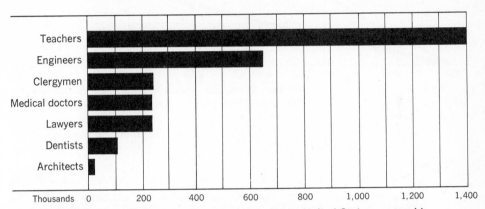

Figure 18.   Approximate number of persons in the United States engaged in selected professional occupations in 1960. The number of public school teachers only approximately equaled the number of persons in six other major professions.

cording to the level as well as the type of work involved, of this tremendously large number of people in the teaching profession. A knowledge of the proportionate distribution of the number involved will give you some idea of opportunities existing within the profession.

In 1960–1961 there were over 1,400,000 public school teachers, over 200,000 private school teachers, approximately 15,000 superintendents, 85,000 principals and supervisors, and over 30,000 consultants, researchers and other specialists in elementary and secondary schools [181: 28]. Approximately 350,000 professional personnel were employed in higher-education institutions. Another 25,000 were employed as staff members in professional organizations, in government offices of education, and in private agencies with educational programs.

The number in the profession will continue to expand for several reasons. The 1960 census revealed the tremendous increase of 42.8 per cent in the population age group of 5–17 years between 1950 and 1960. As this large group moves through the schools and into adulthood, even greater numbers of children may be expected. There is a growing tendency to include kindergartens, nursery schools, and junior colleges in our free public school systems, and this will increase enrollment. Also, educators generally agree that the pupil-teacher ratio in elementary and sec-

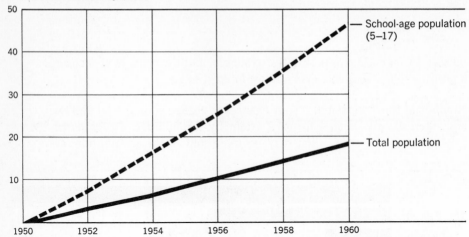

Per cent of increase over July 1, 1950

Figure 19. School-age population is growing faster than the total population. (*Source:* National Education Association.)

ondary schools should be lowered. Increasing numbers of boys and girls are continuing their high school studies rather than dropping out of school.

New demands for comprehensively trained personnel are being heard especially in the scientific fields. The unmet needs in many other fields of instruction, and educational services are equally urgent. There are needs for trained counselors, specialists in remedial reading and speech, and instructors of the handicapped, as well as for teachers of subjects

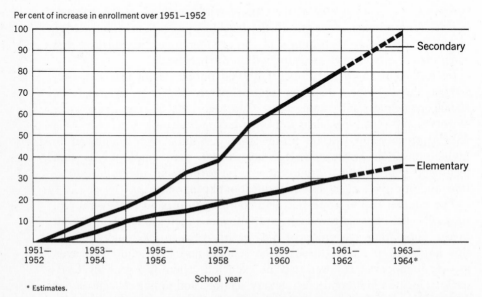

Per cent of increase in enrollment over 1951–1952

School year

* Estimates.

Figure 20. Public secondary school enrollments are increasing more rapidly than elementary school enrollments. (*Source:* National Education Association.)

not now being offered in many high schools. Further demands are being made in the field of adult education, since the span of life is being increased. Thus, the services of the school will extend in many different directions.

Distribution of Men and Women.   The proportion of men and women in any profession is of significance to anyone planning a career. Furthermore, the attitude of members within the profession as well as of society in general toward the existing proportions is important to consider, especially in terms of employment possibilities and long-range plans.

Unlike European countries, where teaching has been considered a man's work, the United States has far more women than men teaching in its public schools. From 1880 until 1920 the percentage of men teachers in our public schools decreased from 43 to 14 per cent. In the 20 years that followed, the percent of men rose to 23 per cent, but during World War II it declined to 15 per cent of the total. Since then there has been a steady increase until, in 1962, it had reached slightly over 29 per cent. In 1961–1962, 14 per cent of the 876,000 public elementary school teachers and 53 per cent of the 578,000 public secondary school teachers were men [42:6]. While the percentage of men teachers in the secondary schools is over three times as great as in the elementary schools, the gap seems to be narrowing. On the college and university level three-fourths of the instructional staff consists of men.

Considerable effort is being made to attract more men into public school teaching, especially into the elementary schools. A teacher-opinion poll conducted in 1961 indicated that 71 per cent of the teachers believed that a higher proportion of men is needed in classroom teaching at the secondary school level, and 57 per cent believed that more men are needed at the elementary level [162:32]. The decided trend toward the establishment of single salary schedules has provided added incentive for men to consider teaching on the lower level, where the opportunities are great. Higher salaries for all public school teachers should encourage more men to enter the profession on all levels. As will be discussed more fully in a later chapter, it has been advocated that teachers with dependents should be given extra compensation. It is maintained that such a plan would attract more men to the teaching profession.

In our society, men are generally considered better administrators than women. Whether this is valid or not, the vast majority of the school administrators, especially superintendents and high school principals, are men. As the size of the school or school system increases, the probabilities of a man's holding the administrative position also increase. Only in elementary school principalships are the number of men and women approximately the same.

Though teaching in the United States has been considered a woman's field, especially on the elementary level, the profession presents great opportunities for both sexes. Young men especially interested in the administrative phase of school work will do well to consider the possibilities of elementary education. In spite of the relatively small number of men in the elementary school, 51 per cent of the elementary school principalships are held by men [42:6].

General Factors Affecting Supply and Demand of Teachers. Broadly conceived, the demand for teachers consists of the total number of teaching positions to be filled in a given year. Demand is created through such factors as death, retirement, disability, dismissal, resignation, and the creation of new positions. Supply is created through the completion of certification requirements and the seeking of teaching positions. Some prospective teachers complete the requirements for certification but decide not to teach. Other teachers, who have left their positions for a different type of work, wish to return to the profession. Conditions vary from one part of the country to another.

It is estimated that the annual turnover of public school teachers throughout the United States is approximately seventeen per cent of the total number of teachers [182:17]. Six per cent move to other jobs and

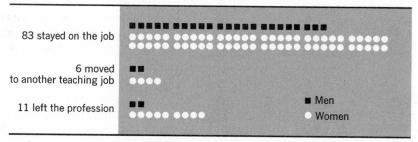

Figure 21.   What happened to 100 teachers between spring and fall, 1959. (*Source:* U.S. Office of Education.)

eleven per cent leave the profession. Of the number who leave the profession each year, about one-third leave for marriage and family reasons, one-sixth retire for age or disability, one-sixth (largely men) enter other types of employment, and one-third leave for miscellaneous reasons including not being reemployed.

School officials often are unable to fill all their vacancies with qualified teachers. As indicated in Chapter 4, these positions frequently are filled with teachers who hold emergency permits and who are not properly trained for their positions. Positions held by these emergency teachers actually constitute a demand for qualified teachers.

A number of people feel that one method of meeting the demand for teachers represented by those holding emergency certificates is to lower certification standards. They likewise feel that raising certification standards will result in an increase in the number of emergency certificates issued. Neither of these feelings is substantiated by facts. In general, the greatest shortages of qualified teachers occur in rural schools, where teachers held 52 per cent of all emergency certificates in 1960–1961; in elementary schools; and in states having the lowest certification standards and lowest salaries. Most states which issue relatively small percentages of emergency certificates not only have high standards but also pay above-average salaries and maintain good teacher retirement systems.

Another factor which affects demand is the number of pupils assigned to a teacher. For example, if 100 rather than 25 pupils were assigned to each teacher, only one-fourth as many teachers would be needed.

Educators generally recommend no more than 25 pupils per teacher. However, some research reveals that, so far as academic achievement in subject matter is concerned, the results obtained in a large class may be just as good as those in a small one. On the other hand, modern education assumes that the teacher contributes to the total growth of the child: emotional, social, and physical growth as well as knowledge of subject matter. "The educational process must be consciously designed to help the student (a) gain meaningful understandings, (b) develop desirable study habits, (c) speak effectively and listen critically, (d) build high ideals, and (e) gain respect and concern for others. In short, education today faces a growing responsibility for the development of habits and attitudes conducive to good adult citizenship in a local, national and worldwide society" [165:20]. In order to accomplish these aims adequately, the number of pupils per teacher, especially on the elementary level, must be lowered.

There are great variations throughout the United States in the pupil-teacher ratio. Generally it is lower (and therefore better) in secondary schools than in elementary schools; lower in areas where the population is sparse; and lower in areas where many one-room schools are found.

There has been a definite trend toward the reduction of the number of pupils assigned to a teacher. The pupil-teacher ratio in 1929–1930 was 30.1; in 1939–1940 it was 29.1; in 1949–1950 it was 27.5; in 1960–1961 it was 26.4. In 1960–1961 the number assigned to elementary teachers was 29.5 and the number assigned to secondary teachers was 21.7 [181:26]. If the very desirable downward trend continues, a sizable number of new teachers will be needed.

The number of children born each year obviously has its effect on the number of teachers needed. During the late 1920s and throughout the 1930s the birth rate in the continental United States decreased. Following World War II the birth rate increased, as indicated in Figure 22. In contrast to previous predictions, there seems to be little evidence that it is going to level off or decrease greatly. Table 4 indicates what may be expected in kindergarten, elementary and secondary school, and college enrollments during the next few years.

The demand for teachers also is affected by the number of pupils who remain in school. For example, the phenomenal increase in the percentage of 14- to 17-year-olds attending secondary school created a great demand for teachers during the past half century. The anticipated increase in pupils attending secondary schools will make demands for additional secondary teachers. Also, as public school opportunities are extended up-

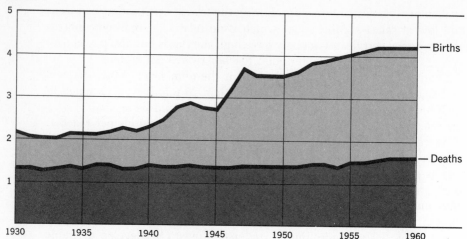

Millions

Figure 22. Births and deaths in the United States, 1930–1960. The number of births have continued to rise much more rapidly than the number of deaths, which has changed the age composition of our population. (*Source:* Association of Collegiate Registrars and Admissions Officers.)

ward to include junior college and extended downward to include kindergarten and possibly nursery school, appreciable demands will be made for teachers qualified to teach on these levels.

Economic conditions affect the demands for teachers. In times of depression, fewer high-salaried positions occur outside the profession to attract teachers, more married women continue to teach, and vacancies in school systems frequently are absorbed by the remaining staffs. In times of prosperity, more teachers leave the profession to accept higher-paying positions, a greater number of married teachers discontinue teaching, vacancies are filled by new teachers, and new positions are often created.

As the nature of the school program changes, the demand for teachers also changes. Certainly the percentage of Latin and Greek teachers is less today than at the time of the Latin grammar school. In recent years new

TABLE 4 PROJECTIONS OF ELEMENTARY, SECONDARY, AND HIGHER EDUCATION ENROLLMENTS IN PUBLIC AND NONPUBLIC SCHOOLS, 1960–1980

School year	Elementary schools	Secondary schools	Institutions of higher education	Total
1960–1961	32,441,000	10,249,000	3,570,000	46,259,000
1965–1966	35,755,000	13,226,000	5,379,000	54,360,000
1970–1971	38,430,000	14,894,000	7,020,000	60,344,000
1975–1976	42,411,000	15,985,000	8,325,000	66,721,000
1980–1981	48,696,000	17,388,000	9,018,000	75,102,000

Source: Statistical Abstract of the United States, 1961, U.S. Department of Commerce, Bureau of the Census, 1961, p. 108.

demands have been made for instruction and services. As the school continues to meet the needs of boys and girls more adequately, new demands may be expected.

Primarily through the aid of medical science, the life span in the United States has been increased considerably. There is every reason to believe that it will be lengthened still further. This means that more children will have time to complete their college as well as their elementary and secondary education.

Years of age

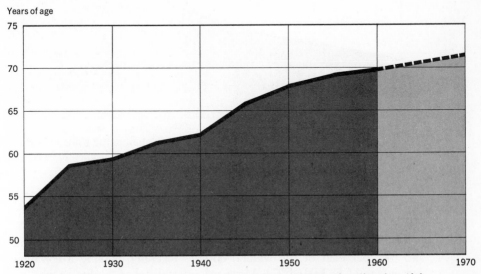

Figure 23.   Life expectancy in the United States. What educational, social, and vocational problems arise from the increasing number of people who are 65 years and older? (*Source:* Bureau of the Census.)

It also means that a greater percentage of our population will be of adult age. If our democratic way of life, which is based upon an enlightened public, is to be improved, increased educational facilities must be made for our adult population. As indicated in Figure 24, it is estimated that the population of the United States, in the year of 2000, will reach the phenomenal figure of 336 million.

Sources of Teacher Supply.   It is extremely difficult to determine accurately the total number of certified teachers who are actively seeking teaching positions. For example, a number of teachers who have not taught for a number of years may desire to return to the profession. There is no precise way of ascertaining how many teachers for any given year will fall into this category. Furthermore, some students who have completed the requirements for teaching may never seek a teaching position or may postpone accepting a teaching position for several years.

Although the loss of certified graduates to the teaching profession seems to be decreasing each year, approximately one in five of the elementary-teacher graduates and three in ten of the secondary-teacher

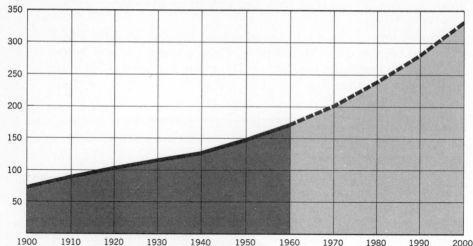

Figure 24. Past and projected increase of population in the United States by decades from 1900 to 2000. (*Source:* National Education Association.)

graduates of 1961 were not available for teaching positions. In all, 82.8 per cent of the elementary school men and 82.1 per cent of the elementary school women accepted teaching positions—a combined average of 82.2 per cent. Of the secondary-teacher graduates, 66.8 per cent of the men and 69.5 per cent of the women entered teaching, making a combined percentage of 68.1 [164:27]. More secondary-teacher graduates who had majored in women's health and physical education, mathematics, music, English, and art entered teaching than those who had majored in agriculture and commerce. Other nonteaching occupations, as might be expected, drew heavily on teachers who had majored in such areas as business education, chemistry, agriculture, and physics. Approximately six per cent of the secondary teachers continued formal study, the majority of whom were in foreign languages, speech, and the science areas. A number of men entered military service upon graduation.

Another factor makes it difficult to determine the supply of teachers. An appreciable number of well-educated people, especially women holding bachelor's degrees and who have not taken teacher training as a part of their undergraduate work, are deciding later to take professional course work to meet certification requirements. A number of teacher-education institutions have developed special fifth-year programs which have academic and professional respectability in order to prepare these people for teaching.

In the light of the variables indicated above, perhaps the most dependable rough indication of the supply of teachers is the number of college students completing standard certification requirements. The Research Division of the National Education Association sponsors studies, directed by C. Ray Maul, that provide estimates of the number who, at the end of each school year (including summer sessions), qualify for standard teaching certificates. Table 5 is an example of the kinds of information which Maul's annual research provides. From this table you can gain a fairly accurate picture of the supply and demand for teachers on various levels and in various subject areas, the relative number of beginning teachers who were assigned to teach full time in their major areas, and the combination of major and minor subject areas to which beginning teachers were most frequently assigned. In studying the various combinations of subject areas for 1961–1962, for example, note that English major assignments were combined most frequently with social studies, foreign-language, or speech minor assignments.

The results of these studies are published annually by the Research Division of the National Education Association. Since some changes occur from year to year in the supply and demand for teachers, consult the most recent reports available to note any trends that may be taking place. Also, check with your college placement officer to see whether these national data are typical of the supply-and-demand conditions in the local area which interests you.

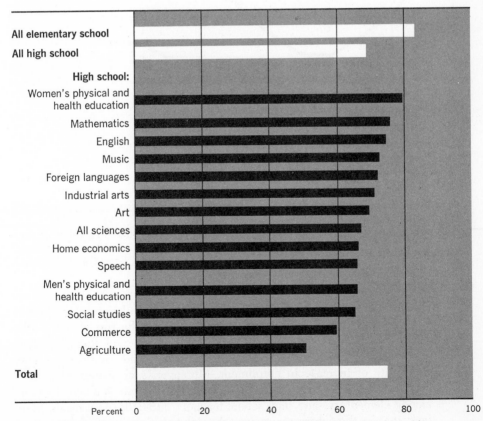

Figure 25.   Per cent of certified graduates of 1961 who entered teaching service. (*Source:* National Education Association.)

Imbalance in the Demand and the Supply of Teachers.   If you examine Table 5 carefully you will note that in some subject areas the number of qualified secondary-teacher graduates exceeds the demand. On the other hand, in certain subjects the supply is far from adequate. Such data would seem to indicate that college students intending to become high school teachers choose their major fields without a thorough knowledge of the number of opportunities and the amount of competition in the various high school teaching fields.

The greatest imbalance, however, is to be found in the relatively small number of elementary teachers that are being prepared. As Maul points out [164:13], the ratio of elementary teachers to secondary teachers has been about 8 to 5 for many years. "In the next decade the ratio of increase

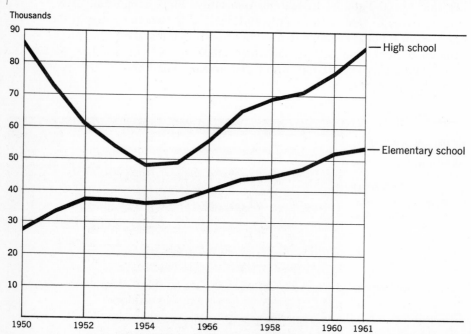

Figure 26.   College graduates prepared to teach. How can a better balance between elementary and secondary prospective teachers be achieved?
(*Source:* National Education Association.)

in enrollment will be somewhat greater in the high schools, but over-crowding is most acute in the elementary grades, and new techniques of teaching will probably find wider application at the top of the public school system. Any increase in pupil-teacher ratio will therefore most likely be at the high school level, and thus will tend to offset the more rapid rate of increase in enrollment. Moreover, such evidence of turn-over as is available substantiates the belief that the rate is about the same among elementary—and high school teachers" [164:13]. As a result, Maul feels that in the future approximately eight elementary teachers will be needed for every five secondary school teachers. Yet the supply is almost

TABLE 5 NEW TEACHERS EMPLOYED IN 1961–1962 AND NEW TEACHERS PRODUCED IN 1960–1961: 29 STATES AND THE DISTRICT OF COLUMBIA

Major subject assignment	Minor subject assignments																				Total demand	Total new supply
	Agriculture	Art	Commerce	English	Foreign language	Home economics	Industrial arts	Journalism	Library science	Mathematics	Music	Phys. ed. Men	Phys. ed. Women	General science	Biology	Chemistry	Physics	Social studies	Speech	Other		
Agriculture	208		1	3	2	1	13	1	5	13	2	5	2	25	26	13		5	1	5	319	615
Art	3	628		38	10	3	3	9	7	3	3	4		8	1			26	3	10	743	1019
Commerce	3	4	1421	144		17	4	97	121	73	42	44	23	14	4	1		118	6	17	1922	3315
English	7	27	82	3936	398	26	2		3	86	3	30	50	78	10	4		765	245	51	6057	4852
Foreign language		1	2	261	914	6				20		4	7	7	3		6	79	2	9	1321	984
Home economics	1	12	14	59	4	1360	1	1	5	7	3		63	102	22	4		38		28	1724	2284
Industrial arts	2	5	4	5		2	881	1	3	57	2	57	2	15	9	5		48		35	1139	1776
Journalism			1	7		1		9		3					1			1			23	29
Library science	4		5	49	8			1	433	5	5		2	5			1	16		4	538	116
Mathematics	6	4	28	80	19	4	31		4	2646	13	104	21	484	46	82	109	140	8	28	3857	3104
Music	2	6	3	71		1	2	1		25	1362	6		9	1		2	77	8	9	1594	2385
Phys. ed. men	4	1	11	15	8		13		1	56	2	893	6	66	32	1	3	142		24	1273	3685
Phys. ed. women		1	13	33	2	11		1	7	15		11	1028	51	23		1	79	4	17	1296	1306
General science	20	6	3	37	1	10	4		2	288	4	97	22	1265	169	80	51	97	1	15	2181	1569
Biology	4	2	2	14	9	1	4			37	1	38	13	171	403	76	20	23		7	822	1464
Chemistry				4	6					43	1	2	2	60	39	126	61	3		3	343	366
Physics				1	2					30		1		17	9	28	45	10		1	145	126
Social studies	11	15	39	411	55	6	12	13	5	104	22	237	44	80	29	9	4	2458	24	70	3648	6184
Speech	1	2	1	70	2		2	3	3	2	1	2	2	1	1			12	160	17	282	969
Other	3	2	8	31	5	3	6	2	3	22	5	10	2	7	3			28	2	1006	1148	742
High school total																					30,375	36,890
Elementary school total																					34,378	22,131

Source: Adapted from "Teacher Supply and Demand in Public Schools, 1962," *Research Report 1962-R8,* National Education Association, Research Division, Washington, April, 1962, p. 23.

exactly in the reverse ratio. For example, in 1961 there were approximately 58,000 high school and 44,000 elementary school qualified candidates who could be expected to teach [164:5].

The excessive imbalance of teachers in the various fields and levels of teaching constitutes a serious problem in the minds of many educators. As a future professional educator you will be affected by this imbalance. How should the problem be solved? Do you feel that no planned attempt should be made to maintain a reasonable balance between the supply and demand of teachers? Do you maintain that it is undemocratic to limit, as does the medical profession, the number permitted to prepare for the profession? Do you maintain that the problem eventually will solve itself? Do you believe that, when the imbalance becomes too great, increased numbers of intelligent students will foresee the lack of job opportunities and therefore will not plan to teach?

Or do you feel that a definite plan should be developed to solve the problem of excessive imbalance in supply and demand? Is there no justification, so far as society is concerned, in allowing everyone to prepare for teaching who wishes to do so? Do you feel that both students and society will profit far more by guiding the less promising students into other occupations in which the probabilities of employment are much greater? Thus, many would avoid the possible bitterness of not being able to secure teaching positions and of having wasted the opportunity to prepare for something else.

A few institutions, especially in the eastern part of the United States, have attempted to limit the teacher supply by accepting only a certain number of candidates. Too often the quota plan does not give adequate attention to quality or probable fitness for teaching. Other institutions have made some attempts to control the number of graduates by raising scholastic requirements. Unfortunately, many students can succeed very well academically and yet be poor teachers. Obviously, many other factors must be taken into consideration in judging probable fitness for teaching.

As you move into your teaching career, you have the opportunity to be concerned with the problem of imbalance in the demand and supply of teachers. Through the efforts of educators and public school personnel, some solution probably will emerge whereby employment opportunities will be decreased for the unfit and increased for those who hold the greatest promise for guiding our youth.

Too often, factors other than fitness operate in the selection of teachers for positions. The intelligent, promising individual who should prepare for teaching may foresee that appointments are not always based upon merit and may abandon the idea of teaching. Consequently, the quality of those preparing for the profession is lowered.

In planning your career in education you have the basic responsibility of securing and taking into consideration all possible available data regarding supply and demand, especially in those areas and/or levels in which you are particularly interested. Personnel in almost all teacher-education institutions today have these data available. They will be able to advise you not only in terms of the national picture but also in terms of the conditions that exist in your specific locale. Since conditions do change from time to time, it is important that you maintain close contact throughout your preparation for teaching with the teacher-employment office which your institution probably maintains.

Analysis of Opportunities in Elementary and Secondary Schools.   Maul feels that, if the school system is to meet its responsibilities to society, the demand for thoroughly competent teachers must be met through (1) replacement of those who quit teaching, (2) accommodation of the increased enrollment, (3) reduction of oversized classes and elimination of half-day sessions, (4) provision of instructional and educational serv-ices not now generally available, and (5) replacement of unqualified per-sons now serving as teachers [165:22]. What, briefly, does each of these demands mean, so far as your opportunities for teaching are concerned?

Maul estimates an annual loss of 8.5 per cent of the public school teachers due to retirement, disability, dismissal, or death. For example, in 1962 it was estimated that 125,000 teachers would be needed to replace those leaving the profession for the above reason. It was also estimated that 35,000 additional teachers would be needed in September, 1962, to provide for the increase in school enrollment. The number of births per year foretells the approximate size of the school population in the years to come. Obviously, the expanding birth rate of the past 20 years indi-cates that elementary schools are already experiencing larger enrollments and these larger numbers of pupils are moving on through the secondary schools. Also, the increasingly greater proportions of pupils remaining

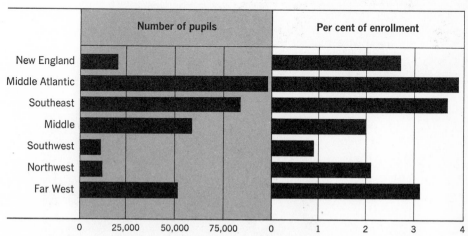

Figure 27.   Elementary school pupils in half-day sessions, November, 1959. Far too many pupils are in half-day sessions. What educational sacrifices are made by children attending these sessions? Can society afford these sacrifices? (*Source:* National Education Association.)

(*Photograph by Carl Purcell, National Education Association.*)

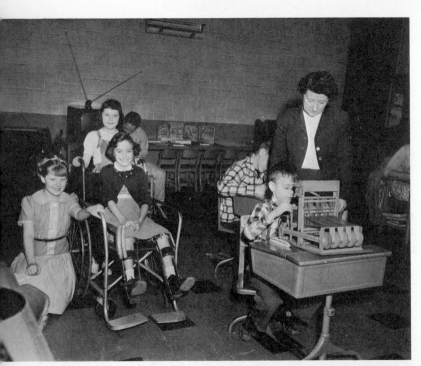

(*Photograph from the National Education Association.*)

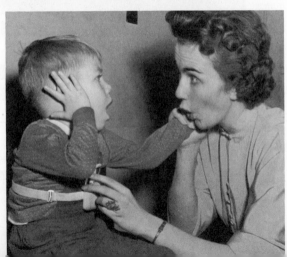

(*Photograph from the Des Moines Hearing and Speech Center, Des Moines, Iowa.*)

(*Photograph by Carl Purcell, National Education Association.*)

In addition to the need for teachers in the various instructional areas, increasingly greater demands will be made in a number of specialized areas. Identify the areas shown.

in the secondary schools will increase the demand for teachers unless the pupil-teacher ratio is increased.

In addition to these two very realistic needs, Maul indicates other needs that have not been met and are likely to continue [165:20–21]. For example, it was estimated that 30,000 teachers were needed in 1962 to relieve overcrowded classrooms and to eliminate part-time sessions. The greatest problem, in regard to overcrowdedness, existed in the elementary schools, where both experience and mature judgment indicates that the effectiveness of the teacher falls rapidly as the 1-to-25 pupil-teacher ratio is exceeded. At the lower grade levels particularly, the immaturity of the child is such that personal attention should not be denied. A nationwide study, however, indicates that 83.3 per cent of the classrooms in all urban school districts in 1962 had more than 25 children each; 50.4 per cent had more than 30 each; 16.4 per cent had more than 35 each; and 2.9 per cent had more than 40 each [165:20].

In 1962, the Research Division of the National Education Association estimated that 330,000 elementary and 270,000 high school pupils, a total of 600,000, were attending half-day or triple sessions. Unfortunately, elementary school children are less able than secondary school pupils to compensate effectively for the loss of individual attention and assistance which results from such part-time emergency measures. It is easy to see that any relief from these educational inequalities will demand the services of a sizable share of the graduates who annually meet elementary- and secondary-teacher certification requirements.

As mentioned earlier, new demands for instruction and services are being made. Much attention is being given to such instructional fields as mathematics, chemistry, and physics. More foreign language is being advocated for elementary and secondary school children. Increasingly greater demands will be made for counseling and guidance services,

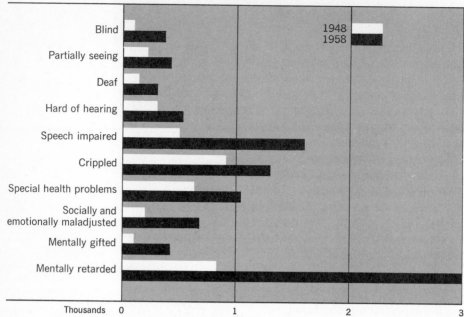

Figure 28. Number of local public school systems reporting enrollments in each area of exceptionality, 1948 and 1958. An increasing number of specialized teachers will be needed to teach exceptional children. (*Source:* U.S. Office of Education.)

library services, vocational education programs, work experiences, health education, recreation and safety, audio-visual materials, speech and hearing therapy, remedial reading, specialized instruction for the mentally retarded and for the physically handicapped, specialized instruction for the gifted, and instruction in subjects not now being offered in many of the smaller schools. Maul conservatively estimated that 25,000 more teachers would be needed in 1962 if this additional instruction and services were to be provided.

Few people would argue the fact that some teachers are not adequately prepared. There is no single answer, however, to the question "When is a person so completely inadequate that his removal from the classroom is justified?" In 1962, Maul roughly estimated that the preparation of approximately 30,000 teachers was so inadequate that they should be replaced [165:21]; on the other hand, it is gratifying to note that, when measured by the number of hours of college credit, much improvement in the preparation of teachers has taken place. For example, between 1948–1949 and 1961–1962 the percentage of elementary teachers having completed less than 60 semester hours of credit decreased from 16.9 to 1.9 per cent, and the percentage having 120 or more hours increased from 49.1 to 79.1 per cent [165:24].

From the above analysis, Maul concluded that 240,000 new teachers were needed in September, 1962 [165:21]. If 106,000 (74.5 per cent) of the 142,547 qualified graduates of 1962 had actually taught, the net estimated shortage of teachers would have been 134,000 teachers.

In terms of the preceding information, you may conclude that the future looks bright for students who wish to prepare for teaching. As has been true in the past, the demand for elementary teachers will be especially great. With careful attention being given to the supply and demand for teachers in the various subject areas, you may look forward with much confidence to teaching in the secondary school area.

Subject Combinations for Teaching in the Secondary Schools. Most secondary teachers begin their teaching careers in small school systems, since city school systems usually demand that their new appointees have a few years' successful teaching experience. Therefore keep in mind, as you plan your preparation for teaching, that you probably will need to teach in two or more subject areas. Even in large school systems many teachers teach in more than one subject area, as you may note from Table 5. Teachers in special areas such as agriculture, commercial subjects, fine arts, home economics, industrial arts, and music are more likely than other secondary teachers to teach in one subject area only.

The ease with which you obtain your initial appointment will depend to some degree on the extent to which the subject combination you select is in demand. A combination that is seldom in demand, such as foreign languages and physical education, is little better than a single subject, while foreign languages with English is demanded more frequently.

Fortunately the combination of subjects tends to follow definite patterns. Unrelated combinations, such as fine arts, agriculture, physics, and English, asked by employing officials in the past are disappearing. Small secondary schools are revising programs of study so that various courses are offered in alternate years. Many small schools are reducing the number of highly specialized subjects that are offered. Furthermore, the trend toward school consolidation, which increases the enrollment and the size of the faculty of each school, means that teachers may be assigned more nearly according to their preparation.

Many studies have been made of the combination of subjects taught by secondary teachers. Your college teacher-placement officer probably makes an annual study of the subject combinations requested by employing officials. Although almost every possible combination may be found, there are certain ones that occur more often than others. You may gain some idea of desirable combinations of subject areas by studying Table 5. You will note considerable demand for such combinations as commerce and social science and/or English; English and social science, foreign languages, or speech; mathematics and general science, social science, or English; music and English; and men's physical education and social science.

The demand for various subject combinations fluctuates from year to year and varies in different sections of the United States. For example, in some states the secondary school candidates are heavily concentrated in certain fields, while in other states they are more widely distributed. Considerable variation in the demand for subject areas may exist between school districts. Your local teacher-placement officer may be of great help in selecting the combination of subjects that seems most desirable for you and most consistent with your abilities and interests.

Opportunities for Teaching on the College Level. You may plan to teach on the college level. A number of individuals value the opportunities that college teaching provides for writing, conducting research, and engaging in other scholarly pursuits. Some value highly the prestige that college instructors have, compared with that of public school teachers. Whatever the reasons may be, they may definitely affect your plans.

In some college departments, especially in the subject-matter areas, a few highly selected graduates are encouraged immediately to work for higher degrees. The students usually are granted assistantships that entail some teaching, supervision of laboratories, or the like, while they continue their studies. The assistantships pay a relatively small amount of money but provide fee exemptions from college work taken by the student. You may wish to investigate possibilities along these lines.

A large percentage of college teachers began their teaching careers in public schools. They pursued graduate work during their summer vacations or returned for full-time study to complete their degrees. Usually they have found their public school experiences to be of great value in their college teaching. A number of years of successful elementary or secondary teaching experience is a prerequisite for securing a position in which you teach education courses.

Opportunities for college teaching will be affected by the extent to which college enrollments increase. The percentage of the group 18 to 21 years old in college has been increasing approximately one per cent a year. In 1960–1961, 38.9 per cent of this group was in college. Taking this trend into account along with the increasing birth rate, it has been predicted that over 9 million students will be in college by 1978—over twice the number attending college in 1961–1962 [48:1–3].

The President's Commission on National Goals [114:90–92] specified that higher-education institutions should be prepared to handle up to 50 per cent of the college-age population by 1970. Emphasis was placed upon the development of junior colleges. By 1970, graduate schools should be producing 20,000 Ph.D.'s annually as compared with 9,360 in 1958–1959.

In studying the demand for college teachers, the Research Division of the National Education Association assumes that withdrawal from classroom service for all reasons will continue at about 6 per cent a year, and that student-teacher ratio will gradually increase from 13 to 1 in 1958–1959 to about 16 to 1 in 1969–1970. If these assumptions are correct, the demand for new college teachers will average about 31,000 per year [53:62].

The shortage of well-qualified teachers to meet the increasing college

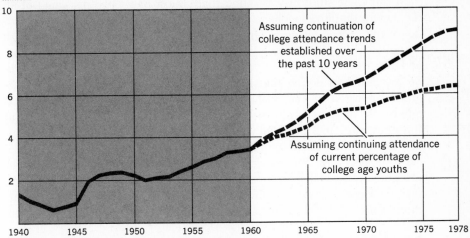

Figure 29. Past and projected enrollments in higher education. (*Source:* The American Association of Collegiate Registrars and Admissions Officers.)

enrollments is reflected in the decrease of formal preparation possessed by the newly employed teachers. In 1953–1954, 31.4 per cent of the new teachers employed held doctor's degrees. Only 25.8 per cent of those employed in 1960–1961 were at this high level of preparation, 20 per cent had completed a full year of graduate study beyond the degree, and 17.4 per cent had not even attained the master's degree [53:62]. In junior colleges, the most frequently accepted level of preparation was the master's degree.

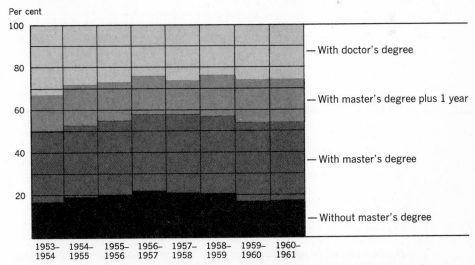

Figure 30. Trend in the employment of new college teachers according to levels of preparation. The demand for college teachers has been so great that the level of preparation of those employed has decreased. What effect may this condition have upon the quality of college teaching and upon research? (*Source:* National Education Association.)

In this same study it was found that almost half (46.3 per cent) of all the newly employed college teachers in 1960–1961 were graduate students the preceding year. One of every eight came directly from high school teaching, one of every ten came from some business occupation, and the rest came from various sources [53:62]. As a teacher you will be interested in noting that in 1959–1960 the number of education degrees conferred at the bachelor's level was 22.8 per cent of the total number of degrees in all fields; at the master's level, 45 per cent; and at the doctorate, 16.2 per cent. This percentage distribution has been approximately the same during the past few years [37:4].

From the above information you may conclude the opportunities for teaching on the college level are excellent. If you are interested, however, plan to become as well qualified as possible. In general, the better opportunities are related directly to the amount of college work you have taken.

Opportunities in Other Areas of Education.   Unfortunately most people limit their concept of the opportunities in the field of education mainly to teaching in the public or private school classroom. It is true that over 80 per cent of those engaged in public school work are regular classroom teachers. On the other hand, there are specialized kinds of instruction and services to be rendered, such as counseling; teaching speech and hearing therapy and remedial reading; teaching the mentally retarded, physically handicapped, partially seeing, hard of hearing, emotionally disturbed, and the gifted; serving as librarian; and teaching driver education and distributive education courses. Attention already has been called to the large number of superintendents, principals, supervisors, and others involved in administrative services.

It would be exceedingly interesting to analyze all the different kinds of work demanding the services of educators and to note the number involved in each. Unfortunately these data are not available. The following listing of the more common educational opportunities may be of interest to you. In no sense is the list complete.

I. Preschool—nursery and kindergarten
   A. Teacher
   B. Supervisor
   C. Consultant in child growth and development
   D. Research worker in child growth and development
   E. Director of a private nursery or kindergarten
II. Elementary schools
   A. Teacher for separate grades or combined grades
   B. Teacher of special subjects such as art, music, or physical education
   C. Teacher of a subject such as arithmetic or geography in a departmentalized school
   D. Teacher of physically handicapped, partially seeing, or hard of hearing children
   E. Teacher of exceptional children—talented, mentally retarded, or emotionally disturbed
   F. Critic teacher in a laboratory or experimental school
   G. General or special supervisor

H. Assistant principal
I. Principal
J. Librarian
K. Speech correctionist and/or hearing therapist
L. Visiting teacher
M. Child psychologist or counselor
N. School nurse
O. Curriculum consultant

III. Secondary schools
   A. Teacher of subjects such as English, foreign language, social studies, or music
   B. Teaching of special subjects such as art, home economics, industrial arts and trades, music, physical education, driver education, speech and hearing therapy
   C. Critic teacher in a laboratory or experimental school
   D. Department head of a subject area
   E. Assistant principal
   F. Principal
   G. Supervisor of a subject area
   H. Curriculum consultant
   I. Athletic coach
   J. Guidance director
   K. Librarian
   L. Visiting teacher

IV. Administrative and special services
   A. Superintendent
      1. Full-time
      2. Part-time
   B. Assistant superintendent—usually assigned a specific phase of work such as finance
   C. Business manager (supplies, purchasing, etc.)
   D. School secretary
   E. Research director
   F. Attendance officer
   G. Director of audio-visual materials
   H. Director of public relations
   I. School psychologist
   J. School psychometrist
   K. Vocational counselor and placement officer
   L. School statistician
   M. Clerical assistant
   N. Cafeteria manager
   O. Dietitian
   P. School physician or dentist
   Q. School nurse or health officer

V. Junior colleges
   A. Teacher of different fields (English, mathematics, science, etc.)
   B. Personnel director
   C. President or dean
   D. Registrar
   E. Business manager
   F. Health service officer

VI. Teachers colleges
   A. Teacher of
      1. Subject such as English, science, etc.
      2. Subject in education

      B. Critic teacher in demonstration schools
      C. Head of department
      D. Head of demonstration or laboratory school
      E. Dean of instruction
      F. School psychologist and director of guidance
      G. Dean of men
      H. Dean of women
      I. Business manager
      J. Registrar
      K. Health service personnel
      L. Alumni secretary
      M. Director of public relations
      N. Director of placement service
      O. President

VII. University positions
      A. Teacher of any subject field included in a large university
      B. Assistant to deans
      C. Dean of a separate college such as liberal arts, education, engineering, agriculture, law, medicine, fine arts, pharmacy, social service, dentistry
      D. Dean of instruction
      E. President
      F. Dean of men
      G. Dean of women
      H. Registrar
      I. Director of guidance
      J. Business manager
      K. Research worker
      L. Director of research
      M. Secretary and/or accountant
      N. Field worker for recruiting students
      O. Field worker for carrying services of university to the people
      P. Placement director
      Q. Health service personnel

VIII. Professional organizations like National Education Association; other national and state educational associations
      A. Director
      B. Executive secretary
      C. Research worker
      D. Field worker
      E. Writer

IX. State departments of education
      A. State superintendent of instruction
      B. Deputy
      C. Special field worker

X. Educational directors or consultants for noneducational agencies
      A. Publisher of newspapers, magazines, films
      B. Manufacturing firms—job training, recreation, testing, etc.
      C. Religious associations
      D. Chambers of commerce
      E. Aviation companies
      F. Service agencies, such as state tuberculosis association

XI. Municipal, private, religious, and civic agencies
      A. City recreation director
      B. Boy and girl camps—director, instructor
      C. Director of youth organization
          1. Boy and girl scouts

2. 4-H club
3. YMCA and YWCA
 D. Teacher in a hospital
 E. Teacher in a church or Bible school
XII. Federal agencies
 A. U.S. Office of Education
 B. UNESCO
 C. Department of Interior—Bureau of Indian Affairs
XIII. Foreign countries
 A. Teacher
 B. Conductor of tours
 C. Consultant
 D. Research worker
 E. War Department appointments—dependent schools, military government

It should be pointed out that many of the different kinds of educational work listed above do not exist in the small schools where you may begin your professional career. Small schools do not have the extensive programs and diversified types of work to be found in large schools. Furthermore, successful teaching experience normally is required for many of the positions not involving classroom teaching.

Do not overlook the educational opportunities that are continuing to develop in the business world. Industries and businesses all over the country need educational directors, would be glad to employ them if they were available, and would give them opportunities for very significant contributions to education in general. The field of educational radio and television is expanding rapidly. Textbook publishers and educational supply firms frequently employ teachers for sales or editorial positions.

As nations throughout the world make increasingly greater demands for better schools, opportunities for educators to teach and to serve as consultants abroad will continue to increase. In this photograph a UNESCO educator is helping Thai educators to relate classroom learning to the daily living environment at Chachoengsao, Thailand. (*Photograph from the United Nations.*)

The unique advantages of motion pictures, educational television, and radio as instructional media offer increased opportunities for new fields for able teachers. (*From the film* Crowded Out *by the National Education Association.*)

The AFL-CIO, the International Ladies Garment Workers Union, some cooperative associations, and the like already have educational directors. There are dozens of national organizations that would have educational directors now if they knew where to find them. Also, as noted previously, the whole field of adult education is barely getting started in this country. There is room for thousands of new jobs in that field for men and women with sound general training, creative imagination, and drive.

For the more adventurous person, the opportunities to work in even the most remote areas of the world continue to increase. In 1962 the Peace Corps estimated that 50,000 teachers could be used in its programs

After a year of teaching experience in Dayton, Ohio, Carol Watkins joined the Peace Corps and was assigned to a teaching position at St. Lucia, Windward Islands, British West Indies. Being a member of the Peace Corps provides an opportunity to render service while getting travel and teaching experience. (*Photograph by Rowland Scherman, Peace Corps.*)

in underdeveloped countries. You may wish to check upon the requirements and opportunities for working in schools in outlying states and areas of the United States, and in schools and programs sponsored by the United States government, such as Dependent Schools Abroad, Information Services, and Act for International Development.

Preparation in the teaching profession certainly presents many different opportunities, and you can engage in the type of activity of special interest to you. If you are willing to prepare yourself well for a particular type of work, the chances of reaching your goal are good.

SUMMARY

The teaching profession is, by a wide margin, the largest of all the professions. Although women predominate on the elementary school level, the number of men is increasing gradually. Increases in salary and continued improvements in teaching conditions may result in larger numbers of men being attracted to teaching in the public schools.

Many factors affect the supply and demand for teachers. In periods of economic depression the supply tends to become greater than in times of economic prosperity. Birth rates, pupil-teacher ratio, turnover and expansion or contraction of educational services rendered by the school affect significantly the demand for teachers.

The elementary schools are faced with an alarming shortage of teachers. The demands for personnel to handle new enrollments, replace teachers who annually withdraw from the profession, reduce the teacher-pupil ratio, and replace inadequately prepared teachers will far exceed the supply of teachers. This means that the educational welfare of many children will suffer.

As the large numbers of elementary school children continue to move into the secondary schools, the demand for secondary teachers will increase greatly. And as the need for secondary school teachers continues to mount, the imbalance in the demand and supply of teachers in the various subject areas will become more crucial. If you plan to teach on the secondary school level, pay careful attention to the imbalance that exists in the subject areas and note any changes that may be occurring in the demand and supply of teachers.

The large majority of positions in the profession involve classroom teaching, for which there is demand in all areas and on all levels, provided the candidate is highly capable and well prepared. In addition to teaching, the profession provides many other opportunities for meeting individual interests and abilities. Explore these opportunities and possibly consider some of them in your long-range plans.

QUESTIONS FOR YOUR CONSIDERATION

1. Many educators feel that more men should be attracted into public school teaching, especially into the elementary schools. Do you agree or disagree? What are your reasons?

2. Some individuals feel that the supply of elementary teachers would increase if the certification requirements were lowered. How could you defend (or deny) this opinion?

3. For what reasons can you expect the number of 14- to 17-year-olds attending secondary schools to increase significantly?

4. How might the percentage of certified graduates accepting teaching positions be increased?

5. What major and minor teaching combinations are in greatest demand? Least demand?

6. What suggestions can you make for solving the problem of excessive imbalance of teachers in the various fields and levels of teaching?

7. What sacrifices are made by pupils when they are forced to attend half-day sessions?

8. What preparation is necessary to teach on the college level? What financial assistance is being offered in an attempt to encourage students to prepare for college teaching?

9. What advantages and disadvantages do you see in teaching on the college level?

10. What solutions can you suggest for solving the increasing shortage of teachers on the college level?

11. If you had to change your subject area or level of teaching, what would you choose? Why?

12. In your opinion, what are the frontier opportunities for teachers in industry, business, and overseas?

ACTIVITIES FOR YOU TO PURSUE

1. Plan a number of visits to more than one school, in which you observe various elementary and secondary school classes. Attempt to decide upon, or further verify, an original decision regarding the subject areas and/or the level in which you may wish to teach.

2. Plan some leadership experiences with children of different age levels to decide upon, or further verify, an original decision regarding elementary or secondary teacher preparation. Experiences as camp counselors, playground supervisors, boy or girl scout directors, and the like should prove very valuable to you.

3. Consult your local superintendent to see if you might serve as an assistant in a school between the time public schools open in the fall and the time your college courses begin. Attempt to gain broad experience both in the classroom and around the school.

Study these experiences in terms of your fitness for teaching, the level on which you should teach, and learning significant for future courses in education.

4. Question a number of teachers whom you respect, especially those teaching on the elementary level, regarding the advantages and disadvantages of preparing for teaching in the subject areas and/or levels which they represent.

5. Consult your local school administrator about the causes of teacher turnover.

6. Consult the adviser and the teacher-placement official in your college concerning the probable supply and demand for teachers when you expect to graduate. Secure from educational literature as much data on this problem as possible.

7. If you do not plan to teach in the locale where you are attending school, secure data on teacher supply and demand for the area in which you expect to begin your work.

8. Examine the organizational setup of a large city school system to discover the different kinds of positions involved. Talk with those individuals who hold positions that may interest you. Discuss such matters as qualifications, duties, advantages, and disadvantages of the work.

9. Discuss with your college adviser any occupational plans other than teaching that you may have in the field of education. Consider specific implications that these plans may have in your preparation for teaching.

RESOURCE SECTION FOR PART I

- A Self-Rating Scale for Determining Fitness for Teaching

- The California Statement of Teaching Competence

- Check List of Important Factors in the Teacher's Personality

- An Inventory of Personal Appearance

- A Check List for Voice and Speech

- Am I a Good Group Participant?

- Suggested Films, Filmstrips, and Recordings

- Suggested Readings

- Figure Credits

• A SELF-RATING SCALE FOR DETERMINING FITNESS FOR TEACHING

	Never	Sel-dom	Some-times	Often	Al-ways
I. Leadership Ability					
1. Have you served as leader in student groups, i.e., have you held an office, taken part in programs, or led discussions?					
2. Do your fellow students respect your opinions?					
3. Do they regard you as a leader?					
4. Do your fellow students ask you for help and advice?					
5. Do you sense how others feel, i.e., whether they approve certain proposals, or like or dislike certain persons?					
6. Do you try to make others happy by listening to what they say, and by being courteous, friendly, and helpful?					
7. Do you succeed in getting others to follow your suggestions without creating friction or ill will?					
II. Health and Physical Fitness					
1. Do you have good health?					
2. Do you have lots of vitality? Can you stand to do hard physical tasks or nerve-racking work?					
3. Can you engage in activities which others in your group customarily do?					
4. Do you give others the impression that you are physically fit, well groomed and attractive in personal appearance?					
5. Do you keep cheerful and even-tempered even when tired or ill?					
III. Good Scholarship					
1. Have you maintained a better-than-average academic record?					
2. Are you interested in the subjects you have taken or are taking?					
3. Do you enjoy studying and find it easy to concentrate when you do study?					
4. Do you express your ideas well before a class or public group?					

Source: E. E. Samuelson and others, *You'd Like Teaching,* Craftsman Press, Seattle, Wash., 1946, pp. 31—35. Materials prepared and published, and permission for use granted, by Central Washington College of Education.

A SELF-RATING SCALE FOR DETERMINING FITNESS FOR TEACHING (*continued*)

	Never	Sel-dom	Some-times	Often	Al-ways
5. Is it easy for you to explain things so that others understand and can follow your directions?					
IV. Intellectual Traits and Abilities					
1. Are school subjects easy for you?					
2. Do you spend time finding out more about a topic discussed in class or covered in an assignment?					
3. Do you read books or magazine articles on current topics?					
4. Do you like to work out ideas on your own?					
5. Do you suggest new ideas or plans which can be carried out by groups?					
V. Emotional Stability					
1. Are you an even-tempered, cheerful, happy sort of person?					
2. Can you "take it" without getting angry or upset?					
3. Do you keep from worrying and feeling depressed?					
4. Are you naturally patient with and tolerant of others?					
5. Are you objectively critical of yourself?					
6. Do you see the humorous side of everyday happenings even when you yourself are involved?					
VI. Social Aspirations					
1. Are you interested in the problems other people meet and do you want to help them solve them?					
2. Are you interested in finding ways by which you can help improve human living?					
3. Do you like people—especially children?					
4. Do you set high social standards for yourself and seek to reach and maintain these standards?					
5. Do you cooperate readily with other people in socially desirable activities?					
6. Are you willing to make sacrifices and endure inconveniences to reach a goal you consider worthy?					

● THE CALIFORNIA STATEMENT OF TEACHING COMPETENCE*

The competent teacher:
1. Provides for the learning of students
   a. Uses psychological principles of learning
     (1) Uses effective and continuing motivation
       (*a*) Recognizes and makes use of the interests, abilities and needs of students
       (*b*) Uses the experiences of students and draws upon life situations and the interests inherent in subject matter
     (2) Provides varied learning experiences
     (3) Uses a variety of teaching procedures, such as discussion, review, etc., effectively
     (4) Plans cooperatively with students
   b. Uses principles of child growth and development in learning situations
     (1) Provides for differentiated activities and assignments to meet the needs and abilities of students
     (2) Knows the health (mental and physical) status of his students and adapts activities to their needs
   c. Maintains an atmosphere in the classroom that is conducive to learning and is marked by a sense of balance between freedom and security
     (1) Maintains an effective working situation
     (2) Helps students increasingly to assume leadership and responsibility
     (3) Provides opportunities for students to cooperate and to exercise leadership in the activities of large and small groups
     (4) Provides opportunity for expression of independent critical thought with emphasis on freedom of expression and open-mindedness
   d. Plans effectively
     (1) Aids the students to define worthwhile objectives for large units, daily class work, and special class activities
     (2) Organizes his teaching well by choosing wisely learning experiences, subject-matter content, and materials of instruction
     (3) Selects and uses a wide variety of materials of instruction (e.g., books, pamphlets, films, bulletin boards, flat pictures, radios, recordings, etc.)
     (4) Uses resources of the school library and the community
   e. Uses varied teaching procedures
     (1) Uses teaching procedures (such as group reporting, discussion, planning with pupils) designed to achieve desired purposes in teaching
     (2) Builds effectively upon the students' participation in class activities
     (3) Develops study skills of students
     (4) Stimulates creative activities of students
     (5) Aids the students to evaluate their own achievements
   f. Uses diagnostic and remedial procedures effectively
     (1) Is familiar with common diagnostic tests in his own and related fields
     (2) Constructs, administers, and interprets diagnostic tests
     (3) Uses other appropriate diagnostic procedures
     (4) Plans and uses remedial procedures
   g. Uses adequate procedures for evaluating the achievement of students
     (1) Uses informal evaluation procedures (anecdotal record, interview questionnaire) for collecting and interpreting needed information
     (2) Uses standard achievement tests
       (*a*) Is familiar with the more common ones in his field
       (*b*) Selects, administers, and interprets the results of tests and uses them in planning

* *The Evaluation of Student Teaching,* Twenty-eighth Annual Yearbook of the Association for Student Teaching, State Teachers College, Lock Haven, Pa., 1949, pp. 6–11.

(3) Uses teacher-made tests
   (*a*) Constructs appropriate tests skillfully
   (*b*) Interprets the results and uses them in planning
(4) Keeps accurate and adequate records, e.g., case studies, cumulative records
(5) Makes effective reports to students and parents concerning the progress of students in their growth

h. Manages the class effectively
   (1) Plans satisfactory routine for the handling of materials, equipment, and supplies
   (2) Uses own and pupils' time effectively
   (3) Is attentive to the physical well-being of students in such matters as heating, lighting, ventilation, and seating

2. Counsels and guides students wisely
   a. Uses sound psychological principles concerning the growth and development of children in guiding individuals and groups
      (1) Maintains objectivity when dealing with behavior that is aggressive and abnormal
      (2) Is sympathetic with and sensitive to students' personal and social problems as well as their academic needs
      (3) Makes adjustments in the curriculum and other requirements in the light of pupils' needs
      (4) Secures sufficient rapport with students so that they come voluntarily for counsel
   b. Maintains effective relationships with parents
      (1) Explains the needs, abilities, interests, and problems of the students to their parents
      (2) Obtains cooperation from parents in helping students with their problems
   c. Collects and uses significant counseling data
      (1) Administers aptitude and intelligence tests
      (2) Interprets the results of such tests
      (3) Uses results collected in counseling with students
      (4) Keeps research suitable for guidance
   d. Uses suitable counseling procedures
   e. Maintains appropriate relations with guidance specialists, recognizing their role and the limitations of his own skill and ability

3. Aids students to understand and appreciate our cultural heritage
   a. Organizes the classroom for effective democratic living
   b. Directs individuals and groups to significant life applications of classroom learnings
      (1) Uses subject fields to develop understanding of social, economic, and political problems
      (2) Develops an understanding of the wide significance of various fields of subject matter
   c. Draws on his own background of experience to elicit the cultural growth of individuals and groups
   d. Helps students to know and to apply in their daily lives the democratic principles which are rooted deep in our historical development

4. Participates effectively in the activities of the school
   a. Plans cooperatively the means of achieving educational objectives
      (1) Shares effectively in curricular revision and is able to evaluate progress toward attaining education objectives
         (*a*) Defines objectives clearly
         (*b*) Collects data efficiently and draws appropriate conclusions from them
         (*c*) Employs appropriate remedial procedures
         (*d*) Shows flexibility in modifying his plans and procedures to fit with those of the entire school

Joseph B. Taylor, S.J.

    b. Assumes his share of the responsibility for school activities
        (1) Carries out effectively the administrative responsibilities delegated to him
        (2) Participates in planning and administering extracurricular activities
    c. Maintains harmonious personal relations with his colleagues
5. Assists in maintaining good relations between the school and the rest of the community
    a. Acquaints himself with available community resources and uses them in classroom activities
    b. Obtains the cooperation of parents in school activities
    c. Aids in defining and solving community problems
        (1) Helps in defining community problems and in developing awareness of them in students and parents
        (2) Draws on available and appropriate resources within the school in attacking community problems
    d. Takes part in community affairs and projects
    e. Observes professional ethics in discussing school problems particularly with lay persons
6. Works on a professional level
    a. Gives evidence of the social importance of the profession to parents, students, and other members of the profession
    b. Adheres to a professional code of ethics
    c. Contributes to the profession by membership in professional organizations and participation in their activities
    d. Assumes responsibility for his own professional growth by planning an appropriate program for professional betterment
        (1) Continues professional study through courses, lectures, institutes, professional reading and other activities
    e. Aids in supervising student teachers and in the orientation and induction of beginning teachers

● CHECK LIST OF IMPORTANT FACTORS IN THE TEACHER'S PERSONALITY

Directions: Consider each of the ten divisions in this list separately. Read each statement under the major headings carefully and underline any of the qualities or traits which obviously are missing in the personality being rated. Before you proceed to the next division, look back over any of the statements you may have underlined and then place a check mark in the column that expressed your general opinion of the person with respect to the particular aspect of personality being considered.

Suggested standard for traits or qualities	Below average	Fair	Good	Excellent
1. *Emotional stability and mental health.* Free from fears, remorses, humiliations, and worries about trivial things; is disposed to make a realistic inventory of his mental resources; not supersensitive to criticism; has a mind stored with wholesome resources for self-entertainment; not easily irritated;				

Source: Raleigh Schorling and Howard T. Batchelder, *Student Teaching in Secondary Schools,* McGraw-Hill Book Company, Inc., New York, 1956, pp. 12–13.

CHECK LIST (*continued*)

Suggested standard for traits or qualities	Below average	Fair	Good	Excellent
is free from excessive shyness and from temper tantrums and daydreams; meets unexpected situations well; adapts readily to changing situations; exercises self-control; is free from complexes of inferiority and superiority; has control over moods, with no sudden shifts in extremes from ups to downs; can take disappointments in life in full stride.				
2. *Personal appearance.* Is dressed appropriately for the occasion; is alert and well poised; is well groomed; gives appearance of being self-possessed; exercises good taste in selection of clothes; impresses one as being refined and cultured; color combinations are harmonious; clothes are pressed and clean; looks to be in good health.				
3. *Health and vitality.* Shows evidence of a "driving force"; is physically and mentally alert; is enthusiastic and cheerful; looks the picture of health; is dynamic; is wide awake to the potential possibilities in every situation; has a happy expression of countenance; has reserve energy.				
4. *Honesty, character, and integrity.* Shows a good sense of values; can be expected to do the right thing under all conditions; is trustworthy and loyal; admits mistakes; keeps his word; is fair and just in his dealings with others; fulfills obligations; is intellectually honest; maintains high standards of conduct.				
5. *Adaptability.* Accepts gracefully and understands quickly suggestions from others; accepts responsibility for making a positive contribution to a situation; is willing to inconvenience self in helping others; is challenged by new situations; is sympathetic and patient in sharing and understanding the thoughts and difficulties of others; says what needs to be said with diplomacy and a minimum of offense; responds readily to necessary routine.				
6. *Cooperation.* Can work with others for attainment of a common end; volunteers services when they are needed; fits in where most needed; welcomes suggestions and tries to improve; places welfare of the group before self; is willing to share in the "extra" tasks; is a constructive worker on a committee.				
7. *Voice and speech.* Shows refinement and evidence of cultural background; is clear and distinct; has proper degree of inflection; is well modulated,				

CHECK LIST (*continued*)

Suggested standard for traits or qualities	Below average	Fair	Good	Excellent
controlled, and adapted to size of group; has an accepted and natural accent; arrests favorable attention; is easy to understand; words are pronounced correctly, speech is free from distracting and irritating mannerisms or defects.				
8. *Leadership*. Commands respect; is self-confident; shows ability in planning, organization, and execution; can persuade others of a proper course of action; can act in emergencies with decision; uses good judgment; inspires others to do their best; shows mastery of a situation; exercises initiative and originality; has the ability to put into words the inarticulate desires of a group; possesses courage to support sound convictions.				
9. *Resourcefulness*. Is prolific in suggestions for meeting a difficulty; is discerning and quick in selection of the most promising solution; can "see around a corner"; has an abundance of reserve energy upon which to draw; is intuitive in "striking when the iron is hot"; suggests power of mental strength and vigor.				
10. *Sociability*. Reveals knowledge of the rules of etiquette sufficient to avoid embarrassing, offending, or irritating others; is unselfishly interested in "just folks"; is a dynamic human spark; is a stimulating conversationalist with a wide range of interests; has a vicarious point of view; puts others at ease; seeks associations of others; is tolerant of the opinions of others, of community life, and in the numerous agencies for social expression; wins and holds his friends; is a good listener; knows when to be playful; creates a comfortable and pleasant atmosphere; sees the humorous element in situations; can jest and frolic at parties and picnics but recaptures his dignity at the appropriate time; is a good sport.				

• AN INVENTORY OF PERSONAL APPEARANCE

Directions: Check each item carefully and place an X in the appropriate column opposite the quality being considered. For example, if your handkerchiefs are always fresh, place an X in the "Yes" column opposite that item. When you have finished, try to determine whether you present an appearance that is pleasing (1) all the time, (2) sometimes, or (3) not at all. Check marks in the two outside columns should serve as reminders or "conscience ticklers" that you still have room for improvement.

Appearance factors	Yes	Some-times	No
Clothing:			
1. Are your clothes always clean, pressed, and free from unpleasant odors?			
2. Do you keep your shoes cleaned, shined, and heels straightened?			
3. Do you attempt to "freshen up" at noon or in the evening?			
4. Are your handkerchiefs always fresh?			
5. Are color combinations in good taste?			
6. Are your clothes becoming to your type and size?			
7. Do you consider quality in clothes when making a selection?			
8. Do you get up early enough to have plenty of time to devote to your personal appearance?			
9. When in question about style do you consult a reliable clothier or a current fashion guide?			
10. Do you adapt clothes and appearance to the time, place, occasion, and your age?			
Skin, Hair, and Nails:			
1. Do you avoid all evidences of dandruff?			
2. Do you visit a barbershop or hairdresser frequently enough to keep looking trim?			
3. Do you wash your hair frequently enough to keep it soft and healthy?			
4. Are you free from skin eruptions? (The cause of such eruptions may be improper cleansing or diet, but see your physician.)			
5. Do you keep your nails trim and clean?			
Health (Physical):			
1. Is your weight about normal (so that you are neither overweight nor underweight)?			
2. Are you alert, free from a tired and worried appearance?			
3. Are you careful about your posture?			
4. Is your breath free from obnoxious odors?			
5. Are your teeth clean and free from cavities?			

Source: Raleigh Schorling and Howard T. Batchelder, *Student Teaching in Secondary Schools,* McGraw-Hill Book Company, Inc., New York, 1956, p. 15.

• A CHECK LIST FOR VOICE AND SPEECH*

There are two ways in which this check list may be useful: (1) you may wish to ask some trained person to evaluate your teaching voice; (2) the results may prove helpful when two or three student teachers rate each other, and later compare notes.

Speech factors	Needs attention	Satisfactory or superior
Quality of voice: Is his voice		
1. Too high pitched?		
2. Nasal?		
3. Strained?		
4. Breathy?		
5. Varied in pitch?		
6. Clear and distinct?		
7. Rich and colorful?		
8. Adapted to the size of the listening group?		
9. Well controlled and modulated?		
10. Resonant?		
Unpleasant Speech Mannerisms: Does he speak		
1. Too fast?		
2. In a drawling manner?		
3. Lispingly?		
4. Gruffly?		
5. Too slowly?		
6. In an uncertain, halting, or stumbling manner?		
7. With an affected accent?		
General Speech: Does he		
1. Pronounce words correctly?		
2. Enunciate carefully?		
3. Use slang inappropriately or excessively?		
4. Keep calm, free from anger and excitement?		
5. Employ concepts adapted to his audience?		
6. Adapt voice to the occasion?		
7. Use proper inflection?		
8. Show evidence of an adequate vocabulary?		

* Only two columns at the right are employed in order to emphasize the items to which the teacher should give remedial attention.

Source: Raleigh Schorling and Howard T. Batchelder, *Student Teaching in Secondary Schools,* McGraw-Hill Book Company, Inc., New York, 1956, p. 17.

• AM I A GOOD GROUP PARTICIPANT?

1. Do I propose new ideas, activities, and procedures? Or do I just sit and listen?
2. Do I ask questions? Or am I shy about admitting that I do not understand?
3. Do I share my knowledge when it will prove helpful to the problem at hand? Or do I keep it to myself?

Source: "Am I a Good Group Participant?" *National Education Association Journal,* vol. 45, p. 168, National Education Association, Washington, March, 1956.

4. Do I speak up if I feel strongly about something? Or am I shy about giving an opinion?

5. Do I try to bring together our ideas and activities? Or do I concentrate only on details under immediate discussion?

6. Do I understand the goals of the group and try to direct the discussion toward them? Or do I get off the track easily?

7. Do I ever question the practicality or the "logic" of a project, and do I evaluate afterwards? Or do I always accept unquestioningly the things we do?

8. Do I help to arrange chairs, serve refreshments, and even clean up when the session is over? Or do I prefer to be waited on?

9. Do I encourage my fellow group members to do well? Or am I indifferent to their efforts and achievements?

10. Do I prod the group to undertake worthy projects? Or am I happy with mediocre projects?

11. Am I a mediator and a peacemaker? Or do I allow ill feeling to develop?

12. Am I willing to compromise (except where basic issues such as truth and justice are involved)? Or do I remain inflexible?

13. Do I encourage others to participate and to give everyone else a fair chance to speak? Or do I sit by while some people hog the floor, and do I sometimes dominate it myself?

● **SUGGESTED FILMS, FILMSTRIPS, AND RECORDINGS**

The number in parentheses following each suggestion denotes the chapter for which it is best suited.

Films (16 mm)
Adult Education   (United World, 19 min). Depicts night classes and activities attended by adults at Bryant School, Woodside, Long Island. Arts and crafts, mathematics classes, shop courses, and other activities are pictured. Students in a public-speaking course describe the benefits of adult education. (5)
Carpet under Every Classroom   (Marion Hoch, 17 min). Shows ways the library and librarians can help to realize objectives of a secondary school. Presents the library as a resource center for students and teachers and demonstrates teacher-librarian cooperation. (5)
Challenge of the Gifted   (McGraw-Hill, 12 min, color). Surveys the program of the Vallejo, California, Unified School District in meeting the needs of the gifted children of the intermediate grades. Shows special classes are taught in the various curriculum areas by specially qualified teachers and points up the selection of gifted children according to several talents and abilities. (5)
Choosing Your Occupation   (Coronet Films, 10 min). Outlines the services that are presently available for helping one choose an occupation; describes various tests to determine one's interests, abilities, and personality pattern, and suggests information which one needs concerning his chosen occupation. (2)
Class for Tommy   (Bailey Films, 20 min). Tells the story of a mentally retarded little boy who cannot go to school with his younger brother and is consequently lonely and left out. After he is given mental maturity tests and a physical examination, arrangements are made for him to enter a special-education class. The activities of the group in the classroom, on the playground, and in the cafeteria are shown. (5)
Day in the Life of a Five Year Old   (Metro School Study Council, 19 min). Pictures young children becoming aware of the world about them at a well-planned and well-equipped kindergarten. Also shows the role of the kindergarten teacher. (5)
Developing Leadership   (Coronet Films, 11 min, color). Describes how to become

a leader and a group member. Shows how the changing pattern of leadership in a democratic group occurs and suggests leadership qualities which individuals should possess. (3)

Distributive Education   (Virginia State Board of Education, 16 min, color). Portrays the nature and the role of the Distributive Education Program in the state of Virginia in preparing students for possible future jobs. (5)

Emotional Health   (McGraw-Hill, 21 min). Shows interviews of a college student with a physician and then with a psychiatrist who uncovers his fears and helps him become emotionally adjusted; uses occasional flash-backs to the boy's childhood. (3)

First Steps   (United Nations Film Board, 10 min). Shows the physical and social therapy being provided children crippled by paralysis. Emphasizes the importance of turning these children's thoughts outward, so that they can become well-adjusted useful adults. (5)

Golden Age   (McGraw-Hill, 27 min). Problems faced during the retirement age are reviewed through the experiences of three men. Each man has a different approach to retirement years. (2)

Good Speech for Gary   (McGraw-Hill, 22 min). Presents Gary, a second grader with a speech defect, as having difficulty adjusting to his new school. Shows the teacher's recognition of the problem and the remedial work conducted through physical and mental tests and consultations with parents. (5)

Guiding the Growth of Children   (McGraw-Hill, 17 min). Shows how a teacher may work to understand each child and to guide him in his growth and development. Deals with seven problem cases and suggests possible ways of handling them. Shows a variety of techniques that a teacher may-use but insists that underlying each technique is the teacher's genuine desire to help plus sympathetic, patient understanding. (3)

Helping Teachers to Understand Children, Part I   (United World Films, 21 min). Points out a need for teachers to understand children and illustrates a variety of ways through which a knowledge of child behavior can be gained and interpreted. Presents a case study of one child and suggests the use of school records, interviews with teachers, the child's writing and art work, home environment, an anecdotal records as sources of information. (3)

How to Conduct a Discussion   (Encyclopaedia Britannica Films, 24 min). Presents the results of a survey of about 50 adult groups to find common elements of a good group discussion. Illustrates the qualities of good leadership by showing various groups in action and exemplifies 11 important elements of effective group discussions. Uses narration and synchronized sound to portray the different groups and summarize the important points. (3)

Introduction to Student Teaching   (Indiana University, 19 min). Dramatizes the experiences of three beginning student teachers. Suggests getting well acquainted with the school, its personnel, and its policies; becoming accustomed to handling routine classroom matters; becoming familiar with a wide variety of instructional materials, their preparation, and their use; learning as much as possible about the pupils. (3)

Maintaining Classroom Discipline   (McGraw-Hill, 15 min). Contrasts situations in which first poor and then good discipline results from the teacher's varied approaches. Emphasizes the importance of stimulation of interest, the teacher's personality, and the handling of minor incidents. (3)

Make Your Own Decisions   (Coronet Films, 11 min). Pictures Jane's frustration when a party invitation tempts her to neglect her homework. Points out that making decisions is a skill that everyone must learn for mature and successful living. Working out her problems, Jane gains confidence in her ability and learns to break down each problem into the following steps: identifying the choice, knowing when a decision must be made, learning what information is needed, deciding and acting. (3)

Not by Chance   (National Education Association 28½ min, color). Traces the general education and the special preparation of a truly professional teacher. (2)

Planning for Personal and Professional Growth   (McGraw-Hill, 17 min). Shows four schoolteachers who have made certain adjustments and achieved success in their teaching to various degrees. A middle-aged woman found teaching dull with many frustrations; she was not aware of her problems and could not adjust satisfactorily. A science teacher made long-range plans for his growth through graduate study, but found that he had to reevaluate his ambitious plans. A foreign-language teacher had conflicts between family life and teaching, but by relating her teaching to life she made a desirable adjustment. An elderly woman is enthusiastic for teaching, loves children, and finds teaching a rich, rewarding experience. (3)

Preparation of Teachers   (United World, 20 min). Uses the experiences of two prospective teachers during their training period to show that teaching is not just the business of getting information across, but includes sharing children's excitement and experiences. Emphasizes the fact that a teacher must have a well-rounded background in order to help children to become useful and responsible citizens. (2)

Teachers for Tomorrow   (University of Wisconsin, 22 min). Shows how prospective teachers are chosen and trained at the University of Wisconsin. Pictures many phases of the student teacher's work with pupils, supervisory teachers, faculty members, and teaching materials. Shows the need for more teachers and presents the values of teaching as a career. (2)

That the Deaf May Speak   (Campus Film Productions, 43 min, color). Illustrates the methods used in developing speech in deaf children and in teaching them school subjects. Shows how, from preschool age through the eighth grade, the children receive individual and group training in speech and lip reading. (5)

Tips for Teachers   (Jam Handy Organization, 18 min). Explains the importance of personality, preparation, and presentation in good teaching. Uses classroom situations to show that a teacher must also use showmanship, salesmanship, and dramatic ability to help speed up the learning process. (3)

What Greater Gift   (National Education Association, 28 min, color). Presents the teacher as a professional person and shows something of the nature of teaching. Stresses that today's teacher needs professional preparation to acquire the understanding and skills essential to good teaching. (2)

What Is a Good Observer?   (Indiana University, 30 min). Considers the differences between a good and a bad observer. Points out that the use of conclusions based on observations of similarities alone results in a limitation of our awareness of the world, while the use of conclusions grounded on observation that also consider differences is a mark of the mature mind. Available for nontelevision use only. (3)

Who Will Teach Your Child?   (National Film Board of Canada, 25 min). Discusses the problem of maintaining high-quality teaching staffs in the public schools. Compares the work of good and poor teachers and suggests ways to attract the best type of young people to the teaching profession. (3)

Why Can't Jimmy Read?   (Syracuse University, 16 min). Follows Jimmy, a nine-year-old with reading difficulties, through successive remedial procedures. (5)

The Workshop Process   (University of California at Los Angeles, 12 min). Follows the step-by-step procedure involved in the organization, operation, and evaluation of a teacher's workshop developed under the guidance of the superintendent of the Montebello School District in California. (4)

Filmstrips

Children in the Primary School   (Association for Childhood Education International, 51 fr.). Describes and illustrates good school experiences for children six through eight years of age. (5)

Counselor's Day   (McGraw-Hill, 29 fr.). Shows the work of a school counselor. (5)

Know Your School   (Stanley Bowmar, 36 fr.). Presents the multitude of educational opportunities for adults in a public school program. (5)

Planned Life   (Visual Education Consultants, 27 fr.). Contains suggestions on how to plan one's life to achieve happiness and welfare and contribute one's share to a democratic society. (2)

Preparing to Teach   (American Council on Education, 56 fr.). Shows how students are preparing for the teaching profession in a representative teacher-education institution in the United States. Includes academic and extracurricular activities, student-faculty relations, and student-community relations. (2)

The Principal   (McGraw-Hill, 40 fr., color). Mary visits the principal's office and becomes aware of the administrative and counseling work done by a principal. (5)

Special Education for Special Needs: The Physically Handicapped   (American Council on Education, 58 fr.). Presents some of the important aspects of special education provided for the physically handicapped. (5)

Tagline for Success   (Bristol-Myers, 25 fr., color). Stresses importance of training, attitude, and grooming in getting and holding a job. (3)

The Teacher   (McGraw-Hill, 33 fr., color). A young boy who moves to a new community finds his adjustment a happy one because of the interest and help given him by his new teacher. (3)

Teachers and Librarians   (Society for Visual Education, Inc., 60 fr.). Depicts the job opportunities available in the teaching and librarian professions. Required qualifications, advantages and disadvantages, and wages are mentioned. (5)

Teaching as a Career   (National Film Board of Canada, 47 fr.). Examines the pros and cons of teaching as a career with special reference to educational requirements, personal aptitudes, specialized training, remuneration, and opportunities for advancement. (2)

Your Future in the World of Work: Selecting Your Life Work and Preparing for It (Society of Visual Education, 49 fr.). Indicates the importance of aptitudes, interests, and personality factors in the selection of your life work. (2)

Recordings

Characteristics of a Good Teacher   (Recording, Educational Recording Service, 33⅓ rpm). Professor A. S. Barr, department of education, the University of Wisconsin, discusses the personal qualities and characteristics of a good teacher. (3)

Critical Issues in Education: How Should America's Teachers be Educated? (Tape Recording, National Tape Recording Project, 40 min). Professor Arthur Bestor, Jr., and Professor Karl W. Bigelow present opposing points of view; each being allowed 20 minutes to make his presentation. (2)

Teachers Are People Too   (Tape Recording, National Tape Recording Project, 15 min). Presents teachers as sincere, cooperative, hard-working individuals. (3)

● SUGGESTED READINGS

The number in parentheses following each suggestion denotes the chapter for which it is best suited.

Alexander, William M.: *Are You a Good Teacher?* Holt, Rinehart and Winston, Inc., New York, 1959. Presents guidelines that may be used by teachers in appraising their effectiveness in the classroom. (3)

Allen, Herman R.: "Observations of a Newsman about College Teaching," *National Education Association Journal,* vol. 51, no. 5, pp. 23–25, National Education Association, Washington, May, 1962. Presents some of the challenge and satisfaction of teaching on the college level. (5)

American Association of School Administrators, Department of Classroom Teachers, and National School Boards Association: *Who's a Good Teacher?* National Education Association, Washington, 1961. Contains an analysis of what research has to say in regard to the evaluation of teacher effectiveness. (3)

Armstrong, W. Earl, and T. M. Stinnett: *A Manual on Certification Requirements for*

School Personnel in the United States, National Commission on Teacher Education and Professional Standards, National Education Association, Washington. (Revised biennially.) Contains an excellent listing of certification requirements for school personnel and indicates trends in certification. (4)

Bernard, Harold W.: *Mental Hygiene for Classroom Teachers,* 2d ed., McGraw-Hill Book Company, Inc., New York, 1961. Chapter 5 discusses the effect of the teacher's personality upon the behavior of pupils. (3)

Bruce, William F., and A. John Holden, Jr.: *The Teachers Personal Development,* Holt, Rinehart and Winston, Inc., New York, 1957. Presents an excellent discussion of the significance of the teacher's experience with people, especially as that experience promotes self-understanding that leads to further understanding of others. (3)

Callahan, Raymond E.: *An Introduction to Education in American Society,* 2d ed., Alfred A. Knopf, Inc., New York, 1960. Chapter 17 discusses the historical development of teacher education in America. (2)

Dale, Edgar: "A Matter of Values," *The Newsletter,* vol. 27, no. 2, Bureau of Educational Research and Services, Ohio State University, Columbus, November, 1961. Discusses the confusion of values in our society. (2)

Distributive Education: Educational Values in Club Programs, U.S. Office of Education Bulletin 294, ser. 31, 1961. Discusses the values of distributive education clubs and the important role distributive education teachers can play in a community. (5)

Hodenfield, G. K., and T. M. Stinnett: *The Education of Teachers,* Prentice-Hall, Inc., Englewood Cliffs, N.J., 1961. Identifies points of conflict and consensus in regard to the manner in which teachers should be prepared. (2)

Hughes, Marie: What is Teaching? One Viewpoint," *Educational Leadership,* vol. 19, no. 4, pp. 251–259, National Education Association, Association for Supervision and Curriculum Development, Washington, January, 1962. Presents the results of research involving verbatim records of what teachers said and did and the responses made by a child or group. (3)

"Inservice Education," *National Educational Association Journal,* vol. 48, no. 5, pp. 18–29, May, 1959. Presents the following featured articles on in-service education: "Highway to Quality Teaching, Some Workshops that Have Worked"; "A Staff Organizes for Inservice Education," "My Paths to Personal Growth," and "Ladder to Professional Improvement." (4)

Jacob, Philip E.: *Changing Values in College,* Harper & Row, Publishers, New York, 1957. Presents the results of an extensive survey of changes in students' beliefs and values while in college. (2)

Jacobi, Fern H.: "Ladder of Professional Improvement," *National Education Association Journal,* vol. 48, no. 5, pp. 29–30, National Education Association, Washington, May, 1959. Discusses some of the steps in professional improvement. (4)

Klausmeier, Herbert J., and Katharine Dresden: *Teaching in the Elementary School,* 2d ed., Harper & Row, Publishers, New York, 1962. Chapter 15 discusses the work of a teacher in regard to the education of various types of exceptional children. (5)

Lambert, Sam M.: "Educational Growth and Change Lie Ahead in the 1960's," *National Education Association Journal,* vol. 49, no. 9, pp. 45–47, National Education Association, December, 1960. Contains predictions, based upon research, of what is likely to happen in education in the next ten to twenty years. (5)

Leese, Joseph, Kenneth Frasure, and Mauritz Johnson, Jr.: *The Teacher in Curriculum Making,* Harper & Row, Publishers, New York, 1961. Chapter 4 is concerned with the personal development of the teacher. (3)

Lindsey, Margaret (ed.): *New Horizons for the Teaching Profession,* National Education Association, National Commission on Teacher Education and Professional Standards, Washington, 1961. Chapter 4 deals with the preparation of professional personnel. Chapter 6 indicates recommendations regarding the certifications of teachers. (4)

McGrath, Earl J.: "The Ideal Education for the Professional Man," in Nelson B. Henry (ed.), *Education for the Profession.* The Sixty-first Yearbook of the National

Society for the Study of Education, Part II, University of Chicago Press, Chicago, Ill., 1962, pp. 281–301. Discusses the elements of education considered to be essential for any profession. (2)

Mackie, Romaine P., and Frances P. Connor: *Teachers of Crippled Children and Teachers of Children with Health Problems,* U.S. Office of Education Bulletin 1960, no. 21, 1960. Discusses the qualifications, preparation, and opportunities of teachers of exceptional children. (5)

Mason, Ward S.: *The Beginning Teacher: Status and Career Orientations,* U.S. Office of Education Circular 644, 1961. Presents the results of an extensive study of the social, professional, and economic status of beginning teachers and of their aspirations, values, and attitudes concerning a career in teaching. (2)

Massey, Harold W., and Edwin E. Vineyard: *The Profession of Teaching,* The Odyssey Press, Inc., New York, 1961. Chapter 16 deals with a number of topics concerning the inservice growth of teachers. (4)

Michal-Smith, Harold: "It Takes Self-understanding," *National Education Association Journal,* vol. 49, no. 4, pp. 37–40, National Education Association, Washington, April, 1960. Stresses the point that to be a really outstanding teacher one must have self-understanding. (3)

New Horizons for the Teaching Profession, National Education Association, National Commission on Teacher Education and Professional Standards, Washington, 1961. Presents the findings and recommendations of a committee concerned with the improvement of teacher education. (2)

Opportunities for Educators with Army's American Dependents Schools Overseas, U.S. Department of the Army (latest issue). Contains detailed information on opportunities for teaching in Dependent Schools Overseas. (5)

The President's Commission on National Goals: *Goals for Americans,* by the American Assembly, Columbia University, Prentice-Hall, Inc., Englewood Cliffs, N.J., 1960. Chapter 3 presents national goals in education. (5)

Ragan, William B.: *Teaching America's Children,* Holt, Rinehart and Winston, New York, 1961. Chapter 2 indicates abilities needed by teachers. (3)

Reilly, William J.: *Life Planning for College Students,* Harper & Row Publishers, New York, 1954. Presents some excellent suggestions for planning a life career. (2)

Ryans, David G.: *Characteristics of Teachers: Their Description, Comparison and Appraisal,* American Council on Education, Washington, 1961. Presents the findings of extensive research on the characteristics of good and poor teachers. (3)

"Special Classes for Handicapped Children," *Research Bulletin,* vol. 39, no. 2, pp. 43–46, National Education Association, Research Division, Washington, May, 1961. Presents the results of a nation-wide survey of special classes for handicapped children and indicates the need for more specially trained teachers. (5)

Stiles, Lindley, A. S. Barr, Harl R. Douglass, and Hubert H. Mills: *Teacher Education in the United States,* The Ronald Press Company, New York, 1960. An excellent treatment of teacher education in America. (2)

"Teacher, Superintendent, Board Members: What Traits Do They Value in Each Other?" *National Education Association Journal,* vol. 50, no. 4, National Education Association, Washington, April, 1961. A symposium discussion on what teachers, superintendents, and board members would like to see in each other. (3)

"Teacher Supply and Demand in Public Schools," *Research Report* (issued annually), National Education Association, Research Division, Washington (latest report). Contains an extensive analysis of the supply and demand for public school teachers and indicates trends. (5)

Thomas, Russell: *The Search for a Common Learning: General Education 1800–1960,* McGraw-Hill Book Co., Inc., New York, 1962. Indicates the many efforts that have been made to arrive at a common corps of learning for all and presents contemporary views on the general education movement. (2)

Turner, Richard L., and Nicholas A. Fattu: "Skill in Teaching, Assessed on the Criterion of Problem Solving," *Bulletin of the School of Education,* vol. 37, no. 3,

Indiana University, Bloomington, Indiana, May, 1961. Presents a synthesis of the technical research in assessing the problem-solving skills of teachers. (3)

"Unusual Teaching Opportunities at Home and Abroad," *National Education Association Journal,* vol. 49, no. 5, pp. 56–57, 60–61, National Education Association, Washington, May, 1960. Contains an extensive list of unusual opportunities and indicates where inquiries may be sent regarding these opportunities. (5)

Van Til, William: *The Making of a Modern Educator,* The Bobbs-Merrill Company, Inc., Indianapolis, 1961. A collection of essays that deal with a variety of educational topics that are of concern to anyone planning to teach. (2)

"What is a Teacher?" *Look Magazine,* Feb. 21, 1956, pp. 29–39. Pictures the teacher as an educator, foster mother, and one of the most important people in our national life. (3)

Wiles, Kimball: *Teaching for Better Schools,* Prentice-Hall, Inc., Englewood Cliffs, N.J., 1959. Part I discusses penalties of effective teachers. Chapter 4 indicates the importance of a teacher's feelings about himself. Chapter 15 discusses the process of becoming a quality teacher. (3)

Williams, Harold M.: *Education of the Severely Retarded Child: Classroom Programs,* U.S. Office of Education Bulletin 1961, no. 20, 1961. Discusses some of the factors in classroom programs for middle-range retarded pupils. (5)

Woellner, Robert C., and M. Aurilla Wood: *Requirements for Certification of Teachers, Counselors, Librarians, Administrators for Elementary Schools, Secondary Schools, Junior Colleges,* University of Chicago Press, Chicago. (Revised annually.) Presents the certification requirements by states for various school personnel. (4)

Wynn, Richard: *Careers in Education,* McGraw-Hill Book Company, Inc., New York, 1960. Chapter 1 presents some good suggestions in choosing a career. (2)

Zirbes, Laura: *Spurs to Creative Teaching,* G. P. Putnam's Sons, New York, 1959. Emphasizes the creative aspects of teaching and attempts to help teachers become more creative in their outlook on life and learning. (3)

● FIGURE CREDITS

Figure 15. (*Source:* "Teacher Supply and Demand in Public Schools, 1962," *Research Report 1962*-R8, p. 29, National Education Association, Research Division, Washington, April, 1962.)

Figure 16. (*Source:* Data from National Council for Accreditation of Teacher Education.)

Figure 17. (*Source:* Adapted from *Public Education and the Future of America,* National Education Association, Educational Policies Commission, Washington, 1955, p. 63.)

Figure 19. (*Source:* "School Statistics: 1960–61," *Research Bulletin,* vol. 39, no. 1, p. 4, National Education Association, Research Division, Washington, February, 1961.)

Figure 20. (*Source:* Data from "Estimates of School Statistics, 1961–62," *Research Report, 1961*-R22, p. 8, National Education Association, Research Division, Washington, December, 1961.)

Figure 21. (*Source:* "What Happened to any 100 Teachers Between Spring and Fall, 1959," *School Life,* vol. 42, no. 9, p. 17, U.S. Office of Education, Washington, May 1960.)

Figure 22. (*Source:* Ronald B. Thompson, *Enrollment Projections for Higher Education 1961–1978,* Enrollment Studies Committee of the American Association of Collegiate Registrars and Admissions Officers, September, 1961, p. xi.)

Figure 23. (*Source:* Data adapted from *Statistical Abstract of the United States,* U.S. Department of Commerce, Bureau of the Census, 1961, p. 54.)

Figure 24. (*Source:* Data from *Manpower and Education,* National Education Association, Educational Policies Commission, Washington, 1956, p. 10.)

Figure 25. (*Source:* "Teacher Supply and Demand in Public Schools, 1962," *Research Report 1962*-R8, p. 34, National Education Association, Research Division, Washington, April, 1962.)

Figure 26. (*Source:* "Teacher Supply and Demand in Public Schools, 1962," *Research Report 1962*-R8, p. 34, National Education Association, Research Division, Washington, April, 1962.

Figure 27. (*Source:* "Class Size in Elementary Schools," *Research Bulletin,* vol. 38, no. 3, p. 91, National Education Association, Research Division, Washington, October, 1960.)

Figure 28. (*Source:* Romaine P. Mackie and Patricia P. Robbins, "Exceptional Children in Local Public Schools," *School Life,* vol. 43, no. 3, p. 15, U.S. Office of Education, November, 1960.)

Figure 29. (*Source:* Ronald B. Thompson, *Enrollment Projections For Higher Education 1961–1978,* Enrollment Studies Committee of The American Association of Collegiate Registrars and Admissions Officers, September, 1961, p. vi.)

Figure 30. (*Source:* "College Teachers: Demand Exceeds Supply," *Research Bulletin,* vol. 39, no. 3, p. 78, National Education Association, Research Division, Washington, October, 1961.)

TEACHERS AND THEIR WORK

The value of your formal preparation for teaching will be enhanced by the extent to which you see clearly the duties and demands made upon you as a professional worker. Chapter 6 discusses the wide variety of responsibilities with which you most likely will be confronted in the classroom, outside of the classroom, and in the school community. Chapter 7 contains suggestions and procedures for you to use in gaining depth and comprehensiveness in your understanding of pupils, and in gaining skill in effectively guiding their educational growth. In Chapter 8 you are confronted with some of the obligations and responsibilities which you will assume as a member of the teaching profession.

6

SCHOOL AND COMMUNITY RESPONSIBILITIES OF TEACHERS

What will be expected of you as a teacher? What will you have to do in school? What particular competencies will you need in order to perform effectively? To what extent will you be able to find interest and challenge in your duties? What will the community demand of you when you become a teacher?

Questions such as these are real and pertinent to anyone actively planning a career in teaching. The answers tend to set the pattern for your professional work and, to some extent, for your future personal life. Many rich rewards come to teachers, but not without cost. Are you willing to pay the price?

CLASSROOM RESPONSIBILITIES OF TEACHERS

It is unlikely that anyone could describe with certainty the precise duties or responsibilities expected of *you* when you report for your first teaching position. Conditions in public schools differ considerably throughout the United States. There are great gaps between what an elementary teacher does in a one-room rural school and what a senior English literature teacher does in a large metropolitan high school. Teachers' lives vary in significant ways. At the same time there are many elements that are common to their work. You should examine these in some detail.

Number of Classes Taught. The number of classes you will be expected to teach varies for several reasons. Elementary teachers generally stay with their particular groups for the greater part of the school day, including the lunch period in many schools. In some school systems, elementary music, art, physical education, special reading, and speech work are taught by highly specialized people who usually move from grade to grade in a single school or in several schools in a district. In addition, many school systems have attempted to provide some time during the school day for elementary teachers to use for planning, attending conferences, or relaxing from the tensions of the classroom.

In the secondary school, teachers generally meet several different classes in one day; the variety of subjects taught by each teacher is usually greater in small schools than in large ones. The number of courses offered in secondary schools has increased considerably over the years. In their attempts to provide for the needs and interests of their increasing enrollments, secondary schools have added many, many subjects. In fact, curriculum workers have viewed with much alarm the tendency to change the secondary school program merely by adding courses. The trend they prefer to encourage is toward reducing these numbers. Curriculum workers have suggested removing courses which are outmoded or inappropriate, combining several closely related courses into one new course, and reorganizing the common learning experiences of pupils in a given school around areas of living which draw upon many subjects and resources.

In attempting to assure reasonable teaching loads in member schools, the North Central Association of Colleges and Secondary Schools has recommended as one of its school accrediting policies that each teacher be assigned at least one conference and preparation period daily [112:14]. In schools operating on a six- or seven-period day this would mean that a teacher should not be assigned more than five classes and/or study halls. In schools using eight or more periods, a teacher should not be assigned more than six classes and/or study halls.

Of course, the number of classes is only one aspect of a teacher's load. Other factors to be considered include the subject being taught, class

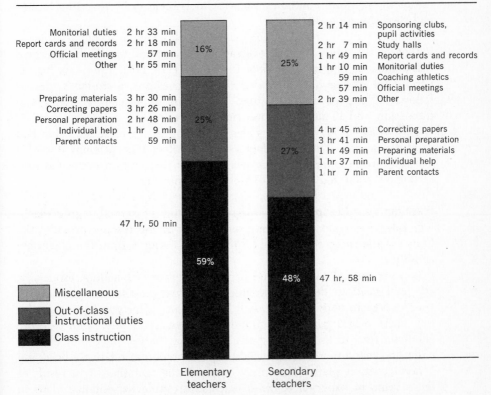

Figure 31. How elementary and secondary school teachers divide an average work week of 47 hours and approximately 55 minutes. (*Source:* National Education Association.) 167

size, length of period, administrative or supervisory duties, assignments in extraclass activities, counseling duties, and length of school day. In addition, more recent approaches to teaching, such as television and other electronic aids, team teaching, and the use of programmed material with or without machines, tend to make "number of classes taught" a less and less accurate description of a teacher's day. Figure 31, therefore, gives only approximate distributions of time for elementary and secondary school teachers.

Size of Classes.   The quality of your work in different teaching assignments will be influenced somewhat by the number of pupils in your classes. As indicated in the preceding chapter, there is no absolute agreement upon the optimum class size for a learning situation. The size is relative to the purposes that are to be accomplished. For instance, it might be possible to handle large numbers effectively in certain courses such as physical education and, occasionally, music classes; on the other hand, it would be desirable to have smaller groups studying foreign languages, laboratory sciences, or remedial reading.

In the earliest experiments with television in the classroom, the usual practice was to use large groups of 100 or more students. However, as use of the medium continues, many schools seem to be reverting to normal class-size groups.

Another type of project which may affect class size in secondary schools is that of the study of staff utilization by a committee of the National Association of Secondary-School Principals [174, 175]. Proposals for experimental studies have included the distribution of a student's time as follows: 40 per cent in large group instruction, 20 per cent in small group discussion, and 40 per cent in individual study.

The whole problem of class size is coming in for close attention and careful research. The many factors which affect the optimum size of a learning group complicate this work a great deal. As an interested professional person, remain alert to these developments.

Planning Your Lessons.   Good lesson planning is essential to good teaching. Likewise, good preplanning on the part of the teacher provides the basis for the most effective pupil-teacher planning within the classroom activities.

In your student teaching and in your first year of teaching, especially, you will need to devote a greater amount of time to the planning of your classroom activities than will be necessary after you have gained a few years of experience. Beginning teachers frequently fail to devote adequate time to the planning of classroom activities, since they observe older and much more experienced teachers preparing relatively brief and general written plans. They may overlook the fact that, as a result of these years of experience, older teachers are able to visualize plans in much detail, and that they have developed great skill in guiding pupils toward the desired objectives.

Advance planning and careful organization are essential for realizing the daily objectives the teacher has in mind. (*From the film* Not by Chance *by the National Education Association.*)

Your lesson plans should: (1) consist of flexible arrangements, procedures, or methods of action for achieving educational objectives which you consider to be desirable; (2) be records of your thinking about desirable school experiences for your pupils; (3) include a description of the specific learning experiences in which they will participate during the time included in the plan; (4) be both long range and short range in nature; (5) give you a sense of security—of knowing where you are going and why—as well as a basis for appraising how well you and your pupils have succeeded. Your written comments concerning the strengths and weaknesses of the plans after they have been used provide a basis for your future growth as a teacher.

Your general plans frequently will involve considerably more than the subject matter you are going to teach. You may need to prepare charts or graphs; secure photographs, maps, films, or records; prepare demonstrations, tests, or reading assignments; arrange for equipment such as projectors and tape recorders; survey library and community resources; study educational-telecast schedules. A field trip may be desirable, in which case you may need to obtain permission from your school principal, make arrangements with the places to be visited, secure transportation, prepare the pupils for the trip, and help them appraise the experience. Many things may be involved and should be planned in order that you may provide your pupils with rich learning experiences.

The specific pattern of written plans that you use will depend considerably on the school system in which you find yourself. There still exist some systems in which a teacher is expected to submit his lesson plans to the principal a week in advance. Usually these are presented in a printed form known as a plan book. In other schools, teachers have greater flexibility in developing their plans.

There may be occasions when you resent the amount of time required to plan activities for your pupils. You may be tempted to feel that the teacher who regularly leaves the school building empty-handed shortly after the pupils have been dismissed is, after all, the wise one. But there is no substitute for the satisfaction of knowing precisely what you want your pupils to achieve, of being able to guide creatively the activities of pupils toward clearly perceived goals, of feeling that your work for the day has been well done. The relationship of good planning and good teaching is amazingly high.

Guiding Each Class Group. Your major responsibility as a classroom teacher is to lead and guide your group. In the modern school this is considered to be a democratic and cooperative process, which respects the dignity of each individual involved. What do the terms "democratic" and "cooperative" mean to you in relation to teaching and learning? It is most important that in your thinking of, and working with, the class group you do not forget each of the individuals who make up that group. Recent studies and publications have served to remind us of this importance of the individual, the source of group strength. There is a danger that the individual will be forgotten within impersonal institutions [121:ix]. In an attempt to ensure recognition for the individual, it has been recommended that in secondary schools each student have an individualized program [32:46].

In guiding your class groups, your chief work as a teacher will involve helping youngsters help themselves. This will mean helping them define their most pressing needs and interests and problems; helping them understand themselves better; and helping them understand their families, their friends, their whole community. Out of this will emerge certain specific objectives the youngsters will consider important to achieve. Your function will then be to help them formulate and appraise their objectives in terms of value to the learners and to the community. It will be necessary to plan ways and means of arriving at those objectives which the youngsters feel are important to them. You should see that the learning experiences grow out of the everyday lives of the learners and that they utilize wisely the available resources—especially people—in the entire school community.

Learning can be sterile unless the pupils relate to their everyday lives the facts they have discovered. This requires numerous deliberate applications and the development of generalizations which makes sense to the learners—which they can use to gain better control over their future behavior. Research seems to indicate that in tests of academic achievement requiring analysis, synthesis, evaluation, and application of knowledge, better results may be obtained through more informal group processes described here rather than through more formal lectures and recitations [146:20]. These are important considerations, so far as your

This teacher knows that learning becomes more meaningful when it is related directly to the everyday lives of pupils. Here a local traffic policeman instructs a class about the rules of safety. (*Photograph from the Audio-visual Center, Indiana University.*)

responsibilities relating to the guidance of learning are concerned. They apply no matter what grade or subject you teach. If you spend time and effort studying these things carefully, you will be much less troubled with what are loosely labeled "discipline problems." There are matters of good leadership in the classroom, of good guidance, of learning experiences, of patience, of acceptance, and of loyalty to yourself, your pupils, your community, and your profession. Failure here inevitably leads to problems in classroom behavior. You will be a far more effective teacher if you look well beneath the surface symptoms of discipline problems and seek out their deeper causes. In attempting to determine these deeper causes in an individual pupil, would you seek information concerning his home conditions? His neighborhood friends? His school friends? His health? His behavior in other classes? His academic ability? His academic difficulties? Would you reexamine your own classroom procedures? Your teaching personality? In a group problem what factors would you try to analyze? The causes of behavior problems will diminish in proportion to how skillfully you guide learning experiences.

Handling Paper Work. There are several kinds of paper work which classroom teachers need to consider. Some of it is clerical and may seem incidental to the real work of teaching, but some of it is highly professional and very important in the teaching-learning process.

It will be necessary to keep a daily attendance record. You may be asked to do this on official state forms which are used in calculating state money allotments to individual school districts. In the secondary school, you may be asked to keep class records of every absence during the day.

Classroom teachers frequently file excuses for absence along with other notes, statements, or records of conferences and observations concerning their pupils. When various materials of this sort are organized so that there is a separate folder for each pupil, they constitute a cumulative record system. In this folder you can keep significant writings and products of the youngsters themselves as well as grades and testing results of all sorts. Reports of home visits, medical histories, health examinations, home and family conditions, scores on standardized tests and rating scales, scholastic achievements, personality traits, participation in extra-class activities, interest inventories, educational and vocational objectives, work experiences, nonschool activities, and any other information which may be useful in helping you and other teachers understand the individual pupils—all of these should become a part of the cumulative records. Your responsibility in recording the information will vary from school to school, depending upon the provisions for clerks, secretaries, or other clerical help.

It is important that you keep accurate written records of any money for which you have collection responsibility. This is good business practice, and it serves as a protection to you as a teacher if any question should ever arise.

Another kind of paper work to which teachers must attend grows out of the planning and conducting of daily activities. Written reports of pupils need to be read and appraised. Drill work needs to be checked. Specific written assignments need to be read, corrections noted, comments given, and sometimes grades recorded. The amount of time required for these duties varies according to subject areas and grade levels. It is important that you schedule such work so that it does not take time unnecessarily from more important phases of your teaching and does not overtax your energy.

Taking Attendance.   Actually, taking attendance is one of the minor clerical tasks for which the teacher is responsible. The way in which the job is done is of some importance. Calling the roll aloud has the advantage of helping fix names and faces for teacher and pupils alike; but it is very time-consuming. For you as a teacher, an ideal situation could be to know the group so well personally that anybody's absence would be detected instantly and recorded without disturbing the learning activity. On the other hand, here is an opportunity to promote pupil growth in the assumption of responsibility by delegating to various youngsters, in turn and under supervision, the recording of attendance.

Evaluating Pupil Progress.   Throughout each learning experience, teachers and pupils must take stock of their progress to see whether the goals are being approached or whether the objectives need revising. They must appraise their procedures and decide whether they are the best that can be used and whether they are being used well. They must take inventory of their available resources to see whether their selection and use have been adequate and wise. These aspects of evaluation may require written reports, committee minutes, anecdotes, check lists, questionnaires, rating scales, personal documents such as diaries, projective techniques, and different kinds of tests. Some of the tests will be formal and standardized, whereas others will be informal teacher-constructed instruments, both essay and objective. In either case, the administering, scoring, and interpreting of the tests will be among your important functions. Where you decide to build the evaluative instrument yourself, whether you use an inquiry form or test, a great deal of help can be gained from your colleagues. Such sources of help should be sought out deliberately. Certainly, the use of a test should not mark the end of learning concerning any phase of school experience. These learnings should be used time and again in future experiences.

Reporting to Parents.   Teachers are expected to keep parents informed about the progress of their pupils. If they do this systematically and regularly, it can prove to be one of the most fruitful avenues for bringing together the public and the schools. This should involve reviewing and summarizing the information you have about each of your youngsters, going over his activities and anecdotal records, looking into his cumulative record, observing testing results of various sorts, and, finally, making an appraisal of each. This should be done in terms of his growth and development toward those desirable purposes which together you have formulated and striven to achieve. It is difficult, at best, to grade pupils. Sometimes it is a heart-rending process for parents, teachers, and pupils alike.

Most of the conventional systems of grading and reporting to parents have serious limitations. Many of them fail to inform adequately, and a few actually misinform parents. Parents, prospective employers, college officials, even the students and the teachers are frequently confused and misled by A-B-C grade reports. Where numerical percentages are used, the situation is even worse. Ability grouping further complicates the picture. Does an A in an accelerated group mean the same as an A in a slow-learning section?

The most common methods of reporting to parents are report cards, parent conferences, and letters to parents. The usual parts of a report card include letter grades, attendance and tardiness records, and a checklist section on personal characteristics [131:27–28]. In a few schools, usually on the elementary level, grades as we know them have been eliminated. However, even in most schools which have abandoned or supplemented the traditional report card, grades remain a part of the total evaluation of pupil progress. In view of the current emphasis on preparation for college and on college entrance requirements, it is probable that such grades will continue to be an important phase of pupil appraisal on the secondary level.

Parent-teacher conferences have gained in frequency, particularly at the elementary level and to some extent at the junior high school level. Research indicates that a preference exists at the elementary school level for reporting through a combination of cards and parent confer- ences [126:25]. It is obvious that parent-teacher conferences are more easily arranged in an elementary school than in a secondary school. In an elementary school such a plan involves perhaps 25 to 35 conferences with parents. In a secondary school such a plan involves conferences with 100 to 200 parents for each report period. The latter plan is practically impossible, and other patterns have been suggested, such as parent con- ferences with the home-room teacher or designated counselors. At any rate the problem is a major one at the secondary level.

Some schools have experimented with letters to parents. However, such letters are time-consuming and frequently become almost as formalized as report cards.

In the final analysis, by far the most common type of reporting is that of the report card, with many schools combining it with parent-teacher conferences and a few using letters to parents. In most schools these re- ports are made either four times a year or more than five times a year [126:25]. In reporting to parents, new procedures and new instru- ments are urgently needed. Perhaps this is an area in which you can make a major contribution to your profession.

Caring for Your Classroom.   You will be responsible for the condition of at least one classroom, although you may not carry on all of your work in one room. Your chief responsibility will be to see to it that the situa- tion in your classroom is healthy, comfortable, and efficient for the de- sired growth and learning of the pupils. This calls for a sense of function and balance in the manipulation and arrangement of furniture and equip-

The development of mutual understandings and cooperation is an important gain of parent-teacher conferences. (*From the film* Who is Pete? *by the National Education Association.*)

In addition to being of much help to you, pupils can gain valuable learning experiences by assuming a variety of responsibilities in caring for the classroom. (*Photograph by Carl Purcell, National Education Association.*)

ment of many kinds. It involves artistic talent and ingenuity as well as certain elementary abilities, at least in working with construction tools and materials.

Strive to keep your room cheerful, tidy, and conducive to good work. No one can teach effectively in a classroom which is dark or cold or poorly ventilated. Alert teachers check quickly to see whether pupil-attention problems rest with the youngsters or with the room itself, and, if with the latter, they correct conditions as soon as possible.

Teachers and pupils working together can provide pleasant learning conditions in almost any classroom through colorful bulletin-board exhibits, interesting displays, growing plants, various types of room decorations, and orderly procedures of neatness and care of property. Even where lighting and ventilation are not satisfactory, careful study of the situation by the teacher, pupils, administrators, and custodians will usually result in suggestions for improvement under any classroom condition.

Seats and desks or tables and chairs need to be adapted to the pupils using them. The modern trend is toward rooms with several sizes of furniture or with adjustable pieces to meet the individual needs of each pupil.

Our early schools developed furniture similar to that which characterized the colonial homes, sometimes modified by demands for economy. The result provided little or no comfort for pupils. Though American homes have undergone radical changes since colonial days, school furnishings have not kept pace. For our living quarters we normally have sought roomy, comfortable, upholstered chairs; tables of every level, size, and description; shelves, cupboards, and so forth to meet the different needs of all the members of the family. Sometimes home furniture is built in to provide more functional use of space. Lighter colors are more popular because they are more cheerful and provide better lighting. Hard plastics are used for covering floors, table tops, and work spaces; soft plastics cover chairs, seats, and other surfaces. Foam rubber is used for padding the seats and backs of modern living-room chairs. New materials, new designs, new sizes, new shapes appear everywhere in the furnishings of the modern home.

Many schools today have equipped their libraries with comfortable chairs, sofas, and excellent lighting, so that youngsters can see and read in comfort. Many offices of administrators and supervisors contain the latest and most functional and comfortable furnishings in their schools. But we have yet to meet the same needs for our pupils. It will be costly. It will take time and effort to help people understand the practical wisdom of such changes. Eventually, when we are willing to spend as much for education as we do for cigarettes and alcohol, our schools will be as comfortable and efficient as our homes, our theaters, or our business offices. To the extent that you as a beginning teacher understand the problem and work toward its solution, you can hasten that day.

One of your responsibilities as a teacher will be to work with parents and lay people generally to help gain acceptance for the newer types of school furnishings. Perhaps more important will be the work you will need to do in this connection with some of your pupils. It will be necessary to help them assume more responsibility for the care of their school equipment. Just glance at the desk tops and walls of almost any secondary school or college, and it seems that many pupils are guilty of vandalism. But this is not the case. Most pupils come from homes where property is considered valuable, and willful destruction is effectively discouraged. Most people, including pupils in school, like attractive and comfortable furnishings and try to care for them properly. Your job as a teacher is to help the small group of youngsters, and sometimes adults, whose sense of responsibility for property needs more development. A positive, constructive approach to problems of helping people assume appropriate responsibility is an unavoidable duty of every teacher. You can usually work effectively through committees of pupils in attempting to promote this attitude of responsibility in your classroom. In the school such a program can be a major activity of the school's student council or of its parent-teacher association.

The seating arrangement of the youngsters in your room needs careful attention. What you can do will be affected considerably by the type of room and furniture you have, by the kind of learning experiences you plan and the way they are approached, and by the needs of the pupils themselves. The traditional system of having desks in straight rows fixed to the floor is still a common arrangement in our schools. But teachers, pupils, and school-board members in more and more schools are realizing that movable furniture is far more convenient. Flexible seating may make it possible for three or four committees to work on separate problems at the same time in the same room. The organization of other groups for different purposes may require drastic rearrangements of the furniture.

Some activities may require that the entire central space in a room be cleared of furniture; others, that the seats be arranged in a broad semicircle for discussion purposes.

Teachers in schools where the furniture is fixed to the floor can often gain permission to remove the screws and place the seats on runners so as to make possible rearrangements that will best accommodate various learning activities.

It should be remembered, however, that movable furniture sometimes complicates living in classrooms. You may have problems to contend with—problems of noise, loss of time required to make the changes, and disagreements as to who is going to move what. Such things require careful attention and planning to ensure smoothness and efficiency in making the changes.

There is much variety in the seating arrangements of pupils aside from the requirements of various learning activities. Some teachers seat their pupils on the first day of class and require that these same seats be retained for the entire semester. Often this is done alphabetically. Frequently the small children are seated in the front and the tall children are seated in the back of the room. Usually special allowance is made for pupils with sight or hearing deficiencies. Permanent seats permit the drawing up of a chart which will help you learn the names of your pupils. That is an important factor. Alphabetical seating will facilitate the collecting and distributing of papers and supplies, the taking of attendance, and the keeping of records in a book or file. On the other hand, if permanent seating is maintained for the entire semester, it has all the disadvantages of fixed seats; it blocks flexibility and variety in learning activities. Only rarely should it be necessary for you to insist that certain pupils sit in certain places. People like to group themselves in different ways for different purposes; they like to be near friends; they like informal and flexible arrangements. And pupils are people.

Ordering Learning Materials.   Every teacher has some part to play in the selection, ordering, and handling of learning materials. Sometimes this means little more than the right to choose between two different state-adopted texts. However, some teachers have a great amount of freedom and responsibility in this regard. Some teachers go without some kinds of materials needed for good classroom instruction because they do not know what to ask for, or they do not bother to ask for them. Know what you want and why you want certain materials. Your principal wants you to do a good job of teaching and will help you secure them.

If you did have unlimited choice in ordering learning materials, what factors would you consider? With respect to text and reference books alone, you would need to be familiar with the most recent and most important ones in your field. You would need to read many books as well as summaries and reviews. Your school's professional library for teachers should be useful to you. Professional journals and the book-review section of newspapers such as the *New York Times* could also prove helpful.

Publishing companies will be glad to place you on their mailing lists, should you so request, and will keep you informed about new materials in your field.

Many learning materials can be procured at little or no cost by paying attention to the "yours for the asking" and similar columns in professional periodicals. Also available at a nominal cost are extensive listings of free and inexpensive materials. Regardless of your teaching field or level, be well informed concerning periodicals, newspapers, maps, pictures, charts, models, motion pictures, filmstrips, slides, records, tape recordings and the like. If you intend to teach such secondary school areas as shop, art, music, home economics, or physical education, your responsibilities may include selecting, ordering, and handling a variety of materials peculiar to those areas. You will be expected to be sufficiently familiar with equipment, brands, qualities, prices, and the like to make purchases that are economical. You will also need to know how to use and care for the equipment and materials so that they may render best returns for their cost to the community. The criteria you establish to help you make decisions of selection and use of materials warrant careful study.

Being Responsible for Visual Materials.   Nearly every classroom has its quota of pictures, maps, charts, and bulletin boards. Your own work as a teacher will probably involve these and other kinds of learning materials.

(*Photograph by Carl Purcell, National Education Association.*)   (*Photograph from the Audio-visual Center, Indiana University.*)

Your knowledge of the uses of instructional materials, ready-made or created, will have many practical applications in the classroom.

A few general principles are worth considering in this connection. Pictures ought to lend a bit of color and beauty to the room. If you inherit a room with pictures that have long since lost their reason for being, see what can be done about replacing them with more appropriate decoration. Some teachers have seen fit to do this even at their own expense. Keep in mind, too, that this is the youngsters' room. Let at least some of the items be suitable to their interests and their level of maturity. Pictures, maps, charts, and the like which are related to learning activities in the classroom need to be pertinent, up-to-date, accurate, and usable in terms of form and pupil comprehension. Bulletin-board displays need careful planning, interesting arrangement, and periodic change. Such materials should be connected deliberately with the learning experiences of the class and should be placed so that pupils can see them. This can be accomplished by holding such materials for pupils to see and by pointing to them and frequently referring to them during discussions. A sure way of gaining pupil interest in such learning materials is to encourage contribution of items by the students' creative efforts or by their bringing in items and helping in their arrangement and display. A student-managed bulletin board seldom wants for an audience, and its message is usually referred to often in the regular activities of the class.

Utilizing Planning or Conference Periods. Many forward-looking schools provide a planning or conference period for each teacher, during which the teacher is unassigned in the daily school schedule. The practice is much more prevalent in secondary than in elementary schools. You will find such a period to be of great value to you in your many school duties. It provides an opportunity for you to hold scheduled conferences with pupils or parents, plan your work for the next few days, preview audio-visual materials, browse through various professional magazines and books, or observe your colleagues in different classes throughout the school. Such observation is being encouraged more and more by both teachers and administrators as an important technique in the improvement of teaching.

In addition to these uses of your planning period, you will always find it most helpful in handling the paper work connected with your classes. Finally, there may be times when the period, or part of it, is needed to provide a time for relaxation from the tension of academic duties. It will prove especially helpful to you as a beginning teacher if you have a planning or conference period.

RESPONSIBILITIES WITHIN THE SCHOOL

In addition to your classroom duties, you will have many other opportunities and responsibilities within the school. Some of these responsibilities, such as home rooms, study halls, and extracurricular activities, are more highly organized in the secondary school than in the elementary school, but the principles involved in working with boys and girls remain the same.

Sponsoring Home Rooms.   It is difficult even to guess what will be expected of you as a home-room teacher in a secondary school. Your duties here will depend largely upon policies and practices that exist in the school in which you teach. In many schools there is no home room at all;

in others, the period appears on the schedule, but the purposes of the home room are poorly conceived or are misinterpreted by the school personnel. Its main purpose, in far too many instances, is to provide only for taking attendance, reading announcements from the principal's office, and conducting other items of school business. In the great majority of schools where the home room exists as an administrative device, it is held the first period in the school day and sometimes the first in the afternoon for periods of 5 to 15 minutes. In many other schools a longer daily home-room period of 20 to 40 minutes is provided, which, on certain days, also serves as an activity period when clubs and other extracurricular activities meet. Too often this longer home-room period becomes merely a study period because teachers and pupils have not planned for purposeful home-room activities.

Rightly conceived, the home room can be one of the most important parts of any school. It is designed for youngsters, not for teachers or administrators. It is meant to be the youngsters' home at school. It should be a place where pupils and teachers grow to know and understand one another. Pupil guidance should take place within an atmosphere of informality and friendliness. In fact, guidance is the chief function of the home room. Since student and teacher come together regularly here and have no special subject to which they must devote their time, opportunities for guidance in the home room are exceptionally good. Plans should develop, under the teacher's leadership, to consider personal-social problems that are important to the pupils. These might best be handled on a discussion basis, through group guidance procedures, and sometimes by personal counseling.

As a home-room teacher, your responsibilities will include studying your pupils carefully, so that you may know each one intimately and be able to counsel wisely. For this reason you will need to exhaust every resource to gain information. Tests will provide certain data, visits to homes will provide more, and conferences or conversations with various people will add still other information. Surely you will want to learn all you can about your pupils. Seek information from parents, other teachers, and, with discretion, from others who know your pupils well. Hold many conferences or conversations with the youngsters themselves. Observe them often and carefully, and keep objective anecdotal records of what you observe.

Much of the information which has already been gained in this way may be found in the cumulative pupil records, if the school uses this system. Where such records are available, study them carefully and use them judiciously. Many school faculties are already functioning on this wisely conservative premise.

As a result of a national study of the American high school, Conant has emphasized a slightly different function for the home room—its role as a social and governmental unit in the school. To promote its purpose in these phases of the school program, it has been suggested that the home-room group remain together throughout the high school years and that the group be composed of a cross section of student abilities and vocational interests. The home room would then serve as the basis for representation on the student council [32:74].

In all these areas of pupil development—educational, vocational, social, and citizenship—the home-room potential is great. However, many improvements are needed—in personnel, training, and especially in financial support—before good home-room guidance can become as widespread as it deserves to be. It must be based on sincere interest and detailed information. How else can you be a real friend to these youngsters? How else can you know them as the unique persons they are? How else can you help them with the pressing personal-social problems which tend to be slighted or ignored in the rest of the school program? How else can you hope to help them gain the best measure of security, the most wholesome adjustments, the highest potential of which they are capable? How else can you provide a home at school?

Supervising Study Halls.   At the secondary level, your assignment may include not only four or five subject groups to teach, but also a study hall to supervise. In some schools the study halls are large rooms seating over 100 students. Here your main responsibilities will be to keep track of the youngsters who are absent, tardy, or truant, and to know who leaves the room and for what reasons. These are mostly clerical details. You will also be expected to keep order in the room so that the efforts of pupils can be devoted to fruitful learning. Wherever possible, you will be expected to render help to individual pupils or small groups.

Your duties are far less complicated and less confining in a small study hall than in a large one. You may even find a few moments for scoring the last test or planning the next day's work for your pupils. In some schools, the study halls are supervised by student monitors chosen from the more capable youngsters. In other schools the teacher in charge may utilize pupil assistance for clerical or other tasks during the study-hall period. In secondary schools the full responsibility for study halls usually falls on the teachers.

Although 86 per cent of the urban senior high schools in 1961 still provided a period of study hall [72:10], it appears that the large study hall is becoming less important in today's secondary school. There are several reasons for this. More high school students are taking more classes. Supervision of study has been recognized as a vital part of teaching itself; thus, study has become a legitimate part of class time. Further, it has been recognized that, if supervision of study is to be most effective, it should be in class-size groups rather than in larger groups. In accord with this point of view, most new school buildings do not include a large study hall.

Supervising Pupils Outside the Classroom.   Besides the management of their own rooms, teachers cooperate in the management of certain aspects of the school as a whole. Hall duty, for instance, may become one of your responsibilities. In some schools this is merely a matter of being on the scene. The school may not be particularly crowded, or traffic may be handled by a designated student traffic squad—often under the supervision of the student council—or it may be that somewhere the youngsters already have learned how to conduct themselves when they leave the adult supervision of classrooms. In other schools the job is quite different. You may be the chief, possibly the only, traffic officer. You may have to keep traffic flowing in proper channels in order to prevent certain youngsters from being hurt and others from disregarding all the school's rules. You may have to inspect passes of all pupils who are in the halls during class periods to see that they are out of their rooms for legitimate reasons. You may even have to patrol the upper corridors and to inspect dark corners to see that a few adventurous youngsters have not paired off for obviously nonacademic purposes of their own.

In similar fashion, teachers often are required to supervise the cafeteria and the school bus. In the lunchroom you can help youngsters learn more about foods, table manners, desirable social customs, and the like. Certainly, the lunchroom is replete with opportunities for valuable learning. Traveling by school bus provides comparable valuable opportunities. It has been said by some that more significant learning takes place in these informal situations than in the typical classroom. At least it is clear that when young people reach the informal atmosphere of the bus, especially if the driver really enjoys youngsters, they are likely to behave as naturally as they know how. Here is one test of the learning which has taken place at home and in the school. Some youngsters who are tense and backward in the typical formal classroom frequently blossom out on the school bus, lose their fears, assert themselves vigorously, and even assume positions of leadership in the traveling group. If you should have opportunities to supervise children under such circumstances, you will find the task richly rewarding in terms of the new knowledge and understanding you gain. Bus duty may be related to athletic trips, class-project excursions, traveling dramatics groups, senior-class annual trips, and the like. Whether by volunteer system or by administrative appointment, teacher duties of this nature are usually proportioned among the staff group so that no undue burden falls upon anyone.

Classroom teachers are also called upon for incidental help with various other school activities. You may be asked to assume responsibility for taking tickets for basketball games or dramatic events. Or you may have to assume. general charge of the auditorium during a public forum. You may need to be on hand when the physical education group or the home economics department put on their annual demonstrations. You may be asked to chaperon parties, picnics, and other social affairs. A total school program is a cooperative undertaking. Other teachers will need to help you in your school activities. Taken in the right spirit, such "duties" can be as relaxing and enjoyable for teachers as they are for pupils. Consider these opportunities seriously and make the most of them.

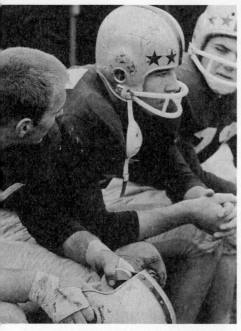 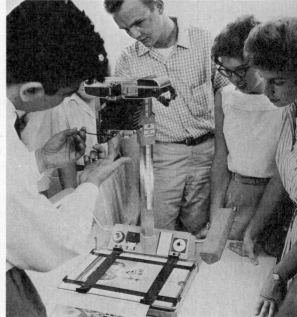

(*Photograph by Carl Purcell, National* (*Photograph by Carl Purcell, National Education Association.*) *Education Association.*)

The teacher is called upon to assume responsibilities in connection with extra-curricular activities such as those shown here. In what kinds of extracurricular activities will you be able to participate, and what could you expect to gain through such participation?

Sponsoring Extracurricular Activities.   Most secondary and many elementary teachers have some responsibilities for the extracurricular program. In the past, many things youngsters wanted and needed from school simply did not appear in the academic curriculum. As a result, these things were gradually brought into the school by the pupils rather timidly and cautiously. At first they were ignored by the faculty, then violently opposed, and eventually accepted. Now they are firmly established. Many educators feel that they should be part of the recognized school program and handled on school time. This is the story of the school band, the dramatics society, the science club, the school paper, the student council, the assembly program, the camera club, the discussion group, the yearbook, the social club, and many other activities not usually accepted in the formal curriculum of the school. It is unfortunate that the conduct of these so-called extracurricular activities is seriously handicapped by lack of adequate time in the regular school day and by lack of adequate financial support. Yet both the youngsters and the teacher-sponsors seem to balance this with high enthusiasm and seriousness of purpose in the pursuit of these activities.

As a professional teacher, consider very carefully the desirable characteristics of the extracurricular activities—the informal atmosphere, the large element of pupil planning and management, the flexibility, the pupil-centered purposes and standards, and the friendly relationships between teacher and group. To what extent does this part of the school program suggest improvements that might well be attempted in the regular curriculum?

In spite of the fact that attendance is voluntary, that meetings are held after school hours, that students often have to lend financial aid to the activities, and that no credit is granted for participation, extracurricular activities retain unusual popularity among students. There must be real and significant values in these activities which are pursued and supported so vigorously. You will experience a new relationship with youngsters and reap rich rewards for yourself by offering your leadership in the extracurricular program of your school. You might be the freshman-class sponsor or the senior-class sponsor, for example. Your duties in this connection would vary from one class to another and from one school to another. In larger schools, the more mature teachers usually gain these responsibilities; in smaller schools, even new teachers are likely to be assigned this role. Sponsorship of upper classes in the secondary school is usually far more complicated than that of the beginning classes. The upper-class sponsor exerts leadership and supervision over such affairs as the class play, the yearbook (seniors usually), participation in school government, class organization, dances, and all other affairs which are peculiar to the separate grade groups in school. Such activities weld strong student friendships and loyalties and build high morale in school. You will be fortunate if the opportunity to sponsor a class group comes your way early in your teaching career.

Meeting Certain Professional Responsibilities.   Classroom teachers have still other duties of a miscellaneous nature which call for careful attention. You will have many letters and professional inquiries which must be answered. You may be asked to review books or to fill out check lists and questionnaires—often from college people or state officials who are conducting serious research. Then too, you must keep alert in your own fields; and one way is to plan a regular time for the reading of professional books, journals, and other materials. Many teachers spend time and effort in educational experiments of their own or in original writings. All these things, and more, are part of the job. They take time, but they are rewarding in terms of professional growth and development. It is necessary to plan and experiment in order to gain efficiency in discharging these miscellaneous duties, but there are various sources of help. Usually some of the more experienced teachers in your school will be glad to discuss these matters with you. You will probably gain useful information about acceptable ways of doing things, about official forms and procedures that should not be neglected, about systematizing and routinizing and possibly delegating various jobs for which you are responsible in school.

Working with Administrators, Supervisors, Fellow Teachers, and Other School Personnel.   When you start teaching you probably will find yourself working with several "team members." It is this skill in human relationships, the ability to work well with others, that quite often determines your success and happiness in teaching.

You will have an administrative superior, a superintendent who is directly responsible to the board of education and to the people of the community for providing a good education for the pupils. While the superintendent is responsible for the activities that take place in all of the classrooms, he usually does not oversee the detailed work of each teacher. Much of his time may be involved in such matters as budgets, employment of teachers, housing facilities, and public relations. He expects the teacher to have considerable freedom in fulfilling his classroom responsibilities and to abide by the accepted policies of the school system in regard to such matters as curriculum organization, teaching procedures, standard report forms, and professional behavior. He depends upon principals and supervisors to ensure the effectiveness of classroom instruction.

The principal is responsible to the superintendent for all of the learning activities that take place in his school building. He works more intimately with the teachers, pupils, and community members within his school district than does the superintendent. Principals are assuming increasing amounts of responsibility for the improvement of classroom instruction. Larger school systems usually employ supervisors whose major reponsibility is the improvement of classroom instruction. It is to your principal and to your supervisor that you should look for assistance on the problems you encounter and for guidance in regard to any wide deviations in existing practices that you may wish to initiate. Look upon these people as your friends who are anxious to help you succeed to the fullest extent possible.

In larger school buildings you may need to work cooperatively with department heads, various kinds of special teachers, many others who are teaching the same grade or subject, health and social workers, business staff members, and custodians, all of whom play important roles in achieving a common goal—the education of boys and girls.

One of the ways in which you will most frequently work with other teachers is in teachers' meetings. The nature of teachers' meetings varies greatly in school systems. Some are democratic and others are not; some are very interesting, constructive, and helpful, and others are not. Regardless of the nature of these meetings, however, you should attempt to participate in them.

You may also be asked to serve on various committees. Some of these committee assignments may involve rather immediate, short-term problems; others, such as curricular improvements, methods of reporting to parents, or evaluation procedures, may be of a long-term nature. As a beginning teacher, welcome the opportunity to serve on these committees, since they enable you to become better acquainted with other staff

Greater skill in group planning and action is required of teachers in today's society. (*Photograph from the National Education Association.*)

members, to become accepted as a coworker, to assist in the solution of common problems, and gradually to assume a position of leadership.

As you approach your first teaching position, discover what the chief aims and purposes of your school are, what the general philosophy of the school is, and what the general patterns of instruction seem to be. It will be largely up to you to get acquainted with the various members of the school community and to learn their major interests, needs, and desires. You will be expected to pitch in and help further the school's program toward the goals they consider important.

Unfortunately, in many schools you, as a beginning teacher, may feel imposed upon rather heavily. Some schools expect the beginning teacher to carry the heaviest class load, the most difficult pupils, the least desirable teaching areas or extracurricular activities, or to work in the least attractive classroom space. Such schools operate largely on a seniority basis. Such practices represent gross inadequacies in administration and supervision. Modern trends are distinctly *away* from this.

Keep in mind that newcomers do not ordinarily turn things topsy-turvy and survive. You will meet a number of people in your work whose ideas toward certain educational matters are very different from yours. They, too, have studied carefully and thought seriously. They may be just as sincere as you are. You will want to proceed cautiously. Control the beginner's zeal which tempts many new teachers to feel that their answers are the only answers, their ways the only ways. Often the same goal can be reached by different paths. Sometimes a path that looks straight and clear at the start becomes devious and confused later on. If you are right on some matter and you know that you are, move slowly and without arousing undue antagonism. Not until you are rather well accepted as a person and as a coworker can you expect to play a very significant role in such matters as developing the school philosophy, changing the curriculum, or resolving basic issues. One of the best ways to gain that acceptance is by being diligent and helpful as you work with all your colleagues in school.

Bill of Rights for Teachers. If you are to fulfill adequately the duties that have already been mentioned you have a right to expect certain conditions to exist. The Pennsylvania State Education Association has developed and adopted a Bill of Rights for teachers which involves many of the duties that have been discussed [171:7–9]:

The Bill of Rights

1. Size of Class and Pupil Load

Each teacher has the right to classes of such size and a total pupil load of such weight that he may develop the maximum interests, capacities, and skills of individual pupils.

2. Time for Planning and Co-ordinating Work of a Professional Nature

Each teacher has the right to a class and activity schedule that will allow time during the school day for a thoughtful and effective discharge of his professional duties and for planning and co-ordinating.

3. Constructive and Sympathetic Supervision

Each teacher has the right to adequate constructive and sympathetic supervision.

4. Good Working Materials

Each teacher has the right to materials and equipment which are of practical necessity to effective teaching.

5. Adequate Physical Conditions in the Building

Each teacher has the right to practice his profession in a school environment that provides physical conditions necessary for good health, good teaching, and good morale.

6. In-service Education

Each teacher has the right to facilities and a program that will encourage in-service improvement, such as a professional library, workshops, group studies, and sabbatical leave.

7. Participation in School Policy and Program

Each teacher has the right to be consulted in the formulation of policies affecting the school and the school program within the framework of the school law.

8. Adequate Contractual Retirement Income

Each teacher has the right to a contractual retirement income based upon the total years of service and total professional earnings, and adequate for him and his dependents.

9. Right to a Position

Each teacher who is properly certified has the right to practice his profession with full contractual status, after an adequately supervised and acceptable probationary period.

10. Right to Engage in Professional Activities

Each teacher has the right to engage in properly recognized professional activities without incurring prejudice.

11. Right to an Adequate Income

Each teacher has the right to receive for his services a financial return, as it becomes due, that will allow him a living standard comparable to that of other professional groups and that will enable him to improve his professional service.

12. Right to Salary When Due

Each teacher has the right to receive his salary when it becomes due.

13. Right to Have Position Defined

Each teacher has the right to have the nature and scope of his professional duties defined.

14. School Day and School Week

Each teacher has the right to decline without prejudice special assignments beyond the normal school day.

15. School Year

Each teacher has the right to proportionate compensation for professional services beyond the minimum mandated school day and/or school term as prescribed by State law.

16. Political Participation

Each teacher has the right to participate in political activities as citizens, consistent with the American way of life, without endangering his professional position.

17. Protection from Discrimination

Each teacher has the right to protection from discrimination on the basis of race, color, creed, sex, political beliefs consistent with American democracy, residence, marital status, economic status, and consanguinity.

Appraising the Quality of Your Teaching.   Every teacher should feel an obligation to review systematically the quality of his teaching. Through frequent self-analysis and appraisals a teacher gains insights with regard to ways in which his teaching may be improved.

In a very practical and informative booklet titled *Are You a Good Teacher?* Alexander [3] has prepared a list of 20 indicators of the quality of teaching. Review the list, which is located in the Resource Section for Part II, as a means of gaining further insight into your role as a teacher. When you begin teaching, check yourself periodically against such a list.

COMMUNITY EXPECTATIONS OF TEACHERS

In planning a teaching career, you naturally are curious about the roles teachers play in the community. The act of teaching alone represents one significant community area where school people assume key responsibilities. In the act of teaching, the community will expect you to show interest in your pupils, to be able to work effectively with them, and to know your subject matter well. Furthermore, when you enter a community as a teacher, you will be expected to show certain attitudes, understandings, and behavior patterns which members of the community have come to associate with teachers. Your work will be considered a public service, paid for at public expense and influenced very decidedly by what the public wants. You will also be considered a leader in the business of helping people grow and learn, of helping whole communities become better places in which to live. Among these important areas of community participation are religion, clubs, and politics.

Religion is an important element in the lives of most people, and, since teachers are expected to set good examples for the young, most communities expect them to be active in church affairs. A national survey indicated that teachers were meeting that expectation. Among teachers, 91.5 per cent were church members, as contrasted with 60.9 per cent of the *total* population [154:32–33]. Although comparisons were not made for the adult population, it seems clear that teachers are above the national average in membership.

Teachers often join social, civic, service, veteran, and fraternal organizations. The frequency with which they do varies greatly from community to community. You may be certain that you will have many opportunities to assume a very active role in community organizations if you desire this kind of activity during your leisure time. The survey mentioned above also listed the types of organizations (other than churches) in which teachers most frequently reported active membership: lodges and related social groups, fraternities, sororities, and alumni groups; health and social-welfare groups; cultural and recreational groups, such as drama, bowling, hobbies; men's and women's business and professional, service, and civic-social clubs; religious-social youth-building groups. Percentages of teachers active in one or more organizations of the various types ranged from 31.8 in religious-social youth-building groups to 41.0 in lodges and related social groups [154:33].

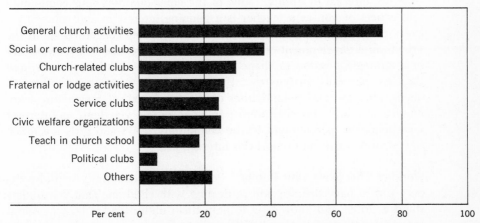

Figure 32. Per cent of teachers regularly taking part in various types of community activities. (*Source:* National Education Association.)

Traditionally the community political activity of teachers has been less extensive than participation in the activities of churches and other organizations. However, teachers seem to be setting an example, at least in the act of voting. The Citizenship Committee of the National Education Association has estimated that nine out of ten teachers voted in the 1960 presidential election [41:6]. Perhaps political activity of teachers is increasing. An opinion poll revealed that half of the nation's classroom teachers thought they should work actively on their own time as members of political parties in state and national elections [161:64]. Regardless of their personal political activity, teachers have an important responsibility to the community in their handling of controversial issues in the classroom.

What is expected of you as a teacher will depend in part upon the community where you happen to be located. In small schools, teachers usually have personal relationships with a relatively large percentage of the total school population. Teachers in small communities come in contact with and are known and appraised by large percentages of the people. Because of the intimacy of these relationships and because of certain folkways of people in small communities in the United States, teachers in such places must anticipate somewhat less liberal attitudes than those they would find in large cities. The situation may be quite different where population centers are dense, where your school may be one of a dozen or two in the large city, where your school may be located in one section and your home in another part of the city. In such a situation, it would be possible for you to work many months without being intimately known by more than a handful of people in your school and another handful in the neighborhood where you live. At the same time, keep in mind that, regardless of its size, location, or essential nature, every community will have certain expectations of its teachers.

Showing Interest in Pupils.   One of the chief qualities your community will expect of you as a teacher is a genuine interest in and concern for every child that you teach. Most parents are deeply concerned about the growth and development of their children. They realize that teachers are in a strategic position to shape the course of their children's lives, and they are naturally anxious that the course be in keeping with the real needs, interests, and potentialities of the pupils and of their entire community. Through sincere interest in your pupils you help to interpret your school to parents and to the community. Boys and girls are quick to feel, appreciate, and report this interest.

Working Effectively with Pupils.   People in the community will also expect you to have definite skill in dealing with children. That you understand children and know how to help them understand you is a general assumption. One of the great challenges in the classroom is that of establishing a climate for learning which is based on mutual respect and confidence between pupils and the teacher. What emotional needs will be yours in teaching—affection, recognition, a sense of security, a measure of success, a spirit of fun and adventure in learning? Pupils in your classroom have the same needs! In the succeeding months, your professional education program will provide both training and experience to help you in developing these understandings.

Knowing Subject Matter.   As a teacher, you will need to possess adequate competence in certain subject-content areas. Demands here will vary somewhat with the community and with the level at which you teach. High school teachers usually handle four or five different classes, and, especially if you begin teaching in a relatively small community, you may need to be prepared to handle three or four different subjects. In general, a higher degree of knowledge of particular subjects is expected in the larger cities where larger schools with expanded programs permit greater specialization on the part of teachers. To be sure, no parent or community wants youngsters poorly educated or misinformed. That is one reason why the state requires that you be licensed before you may teach, why most licenses require college graduation and some require even a master's degree. The long years of required training were deliberately conceived to fit you for recognizing teaching responsibilities.

Another responsibility in the various subject-matter areas is that of helping boys and girls to understand the role of knowledge in solving problems and in considering controversial issues. Only in the light of sifting all the facts can people come to intelligent decisions.

Traditionally, teachers in the United States have been expected to be completely neutral in the classroom on controversial issues. It has become increasingly clear to teachers in America, however, that the discussion of controversial issues cannot be divorced from our schools. Education is always a matter of a particular time and a particular place. Controversial issues are being considered by the people every day. The democratic system demands freedom to learn and freedom to communicate. Failure on the part of teachers to consider controversial problems and to study and help others understand the facts involved represents serious reluctance to discharge their responsibilities as teachers and citizens.

Providing Exemplary Behavior.   One of the most challenging aspects of the teaching profession is that most communities expect teachers to be laudable examples of personal-social living. This is further recognition of the significant influence teachers wield in the lives of their pupils. Most parents insist that this influence be of a desirable nature. You should recall again that there is wide variation in expectations of teachers from one community to another.

Parents often expect teachers to be better examples for children than parents themselves choose to be. In some communities teachers are not expected to smoke or drink alcoholic beverages in public places, and smoking or drinking, even in a teacher's own home, would be highly criticized by the public. However, the teacher in many other communities enjoys as much freedom in personal matters as any other professional person.

If you were to call upon a lawyer or a medical doctor for business reasons, either would be likely to appear before you carefully groomed and would display behavior considered appropriate to his profession. The same is expected of teachers. The teaching profession carries with it certain obligations with respect to behavior. Yet there is no need to be strait-laced about these matters either. As a new teacher in the community, it is better to discover exactly what the expectations are and to heed them carefully. After you are somewhat more experienced, better established in many groups, and well known as a capable teacher and respectable person, you can expect more freedom in matters of this sort. At the same time, remember that attitudes toward the personal behavior of teachers are slowly changing for the better. As a teacher, you could further this improvement by conducting yourself in a highly professional and respectable manner.

If you exercise good judgment it is unlikely that you will feel that your personal life is seriously restricted. In a nationwide study involving nearly 6,000 teachers [154:32–33], almost two-thirds of the teachers reported that their personal lives were not restricted in any way, and almost one-third indicated that their lives were restricted but not seriously. Only 2.1 per cent reported serious restrictions on their personal lives. As you might expect, the young teachers in small school systems felt that they had to exercise more caution than teachers in large cities. Single men seemed to feel a greater amount of restriction than did any other group of beginning teachers. Nearly 46 per cent of the single men reported that their behavior was somewhat restricted but not seriously, and 3.4 per cent reported serious restriction. Unmarried women did not feel quite as free of restrictions as did married women. A slightly higher percentage of teachers in secondary grades than in the elementary grades reported restrictions on their personal lives.

Living in the Community. People normally expect teachers to live in their school community. If you should have a job within commuting distance of your own home, you might be tempted to race out of town after school on Friday afternoons to enjoy the week ends at home. Most communities discourage this practice, and with much reason. The week end provides one of the best opportunities for you and the community folks to get better acquainted and to work together. There is time then for informal recreation, for friendly visits, and for playing a more responsible role in various community organizations.

You can reasonably look forward to acceptance into the social life of the community in which you are teaching. The survey referred to in the above sections also sought answers to this question of social acceptance. More than 88 per cent of the teachers in the study reported acceptance, more than 11 per cent reported partial acceptance, and less than 1 per cent reported being ignored or rejected [154:31–32].

Choosing Desirable Companions.   Another group of community expectations relates to your friendships and social relationships. Most communities will observe a teacher's friends and companions very keenly. Naturally you should choose your associates with some degree of care and with due regard for the same high personal qualities that people expect of teachers themselves. Most people would object rather strenuously to your dating pupils in school. People in small communities particularly would look askance upon your showering attentions upon a wide circle of friends of the opposite sex. On the other hand, most communities approve of teachers having serious relationships, especially between a teacher and a community member, where such relationships often lead to love, courtship, and marriage.

Married men as teachers are readily accepted in most areas. They usually settle down in the school community, rent or buy a home, spend regular sums for food, clothing, amusements, and the like. They join churches and other community organizations. They let their roots run deep. As noted in Chapter 1, married women are gaining more and more approval, as is evidenced by the increasing number of communities which hire or retain them. Today, a great many communities reveal a healthy attitude toward married women teachers and provide maternity leave from three months to three years for expectant mothers. Teaching has become a career which women can combine with homemaking.

Working in Other Community Agencies.   The smaller communities, particularly, may expect you to attend church on Sunday. A few may feel that you should attend Sunday school or conduct Sunday school classes or sing in the choir. However, the fact that you are a teacher should not fix upon you specific responsibilities in these areas. Neither should it preclude your active participation. These tasks need doing. They carry rewards. They serve important community purposes. Teachers who have the ability, the time, the energy, and the interest to assume various church responsibilities often weld strong bonds between themselves and other persons and groups in the community. The same results accrue for work teachers may do to assist the Young Men's or Young Women's Christian Association, the Red Cross, the United Fund, the Child Welfare Agency, the Country Club, the Grange, the Farm Bureau, Boy Scouts, Girl Scouts, and various service clubs such as Exchange, Kiwanis, Lions, and Rotary or any other community organization.

However, neither membership nor participation in any of these organizations should be decided by the fact that you are a teacher. If any teacher should be forced by circumstances to decline a request of any community agency, his reply should be accepted with the same degree of finality and the same good grace as the reply of a banker, a lawyer, a carpenter, a plumber, or anyone else.

Teachers are often expected to take part in problem-centered groups directed toward community improvement. You might be asked to join a community council whose attention is centered on problems like housing, health and hospital services, local libraries and museums, slum clearance, annexations, parking, schools, or parks and recreation centers. As a teacher you will be well qualified to help study these matters and to promote desirable improvements. Intimate contact with such problems will provide an understanding of the community that will be invaluable as you work with your pupils in school.

Promoting Good School Relationships.   In the preceding discussion it is obvious that the classroom teacher, whether purposefully or incidentally, helps shape public attitudes toward schools. In fact, the classroom teacher functions as the primary agent in the establishment of school public relations—whether they be good or bad.

The school today needs the understanding and positive support of the public more than ever before. Many teachers engage in a variety of activities in an attempt to promote lay interest and participation in schools. Too many, however, are not doing as much as they should.

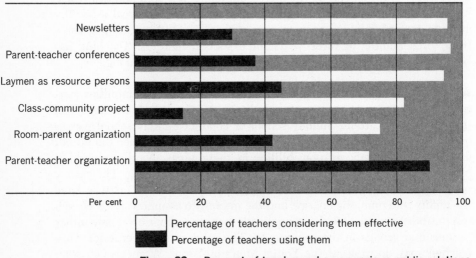

Figure 33.   Per cent of teachers who use various public relations techniques and who consider these techniques to be effective. Are there other techniques that should be used? (*Source:* National Education Association.)

The Research Division of the National Education Association has constructed a check list for teachers so that they may appraise themselves on how well they are accomplishing their public relations function. Review this check list, which is located in the Resource Section for Part II, as a means of gaining further insight with respect to ways in which you may promote effective school-public relationships.

SUMMARY

Very few aspects of the teacher's work are purely mechanical. While the classroom and other responsibilities within the school that have been described may seem somewhat tedious at times, they are part of the main stream of teaching and learning. Frequently they set the stage so that effective learning can take place. Often they present opportunities for rich learning experiences for pupils and teachers alike. In every case they require technical and professional know-how for their best management, as well as a sincere interest in and knowledge of youngsters—how they grow and develop, how they live and learn.

As you reflect upon the community expectations that have been presented in this chapter, remember that they exist for good reason. They have changed somewhat through the years and will continue to change. By your own attitudes and behavior you may accelerate the change in desirable channels. Teaching is an intimate social work. It is a powerful molding force. It is small wonder that those who hire you for such work should scrutinize you carefully and set certain standards which they feel must be upheld. Such concern should be interpreted as a tribute and a challenge—a tribute to the significant role of teachers and a challenge to lead the community and all its people to a higher level of living. When you understand your school and your role in that school, when you understand your community and your role in that community, then you can be most effective in interpreting the school to the community—a responsibility of all teachers.

QUESTIONS FOR YOUR CONSIDERATION

1. It has been said that a teacher should know his subject matter, his pupils, himself, and how to organize these into learning situations. Do you agree? Do you feel that there is any priority among these items?

2. Do you believe that teachers are forced to spend too much time in routine details? What suggestions can you make for relieving the situation?

3. In your opinion how should the progress of pupils be evaluated?

4. How should the progress of pupils be reported to parents?

5. How can extracurricular activities help pupils develop greater interest in the curricular activities of the school?

6. Some parents feel that too many extracurricular activities are being sponsored by schools today. How do you account for this feeling? What is your opinion?

7. In what ways does the work of a teacher in a large school differ from the work of a teacher in a small school?

8. To what extent do teachers enjoy the privileges expressed in the *Bill of Rights* developed and adopted by The Pennsylvania State Education Association?

9. It is frequently pointed out that most teachers who lose their jobs do so not because of lack of knowledge in their teaching fields but because of lack of ability in working with others: What are some of the personal qualities involved in working successfully with others?

10. Many prospective teachers feel that there may be many restrictions on their personal lives. Do you feel this way? Why?

11. Parents often expect teachers to be better examples for children than parents themselves choose to be. Do they have any right to make such demands of teachers?

12. How important is the teacher as a public relations agent? When does he serve as such an agent?

ACTIVITIES FOR YOU TO PURSUE

1. Spend as much time as you can for two or three days in succession observing the same teacher and class in school. Make a careful record of the duties the teacher performs. Try to identify those responsibilities which are most important. Examine those selected to determine whether they are of the mechanical or the leadership and human relations type.

2. Compare the daily schedule of classes of a small high school with that of a large high school. What differences do you observe in the number and variety of offerings? Consider both the regular curriculum and the extracurricular activities. How do the educational opportunities for pupils in the two schools compare in terms of available offerings? Which areas of teaching and learning appeal to you most? Why?

3. Become acquainted with a social or religious organization which serves children or youth in your community. Make several observations of the group at work. What relationships do you observe between the youngsters and the adult leaders of the group? Between the adult leaders and the parents of the youngsters? What similarities do you find between this situation and teaching in the public schools?

4. Organize student panel discussions in which you explore such topics as: What kinds of home rooms fulfill their function in a modern secondary school? What are some modern trends in reporting to parents?

5. Study the student handbook of a junior or senior high school. What opinions do you form concerning the school as a result of this study? What questions do you have?

6. Visit a number of modern classrooms and note improvements in the construction of school plants and equipment. Discuss with your colleagues how these improvements may help the teacher in meeting the educational needs of pupils today.

7. Through the use of the check list in the Resource Section for Part II, appraise one or more of your former teachers to see how well he fulfilled his public relations function.

7
LEARNING TO GUIDE THE GROWTH OF PUPILS

When a teacher first meets his class at the beginning of the school year, he begins the cycle that makes up the main portion of his responsibilities —the task of guiding the growth of his pupils. Here before him is the class waiting for—for what? As the person immediately responsible for the direction in which these young people will grow during the coming year, the teacher will have already asked himself that question, "For what?" And immediately the next question arises—"How?" Whether the pupils are first graders or high school seniors these same questions are to be answered. *What* are the goals and how are these particular pupils to be helped to attain these goals?

Perhaps the latter question presents greater concern for you at this stage of your preparation for teaching. The question would not appear to be so troublesome if you were to deal with only one pupil. But you will be responsible for a number of pupils, each quite different physically, psychologically, and socially. As a teacher, you will be concerned with each pupil and his total growth. Although it would be a dull world indeed if all persons were the same, the fact that individuals within one class-room can vary to a high degree poses problems for you. Some variations among pupils, however, will not be so great as to interfere with learning progress, while others must be dealt with individually.

The well-worn axiom "Start where the pupil is" sums up the point that

In what ways do these children seem to be different? In what ways to they seem to be alike? How should the school attempt to meet their differences as well as their likenesses? (*Photograph from the National Education Association.*)

you must deal with the pupil at his present stage of educational, social, and psychological development, and must plan for him and with him the program that will best help him to attain the goals expected of him. In other words, to adjust instruction to the pupil's present state, you must know the individual pupil; and, through the combined efforts of teacher and pupil, you can be much more successful in fulfilling your function.

Learning to Understand Pupil Behavior. Many beginning teachers fail to recognize the cues from a pupil's behavior that signal "Attention needed." If Mary fails to do any of the subtraction problems correctly because she subtracts the smaller digit from the larger regardless of position, it is obvious at this stage that she does not understand the process of subtraction. But what earlier signals did she give that indicated she was not understanding the process and, as a result, must now unlearn and then relearn? The experienced teacher might recognize that, as soon as Dick begins to tap his pencil, it is a signal that learning for him has ceased and that his attention is now directed to more playful pursuits. But in Bob's case, pencil tapping signals only that he is releasing some youthful energy while attending fully to the task at hand.

How can you become expert at understanding individual behavior? It is a process that one continues to learn throughout a lifetime. An infant soon learns the meaning of many of his mother's actions. A college student already has learned to interpret the meanings of many kinds of behavior. One familiar example is that of the student wanting a raise in allowance. He observes his parent's behavior very closely for signs of a propitious moment to bring up the subject and, once having opened up the matter, seeks further signs to learn how well things are going. This same procedure should underlie your approach to understanding pupil behavior. Be a close observer.

The professional training that you receive includes course work and opportunities to gain skill in effective observation. Basic courses in educational psychology, child development, and adolescent development serve to provide the general principles underlying human behavior. Early practice in applying these principles will enhance later performance when you are actually responsible for guiding pupils toward educational goals.

Through many observations of boys and girls and discussion about their behavior, you will be able to gain greater depth of understanding of behavior, build confidence, and achieve competence as a teacher. Your immediate goal is to develop a sensitivity to significant cues. This means that you must be sensitive to cues in general and to be able to discriminate which are the significant cues for the purpose.

Unless observation is systematic, little useful information will be obtained. You cannot observe the total environment at one time. In a class- **199**

Through repeated observations of boys and girls you will be able to gain greater understanding of their behavior and insights into their abilities and interests.

room context, the total environment includes not only the pupils but also the teacher, the materials, and the physical structure. Without an underlying system, you tend to observe whatever attracts your attention strongly enough. With guides for observation formulated in advance, you can observe for specific purposes. While the experienced teacher will be able to keep several purposes in mind; initially, you will probably gain more from your observation by attempting to answer only one question, say, "What was the general response of the class to the kinds of materials used during the observation period?"

To find answers to the question, observe in terms of the actual behavior of pupils. If the conclusion was made that the group responded well to the instructional materials selected by the teacher, the evidence for that conclusion would be in terms of actual behavior. What did the group do? Were there enthusiastic comments such as, "Good! I like this book?" Were there eager anticipations of receiving the material, such as clearing a space to accommodate the books? Were the boys and girls alert in their facial and body expressions? On the other hand, did some pupils grumble and slump back in their chairs as if to say "That old thing again?"

While the questions to be answered during an observation might well be posed in general purposes and in abstract terms, the answers can only be made in terms of observed behavior. In answering the question, "How is day-to-day instruction being adapted to individual differences?" for example, the teacher's behavior might be observed in terms of group management. If you are observing a reading lesson, are small groups made so that the wide differences within the whole group are lessened in order to meet the common needs represented by the smaller groups? After getting the small groups started, are there one or two individuals needing special help? Does the teacher find time to help these individuals? Are instructional materials selected from various levels of difficulty, or must all pupils, regardless of present achievement level, use the same material?

Perhaps there is a pupil who needs guidance and help because social or psychological factors are interfering with his achieving educational goals. For example, a boy may aggressively be seeking attention. He also may be interfering with the learning of other class members. Does the teacher use means that will permit him to receive attention for doing constructive instead of disruptive work?

Remember one caution in drawing conclusions from observations: one instance is not a sufficient basis on which to make general statements. Observations must be made many times to discover the patterns of behavior which constitute the reliable signals or cues on which a teacher operates.

Opportunities for informal observation are constantly at hand. All kinds of situations may be used to observe the behavior of boys and girls. You may observe them on the street, on a playground, at church, or at a basketball game. These situations provide excellent sources for you to use in gaining skill in observing behavior. In other words, observe the people you want to understand under all conditions available to you. Classroom observation is more formal. On the other hand, it provides the context in which the teacher works. An alertness to the influence on classroom behavior of factors coming from outside the school room, however, should enable you to have a better understanding of behavior observed in the classroom.

In learning to be a close observer, select only a few individuals and watch them in terms of only one general question. With a little practice, more individuals can be included as well as more questions. As a help toward systematic observation, a guide sheet is presented below. For each of the first six questions included on this sheet, space is provided for you to record relevant observed behavior and to answer the question.

Learn to identify the psychological and social needs of pupils rapidly. These needs are as important as their intellectual needs and affect academic progress greatly. (*Photograph from the* Planning for Teaching *series of motion pictures.*)

Guide sheet for observing classroom teaching

1. What are some of the positive techniques used in working with pupils?
   _____
   _____
   _____

2. How is day-to-day instruction being adapted to individual differences?
   _____
   _____
   _____

3. What are some evidences that the teacher is alert to physical, social, and psychological needs of individual pupils?
   _____
   _____
   _____

4. What are some evidences of pupil-teacher planning?
   _____
   _____
   _____

5. What are some evidences of a rich educational environment?
   _____
   _____
   _____

6. What is the place of the teacher in the group?
   _____
   _____
   _____

7. What questions from your observation do you wish to discuss with your college teacher?
   _____
   _____
   _____

Every day offers opportunity to learn to know youngsters. A ride on the city bus at school time or a place at the football game may reveal many things about how high school youngsters react in group situations. A child playing alone in the mud paints a picture of his personality in the things he does and says. To know boys and girls is to know how they work and play, how they react to various situations and people, and what makes them individuals.

As a teacher, you will have many opportunities to observe youth. Be alert to them in the cafeteria, on the playground, and at club meetings. Plan your classwork so that you may sometimes be on the side lines watching as your groups work. Find occasions outside the school—at church, in the park, on the street—to see boys and girls as they really are. The efficient teacher records his observations for further study. He devises a simple scheme for collecting and organizing his information about individuals or groups. He then teaches himself to be objective in using his plan. Although the observations which you make now will be somewhat different from those you will make of your pupils when you begin to teach, recording the things you observe as you come in contact with youngsters will help you to become expert in gathering data and will afford practice in finding meaning in your observations.

Understanding the Needs of Pupils.   From experiences in learning to know boys and girls, teachers grow in their understanding of what is required for growth and happy living. There is no real substitute for this insight and skill.

The needs of youth are of several kinds. Perhaps the first that must be satisfied are those that relate to good physical condition and health. All individuals need adequate food and clothing, freedom to be active, a place and time for rest, and immunity from disease. The physical organism demands all these things. If these persistent needs are not met, individuals sometimes react in undesirable ways.

Every morning about eleven o'clock John became a trouble spot in the fifth grade. He began to disturb his neighbors, to push and shove, to whine and fuss. Something was sure to go wrong in a short time; John seemed to be always in the center of it. This deviation from his normal behavior sent his teacher exploring. It did not take long for her to discover that John left his farm home quite early each morning on the school bus, having had his breakfast half an hour before. By eleven it was time for food again, and the rebellious John began acting up. A midmorning lunch for John solved the problem. Some teachers would have said that John was just a troublemaker.

Another example, directly related to school work, is the case of a child who has trouble in reading because of a specific visual defect. You will be amazed at the number of experienced teachers who frequently fail to detect visual defects in children. While most children have normal vision, there are special cases, and the observant teacher is alert to possible physical factors which might interfere with progress. Does the child habitually squint his eyes? Does he hold his book at an unusual angle? Does he always turn his head slightly when listening? Is it because one ear is defective and he is adjusting for that defect? Early observance of physical needs of pupils can permit early treatment and adjustment.

Mental and psychological needs are as important as physical ones. All individuals experience them—the need to feel secure in the affection of someone, the need to be a part of the group, and the need to be a creative member of society. The understanding teacher keeps these needs always in mind. He demonstrates constantly that he likes boys and girls. He finds a way for each pupil to do something well every day. He explores with them many opportunities to be creative. He plans to help each pupil find a place in the group, and each group widen its circle of friendships. He knows how important it is to be one of the team.

Meeting the mental or psychological needs of pupils will help them satisfy their social needs, too. But social needs require special skills and techniques which boys and girls have to learn. They need to know how

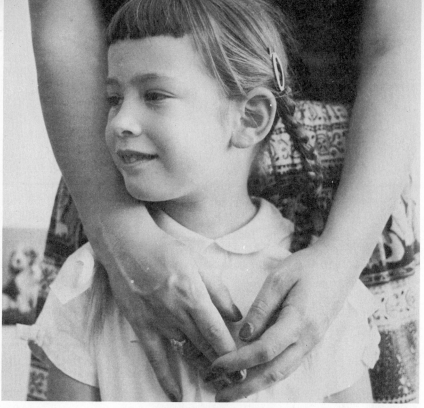

All individuals need to feel secure in the affection of someone. How will you attempt to meet this need in your classroom? (*Photograph by Carl Purcell, National Education Association.*)

to do things, how to express themselves clearly, how to meet situations with poise, and how to win acceptance from others in the group.

As a teacher you may meet an adolescent girl like Lydia, who was trying to find a place for herself in her group. An alert teacher recorded her observations of Lydia's struggle to learn the techniques that would satisfy her need to belong [58:44–45].

October

During the next several weeks Lydia came in frequently crying and saying: "I don't like it here. The girls don't like me." Each time I persuaded her to try it again and to try to get better acquainted with some of the teachers who might help her.

November

Lydia came to me several times complaining that the girls in her home economics class didn't like her. She even asked that I call some of them to my office to talk to them about it. I tried to bolster her self-confidence by helping her to see that the girls who worried her weren't too successful themselves and might be only trying to tease her. . . .

January

Two weeks later Lydia again complained. "The girls in home economics class don't like me. They sit and talk about me. I'd like to drop the course. Could I transfer to Girls' Technical High?"

End of January

Shortly after this Lydia turned in an excellent notebook in her home economics class and received the best grade in the class. This seemed to give her the confidence she needed. She told me about it and said maybe she really did know as much as the other girls in the class. She never again complained of their not liking her.

November

Lydia came in after morning club period (she belongs to "white-collar girls"— anyone may join until the quota is filled). She had on a white blouse and checked skirt and looked very neat. She smiled pleasantly and asked, "Miss Jones, may I come in to talk to you during the sixth period today?"

I had to tell her that I was attending a conference this afternoon, but could see her tomorrow if it were something that could wait. "Oh, tomorrow will be all right," she replied rather airily. She carried a white crepe paper bow and, holding it up, said, "We white-collar girls have to wear one of these today." I said, "Oh, you are a white-collar girl. I imagine you enjoy that." She answered, "I was in study hall last year and I didn't want that again."

December

One day Lydia stopped in my office for a needle and thread to sew up a small rip in her skirt. She said, "Miss Jones, do you notice how much I've gained since last year?" I answered, "Well, your face looks fuller and it is becoming to you." She answered, "Oh, I feel better than I did last year. I laugh a lot now. You know some of those girls I thought didn't like me in home economics class are my best friends now."

Teachers like Miss Jones see their pupils as real individuals. They realize they cannot use the same educational program and the same educational measuring stick for all. They know that their pupils are maturing at different rates and in different directions, just as they read varying levels of books, have diverse creative abilities, and have widely different problems to meet.

The teacher must discover the individual differences which exist within his group. He must identify Dick who, although very brilliant, is too socially young for his class. He must uncover Patricia's talent for art and put it to work to help her make a place for herself among her companions. He must appreciate the fact that Carol should begin her new work in arithmetic where she left off last year and that she may not be ready to begin the assigned work of her grade. He must recognize that, even though David and Bill seem to be of about equal maturity and ability, the wide differences in their backgrounds and out-of-school experiences mean that the school day must be planned differently for each of them.

You are probably saying, "Do you mean that when I teach school I'll be expected to make a special plan for each of the 40 pupils I'm likely to have? That's impossible!" Of course, you are right. It is not the purpose of the school to teach its pupils one at a time. As a resourceful teacher you will find many occasions when it will be highly desirable for the whole group to share an experience and to learn from one another. Small collective enterprises will help your boys and girls who have similar needs and who are of similar ability to work profitably together. Still other groups will bring together pupils who have common interests but who

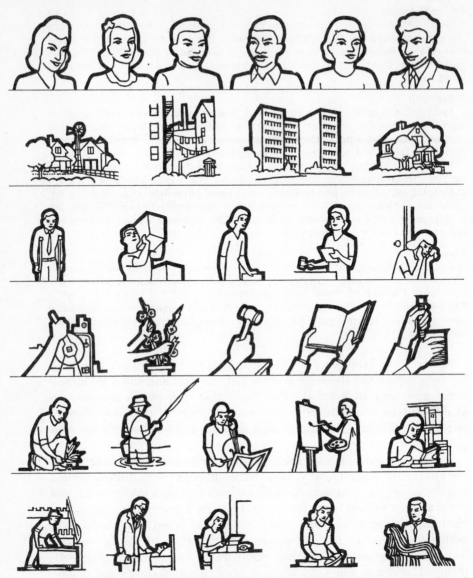

Figure 34. The school is confronted with the task of meeting a wide variety of individual differences. What are the major groups of differences suggested in this illustration? How will you attempt to meet the great diversification of needs of pupils? (*Source:* National Education Association.)

may be at different levels of maturity. Sometimes boys and girls from several grades will cooperate on worthwhile activities. In all this interchange, individual differences will come into play, and youth will have opportunities to satisfy their physical, intellectual, and social needs.

Can you begin now as you plan your career to become alert to youth and its needs? Your observations will help you recognize many of their interests and problems.

Young children especially, reveal some of their characteristics, thoughts, and feelings through their creative activities. (*Photograph from the Audio-visual Center, Indiana University.*)

Understanding How Learning Takes Place.   The word "learning" is commonplace in our language, but, like the word "think," it is difficult to define precisely. As you proceed in your preparation for teaching you will devote much study to its precise meaning and implication for your work.

A teacher observes performance rather than learning, and infers from it that certain learnings have taken place. Learning involves some change or modification in the behavior of a pupil. For example, suppose that a pupil has written a theme containing the sentence, "They, was also going to make the trip." Two errors in performance were made—the comma and number of the verb. When these errors have been called to the attention of the pupil and explained, future performances will be checked to discover whether or not these particular behaviors have been modified. If commas are no longer misplaced and plural subjects are accompanied by plural verbs, then it is inferred that this bit of learning has taken place.

As you observe boys and girls you become more and more aware of the fact that there are times when learning becomes especially meaningful to pupils. There probably is one best time to teach everything, if teachers could only know that time. There are no magic or scientific formulas yet available for determining these exact moments when students should be taught. Your preparation for teaching will help you in determining when teaching will become most significant. Certain conditions, however, can be cultivated or arranged which foster effective learning. From their many contacts with boys and girls teachers know that pupils learn when they are motivated by their own need and challenged to put forth their best effort. They know that pupils learn best when learning is closely related to and grows out of past and present experiences. They know that pupils who have opportunities to plan their activities and to

This garden project of the Madison School in Phoenix, Arizona, enables the pupils to relate specific principles to practical life situations. What other types of projects would encourage this kind of learning? (*Photograph from the National Education Association.*)

select their materials under the guidance of a wise and resourceful teacher are learning far more than those who must follow the direction of a classroom autocrat. Good teachers help boys and girls to experience in a great variety of ways, to use what they are learning, to evaluate the success of their plans, and to see real progress toward a goal.

The important conditions for learning were vividly apparent in a fifth grade that embarked on a camping project. When Ted, Ralph, and several others returned to school in the fall they talked of nothing else but their summer at a boys' camp. There was no doubt about what they had learned. Every sharing period sooner or later turned to the topic of life out of doors. The enthusiasm of the class was quickly kindled, and many looked longingly ahead to camping a year hence. But an alert teacher saw opportunities for putting the conditions of learning to work. He suggested the prospect of several days in the woods, not next summer, but right now, this fall. The pupils were wild with interest.

Everyone went to work. The teacher enlisted the help of the community recreation department and the parents. The boys and girls worked with a will at their responsibilities. They planned shelters to use during their outing; they planned menus for the noon and evening meals; they outlined the study activities to be carried on in their nature classrooms. They gathered together the materials they would take, practiced the various camp skills they would need, and generally made ready for the exodus from school.

The outing was exciting and successful, the youngsters enthusiastically agreed. What did the teachers and the parents say? Were there real learnings in this new experience? What did it contribute to the well-being of children and to their ability to live and to work together? No brief report can record all the values. Skills of many kinds, from reading to handicrafts, were utilized in real-life situations. The scenes of their learning were real—the woods, the cookhouses, the shelters, and the lake. The activities—the bird hikes, the building of a campfire, the story and stunt hour, the study of a live bat, the making of leaf prints—were real as well. The pupils saw sense in what they were doing. Here was a reason for learning and a real nature laboratory in which to find out things.

The pupils brought home much of their new learning to the classroom to be preserved in memory and to be applied to new tasks at hand. They took stock of what they had done, analyzed their methods of working together, tried to locate weaknesses in their handling of reading, writing, and arithmetic, thought through again some of the ways in which they had solved their problems, and then took a look ahead to see how all these experiences would contribute to the winter before them.

Selecting and Guiding Learning Experiences.   Choosing the learning experiences which pupils should have may seem to you to be a big job for a young teacher. There are so many things boys and girls may do, so many choices to make. How does a teacher know in what directions to guide his pupils?

Modern teachers have many aids, one of the most important of which lies in the needs and interests of pupils. The knowledge of these needs, as you already know, comes from constant observation and careful study. Each activity leads the way to the next, pointing to new experiences which particular individuals need. Today's teachers, by their awareness of the community in which they live and by their understanding of the influences which affect young people, are able to help youth make wise choices. An appreciation of the demands of democratic living enlarges even more the teacher's vision of the kinds of goals for which youth should be reaching.

Leaders in education are pretty well agreed upon the kinds of experiences boys and girls need in order to participate fully in living today and in the future. These experiences include developing efficiency in the basic communication and mathematics skills, learning techniques of group planning and problem solving, making and taking responsibility for decisions, developing a knowledge of themselves and of other people that will contribute to better group living, and developing a knowledge and understanding of the environment in which all these activities take place. To these must be added participation in community activities, efforts to promote critical thinking, evaluation of experiences, building a wide range of interests that will contribute to the making of a well-balanced individual, and the development of personal and social values. (See Chapter 14.)

These are the kinds of experiences that teach the cooperation that is so increasingly necessary in today's world; they help each individual reach his highest potentialities. Do you find it difficult to see the traditional teacher as an educative force in such surroundings? Where is the teacher who merely assigns pages in a textbook, listens to the recitation of what has been read, gives a grade, makes the next assignment, and begins the cycle all over again?

The modern teacher is not only a good group leader but also a most resourceful one. He knows how to do things and where to find information. Pupils call upon him for technical aid in many situations. He is a sympathetic adult who does not berate them for not knowing. When group planning becomes bogged down, he is the one who can pull it out of the mire.

The teacher facilitates the experiences of his pupils. He senses the direction of their thinking and planning and can smooth the way to success. He helps them just enough, but not too much. He saves them from failures they cannot understand. He promotes good group relationships by

In the modern school, the value of the sharing of learning experiences is emphasized. This pupil's report is obviously of interest to her classmates. (*Photograph from Department of Elementary School Principals, the National Education Association.*)

foreseeing personality clashes and by helping them to accept each other. Oiling the machinery is an important job for the teacher.

The teacher helps boys and girls to evaluate their group work and aids each pupil in judging his own efforts in the light of his needs and ability. In a relaxed, friendly atmosphere youth face their mistakes and short-comings frankly and make plans for improvement. Failing to reach the goal the first time merely motivates a second and better try. Pupils individually and as groups ask and seek answers to such questions as these: "Did we accomplish what we set out to do?" "What part of our work did we do well?" "Why did some of our efforts fail?" "What shall we do differently next time?" "Were all group members participating?" "Did I do my part?" "How did I feel about my part of the job?" "What new things were learned?" "How can these new ideas be used?" "What new problems came up that need to be solved?" Surely these are more important than to ask, "What grade did I get?"

The teacher is concerned that each individual, whether he be working alone or in a group situation, has maximum opportunity to develop his interests and abilities. He recognizes that the strength of a democratic society is dependent upon the full development of each individual's talents. Within a group situation the development of these talents not only provide for individual self-realization but also for the enrichment of the entire group. For example, as the teacher helps a pupil develop his special abilities in science, the pupil moves toward self-realization, assumes roles of leadership within the group, and enriches the lives of others through his contributions to the group. His life, in turn, is enriched through the sharing of unique interest, and abilities possessed by other members of his group.

How will you select the activities in which your pupils engage? Experiences are not of equal educative value, and pupils can engage in only as many experiences as time will allow. You therefore need some yardstick of values against which you can make selections. This yardstick consists of the values which a democratic society prizes and covets. The following statement of principles should aid you in making these choices [adapted, 62:25–27]:

1. *The experience must begin and grow out of the needs of the pupils as they see them and as society sees them.* Such needs tend to be needs which the pupils themselves recognize or can be made aware of. They may be needs for knowledge, skill, expression, the satisfaction of an interest—any one or a pattern of needs.

2. *The experience must be managed by all of the learners concerned—pupils, teachers, parents, and others—through cooperative, democratic interaction.* Experiences in the modern school frequently draw in many people who do not give full time to the school. Parents contribute in many ways, as do many civic authorities, merchants, and others.

3. *The experience must take on meaning and unity as the pupils' purposes become clearer and their work moves through one stage after another toward completion.* At times pupils may purpose to do things which have relatively little meaning to them because of their meager experience, but as work progresses new understandings are added, horizons are pushed out, and the whole matter assumes new and lasting values.

4. *The experience must aid each pupil in improving his purposes and increasing his power to make intelligent choices.* Pupils' original choices may be trivial and of slight value because of their lack of experience and insight. As their work progresses, guided by a skillful and understanding teacher, the inherent values and meanings become apparent to the pupils and they purpose more and more wisely as their knowledge and insight grow. One of the major goals of all education is that of guiding the individual into ever higher and finer purposing, ever better and more worthy choices.

5. *The experience must aid each pupil to integrate past experience with present experience, making all available for future use.* Often, in the traditional school, learning has been of little permanent value because each skill or item of content was learned as a separate entity; the pupil failed to utilize past experience to solve present problems. As a result he saw little or no application of present learning to his own out-of-school experience, and the life value of the learning was negligible.

6. *The experience must increase the number and variety of interests which each pupil consciously shares with others.* One of the school's major tasks is that of opening up new and untried avenues of experience. A democratic society is one in which the genius of one individual can be utilized to enrich the entire mass and in which the level attained by the society as a whole is the aggregate of the levels attained by the interacting individuals within the society. Therefore it follows logically that the pupils need many leadership opportunities in cooperative interaction and sharing of experiences. When these shared experiences widen horizons and increase the number and variety of interests, their service is twofold.

7. *The experience must help each youngster build new meanings and refine old ones.* Real learning is forever a matter of adding new meanings and modifying old ones. If the addition and modification refine, enrich, and enlarge the total fund of meanings which the pupil possesses, they add substantially to the working material which the pupil draws upon to understand and interpret other experiences.

8. *The experience must offer opportunity for each pupil to use an ever increasing variety of resources for learning.* Resources for learning in life outside the school include people, first-hand and vicarious experiences, books, magazines, television, radio, movies, and many other avenues. The more resources a youngster learns to use under the guidance of the school the more readily and independently he will learn in his life outside of the school.

9. *The experience must help each pupil to use a variety of learning activities which are suited to the resources he is using for learning.* Pupils need to do wide reading and intensive reading, to work alone and in groups, to learn many skills and develop many abilities, and to use those skills and abilities in many ways.

10. *The experience must aid each pupil to reconstruct his past experience creatively as the new learning situation develops.* Again, it is a matter of helping pupils to draw upon their past experience to understand their present experience, and in so doing to enlarge and enrich the total concept.

11. *The experience must challenge the thinking and call forth the effort of the youngster to bring it to a satisfactory conclusion.* Any really valuable experience is broad enough in the scope of its possibilities to provide worthwhile experience for the slowest learner and still challenge the more able learner and cause him to exert himself willingly to solve the necessary problems and carry on the work. Youth enjoy work which calls for effort and energy when they feel a need for it and understand its values.

12. *The work must end with a satisfying emotional tone for each pupil.* To work hard and intensive and to reach one's goal is highly satisfying to youngsters as well as adults, and that satisfaction provides a solid foundation for future work.

Are you wondering how you can prepare to be the kind of teacher described here? Take every opportunity to build a wide background of information and experience for yourself. Choose your college electives with a view to broadening your contacts with several areas of learning. Explore the community in which you live; try to identify the aspects of community living which will make worthwhile experiences for boys and girls. Build personal interests and hobbies in the areas which will contribute to your work with pupils. Read widely. Your college library is a resource you may never be able to duplicate later. If you are working with young people, utilize some of your ideas in guiding their experiences; try to be the kind of leader now that you want to be later as a teacher.

Planning with Pupils.   Out of experiences with youth grows the curriculum of the modern school. From the circumstances of daily living at school and in the community come the plans which teachers and pupils make for the learning ahead. This planning is essential if pupils are to follow their own purposes and engage in learning that is meaningful to them. The teacher must help them clarify their aims and set up their goals. "What are we trying to find out?" "Why do we need this information?" "What are the resources for finding out?" "How will we know when we have found what we are seeking?" These and other questions will be answered cooperatively by pupils and teacher.

Learning the skills of problem solving is an integral part of planning with pupils. The teacher acts as an adult resource person who, because of his experience and wider knowledge, can advise and guide pupils through the steps needed to solve a problem. Teacher-pupil planning means that pupils and teachers actually plan together. It means that they identify the problems that are pertinent to them and the questions that they need to answer. The teacher as a group leader contributes his ideas and questions. Together they apply the scientific method to the solving of the problem, and critical thinking to the answering of the questions. They go about this work systematically, with the teacher helping the group direct its efforts profitably. They plan how and where to locate necessary information. They exchange opinions and ideas and try to locate all the resources within the group. They organize themselves for effective work and evaluate the progress they make. The teacher encourages the reticent, helps leaders to permit others to lead sometimes, and guides those who find it difficult to assume responsibility. Pupils and teachers work through their problems to a satisfying conclusion.

Does the concept of teacher-pupil planning, as indicated above, seem difficult for you? Would it not be easier just to tell your pupils what to do as perhaps you were told when you were in school? As you explore the kinds of responsibilities which citizens of the world face today, can you see that planning is important? Locating problems that need to be solved and knowing how to go about solving them are essential skills in democracy.

During your college days you may have opportunities to participate in group-planning experiences. These will be invaluable to you later, if you take time to observe how people work together, how leadership emerges, how resources are utilized, and how conclusions are reached. If you are working with young people's groups, encourage them to do their own planning and help them appreciate the fact that this is in itself a vital experience.

Building Relationships with Pupils and Parents.   As you look forward to teaching, you may be most concerned about getting along with people. Managing a classroom of active pupils may seem one of the biggest challenges a teacher faces. You are no doubt remembering some of the experiences your own teachers had with students. As you prepare for teaching, your training experiences will help you to meet this challenge. Just now, while you are making plans for the future, it may be well to explore how good relationships with others are built.

You can see that the kind of teacher described in this chapter is well on the way to happy experiences with youngsters. Boys and girls who are interested in following their own purposes, who are working at their own level of ability, and who see the why of what they are doing have little desire to exhibit resistive behavior. An important study of teachers and their relationships to pupils has developed some revealing phrases to describe effective and noneffective teachers. Here are some of the most telling items [adapted, 12:33–35]:

Building good relationships with pupils is important for success in teaching. How well are you able to relate to pupils? (*Photograph by Marie Fraser.*)

Effective teachers	Noneffective teachers
Having the ability to remain self-controlled in the midst of conflicting demands.	Displaying an inadequacy to classroom demands, easily disturbed.
Habitually quiet, poised, and courteous in relationships with children.	Demanding, imposing, impatient in relations with children.
Constructive and encouraging in comments and manner.	Resorting to threats and punishments, sarcastic, cross.
Enthusiastic about pupils and teaching.	Harassed, disturbed, unsure, with no interest or enthusiasm.
Possessing sufficient self-restraint to allow children to work through their own problems.	Imposing directions and requirements upon pupils, oblivious of pupil initiative and resourcefulness.
Ingenious in utilizing opportunities for teaching.	Unaware of opportunities for vitalizing classroom teaching.
Careful in planning with pupils and in guiding them to successful completion of undertakings.	Expecting children to know what to do and seemingly satisfied if they keep busy.
Skillful in directing pupils to evaluate their own work.	Failing to help pupils set up standards of their own.
Interested in pupils as persons.	Interested only in each child's academic progress.

As you go about visiting classrooms to observe teachers and pupils, try to identify the characteristics of the teacher who has established wholesome relationships with children. What do you think the teacher in the following situation is building for?

"If you don't finish your arithmetic, you'll have to stay in at recess. I've warned you for the last time."

"It doesn't make any difference how you did it last year. You're in the eighth grade now, and I'm the teacher."

"I can't imagine what your mother's thinking of, to let you read such things."

"The children in this group are the most trying I've ever had. Honestly, I think I'll shut the door and never come back."

"Don't you know any better? Only stupid folks have to be told as many times as I've told you."

"If you'd put as much effort on your lessons as you do on those model planes, you'd be better off."

Be on the alert for teachers of another kind. What are they saying to their pupils?

"If your idea works out well, there's no reason why we shouldn't try it together."

"Do you feel that this is the best you can do now? What do we do next to help you improve?"

"We all make mistakes, you know. It would be a pretty dull world if everyone were perfect."

"Let's skip the spelling until tomorrow. Then you'll have time to finish planning for the assembly."

"School wouldn't be much fun without the pupils. Every day is different, new, and exciting."

Building fine relationships with pupils is easiest when teachers and parents are well acquainted. The teacher, of course, cannot know his boys and girls completely nor guide their learning experiences adequately unless he himself looks beyond the classroom to the home. How are such relationships established?

When you meet a parent you will be able to sense that foremost in his mind is the question "How is my child getting along in school?" He expects you to say something about the youngster. Remember that children are the most precious possession of parents. This concern represents a point of departure for your conversation with a parent.

It is important for you to evidence a sincere and genuine interest in the welfare of the youngster. It also is important to recognize that the parent is more intimately acquainted with him than you, that he has known the child from birth. Through the cooperative sharing of concern for the youngster you can develop a team approach that is in the best interest of the child and out of which may grow respect and understanding for you as a teacher.

In preparation for the day when you will be meeting the parents of your pupils, take every opportunity now to know the people of your community. Learn about their interests and problems. Practice the techniques of meeting adults with courtesy and thoughtfulness. Try to be skillful in the handling of controversial topics in the groups with which you meet. Learn to put yourself in the other person's place. Building good relationships with school patrons requires the same kind of skill that puts you at ease in any adult group. This skill plus your genuine interest in each pupil's welfare will see you safely through.

Creating a Happy School Environment.   Because people are so much the products of their environments and because their reactions are greatly influenced by the setting in which they work and play, an attractive school home is essential. How does the modern school create its setting?

Teachers and pupils work together to build the physical surroundings. They plan cooperatively ways in which they can make the room a pleasant place in which to work. They take responsibility for keeping the bulletin boards up to date. They share the duties of keeping the classroom in working order. Because pupils have a part in making the room a comfortable place in which to study and carry out activities, they come to feel that it is truly their own. They are happy to be there and proud to show it to visitors. "My room at school" becomes a real part of living.

Many of you will someday walk into classrooms that you will say are hopeless. But you will be surprised to see what an energetic teacher and enthusiastic youngsters can do as a result of their imagination and perseverance. The fun of the doing will pay dividends in helping pupils to share a common task and to learn to work together for the good of the group. A happy school environment is not necessarily found in the newest and most costly school building; it may be found in the drab, barren room which boys and girls inherited and fixed up all by themselves.

Desirable relationships among teachers, parents, and youth grow best in environments that are suited to the activities of the modern school. How difficult it is to put new ideas to work in surroundings that were made for a different kind of education! Today's schools are "doing" schools; there must be places for pupils to do things. Today's schools are interested in individual children; there must be good light, suitable furniture, and proper heat and ventilation. Today's schools spill their activities out over the entire community; neighborhoods both close and far away contribute their part to the school's environment. Today's schools build for cooperation and social competency; there must be room to work and play with others.

A happy school environment, of course, goes far beyond matters of physical setting. The tone of the principal on the phone, the way the pupils greet their visitors, the look on the teacher's face when plans are unexpectedly changed are all evidences that suggest the atmosphere of the school. Even a short visit will reinforce these first hints and will indicate the measure of happiness that adults and pupils experience in working together in satisfying ways.

Was your school like the modern school described here? Find an opportunity to visit the schools in your own community. Can you feel the atmosphere of the school almost from the moment you step through the door? What evidences do you see of conscious efforts to create a real school home for young people?

Learning to Use Newer Instructional Techniques and Procedures.   If all of the tasks and responsibilities required of teachers were listed together, the result would add up to formidable proportions. But aids in an increasing variety and in increasing excellence are being offered. Teaching machines, television, teacher aids, and team teaching are all examples of newer techniques to make teaching more effective and more efficient. Other techniques will be devised and made available. But new techniques are often confusing and are abused when not correctly understood. *None of the new instructional devices is designed for the purpose of replacing a classroom teacher, but rather to free the teacher for matters that require personal presence and judgment.* The intention of these newer devices is to provide better utilization of our teachers and other education resources.

B. F. Skinner, an eminent psychologist, has described the present educational process as one in which methods of imparting knowledge have changed scarcely at all [145:91]. Our school systems have been criticized because too many young people come through the process without adequate command of basic subjects. In addition, too many of our young people become discouraged and leave school as soon as the law permits, while others hang on bravely but find the process in many ways a punishing ordeal. These newer techniques and instructional devices take advantage of our advancing technology and of findings from behavioral sciences to improve the process of imparting knowledge and avoiding some of the consequences of school failures.

Teacher aides are among the various techniques used in order to increase the effectiveness of the school. By employing housewives or other nonprofessional personnel to handle noneducational tasks (collecting lunch money, keeping records, and preparing equipment), the teacher is freed to do what he was trained to do: teach. When the teacher has help for nonteaching chores and can devote his attention and time to instruction, results are most satisfying. The use of teacher aides, launched in Bay City, Michigan, in 1952, has been tried and proved effective in communities throughout Michigan and in Colorado, Connecticut, Iowa, Minnesota, Massachusetts, and Utah. This plan has also been tried in Chicago, Detroit, and New York.

An interesting outgrowth of the teacher-aide plan is team teaching. Just as the team approach has been used in clinics and in business organizations, a team-teaching situation permits teachers to do what they can do best. Instructional teams are organized to take advantage of the individual talents and special training of the teachers. Pupils gain a much broader experience from the team than is possible from teachers working alone with small groups. Eurich [50:4] points out that, apart from pupil gain, the team approach has suggested a new career pattern in public education that should encourage outstanding teachers to stay in the profession. By becoming team leaders they usually can qualify for higher salaries. In the past about the only future for teachers seeking advancement was to move out of the classroom and into administration or supervision.

The use of television for regular instruction has perhaps expanded more rapidly than any other of the newer techniques. Its use is viewed with mixed feelings, ranging from disdain to great enthusiasm. Actually, television, like films, books, and radios, is a communication medium and not a teacher. As an instructional device its worth depends on the quality of the teacher who is planning and presenting the material and on the planning and coordination of the classroom teacher who is viewing the lesson with his pupils.

Continental Classroom has been an outstanding example of direct teaching of full year courses to individuals by television. Outstanding instructors, including Nobel Prize winners, have taught physics, chemistry, mathematics, and government to millions. During the American Government course, for example, political leaders appeared for interviews or to lecture along with the regular instructor. Such facilities are not available to the individual school.

An example of coordinating television instruction with the usual class-

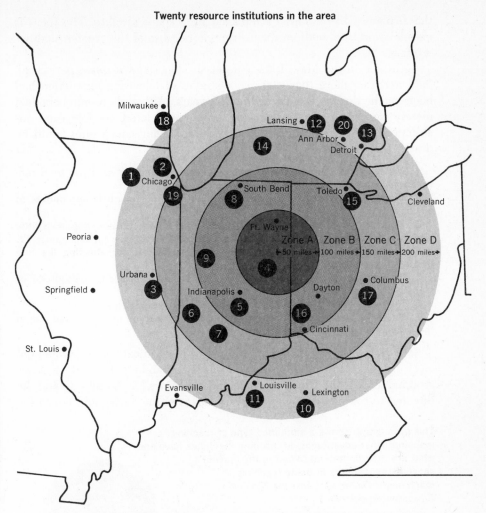

Figure 35. Service area and resource institutions involved in the Midwest Program on Airborne Television Instruction. What are some of the potential values of such an experiment? (*Source:* Midwest Program on Airborne Television Instruction.)

room has been the airborne TV courses starting in 1961 in the Middle West. An airplane has circled over northern Indiana broadcasting TV courses to elementary, secondary, and college students in an area including parts of Illinois, Indiana, Kentucky, Michigan, Ohio, and Wisconsin, reaching a potential audience of 5 million students in 13,000 grade schools, high schools, and colleges. Use of this medium brings to pupils in small, understaffed schools top-flight teachers heretofore unavailable to them. Through coordination of plans, the classroom teacher can prepare his class for the lessons and be present for discussion on an individual basis. The airplane was used because of transmission techniques available at the time. As the transmission of television signals improves, the airplane will perhaps be replaced by a space satellite. The focus is on television as a medium for instruction because of the greater facilities it offers.

An article in the May, 1962 issue of the *Phi Delta Kappan* periodical, indicated that more than 400 major studies of television instruction had been made during the preceding 15 years. Although researchers had merely scratched the surface of problems related to television instruction, the research indicated that the following conclusions could be drawn [177:329]:

1. Much information can be learned as effectively from TV as it can from conventional instruction.
2. Students of varying ability learn from TV; it is not uniquely appropriate to any specific ability level.
3. Students' and teachers' attitudes toward TV vary greatly. We have little evidence that learning is affected by the student's preference for or against TV.
4. Class size does not appear to be an important factor affecting learning by TV.
5. No subject matter area or grade level is either especially appropriate or inappropriate for TV.
6. Recorded programs are about as effective as live presentations.
7. Students prefer an experienced instructor on TV to an inexperienced one in the conventional classroom.

As with television instruction, the use of mechanical and electronic devices also has a history of abuse and misunderstanding. These devices are grouped under the label of "teaching machines." Attention should be directed to the program presented by means of the device and not to the

This photograph shows a simplified type of teaching machine. What advantages do teaching machines have and what are their limitations? What is the teacher's special responsibility in using teaching machines? (*Photograph from the National Education Association.*)

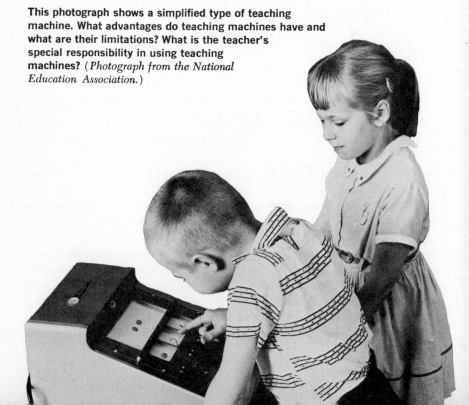

device itself. Teaching machines range from printed cards to elaborate electronic devices combining printed material with illustrations and some means of giving individual guidance to the student making errors. Selection of the means of presenting programmed material must be left to the purpose and budget of the users.

The classroom teacher has often devised special practice materials for pupils or has selected appropriate exercises from available workbooks for pupils needing additional work. This is not new, nor is recognition of the fact that pupils need to know the immediate results of their work in order to make corrections and proceed effectively. Textbooks and workbooks with answers in the back of the book are not new. Having such material already prepared in a systematic way, based on principles coming from the experimental laboratories and available to the student to use independently, is new in the sense that machine-type instruction has now been put to wide use. Allowing students to proceed at their own pace for drill work or even original instruction from programmed material frees the teacher to do what he can do best in person: guide discussions and work

Many schools have installed language laboratories. How have they improved language instruction? For what other instructional purposes may they be used? (*Photograph from Robert Mossholder.*)

with individual pupils. The programmed material is not something that just happened; outstanding teachers can write a program just as they can instruct in person. What else in essence is a textbook?

Much of the time now spent by the classroom teacher covers material that the pupil could learn independently if it were properly presented. Imaginative uses of such devices frees the classroom teacher to help students discuss and pursue ideas encountered in the material—and this can be the essence of teaching.

The point cannot be made too strongly that these innovations in teaching and learning aids are not gimmicks to provide miracle cures nor to replace rigorous learning and teaching with synthetic substitutes—they are a means to the end of better education. During your preparation for teaching you will want to become thoroughly familiar with these newer techniques, to know their limitations, and to gain skill in using them effectively.

SUMMARY

Study boys and girls, not only in the classroom, but in their out-of-school activities. Become acquainted with them in their homes, if possible. Try to find out how each works and plays, how he reacts to various situations and people, and in what ways he is different from other youngsters.

Every pupil has physical, psychological, and social needs. Physically, he must have sufficient food and clothing; he must have an opportunity to be active; and he must have proper rest. Psychologically, he needs to be loved, to feel he is a part of the group, and to have confidence in himself as a creative member of society. Socially, he needs to know how to do things, how to express himself clearly, how to meet situations with poise, and how to win acceptance from others in the group. Help each pupil fulfill these needs. Discover in what way he is different from the others, and then plan his play and work accordingly.

It is difficult for a young teacher to know how to choose the learning experiences which pupils should have. To do this he must have a rich background of experience himself—experience that has taught him cooperation and helped him develop fully. The teacher must therefore read widely, have broad contacts, and build up personal interests and experiences that help him understand and promote desirable characteristics in his pupils. He must encourage pupils to cooperate with him in building a happy school environment, and, above all, he must become a good group leader who plans with pupils and helps them clarify their aims, establish desirable goals, and devise effective ways of reaching these goals.

Various types of instructional materials are becoming available to teachers. In order to meet educational challenges of the future, gain skill in the effective use of such equipment and techniques. They will never replace the teacher. Their effective use depends upon the creative imagination and ingenuity of the teacher in providing rich learning experiences for his pupils.

QUESTIONS FOR YOUR CONSIDERATION

1. Why is a knowledge of psychology so important for teachers?

2. What are some of the psychological and emotional needs of pupils and how can a teacher best meet these needs?

3. What are some of the social needs of pupils and what can the school do in order to meet these needs?

4. To what extent are schools helping boys and girls develop good human relationships? What are some of the effective means that are being used?

5. Account for the fact that many pupils lose interest in school and drop out before graduating. How has the school failed to fulfill its function in regard to these pupils?

6. What criteria will you use in selecting activities or learning experiences in which your pupils will engage?

7. What are some of the campus activities in which you can gain further skill in group participation and leadership?

8. Why should Skinner feel that "the present educational process is one on which methods of imparting knowledge have changed scarcely at all?"

9. How does the use of such instructional devices as teaching machines and television affect the role of the teacher? What new skills will be required of you? How may these devices affect organization for classroom instruction?

ACTIVITIES FOR YOU TO PURSUE

1. Observe closely some of the boys and girls with whom you come in contact during the week. What can you find out about their interests, their needs, and their abilities?

2. Accompany a youngster you know well to a special event—a movie, a football game, church. Study his reactions to the various happenings. How does he identify himself with the things he sees? What does he talk about after the event? Does the presence of you as an adult seem to make a difference? Compare your knowledge of this child with descriptions which you may find in your reading.

3. Keep an anecdotal record of the successive activities and the conversation of a child whom you are able to observe unnoticed for a period of an hour or two. Try to be as objective as possible.

4. Visit an elementary classroom where children draw and paint freely. Study their art work. Is there splash and verve, or just timid daubs here and there? What differences can you see among children just from observing what they put on paper? Ask them to tell you the story of what they have painted.

5. Study the group process at work in the next group in which you participate. Who is the leader? What qualities does he exhibit? Is he a democratic or an autocratic leader? How does he motivate the group to work?

6. Visit an unattractive classroom in your community. Plan ways in which you could create a happy learning environment there.

7. Work in a leadership capacity with a group of boys and girls either in school or out. Help them initiate plans for an activity, encourage them to carry out their plans, and lead them to evaluate their experience. Analyze carefully your own part in the planning process.

8. Visit often in a classroom where the teacher seems to function in the manner described in the preceding chapter. Note how teacher-pupil planning takes place and how the basic needs of the pupils are being met.

9. Observe classroom situations in which team teaching, teaching machines, and television are being used very effectively. List the specific abilities you will need in order to use these devices effectively.

8
PROFESSIONAL ORGANIZATIONS AND PUBLICATIONS

What constitutes a profession? To what extent is teaching a profession? In what ways does it differ from other occupations? What different organizations exist in the teaching profession? In what ways may these organizations benefit you? Through what organizations can you contribute most to the profession?

It is only as individual teachers give serious consideration to questions such as these that the teaching profession can continue to advance and to assume its deserved role among the great professions.

THE TEACHING PROFESSION

When you become a teacher you become a member of a profession with responsibilities for improving the status of that chosen profession. As a professional person you may find it difficult at times to differentiate among your professional services, your personal life, and your activities within the profession itself. Perhaps this sense of dedication is one of the distinguishing characteristics of a professional person. At any rate, in this chapter you are asked to think carefully about your role in the profession and its organizations.

Characteristics of a Profession. How would you define a profession? Many scholars and many scholarly groups have given careful thought to formulating an answer to this question. The professions have studied themselves in attempts to enlighten their own members and the public concerning the characteristics and role of a profession. Although these various statements have differed in many details, there seems to be consensus concerning some of the major practices descriptive of a profession.

A profession requires that its members:

1. Commit themselves to the ideal of service to mankind rather than to personal gain.
2. Undergo relatively long periods of preparation, meet established qualifications for admission or certification, and keep up-to-date through in-service growth.
3. Establish and adhere to codes of ethics regarding membership and practice.
4. Form organizations to improve the profession, its services, and the economic well-being of its members.

A profession is further described as demanding intellectual activity, based on a body of specialized knowledge accorded high status by the public, providing opportunities for advancement and specialization, and encouraging a life career and permanent membership on the part of its members.

Certainly there are differences among the requirements and characteristics of manual labor, skilled labor, the subprofessions, and the professions. However, in many cases it is not a simple task to differentiate between the subprofessions and the professions. The professions of medicine, law and the ministry have long been recognized. But what of the additional groups that have sought recognition as professions—nurses, teachers, engineers, journalists, and many others? Although it is obvious that at present teaching is considered a profession, it is only fair to point out that this status is challenged by many persons.

Status of Teaching as a Profession.   Teaching is actually one of the oldest professions. It is true that the requirements for entrance into the teaching profession have not always been as high as those for some other professions. It is also true that in the profession of teaching there are some members who have not lived up to desirable levels of conduct and service. Furthermore, many persons have used teaching as a stepping-stone to other professions. Finally, there are major differences between teaching and the other professions. However, these aspects of teaching and teachers do not deny to teaching its status as a profession.

In what ways does teaching differ from other professions? These differences lies in the control, support, size, and in the ratio of the sexes [73: 66–70]. The legal control of education belongs to the public, not to the profession itself. Thus, the members of the teaching profession must work constantly to inform the public and must participate extensively in public concerns. Public school teachers are paid from tax money, which presents certain limitations and problems not inherent in other professions.

The need for large numbers of teachers affects the policies of recruitment and selectivity within the profession, and the fact that women outnumber men in the teaching profession differentiates it sharply from law, medicine, and the ministry. Nevertheless, these differences should not be considered to prevent teaching from being accorded professional status.

What are the conditions and characteristics which support teaching as a profession? Among them are the following:

1. Most teachers are working for the sake of giving service to mankind rather than for great personal gain. Naturally there are some people employed in our schools, as is true in any other profession, who work against the progress of teaching as a profession. Consider the tremendous personal differences to be found among nearly a million and a half teachers, the wide variations among our thousands of school districts, the meager resources of some communities, and the relative newness of education as a broad-scale organized enterprise in America. When these factors are considered, the fact that there are "problem members" in the profession can be understood. Such conditions represent a challenge which must be taken up by teacher-education institutions and by leadership in the public schools at every level. The actions of a few should not be allowed to detract unduly from the ideals of service held by the profession.

2. Teachers are required by law to complete certain requirements for certification and entrance into the profession.

3. Teaching requires careful skills and understandings.

4. Teachers have "trade journals" to help keep them up to date.

5. They attend summer school, extension classes, workshops, conventions, and institutes. Then engage in a wide variety of in-service education activities.

6. Teachers have their standards and ethics operating through the National Education Association and through state and local departments of education. Teachers' rights are defended by these organizations, with the National Education Association as a body of ultimate appeal.

Through the help of teachers like yourself the profession of teaching can be further strengthened as it strives to accomplish the tasks of education and as it attempts to exemplify to an even greater extent the characteristics of a profession.

PROFESSIONAL ORGANIZATIONS

Many years and the efforts of countless people have been involved in the development of the teaching profession in America. During this time the profession has developed a system of purposes, refined its procedures, set standards relating to training, and reduced to a definite code certain important elements in the behavior of its members.

One of the important conditions of professionalism is membership in various organizations. By sharing ideas and experiences with others through these organizations, teachers can improve the general level of their performance and exert their collective influence in bringing about more desirable conditions for work. A great portion of the improvements in education have resulted from the work of these organizations. In this world of special-interest groups, there is a very real need for teacher organizations.

In considering the services and characteristics of professional organizations, the Educational Policies Commission of the National Education Association, itself a professional organization, has suggested that they should aim to do the following [117:27–54]:

1. Encourage members to cherish education's distinctive knowledge and insight
2. Aid in disseminating information and understanding throughout the profession
3. Promote research, support research, encourage research by members, and foster the application of research findings
4. Help improve teacher education
5. Safeguard teachers' basic freedoms
6. Meet members' personal needs
7. Improve teaching loads and school environment
8. Seek adequate salary provisions
9. Promote professional ethics
10. Inform the public
11. Take positions on issues affecting education
12. Cooperate in counseling the public
13. Influence public policy
14. Cooperate with interested lay groups

Since the organizations for teachers are considerable in number and vary in scope of membership, purpose, and procedure, a few of the more important ones should be discussed.

Local Education Association. Local associations provide opportunities for teachers to consider matters that are of concern to the immediate community and teacher group. Through the association, teachers are able to participate in the formulation of local school policies, keep the community informed regarding educational matters, and influence the policies of their state and national associations. Local groups usually are represented in their respective state associations and participate in the election of state-association officials.

Local teacher organizations differ considerably in form. Generally they include all the school personnel within a school system. The number as well as the nature of the meetings held each year varies. Frequently, the organizations are very strong in nature, and the members are vitally concerned with problems common to the group. Various subgroups may be working on such problems as reporting to parents, textbook selection, curriculum reorganization, and evaluation. Participation in these groups usually provides an excellent opportunity for a teacher to be professionally stimulated and to work constructively with his colleagues.

State Education Association. Educational workers are also organized at the state level. Membership in a state group is larger than that in the local groups. Dues are required. A journal is published, usually monthly, to keep teachers in the state informed on problems, trends, and events in education. Meetings of the total membership are arranged usually once or twice a year. Public schools may be dismissed for about two days, so that public school educators may attend the state convention. The state educational meetings generally are held in the capital city, and, if the state is large, in selected regional cities. Participation of many teachers and administrators is required in order to make these conventions successful and to carry on the activities of the association throughout the year. The typical state education association has a large and competent central office and staff, a comprehensive organizational plan, a constitution, and a set of bylaws. Often significant experimentation and research are centered there, and the results are communicated to the entire professional body. State teacher associations frequently know of important job opportunities within the state, and some provide placement services. Some state associations also provide for members a program of term life insurance at rates lower than normally available to an individual.

Most state organizations provide legal protection for individual teacher members against unfair or unjust practices which may arise in local situations. Few individual teachers would be able to wield much influence or stand the expense involved if such a problem should need to be carried far in the courts. It is comforting for teachers to know that there is an organization ready and able to fight for their cause.

Since the central legal responsibility for education rests with the separate states in America, the state organization usually sets minimum standards for teacher certification, school facilities, instructional programs, and the like. Some of the most significant laws relating to education in the

State and national education association meetings further the development of various aspects of professional education. At these meetings teachers and administrators have an opportunity to exchange information in small groups . . . to hear outstanding educators such as Dr. James B. Conant . . . to visit exhibits and demonstrations . . . and to attend sessions dealing with their special interests.

several states are created and promoted by the state education associations. The securing of favorable legislation and the improving of conditions in the schools are primary functions of state education associations. They warrant your enthusiastic support.

National Education Association. Medical men have the American Medical Association to represent them. Lawyers have the American Bar Association. Teachers have the National Education Association, usually referred to as the NEA, which is the oldest teacher organization in the United States. It began in 1857 when 43 educational leaders from 12 states and the District of Columbia met in Philadelphia to establish the

National Teachers Association for the purpose of elevating the character and advancing the interests of the teaching profession and promoting the cause of popular education. From 1870 to 1907 the organization was known as the National Education Association, and the present name was adopted in 1907 when the association was chartered by the Congress of the United States.

The association grew slowly at first. After World War I, teachers sought a more active role in the national organization. This was achieved through a reorganization of the association, whose control was then vested in a representative assembly made up of elected delegates from state and local teacher organizations that held membership in the NEA. At about the same time, a building in Washington, D.C., was secured to house the national headquarters. The NEA has grown in membership and influence to such a point that it approaches the status of being the official spokesman of the public school people of America. At least half of the teachers in the United States belong to the NEA. By 1961, the association was made up of more than three quarters of a million members; and through affiliation of the local, state, and territorial associations, the NEA probably represented 1,500,000 teachers [98:3].

A recent change in the membership qualifications provided that after August 31, 1964, eligibility for membership in the NEA would include an earned bachelor's degree or a higher degree [98:30].

The annual dues for membership are only $10, payment of which permits you to attend the annual meeting, to call upon various divisions for assistance and services, and to participate in a term life insurance program at substantial savings on premiums. Life membership is available for a cash payment of $225 or $25 per year for 10 consecutive years. In addition to the benefits described above, your membership also includes a subscription to the *National Education Association Journal*. The wide variety of articles published in the *Journal* helps teachers to keep abreast of recent developments in school programs and educational thought.

The services performed by the NEA are of tremendous variety and scope, but in order to gain some understanding of the total program and activities these services can be listed under the following broad categories: professional growth, public relations, defense of the teaching profession, research, professional standards, teacher welfare, Federal relations, curriculum and instructional development, international education, selective teacher recruitment, and publications [156:118–125].

In its continuous efforts to elevate the standards of the teaching profession, the NEA provides services to local associations as well as to individual teachers. These services include various publications, consultative services, conferences, a clearinghouse for ideas, and special materials to local committee chairmen. An example of such service is that of the Research Division of the NEA. This division renders a real service to teachers, associations, and government officials by collecting and publishing nationwide data on such problems as teacher load, salaries, tenure, certification, retirement, finance, legislation, welfare, and status. These data have been of much help to teachers and teacher associations in appraising the status of local conditions in comparison with the status in the United States as a whole.

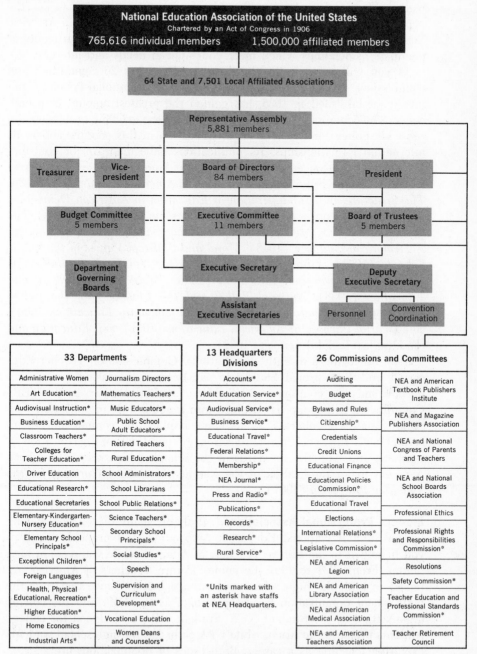

National Education Association of the United States
Chartered by an Act of Congress in 1906
765,616 individual members   1,500,000 affiliated members

64 State and 7,501 Local Affiliated Associations

Representative Assembly
5,881 members

Treasurer   Vice-president   Board of Directors 84 members   President

Budget Committee 5 members   Executive Committee 11 members   Board of Trustees 5 members

Department Governing Boards   Executive Secretary   Deputy Executive Secretary

Assistant Executive Secretaries   Personnel   Convention Coordination

33 Departments		13 Headquarters Divisions	26 Commissions and Committees	
Administrative Women	Journalism Directors	Accounts*	Auditing	NEA and American Textbook Publishers Institute
Art Education*	Mathematics Teachers*	Adult Education Service*	Budget	
Audiovisual Instruction*	Music Educators*	Audiovisual Service*	Bylaws and Rules	NEA and Magazine Publishers Association
Business Education*	Public School Adult Educators*	Business Service*	Citizenship*	
Classroom Teachers*		Educational Travel*	Credentials	NEA and National Congress of Parents and Teachers
Colleges for Teacher Education*	Retired Teachers	Federal Relations*	Credit Unions	
	Rural Education*	Membership*	Educational Finance	
Driver Education	School Administrators*	NEA Journal*	Educational Policies Commission*	NEA and National School Boards Association
Educational Research*	School Librarians	Press and Radio*		
Educational Secretaries	School Public Relations*	Publications*	Educational Travel	
Elementary-Kindergarten-Nursery Education*	Science Teachers*	Records*	Elections	Professional Ethics
Elementary School Principals*	Secondary School Principals*	Research*	International Relations*	Professional Rights and Responsibilities Commission*
		Rural Service*	Legislative Commission*	
Exceptional Children*	Social Studies*		NEA and American Legion	Resolutions
Foreign Languages	Speech			Safety Commission*
Health, Physical Educational, Recreation*	Supervision and Curriculum Development*	*Units marked with an asterisk have staffs at NEA Headquarters.	NEA and American Library Association	
Higher Education*				Teacher Education and Professional Standards Commission*
Home Economics	Vocational Education		NEA and American Medical Association	
Industrial Arts*	Women Deans and Counselors*		NEA and American Teachers Association	Teacher Retirement Council

Figure 36.   Organizational chart of the National Education Association. The National Education Association is the only organization that represents or has the possibility of representing the great body of teachers in the United States. (*Source:* National Education Association.)

As may be noted in the organizational diagram, Figure 36, there are now 33 different departments and associations within the NEA. Each one serves a particular level or other special concern of its members. As a responsible member of a significant profession, you will want to join the parent body and promote the work of improving education in America. You also should consider joining one or more of those departments or members associations which meet your special needs and interests.

As you will note on the diagram, the NEA has 26 committees and commissions. Of the commissions, perhaps the Educational Policies Commission, established in 1935, has gained the greatest amount of prominence. The commission considers issues facing the teaching profession and proposes policy for the conduct of education in this country and in its international relationships. Its publications have made major contributions to thinking on educational problems. Among these are the following: *The Unique Functions of Education in American Democracy* (1937), *The Structure and Administration of Education in American Democracy* (1938), *The Purposes of Education in American Democracy* (1938), *The Education of Free Men in American Democracy* (1941), *Education for All American Children* (1948), *Moral and Spiritual Values in the Public Schools* (1951), *Education for All American Youth: A Further Look* (1952), *Manpower and Education* (1956), *Mass Communication and Education* (1958), *National Policy and the Financing of the Public Schools* (1959), *Contemporary Issues in Elementary Education* (1960), *The Central Purpose of American Education* (1961), and *Education and the Disadvantaged American* (1962).

Established more recently, the National Commission on Teacher Education and Professional Standards has become increasingly more important since its creation in 1946. More familiarly known as the TEPS Commission, this group has evolved into a nationwide organization with parallel state commissions. As its name implies, the commission is concerned with the recruitment, selection, preparation, and certification of teachers, and with the standards of the schools which prepare teachers. A recent major publication of the commission is *New Horizons for the Teaching Profession* (1961).

Student Professional Associations.   Probably many of you now belong to the Student National Education Association, and probably many of you belonged to the Future Teachers of America while you were in high school. From 1937 to 1957 the name "Future Teachers of America" referred to both the high school and college groups. Since that time the high school organization has been known as the FTA and the college organization as the Student NEA. Student NEA is designed for college students preparing to teach, while FTA clubs are for high school students exploring teaching as a career. Both types of organizations are assisted in their work by the National Commission on Teacher Education and Professional Standards of the NEA.

Any student who is enrolled in a teacher-education program in a properly accredited college or university may become a student member of the NEA, provided he joins through a chartered chapter [157:8]. Membership in the Student NEA carries with it enrollment in the NEA and in the respective state teacher association in which your college or university is located. Members also receive the *National Education Association Journal* and the journal of the state education association. In addition, student members are eligible to participate in the life insurance program of the NEA.

You may gain valuable experiences from your membership in the Student National Education Association. Here students and faculty members are viewing an exhibit on professional opportunities and requirements in education. (*Photograph from the Audiovisual Center, Indiana University.*)

The Student NEA provides its members with opportunities in the following areas [157:8]:

(1) Personal and professional growth; (2) development of leadership skills: (3) understanding of the history, ethics, and programs at state and national levels; and (4) participation in professional activities at local, state, and national levels.

As an organization, the Student NEA should deepen the interest of capable students in teaching as a career; encourage the careful selection and guidance of persons admitted to teacher education programs; and, through higher standards of preparation and the dissemination of information, contribute to a reasonable balance in teacher supply and demand.

The Student Education Association chapter on your campus offers you many opportunities to participate in professional activities and to begin to assume the responsibilities of your chosen profession. A record of your membership and participation can be an important part of your placement credentials.

Perhaps some of you may become the faculty sponsors or advisers to the FTA in the high school in which you begin your teaching. If so, you will have an opportunity to encourage the finest boys and girls in school to enter the teaching profession. And in this capacity you will have close association with the local, state, and national professional units, and have an opportunity to become a leader in your profession.

The official purposes of the FTA are as follows [98:93]:

FTA seeks to enable its members (a) to study and to identify the qualities, traits, and aptitudes which are basic or related to successful teaching; (b) to acquire an understanding of the history and development of our public schools and their purposes and objectives and an appreciation of the contributions they have made to our democratic society; (c) to secure accurate information on vocational opportunities in education and the special competencies required, to aid in self-evaluation; and (d) to participate in prevocational activities which are both exploratory and developmental in nature.

FTA seeks to enable the profession: (a) to develop selective recruitment programs to identify capable candidates for teaching and to motivate them to choose appropriate fields of preparation; (b) to offer potential teachers appropriate experiences to help them develop readiness for college programs of teacher education; and (c) to achieve and maintain a balanced supply of qualified teachers.

American Federation of Teachers.   Another organization with which you should be acquainted is the American Federation of Teachers, an affiliate of the American Federation of Labor-Congress of Industrial Organization, with its national office in Chicago. The AFT originated in 1916 and, until the merger of AFL and the CIO in 1955, was affiliated with the AFL. After considerable difficulty in getting started, it has experienced an appreciable increase in membership in the past 15 years, especially in some of our biggest cities. The total membership exceeds 62,000 in over 460 local organizations. In Chicago, for example, 8,400 teachers, or nearly 55 per cent of the total, are members of the AFT. The official journal of the AFT is *The American Teacher*. The chief objectives of the federation include improving the educational situation for the nation as a whole, with special emphasis on securing money for schools, better pay and working conditions for teachers, and an improved and more democratic education for all youngsters. More specifically, the AFT has vigorously promoted integration within the schools, supporting the idea of equal educational opportunities for all. It has opposed any form of a merit-rating salary plan as educationally unsound. Although affiliated with the AFL-CIO, the AFT is a legal entity in its own right. It need not join the AFL-CIO in any specific action.

Without question, organized labor has been a staunch friend of education in America. On the other hand, there are many persons who consider it unwise for teachers to join forces with labor. They insist that there is a distinct difference between the public service rendered by teachers and the work for pay rendered by labor. They have grave fears of becoming involved in broad labor strikes and of being forced to join the union. They do not favor collective bargaining as does the AFT. They are not impressed by the fact that membership in the AFT is voluntary for each teacher and that teacher union strikes (really nonstriking violations) have been infrequent—in fact, they have been far less in number than the strikes conducted by nonunion local teacher organizations. Those who oppose the teachers' union feel that it produces needless division of the ranks. There is a broad, national professional organization in the NEA.

If teachers lend their full support to that body—in time, energy, and money—they may achieve such solidarity and influence in this organization as medical doctors or lawyers enjoy in theirs.

International Educational Organizations.   As the nations of the world grow closer together, educators find that they have many common interests. In the first place it is the desire of the free world to have peace and security. The best way to ensure this peace and security is through the development of international understanding, which is a crucial task confronting teachers throughout the world. In the second place, because of the increasing relatedness of nations today, the welfare of the teachers in any nation becomes the concern of teachers in all other nations. For these reasons efforts have been made to develop an organization for the educators of all nations.

The World Confederation of Organizations of the Teaching Profession was established in 1952 as a result of a merger of various international organizations, including the World Organization of the Teaching Profession which originally had been founded in 1946 at the invitation of the National Education Association. The confederation seeks "to foster a conception of education directed toward the promotion of international understanding and good will, with a view to safeguarding peace and freedom and respect for human dignity; to improve teaching methods, educational organization, and the academic and professional training of teachers so as to equip them better to serve the interests of youth; to defend the rights and the material and moral interests of the teaching profession; to promote closer relationships between teachers in the different countries" [98:309].

There are more than 100 national member associations in the WCOTP. Representatives of these member associations meet annually to consider a theme such as the following: Education for Teaching, The Status of the Teaching Profession, Public Support for Education, Teaching Mutual Appreciation of Eastern and Western Cultural Values, Child Health, and the School and Education for Responsibility. WCOTP activities include leadership training seminars, research studies, and an extensive multilingual information program. In addition to its permanent committees for Asia, Africa, and the Americas, the WCOTP maintains committees in such fields as adult education, rural education, education for handicapped children, educational journalism, and technical and vocational education [23:24–25].

Although not all nations belong to the WCOTP, progress is being made in bringing about common understanding, in resolving prejudices, and in opening up the channels of communication by means of which teachers throughout the world become better informed about educational needs, interests, and problems. The WCOTP holds great potentialities for improving the status of the teaching profession internationally and, by greater universal educational opportunities, for promoting world understanding and peace.

An American **UNESCO** technician demonstrates to a Pakistanian the operation of an instrument used in the study of artificial rain making. Such cooperation between individuals can improve the welfare of nations. (*Photograph from the United Nations.*)

UNESCO (United Nations Educational, Scientific, and Cultural Organization) was created in 1945 by the United Nations. According to the constitution of UNESCO, its purpose is "to contribute to peace and security by promoting collaboration among the nations through education, science, and culture in order to further universal respect for justice, for the rule of law and for the human rights and fundamental freedoms which are affirmed for the peoples of the world, without distinction of race, sex, language or religion, by the charter of the United Nations." Each year, delegates from countries that belong to the United Nations convene in order to share their ideas, to pool their thinking, and to develop plans for bringing about mutual understanding among the peoples of the world.

Within the framework of these purposes, UNESCO has engaged in many different types of activities. Those most closely related to education have included the organizing of educational missions to assist underdeveloped countries, the dissemination of educational materials, the holding of international conferences and seminars, the planning of programs of fundamental education to combat illiteracy, the promotion of international understanding, and the carrying on of research in world educational problems. An example of the last type of activity has been the *World Survey of Education*. The first volume of this extensive study, an over-all view of education in the world, was published in 1955; and the second volume, devoted to primary education, in 1958. The third and fourth volumes, devoted to secondary education and higher education, respectively, are scheduled for publication at three-year intervals.

In essence, the United Nations Educational, Scientific, and Cultural Organization attempts to further world peace by encouraging free interchange of ideas and of cultural and scientific achievements; by removing social, religious, and racial tensions; and by improving and expanding education.

Other Education Associations.   The *Education Directory*, issued regularly each year by the U.S. Office of Education, lists many national, regional, and state educational associations in addition to the few that have already been discussed. A good share of these are designed to meet the needs of various specialized groups of educators. Some of them are departments of the NEA, but many others are not.

If you teach in an elementary school, you may wish to become a member of an association such as the Association for Childhood Educational International (ACEI), which is "concerned with children 2–12"; the Department of Kindergarten–Primary Education of the NEA; or the state, regional, or national association in a subject area in which you are especially interested. If you teach in a junior or senior high school, each subject area has its own national association, such as the National Council for the Social Studies, the National Council of the Teachers of English, the National Council of the Teachers of Mathematics, and many others.

Looking further into the future, some of you may wish to become a curriculum supervisor or consultant. In that case you will certainly want to be affiliated with the national association in your subject area and perhaps with the Association for Supervision and Curriculum Development (ASCD). Some of you may become principals or superintendents. If so, in addition to the associations already mentioned, you will want to become a member of the Department of Elementary School Principals (DESP); the National Association of Secondary School Principals (NASSP); or the American Association of School Administrators (AASA).

As some of you advance in graduate work, as your interests become more highly developed, or as you move into college or university teaching, you may wish to become a member of a more specialized group, such as the National Society for the Study of Education, the John Dewey Society, the American Educational Research Association, or the American Association of University Professors.

The associations mentioned in this section are only a few of those in the field of education. The important point is that, regardless of your position and interest, there is a professional association composed of other persons with like positions and interests with which you can affiliate. Furthermore, it is the journals and yearbooks of these associations that provide much of the professional literature in education.

Honorary Educational Associations.   While you are in college you may want to work toward such professional and honorary groups as Pi Lambda Theta (for women) and Phi Delta Kappa (for men), or Kappa Delta Pi (for both men and women).

Pi Lambda Theta is open to undergraduate and graduate women students and women faculty members who meet the necessary qualifications. General qualifications include evidence of high professional standards, qualities of leadership, and ability to live and work with others. In addition, there are more specific requirements for both student and faculty eligibility for membership. For example:

The purpose of Pi Lambda Theta is to maintain the highest standards of scholarship and professional preparation and to foster professional spirit and fellowship by: working actively to further the cause of democratic education; cooperating in the solution of problems which interpenetrate various fields of knowledge; encouraging intercultural understanding; striving for a clear understanding of local, state, national, and international problems and stimulating active participation in their solution; encouraging graduate work and stimulating research [110:5].

Membership in Phi Delta Kappa is by chapter invitation to male graduate or undergraduate students who have completed at least 90 semester hours toward the baccalaureate degree, who give promise of success in a professional career in education, and who will contribute to the purposes of Phi Delta Kappa. Additional requirements include 15 semester hours of courses in education, scholarship acceptable for admission to candidacy for a graduate degree, and commitment to a life career in educational service.

The chief purpose of Phi Delta Kappa shall be to promote free public education as an essential to the development and maintenance of a democracy, through the continuing interpretation of the ideals of research, service and leadership. It shall be the purpose of Phi Delta Kappa to translate these ideals into a program of action appropriate to the needs of public education [76:n.p.].

Membership dues in the organization includes a subscription to the *Phi Delta Kappan*, which is published monthly, October through June of each year. This journal carries many articles, reviews, and features of special interest to educators.

Kappa Delta Pi is open to both men and women and is composed of outstanding junior and senior undergraduates, graduate students, and faculty members. In addition to the functions commonly performed by honorary educational organizations, Kappa Delta Pi has contributed to the general cause of education by issuing several significant publications. These publications include *The Educational Forum, The Kappa Delta Pi Lecture Series,* and the *Kappa Delta Pi Research Publications.*

These honorary educational associations exert positive influences upon the profession. You doubtless will be bountifully rewarded if you should gain membership to any one of them and join forces toward a worthy cause.

Parent-Teachers Association.   An opportunity for parents and teachers to work together effectively on both local and national levels is provided through the Parent-Teachers Association. Teachers are usually expected to take an active part in this association in those communities where it is established. All official local PTA groups are members of the National Congress of Parents and Teachers. The objects of this group of more than 12 million members are as follows [102:ii]:

To promote the welfare of children and youth in home, school, church, and community.
To raise the standards of home life.
To secure adequate laws for the care and protection of children and youth.

To bring into closer relation the home and the school, that parents and teachers may cooperate intelligently in the training of the child.

To develop between educators and the general public such united efforts as will secure for every child the highest advantages in physical, mental, social, and spiritual education.

In communities the PTA takes its work seriously, studies its problems realistically, and wields tremendous power in shaping trends toward better schooling. Unfortunately, some teachers feel that PTA work requires too much of their time. Some administrators feel that it provides another unnecessary opportunity for people to meddle in school affairs.

In most PTA groups, mothers far exceed fathers in number. Many PTAs fail to reach those parents in the community when response would be most advantageous to themselves, to their children, and to the improvement of the instructional program in school. These are typical problems which, through planning, hard work, and cooperation on the part of parents and school people, have been largely solved in individual communities.

You will have noticed in the organizational diagram, Figure 36, that the National Education Association recognizes the value of the PTA through a joint committee called the NEA and National Congress of Parents and Teachers. *The PTA Magazine* has won the School Bell Award of the National School Public Relations Association for distinguished service in the interpretation of education.

A parent-teacher association is the most natural group imaginable where important common concerns exist, because both parties usually have the best interests of the children at heart. You will be fortunate to work in a community where the PTA is a live and going concern. If this is not the case, you will be faced with the challenge of helping to make it so.

Code of Ethics for the Teaching Profession.   Besides joining and working earnestly to promote the purposes of various professional organizations, every teacher is expected to conduct himself and manage his work affairs in such ways as are approved by the profession at large. Should you tutor your own pupils for pay? Should you leave a position suddenly in the middle of a semester? Is it legitimate to make political speeches favoring your party in classrooms? If your father is superintendent of schools back home, should you accept a position under his administration? The acceptable modes of behavior along these lines, and many others, are well established in professional codes of ethics. Medical doctors have such codes, lawyers have them, teachers also have them. These codes are not legal enactments. Sometimes they are not even written down. Nevertheless, they are definite and well understood by the great body of the profession. It behooves you as a prospective teacher to become well acquainted with the code of the teaching group.

The NEA has spent a great amount of time and effort in developing and revising a "Code of Ethics for the Teaching Profession" designed to be acceptable to all workers in education in all parts of the nation. The first national code of ethics for teachers was adopted by the NEA in 1929 and revised in 1941 and 1952. The last revision is presented here for your study [98:326–328]:

WE, THE MEMBERS of the National Education Association of the United States, hold these truths to be self-evident—

—that the primary purpose of education in the United States is to develop citizens who will safeguard, strengthen, and improve the democracy obtained thru a representative government;

—that the achievement of effective democracy in all aspects of American life and the maintenance of our national ideals depend upon making acceptable educational opportunities available to all;

—that the quality of education reflects the ideals, motives, preparation, and conduct of the members of the teaching profession;

—that whoever chooses teaching as a career assumes the obligation to conduct himself in accordance with the ideals of the profession.

As a guide for the teaching profession, the members of the National Education Association have adopted this code of professional ethics. Since all teachers should be members of a united profession, the basic principles herein enumerated apply to all persons engaged in the professional aspects of education—elementary, secondary, and collegiate.

First Principle: The primary obligation of the teaching profession is to guide children, youth, and adults in the pursuit of knowledge and skills, to prepare them in the ways of democracy, and to help them to become happy, useful, self-supporting citizens. The ultimate strength of the nation lies in the social responsibility, economic competence, and moral strength of the individual American.

In fulfilling the obligations of this first principal the teacher will—

1. Deal justly and impartially with students regardless of their physical, mental, emotional, political, economic, social, racial, or religious characteristics.

2. Recognize the differences among students and seek to meet their individual needs.

3. Encourage students to formulate and work for high individual goals in the development of their physical, intellectual, creative, and spiritual endowments.

4. Aid students to develop an understanding and appreciation not only of the opportunities and benefits of American democracy but also of their obligations to it.

5. Respect the right of every student to have confidential information about himself withheld except when its release is to authorized agencies or is required by law.

6. Accept no remuneration for tutoring except in accordance with approved policies of the governing board.

Second Principle: The members of the teaching profession share with parents the task of shaping each student's purposes and acts toward socially acceptable ends. The effectiveness of many methods of teaching is dependent upon cooperative relationships with the home.

In fulfilling the obligations of this second principle the teacher will—

1. Respect the basic responsibility of parents for their children.

2. Seek to establish friendly and cooperative relationships with the home.

3. Help to increase the student's confidence in his own home and avoid disparaging remarks which might undermine that confidence.

4. Provide parents with information that will serve the best interests of their children, and be discreet with information received from parents.

5. Keep parents informed about the progress of their children as interpreted in terms of the purposes of the school.

Third Principle: The teaching profession occupies a position of public trust involving not only the individual teacher's personal conduct, but also the interaction of the school and the community. Education is most effective when these many relationships operate in a friendly, cooperative, and constructive manner.

In fulfilling the obligations of this third principle the teacher will—

1. Adhere to any reasonable pattern of behavior accepted by the community for professional persons.

2. Perform the duties of citizenship, and participate in community activities with due consideration for his obligations to his students, his family, and himself.

3. Discuss controversial issues from an objective point of view, thereby keeping his class free from partisan opinions.

4. Recognize that the public schools belong to the people of the community, encourage lay participation in shaping the purposes of the school, and strive to keep the public informed of the educational program which is being provided.

5. Respect the community in which he is employed and be loyal to the school system, community, state, and nation.

6. Work to improve education in the community and to strengthen the community's moral, spiritual, and intellectual life.

Fourth Principle: The members of the teaching profession have inescapable obligations with respect to employment. These obligations are nearly always shared employer-employee responsibilities based upon mutual respect and good faith.

In fulfilling the obligation of this fourth principle the teacher will—

1. Conduct professional business thru the proper channels.

2. Refrain from discussing confidential and official information with unauthorized persons.

3. Apply for employment on the basis of competence only, and avoid asking for a specific position known to be filled by another teacher.

4. Seek employment in a professional manner, avoiding such practices as the indiscriminate distribution of applications.

5. Refuse to accept a position when the vacancy has been created thru unprofessional activity or pending controversy over professional policy or the application of unjust personnel practices and procedures.

6. Adhere to the conditions of a contract until service thereunder has been performed, the contract has been terminated by mutual consent, or the contract has otherwise been legally terminated.

7. Give and expect due notice before a change of position is to be made.

8. Be fair in all recommendations that are given concerning the work of other teachers.

9. Accept no compensation from producers of instructional supplies when one's recommendations affect the local purchase or use of such teaching aids.

10. Engage in no gainful employment outside of his contract, where the employment affects adversely his professional status or impairs his standing with students, associates, and the community.

11. Cooperate in the development of school policies and assume one's professional obligations thereby incurred.

12. Accept one's obligation to the employing board for maintaining a professional level of service.

Fifth Principle: The teaching profession is distinguished from many other occupations by the uniqueness and quality of the professional relationships among all teachers. Community support and respect are influenced by the standards of teachers and their attitudes toward teaching and other teachers.

In fulfilling the obligations of this fifth principle the teacher will—

1. Deal with other members of the profession in the same manner as he himself wishes to be treated.

2. Stand by other teachers who have acted on his behalf and at his request.

3. Speak constructively of other teachers, but report honestly to responsible persons in matters involving the welfare of students, the school system, and the profession.

4. Maintain active membership in professional organizations and, thru participation, strive to attain the objectives that justify such organized groups.

5. Seek to make professional growth continuous by such procedures as study, research, travel, conferences, and attendance at professional meetings.

6. Make the teaching profession so attractive in ideals and practices that sincere and able young people will want to enter it.

Most states and even local schools and communities have established their own codes of ethics or have adopted the NEA code. It is a most worthwhile experience for the smaller local units to formulate such codes or to study established codes. The Professional Ethics Committee of the NEA publishes materials which serve as guides for the ethics committees of local associations in their activities and studies.

Appraising Your Professional Ethics.   Every teacher periodically should ask himself the question "How professional am I?" Rather than read the lengthy statement of a code of ethics, he may find the self-appraisal form titled "How Professional Am I?" which is located in the Resource Section for Part II, to be more helpful. Even though you are not actually teaching, you should find a number of the questions to be appropriate as you prepare for teaching. For example, do you speak proudly of the importance of education to society?

Not only will you be expected to live up to a professional code of ethics, but you will also be expected to promote the best interests of the profession on every possible occasion. If you are serious about your vocation, this will be the natural thing to do anyway. Teachers should be well informed about their schools, their pupils, and their patrons. They should be enthusiastic about their work and should talk and look and act as if they are. Feigned interest is easily detected and ill-advised. Neither is it sensible for a teacher to speak poorly of his profession and to complain about his lot continually without taking studied action to improve what needs to be improved, or without seeking what for him might be a happier situation in another line of work. If you want to be worthy of your profession, you will never lose an opportunity to tell its merits, its deep satisfactions, its real purposes. You will defend it against malicious gossip and distorted statements of all sorts. Yet you will not be blind to its shortcomings or to the whole range of its inadequacies. These, too, you should discuss constructively and professionally with your fellow workers and lay people so that a better understanding of problems may be achieved. Often it is because the heart of a problem goes unrecognized by a community that no action, or possibly the wrong action, is taken. Positive attitudes and wholesome public relations lead not only to better understanding of the significance of teachers and schools but to a realistic appraisal of the local educational situation, to mutual esteem and cooperation between school and lay people, and to improved conditions for living and learning. These things are worth planning for, working for, and so conducting our professional lives that they may soon come to pass.

SUMMARY

The advancement of teaching as a profession depends in great degree upon the professional organizations and their membership. It is probable that as an individual you can contribute most to your profession and your own welfare through professional organizations. Within the field of education there are professional organizations based on geography—local, state, regional, and national in scope. There are organizations based on types of duties—teaching, counseling, administration. There are organizations based on level of teaching—elementary, secondary, higher. There are organizations based on subject-matter specialties. And there are organizations that are comprehensive in nature and include all of these types. Choose your organizations carefully.

Teachers need to support one another and to work together cooperatively for the good of their schools and their pupils. Joining forces in professional organizations of various sorts, studying their purposes and procedures, and playing a responsible part in those groups is one way of accomplishing the necessary cooperation. This you will want to do at the local, state, and national levels. Your activities in these organizations and in all other professional affairs, whether in the school or not, should always conform to the rules and regulations set down in the code of ethics for the teaching profession. This is your professional responsibility to your pupils, to your fellow teachers, to your entire school community.

QUESTIONS FOR YOUR CONSIDERATION

1. What is meant by the statement that "education is the mother of all professions"?

2. How does teaching as a profession differ from other professions?

3. What are the chief differences between the NEA and the AFT with respect to policies, services, and potential contributions to the improvement of education in the United States?

4. Is it reasonable to expect a teacher to give some of his time to the profession itself? Would you accept a committee responsibility or an office?

5. Should teachers be required to join one or more professional organizations?

6. There are many opportunities today for teaching abroad. What values usually come to the teacher who participates in such a program? What special responsibilities does he have?

7. Why do you suppose the Parent-Teachers Association has usually been more successful at the elementary level than at the secondary level?

8. What procedures may the teaching profession ethically use in attempting to gain higher salaries and better working conditions?

9. What are the values of a code of ethics for you as a teacher?

10. Consider the teachers whom you have had. To what extent did they seem to be aware of a code of ethics? To what extent did they seem to practice the provisions of this code?

ACTIVITIES FOR YOU TO PURSUE

1. Attend one or more local and state teachers' meetings. Make a careful study of the problems discussed and the values gained by teachers as a result of these meetings.

2. Investigate your campus chapter of the Student National Education Association. Secure information concerning its major purposes and its program.

3. Visit the Future Teachers Association chapter of the local high school or arrange to talk with the sponsor about the activities of the group.

4. Study the NEA code of ethics. Arrange student presentations of specific problems or questions related to application of the code.

5. Arrange a panel to discuss the meaning and value of a professional code of ethics. If possible include on the panel a clergyman, a medical doctor, a lawyer, an engineer, and a school superintendent.

6. Through the use of the check list in the Resource Section of Part II, appraise one of your former teachers to determine how professional he was.

7. Watch the newspapers for a month for all NEA news releases. Try to classify the items as to types and purposes.

8. Study the *National Education Association Journal* and the publication of your state teachers association. Compare and contrast the contents and purposes of these publications.

9. Examine some of the publications of the various departments, divisions, and commissions of the NEA. How will they help you in your teaching?

10. Invite representatives of various honorary groups in the teaching profession to explain the purposes and programs of their organizations.

11. Carefully review the code of ethics for the teaching profession. Do you find any omissions or points with which you disagree?

RESOURCE SECTION FOR PART II

- Twenty Indicators of the Quality of Teaching

- How Well Are You Doing in Public Relations?

- How Professional Am I?

- Suggested Films, Filmstrips, and Recordings

- Suggested Readings

- Figure Credits

- **TWENTY INDICATORS OF THE QUALITY OF TEACHING**

	Indicating a high quality of teaching	Indicating a low quality of teaching
Work with individual pupils:		
Assignments	Varied for individuals	Uniform for all
Pupil-teacher relations	Friendly; personalized	Very formal or very flippant
Pupil-teacher conferences	Frequent, to help pupils	For disciplinary purposes only
Pupils' work	Carefully reviewed, promptly returned	Carelessly handled; errors not checked
Planning and Preparation:		
Daily continuity	Each day built on one before	Work unrelated from day to day
Teacher's knowledge	Well-informed teacher supplements books pupils use	Unable to answer simple questions
Lesson plans	Plans on blackboard or otherwise obvious	No evidence of plans
Advance arrangements	Necessary materials at hand	Necessary materials lacking
Use of teaching aids:		
Use of books	Pupils know how to use books	Pupils unacquainted with special features of books they use
Use of library tools	Pupils use effectively card catalogue, reference guides, other tools	Pupils unable to get information in the library on their own
Use of audio-visual aids	Aids carefully related to work of class	Little advance explanation or follow-up of aids used
Use of field trips	To introduce or supplement class study	Used as holiday from class
Involvement of pupils in varied learning experiences:		
Types of experiences	Many different types used	Experiences mostly of one type
Pupil-teacher planning	As their maturities permit, pupils help in planning	Pupil participation or reaction not sought
Responsibilities of pupils	To prepare their own work and to help class as a whole	Only to prepare own assignments
Techniques of motivation	Work made interesting and important to pupils	Threats and criticisms only
Active leadership of the teacher:		
Use of pupil leaders	To give leadership experiences under supervision	To rest the teacher
Use of play or entertainment experiences	To provide a balanced program under teacher guidance	Also to rest the teacher
Handling behavior problems	Disturbers promptly and consistently dealt with	Inconsistent leniency, harshness
Discussion	Genuine and general participation	Drags or dominated by a few

Source: William M. Alexander, *Are You a Good Teacher?*, Holt, Rinehart, & Winston, Inc., New York, 1959, p. 26.

• HOW WELL ARE YOU DOING IN PUBLIC RELATIONS?

Note: When you become a teacher you should check yourself periodically on this check list. You will be doing very well if you can answer "yes" to all the following questions:

Do you believe that public relations activities should foster lay participation in the educational program?   _____

Do you really enjoy talking and working with children?   _____

Do you really enjoy talking and working with adults?   _____

Are you genuinely proud to be a teacher?   _____

Do you believe that good public relations are your responsibility?   _____

Do you regularly visit your pupils' homes?   _____

Do you ever send newsletters home to parents?   _____

Do you ever send notes to parents concerning things other than problem behavior?   _____

Do you ever send home complimentary notes concerning your pupils who are not outstanding students?   _____

Do you encourage your pupils' parents to visit you and the school?   _____

Do you schedule regular conferences with parents?   _____

Do your contacts with critical parents tend to placate them rather than increase their irritation?   _____

Do you have a room-parent organization?   _____

Does your school have a parent-teacher organization?   _____

Do you regularly attend parent-teacher-organization meetings?   _____

Does your school foster parent participation in planning class work and activities?   _____

If so, do you personally take advantage of this policy to involve parents in your classroom planning activities?   _____

Do you ever enlist the help of parents in the performance of routine clerical tasks?   _____

Would you recognize the parents of most of your pupils if you met them on the street?   _____

Do you encourage your classes to invite laymen to share their experiences with the class?   _____

Do you make an effort to bring school matters of public interest to the attention of appropriate officials or news media?   _____

Do your classroom activities ever involve community problems and contacts with laymen?   _____

Do you willingly accept invitations to address groups of laymen, either on school matters or on other subjects?   _____

Do you take an active part in church, political, civic, or fraternal organizations in your community?   _____

Do your personal actions reflect credit upon your profession?   _____

Do your remarks in the community tend to present a constructive view of teaching and of your local school situation?   _____

Source: Glen E. Robinson and Evelyn S. Bianchi, "What Does PR Mean to the Teacher?", *National Education Association Journal*, vol. 48, no. 4, p. 14, National Education Association, Washington, April, 1959.

● HOW PROFESSIONAL AM I?

In using this instrument, indicate your self-appraisal on each item by placing a dot on the line to the right somewhere between "Low" and "High." When you have finished, connect the dots with straight lines.

	Low	High

I. Teacher-pupil relationships:
Do I—
1. Individualize pupils in my teaching?
2. Try to find out their capacities and abilities?
3. Refrain from the use of sarcasm?
4. Avoid embarrassing a child before the group?
5. Create an atmosphere of friendliness and helpfulness in the classroom?
6. Provide for democratic participation of pupils?
7. Try to improve my methods?

II. Teacher-teacher relationships:
Do I—
1. Recognize accomplishments of colleagues and tell them so?
2. Refrain from adverse criticism of a colleague's method or work except when requested by a school official for the welfare of the school?
3. Refrain from blaming the previous teacher for inadequate preparation of pupils?
4. Avoid letting jealousy of a good teacher adversely affect my personality development?
5. Avoid unkind gossip *of* and *among* colleagues?
6. Have a respectful attitude toward the subject matter and work of other fields?
7. Refrain from interfering between another teacher and pupil unless called upon for advice or assistance?
8. Avoid criticism of an associate before his students and before other teachers?

III. Teacher-administrator relationships:
Do I—
1. Talk things over with the administrator next above me?
2. Support the policies and programs of my principal and superintendent?
3. Avoid criticism of my principal and superintendent in public?

IV. Teacher-board of education relationships:
Do I—
1. Support the policies of my board?
2. Have the goodwill of my board as a person of professional integrity?
3. Respect my contract obligations?
4. When contemplating a change of position, make a formal request thru my superintendent to the board of education for release from my contract?
5. Give sufficient notice when asking for release from my contract?
6. Use my local professional organization to convey constructive suggestions and criticisms to the board thru my superintendent?

	Low	High

V. Teacher-public relationships:

Do I—

1. Remember that I am a public servant? _____
2. Try to exemplify to the public the best qualities of a teacher? _____
3. Participate in community activities that are not directly connected with my profession? _____
4. Contribute of my time and/or money to the various community drives? (Community Chest, and the like.) _____
5. Show by my life that education makes people better citizens and better neighbors? _____

VI. Teacher-profession relationships:

Do I—

1. Keep myself informed about best practices in my field? _____
2. Belong willingly to my professional organizations—local, state, national? _____
3. Contribute of my time and talents to my professional organizations? _____
4. Accept responsibility in my professional organizations? _____
5. Help to make possible a democratic approach to school administrative authorities thru teacher organization channels? _____
6. Speak proudly of the importance of the service of education to society? _____
7. Maintain my efficiency by reading, study, travel, or other means which keep me informed about my profession and the world in which I live? _____
8. Dignify my profession? _____
9. Encourage able and sincere individuals to enter the teaching profession? _____
10. Avoid using pressure on school officials to secure a position or to obtain favors? _____
11. Refuse compensation in the selection of textbooks or other supplies in the choice of which I have some influence? _____
12. Refrain from sending for sample copies of texts merely to build up my own library? _____
13. Refrain from accepting remuneration for tutoring pupils of my own classes? _____

Interpretation: If your profile is reasonably straight and close to "High," you are professional and your school and community should be very proud of you! If your profile zigzags and is close to "Low," then you probably need remedial exercises in ethical practices to improve your professional outlook. You should: (1) Concentrate on the ethical principles on which you rated yourself the lowest. (2) A few months from now take this test again, using a different color to draw the connecting lines. Check to see whether you have improved. "Live good ethics everyday; check your ethics profile at least twice a year!"

Source: Grace I. Kauffman, "How Professional Am I?", *National Education Association Journal,* vol. 39, no. 4, p. 286, National Education Association, Washington, April, 1950.

● SUGGESTED FILMS, FILMSTRIPS, AND RECORDINGS

The number in parentheses following each suggestion denotes the chapter for which it is best suited.

Films (16 mm)

Effective Learning in the Elementary School   (McGraw-Hill, 20 min). Shows a fifth-grade class planning their daily work with their teacher and their study of a unit on pioneer life. They decide what should be studied. The teacher gathers materials for pupil use. As the children work individually and in committees, attention is given to reading, writing, and arithmetic. A mural is constructed and maps and models are made. Folk songs and dances are practiced. As a culminating activity, a play is put on for the children's parents and teachers. (6)

Elementary School Teacher Education Series: Curriculum Based on Child Development   (McGraw-Hill, 12 min). Shows how a fourth-grade teacher plans a curriculum based on the developmental characteristics of her pupils. Reviews the behavioral patterns of eight- and nine-year-olds and shows materials for learning and classroom activities that are based on their interests, abilities, and group needs. Illustrates how the teacher encourages respect for other points of view in a discussion. (7)

Elementary School Teacher Education Series: Elementary School Children, Part II, Discovering Individual Differences   (McGraw-Hill, 25 min). Uses individual cases to show how an elementary school teacher systematically investigates the differences in backgrounds, activities, and needs of the pupils in her class. Outlines steps in investigation, including casual and controlled observations, consulting records, conferences with teachers, parent-teacher interviews, and staff conferences. Illustrates the need for resourcefulness and understanding in improving the education and social adjustment of pupils. (7)

Guiding the Growth of Children   (McGraw-Hill, 17 min). Shows how a teacher may work to understand each child and to guide him in his growth and development. Deals with seven problem cases and suggests possible ways of handling them. Shows a variety of techniques that a teacher may use but insists that underlying each technique is the teacher's genuine desire to help plus sympathetic, patient understanding. (7)

And Gladly Teach   (National Education Association, 28 min, color). Discusses teachers and "the company they keep." Points out the satisfactions and opportunities in teaching. (6)

Helping Teachers to Understand Children, Part I   (United World Films, 21 min). Points out a need for teachers to understand children and illustrates a variety of ways through which a knowledge of child behavior can be gained and interpreted. Presents a case study of one child and suggests the use of school records, interviews with teachers, the child's writing and art work, home environment, and anecdotal records as sources of information. (7)

Helping Teachers to Understand Children, Part II   (United World, 25 min). Summarizes a summer workshop in which six aspects of a child's life were studied—physical, affectional, cultural, peer group, self-developmental, and emotional. (7)

The Hickory Stick   (Mental Health Film Board, Inc., 25 min). Shows how a teacher maintains an orderly atmosphere for learning and at the same time helps her youngsters cope with their behavior and learning problems. She doesn't need a hickory stick to build character, with firmness and understanding she can help children control their feelings and accept authority. (6)

Learning and Growth   (Encyclopaedia Britannica Films, 11 min). Clarifies some of the principles which govern the learning process. Describes the possibilities and limitations of training infants from 24 to 48 weeks of age. Relationships between age, growth, and learning are indicated. Several learning problems are analyzed with reference to the effect of maturity. Points out laws which determine learning in older children. (7)

Learning is Searching   (New York University Film Library, 20 min). Shows how a third-grade class carries out its studies of a unit on man's use of tools. After defining the terms that will be used through direct experiences and field trips, the group sets up the problem it wants to consider. The pupils then search for solutions and try out tentative ones. In accomplishing this they have many direct experiences, prepare a textbook, and correlate these activities with other subject areas. Further activities involve projects based on previously discovered knowledge. Finally, culminating exhibits and presentations are made. (7)

Learning to Understand Children: Part I, A Diagnostic Approach (McGraw-Hill, 22 min). Presents a case study of Ada Adams, an emotionally maladjusted girl fifteen years of age. Ada's teacher diagnoses her difficulties by observation of her behavior, study of her previous record, personal interviews, home visits, and formulation of a hypothesis for remedial measures. (7)

Learning to Understand Children: Part II, A Remedial Program (McGraw-Hill, 25 min). Continues the case study of Ada Adams. An interest in art improves her self-confidence and interest in schoolwork, although some of her problems cannot be solved by the efforts of her teacher. (7)

Meeting Emotional Needs in Childhood (Vassar College, 32 min). Shows how the home and the school can meet children's emotional needs for security and independence. Pictures the behavior of emotionally maladjusted children and adults, and contrasts their home situations with good home situations. Also illustrates children's efforts to achieve independence. (7)

Practicing Democracy in the Classroom (Encyclopaedia Britannica Films, 21 min). Shows a teacher explaining to parents his method of teaching social studies. Depicts students selecting discussion topics with the guidance of the teacher, establishing goals, working as committees in contacting groups and leading citizens of the community, and reporting their experiences to the class. Explains that such teaching methods improve pupils' understanding of the meaning of democracy. (7)

Promoting Pupil Adjustment (McGraw-Hill, 20 min). Shows that a teacher must be alert and sensitive to student problems if classroom learning is to be effective, and illustrates ways by which teachers can facilitate pupil adjustment. Portrays a teacher's concern for the intellectual, social, and personal needs of her students and how she can cope with problems posed by individual differences. Follows the case of a student who feels unwanted until the teacher guides him to the point where he improves his adjustment. (7)

Providing for Individual Differences (Iowa State Teachers College, 23 min). Indicates the ways in which the classroom teacher can adjust the learning environment to meet the individual differences among her pupils. Depicts a college class discussing the methods of adjustment to individual differences that they have observed on visits to an elementary school and a high school. (7)

School (Office of Inter-American Affairs, 21 min). Shows one day's activities in an elementary school in an Ohio town. Pictures the janitor opening the building, children on their way to school, the first grade studying and playing, and a PTA meeting in the evening. (6)

The Second Classroom (National Education Association, 25 min). Shows the contribution educational television can make, presenting seven samples of programs currently available through this media. A TV producer acts as a narrator in introducing each of the seven selected programs, characteristic of educational television, which include second-grade music, biological science, teacher education, and an interview with a U. S. Senator. Concludes by reviewing the potential contributions of this form of educational media. (7)

Skippy and the Three R's (National Education Association, 30 min, color). Follows a first-grader from his first day at school, through his school experiences guided by the teacher and her teaching methods, to the point where he is learning through self-motivation. Shows the method of motivating the desire to read, write, and do number work and illustrates how a teacher utilizes the interests of pupils to encourage the learning of fundamental skills in schoolwork along with the social skills of living. (7)

Task Ahead   (Association Films, 19 min). Traces the growth of UNESCO during its first five years, and shows some of the work it sponsors. Includes book programs, international work camps, children's communities for cripples and orphans, training of Arab refugees, and the fundamental education program in Haiti. (8)

The Teacher   (Encyclopaedia Britannica Films, 13 min). The story of Julia Wittaker, a middle-aged fourth-grade teacher, is used to explain the role of the teacher in the community, her professional and personal life and contribution to the furthering of education after extensive preparation and study. (6)

Teacher as Observer and Guide   (Metropolitan School Study Council, 22 min). Six school situations illustrate the following concepts: guiding pupils to better ways of solving their problems, developing artistic talents, promoting the growth of character and citizenship, and providing needed assistance for slow learners. (6)

Teaching Machines and Programmed Learning   (United World, 28 min). Presents Drs. B. F. Skinner, A. A. Lumsdaine, and Robert Glasen as each in turn discusses teaching machines and programmed learning. (7)

We Plan Together   (Columbia University Teachers College, 21 min). Eleventh-grade pupils at the Horace Mann-Lincoln School, New York City, are shown planning cooperatively a core program. A new student tells of his experiences and changing viewpoint as he becomes a part of the program. (6)

Willie and the Mouse   (Teaching Film Custodians, 11 min). Contrasts Willie's father's education, in which facts were learned by repetition, with Willie's education, in which life situations are dramatized in the classroom. Various experiments with white mice demonstrate that some mice learn by sight, others by ear, and still others by touch. Shows how such experiments as these have caused individual differences to be recognized in the classroom. (7)

Filmstrips

Achieving Classroom Discipline   (Wayne University, 47 fr.). Shows some of the more important techniques which help produce desirable action patterns in children. (6)

Bringing the Community to the Classroom   (Wayne University, 45 fr.). Illustrates how teachers in various curriculum areas may bring community resources to the school so that instruction may be of maximum effectiveness. (6)

Community Resources Workshop for Teachers   (American Iron and Steel Institute, 59 fr., color). Explains how to plan and operate community resources workshops where teachers can learn to utilize their communities as laboratories for improved teaching. (6)

Core Curriculum Class in Action   (Wayne University, 50 fr.). Follows a typical ninth-grade core class from its first class meeting through various teacher-pupil planned activities and the final evaluation of the work done. (6)

Country School   (Curriculum Films, Inc., 26 fr., color). A typical day in the life of country children. Shows the advantages and disadvantages of the one-room country school. (6)

Grading Student Achievement: Some Basic Grading Principles   (Educational Filmstrips, 49 fr., color). Describes some basic principles of meaningful evaluation of student achievement, and suggests definitions for the grades of achievement. (6)

Grouping Students for Effective Learning   (Bel-Mort Films, 44 fr., color). Considers grouping students on the basis of age, ability grouping, and flexible grouping. (6)

How Pupils and Teachers Plan Together   (Wayne University, 48 fr.). Presents the details of teacher-pupil planning in a number of representative school situations. Intended primarily for teacher education purposes. (6)

Individual Differences   (McGraw-Hill, 49 fr.). The case study of a shy, slow child who is different from his classmates and from his older, socially adept brother. Points out that individual differences must be met in terms of individual interests and capabilities, that it is the job of the school to shape education to individual needs. (7)

Lesson Plan   (Jam Handy Organization, 60 fr.). Indicates that all lessons are more effective if they follow definite plans. Clearly stated aims tend to limit the scope and keep the teacher within the limits of the lesson. (6)

PTA at Work (Visual Education Consultants, 34 fr.). Explains many activities and functions of the Parent-Teachers Association that are unknown to new members. (8)
Story of UNESCO (Nestor Productions, 45 fr., color). Explains the ideals and concepts of UNESCO and opens the door to participation by students and others in its work. (8)
Teacher and Public Relations (National Education Association, 50 fr.). How to build an appreciation of the professional skills and achievements of teachers, why we teach what we teach, how we teach, homework assignments, reports to parents, public relations values of cocurricular activities making parents partners, and working with community groups. (6)
Teaching by Television (Basic Skills Films, 51 fr., color). Summarizes the research on what is known about teaching by television in relation to what television teaching can do, how to use television in the classroom, and how to teach over television. (7)
Teaching Machines (Basic Skills Films, 64 fr., color). Tells what teaching machines are, the types of teaching machines, what a teaching-machine program is like, and the educational role of teaching machines. (7)

Recordings
I Do Not Walk Alone (University of Illinois, 12 min). Walter E. Englund indicates the value of membership in the Minnesota Education Association. (8)
New Horizons in AV Education (National Tape Recording Project, 60 min). Mr. Mitchell tells of the unlimited possibilities of audio-visual aids in education in the future. (7)
New Methods of Reporting Pupil Progress (Recording, Educational Recording Service, 33⅓ rpm). Virgil M. Rogers, dean of education, Syracuse University, discusses ways in which improvements can be made in reporting to parents. (6)
Principles of Teaching and Learning of the Secondary School Level (Recording, Educational Recording Service, 33⅓ rpm). Hugh M. Shafer, professor of education, University of Pennsylvania, discusses effective ways of guiding the educational experiences of secondary school pupils. (7)
Teacher-Pupil Planning Techniques (Recording, Educational Recording Service, 33⅓ rpm). H. H. Giles, professor of education, New York University, discusses various techniques which teachers may use in effectively planning educational experiences with pupils. (6)

● SUGGESTED READINGS

The number in parentheses following each suggestion denotes the chapter for which it is best suited.

Anderson, Robert H.: "Team Teaching," *National Education Association Journal,* vol. 50, no. 3, pp. 52–54, National Education Association, Washington, March, 1961. Presents examples of practices in team teaching, and indicates research findings relative to these practices. (7)
Association for Supervision and Curriculum Development: *Perceiving, Behaving, Becoming: A New Focus for Education, 1962 Yearbook,* National Education Association, Washington, 1962. Discusses the psychological, social, and philosophical aspects of guiding the growth of pupils. (7)
Becker, Harold S.: "The Nature of a Profession," in Nelson B. Henry (ed.), *Education for the Professions,* The Sixty-first Yearbook of the National Society for the Study of Education, Part II, University of Chicago Press, Chicago, Ill., 1962, pp. 27–46. Indicates the symbols associated with a profession, and suggests ways in which teaching may be identified more clearly as a profession. (8)

Bent, Rudyard K., and Henry H. Kronenberg: *Principles of Secondary Education,* McGraw-Hill Book Company, Inc., New York, 1961. Presents a comprehensive view of the work of secondary school teachers. (6)

Bernard, Harold W.: *Mental Hygiene for Classroom Teachers,* 2d ed., McGraw-Hill Book Company, Inc., New York, 1961. Chapters 2 and 3 discuss the basic needs and tasks of children and adolescents. Chapter 6 is concerned with teachers understanding and helping pupils with problems. Chapter 20 discusses the teacher's responsibilities to pupils, administrators, fellow teachers, and to the community. (7)

Brown, Edwin John, and Arthur Thomas Phelps: *Managing the Classroom,* 2d ed., The Ronald Press Company, New York, 1961. Indicates the administrative role of the teacher in the classroom and in the school as a whole. (6)

Bruce, William F., and A. John Holden, Jr.: *The Teacher's Personal Development,* Holt, Rinehart and Winston, Inc., New York, 1957. Chapter 12 emphasizes self-awareness and interpersonal relations as a teacher works with learners. Chapters 13 and 14 emphasize self-awareness and interpersonal relations as a teacher cooperates with professional associates and as he lives in a community. (6) and (7)

"Building a Classroom Climate for Learning," *National Education Association Journal,* vol. 39, no. 4, pp. 34–38, National Education Association, Washington, December, 1961. Presents a number of excellent examples of good climates for learning. (7)

Callahan, Raymond E.: *An Introduction to Education in American Society,* 2d ed., Alfred A. Knopf, Inc., New York, 1960. Chapter 18 discusses the teaching profession in present-day America. (8)

Carr, William G.: "World-wide Co-operation Among Teachers," *National Education Association Journal,* vol. 50, no. 5, pp. 24–25, National Education Association, Washington, May, 1961. Discusses the founding, growth, and activities of the World Conference of Organizations of the Teaching Profession. (8)

Classroom Teachers Speak on Teaching as a Profession, National Education Association, Department of Classroom Teachers, Washington, 1960. Discusses the marks of a profession and how the status of teaching as a profession may be improved. (8)

Conditions of Work for Quality Teaching, National Education Association Department of Classroom Teachers, Washington, 1959. Consists of a guide for the continuous development of effective local policies in regard to the working conditions of teachers. (6)

Drummond, Harold D.: "Team Teaching: An Assessment," *Educational Leadership,* vol. 19, no. 3, pp. 160–165, National Education Association, Association of Supervision and Curriculum Development, Washington, December, 1961. Analyzes the advantages and disadvantages of team teaching. (7)

Ford, Edmund A.: *Rural Renaissance: Revitalizing Small High Schools,* U.S. Office of Education Bulletin 1961, no. 11, 1961. Discusses experimentation in small schools with the use of teaching machines, airborne television, teaching assistants, and team teaching. (7)

A Guide to Programmed Instructional Materials, U.S. Office of Education Bulletin OE 34015, 1962. Presents information on the various types of programmed materials available to teachers. (7)

Haskew, Laurence I., and Jonathan C. McLendon: *This is Teaching* (revised edition), Scott, Foresman and Company, Chicago, 1962. Chapter 3 provides helpful suggestions for studying and understanding learners. Chapter 6 discusses what teachers do in school. (7)

"How Long Is a School Day?" *Research Bulletin,* vol. 36, no. 1, pp. 8–10, National Education Association, Research Division, Washington, February, 1961. Presents the results of an extensive study of the length of day for teachers, number of class periods taught, and responsibilities for home-room periods, lunch periods, and study halls. (6)

Hutchinson, Joseph C.: *Modern Foreign Languages in High School: The Language Laboratory,* U.S. Office of Education Bulletin 1961, no. 23, 1961. Explains the various types of equipment being used in teaching foreign languages and gives helpful suggestions for the use of this equipment. (7)

Hymes, James L., Jr.: *Behavior and Misbehavior*, Prentice-Hall, Inc., Englewood Cliffs, N.J., 1955. Presents an excellent discussion of discipline problems and suggestions for dealing with these problems. (6)

Klausmeier, Herbert J., and Katherine Dresden: *Teaching in the Elementary School*, 2d ed., Harper & Row, Publishers, New York, 1962. Chapters 2 and 3 represent an excellent discussion of child development and the learning process. Chapter 15 deals with mental health and problems of discipline. (7)

Learning and the Teacher, National Education Association, Association for Supervision and Curriculum Development, Washington, 1959. Pulls together many of the recent research findings regarding learning and presents many excellent suggestions on how the teacher may facilitate effective learning. (7)

Lee, J. Murray, and Dorris M. Lee: *The Child and His Curriculum*, 3d ed., Appleton-Century-Crofts, Inc., New York, 1960. Consists of a comprehensive treatment of teaching in the elementary school. (6)

Leese, Joseph, Kenneth Frasure, and Mauritz Johnson, Jr.: *The Teacher in Curriculum Making*, Harper & Row, Publishers, New York, 1961. Chapter 7 indicates how the teacher plans for effective learning experiences. (6)

Morse, Arthur D.: *Schools of Tomorrow*, Doubleday & Company, Inc., Garden City, N.Y., 1960. Chapters 1, 4, 5, and 8 report on educational experiments with team teaching, teacher aids, and educational television. (7)

N.E.A. Handbook for Local State and National Associations, National Education Association, Washington (latest issue). Contains much information about the National Education Association. (8)

Perden, Philip W.: *The American Secondary School in Action*, Allyn and Bacon, Inc., Englewood Cliffs, N.J., 1959. Presents a realistic description and interpretation of modern practices in secondary schools. (6)

Priwer, Jane: "Busy as a Classroom Teacher," *National Education Association Journal*, vol. 48, no. 3, pp. 29–32, National Education Association, March, 1959. Depicts the busy productive life of a classroom teacher. (6)

Professional Organizations in American Education, National Education Association, Educational Policies Commission, Washington, 1957. An excellent statement of the characteristics of professional organizations within American education. Suggests basic criteria for organizational activities which should be carefully considered by all members and prospective members of the education profession. (8)

Rothney, John W. M.: *Evaluating and Reporting Pupil Progress*, What Research Says Series, no. 7, National Education Association, Department of Classroom Teachers, American Educational Research Association, Washington, 1960. Presents an excellent discussion of the problem of evaluating pupil progress, and indicates research evidence in regard to the various techniques that might be used. (6)

Sherman, Mendel: "MPATI's Promise: A Summing Up," *Phi Delta Kappan*, vol. 43, no. 8, pp. 326–330, May, 1962. Summarizes the educational strengths and weaknesses of the Midwest Program on Airborne Television Instruction. (7)

Smith, Louis M.: *Group Processes in Elementary and Secondary Schools*, What Research Says Series, no. 19, National Education Association, Department of Classroom Teachers, American Educational Research Association, Washington, 1959. Contains research materials on teaching group processes in elementary and secondary schools. (6)

Stinnett, T. M.: *The Teacher and Professional Organizations*, National Education Association, Washington, 1956. Contains an excellent discussion of the role that teacher organizations play in the profession. (8)

Student NEA Handbook, National Education Association, National Commission on Teacher Education and Professional Standards, Washington, 1961. Contains many suggestions that should help Student NEA members fulfill their duties and responsibilities. (8)

"Teacher-aides: Current Practices and Experiments," *Educational Research Service*, Circular 5, National Education Association, Research Division, Washington, July, 1960. Presents the results of a study of practices in the use of teacher aids. (7)

"Teaching Machines and Programmed Learning," *National Education Association Journal*, vol. 50, no. 8, pp. 15–30, National Education Association, Washington, November, 1961. Presents a series of articles on mechanization of learning, psychological bases for the use of teaching machines and what schools are doing in the use of teaching machines. (7)

Trump, J. Lloyd: *Images of the Future: A New Approach to the Secondary School,* National Education Association, Commission on the Experimental Study of the Utilization of the Staff in the Secondary School, National Association of Secondary-School Principals, Washington, 1959. Suggests a number of new approaches to educating secondary school pupils which will affect the work of a teacher. (6)

Trump, J. Lloyd and Dorsey Baynham: *Guide to Better Schools: Focus on Change,* Rand McNally & Company, Chicago, 1961. Presents many excellent suggestions on ways in which greater flexibility and better methods of teaching may be provided in secondary schools. (6)

Washburne, Carleton: *What Is Progressive Education,* The John Day Company, Inc., New York, 1952. Presents a very excellent and brief down-to-earth discussion of the meaning of progressive education. (7)

Wiles, Kimball: *Teaching for Better Schools,* 2d ed., Prentice-Hall, Inc., Englewood Cliffs, N.J., 1959. Chapter 8 indicates how teachers may provide for individual differences in pupils. Chapter 10 indicates how a stimulating intellectual climate may be created. Chapters 13 and 14 indicate how a teacher exerts leadership in the school and in the community. (6) and (7)

Wingo, G. Max, and Raleigh Schorling: *Elementary School Student Teaching,* 3d ed., McGraw-Hill Book Company, Inc., New York, 1960. Chapter 3 discusses individual differences in children and suggests how a teacher may deal with these differences. (7)

● FIGURE CREDITS

Figure 31.   (*Source:* Materials from the National Education Association, Research Division, Washington.)

Figure 32.   (*Source:* "Teachers View Public Relations," *Research Bulletin,* vol. 37, no. 2, p. 40, National Education Association, Research Division, Washington, April, 1959.)

Figure 33.   (*Source:* "Teachers View Public Relations," *Research Bulletin,* vol. 37, no. 2, p. 39, National Education Association, Research Division, Washington, April, 1959.)

Figure 34.   (*Source: Planning for American Youth,* National Education Association, National Association of Secondary School Principals, and the Educational Policies Commission, Washington, 1951, p. 9.)

Figure 35.   (*Source:* Philip H. Coombs, *Airborne Television Instruction and Better Quality Education,* Midwest Program on Airborne Television Instruction, Lafayette, Ind., December, 1960, n.p.)

Figure 36.   (*Source:* National Education Association.)

III

ECONOMIC ASPECTS
OF TEACHING

The economic aspects of any occupation affect not
only the manner in which an individual views his
work but also his attitude toward life in general.
Many people have erroneous ideas in regard to
various economic aspects of teaching. Effective
planning necessitates that you become quite well
informed about such matters so that your plans
may be realistic, comprehensive, and meaningful.

The welfare of our nation is, to a considerable
extent, dependent upon a large number of our most
able young people being attracted to the teaching
profession. The economic status of teachers will
have some bearing upon the extent to which these
people will be interested in such a career. As a
future member of the profession, you will want to
work effectively toward the further improvement of
the economic status of teachers. Through such
efforts, you will improve your own status and make
the profession increasingly attractive to others.

Chapter 9 explores the current and probable
future status of salaries in public elementary and
secondary schools, and on the college level.
Chapter 10 is concerned with such nonsalary
benefits as teacher tenure, leaves of absence, group
insurance, credit unions, and retirement benefits.

9
SALARIES OF EDUCATORS

How high a salary can you expect as a beginning teacher? How fast will your salary increase? What does the future hold so far as teacher salaries are concerned? What kind of salaries are paid to others, such as principals, supervisors, superintendents, counselors, special fields, and college teachers? Are there other sources of income for teachers? These are important questions to consider as you plan your career in education.

The salary status of teachers, especially since World War II, has been a matter of increasing concern both nationally and locally. The great shortage of teachers, especially in the elementary schools, no doubt has contributed to this concern. Since teachers require the same basic necessities of life and have the same desires as all other normal people, it is not possible for them to render maximum service, regardless of ability and preparation, if their income is not sufficient for them to feel economically secure.

Various attempts have been and are being made to increase the salaries of teachers. Data on salaries for any one year, therefore, may be obsolete the following year. Check carefully on current salaries and examine conditions, especially in your local situation. Also be careful in your interpretation of salaries, for the mere number of dollars earned per year does not take into account other factors such as a variation in overhead expenses between those in the teaching profession and those in certain other professions.

Standard of Living Maintained by Teachers. Salaries need to be considered in terms of general standards of living fixed by society for different occupations. For example, professional people are expected to maintain higher standards of living than are unskilled laborers. Obviously it requires more money to maintain a higher standard of living. Unfortunately, the American public has never been too clear in its thinking as to whether the teacher belongs to the wage-earner or the professional class of workers; it seems to place him somewhere in between. When you study the historical development of education in America, it is easy to understand why there has been confusion as to the status of teachers. The work of their national, state, and local organizations, however, is contributing much to the establishment of teaching as a profession in the minds of the general public. It is reasonable to believe that the teacher will be accorded higher status and therefore will be expected to maintain the standard of living generally associated with professional people.

If you are to be a professional worker, you will need more than the basic necessities of life in order to fulfill your function in society. You will need a salary adequate to continue your professional study, to travel, and to provide for your cultural, recreational, and civic needs in order to bring to the classroom increasingly richer experiences.

Relationship Existing between Income and Standard of Living. The money required to maintain a certain standard of living varies with respect to the community in which you live. The incomes of people in a given area largely determine the local standards of living and the standards that will be expected of you. If you live in a very wealthy community, you will find it necessary to maintain better housing facilities and to do more entertaining than if you settle in a rural section where a more simple mode of living is practiced. Generally speaking, the cost of food, rent, and services is cheaper in rural areas. A beginning salary in a nonurban community may be more favorable economically than an appreciably higher salary in a city, and a lower salary in one section of the United States may be equivalent to a higher salary in a similar community in another section.

The value of money also fluctuates from year to year. Consider the extent to which salaries in various occupations are affected in periods of economic recession and prosperity. Since World War II, the purchasing power of the dollar has dropped. Continued inflation will decrease the teacher's salary unless corresponding raises are made.

The Research Division of the National Education Association periodically analyzes the income of teachers in terms of the purchasing power of the dollar. Consult the most recent publications of this division to determine trends in the economic status of the teacher.

Some Factors to Consider in Comparing the Income of Teachers with Incomes in Other Occupations. Some students may be impressed with the huge income earned by men in business. No one ever learns of a schoolteacher who falls into comparable income brackets. It is true that this is the land of opportunity; on the other hand, consider carefully the probabilities of becoming the outstanding railroad magnate or business tycoon. With the unusually successful businessman you must balance the hundreds who barely make a decent living, who just manage to keep above bankruptcy, or who fail.

You also have read of the huge earnings of movie stars, prize fighters, professional football and baseball players, and the like. Unfortunately, their productive years are often exceedingly short, while the productive part of a teacher's life continues for many years.

Since World War II there has been considerable increase in the wages of semiskilled and skilled labor. The bricklayer, house painter, or coal miner may seem to be earning more than the professional worker. Though these laborers may be receiving extraordinarily high hourly rates, the total number of hours that they work per year often is relatively small. Regularity of income, therefore, is an important factor to consider in comparing the relative attractiveness of occupations.

The gross income in some occupations seems to be large. On the   259 other hand, considerable operating expenses are incurred. Doctors and lawyers must maintain offices, employ secretaries and assistants, and buy supplies. Teachers are relatively free of such expenses. The only comparable ones incurred by the teacher are those that provide for his professional growth.

In considering teaching as a profession, recognize the fact that a definite income is assured once you accept a position, for which you are eligible upon completing the requirements for a certificate. You do not need to incur heavy capital investments in equipment and supplies in order to begin your business. Furthermore, you do not encounter the problem of developing a clientele, from which little or no net profit may accrue during the first few years, as does the doctor, dentist, and lawyer.

The average income reported for any vocation does not give a true picture of the situation. For a number of reasons, this is particularly true of teaching. Only a relatively small percentage of teachers have made teaching a life career. As a result, a large number of the teachers are either beginners or those with limited amounts of experience. Obviously these salaries are low. Over 70 per cent of the teachers are women, and women tend to be paid less than men. Some teachers in the elementary schools have no more than two years of college training, since they earned life teaching certificates a number of years ago when standards for certification were low. These teachers are paid appreciably less than those with four and five years of preparation, such as the more recently trained teachers. In other words, the heterogeneous background of teaching personnel makes it unwise to compare their income with incomes in other occupations, such as law and medicine, where the professional background is more homogeneous. The beginning teacher today is generally better trained than his predecessors and will consequently have a greater earning capacity.

Over half of the school children and teachers in the United States are located in rural areas. In the past, rural teachers' salaries were considerably lower than urban salaries although there has been a tendency for this gap to be lowered. Furthermore, rural schools have been forced to employ more teachers with substandard qualifications, especially in the elementary schools. These teachers are paid proportionately less salary.

Salary Trends in Teaching and Other Occupations. For a number of reasons it is difficult to indicate accurately the salary trends in many occupations. Only scattered information is available. We do know that since World War II considerable change has resulted in the earnings, especially of unionized labor and professional workers who are not on regular salaries. Wages in some occupations fluctuate rapidly according to the cost-of-living index; whereas other occupations remain relatively constant in earning power. With the teaching profession, however, much information on salaries is available. A report of the Research Division of the National Education Association indicates that, during the 10-year period from 1950–1951 to 1960–1961, the public school median starting teaching salary for college graduates increased from $2,500 to $4,300, and the top maximum moved from $4,700 to $7,630 [169:52–53]. When these increases are converted into constant dollars, using the value of the

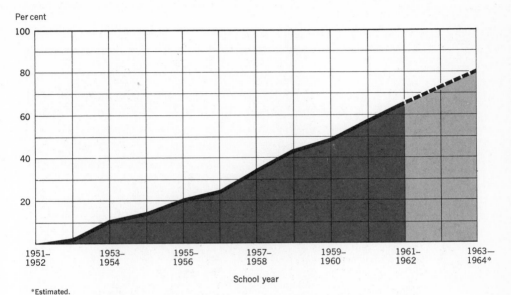

Per cent

School year

*Estimated.

Figure 37.   Per cent increase over 1951–1952 in the average salary of public school instructional staff members. (*Source:* National Education Association.)

1950 dollar as a base, the salaries represent an average gain in purchasing power of about one-third over a 10-year period. This amount represents a potentially higher standard of living for teachers [169:53].

Since the earnings of all persons working for wages and salaries establishes the movement of wages in the economy as a whole, it is important to compare the gains of teachers with those of all employed persons. Disregarding losses due to price changes, the earnings of all wage earners increased 57.4 per cent from 1950 to 1960, and the increase for teachers was 62.4 per cent [69:54]. Actually, from 1949 to 1959 the increases in the average earnings of teachers have exceeded the annual gains of all employed persons [55:49]. In terms of purchasing power, the gain in average earnings during this 10-year period was 31 per cent for all employed persons and 41 per cent for teachers.

A number of studies have shown that the average earnings of professional workers are substantially higher than the salaries of teachers. The Research Division of the National Education Association, for example, compared the economic status of teachers in 1959–1960 with that of workers in 17 other professions in which four years of college training was involved (architects, chemists, clergymen, dentists, dietitians, engineers, foresters and conservationists, lawyers and judges, librarians, natural scientists, optometrists, osteopaths, pharmacists, physicians and surgeons, social and welfare workers, social scientists, and veterinarians). It was found that the median earnings in the teaching profession were 59 per cent of the median earnings of the 17 other professions. The average (arithmetic mean) earnings, however, were only 47 per cent.

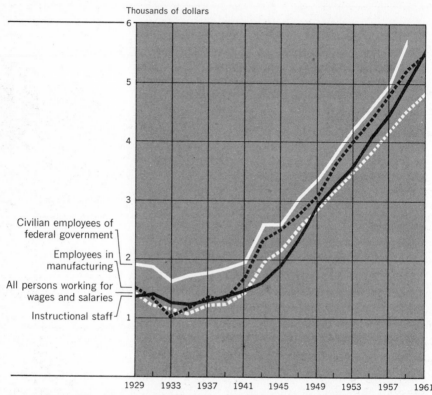

Thousands of dollars

Civilian employees of federal government

Employees in manufacturing

All persons working for wages and salaries

Instructional staff

1929   1933   1937   1941   1945   1949   1953   1957   1961

Figure 38.   Trends in earnings of instructional staff in public elementary and secondary schools compared with earnings of certain other groups. In recent years teachers' salaries have risen to a level about 14 per cent above the earnings of all wage-and-salary workers. (*Source:* National Education Association.)

The Committee on Educational Finance of the National Education Association in 1961 expressed the feeling that salaries would average about $10,400 for classroom teachers and $10,750 for all teachers, including principals and other instructional personnel if the National Education Association salary goals were to be in effect [118:18]. They indicate that the 1960–1961 total of $8.2 billion for teachers' salaries was about 1.6 per cent of the Gross National Product of 1960. They feel that 3.8 per cent of the Gross National Product should be used in order to provide smaller classes and to pay appropriate professional salaries to teachers.

Trends in Teachers' Salaries in Various States.   Figure 40 gives you an idea of the great range in the average salaries paid in the various states. As you study this figure keep in mind that the average state salaries

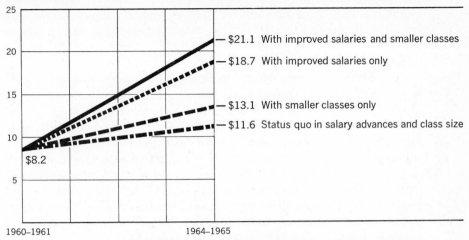

Figure 39. In order to improve conditions and raise the salaries of teachers to a more professional level, expenditures for teachers' salaries would more than double. (*Source:* National Education Association.)

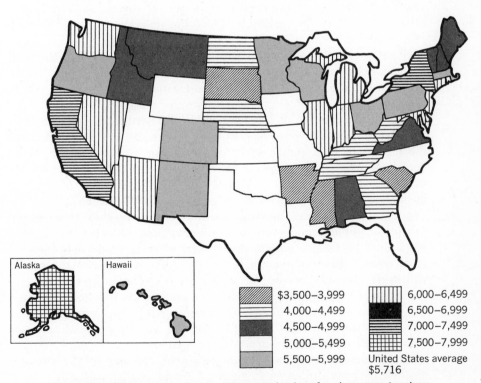

Figure 40. The range in the average annual salary for classroom teachers within the United States is great. The average salary for each state is more meaningful than an average salary for the United States. (*Source:* National Education Association.)

are subject to all the weaknesses indicated previously. Naturally, the averages change from year to year, and you should consult current data from the Research Division of the National Education Association to determine the current average salaries for the states in which you are interested.

The extreme range shown in this figure points up a very crucial problem in education. Differences in the cost of providing the basic necessities of life for teachers cannot account for the variation in average salaries. As will be explained more fully in Chapter 17, the differences result more from the lack of taxable resources for financing schools than from the willingness of the states to pay for education. The inequalities are so great that there seems to be little hope of rectifying them without some form of Federal assistance. Generally speaking, the Northern and Western states, where there are greater financial resources, have higher average salaries than the Southern states, where the financial resources are more limited. This has been true for many years.

Teachers, like individuals in other occupations, tend to gravitate toward areas in which high salaries are paid. Many of the able teachers leave the poorly paying states and find teaching positions elsewhere. Wealthier states can demand better professional training, and many large school systems have well-organized personnel divisions which select incoming teachers very carefully. Thus, the states having low teachers' salaries are left with a relatively high percentage of inferior teachers as well as of inadequate equipment. Educationally speaking, the rich become richer and the poor become poorer. Some provision must be made to equalize the educational opportunities of *all* American youth.

Trends in the Salaries of Teachers within Different-sized Communities.
A direct relationship seems to exist between the size of communities and the salaries of their public school teachers. For example, in the school year 1960–1961, public school teachers in cities of 500,000 or over had an average salary approximately 37 per cent greater than that of teachers in districts having a population of fewer than 5,000 [123:68].

A number of things account for the differences that exist in the salaries of public school workers in different sizes of cities. Teachers in large cities have been able to group together more easily than those in rural areas, and consequently have been able to acquaint the public with their economic needs. The very large city schools often have been able to afford a public relations division whose main function is to keep the public informed of their educational needs. Cities usually possess more property than rural areas that may be taxed for school purposes without causing undue strain on the population.

The tendency for salaries to increase with the size of the city has resulted in a high turnover in rural areas and small towns. Great rural shortages of well-trained teachers have resulted. This condition has presented a real national problem, especially when you consider that

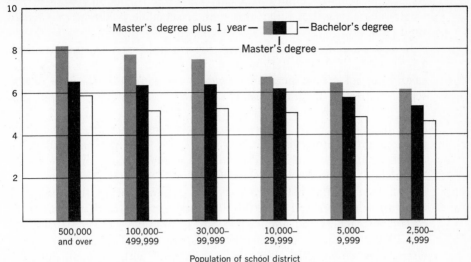

Thousands of dollars

Master's degree plus 1 year — ██ □ — Bachelor's degree

Master's degree

Population of school district

Figure 41. Average salaries of classroom teachers vary with the level of preparation and the size of the school district. (*Source:* National Education Association.)

approximately one-half of the school population resides in cities having a population of 2,500 or less, or in the open country. The National Education Association has been increasingly concerned in recent years with the problem of providing equal educational opportunities to rural and city boys and girls.

There has been a tendency, however, for the differences in the salaries paid in various communities to decrease. For example, in 1930–1931 the median salary paid to teachers in cities having a population over 500,000 was 90.7 per cent higher than that paid to teachers in towns having a population range of 2,500 to 5,000. As noted above, this difference had decreased to 37 per cent. It seems likely that this trend will continue.

Trends in the Salaries of Various Types of School Employees. Throughout the history of education, elementary teachers have received less salary than have secondary school teachers. There are a number of reasons for this, but the following two stand out: Lower standards of training have been required for teaching in the elementary schools. Also, a higher percentage of teachers in the elementary schools than of those in the high schools have been women, and our society pays women lower salaries.

As early as 1918, however, cities began to establish single-salary schedules. This kind of schedule specifies the same salary to teachers, regardless of sex, with equal training and experience when assigned to regular positions in elementary, junior high, and senior high school. Progress at first in the adoption of a single-salary schedule was slow, even though it had been urged by the National Education Association as early as 1920.

As late as 1940–1941 only 31.3 per cent of the schedules were of the single-salary type, but today this type of schedule is almost universally used [134:19].

If you examine the most recent reports published by the Research Division of the National Education Association, you will note that the salaries of all school personnel tend to increase with the size of the school district. The principalship salaries in cities having a population of 500,000 or above are almost twice as high as those in the 2,500 to 5,000 population class; whereas the superintendencies are almost three times as great. However, the size of the city does not make so much difference in the salaries of directors, assistant directors or supervisors.

Members of the Research Division of the National Education Association have found that there has been a trend toward the closing of the gap which existed in 1930–1931 between the median salaries of classroom teachers and administrators. For example, between 1940–1941 and 1960–1961 the average salaries of classroom teachers in urban school districts increased 191.5 per cent as compared with approximately 183 per cent for school administrators [123:70]. As reasons for this trend, the association has pointed to the extreme shortage of teachers, especially in the elementary schools after World War II; and the rising cost of living, which necessitated placing additional funds toward the salaries of classroom teachers. Many states increased the amount of state aid for school-salary purposes and raised minimum salaries for inexperienced teachers more rapidly than maximum salaries.

There also seems to be a change taking place in the manner of determining salaries for principals [136:99–103]. The older practice involved a dollar differential, a fixed sum of money above the amount the principal would receive if he were a classroom teacher. For example, an elementary school principal might receive $1,000 more than the teaching maximum for his level of preparation, plus $500 for each year of administrative experience up to four years. From a study conducted by the Research Division of the National Education Association [136:100] it was found that the ratio-differential method of determining a principal's salary was growing in popularity. The salary that a principal receives is stated as a percentage in excess of the salary he would receive if he were classified as a classroom teacher. For example, an elementary principal may receive 120 per cent of the maximum salary for a master's degree on the teachers' salary schedule, plus 5 per cent for each year of administrative experience up to five years. This method of compiling the salaries of principals would seem to have definite merit. It is highly probable that it will be used increasingly in determining the salaries of other central administrative officers, such as supervisors, consultants, directors, and coordinators. The practice of using the same salary schedule for elementary and secondary school principals in a school system still is rare—occurring in about 27 per cent of the very large school systems and less frequently in the smaller school system [92:121]. This situation is understandable since elementary schools tend to be smaller, and elementary school principals frequently are paid for fewer months of service than secondary school principals.

Trend toward Minimum Salaries for Teachers.   As early as 1904, laws regarding the minimum salaries to be paid to teachers were enacted by several school systems. At the beginning of the school year 1960–1961, public school teachers in 34 states were employed under the minimum-salary laws [149:5]. These laws differ greatly in requirements as well as in amount of salary. Some states only guarantee a flat-rate minimum. Other states specify only minimum salaries for beginning teachers, according to the amount of preparation; whereas other states specify a minimum salary both for beginning teachers and for teachers who have a maximum amount of teaching experience for which credit is received.

Each year the Research Division of the National Education Association prepares a release on the current state minimum-salary requirements for classroom teachers. This release indicates for each state the minimum starting salary for teachers holding the lowest certificate recognized, the bachelor's degree or four years of training, and the master's degree or five years of training. You may wish to secure this list from your library in order to study the current conditions in states where you may be interested in teaching.

There are a number of advantages in having minimum-salary laws. For example, they protect children against boards of education which would be willing to employ poorly qualified teachers at low rates of pay. Some boards of education have been willing to sacrifice quality in order to keep the local school budget as low as possible. Minimum-salary laws also improve ethics in the employment of teachers. Heretofore, a process of salary bargaining was in practice, especially for teachers in overcrowded subject areas. Wherever a minimum wage is stated, both the employee and the employer are operating on a higher professional plane. A state's adoption of a minimum-salary law in no way threatens local control of the school, and a community is free to pay teachers above the minimum to whatever extent it so desires.

Trend toward Definite Salary Schedules.   If teachers' salaries are to be placed on a professional basis it is necessary to establish a definite classification of them with respect not only to minimum salaries but also to yearly increments and maximum salaries.

A definite salary schedule is desirable for a number of reasons. When a teacher is able to determine definitely the income that he will receive during and at the end of the next 10 or 20 years, he is able to do long-range financial planning. A teacher is relieved of trying to get as much money as possible, sometimes having to resort to unethical practices; an administrator is not tempted to pay a teacher as little as possible. The tensions between teachers are relieved, since the initial salaries and the yearly increases are known to all. The administrator cannot be accused of playing favorites by giving unwarranted raises. Administrators and school-board members can calculate budget needs more easily when a definite salary schedule is at their disposal.

You may wish to examine salary schedules that are used in various school systems. Superintendents of schools normally are happy to provide prospective teachers with these schedules. Some state departments of education publish the salary data of the major school systems in the state. The placement officer in your college will probably have copies of such data for various school systems. Study the schedules and try to discover the strengths and weaknesses of each.

A salary schedule usually contains from two to four columns, representing various levels of preparation, such as the bachelor's, master's, sixth-year, and doctor's degree; and 12 or 13 steps representing annual increments for each year of experience [75:108]. You will be especially interested in the size and the number of increments that are provided. For teachers having a bachelor's degree the typical number of increments is 12, with relatively few schedules providing less than 9 or more than 16. The number of increments usually is greater for teachers who have more than the bachelor's degree. The basic weakness in the use of salary increments is that the increment is not primarily a reward for increased efficiency or competence on the part of the teacher. No provision is made for merit raises because of outstanding work. If the increments do not extend over a long period of time, a teacher reaches a maximum salary early in his career and faces the prospect of 20 or more years of service with little chance of a raise unless he is able to obtain another position as a teacher, a supervisor, or an administrator. On the other hand, if the teacher is delayed too long in reaching a maximum salary, he may experience great hardships in the early part of his career as his dependency responsibilities expand. A few schools have followed the practice of granting large increases during the first few years of a teacher's service and smaller increments in the remaining period until he has reached the maximum.

An increasing number of school districts have been using an index or ratio to determine the salaries of teachers. This kind of schedule typically uses the bachelor's degree with no experience as its base of 100. or 1.00. Increments for years of experience and for additional preparation beyond the bachelor's degree are calculated as per cents in addition to the base. For example, the annual increment may be 6 per cent of the base, and an inexperienced teacher with a master's degree may receive a salary 10 per cent above the base. The index schedule has the advantage of establishing salary-step relationships that remain constant even though the dollar amounts change. If the base salary is raised, the increments increase, and the relative distance between the minimum and maximum salaries is not reduced [75:108].

One of the very thorny problems with which teachers and school administrators are confronted involves rewards and penalties for quality

	Salary step	Bachelor's degree	Master's degree	Sixth year M.A. + 30	Doctor's degree	
			Base: $ _ _ _ _ _ _ ◄———————			Base amount to be reviewed annually; NEA recommends $6,000
Uniform increments; 6 per cent of the bachelor's degree minimum	1	1.00	1.10	1.20	1.35	10 per cent above base for each additional year of professional preparation; 15 per cent for doctor's degree
	2	1.06	1.16	1.26	1.41	
	3	1.12	1.22	1.32	1.47	
	4	1.18	1.28	1.38	1.53	
	5	1.24	1.34	1.44	1.59	
	6	1.30	1.40	1.50	1.65	
	7	1.36	1.46	1.56	1.71	
12 increments for bachelor's degree class and 13 for master's degree class; typical of present practice	8	1.42	1.52	1.62	1.77	
	9	1.48	1.58	1.68	1.83	
	10	1.54	1.64	1.74	1.89	
	11	1.60	1.70	1.80	1.96	
	12	1.66	1.76	1.86	2.02	Twice the bachelor's degree minimum
	13	1.72	1.82	1.92	2.08	
	14	......	1.88	1.98	2.14	
	15	......	....	......	2.20	

Figure 42. Hypothetical index salary schedule.
(*Source:* National Education Association.)

of service. A salary schedule based entirely upon the amount of training and years of experience does not reward the teacher who is doing superior work, or penalize the teacher who is doing an inferior job. Many educators feel that such an arrangement gives teachers little incentive to do their very best in fulfilling their professional obligations to boys and girls. In a survey concerning quality-of-service policies conducted by the Research Division of the National Education Association, it was found that, from a sampling of 701 schedules from school districts of 30,000 or more in population in 1960–1961, 8.3 per cent authorized or required that superior service be rewarded with higher salaries [184:63]. Some people feel that merit rating tends to lower teacher morale, creates professional jealousies, destroys a spirit of cooperation between teachers and administrators, violates the principles of democracy by forcing compliance, undermines the single-salary schedule, etc. You might be interested in reading some of the current educational articles in which this very controversial issue is being debated.

Trends in the Salaries of Men and Women Teachers. Statistics on average salaries indicate that men teachers receive higher salaries than do women teachers. It should be pointed out, however, that the discrimination against women teachers is not as great as it may seem. An appreciable number of women in the elementary schools still have far less than a college degree. A large number are teaching on substandard permits because of the shortage of elementary teachers. The great majority of men, however, teach on the high school level, where a degree is required. Furthermore, a high percentage of the administrative positions are filled by men. The fact that men are better trained, for which a higher salary is paid, and that they fill a majority of the administrative positions may give the impression of higher discrimination against women than actually exists in the teaching profession. Actually, studies show that there is less inequality between men and women in teaching than in other professions [55:53].

The battle for equal pay with the same training and experience, especially on the college level, is not over. Basically, almost all would agree that the theory is sound, based on the assumption that teachers with the same amount of training and experience are making the same contributions to society. Furthermore, the idea is in harmony with democratic concepts. Any policy that fosters discrimination among a group of individuals who are equals is undemocratic. Teachers, above all, need to demonstrate concepts of democracy.

The advocates of a dual-salary schedule in regard to sex, however, feel that there should be more men teachers, especially in the elementary schools, than there are at present. Since the opportunities for men in industry are greater than those for women, schools should pay higher salaries to men in order to attract them to teaching. Advocates of the dual schedule also feel that equal pay provokes undue hardships on men teachers, who generally have more dependents than women. Some school systems have solved the problem of dependents partially by adopting a policy similar to one used in computing income tax; that is, all teachers are given allowances for the number of dependents.[1]

Period of Time Teachers Receive Pay. The predominant practice in paying teachers is to distribute their salaries monthly over the period in which school is in session. For example, if you teach in a school that is in session for nine months during the year, you may expect to receive one-ninth of your pay at the end of the first month of service. A small percentage of school systems have adopted the policy of paying teachers semimonthly.

There seems to be a trend, however, for schools to distribute the pay of teachers over a 12-month period for services rendered while school is in session. This helps teachers to budget their salaries throughout the year. Otherwise they often find it necessary to borrow money during the summer vacation.

An increasing number of school systems are adopting a policy of expanding the period in which teachers are employed during the year.

[1] "Extra Pay and Dependency," *National Education Association Journal,* vol. 49, no. 8, pp. 52–54, November, 1960.

Some states—Florida, for example—employ teachers for an extra month of work. This enables the school staff to plan before schools open in the fall and after they close in the spring, providing a much-needed time for teachers to work together to improve their teaching.

Approximately 5 per cent [181:28] of the urban school systems hire teachers on a year-round basis and adjust the work accordingly. The school is organized so that teachers work in the classroom for the traditional 10-month school year. During the summer they work in the recreation program, take part in workshops to improve teaching techniques, study, or travel, and then have one month's vacation with pay. Advocates of this year-round employment plan feel that teachers should have regular duties connected with improving the educational program and with providing recreation and new opportunities for the children. They also point out that administrators are usually employed on a year-round basis, which accounts in part for their salaries being higher than those of classroom teachers in comparable school systems. The year-round school idea, however, will probably take more of the form of a greatly expanded summer school [47:45].

Extra Earnings of Teachers. "Extra pay," "additive salaries," "off-schedule salaries," or "compensation for irregularities" are terms used to identify provisions for paying teachers for assignments beyond the regular school day or term. The most common activities that fall within the range of the definition are coaching athletics, directing bands, directing choirs, directing dramatics, and sponsoring school publications.

A study conducted by the Research Division of the National Education Association [52:1–32] revealed that a scale of flat rates usually was provided in salary schedules as extra pay for specific coaching duties or other supervisory assignments outside of school hours. The amount varied somewhat according to the size of the school. The highest pay was reported for head football coaches, whose extra compensation ranged from $250 to $2,800 [52:3]. Head basketball coaches were the next highest paid, while head baseball and track coaches were paid about equally. Extra compensation for supervisory assignments involving dramatics, band, newspaper, or yearbook approximated $250.

A number of educators feel that the total educational program is undermined by extra-pay policies which encourage teachers to assume duties requiring time that should be devoted to teaching responsibilities [52:1]. Some feel that it is a type of exploitation, since it would cost far more to employ enough teachers to do the extra work. There is no question that limited budgets and teacher shortages are forcing many school districts to depend upon extra-pay practices in order to provide for these extra duties.

During the past few years more school districts have been providing summer sessions. They have been doing so largely because they have a new concept of the scope of the summer program. The emphasis in summer school is shifting from helping only the slow students to a broader concept in which all students may gain value from attending summer school. In many schools, advanced or highly talented students may take either accelerated courses or more advanced courses in such areas as mathematics and science that cannot be offered economically during the regular school year. The length of the summer school programs at both elementary and secondary levels ranges from four to ten weeks.

Figure 43 shows the results of a study, conducted by the Research Division of the National Education Association, of summer school pro-

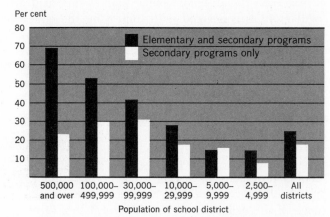

Figure 43. Extent of summer school programs, 1959. To what extent do you feel summer school programs should be promoted? (*Source:* National Education Association.)

grams [158:23–24]. As more schools offer summer school programs, more teachers will have opportunities to increase their annual earnings. Dr. Lambert of the Research Division of the National Education Association predicts that by 1970 or 1980 as many as 50 per cent of all pupils will be attending summer sessions [47:45].

Other types of extra-pay activities involve a very wide range of jobs in which teachers engage outside the school hours and especially during the summer months. During the school year these jobs usually relate in some way to the specialized field of the teacher, such as privately teaching music, giving public lectures, sewing, serving as a consultant to a business, etc. At least 16 per cent of the urban school districts impose limitations on the employment of teachers outside school [181:29]. The most common requirement is that outside employment does not interfere with teaching duties. During the summer months the distribution of jobs for teachers who work falls approximately within the following categories: professional or semiprofessional—30 per cent; managerial or self-employed—7 per cent; clerical or sales worker—13 per cent; skilled or semiskilled worker—27 per cent; unskilled worker—15 per cent; farmer—8 per cent [154:22]. No accurate data on the amount earned are available.

Trends in Salaries for College Teachers. It is more difficult to present precise salary schedules for college teachers than for public school teachers because of the fluctuation of college salaries based on the supply and demand for instructional personnel. Approximately one in every eight colleges and universities have clearly defined salary schedules with designated increments. It is apparent, however, that improvements in college-salary practices have lagged behind those in the public schools.

The most common type of college salary schedule utilizes maximum and minimum salaries according to rank; i.e., instructor, assistant professor, associate professor, and full professor. The limits as well as the average salaries within each of these ranks vary considerably among institutions as well as among departments within institutions. For example, the average salary received by a full professor in a small private college may be more than the salary received by a teacher of comparable rank in a large university, or vice versa. Also, the full professor in the English department of a large university may be receiving a lower salary than a full professor in the law college. The teachers in the college, school, or department of education in larger institutions generally receive slightly higher salaries than other college personnel in all ranks because of the amount of public school experience required and competing salaries in public school work.

The Research Division of the National Education Association completed, in 1962, a very thorough study of salaries in almost all the degree-granting institutions in the United States [135:5–58].

Table 6 indicates the median salaries, according to rank, for *nine* months of full-time teaching in all colleges and universities included in the study. It also indicates the per cent of increase for a period of two years.

TABLE 6   MEDIAN SALARIES FOR NINE MONTHS OF FULL-TIME TEACHING IN COLLEGES AND UNIVERSITIES, 1959–1960 AND 1961–1962

	Median salaries		
	---	---	---
Rank	1959–1960	1961–1962	Increase, Per cent
Professor	$9,107	$10,256	12.6
Associate professor	7,332	8,167	11.4
Assistant professor	6,231	6,900	10.7
Instructor	5,095	5,582	9.6

Source: Adapted from "Salaries Paid and Salary Practices in Universities, Colleges, and Junior Colleges, 1961–62," *Research Report 1962-R2,* National Education Association, Research Division, Washington, February, 1962, p. 9.

The salary range for each of the ranks was wide. For example, the salaries paid to full professors ranged from $2,000 to more than $18,000 [135:12]. The highest median salaries for all college teachers were paid in municipal universities, followed by state universities, nonpublic universities, land-grant colleges, state colleges, teachers colleges, nonpublic colleges of over 1,000 enrollment, and small nonpublic colleges. In terms of geographic regions, the median salaries for all full-time college teachers were highest in the Far West, followed by New England, Middle West, Middle Atlantic, Northwest, Southwest, and Southeast in the order named.

Median salaries for nine months of full-time teaching in public and nonpublic junior colleges, in 1961–1962 were $6,811 [135:53]. The median salaries for public junior colleges ($7,212) were higher than those in nonpublic junior colleges ($5,074).

In addition to the actual salaries paid, almost all institutions provide various types of fringe benefits such as health, accident, and life insurance, and contributions to retirement funds. Although the range is considerable, these benefits may be equivalent to approximately 11 per cent of the actual salaries paid.

The study also included the median 12-month salaries of various college administrative officers. The results are indicated in Table 7.

TABLE 7   MEDIAN SALARIES OF CERTAIN ADMINISTRATIVE OFFICERS IN COLLEGES AND UNIVERSITIES, 1959–1960 AND 1961–1962

| Office | Median salaries | | Increase, Per cent |
	1959–1960	1961–1962	
President	$13,827	$15,375	11.2
Vice-president	14,154	16,000	13.0
Dean of the college	10,723	12,230	14.1
Dean of students	8,796	9,592	9.0
Dean of men	7,280	8,202	12.7
Dean of women	6,638	7,399	11.5
Dean of admissions	7,680	8,636	12.4
Registrar	6,340	7,312	15.3
Business manager	8,536	9,405	10.2
Head librarian	7,078	8,163	15.3
Director of athletics	8,104	8,930	10.2
Head football coach	7,824	8,554	9.3
Head basketball coach	6,888	7,770	11.8

Source: Adapted from "Salaries Paid and Salary Practices in Universities, Colleges, and Junior Colleges, 1961–62," *Research Report 1962-R2,* National Education Association, Research Division, Washington, February, 1962, p. 29.

Practically all multipurpose institutions, state colleges, and teachers colleges have summer instruction programs in which approximately one-half of the regular full-time teachers have an opportunity to supplement their salaries by offering courses [135:22–23]. Some college teachers are able to earn an appreciable amount of money by writing for publication; or by serving as consultants in school systems, in businesses, or in industries.

The demand for college teachers in the future will be very great. From both an instructional and an administrative standpoint the way is open to substantial rewards if you are willing to undergo the rather rigorous task of preparing yourself for teaching on the college level.

Minimum-salary Standards. The National Education Association has fought vigorously for many years for higher salaries for teachers. In commenting on the need for better pay scales in order to attract teachers of high professional caliber, one spokesman has said: "A community which employs teachers of less than professional quality condemns many of its children to lifetimes of mediocrity or perhaps of frustration and maladjustment. The price of poor teaching is prohibitive. The cost of adequate salaries is much less" [88:662].

In July, 1960, the Representative Assembly of the National Education Association recommended that "the salaries of beginning qualified teachers should be at least $6,000 and salaries should range to $13,000 and higher" [98:58]. Further recommendations include the following [98:57]:

A professional salary schedule should—

a. Be based upon preparation, teaching experience, and professional growth.

b. Provide a beginning salary adequate to attract capable young people into the profession.

c. Include increments sufficient to double the beginning salary within ten years, followed by continuing salary advances.

d. Be developed cooperatively by school board members, administrators, and teachers.

e. Permit no discrimination as to grade or subject taught, residence, creed, race, sex, marital status, or number of dependents.

f. Recognize experience and advanced education, through the doctor's degree.

g. Recognize, by appropriate salary ratios, the responsibilities of administrators and other school personnel.

h. Be applied in actual practice.

It is encouraging to note the amount of progress that is being made in school systems throughout the nation in their efforts to prepare salary schedules based on the principles recommended by the National Education Association. As continued changes are made toward the achievement of these minimum- and maximum-salary recommendations, teachers certainly will gain greater professional status.

Appraising Salary Schedules. As a part of this course, you may wish to study the salary schedules of various school systems. The check list located in the Resource Section for Part III of this book should help you in appraising the schedules. When you seek a position in the years to come, you should find the check list to be of much value to you.

Teachers' Responsibilities for Improving Salaries. Low teachers' salaries in the past have been excused somewhat upon the grounds that teachers love their work and therefore are willing to receive low salaries. This thesis is no longer acceptable, and teachers have a responsibility for correcting this outmoded philosophy. It is thoroughly respectable for a professional group to work ethically toward the improvement of salaries. The public must realize that, as is true in virtually everything in life, there is a direct relationship between quality and price. Quality education is expensive. On the other hand, in this day and age, poor education

Teachers have a responsibility to work ethically toward the improvement of their salaries. The general public may need help in understanding that poorly paid teachers constitute poor economy in terms of the future welfare of our nation. (*Photograph from the National Education Association.*)

is even more expensive in terms of the welfare of our society. This the public must understand, and you, as a teacher, have an obligation to help the public in gaining this understanding.

SUMMARY

Although some very definite improvements have been made during the past several years, the average salaries of teachers are low compared with those of other professions requiring comparable training. *Any average salary listed must be interpreted carefully in the light of all factors that enter into the establishment of an average.* It would be desirable for you to view teaching in terms of existing and probable future salary schedules for beginning teachers.

There is positive evidence that the general public is becoming increasingly concerned over the economic welfare of teachers. Because of the organized efforts of educators and others, the prospects of improving teacher salaries look promising.

Some positive trends are to be noted in the scheduling of teachers' salaries: the establishment of minimum salaries for beginning teachers, definite yearly salary increments, the same pay for men and women who have equal training and experience, and a single-salary schedule for elementary and secondary teachers. Unfortunately, the practice of having salary schedules on the college level has lagged behind that of salaries in the public schools.

Improvements in the scheduling of salaries should encourage competent teachers to remain in the profession for a longer period of time, attract more people with promise into the profession, and enable educators to be more selective of those who are prepared, certified, and employed as teachers. As these factors operate, the level of the teaching profession will be raised; this, in turn, will tend to raise the salaries.

QUESTIONS FOR YOUR CONSIDERATION

1. What factors should be kept in mind as you interpret average salaries of teachers?

2. Can you think of any teachers who are being overpaid? If so, upon what grounds do you base your judgment? What should the school board do about these situations?

3. How can you defend equal pay for men and women teachers, providing they have equal training and experience?

4. How do you account for the fact that public school teachers are not as well paid as members of other professions? What should be done in order to obtain salaries comparable to the other professions?

5. What are the advantages and disadvantages of a salary schedule that is based entirely upon the amount of training and experience of teachers?

6. In your opinion, how should superior teachers be rewarded?

7. To what extent do you feel that teachers should be given salary allowances for the number of dependents they have?

8. Are you in favor of the trend for schools to distribute the pay of teachers over a 12-month period for services rendered during a 9- or 10-month school year? Why?

9. What advantages and disadvantages do you see in the year-round employment plan for teachers? Should schools be operated on a 12-month plan?

10. Do you favor a plan whereby teachers receive extra pay for school assignments beyond the regular school day or term? What are the weaknesses and strengths of such a plan?

11. Some teachers work on jobs during after-school hours and on week ends. Do you favor such practices? Upon what grounds might a school board specify that teachers are not to engage in such practices?

12. How can you account for the wide range in the salaries of college teachers? To what extent and by what means should these salaries be made more equitable?

13. How might you work positively toward the improvement of salaries for teachers?

ACTIVITIES FOR YOU TO PURSUE

1. Consult your home-town superintendent of schools regarding the bases upon which his teachers are paid. Discuss with him the problems of salary schedules.

2. Secure information on the salary schedules for all school systems in which you might like to secure a position. Compare them in terms of minimums, maximums, number and size of increments, credit for previous teaching experience, credit for advanced professional work, provisions for recognition of outstanding work, and the like.

3. Compare the salary schedules of school systems in various types of communities, sections of the United States, and foreign countries.

4. Make a careful study of different kinds of occupations to discover the extent to which the salaries or wages of men differ from those of women who possess equal training and experience.

5. Discuss teacher salaries with community members in various types of work to determine how they feel about the subject.

6. Discuss with lawyers, doctors, dentists, engineers, and other professional workers the satisfactions they receive from their work and earnings. Have them compare and contrast the work and the earnings of teachers with their professions. Consult the latest issues of *Economic Status of Teachers*, National Education Association, Research Division, to determine how teachers' salaries compare with salaries in other occupations. Report your findings to your colleagues.

7. Estimate, by referring to a typical salary schedule, your yearly earnings for the period you plan to teach. Consider carefully the extent to which you would be able to develop an adequate budget in terms of your wants.

8. Read some articles in current professional magazines regarding the advantages and disadvantages of merit raises. Report your findings to your colleagues.

9. For what extra duties should a teacher be paid? What should be the basis for the amount of pay? Discuss these questions with your colleagues.

10. Organize a panel to discuss the controversial issue of Federal aid for teacher salaries.

11. Use the check list in the Resource Section for Part III and attempt to appraise the salary schedule in your home community.

10
OTHER ECONOMIC BENEFITS

Practically everyone wants to be economically secure. But what does it mean to *you*? Just a high salary? Or are there other factors to be taken into consideration as you plan your life? Do you want to be reasonably certain of steady employment; of not losing your job unjustifiably? What would happen to you and your dependents if you should become ill or disabled? What are your resources if you need money quickly? There are always the possibilities of accidents, medical operations, and other personal calamities. Effective planning takes into consideration these emergency situations.

What provisions are made for retirement? Yes—you are young, and it may seem unnecessary to be thinking about retirement before you are out of college. Naturally, you are more interested in preparing for a career in teaching rather than in ending it. You feel young, energetic, ambitious, and healthy; and retirement seems far away. You are right. But time passes quickly. In a few years you will most likely be assuming heavier obligations—marriage, dependents, a home, and various other financial obligations. Under such circumstances provisions for retirement become much more real. Effective long-range career planning involves all of these factors—including retirement. You owe it to yourself and to your loved ones. The thought of dying virtually penniless frightens almost everyone.

This chapter should help you plan in terms of certain extra benefits inherent in a teaching career. It will contain a brief discussion of teacher tenure, leaves of absence, group insurance, credit unions, and retirement benefits.

TEACHER TENURE

The term "teacher tenure" often is used in referring to the length of time that a teacher remains in a particular school. In this regard it is a well-known fact that teachers, especially in rural areas where the salaries are low, tend to change positions frequently. It is not uncommon for a third or more of the teachers in a rural school to be new each year. Although adequate data are not available, it is believed that over 90 per cent of the changes that occur in these situations are voluntary on the part of teachers, many of whom move to better teaching or administrative positions. A large percentage of the women marry and discontinue teaching. Some teachers leave the field and do other types of work. A few are judged by boards of education to be unsatisfactory and are not reemployed.

Teacher tenure, in another sense, refers to the prospects that a competent teacher has of remaining in a position without being dismissed for unjustifiable reasons. It refers to the amount of protection that a teacher has against losing his job.

Teacher Tenure in the Past.   Teacher tenure has not always been as strong as it is today. It was once common practice to dismiss competent teachers from other areas in order to make room for those in the town. The sons and daughters of the important people of a community who wanted teaching positions usually were successful in easing out others who did not enjoy such parental affiliations. School-board members have fired competent people and hired others who were willing to be bribed. Hiring and firing of teachers depended more upon a school official's liking for a teacher than upon a careful examination of the person's competency for teaching. In these circumstances most of a teacher's energies were directed toward cultivating and maintaining the good will of the community members in whose hands the security of his position rested. He was careful of his political and religious affiliations. He taught that the earth was square if it seemed desirable to teach that way. Special attention was given to pupils who were sons or daughters of the influential people. Great care was taken to avoid a discussion of any local problem or controversial issue that might incur the disapproval of some community member. The teacher's position often was subject to the whims, selfish interests, or ignorant and unscrupulous motives of those who had little or no concern for the welfare of children.

Reasons for Teacher Tenure.   For a number of years the general public has recognized that civil employees need protection against prejudice and pressure groups if they are to handle their jobs effectively. In government work this protection is provided through civil service appointments. The public now realizes more thoroughly the importance of the job of the teacher in our society and the need for position security because of the peculiar nature of teaching. The teacher has the task of transmitting and professionally refining the culture, and of promoting understanding of the problems and purposes of modern group living. In order to accomplish this task the teacher must be protected from having to move from one job to the next and from vacillating public opinion; otherwise children suffer in the long run and the schools are no longer instruments of *all* the people.

Professional organizations, spearheaded by the National Education Association, have been successful in securing considerable legislation for the protection of teachers. On the assumption that a better teacher means a better school and that the betterment of teaching depends in part on the improvement of teaching conditions, the Committee on Tenure and Academic Freedom of the NEA has set forth the following reasons for tenure [5:6–7]:

1. To protect classroom teachers and other members of the teaching profession against unjust dismissal of any kind—political, religious or personal.
2. To prevent the management or domination of the schools by political or noneducational groups for selfish and other improper purposes.
3. To secure for the teacher employment conditions which will encourage him

to grow in the full practice of his profession, unharried by constant pressure and fear.

4. To encourage competent, independent thinkers to enter and to remain in the teaching profession.

5. To encourage school management, which might have to sacrifice the welfare of the schools to fear and favor, to devote itself to the cause of education.

6. To set up honest, orderly, and definite procedures by which undesirable people may be removed from the teaching profession.

7. To protect educators in their efforts to promote the financial and educational interests of public school children.

8. To protect teachers in the exercise of their rights and duties of American citizenship.

9. To enable teachers, in spite of reactionary minorities, to prepare children for life in a democracy under changing conditions.

Kinds of Tenure Provided for Teachers. An analysis of contracts and tenure laws reveals many differences in the degree of security provided for teachers. These differences are understandable when you realize that in the beginning each school system was largely responsible for developing its own policies. Through the work of professional organizations and state legislation, however, policies are becoming more standardized.

Generally speaking, tenure provisions for teachers may be classified into the following types: annual contracts, contracts that extend for a definite number of years, continuing contracts, and protective continuing contracts.

You should understand the general provisions of the various types of contracts and laws indicated above, since they may have a significant influence upon where you accept a teaching position.

Annual contracts. A beginning teacher usually is given a one-year contract which gives him a legal right to teach in a school system, usually for one year only. A school year generally is considered to be that period of time between the opening of school in the fall and the closing date in the spring or summer. The teacher cannot be dismissed by the board of education during this period without justifiable cause. In some states, the bases for dismissal are written into the contracts given to the teacher and in some they are found in the state statutes governing schools. The term "justifiable cause" generally involves incompetence, inefficiency, immorality, insubordination, neglect of duty, unprofessional conduct, and physical or mental disability. Some laws specifically include intoxication, dishonesty, and commission of a felony. A few states require that the causes for dismissal be indicated in writing. The teacher may have a right to contest a dismissal, either in court or through the professional organizations. At the close of the school year a board of education has no obligation to reemploy a teacher for another year.

In return for the protection that the annual contract provides, the teacher has an obligation to the employing officials. It is often difficult to locate a competent teacher to replace one who decides to discontinue teaching. In order to protect the welfare of the children in the school, the teacher who wishes to terminate his services usually is required to give 30-day notice of his intention to resign, whether that resignation is before the beginning of school or during the school year, and to secure the consent of the board of education. It is true that there is nothing to prevent a teacher from just quitting his position. If he does this, however, his certificate for teaching probably would be revoked by the state board of education, in which case he would be unable to secure another position in that state.

Contracts for a definite number of years.   In the states of Mississippi, Texas, and Utah it is permissible by law to issue contracts for more than one year upon the initial assignment of a teacher. These contracts definitely specify the maximum term of employment. They usually extend for only a reasonable period of time beyond the term of office of the employing officials. They may be renewed for another definite number of years.

Continuing contracts with spring notification.   A teacher employed on an annual contract might not know whether he is to be reappointed until it is too late in the year to find a position elsewhere. In order to improve this situation, a number of states have what is called the "spring notification type of continuing-contract law." This type of contract provides for a teacher to be automatically reemployed for the next year unless notified of dismissal before a specified date. The date, such as April 15, is early enough for the teacher to find a position elsewhere, if necessary. Usually there is no obligation on the part of the school board to renew any contract. Illinois, Maine, and West Virginia require a statement of the reasons for not reemploying a teacher. In reality, "the typical continuing contract law offers limited protection to teachers except that it prevents dismissal after the season for employment of teachers and provides a weak sort of protection against unfair dismissal during the school year" [5:20].

Protective continuing contracts.   Some of the states have a protective type of continuing contract. With this type of contract a teacher is employed from year to year without being dismissed except by a prescribed procedure to be followed by the board of education in regard to the notice, the statement of changes, and the right to a hearing. This type of contract gives teachers virtually as much protection as a true tenure law. A probationary period of three years normally is required before a teacher is granted this type of contract. During this probationary period, the teacher's annual contract is not renewed if he does not measure up to the standards held by the school system. This probationary period protects the school from becoming overloaded with incompetent teachers.

Many school officials follow the practice of warning the teacher who has a protective-type continuing contract that his contract will not be continued unless certain conditions are improved. This practice seems to be in harmony with good school administration. The teacher is given the added assurance that he will not lose his position without having a chance to improve any unsatisfactory aspects of his work.

In order to dismiss a teacher who is employed on a protective-type continuing contract the board of education must notify the teacher at an early date of its intentions and must state the reasons for dismissal. The teacher is provided an opportunity for defending himself if he so desires.

Permanent tenure.   The greatest amount of tenure that you may be able to gain will be in a situation that provides for what is commonly called "permanent tenure." After serving a probationary period ranging from one to five years, the continuous employment of a teacher is assured, provided he renders efficient service and shows appropriate conduct.

The procedure for dismissing a teacher on permanent tenure is very similar to that required by the protective-type continuing contract. The employing officials must establish good cause for dismissal with higher authorities. Usually the bases upon which teachers can be dismissed are written into the tenure laws. A teacher has the right to request a formal review or trial of the case before a special committee or court, provided he feels that inadequate reasons for his dismissal can be shown. Permanent tenure differs primarily from tenure under continuing contracts in that under the former arrangement the case normally is not tried before the employing officials. Many teachers feel that the teacher who is to be dismissed is at an unfair advantage if he has to appeal his case to employing officials who serve as both accusers and judges.

Characteristics of Good Tenure Laws.

In 1960, 37 states and the District of Columbia had teacher tenure laws, either on a state-wide basis or in certain designated areas that apply to teacher contracts. An analysis of the provisions of these laws indicates considerable variation. You may find the following characteristics of good tenure laws, formulated by the National Education Association [adapted, 166:9–11], to be helpful in appraising tenure laws in the various states in which you may be interested in teaching:

1. A teacher should be employed on a probationary basis for a definite number of years—possibly a three-year period. The law should specify whether this employment is to be on an annual- or a spring-notification type of continuing contract, and should indicate the conditions and procedures regarding dismissal that are contained in the contract.

2. After the teacher has successfully completed the probationary period, the law should specify that the superintendent is required to recommend the teacher for tenure status.

3. The law should establish definite, orderly, legal procedures for dismissing unsatisfactory teachers by requiring that there be:
    a. Adequate notice given to the teacher.
    b. Charges stated in writing and including a record of criticism and aid offered.

   c. A hearing before the entire board, either private or public, as the teacher may request.

   d. Benefit of counsel and witnesses.

   e. Safeguard of salary rights during suspension.

   f. Final appeal to higher educational authorities or to the courts.

4. In cases of demotion or suspension, the law should make virtually the same provisions as for a dismissal case.

5. The tenure law should apply to all teachers, whether in rural, village, or city schools and without regard for race or color. Any less comprehensive law is discriminatory and divisive.

6. In cases of economic emergencies or depletion of school enrollments, a tenure law should provide for the fair and systematic dismissal of teachers along the following lines:

   a. A qualified tenure teacher should replace a probationary teacher.

   b. Tenure teachers should be dismissed in reverse order of seniority.

   c. Dismissed teachers should be reemployed in order of length of service and tenure status.

7. The law should define the status of the temporary teacher.

As you seek a position, check upon the provisions of the tenure law, if any, that apply to the position in which you are interested, as well as practices with respect to the placement of teachers on tenure.

Status of Teacher Tenure. Figure 44 will give you a fairly accurate picture of the status of state tenure or contract provisions in effect at

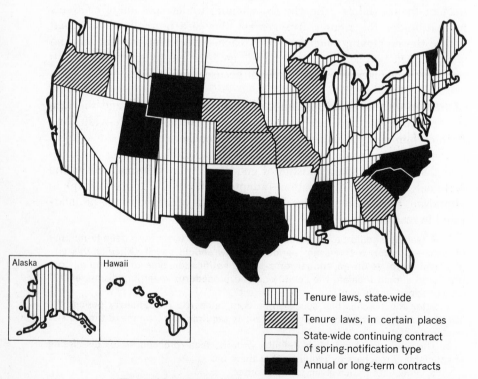

Alaska   Hawaii

||||||| Tenure laws, state-wide

▨ Tenure laws, in certain places

▢ State-wide continuing contract of spring-notification type

■ Annual or long-term contracts

Figure 44. Types of state tenure or contract provisions in effect in various states, 1961. (*Source:* National Education Association.)

the beginning of the 1960–1961 school year [167:83]. Some exceptions should be noted in the 37 states and in the District of Columbia that have state-wide tenure laws. In Colorado, tenure laws are subject to local adoption in small districts. In Michigan the laws are subject to local adoption throughout the state. Separate local tenure laws govern certain cities or counties in Connecticut and Florida. The state tenure laws do not apply to small districts in Illinois, Indiana, and New York. Annual contracts are the usual practice in the nontenure areas of Georgia and Kansas. Continuing contract laws of the spring-notification type apply to the nontenure areas of Missouri, Nebraska, Oregon, and Wisconsin. Of the 13 states without tenure laws, 5 have mandatory state-wide continuing laws of the spring notification type. In Virginia such provisions are subject to local adoption. Provisions for annual or long-term contracts are found in the other seven states.

In general, the tenure laws include supervisors, principals, teachers, and other school personnel. The types of employees covered are specifically mentioned in many tenure laws. A few laws extend tenure status to classroom teachers alone, or only to teachers and principals. Twelve laws explicitly include superintendents, and in five states superintendents are definitely excluded [167:82].

A number of states grant school superintendents contracts that extend for three, four, or five years. The recognized head of a school system is especially vulnerable to the shifting attitudes and reactions of community members; hence, it is felt that he should be granted more protection than is afforded in a one-year contract.

There are several sources of specific information about various provisions for teacher tenure. The Research Division of the National Education Association periodically publishes reports on the status of tenure in the various states. Your college library probably has copies of these reports. You may also secure information by writing to the department of education of the particular state in which you are interested.

Tenure in Institutions of Higher Education. Colleges and universities generally have been free to develop their own policies regarding tenure. As a result, considerable variation exists among the institutions. The continuing contract seems to be the favored type of tenure. The college teacher who is new to an institution usually serves a probationary period before he is granted tenure status. The length of the probationary period varies among, as well as within, institutions. Variations within are governed largely by the rank of the teacher. The instructor serves approximately five years before being placed on tenure; whereas the assistant, associate, and full professors serve respectively shorter periods.

The American Association of University Professors acts as a board of appeals to a college teacher who is in danger of being dismissed. An investigation is conducted by an appointed committee of the AAUP. If, in the judgment of the committee, the college or university is using unjustifiable procedures in dismissing staff members, the association usually places it on its black list until such procedures are changed. The black listing of an institution gives it unfavorable publicity with the general public and weakens its standing among other colleges. College teachers are hesitant to accept positions in such institutions. As a result, a college or university does not wish to incur the disfavor of the association.

Objections to Teacher Tenure.   There have been some objections, of which you should be aware, raised by community members and some school officials to placing teachers on tenure. The fact that 13 states still do not have tenure laws indicates that, even though great strides have been made, the battle for tenure laws is far from won.

It is maintained by some that competent teachers do not need tenure protection. The argument is true, no doubt, for a vast majority of teachers. The relationships of schools and communities in some sections, however, may not have reached a level at which the "spirit of the law may function without the law." For example, in some cases the employing officials, particularly those in small schools, follow the practice of never permitting teachers to gain permanent-tenure status, and in this way they avoid problems of having to dismiss tenure teachers. They have the feeling that it is too difficult to collect objective evidence to show incompetence, and that unpleasant publicity might result from having to dismiss a tenure teacher. As a result, they fail to reemploy a teacher just prior to the time that tenure status would be granted. Hence, these teachers expect to remain in a school system no longer than the probationary period, regardless of their competency.

Before you accept a position, investigate the practices used by a specific district in placing teachers on tenure. The chief sources of information will be the employing officials, teachers already in the school system, your college instructors, teacher-placement personnel, and the state office of the state education association.

Many maintain that incompetent teachers on tenure are too difficult to dismiss. This argument is advanced especially against permanent tenure. Perhaps the basic weakness lies in the administration of the tenure law rather than in the law itself.

It is claimed that a teacher on tenure has little or no incentive to grow professionally. Undoubtedly, there are far too many tenure teachers for whom this objection is justified. Some school systems counteract this tendency by requiring teachers every five or more years to show evidence of professional growth. Reviews of a teacher's work should be made periodically. If the teacher has made no improvement, he should be placed on probation for a period of time adequate for the situation to be corrected. If he fails to make the desired improvement, he should be dismissed. All teachers must assume the obligation of continuing to grow in order to be deserving of tenure rights and privileges.

As long as you remain in the teaching profession, continue your study of teacher tenure laws with a view of discovering their weak spots and to proposing corrections that should be made. In the states where there is no teacher tenure, attempt to obtain statewide tenure laws that will provide the best possible protection for teachers.

LEAVES OF ABSENCE

Regardless of the type of work you do, it is highly probably that you will be ill at some time before you wish to retire. Or family emergencies such as sickness and death will make unforeseen demands upon you. Or you will need, for your professional growth as a teacher, to attend professional meetings—particularly educational workshops—visit other schools, and engage in various projects which will enrich your work in the classroom. In teaching, these kinds of absence from regular classroom duties, may be classified as temporary or as sabbatical leaves.

Provisions for Temporary Leaves.   Teachers generally enjoy good health, and the job is less hazardous, from the standpoint of accidents, than many other types of work. However, teachers occasionally do become ill or have other reasons for being absent from their work. If the teacher who is ill is encouraged to work in order to avoid loss of pay, he endangers the welfare of the pupils through both his inefficiency and his poor health. Thus, sick leaves are granted by school systems more frequently than leaves from any other cause. There are, however, a number of other reasons widely accepted for absence from the classroom. They have been classified under the following three headings [160:2]:

A. Personal and Family
   1. Personal illness or injury
   2. Maternity
   3. Religious holidays
   4. Death in immediate family
   5. Illness in immediate family (including quarantine)
   6. Wedding or birth in immediate family
   7. Moving from one domicile to another
   8. Emergencies
B. Professional
   1. Attending or participating in educational meetings
   2. Visiting other schools
   3. Studying at colleges and universities
   4. Traveling for professional improvement
   5. Exchange teaching
   6. Serving the organized teaching profession through a local, state, or national education association as an officer, committee member, speaker, or legislative agent
C. Civic
   1. Answering a court summons
   2. Serving on a jury
   3. Voting; serving as an election official
   4. Serving in an elective office
   5. Participating in community-sponsored projects (fund drives, civic celebrations, etc.)
   6. Military duty

According to a survey conducted in 1961 [150:94–95], the laws of 33 states and the District of Columbia make specific references to teachers' sick leaves. Almost all of the modern school systems grant sick leave. It is unfortunate that practices in rural sections have lagged behind those in cities.

Plans for granting temporary leaves vary greatly. In some cases a teacher may be absent for a certain number of days at full pay or at part pay each year. Ten days' full-pay leave per year is the most common [150:9]. A few states provide for leave on an annual basis with no carry-over being allowed. The more typical plan, however, calls for an accumulation of unused leave from year to year, up to a specified total amount usually ranging from 20 to 60 days. On the other hand, California, Hawaii, and New Jersey do not place any limit upon the amount that may be accumulated. There is a definite trend in favor of the accumulation of leave time, up to a maximum, since it provides teachers with greater protection during extended periods of illness.

As is the case in any occupational group, a few individuals are inclined to abuse provisions that have been made for such matters as sick leave. For this reason, many school officials require teachers to provide written statements declaring that personal illness necessitated their absence from teaching. Usually a doctor's statement is required if the illness extends over a period of two or more days.

Provisions for maternity leaves are becoming quite common. As a rule

Many school systems now provide for maternity leaves. This enables many young women to remain in the teaching profession. (*Photograph by Carl Purcell, National Education Association.*)

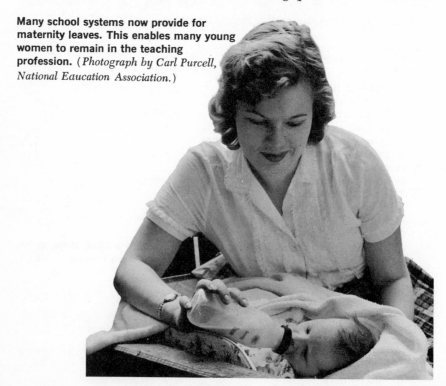

such leaves are without pay. School boards generally require teachers to apply for maternity leaves four to six months before confinement. The period of leave granted after delivery ranges from three months to three years [160:7–8].

Provisions for extended leaves of absence to teachers for exchange teaching in the United States is becoming more common, especially in urban school districts. A number of teachers have been granted extended leaves for teaching as exchange teachers in foreign countries in an effort to broaden culture, ease international tension, and improve the skills of all people. Financial assistance has been given to those who go to other countries as well as to those who come to the United States. School districts normally give their exchange teachers credit for salary increments for the year they teach abroad.

School districts normally grant extended leaves of absence without pay to teachers who wish to teach in Overseas Dependents Schools. Such opportunities enable teachers to have contact with teachers and pupils from all sections of the United States and, at the same time, to learn about other countries—frequently those in remote places of the world which normally are not visited on standard travel tours.

Provisions for temporary leaves in colleges and universities tend to be less formal than in public schools. It is generally assumed that the college teacher will occasionally be absent in order to attend professional meetings, lecture, consult with public school teachers, and the like. By virtue of the nature of the work, it is easier to provide for the temporary absence of college teachers than that of public school teachers.

Teachers for whom temporary leaves are provided are more fortunate than many other types of workers. Doctors and lawyers, for example, lose their fees and possibly some of their clientele when they are absent from their offices. When a person's income depends upon the amount of work he performs, he does not enjoy the same protection that teachers do when on temporary leave.

Provisions for Sabbatical Leaves.   The granting of sabbatical leave is a very common practice on the college level of teaching. The term originated from the practice of granting an extended leave to teachers every seventh year, and the seven-year period of service is usually a requirement today for sabbatical-leave eligibility. The purpose of the leave is to provide an opportunity for the teacher to improve himself professionally. The amount of time granted varies among institutions from a semester to a full year. The salary received on leave varies from full pay in a few cases to a fraction (usually one-half) of the teacher's regular earnings.

The practice of granting sabbatical leaves in colleges and universities probably has had some influence on granting extended leaves to public school teachers. A growing number of public school systems provide for sabbatical leave. The amount of pay varies from one-half of the regular salary to none at all. In some cases the teacher receives the difference between the cost of a substitute and his regular salary. It is fairly common to grant extended leaves without pay to public school teachers who wish to continue their studies toward advanced degrees. By receiving the advanced degree, the teacher may place himself in a higher salary bracket, and although he suffers a temporary loss in salary, he is able to gain financially in the future. The teacher who is granted an extended leave of absence also has the assurance of his position upon his return.

GROUP INSURANCE

Business and industry have shown increasing concern for hospitalization and life insurance protection for their employees. In view of the competition for teachers, it is not surprising to find public school systems and various state and national teacher organizations becoming increasingly interested in making possible such nonwage benefits to teachers.

A number of group life insurance programs have been arranged so that teachers may obtain life insurance at rates appreciably lower than those of individual policies. Group insurance calls for no medical examinations, and teachers usually pay until they reach the age of 65. The plan operates on the same sound principles of an insurance company with which it is affiliated.

Group insurance is very common among colleges and universities, where it is often made compulsory for the teachers. A college or university may have its own group plan or have arrangements with a well-established insurance company [64:92].

A survey conducted in 1961 by the Research Division of the National Education Association revealed that 16 per cent of the reporting school districts of 30,000 or more population assumed some responsibility in paying group life insurance premiums for teachers [64:92–93]. A few districts paid the entire premium. Group health and medical insurance premiums were paid for, at least in part, by more than one-fifth of the school districts. More of the larger districts than of the smaller ones paid part of the premium. Many of the districts had workman's compensation insurance for their employees, especially those engaged in maintenance.

Although some state teachers associations feel that efforts at this time should be centered on raising the salaries of teachers rather than on securing fringe benefits, it is highly probable that increasing numbers of school districts will be granting such benefits to teachers. The competition for teachers, even among school districts, is great enough to provide considerable incentive for making these benefits increasingly attractive to teachers.

CREDIT UNIONS

Many teachers have found credit unions to be exceedingly helpful to them in managing their salaries and in meeting financial obligations. This fact is reflected in the growth of the number of credit unions. In 1960, more than 1,250 teacher credit unions had been formed in school systems and colleges, more than twice the number that had existed in 1950 [35:1].

A teacher's credit union is a cooperative savings and loan organization that is owned and operated by and for its members. The Federal government has legalized the establishment of teacher credit unions. In order to form a credit union, a charter must be obtained which limits the operation to the members of the group. Its records and operations are subject to annual examination either by state or Federal authorities. Its management is under the direction of a board of directors chosen from the members of the group. In order to become a member of a credit union, you have to pay an entrance fee (usually 25 cents) and to purchase at least one share of stock (usually costing $5). In order to borrow from a credit union you must be a member.

Credit unions offer several advantages to teachers, including encouraging them to save some of their salary [141:14]. About half of the unions provide for payroll deductions, which make it easier for teachers to save. The savings are invested in loans to members, in United States bonds, or in other investments of a trust-fund type. The dividend rate compares very favorably with the cash return from many other types of investments. More than three-fourths of the teacher credit unions carry life insurance for each member, which represents a substantial addition to the annual dividend. Loans are made to credit-union members so that they can pay cash for needed items rather than resort to an installment plan which usually is decidedly more expensive. Personal counseling on economic problems is provided to members.

The teacher has an obligation to his profession to be economically efficient. Since the salary is not excessive, you owe yourself the best possible use of your financial resources. A good financial beginning normally results in greater happiness and success in life.

TEACHER RETIREMENT

A democratic society has an obligation to see that no one dies by virtue of his inability to provide the basic necessities of life. When a man becomes so old that he is unable to earn a living, he presents a charge to society unless he has made previous arrangements. In spite of all the efforts of some men during their productive years, it is impossible for them to make adequate financial arrangements for their declining years. For many years large industrial concerns and railroads have felt a responsibility for providing pensions for their employees when they become too old to work. An increasing concern through the years has been shown by the general public for the old-age welfare of all people. The most monumental evidence of this concern is to be found in the Federal Social Security Act passed by Congress in 1935. It can be safely assumed that the practice of safeguarding the basic needs of the old is an accepted practice in our society.

Need for Teacher Retirement.   In earlier days teachers had little interest in a teacher-retirement system, since very few expected to teach for the rest of their lives. Today an increasing number of young people are planning to make teaching their life careers; hence the significance of a sound retirement system becomes important to them.

A sound retirement system for teachers has the following advantages [163:1]:

1. It provides a dignified existence from active service after usefulness has diminished seriously through age or permanent disability.
2. It gives children the advantage of instruction from younger and more efficient teachers.
3. It increases the health and efficiency of teachers by removing worry and fear of a destitute old age.
4. It keeps good teachers in service.
5. It attracts capable, foresighted young people into the teaching profession.

A good retirement system provides a sense of security for teachers in service and a dignified existence from active service after usefulness has diminished through age or permanent disability. In this photograph of retired teacher, Emma Belle Sweet, who was awarded the Gold Key in recognition of her influence in shaping the career of an American leader, Ralph J. Bunche, undersecretary of the United Nations, you note a feeling of dignity and security. (*Photograph by Carl Purcell, National Education Association.*)

Extent of Teacher-retirement Systems.   Since 1946 all states and territories of the United States have had at least one law providing retirement benefits for teachers who have reached a stated age or have served for a stated length of time. There is considerable variation in the provisions of the laws. A complete analysis of each of the laws would be of little interest. A general idea of their provisions, however, may be gained from a study of materials periodically published by the Research Division of the National Education Association. Details regarding provisions in any particular state may be secured from its department of education.

In spite of the decided trend toward state-wide retirement programs, a number of cities have their own plans. The local systems are confined mainly to large cities, such as New York and Chicago, where the programs operate independently from the state-wide program or under permissive legislation of the state concerned.

Provision of Funds for Retirement.   There are two general types of provisions for aged and disabled teachers: pensions and retirement allowances. In pension plans in Delaware and New Mexico, the teacher makes no contribution from his salary. The pension is usually paid from a fund set aside by the state government or by the local school district. The remaining states have some form of a retirement allowance to which both the teacher and the state or school system contribute. It is commonly referred to as a "joint-contributory plan." From his active salary the teacher contributes a flat rate or a given percentage (usually 4 or 5 per cent) to the retirement fund, and this amount is usually matched by the local school system or the state.

It is important to remember that courts have held that pensions such as those granted by Delaware and New Mexico are gratuities, and that gratuities may be diminished or withheld at the will of the grantor. The beneficiary of a pension has no legal right to claim pension allotments. In contrast, the courts have held that in a joint-contributory retirement plan, retirement allowance must be paid to the retired teacher or his beneficiary.

Colleges and universities may belong to the retirement system provided by the state for public school teachers, may have their own system of retirement, may belong to an association such as the Teachers Insurance and Annuity Association, or may have no provisions at all for retirement. Virtually all the larger colleges and universities provide for the retirement of the staff members, although the plans differ greatly.

Some critics of retirement systems maintain that the teacher really pays for all the retirement benefits, that the amount which the state or local school sysem pays is rightfully a part of the teacher's salary. They fear that such an arrangement encourages teachers to accept lower salaries than they would otherwise. Statistics regarding teacher salaries and retirement benefits fail to substantiate this fear but, rather, indicate that an increase in one tends to accompany an increase in the other.

Trends in Providing Retirement Benefits.   Although the provisions for retirement vary considerably among the states, there seem to be certain trends in evidence. For example, a number of states have established plans whereby a teacher may retire voluntarily without meeting the full requirements and receive proportionately less retirement benefits. In some cases the teacher may retire voluntarily at an early date and receive full retirement benefits by paying the total amount that he and the state would have paid, had he met the regular requirements for retirement.

There is a tendency for retirement laws to specify the age when a teacher is compelled to retire, regardless of the amount of time the teacher has taught. This age usually ranged between 60 and 70.

When the requirements for retirement have been met, most systems now specify a formula for computing the allowance given the teacher. The amount usually depends on a certain percentage of the teacher's average salary during the last five or more years of his service. Normally, the yearly retirement allotment is approximately one-half of the average salary, payable until the recipient's death. Attempts are being made to increase the amount given so as to provide a more comfortable living for the teacher during his retirement.

Virtually all states now require all new teachers to participate in a retirement program. This procedure seems justifiable since otherwise many teachers would delay making adequate provisions for their retirement, and the welfare of children would be jeopardized.

Almost all retirement systems provide some sort of credit for service in the Armed Forces. In order to gain credit, however, the teacher usually must serve during a time of war or national emergency or be drafted or called as a reservist. Few systems provide retirement credit for overseas teaching unless the teacher is on exchange and is being paid by his American employer.

Many retirement plans are expanding the optional benefits for the retiring teacher so that he may choose the method of payment of benefits best suited to him.

Almost every state makes provisions for early retirement with compensation if the teacher becomes permanently disabled prior to normal retirement. Most of the laws, however, state that the teacher must have a specified minimum number of years of service before he is eligible for disability benefits. The amount of benefit to be received depends upon the amount of service that the teacher has had or upon a fixed sum specified by policy or law.

Withdrawal after Limited Service.   You normally will be entitled to a percentage of the amount of money which you have contributed toward retirement if you withdraw from teaching prior to the minimum time required for retirement. This percentage increases with the length of service. Usually after 10 years of service you would be refunded 100 per cent for the amount you contributed. A few systems refund the total amount regardless of when you withdraw. In many cases you will not be forced to withdraw your money if you leave the profession. Unless you are in great need, it will be wise for you to leave the sum intact. The capital usually accumulates at a high rate of interest. Furthermore, you may wish to return to teaching, in which case you will have to your credit the money contributed during the previous years of service.

Death of the teacher concerned naturally constitutes a withdrawal from teaching. In this case, the amount of money due would be paid to beneficiaries. Death benefits vary greatly from one state to another.

Transfers from One State to Another.   Unfortunately, if you transfer from one state to another, you may lose some or all of the retirement benefits that you have accumulated. The states vary considerably with respect to the number of years of credit that may be transferred. Usually an experienced transfer teacher must contribute a sum equal to the amount he would have contributed if he had taught in the state the credited number of years. Efforts are being made whereby a teacher's retirement account may be transferred from one state to another without any loss of benefit. However, a number of years may be required before this practice becomes commonplace.

Social Security Benefits for Teachers.   Prior to January 1, 1955, teachers, like all public employees, were not affected by the National Social Security Act. At the time the original act was being considered, in 1935, much attention was given to the possibility of its including all types of people. Teachers as a group, however, did not wish to have their own systems of retirement abolished in favor of the conditions prescribed by the act; most teacher-retirement benefits were appreciably higher. Furthermore, since social security benefits were financed by a tax on both employer and employee, there was a question as to whether the Federal government legally could impose a tax on the states or local governmental agencies or their employees.

In 1950, Congress amended the Social Security Act, permitting states to make agreements with the Social Security Administration so that state employees would be covered. By such a voluntary arrangement, the Federal government could not be accused of taxing a state or its agencies.

In 1954 Congress extended greatly the benefits to be derived from the Social Security Act and also made it possible for public employees to obtain social security benefits without abandoning any existing public employee retirement system. As a result, government employees, as of January 1, 1955, could become eligible for social security benefits if the members, after having had 90 days' notice of the referendum, voted in favor of it. The teachers in a number of states took advantage of this opportunity.

The states that have adopted social security have used various formulas for accomplishing this purpose. In some states, teachers have social security coverage in addition to their retirement benefits. In other cases the social security benefits are coordinated or are integrated with the retirement benefits.

Social security has certain advantages that are not present in many teacher-retirement laws. Since it is nationwide in scope, a teacher does not run as much danger of losing his benefits in moving from one state to another as he does in the case of state retirement plans. There is no compulsory retirement age in the Federal plan, although there is a limitation on the amount an individual can earn between the ages of 65 and 72 and yet draw full social security benefits during those years. If a man wishes, he may retire as early as 62, but the benefits per year are proportionately less. A wife, if she is 65 or more years old, receives an additional one-half of her husband's benefits (or less if she wishes to begin receiving it at age 62), while the husband collects the full amount. Survivors' benefits are provided for widows over 62, children under 18, and widows of any age caring for the deceased's children.

In 1961, about 50 per cent of the public school teachers were covered by social security, including some or all of the teachers in 38 states [147:113]. Under the social security plan a teacher and the school system in which he works each contribute a percentage of his salary, up to $4,800, toward social security. The rate is to increase in the future: $3\frac{5}{8}$ per cent from 1963 through 1965; $4\frac{1}{8}$ per cent from 1966 through 1967; $4\frac{5}{8}$ per cent from 1968 and thereafter.

Check List for Evaluating a Teacher Retirement System. You may be interested in teaching in a state other than the one in which you are being prepared to teach. Likewise, your teaching career may involve retirement plans in two or more states. For these reasons you may find the "Check List for Appraising a Teacher Retirement System," which is located in the Resource Section of Part III, to be of help to you. For the present, the check list should assist you in summarizing the characteristics of a good teacher-retirement system.

SUMMARY

In this chapter you have looked into some of the important factors other than salary that affect the economic security of teachers. Although practices and provisions vary throughout the United States, much progress has been made in providing security through tenure for the competent teacher by means of which he is better able to fulfill his professional responsibilities to youth. The reasons for, the kinds, the present status, and the characteristics of good tenure laws were examined. Increasingly liberal provisions for leaves of absence are being developed. As in the case of business and industry, school officials are showing increasing concern for hospitalization and life insurance protection for their employees. Many teachers are finding credit unions to be exceedingly helpful to them in managing their salaries and in meeting financial obligations. The need for teacher retirement, the extent, provisions, trends in regard to retirement systems were carefully examined. Social security benefits for teachers were also noted.

These added benefits to teachers have come primarily through the concerted efforts of various local, state, and national professional teacher organizations in an attempt to place careers in the field of education on a truly professional level. Continued efforts on the part of all should bring about even further benefits.

QUESTIONS FOR YOUR CONSIDERATION

1. What are the advantages and disadvantages of tenure as it relates to annual contracts, contracts extending for a definite number of years, continuing contracts, and protective continuing contracts?

2. How do you account for the fact that a number of states still do not have tenure laws and that in some states the laws do not apply to all teachers?

3. In what ways may permanent tenure be misused professionally?

4. How may teachers on tenure be encouraged to continue their professional growth?

5. What are the advantages and disadvantages of superintendents not having permanent tenure?

6. What leave-of-absence provisions should a school system make for teachers?

7. To what extent should school districts provide group life insurance programs for teachers?

8. Is a joint-contributory retirement plan more desirable than a pension plan? Why?

9. What, in your opinion, is the most desirable retirement plan which will prevent the migratory teacher from being penalized?

10. What are the advantages and disadvantages of a law which compels teachers to retire upon reaching a certain age?

11. Do you feel that all teachers should be eligible for social security benefits? Why?

ACTIVITIES FOR YOU TO PURSUE

1. Study as many occupations as possible in terms of the provisions preventing an individual from losing his job unfairly. Compare and contrast these occupations with teaching.

2. If you know of a teacher on permanent tenure who seems to be shirking his job responsibilities, analyze the personal factors or values that may be involved.

3. If you were a superintendent of schools, what would you do

if parents reported one of your teachers on permanent tenure as incompetent in the classroom?

4. Study in detail the retirement plans in three or more states in which you may be interested in teaching.

5. Investigate the amount of social security benefits you might receive upon retirement.

6. Investigate various occupations in terms of provisions for emergency leaves. Compare and contrast these provisions with those in your home school system.

7. Compare the rates for group life insurance for teachers with rates for other types of insurance.

8. Assume you wish to borrow money to buy a new automobile. How would the total cost of the automobile, if financed through a credit union such as the Teachers' Credit Union, compare with its cost if financed through a regular loan company?

9. Investigate the fringe benefits for teachers in a large and in a small school system. What differences, if any, exist?

10. Use the check list in the Resource Section for Part III and attempt to appraise the retirement system for teachers in your home state.

RESOURCE SECTION FOR PART III

- Check List for Appraising a Teacher Salary Schedule

- Check List for Appraising a Teacher Retirement System

- Suggested Filmstrips and Recordings

- Suggested Readings

- Figure Credits

• CHECK LIST FOR APPRAISING A TEACHER SALARY SCHEDULE

If you can answer "yes" to each of the following questions, you may be certain that the salary schedule is a good one.

Item	Yes	No

Rules and Regulations
1. Are the following requirements for employment specified: a degree; graduation from an institution accredited for teacher education; full professional certification?
2. Are safeguards provided against arbitrary denial or withdrawal of increments?
3. If "professional growth" requirements are utilized are increases based on clearly defined qualifications which can be reasonably expected of all teachers?
4. Is the application clear and equitable with regard to: credit for prior service outside the district; credit for military service; placing teachers on steps; advanced warning and follow-up supervisory help if increments are denied?
5. Is discretionary initial step placement prohibited?

Starting Salaries
1. Is the B.A. minimum competitive in respect to beginning salaries offered to college graduates?
2. Does this minimum make it possible for teacher to invest in advanced preparation?
3. Does this minimum permit a professional living standard?

Experience Increments
1. Is each increment at least five per cent of the B.A. minimum?
2. Does the B.A. scale have less than twelve steps (eleven increments)?
3. Is the increment structure devised to reduce teacher turnover and to promote in-service growth?

Training Differentials
1. Is the extent of recognition sufficient to include:
   a. A class for the master's degree?
   b. A class for sixth year of college preparation?
   c. A class for the doctor's degree or a seventh-year preparation level as a substitute for the doctoral class?
   d. Intermediate preparation levels for at least each half-year of graduate credit?
2. Are differentials adequate in amounts so as to:
   a. Be an incentive for voluntary professional growth?
   b. Allow teachers with advanced preparation and professional growth credits a salary potential at least $1,000 above the regular B.A. scale?
   c. Reimburse teachers with a reasonable period (not more than ten years) for their investments in advanced preparation?

Source: Taylor, Eula May, and Erwin L. Coons, "Salary-Scheduling Check List," *National Education Association Journal,* vol. 49, no. 7, p. 33, National Education Association, Washington, October, 1960.

CHECK LIST FOR APPRAISING A TEACHER SALARY SCHEDULE (*continued*)

Item	Yes	No
Maximum Salaries **1.** Excepting super-maximums, are they attainable in a reasonable number of years (ten to fifteen)? **2.** Is the B.A. maximum at least sixty per cent above the B.A. minimum?		
Extra Compensation **1.** Are higher salaries based on differences in qualifications, avoiding such discriminatory practices as sex differentials; and subject or grade-level differential? **2.** Are salary differentials allowed for work beyond normal load? **3.** If extra pay is granted, is a schedule of payments included in the salary policy or personnel policies? **4.** Has "extra pay" been abolished in favor of a balanced load for all teachers?		
Other Considerations Related to Quality **1.** Is the schedule a 'booster" rather than a "buster" of teacher morale? **2.** Does the schedule enhance the professional standing of the teaching staff? **3.** Does the schedule generally provide freedom from financial worry? **4.** Does the schedule indicate that teachers are to devote full time to teaching? **5.** Are teacher-supervisor relations for improvement of instruction kept on a high plane of co-operation? **6.** Are irregularities which tend to tear down teachers' prestige, self-confidence, and status avoided?		

• CHECK LIST FOR APPRAISING A TEACHER RETIREMENT SYSTEM

You may be satisfied that the retirement system embodies good features if you can answer "yes" to each of the following questions:

Questions	Yes	No
1. Is the system joint-contributory? **2.** Are investments of the reserves safeguarded? **3.** Is the system administered by a board separate from other governmental bodies?		

Source: Adapted from *Teacher Retirement*, National Education Association Discussion Pamphlet No. 2, Department of Classroom Teachers and Research Division, Washington, November, 1957, pp. 21–22.

CHECK LIST FOR APPRAISING A TEACHER RETIREMENT SYSTEM *(continued)*

Questions	Yes	No
4. Are teachers represented on the retirement board?		
5. Are all types of professional positions covered by the retirement system; that is, administrative and supervisory as well as classroom teaching positions?		
6. Is membership in the retirement system compulsory for teachers employed since the establishment of the system?		
7. Are the contributions sufficient to pay a reasonable retirement allowance?		
8. When a teacher withdraws from the profession or dies in active service, are all his own contributions refundable and with interest?		
9. Are benefits payable to surviving dependents of a deceased member?		
10. Does the teacher who withdraws before retirement have the option of leaving his money in the system and taking a deferred annuity policy instead of a cash refund?		
11. Is out-of-state service credited toward years of service required for retirement?		
12. Does the system give a teacher about to retire a choice of several ways of receiving his allowance?		
13. Are there retirement benefits for a teacher who is disabled prior to meeting requirements (age and years of service) for regular retirement?		
14. Is a teacher who is absent on military leave given credit toward retirement for the time he is in service?		
15. If social security coverage has been extended to the members of the retirement system, has the over-all protection been improved?		

• SUGGESTED FILMSTRIPS AND RECORDINGS

The number in parentheses following each suggestion denotes the chapter for which it is best suited.

Filmstrips
Let's Take a Look at Teaching   (Wayne University, 50 fr.). Gives an overview of the teaching profession and what it has to offer in terms of salary, tenure, working conditions, opportunities for travel, and individual interests. Pictures a typical school day showing the varied demands on the teacher, and her responsibilities. (9)

Recordings
Developing Salary Schedules for Teachers   (Educational Recording Service, 33⅓ rpm). Two teachers, Irving R. Melbo, dean of education, University of Southern California, and D. Lloyd Nelson, professor of education, University of Southern California, present suggestions for the development of salary schedules for teachers. (9)
Teacher Salary Schedule   (National Tape Recording Project, 15 min). Discusses the importance of a salary schedule in attracting good teachers and in improving education. (9)
Teacher Tenure   (National Tape Recording Project, 15 min). Discusses how to avoid the fear that results when cheap politics invades the classroom. (10)

• SUGGESTED READINGS

The number in parentheses following each suggestion denotes the chapter for which it is best suited.

Cooke, Blaine: "Merit Pay for Teachers," *Saturday Review,* Dec. 16, 1961, pp. 46, 47, 61, 62. Discusses the pros and cons of merit pay for teachers. (9)

Credit Unions for Teachers, National Education Association Discussion Pamphlet 6, Research Division and Department of Classroom Teachers, Washington, August, 1960. Contains an excellent discussion of the purposes, operation, and advantages of credit unions for teachers. (10)

Economic Status of Teachers, National Education Association, Research Division (latest issue), Washington. Presents much information on factors affecting the economic status of teachers. (9)

"Extra Pay and Dependency Allowances—Are They Fair?" *National Education Association Journal,* vol. 49, no. 8, pp. 52–54, National Education Association, Washington, November, 1960. Consists of a symposium discussion concerning extra pay for extra work, as well as allowances for dependents. (9)

Extra Pay Provisions in 1959–1960 Salary Schedules, National Education Association Circular 4, Research Division, Washington, 1960. Presents information on the kinds and extent of extra pay provisions in public schools. (9)

Lambert, Sam M.: "Educational Growth and Change Lie Ahead in the 1960's," *National Education Association Journal,* vol. 49, no. 9, pp. 45–47, National Education Association, Washington, December, 1960. Contains predictions, based upon research, of what is likely to happen in education in the next ten to twenty years. (9)

Lillywhite, Ray L.: "Trends in Teacher Retirement," *National Education Association Journal,* vol. 50, no. 2, pp. 45–46, National Education Association, Washington, February, 1961. Presents some immediate and future teacher retirement problems and some possible solutions to them. (10)

McNamara, Pat: "Why Federal Money for Teachers' Salaries?" *National Education Association Journal,* vol. 50, no. 2, pp. 12–14, National Education Association, Washington, February, 1961. Presents a senator's view on Federal money for teachers' salaries. (9)

"Proper Use of Sick Leave," *National Education Association Journal,* vol. 51, no. 5, p. 11, National Education Association, Washington, May, 1962. Presents an interpretation of the NEA Committee on Professional Ethics in regard to the proper use of sick leave. (10)

Salary Schedule Maximums for School Administrators, Urban Districts 100,000 and Over in Population, National Education Association Research Division, Washington (latest issue). Indicates the maximum salaries scheduled for school building administrators and central-office administrators. (9)

Stover, William R.: "The What and Why of Tenure," *National Education Association Journal,* vol. 50, no. 3, pp. 47–48, National Education Association, Washington, March, 1961. Indicates the bases and values of tenure. (10)

Teacher Leave of Absence, National Education Association Discussion Pamphlet 7, Research Division and Department of Classroom Teachers, Washington, May, 1961. Contains an excellent discussion of all types of leaves of absence and presents the results of a nationwide survey. (10)

Tickton, Sidney G.: *Teaching Salaries Then and Now—a Second Look,* The Fund for the Advancement of Education, New York, 1961. Presents a number of tables comparing salaries over the years and with other occupations. (9)

"Why Few School Systems Use Merit Ratings," *Research Bulletin,* vol. 38, no. 2, pp. 61–63, National Education Association, Research Division, Washington, May, 1961. Indicates that unsatisfactory plans for evaluation have led to discontent and misunderstanding of merit pay. (9)

Year-round School, National Education Association, American Association of School Administrators, Washington, 1960. Presents various plans for the year-round use of schools and indicates how the life of a teacher would be affected. (10)

● FIGURE CREDITS

Figure 37. (*Source:* "Estimates of School Statistics, 1961–62," *Research Report* 1961-R22, p. 12, National Education Association, Research Division, Washington, December 1961.)

Figure 38. (*Source:* "Economic Status of Teachers in 1961–62," *Research Report* 1962-R7, p. 19, National Education Association, Research Division, Washington, May, 1962.)

Figure 39. (*Source: Professional Salaries for Professional Teachers,* National Education Association, Committee on Educational Finance, Washington, 1961, p. 19.)

Figure 40. (*Source:* "Estimates of School Statistics, 1961–62," *Research Report* 1961-R22, p. 26, National Education Association, Research Division, Washington, December, 1961.)

Figure 41. (*Source:* "Reduced Progress in Urban Teachers' Salaries," *Research Bulletin,* vol. 39, no. 3, p. 69, National Education Association, Research Division, Washington, October, 1961.)

Figure 42. (*Source:* "Index Salary Schedules for Teachers," *Research Bulletin,* vol. 39, no. 4, p. 111, National Education Association, Research Division, Washington, December, 1961.)

Figure 43. (*Source:* "Summer School—Opportunity," *Research Bulletin,* vol. 38, no. 1, p. 24, National Education Association, Research Division, Washington, February, 1960.)

Figure 44. (*Source:* "Tenure and Contracts," *School Law Series,* National Education Association, Research Division, Washington, November, 1961, p. 3.)

PART IV

OUR EDUCATIONAL HERITAGE

The development of our schools antedates even the earliest immigrants to this country. How these early settlers felt and what they did about education for their children is clearly reflected in certain conditions in school today—conditions that will affect *you* as a teacher.

The extent to which you are able to assess accurately the present status of education will depend in part upon how thoroughly you understand the historical development of schools in America. As you become fortified with this knowledge, you will be more effectively able to aid in the improvement of school practices and procedures.

Chapter 11 attempts to acquaint you with major developments in our school system as they occurred during three rather clearly defined periods. Chapter 12 briefly explores the development of some modern concepts of education. An understanding of the contributions of various outstanding thinkers should aid you considerably in gaining value from subsequent courses in education.

11
HISTORICAL DEVELOPMENT OF OUR SCHOOLS

The American school system is the expression of the hopes, desires, ambitions, and values held by those who have made our nation what it is today. It represents, in fact, one of the most noble and visionary experiments ever attempted by mankind. The story of how it came into being and developed through the years is, as you might expect, a unique and fascinating one.

A really competent educator has a good understanding of how our schools have developed, understands what influenced them to develop in this manner, and takes hold at every opportunity to move them forward to what they can best become. As you gain insights and understandings concerning the background out of which the school of the present has evolved and the forces and conditions which have made it what it is, you will be better qualified to carry on its activities and to direct its future.

As you read this chapter, apply the understandings you have gained from courses you have taken in high school and in college that have been concerned with the development of the United States. These understandings, accompanied by brief descriptions of religious, social, economic, and political forces and factors, should help you in studying the major periods in the development of our schools. As you continue in the field of education, you will achieve a deeper understanding of the historical backgrounds of education. Through such efforts you, as an American citizen concerned with our nation's schools, will be less likely to repeat yesterday's mistakes and be more able to attain tomorrow's aspirations.

EDUCATION DURING THE COLONIAL PERIOD (1620–1779)

The early settlers in the New World brought with them their respective political traditions, religions, styles of architecture, and social customs. When they were faced with problems, it was natural for them to do the same thing that men have done throughout the ages—they drew upon the experiences with which they were familiar. As a consequence, institutions in the New World were built on the foundation of the life and customs of the Old World. Essentially, it was a process of transplantation. Early schools, therefore, were patterned in the European tradition, and the attitudes toward education followed European beliefs.

European education had been influenced greatly by the Greek and Roman concepts of the cultured man which were revived during the Renaissance and given religious emphasis after the Reformation. The need for education was produced by the feeling that each individual should be able to read the word of God. Likewise, a rigid class structure was mirrored in seventeenth-century European education. It was a stratified society in which each individual, generally at birth, found his role in life assigned to him [22:110]. Emphasis was placed upon the stability and maintenance of the society in which each person had his rights and responsibilities for operating within the group. It was rare indeed to find any individual advancing through this stratification to a higher class status.

Since education was considered to be important in meeting the religious needs of individuals, schools were the primary concern of the church or the parents or of both, but not of the general public. The influence of the church upon education in colonial days can scarcely be overestimated.

Since the early colonists came from different countries in Europe, their backgrounds and beliefs differed from group to group and so did their views on education. As a result, it is possible to distinguish three major attitudes toward education centered in three loosely defined areas —New England Colonies (primarily Massachusetts, Rhode Island, Connecticut, and New Hampshire), Middle Atlantic Colonies (principally New York, New Jersey, Delaware, and Pennsylvania), and Southern Colonies (mainly Virginia, Maryland, Georgia, North Carolina, and South Carolina). These attitudes provided bases from which the ultimate structure of our educational system grew.

The New England Colonies. Religious and political freedom were the strong motivating forces which led the early New England settlers to make their journey to the New World. Their strong religious attitude was well set forth in a quotation from a pamphlet titled *New England's First Fruits* [99:242]:

> After God had carried us safe to New England, and wee had builded our houses, provided necessaries for our liveli-hood, rear'd convenient places for God's worship, and settled the civill government: One of the next things we longed for and looked after was to advance learning and perpetuate it to posterity; dreading to leave an illiterate ministry to the churches, when our present ministers shall lie in the dust.

This strong emphasis upon religion required that the individual be equipped to read and understand the word of God as set forth in the Bible. Salvation was a constant concern of the people. Therefore, these early colonists felt a distinct obligation to teach their children to read, so that they might know the Bible and take the first step toward saving their souls.

Another motivating force in the development of education in New England was that a number of the early settlers were highly educated. Estimates have been made which indicate that approximately 3 per cent of the adult men were university graduates. Without a doubt they were highly influential in promoting interest in education. This influence can be appreciated when we consider the fact that by 1635 the Pilgrims, who landed at Plymouth Rock in 1620, had established Boston Latin School.

The Latin grammar school.   The Boston Latin School was the first successfully organized school of any kind in America. It was a so-called Latin grammar school, copied directly from the type developed in England. Its central purpose was to prepare boys for college. Because colleges were concerned primarily with the preparation of ministers, the curriculum consisted chiefly of Latin, Greek, and theology. Pupils entered usually at age seven, having previously learned to read and write, and completed the course in about seven years.

The Latin grammar school provided the framework of secondary schools in America. Although it was essentially a select school—reserved

The Boston Latin School was copied from a so-called Latin grammar school of the type developed in England. (*Courtesy of New York* Herald Tribune.)

for the wealthy and elite and aimed solely at preparation for college—it had some occasional public financial support. This type of school spread slowly throughout New England and further along the coast. There is some evidence that such a school was planned by the Virginia Company in 1621, but the colony was wiped out by the Indian massacre of 1622.

The Latin grammar school was prominent until the Revolutionary War, when it was challenged by another type of secondary school, but some of its influences are still to be found in public schools. The classical emphasis in many high school programs, the persistence of Latin as a general requirement, the rigid graduation specifications which are so often pointed toward college preparation, the emphasis upon logical order per se and rote learning—these are some of the conspicuous influences of the Latin grammar school which have persisted in many public secondary schools to this day.

It should be kept in mind that the Latin grammar school was a private school which charged tuition. This fact alone made it impossible for many boys to attend grammar school in order to prepare for college. Furthermore, practically no relationship existed between what might be called colonial elementary schools and grammar schools. The educational ladder which is so distinctly a part of the American school system had not yet come into being.

Dame school. In the early days of New England it was felt that each family should bear the responsibility for the elementary schooling of its children. Many families, not feeling equal to this responsibility, sent their children to the famous "dame schools" or to private tutors. The dame school was simply a private home where a group of children met under the leadership of a housewife or mother and where opportunities were provided for the children to learn their ABC's, the catechism, and at times a little simple arithmetic. The teacher usually charged tuition for her services. Occasionally a group of parents would engage a schoolmaster to give the same type of instruction which the dame school provided.

Massachusetts school laws. It soon became evident that the dame schools and the private tutors did not guarantee that all children would attain the basic requirements of literacy which the Puritan societies required. By 1642 there had grown a deep concern about "the great neglect of many parents and masters in training up their children in learning and labor." This condition prompted the Massachusetts Bay Colony to enact the Massachusetts School Law of 1642. The law charged the local magistrates in each town with "the care and redress of this evil." These local officials were to take note periodically of what had been done in educating the children, and if their education had been neglected, the magistrates could require that the children be sent to school. Actually this law did not provide for the establishment of schools but, through fines, attempted to enforce upon parents their responsibilities for having their children learn to read.

During the five years following the enactment of the 1642 legislation, it became evident that the law was not being strictly enforced. The feeling grew that government must do more than merely *insist* upon education. It must *make provisions* for education, if children were to be properly educated. Thus in 1647 Massachusetts passed a new law which became known as the "Old Deluder Satan Law." As the name implies, the Massachusetts Law of 1647 reveals a definite church influence. An excerpt (in modernized spelling) follows:

> It being one chief object of that old deluder, Satan, to keep men from the knowledge of the Scriptures, as in former times, by keeping them in unknown tongue, so in these latter times by persuading from the use of tongues, that so at least the true sense and meaning of the original might be clouded by false glosses of saint-seeming deceivers, that learning may not be buried in the grave of our fathers in the church and Commonwealth, the Lord assisting our endeavors . . .

This "mother of all school laws" required that each town of 50 families provide a teacher to instruct the children sent to him. The teacher was to be paid by the parents, by the church, or by the inhabitants in general, as those who managed the affairs of the community might decide. The law also stipulated that every town of 100 families should provide a grammar school to prepare boys for college. This law, therefore, established a common school to teach the rudiments of learning and a preparatory school to qualify young boys for college.

Another part of the law of 1647 stated that any town would be subject to an annual penalty of five pounds if it neglected to establish these schools. Unfortunately some localities found it cheaper to pay the penalty than to observe the stipulations of the law.

New England, in general, was unique in the fact that its governments were the first in the New World to accept any responsibility for educating the young. No such effort was put forth in the other colonies along the

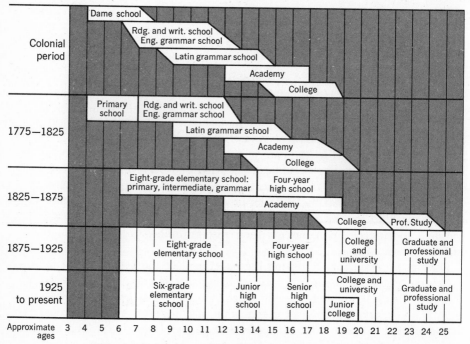

Figure 45. Various types of schools predominated in the development of our educational system. (*Source:* The Ronald Press Company.)

Atlantic seaboard. As the first serious attempt to establish schools by legislation, the law of 1647 was the cornerstone of our free public school system.

Remarkable though the New England achievement was, it would be erroneous to believe that the Massachusetts school was synonymous with the American school as we know it today. The former was substantially a parochial school, even though it operated under the authority of the state rather than of the church. It is well to remember that the religious motive was very strong in the establishment of education in the New England colonies and that what the church wanted could easily be enacted into law. Gradually, as church and state separated in this country, the state supplanted the church in the educational field until ultimately the principle of state obligation and state sovereignty was born.

The Middle Atlantic Colonies. The development of education in the Middle Atlantic or Middle colonies differed considerably from that in the other colonies. There were the Dutch in New York, the Swedes along the Delaware River, and the English Quakers in Pennsylvania. These people came to the New World with different ideals and customs, different languages, different styles of architecture, and different types of Christianity.

Of these groups, possibly the Dutch in what is now New York were the most advanced in their educational thinking. By the 1630s there was some evidence that they had established schools under the authority and the supervision of the government. It is to be remembered, however, that all schools in that day were vitally interested in teaching religion. With all the ethnic and religious differences to be found in the Middle colonies, the only solution to the educational problem was to have each church organize its own school and teach its own beliefs.

The typical school of the Middle colonies, then, was the parochial school—the school of the church parish. Parents were expected to pay tuition for their children, but, if they could not pay, the church sometimes permitted the child to attend nonetheless. In later years, the more common custom was for local authorities to pay tuition for poor children out of the "poor fund."

When the English took over New Amsterdam (New York) in 1664, they added to the complications already in existence. The English, at this time, were more backward than the Dutch in matters of education. Historians agree that in the later colonial period schools in and around New York deteriorated under English rule.

With the heterogeneity of cultural backgrounds and religious beliefs represented in the Middle colonies, attempts to weld such great differences into a sound educational pattern presented a baffling problem.

The Southern Colonies. Virginia was the most important of the Southern colonies, and the development of education here was fairly representative of the colonies in this area. The Virginia settlers came to the New World not primarily because of discontent with the social and political system of the home country but to better their fortunes. They had no particular quarrel with the English way of doing things. The English had developed an aristocratic society whose government took little or no interest in education.

The South was characterized by an agricultural society in which slaveholding was a common practice. Education was not considered to be a function of the government. Rather, parents were expected to attend to the education of their own children. As a result, schooling in the Southern Colonies was almost entirely the private-tutor type. A few schools were established, but these were mainly for youngsters of wealthy plantation owners. Many of the sons of these plantation owners were sent back to England for a large part of their formal schooling. Those who could not afford to do this had very little opportunity to secure an education.

There were, however, several free schools in the colony, which were established through the private contributions of public-spirited citizens. In order to send their children to these free schools, families had to declare themselves publicly to be paupers. The schools became known as "pauper schools." Many parents who could not pay the rates charged by the private schools and who refused to advertise themselves as paupers had no alternative but to keep their children out of school. Thus a large proportion of young people grew up illiterate.

Virginia, like many of the other colonies, followed the European custom of apprenticing orphans or the sons and daughters of very poor families. The law provided that the local magistrate could apprentice such a child to a master craftsman, who would teach the child his trade, give him board and lodging, and provide instruction in reading, writing, and religion. The child in turn agreed to help his master unquestioningly in his work. From reports of this type of vocational education, it was found that far too often the masters were more interested in the services which their apprentices could render than in providing good basic learnings for the child.

Early Elementary Schools.   Educational practices in the early colonial period provided little in the way of an organized pattern of elementary education. Dame schools, early parochial schools, private tutors, apprenticeships, and pauper schools developed quite independently of one another. This condition was due in part to the fact that parents were expected to care for the rudimentary education of their children. Conditions were different from those of today in that the government felt no responsibility for the education of the young.

The common school.   Gradually, various systems were developed for teaching the three R's to youngsters. There were reading schools and writing schools, and often the two were combined into one. The pupils could attend one school in the morning and the other in the afternoon. These became the common schools that spread first through the New England area. There were no rigid regulations about entrance or attendance or withdrawal. The common schools served the masses of youngsters, most of whom did not attend the Latin grammar school or college.

Life in and around these early schools was very different from that in our modern public schools. It is very difficult to visualize the conditions under which colonial settlers struggled to obtain an education. In place of the modern, large, well-lighted, and heated building, they had a single bare, unattractive room. The room might be in a residence, a vacant store building, or a rough log structure [91:48–66]. A few of the better school buildings had glazed windows. In log structures which were designated

This typical early American schoolroom is a far cry from the attractive well-heated and well-lighted schoolroom we know today. (*Photograph from the Library of Congress.*)

solely for the use of education, the usual practice was to leave a log out of one side of the building in order to provide both light and ventilation.

More often than not a rough plank served as the teacher's desk. Long, rough, backless benches were provided for the pupils. Often the feet of the young children did not touch the floor. Equipment was quite meager. Along one side of the room, there would occasionally be a long shelf where students would practice such activities as penmanship, using quill pens. A great stone fireplace furnished the only heat by which the chil-

The hornbook takes its name from the thick sheet of transparent horn used to protect the paper from dirt. (*Photograph from Ruth G. Strickland.*)

dren could keep warm. As with many a present-day fireplace, those who were close to its blazing hearth were likely to get scorched while those farthest away shivered with the cold. Considering many reports of complaints which were recorded and passed down to posterity, it was evident that most of these rooms and buildings were in sad need of repair.

It was in this kind of atmosphere that the hornbook was used. This aid to learning consisted of a piece of wood shaped like a paddle to give a convenient handle. Fastened to the thin board was a sheet of paper on which was printed the alphabet, some syllables, and usually the Lord's Prayer. Various primers were used along with the hornbook.

The New England primer.   This first appeared in 1690 and was one of the more famous primers. During a period of more than a hundred years, this book dominated the curriculum of the elementary schools and 3 million copies were sold. The primer was a crudely printed 90-page booklet, with pages about one-fourth the size of those in our present textbooks. The primer contained the alphabet, syllables, and a few spelling lists. A large part of its contents consisted of two catechisms: John Cotton's *Spiritual Milk for Boston Babes . . . Drawn Out of the Breasts of Both Testaments for Their Souls' Nourishment* and the *Westminster Shorter Catechism.* This reading material was made of doleful admonitions such as the following:

> Tho' I am young, yet I may die,
> And hasten to eternity;
> There is a dreadful fiery Hell,
> Where wicked ones must always dwell;
> There is a heaven full of joy,
> Where Godly ones must always stay;
> To one of these my soul must fly,
> As in a moment when I die.

Teaching methods and materials in these early schools were almost as crude as the buildings in which they were housed. Except for the "spell-downs," each pupil was called before the teacher and recited individually. This practice was largely necessitated by the lack of books, writing paper, pens, and ink. It was common for some of the smaller children to receive only 15 to 20 minutes of individual attention from the teacher during a school day of six to eight hours. During the remainder of the time they were expected to sit quietly on their rough, uncomfortable benches. Slow children might take as long as three terms to master the alphabet. Since arithmetic books were rare, pupils made copy books and sum books by folding sheets of rough paper and sewing them along one edge.

Crude, poorly lighted and heated structures, limited teaching methods, and a dearth of teaching materials were all typical of our early elementary schools. Yet in these schools, while engaged in the consuming task of building a new world, our forefathers preserved the rudiments of learning.

As the population continued to increase, people began moving away from the towns to develop new farming areas. Their children had to travel longer and longer distances to attend school until it became quite difficult for them to get there at all. In some instances school would be held in one part of the township during one term and in another during the next term. This rotation of schools gave rise to the famous "moving school" of early New England days.

Because of the limitations of educational facilities, people in outlying districts organized their own schools, one for each extended neighborhood. Thus were born the "district schools," a term not uncommonly used today. Here there was usually one teacher, often with as many as 50 pupils or more. The counterpart of the district school persists to this day all over the nation.

Higher Education.   The religious influences and English collegiate tradition imported from abroad were dominant factors in the establishment of our first colleges. Harvard University, founded in 1636, was a copy of Emmanuel College, Cambridge University, England. Practically all of our early American colleges were developed under the auspices of some church in order to provide means for perpetuating a literate ministry for

Present name	Date	Religious affiliation
Harvard University	1636	Congregational
College of William and Mary	1693	Episcopal
Yale University	1701	Congregational
Princeton University	1746	Presbyterian
Columbia University	1754	Episcopal
University of Pennsylvania	1755	Episcopal
Brown University	1765	Baptist
Rutgers University	1766	Dutch Reformed
Dartmouth University	1769	Congregational
Washington College	1782	Episcopal
Washington and Lee University	1782	Presbyterian
Hampton-Sidney College	1783	Presbyterian
Transylvania College	1783	Presbyterian
Dickinson College	1783	Presbyterian
St. John's College	1784	Episcopal
University of Georgia	1785	None
College of Charleston	1785	Episcopal
Georgetown University	1786	Catholic
Franklin and Marshall College	1787	German Reformed
University of North Carolina	1789	None
University of Vermont	1791	None
Williams College	1793	Congregational
Bowdoin College	1794	Congregational
Tusculum College	1794	Presbyterian
University of Tennessee	1794	Presbyterian
Union University	1795	Presbyterian

their churches. It was not until the establishment of the University of Pennsylvania in 1749 and of Kings College (now Columbia University) in 1754 that institutions of higher learning were sponsored by civil groups instead of the church. Growth of universities was slow during the colonial period. As you may note in the preceding list [113:201] only nine universities had been established by 1775.

EDUCATION IN EARLY AMERICA (1779–1865)

The development of an organized system of education received relatively little attention for several years following the Revolutionary War. This was a period of transition in which the thoughts and energies of people were concerned primarily with such matters as the formulation of a constitution, the establishment and operation of an organized system of states, and the fighting of the War of 1812.

At first, other factors tended to push education into the background. The rapid development of industry in America encouraged many children to work in mills, stores, and shops rather than to attend schools. Many families, especially immigrant families, were so poor that they needed whatever money their children could earn. The need for earning a living in order to survive was so great that education tended to be considered a luxury. Also, the extreme mobility of settlers who continued to push westward made the task of establishing permanent schools difficult. There was little time for education in the rugged life of the pioneer. Teachers were scarce and the sparse settlements across the land were not conducive to the establishment of school districts.

During this critical time, however, new meanings and values were emerging in the minds of people. Greater attention was being given to concepts of democracy, freedom, equality, individual rights, and faith in the common man. As noted in Chapter 1, the Bill of Rights and other important documents made specific reference to such matters. In 1785, Congress adopted an ordinance relative to the Northwest Territory to the effect that "there shall be reserved the lot number sixteen of every township for the maintenance of public schools within the said township," and in 1787 the following important statement appeared in the famous Northwest Ordinance of 1787: "Religion, morality, and knowledge being necessary to good government and the happiness of mankind, schools and the means of education shall be forever encouraged." These documents as well as the thinking of a number of outstanding leaders, did much to lay the foundation for more rapid educational developments to follow.

By approximately 1825 our nation had achieved a certain amount of national stability and had begun to develop rapidly. The population was increasing, with much of the increase coming from the large streams of immigrants arriving in America. Industry was growing rapidly, and labor associations were beginning to be formed. The economic and social status of the common man was beginning to improve.

The Fight for Common Schools.   Prior to the 1820s, the idea that the government should provide schools for all children had not been widely accepted outside of New England. The growing concern for the equality of man led, however, to an intense fight for free public schools. Public school societies were organized in various cities. Public-spirited citizens became members of these societies, contributing sums of money annually to carry forward the educational program.

The most famous and probably the most efficient of these organizations was the New York Public School Society, which for 40 years was New York City's chief agency for educating the children of the poorer classes. After the city began establishing public schools, about the middle of the nineteenth century, the society transferred its buildings and other property to the municipal government, to become a part of the public school system.

Changes in School Practices and Building Construction.   As social and economic advancements were made, the educational needs for boys and girls expanded. As a result, the curriculum of the elementary school was expanded beyond the teaching of reading, spelling, arithmetic, and religious instruction which characterized the early elementary schools.

Pupils originally were not grouped into grades, as they are today. At approximately the beginning of the nineteenth century, a rudimentary type of grading was attempted in the large schools by roughly dividing the pupils into age groups and assigning the groups to different assistants. Such a system of grading suggested the desirability of having a room for each group, and led to a new type of school building.

In 1848 a forward step was taken in school architecture; a new type of building had been designed. It was three stories high, and on each story— except for the top one, which was one large assembly room—there were four separate rooms designed to accommodate approximately 50 children. Cloak rooms were substituted for the usual small recitation chambers which adjoined the large room. This type of building became standard for a large part of the country. In almost any city established prior to the twentieth century, school buildings constructed on this general plan can still be found.

The Lancastrian System.   The financing of schools enrolling several thousands of children presented a problem of staggering proportions. Fortunately, a new plan of school organization and management was introduced from England to New York City in 1806, which tremendously reduced the cost of educating a child. Most of the society schools rapidly adopted this new plan. It was known as the Lancastrian system, named after its founder, Joseph Lancaster, an English schoolmaster. In this system, one teacher, by using his brightest pupils as monitors to teach about 10 pupils each, might himself be in charge of from 200 to 600 pupils. The schoolmaster taught the monitors who in turn taught their groups. Everything was rigidly organized in a somewhat military fashion.

Each group was marched to its station along the wall of a large class-room, where the monitor presented the lesson. Lancaster himself thought that a real master teacher could take care of 1,000 pupils. With such a high pupil-teacher ratio, it was reported that the per capita cost of operating a school was reduced to $1.25 per year per pupil.

Because of the great public service the school societies were rendering, they felt justified in asking the government for aid in carrying out their program. In some instances this was given. Both the state and city governments in New York regularly contributed substantial sums to the New York society to help support their schools. New York City in 1832 was the first city to establish free public elementary schools. Gradually the public mind became accustomed to the idea of governmental support of schools, and the low cost of the Lancastrian system began to suggest that this way of supporting schools might not be prohibitive. While the system passed away within a few decades, it did much to advance the cause of free public education.

The Primary School.   In 1818 another school was introduced in Boston which became known as the "primary school." Children of ages four through seven were admitted to this school. At first the primary schools were distinctly separate from other schools in the city. They were open all year and prepared children for admission to the city schools, which by this time were known as "English grammar schools." The primary schools had their own buildings and teachers and were quite different from the dame schools, which had previously prepared the pupils for entrance to the grammar schools.

It was not until the latter half of the nineteenth century that primary schools were made a part of the general school system. It often has been pointed out that this origin of the lower grades led to a distinction between primary and grammar grades—a distinction which may be found even today.

The Kindergarten.   Although an infants' school was established in Boston as early as 1816, the kindergarten as conceived by Friedrich Froebel, its founder, was not introduced into America until 1855. Mrs. Carl Schurz, who established this kindergarten in Watertown, Wisconsin, was a strong advocate of Froebel.

During the next 15 years about 10 private kindergartens were organized in German-speaking communities. In 1860 the first English-speaking private kindergarten was opened in Boston, and eight years later a teacher-training course for kindergarten teachers was established in Boston. Under the auspices of Superintendent William T. Harris of St. Louis, the first public school kindergarten in the United States was opened there in 1873.

There has been considerable misunderstanding regarding the role of the kindergarten in our educational system. Many people feel that what the kindergarten features in its program is already included in a good primary school program. Since the kindergarten is a relatively new rung in our educational ladder, it has had to compete with other schools for public support. As a result of these attitudes and forces, the establishment of kindergartens as an integral part of public schools throughout the United States has been greatly retarded—so much so that many of our children never attend a kindergarten.

The Academy.   At about the time of the Revolutionary War, there was a strong demand for a more practical kind of education beyond the three R's. Men who tilled the soil, fought Indians, sailed ships, developed commerce, and started industries in America began to question the appropriateness of the narrow and rigid college-preparatory curriculum of the grammar school to train youngsters for a practical world. Such men were led by Benjamin Franklin, who established the first public academy in Philadelphia in 1751.

This academy was essentially a private tuition school, though some academies gained public support and eventually became public schools.

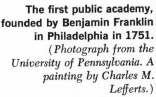

The first public academy, founded by Benjamin Franklin in Philadelphia in 1751. (*Photograph from the University of Pennsylvania. A painting by Charles M. Lefferts.*)

In the academy, English as a language was emphasized; girls were admitted to study; school libraries were established; American history and natural science were introduced; mathematics, especially algebra, navigation, and astronomy, were emphasized; and logic, ethics, and psychology, as well as commerce, surveying, debating, dramatics, and athletics were given attention. The academy movement led to deeper concern for human progress and higher respect for human worth. It stimulated better teaching in the elementary school and provided good educational opportunity for the emerging middle class in America—the substantial farmers, businessmen, tradesmen, and government workers. The movement spread rapidly over the United States.

The academy started out with three particular curricula: the English, the Latin, and the mathematical. A fourth was soon added—the philosophical. The teachings of the Latin and philosophical divisions were geared to prepare youngsters for college. Eventually the college-preparatory aspects of the academy involved more and more of the time and energy of teachers and pupils alike. By the turn of the nineteenth century, the academy aquired most of the characteristics of the Latin grammar school against which it originally protested. It became narrow, rigid, select, essentially classical, and college preparatory in nature.

The academy movement enjoyed wide prosperity, reaching a peak at about the time of the Civil War. While the number of Latin grammar schools never grew large, there were over 6,000 academies in the United States by 1850. Many of these are still in existence and hold a distinctive position among private college-preparatory schools. Some academies such as Franklin's original one, which became the University of Pennsylvania, have contributed significantly to higher education.

The Early Public High School.   Many people were not satisfied with the academy, even though it represented certain important improvements over the Latin grammar school. People whose children had completed the common schools but could not or would not attend the expensive aristocratic private academies insisted increasingly upon more education of a practical sort at public expense. Their efforts bore fruit in 1821, with the establishment of the Boston English Classical School, which soon after was called the English High School. But this type of high school devel-

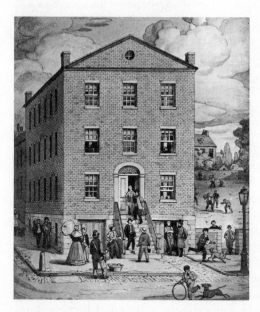

The first English classical high school which was founded in Boston in 1821 to give more education of a practical type at public expense. (*Photograph from the First National Bank of Boston.*)

oped slowly. In 1840 there were no more than 50. Except for the omission of Greek and Latin, the programs offered by these high schools were at first very similar to those of the original academy. Pupils were admitted upon examination at the age of 12 for a three-year course. The high school was free to all the pupils.

Strengthening of State Departments of Education.   During the first part of the nineteenth century a number of people became concerned over the great variation among communities in the extent to which they provided for the education of the young. It was felt that, if a local school district were left free to provide a poor education or no education at all for its children, the welfare of the state would suffer. Furthermore, these children would be denied their birthright to an education that would prepare them for effective citizenship.

There was a gradual growth in the feeling that each state must exert more authority to ensure educational opportunities for all of its children. As a result [21:38], New York State created the office of state superintendent of schools in 1812. Massachusetts established a state board of education in 1837 with the distinguished Horace Mann serving as secre-

Horace Mann (1796-1859) is credited with being the father of American public education. As the first secretary to the Massachusetts Board of Education, he campaigned vigorously, with his brilliant oratory for better schools and better teachers. Among his many contributions, he helped establish the first normal school in Lexington, Massachusetts. (*Photograph from the Library of Congress.*)

tary. Henry Barnard became the first secretary of the state board of education established in Connecticut in 1839. Other states followed. As Butts [21:38] pointed out in his excellent article, "Search for Freedom," "these state agencies could then set minimum standards for all the schools of the state. Meanwhile, the direct management of schools would be left in the hands of locally elected school boards, local superintendents, and locally appointed teachers. Local management served the cause of flexibility, diversity, and freedom.

"This arrangement was designed to assure that schools would serve the whole *public* and would be controlled by the *public* through special boards of education, not through the regular agencies of the state or local governments. This is why in America we use the term public schools, not simply state schools or government schools, as they are often called in those countries that have centralized systems of education."

A number of outstanding leaders emerged to help fight the battle for free schools. Particularly noted among them were Horace Mann of Massachusetts, who became known as "the father of the common school," Henry Barnard of Connecticut, Thaddeus Stevens of Pennsylvania, and Lyman Rucker and Calvin Stowe of Ohio. In general, it was maintained that these common schools should be: (1) free and open to all since no other system, least of all the dual system used in Europe, was acceptable for a democracy; (2) of such excellent quality that all parents would be willing to send their children to them; (3) common in the sense that all children would attend and that it would serve as a unifying force to weld communities together; (4) publicly supported through taxation of the whole community; (5) publicly controlled through elected or appointed public officials responsible to the whole community and not to any particular political, economic, or religious group; (6) and nonsectarian in character and should (7) provide the basic knowledge and skills essential to enable students of diverse backgrounds to assume responsibilities of citizenship in the young Republic [adapted, 22:127–128].

The men who fought for public schools marshaled their arguments along the following lines [adapted, 22:128]:

1. Suffrage had been extended to include all men, and if men were going to vote they had to be educated.

2. Pauper schools and the private and religious schools were inadequate because (a) the pauper schools had a social stigma which kept many children from attending; (b) fees charged by private schools kept some children from attending school; and (c) religious schools might force certain religious teachings upon children.

3. Education was essential to preserve the well-being of the state by preventing pauperism and crime and by reducing poverty and distress.

4. Schools would help prevent a class society from forming.

5. Education serves to increase productivity.

6. Education is the God-given right of all children.

The heated battle for free public schools continued for many years. Although less intense, the fight for free public schools is still with us. Even today there are some who question the right for everyone to be taxed for the support of schools.

Developments in Higher Education.   In order to meet the growing needs of a young nation and to provide an educational outlet for the liberalism which developed during the revolutionary period, more colleges and universities were established. Twenty-six, having a combined enrollment of 2,000 students, had been established by 1800, and the number continued to increase. Little opposition to these new colleges was encountered in those sections where colleges had not already been established. However, when some of the older states attempted to turn the already existing colleges into nonsectarian state universities, friction resulted. The climax was reached in the famous Dartmouth College Case in 1819. The decision which was handed down specified that states could not modify the charter of a college without the consent of the institution's authorities. Although this decision terminated the attempts of a number of states to transform private colleges into public ones, it did provide the stimulus for the establishment of state universities and more private colleges. Since then private and denominational institutions have undergone many changes, so that in many ways it is difficult at the present time to distinguish them from state or public institutions.

Shortly after 1862 Congress passed the Morrill Act, which eventually led to the establishment of land-grant colleges. This legislation gave 30,000 acres of public land to each state for every representative and senator the state had in Congress. This land and the proceeds from its sale were to be used to endow colleges or universities which would teach agriculture and the mechanical arts in such a manner as the legislatures of the respective states prescribed. Scientific and classical studies and military tactics were not to be excluded from the curriculum. In general, the states were to promote the liberal and practical education of the industrial classes. To date, a total of almost 11,400,000 acres of public land has been given for endowment of these colleges by the Federal government.

Prior to 1860 higher education in our country was dominantly the concern of denominational and private colleges, while after 1860 the state universities and land-grant colleges increased rapidly in number, size, and influence. As this happened, the character of many of the private and denominational schools changed so markedly that the pattern of higher education as we know it today began to evolve.

Teacher-education Institutions.   The first institutions to undertake the preparation of teachers in our country were the academies. Although there were a few sporadic efforts to train teachers for special assignments, such as the infants' school and the kindergarten, these were isolated attempts and did not foster the whole idea of teacher preparation. Although teacher training was not one of the more important functions of the academy, it provided some of the initial impetus to the movement. Actually, the academy provided preparation only in the subject-matter fields. Methods, techniques, observation, and student teaching were not included in the curriculum.

Before the establishment of the first public normal school in America at Lexington, Massachusetts, in 1839, teachers seminaries existed in Germany, where they offered a rich background in subject matter and courses in the professional preparation of teachers. There is considerable controversy among historians of education as to whether the concept of teacher preparation had originated from these German seminaries or was indigenous to America, but some of the features of the American normal school were definitely unique. It should be noted, however, that the American normal schools and the German seminaries both had as their point of origin an extension of the academy. Regardless of the exact origin, normal schools were the most influential type of American teacher-training institutions for almost a hundred years.

The teacher-training programs of the early normal schools were usually one year in length. Gradually this practice gave way to a two-year course of study, and, shortly before the teachers college development, a few normal schools had developed strong four-year programs. In addition to a review of the common branch subjects—reading, writing, arithmetic, spelling, and grammar—the normal school also taught the science and art of teaching and classroom management. Often there were opportunities to do practice teaching in a "model" school.

Normal schools, usually with a two-year or four-year curriculum, are still functioning in our country; however, these non-degree-granting schools are fast disappearing from the American school scene.

EDUCATION AFTER THE CIVIL WAR (1865 TO THE PRESENT)

Following the Civil War, rapid progress was made in the industrialization of America. This progress was fostered through advancements in science and technology. More power became available; new machines were invented; and transportation facilities were improved. Through the application of mass production and specialization, America was destined to become an industrial giant.

Industrialization brought about the formation of corporations, new methods of management, and an increased amount of urbanization. With these changes, the demands for more and better education arose. Progress in medicine and sanitation reduced the rate of infant mortality and increased the life span. Immigrants continued to stream to our shores. As a result more children needed to be educated. More and better teachers had to be trained. More and better schools had to be built. More educational opportunities at the higher levels had to be provided.

Change and the complexity of problems resulting from rapid industrial progress fostered the development of new thoughts and practices in education. The ideas of men like Rousseau, Pestalozzi, Froebel, G. S. Hall, William James, John Dewey, and others to be discussed in Chapter 12, were exerting decided influence upon our schools. Responsible citizens were demanding more and better education for youth in order to meet the growing demands and increasing complexity of life.

Progress in Secondary Education.   Initially the progress of the free public high school (English High School) was slow because many people considered it to be unnecessary and maintained that it would be too costly for the government. Many were unwilling to pay additional taxes when they had no children in school. A test case of public-supported schools developed in Kalamazoo, Michigan, in 1874. The State Supreme Court ruled that the city could levy taxes to support free public secondary schools. Similar decisions and laws followed rapidly in other states, and our free public secondary schools began to prosper. By 1890 there were approximately 2,500, and at the turn of the century the number had increased to about 6,000.

Schools and pupils were becoming so numerous that organizational problems became acute. Colleges were much concerned over the diversity in the high school programs and over the possibility that too much elementary work was being duplicated in the high school. National committees wrestled with problems like these and made various recommendations. Largely as a result of these problems, the Carnegie Unit was established and college entrance examinations were developed. Together, they shackled the free public secondary schools with such a rigid college-preparatory program that even today teachers and pupils are still trying to break away from it.

Just after the turn of the century, several happy developments occurred. People began thinking seriously about the interrelationships between the main levels in the American educational ladder, about possible patterns of reorganization, and about experimentation in school content and method. At this point occurred the beginning of the progressive education movement, and the junior college and the junior high school movement.

Shortly after these movements began, the Commission on the Reorganization of Secondary Education issued its momentous report (1918), the *Cardinal Principles of Secondary Education,* reorienting people to the central purposes of education in a free society. As a result, teachers were faced with the problem of deciding whether they wanted secondary schools to be narrow college-preparatory institutions for the select few, or whether they intended them to be truly free to all youngsters, furthering the highest potential of the social group and yet offering each child equal opportunity to meet his own needs, interests, and capacities. This decision is not yet permanently made. It is not easy to accomplish. Thinking here is bound up in tradition, clouded by custom, diverted by vested interests, and faulty for want of accurate information.

The Junior High School.   The junior high school represents a fairly new development in American education. Several eminent educators had become dissatisfied with the graded elementary school as it was set up during the 1850s. Their dissatisfaction was called to the public's attention by an address delivered by President C. W. Eliot of Harvard University in a meeting of the Department of Superintendents of the National Education Association in 1888. Shortly after this address, several committees were appointed by the NEA and they began to study the situation. One of the more famous of these groups, the Committee of Ten, made specific recommendations concerning problems affecting elementary, secondary, and higher education. Early reports from this and similar committees favored a 6-6 plan, i.e., six years of elementary education and six years of secondary education. Numerous subsequent reports suggested that the secondary school be divided into two separate institutions—one to be known as the junior high school and the other as the senior high school, i.e., the 6-3-3 plan.

In 1909, junior high schools were established at Columbus, Ohio, and Berkeley, California; there has always been considerable controversy as to which one was first established. Principles upon which the junior high school was founded included [101:4]:

1. Articulation—helping children to go from elementary school through junior high school into senior high school with as little difficulty as possible.
2. Exploration—giving young teen-agers a chance to find out through brief experiences what some of the high school courses were like, with the expectation that this would help them to choose their senior high school courses more wisely.

3. Educational guidance—helping pupils to choose from among elective subjects offered in the junior and later in the senior high school.

4. Vocational guidance—helping pupils to make decisions about jobs and careers.

5. Activity—providing social and athletic experiences and giving the students a chance to participate in administration and control of the school.

The junior high school movement spread very rapidly from its inception. By 1928 there were over 1,500 junior high schools, and since that time thousands more have come into being. It is only fair to point out, however, that many of the noble purposes which the early advocates of this movement had in mind are not being fully realized. The junior high school is still in a state of flux, and in parts of the country it is still nonexistent.

Junior College.   During the latter part of the nineteenth century considerable demand was being made to extend public secondary school programs into the thirteenth and fourteenth grades. A few private junior colleges already had been organized. For example, New London Seminary in New Hampshire, founded in 1837, became Colby Junior College. Decatur Baptist College, founded in Texas in 1891, was reorganized into a private junior college in 1898.

Through the encouragement of President William Rainey Harper of the University of Chicago, the public high schools of Joliet, Illinois, established a separate educational unit in 1902 that included grades 13 and 14. This became the first public junior college in America. President Harper agreed that the University of Chicago would accept any credits earned by students attending this junior college. He reorganized the program at the University junior and senior college with the hope that the University eventually would not need to provide freshman and sophomore course work.

The junior college, a truly American idea, grew slowly at first, but since World War I its growth has been phenomenal. Junior colleges now exist in almost every state of the nation.

At first, junior colleges attempted to offer the same courses as those offered during the freshman and sophomore years of regular colleges and universities. Later a number of the junior colleges began to adapt their programs to the needs of their respective communities and were called "community colleges." Regardless of whether or not students planned to transfer to a regular college or university, these colleges provided terminal programs, designed to prepare students for occupations primarily in their communities. Frequently late-afternoon and evening courses were offered especially to serve the needs of adult members of the community.

Other types of junior colleges, both public and private, have developed. Some of them offer special kinds of programs, such as business courses or technological training. The two-year pattern is predominant among junior colleges even though some offer more and some offer less than two years.

Progress in the Preparation of Teachers.   As the normal-school movement gradually gave way to the teachers college movement, the number
of students in teacher-training institutions increased enormously. Usually
these schools are four-year degree-granting institutions, but during this
past decade many of them have added a fifth-year program leading to
the master's degree.

Other types of institutions have developed teacher-training programs.
In the area of teacher education, the teachers colleges in some states are
being superseded by the state colleges, where the handling of the professional courses is greatly influenced by the practices of the department
of education in the state university.

A large portion of the nation's high school teachers and an increasing
number of its elementary teachers are receiving their training in liberal
arts colleges. As noted in Chapter 2, this development in teacher training has given rise to some antipathy between professional schools for
teachers and the liberal arts colleges, with each criticizing the programs
and methods of the other. It is not our purpose to pursue this controversy.
It is sufficient to note that it does exist.

The place of the university schools of education in the picture of
teacher-education institutions is not well defined. Typically, universities
possess a college of education where the professional work is concentrated, and the general education and advanced work in subject-matter
fields are offered in other divisions of the university. It is obvious that the
university has peculiar advantages and problems of its own.

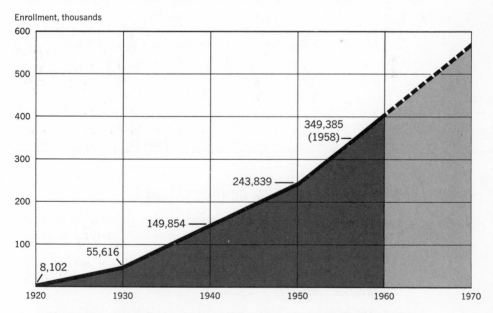

Figure 46.   Enrollment in junior colleges excluding institutions classified as
technical institutes and semiprofessional schools which do not offer
programs consisting wholly or principally of work creditable toward a
bachelor's degree. (*Source:* Bureau of the Census.)

SUMMARY

During the early colonial period in America, many and varied educational attempts were made in the quest for literacy and learning. Basically a dual school system developed in which the common or district schools, offering the three R's, attempted to serve the educational needs of the masses, and the grammar schools were reserved for the wealthy, the select, the elite. Actually the development of the grammar school preceded the development of the common school. Completion of the common school in the early period did not lead to entrance into the grammar school but marked the end of the educational career of the common school pupil.

Academies arose in order to meet the demands for a more practical type of education than was being provided in Latin grammar schools. Public high schools were established when the curriculum of the academies failed to meet adequately the needs of the people, when large numbers of children wanted to extend their education, and when the concept of governmentally supported schools became a part of the thinking of the general public.

During the nineteenth century and in the early part of the twentieth, many improvements were made. The various units of our educational system were welded into a definite pattern. The kindergarten, the junior high school, and the junior college came into being. Professional education for teachers was initiated in normal schools, colleges, and universities. Educators began to appraise their efforts critically, to experiment, and to bring about desirable changes and improvements.

It would be erroneous to assume that the educational system which our forefathers bequeathed to us has reached its fullest and last stage of development. Our American public school system derives part of its dynamic character from the concept of continuous evolution and progress.

As you explore and study the educational situation, you will need all the understanding you can gain from studying the historical backgrounds of our American school system. Study carefully, learn much, and apply what you gain toward the improvement of learning and living for all people everywhere.

QUESTIONS FOR YOUR CONSIDERATION

1. Why does the American school system represent one of the most noble and visionary experiments ever attempted by mankind?

2. In order to become a craftsman in a number of trades today, an individual first must serve a period of apprenticeship. Where did this practice originate?

3. What elements in the typical high school of today reflect back to (a) the Latin grammar school, (b) the academy?

4. If a school is to survive, it must meet the changing needs and

demands of the public. What historical evidence can you give that supports this statement?

5. How do you account for the fact that free, public, tax-supported schools developed first in the New England colonies?

6. Do you know of any individuals today who question the right for everyone to be taxed for the support of schools? What seem to be their reasons?

7. What are the major effects of industrialization on education? How does educational advancement affect industrialization?

8. Why are kindergartens not a part of the public school system in many school districts?

9. What were some of the reasons for the appearance and development of the junior high school?

10. If such a decision as the Dartmouth College Case in 1819 had never been made, how might the development of colleges in America have been affected?

11. Why has the growth of the junior college been so great in recent years? Do you feel that this growth will continue? Why?

12. How do you account for the fact that teachers colleges in some states are being superseded by the state colleges.

13. What contributions have church or denominational colleges made to American education?

ACTIVITIES FOR YOU TO PURSUE

1. Develop in outline form the European influences which affected our American public school system.

2. Imagine that you are a student in one of the American common schools in the eighteenth century. Develop a detailed account of a day in your school.

3. Analyze the various types of schools which attempted elementary education in early days and show how they became part of the present elementary school.

4. See what you can learn about the early history of your local high school.

5. Consult a directory of colleges and universities and identify some institutions that were established under the Morrill Act of 1862. How do these institutions differ from other colleges or universities?

6. Study carefully the "Calendar of Some Important Events in Education" which appears in the Resource Section for Part IV. Memorize some of these dates.

12

THE DEVELOPMENT OF MODERN CONCEPTS OF EDUCATION

What do people mean when they speak of modern practices in education? Do they mean that pupils do as they please in school? Are pupils all promoted regardless of how little they learn? Are they learning less today under the modern approach (sometimes called progressive education) than they learned under the older practices (sometimes called traditional or conventional education)?

As you consider these questions, perhaps other aspects of the educational picture come to mind. What is the teacher's role in discipline? What are the most prevalent learning theories? What is your concept of authority, freedom, and guidance? What is the purpose of a textbook? What is your philosophy of education? These and a myriad of other questions seem to come to the fore whenever modern practices in education are mentioned.

In preparing to teach, it is important for you to develop a clear understanding of what is meant by modern concepts of education and to know how they differ from older ones. To do this you must make a brief study of the development of certain educational attitudes and know their implications for classroom practices. The development of a thoroughly reasoned concept of the school's function and the teacher's role in achieving this function is a major task in planning for a career in education.

One of the convenient ways of gaining an understanding of the differing theories of education is to study the contributions of outstanding individual thinkers and the conditions of society that fostered such thought. Thus it is possible to look at conventional and modern theories and to note the differences in classroom practices which each implies. In the following summary it will not be possible to present all the contributions of all the great men for the past 40 centuries, but some of the sources which have influenced the development of certain important concepts in education can be identified.

CONTRIBUTIONS OF SOME EARLY OUTSTANDING THINKERS

Plato (428–347 B.C.). Over 2,000 years ago, Plato, in his writings about a Utopian society, stated that the role of education is "the drawing and leading of children to the rule which has been pronounced right by the voice of the law, and approved as truly right by the concordant experiences of the best and oldest men." Why is it that Plato would have such an idea about education? It has been said that Plato's ideas were greatly influenced by his master teacher, Socrates. Socrates held a rather democratic point of view. He believed that universal ideas emerged from the common social life and that every man could make an equal contribution to his society.

But Socrates was not living in a society of conflict, as was Plato. Plato grew up in a chaotic period when the great struggles between Athens and Sparta were dividing the loyalties of men who were creating conflicts throughout the Greek world. Plato had been impressed by the military superiority of Sparta and by the excessive individualism that prevailed in Athens. Therefore it was no great wonder that when Plato wrote his *Republic* he was dreaming of setting up an ideal state that would do away with factional conflict.

In his desire to set up an ideal state, Plato believed that all individuals should be strictly subordinated to the state. Since he wanted to operate his ideal state on a principle of efficiency, he divided all people into three classes, each person doing the job that he was best fitted to do, which would provide justice to each. In his stratification of citizenship, he did not overemphasize or underemphasize any individual's role in society. According to him, to be a good citizen the individual had to do the state's bidding, whether it be to work, to fight, or to rule.

Plato, in his effort to set up the ideal state, did both a service and an injustice to education. As a service, he showed that a system of education is integral with the welfare of the state, but he did a great injustice to democracy in emphasizing the rule of the elite in which the "best and oldest men" decided the welfare of others. He advocated a very authoritarian type of education, which is the antithesis of democratic education.

Aristotle (384–322 b.c.). Aristotle, like Plato, had no particular loyalty to democracy. He felt that a good monarchy or a good aristocracy was just as acceptable as a good democracy, depending on which could promote the welfare of the state to the highest degree. Aristotle's basic thesis was that man was a "political animal."

To Aristotle, education was the development of the well-rounded individual divorced from the mechanical, practical areas of vocational or professional training. Further, Aristotle held that the highest form of virtue was speculation, contemplation, and the exercise of intellectual ability. In this scale of reasoning, a man as a knower was higher in the scale of worthy citizenship than was man as a practical citizen.

In Aristotle's day, a liberal education was the education that was deemed best suited to Greek free men. Aristotle, like Plato, did not advocate the same education for all people. Rather, there was a general education for the citizenry, additional education for the warriors, *and* an even higher education for the leaders. Rediscovered during the time of the Renaissance, both Aristotle's and Plato's concept of education provided much of the basis for the classical tradition in education. As mentioned in Chapter 11, our early colonial forefathers imported this tradition from abroad. Many aspects of the educational practices in our American public schools today can be traced to this classical tradition.

Vergerius (1349–1420). A fifteenth-century humanist, Pierre Paolo Vergerius, formulated certain goals for education and set forth a basic theory of formal discipline to which many people today still adhere. He wrote as follows [61:126]:

> We call those studies liberal which are worthy of a free man; those studies by which we obtain and practice virtue and wisdom; that education which calls forth, trains, and develops those highest gifts of body and mind which ennoble men and which are rightly judged to rank next in dignity to virtue only, for to a vulgar temper gain and pleasure are the one aim of existence, to a lofty nature, moral worth and fame.

Vergerius was the proponent of a doctrine of a *limited* body of subject matter which he felt had some special power to train the mind. Evidences of this doctrine can still be found in American schools today.

Locke (1632–1704).   Three hundred years after Vergerius formulated his theory of formal discipline, John Locke further developed the theory. John Locke introduced a new element at this point, his concept of the nature of the learner. This is commonly known as the *tabula rasa* doctrine, which held the mind, at birth, to be like a smooth tablet upon which nothing yet had been written. Locke put greater emphasis on educational methods that would develop all of the senses of the child, not merely through reading, but through the senses of sight, taste, smell, touch, and hearing. In line with this point of view, Locke laid great stress on the importance of the physical development of the body. He felt that education, through sense impressions, should supply all the data used in thinking, as well as provide training in thinking. He advocated difficult intellectual exercises for disciplining the mind and severe tasks for disciplining the body. He saw education as a great power to make men good. But what are the factors that would cause Locke to view education as a great power?

Since this was the period of Newtonian physics, the scientists and mathematicians were prominent in expanding the horizons of knowledge. Knowledge made evident by the sciences and mathematics was a knowledge that was empirically observable. In the biological sciences, an enormous mass of facts was gathered; and the status of the social sciences began to improve in this eighteenth century. Even historical documents began to be treated as though they were scientific data to be gathered, classified, and criticized. This was the time of Voltaire and his Encyclopedists. The job of the Encyclopedists was to simplify knowledge into factual statements that could be recorded in encyclopedia form; they worked for freedom of thought, reform of harsh and unjust laws, elimination of poverty, disease, slavery, and war. These were just a few of the influences that gave John Locke theoretical justification for sense realism in education. It would appear that he, like Plato and Aristotle, seemed to view education in terms of a select group of people only. His human-istic doctrine and advocacy of the formal discipline theory gave further impetus to these conceptions of education.

INFLUENCES OF PRESCIENTIFIC THEORIES

Out of the past fraught with myth and superstition, various theories de-veloped concerning the soul, mind, and body of man, which influenced early concepts of education. Although these superstitions and theories have largely been cast aside as the result of scientific investigations, they still seem to have some influence upon present-day practices in education.

Faculty Psychology. Various theories concerning the mind and body of man have played enormously significant roles in educational practices. According to early theories, mind and body were in sharp contrast. Mind was considered to have spontaneity, initiative, and independence of ac-tion. Body was considered inert and passive.

Out of this dualistic theory of mind and body grew a type of psychol-ogy which became known as "faculty psychology." This theory was based upon the hypothesis that the mind was composed of many mental facul-ties, such as reasoning and memory, and that these faculties were localized in the cerebral hemisphere. It was further theorized that the faculties could be strengthened through exercise, like muscles. The problem for educators who endorsed faculty psychology was to isolate subject matter that would best exercise the muscles. This again, in most cases, reverts to the old classical trivium and quadrivium. Subjects in the trivium in-cluded rhetoric, grammar, and logic. Subjects in the quadrivium were algebra, geometry, music, and astronomy. This, of course, has been modi-fied in different countries and in different centuries; however, the princi-ple of exercise through difficult subjects still remains the same. Since the more difficult subjects, such as classical language and mathematics, were supposed to provide the best type of exercise for the mind, these subjects were looked upon with great favor. Rote memorization became a favorite technique, for it provided the necessary exercise of the faculty of mem-ory. With this doctrine no justification for learning needed to be given other than the training of the mind.

Physiological Psychology. For a long time the doctrine of faculty psy-chology was the dominant educational theory. Then a group called "physiological psychologists" challenged this doctrine by producing evi-dence that certain areas of the brain controlled different body functions.

Using the evidence provided by these psychologists, a pseudoscientific cult of phrenologists advanced some rather unusual theories. The phre-nologists contended that, since different faculties of the mind had their "seat" in specific areas of the brain, the development of these faculties could be determined by an examination of the bumps of the skull.

Under the doctrine of faculty psychology, only abstract qualities of mind had been considered as aspects of the brain. Then, from the work of the physiological psychologists and the limited contributions of the phrenologists, the concept of the brain was expanded to include the "seat" of behavior traits. Emphasis still was placed on the training of the mind.

SOME IMPLICATIONS OF EARLY CONCEPTS OF EDUCATION

In studying these early concepts of education and early theories about the mind, you will find that many questions come into focus. What are the implications of the classical tradition, the humanistic viewpoint, and the doctrine of faculty psychology for educational practices?

Knowledge.   According to the classical tradition, knowledge (acquiring facts) is education. On the basis of this concept of education, teaching becomes a matter of acquiring the techniques of getting pupils to learn established content. The business of the teacher, according to this viewpoint, is to teach the subjects of the curriculum, generally by assigning pages in a textbook, by hearing a recitation consisting of the answers to the teacher's questions, and by grading papers and examinations in which boys and girls reveal their mastery of the formal content of the subject. The teacher also needs to learn the methods by which law and order are preserved in a classroom, so that academic learning may be accomplished.

To those who hold this viewpoint, the student who acquires the most knowledge is the student who is best educated. Where knowledge becomes the end rather than the means to an end, students must learn great masses of material. Isolated, factual information becomes important because it increases the learner's reservoir of knowledge. Page-by-page assignments in textbooks lend themselves well to this concept of education. Little concern is felt about how the students learn as long as they can "parrot" back what they have read or heard. Thus the mark of a cultured person is the knowledge which he has concerning his own culture and the cultures of the past.

Preparation.   Early thinkers generally considered children as miniature adults. Young minds were like Locke's "smooth tablets" upon which an education must be imprinted as a preparation for life. Where preparation becomes the major emphasis in education, certain practices seem to follow. The teacher attempts to get boys and girls to learn something because it will help them when they "grow up." Since the teacher is not necessarily appealing to children's interests, he must resort to ways of getting the work done. Artificial techniques, such as gold stars as rewards, threats in the form of demerits, and additional assignments as punishment, are some of the more familiar techniques which teachers use. Competition between pupils is one of the procedures used by many teachers to motivate pupils to learn. Since competition supposedly exists at a rather high level in adult life, teachers feel that they should provide competitive experiences which will prepare their students for adult society. Some of the more familiar kinds of competition are "spelldowns," oratorical contests, and speed drills in arithmetic. Competition is carried into the realm of evaluation, where students compete for grades on examinations and on their report cards.

With the emphasis on preparation, most of the materials of instruction are slanted toward adult problems. Textbooks use adult situations as the context within which children work. It was believed that the more difficult these materials and problems, the better prepared students would be to face the realities of adult life. Perhaps some of you experienced teaching of this kind in some of your classes in school.

Preparation for the future has been a dominating concept of education throughout history. How often have you heard teachers say that they must prepare their boys and girls for the next grade? An underlying theory which pervades many a school system is that the elementary school prepares for the high school and that the high school prepares for college. This theory is in contrast to the one stated so aptly by Dewey: "The future which grows out of the present is surely taken care of" [38:65].

Training the Mind. Under the doctrine of the faculty psychologists and phrenologists, *exercise* of the different faculties of the mind was of major importance in teaching. Thus, the harder the subjects were for the pupils, the better they fulfilled this purpose. Teachers chose not only hard subjects but also the most difficult subject matter within each subject. After the material was chosen, drill techniques were used. The teacher's purpose for constant drill and resulting rote memorization was not to facilitate understanding of the material studied but rather to exercise the faculty of memory. Long lists of historical dates, names of presidents and vice presidents, and names of state capitals were favorite drill exercises.

Certain types of subject matter were included in textbooks to exercise the powers of reasoning. This typical problem found in an old arithmetic book demonstrates this kind of teaching material:

A man went into an orchard which had seven gates and there took a certain number of apples. When he left the orchard, he gave the first guard half the apples that he had and one apple more. To the second, he gave half his remaining apples and one apple more. He did the same in the case of each of the remaining five guards and left the orchard with one apple. How many apples did he gather in the orchard?

How did an education which trained the mind prepare students for life outside the school? Faculty psychologists explained this through the theory of the transfer of training. This theory postulated that, if the faculty of memory or reasoning was trained by such subjects as foreign language or mathematics, you would be able to remember or reason in every situation in which you encountered such activities.

According to this concept, educators need be concerned only with a limited curriculum. Those few subjects which best train the faculties prepare the student for any eventuality. Teachers do not have to be concerned with teaching methods and techniques which integrate knowledge and understanding. This integration automatically takes place from one subject to another, one situation to another, and one skill to another. A prime example of this kind of teaching is found in the area of arithmetic, where number computations are learned and practiced in isolation. These skills are then supposed to transfer automatically to the solving of verbal arithmetic problems.

The field of educational psychology has produced experimental evidence which raises many questions about the validity of a general transfer of training. Yet many educational practices are based upon this theory.

It would seem that casual observations might raise some questions about this general transfer-of-training theory. How would you explain a situation in which a person with a prodigious memory for dates and names in history cannot remember the names of people he meets? Or how would you explain the situation of the great theoretical mathematician who could not balance his checkbook? Through these and many other casual observations this theory seems to break down.

CONTRIBUTIONS OF LATER OUTSTANDING THINKERS

As early as the sixteenth century, there were rumblings of disagreement and dissent with educational practices. Great thinkers began to question existing theories and to formulate different concepts of education.

Comenius (1592–1640). John Amos Comenius made his education contribution in the seventeenth century which was a period when many cultural forces were striving for the loyalties of man. This was a time of great religious conflict between Catholic and Protestant churches, and a time of new outlooks characterized by science and the scientific method. In this setting, a two-track system of universal education emerged. Because of the class structure of society which was deeply ingrained in all the countries of Europe, differences were made in the amount and kind of education provided to the various classes. The upper classes received a classical secondary education, whereas the lower classes received a vernacular elementary education.

Comenius was one of the severest critics of the schools of his day. He called them "the slaughter houses of the mind where ten or more years are spent in learning what might be acquired in one." He felt that schools were attempting to teach children solely with words and fought against this verbalistic approach. He sought to make learning more concrete and tangible. To do this he advocated the use of pictures and prepared a pictured encyclopedia called *Orbis Pictus*. Here each word was defined and illustrated. He also produced textbooks which for his time were profusely illustrated. Comenius helped to set forth a concept of education less austere and remote and more interesting to the learner.

Comenius was a strong advocate of general universal education. At the time this was in sharp contrast to the views of other educators. But Comenius felt that all children, rather than a select few, should have an opportunity to learn. He also believed that education is a natural process and that educational practices should therefore be in harmony with the nature of the learner. He expressed a desire for a "kindlier" discipline which would be consistent with his view of the natural process of education.

Rousseau (1712–1778).   Jean Jacques Rousseau was an extreme critic of the humanist, formal-discipline theories of education. He believed in the child's right to freedom in development, and his concept of education was based on the premise that it should be "according to nature." Rousseau has been termed by many as an anti-institutionalist. He believed that man was basically good and that it was only under the influence of evil institutions that man became corrupt.

The description of a mythical school in his book *Emile* set forth several principles which have heavily influenced modern concepts of education, such as the idea that the curriculum and teaching methods should be planned in terms of the needs of the pupil, that authority should be replaced by reason and investigation, and that the natural interests, curiosity, and activities of children should be used in their education.

Rousseau was one of the first to propose a "child-centered" school. He would not accept the notion that the child is a miniature adult, and conceived the child to be a growing, developing organism. From Rousseau's contributions it is possible to catch the first glimmerings of the study of child development.

Pestalozzi (1746–1827).   Utilizing some of the best thoughts of the twentieth century, a Swiss educator, Johann Pestalozzi, became a true pioneer in the development of education. He stated in his masterpiece, *Leonard and Gertrude,* that the aim of education is the natural and systematic development of all the powers of the individual. He felt that children develop according to definite laws, and that the role of the school is to further these laws. His "doctrine of interest" to provide the motivation for learning caused a great deal of furor in his time. He insisted that "learning should be a pleasant experience." Other educators felt that this would eliminate the distastefulness of school and might be bad for character development.

Pestalozzi put his ideas into practice in five different schools in Switzerland, the most famous of these being his Neuhof School. Neuhof was actually an orphanage, as was his school at Stanz. These schools were for poor children whose fathers had been killed in the wars. Since most of the children enrolled were children of broken homes, Pestalozzi tried to recapture the ideals of a sound family life with emphasis being given to mild discipline, loving care for children, and religious and moral inspiration.

The work in his schools emphasized sense perception and object les-

A statue of Johann Heinrich
Pestalozzi at Aargon, Switzerland
honors his contribution to
education. (*Photograph from the
Library of Congress.*)

sons. This and his analysis of various teaching methods may be considered the foundation upon which the scientific investigation of similar
educational problems has been undertaken.

Froebel (1780–1852).   Frederick Froebel taught with Pestalozzi and
conducted his own schools in Switzerland and Germany. Froebel was
very impressed with Pestalozzi's sense of realism, but he also leaned
heavily upon the idealistic philosophy of his day. Froebel looked on the
world as a great unity where there was no division between the realm of
that which was spiritual and that which was natural, or between the
individual and society. In his opinion all things found their unity and
their essence in God and His will unfolded on earth.

Froebel looked upon the child as an agency for the realization of
God's will in human nature. It was through education that the child's
spirit became linked with the spiritual unity of God. Froebel believed

that the child had latent powers that were to be unfolded as he entered into the spiritual union with God. Education, then, would be a process of spiritual activity, a process that was creative and morally good.

Since the educative process was so dedicated to the development of the child, Froebel felt that his process should start with the small child of three or four years. He called his new school the kindergarten, a garden where children grow. In his garden, Froebel introduced a new method of teaching that was designated the method of play activity. Froebel felt that play was a natural and appropriate activity for small children, and therefore he wanted to capitalize on the child's interest in play activity. This activity, however, was structured and involved drawing, clay modeling, painting and coloring, singing, dancing, telling dramatic stories, manipulating blocks, paper and cardboard objects, balls, and other objects. As the children played, Froebel tried to teach symbolic meaning in the objects with which they were playing, such as the ball meaning perfect unity in matter. Even in the absence of the symbolic attachment that Froebel gave to play activity, the new emphasis on respect for the child, for his individuality, for the active qualities of learning became influential in American education. An important foundation for the later concept of the child-centered school was laid by Froebel's kindergarten.

Herbart (1776–1841).   Whereas the two European men who preceded Herbart had greatly influenced elementary and preschool education, Johann Herbart's theories found acceptance largely among secondary school and university teachers. In keeping with his times and with his societal emphasis, Herbart laid great stress upon the social and moral character of education. To this end, he insisted that education should be primarily moral in its outlook and intent. To Herbart, morality was not necessarily religious in character but was a matter of relevance to a particular society.

Herbart was greatly concerned that the individual be well adjusted to his society. He believed that the school should be concerned with historical and literary studies and that all other studies should be correlated with them.

Herbart stressed the learning theory termed "associationism," in which great stress was placed upon the development of clear ideas in students. All qualities of man were considered to be secondary to that of the association of ideas in the mind. To guarantee the best association of ideas, Herbart developed the "five formal steps" of learning and teaching: (1) preparation, (2) presentation, (3) association, (4) generalization, and (5) application.

These steps were introduced at a time when reading, memory, and recitation were the principal methods of teaching. Because of the emphasis that society was placing upon scientific and mathematical developments, these steps in the teaching-learning process became vastly popular. His "formula" for teaching spread rapidly through elementary and secondary schools in both Europe ,and the United States. It was not until the twentieth century that a new concept of education was able to shadow the influence of Herbartianism in educational practices.

Parker (1837–1902).   Francis Parker, a teacher and an administrator who has been called a leader of the progressive-education movement in America, ranked high among the pioneers. His theories were geared toward making the school less artificial and conventional. He advocated field trips in science and geography. He felt that children should come into closer relationship with their natural environment.

As principal of the Cook County Normal School at Chicago, Parker trained many teachers. These teachers became disciples of his ideas and spread them throughout America. It has been said that his teachings, his writings, and his speeches laid the groundwork for a large part of John Dewey's concepts of education.

Dewey (1859–1952).   Many people who are acquainted with John Dewey's work in education recognize that, in formulating his point of view, Dewey drew upon three centuries of educational thought. This fact should in no way detract from his significant contributions to modern education. His knitting together of a consistent system from the ideas advanced by his predecessors is in itself a prodigious undertaking.

Dewey early established a laboratory school in Chicago. Here teachers were encouraged to experiment. This was a testing ground for the concepts of child development advanced by Rousseau and for the direct investigation of actual objects as a method of teaching, which had been advocated by Comenius and Parker. As a result of this experimentation, better teaching methods were developed. The experimental attitude found in his school spread to hundreds of teacher-training institutions.

While at the University of Chicago, Dewey published *School and Society*, about education suitable for a democratic society. He pointed out the importance of the individual within the context of a democracy, placing emphasis on the school's role in developing self-discipline for true democratic participation. Throughout the years this book has had a marked effect upon the functions of the American public school. Some of the books which followed his first publication include *Interest and Effort, Democracy and Education,* and *Experience and Education.*

To John Dewey, the learner rather than the subject matter was the prime concern in the educational process. Activity or experiences of the learner became the focal point of emphasis instead of books and verbalisms. Dewey considered the teacher a guide to the learner rather than a "walking encyclopedia." He felt that education should be practical. He favored the attainment of ends that had a direct, vital appeal to the learner, rather than the acquisition of isolated skills and techniques through drill. He felt that pupils should make the most of the opportunities of their present life rather than prepare for a more or less remote future.

Obviously, it is impossible to present a complete expression of John Dewey's philosophy in this brief description of his contribution. In fact, many people today form different interpretations of his writings and of his thinking concerning education.

Kilpatrick (1871–   ).   William Heard Kilpatrick has been one of the leaders in the "progressive" movement who has attempted to interpret the work of John Dewey. In addition to being a philosopher in his own right, Kilpatrick has made a significant contribution to a modern conception of education with his interpretation of Dewey's thinking. The "project" method of teaching is one of Kilpatrick's many contributions to education. Like Dewey and Pestalozzi, he developed schools where his ideas could be tested. His work with these schools and as a professor of education at Teachers College, Columbia University, convinced Kilpatrick that "pupil purposes" are the key to pupil learning. He set forth the idea that pupils might learn to behave certain ways on the outside but not learn to behave that way inside. As a consequence, he became very much concerned about the development of character through education.

In his work at Columbia University, Kilpatrick influenced the thinking of thousands of elementary and secondary schools teachers who attended his classes. This influence has been reflected in the practices which these teachers used in their own schools. In addition, through his books, *The Project Method, Foundations of Method,* and *Source Book of Philosophy,* Kilpatrick has reinforced the concept of instruction through life activities and has placed emphasis upon methodologies which use the concept of living as learning.

Bode (1873–1953).   Boyd Henry Bode was an exponent of progressive education. At the same time he also was a friendly critic of some of the practices which grew out of a part of the so-called progressive movement. He felt that attention merely to children's individual needs and interests as a program of education could become chaotic. This by no means meant that he negated the more modern concepts of education advocated by his predecessors. Rather, he placed emphasis on the use of common interests and on making democracy in the schools a way of life.

While professor of education at Ohio State University, Bode published a book, *Conflicting Psychologies of Learning.* He was concerned here with the question of mind and its relationship to the whole program of education. He reiterated Dewey's concept that "the cultivation of thinking is the central concern of education" [38:179]. Bode further pointed out that this makes the pupil the starting point in any educational program. He advocated individual initiative along with continuous social development. In the area of teaching methodology he was a firm believer in flexible methods to take care of individual differences. His book, which set forth a pragmatic point of view, was a major contribution to educational thinking in the late 1920s. Through his teaching and writing, which included such books as *Fundamentals of Education* (1922), *Modern Educational Theories* (1927), *Democracy as a Way of Life* (1937), *Progressive Education at the Crossroads* (1938), and *How We Learn* (1940), Bode made a major contribution to educational thinking.

CONTRIBUTIONS OF THE SCIENCES

During the past century and a half science has contributed new understandings of human growth and development. Beginning with the work of the empirical psychologists, later scientific investigations in the areas of individual differences, measurement, and learning have contributed much to the improvement of educational practices. What are a few of the contributions of science to modern concepts of education?

Empirical Psychology. In 1831, Johann Herbart, who was discussed earlier in this chapter, published a volume entitled *Letters Dealing with the Application of Psychology to the Art of Teaching.* By many psychologists he was considered the originator of a movement which eventually laid the foundation for a field of psychology, called "empirical psychology," that was based upon the results of experience and observation. However, it was long after Herbart's day that either empirical psychology or the science of education gained any great momentum.

G. Stanley Hall established a center for applied psychology at Johns Hopkins University in 1884. This center devoted its efforts to the study of children's mental development. Hall is often referred to as the founder of child study. This early movement, frequently called the "child-study movement," did not prove effective in establishing a science of education. It did, however, inject into the schools of this country a new spirit of conscious, critical consideration of methods and results of classroom procedures. It opened the door for a later, more scientific system of child study, which proved of great value in the development of sound educational programs.

Human Growth and Development. Growing out of the early work in empirical psychology and child study came a great deal of interest in all aspects of human growth and development. Research into the relative effects of heredity and environment set the stage for many investigations. As a result, educators began to learn more about which aspects of human growth are determined by heredity and/or environment.

Research provided information about the processes, patterns, and rates of human growth. Investigations indicated that the process moved from generalized mass activity to specialized local activity. These findings became extremely influential in the selection of learning experiences for boys and girls at different age levels. The fact was finally established that children are not miniature adults; they are qualitatively and quantitatively different.

Along with the foregoing concepts of growth and development came better understandings of the differences between maturation and learning. Through research it was found that children mature at different rates. It was also found that it is necessary for children to reach certain levels of maturity before they can benefit the most from the experiences provided for them. What an overwhelming effect these findings proved to have on education! They opened the way for a complete reevaluation of existing experiences for various age and grade levels.

On the basis of the research in this area, one thing became clear: Education must be geared to the growth and development of pupils.

Individual Differences.   The fact that people are different was not a very startling revelation. Since the dawn of history people have observed physical differences which existed within their own groups. The startling fact was the extent of these differences.

The extent of differences was discovered quite by accident. Two astronomers could not agree upon their observations. A group of astronomers investigating this phenomenon brought to light the idea that people differ in speed of response to a given stimulus. This led to many experiments in the latter part of the nineteenth century, the results of which indicated the tremendous number of ways in which individuals vary.

A major finding of these scientific investigations was that measured specific characteristics of individuals could be shown to assume a pattern called "a curve of normal distribution." This exploded older concepts of types and averages. No longer could a teacher consider a whole group of students average, dull, lazy, and the like. A range of abilities, attitudes, achievements, and physical characteristics existed in every classroom. Therefore a teacher no longer could expect every child to participate in a learning situation and achieve the same results as every other child. Methods had to be developed to accommodate these differences. The concept of grouping for learning grew directly out of these scientific investigations.

Measurement.   During the period when Dewey and Parker were generating enthusiasm for the study of education, a new note was sounded by J. M. Rice, who was editor of the magazine *Forum*. Rice felt he needed more objective evidence on which to base his description of the school systems of various cities. He devised a method of testing the results of teaching methods. One of his tests consisted simply of a list of common spelling words which he asked children of several cities to spell. This idea, which now seems so simple, was revolutionary at the time. The use of a definite objective test rather than mere observation was a distinct step in the direction of scientific evaluation. These first attempts by Rice to evaluate methods of teaching were scathingly denounced by leading educators of his day [7:85–86].

While Rice was concerned with measuring achievement, Binet, a nineteenth-century Frenchman, was working on a series of tests to use on feeble-minded children in the schools of Paris. From his early efforts grew some of the first instruments to measure intelligence.

The importance of the work done in achievement and intelligence tests can hardly be overestimated for subsequent educational practices.

The measurement movement did not end with the above-mentioned tests and procedures. It included aptitude and personality tests as well. From the elaboration of these instruments and techniques of measurement grew many studies in education. Contributions of the science of statistics and subsequent refinements of statistical methodology enabled educators to use more exact measuring devices for gaining insight into the development of individual students.

Learning.   There were no major problems concerning learning when educators accepted the theories of faculty psychology. But as experimental evidence pointed out the need to replace the older doctrines, scientists hurried to fill the gap. Out of their efforts developed various schools of psychology based on differing theories of learning. Study the results of the many scientific investigations which various schools of psychology have contributed to education, and think of them in terms of some of the following psychological principals:

1. Learning is facilitated when there is a felt need on the part of the learner.
2. Learning is facilitated by meaningful repetition.
3. Learning is facilitated when two or more senses are used at the same time.
4. Learning is facilitated by active participation.
5. Learning is facilitated when the conditions for it are real and lifelike.
6. Learning is facilitated when the learner is in good physical condition.
7. Learning is facilitated by a cheerful, comfortable learning environment.
8. Learning is facilitated when it proceeds from the whole to the parts.
9. Learning is facilitated by interest.
10. Learning is facilitated when it is based on the readiness of the learner.
11. Learning is facilitated when it proceeds on the basis of the individual's own rate.
12. Learning is facilitated when it is based on the maturation level of the learner.
13. Learning is facilitated when it considers the basic needs of the individual.
14. Learning is facilitated when there is emotional stability.
15. Learning is facilitated by praise.

IMPLICATIONS FOR EDUCATION

As has been said the newer viewpoints of outstanding educators and the contributions of science have helped develop the modern concept of education. These ideas have implications for specific educational practices.

The Physical Environment.   "Learning by doing" connotes the use of a learning laboratory. Thus a special learning environment was advocated by Dewey, Kilpatrick, and others. The rather drab, formal recitation halls of the past did not lend themselves to "learning by doing." In their place is to be found a different kind of working environment. Gone are the long rows of screwed-down seats, exchanged for comfortable, flexible furniture which lends itself to different working arrangements which meet the needs of individuals and groups. Centers of interest provide many challenging and stimulating sources for additional learning experiences.

Since the development of the whole child is considered, lighting and ventilation are given careful attention. Experiments show that a colorful, cheerful environment promotes learning. Dingy greens and nondescript tans and browns have been abandoned, and in their place are soft, harmonizing pastel colors. Sight-saving devices such as green chalkboards replace the older light-absorbing blackboards. Bright, colorful furniture with special work areas replaces the furniture with easily marred surfaces. With the cooperation of parents and teachers even the oldest classroom can be transformed into a cheerful working environment.

The Curriculum. What we know about the optimum conditions for learning suggests that the curriculum be cooperatively planned rather than determined by textbooks or specialists. The unified program found in the elementary school is extended into the secondary school within a core-curriculum approach. Functional units at both levels integrate and correlate learnings. Thus the modern curriculum, which will be discussed at length in Chapter 14, has a broad, general scope and sequence within which students and teachers plan learning experiences.

Teaching Materials. The modern emphasis on the development of the intellectual, physical, emotional, and social growth of the individual pupil implies more than the use of subject-matter textbooks. The program uses a multiplicity of teaching materials. As has been shown, Comenius early advocated utilizing more than verbalisms in teaching. Later, men like Parker and Dewey proposed considering the child's total environment as a source of learning experiences.

It is a well-known fact that we are in a period that could be labeled a "knowledge explosion." Underlying this label is the multifaceted implication that the student must learn as much as is humanly possible in the relatively short period of time that he is in school. At the same time, he has the urgent need to gain skill in problem solving and to assume the attitude of a learner as he faces life. Today's concept of the development of each individual to assume an active, participating role in society imposes on each individual the task of greater adjustment in the same period of time. Therefore, all possible means must be utilized in his task to aid the student.

Through research, scientists have found that learning is facilitated when materials of instruction appeal to more than one of the senses; also, that learning moves from the concrete to the abstract. Therefore, today's school uses—along with library and reference books and works on various levels of difficulty—films, filmstrips, records, and tape recordings, which

In this research laboratory classroom at the University of Michigan, various educational theories, as well as materials and equipment, are tested. (*Photograph from Hedrich-Blessing.*)

are available from central sources. A wide variety of art materials provides opportunities for self-expression, creativeness, and development of skills. Materials from the natural environment provide learning experiences in science, and tangible aids in mathematics help to make the specialized area of numbers and symbols a more meaningful language. Radio and television keep the students in constant touch with living history. Only the initiative and imagination of the school administrator, teachers, parents, and students limit the number of valuable teaching materials which can be used in the modern education program.

Grouping. The concept of grouping is not a new one. The most conventional schools have used grade groupings, based on chronological age, for many decades. Actually, this is only one of the ways in which students may be grouped to facilitate instruction. Conceivably, the grouping techniques could be used for every aspect of physical, emotional, intellectual, and social growth characteristics. It was not until the limitless range of individual differences was noted by educators and scientists, however, that other aspects of grouping for instructional purposes were given consideration. Two of the more common types are ability grouping and interest grouping.

The modern classroom teacher, using standardized test results, careful observations, and records of past performances, gains insight into each student's level of ability. The teacher places those of somewhat similar abilities together for certain learning experiences. However, these groupings are flexible, and, as students grow in their abilities, they move from one group to another. Through careful observation, teachers are often able to select groups with similar interests. Group interests may be used to solve mutual problems or to act as a motivating force for further learning. Grouping is only one of many teaching techniques which the modern teacher uses to individualize instruction.

Drill. Scientific investigations have shown that learning is facilitated by meaningful repetition, which indicates that drill has a place in the modern concept of education. It is the word "meaningful" which differentiates the modern concept of drill from the conventional concept of drill. Under the earlier system, drill was a means of training the mind or acquiring knowledge for its own sake; today it is a means of automatic mastery of certain information to facilitate the solution of problems. Drill in the latter sense is effective only when the student appreciates the importance of the material he is attempting to master and fully understands it. Thus, emphasis is placed not on rote memorization of dates and facts, but on pupil purpose for learning.

Since individuals differ in their rates of learning and achievement levels, these differences are taken into account in the modern concept of drill. No single textbook page or workbook page for everyone in the class at the same time will be satisfactory. Therefore, the modern drill theory makes use of a variety of teaching techniques and aids which stimulate interest and understanding. It is not *whether* you will use drill techniques; it is *how* and *when* you use them that is the important consideration.

Discipline. The more conventional concept of discipline centers around order in the classroom, techniques of maintaining that order, and means of punishment. The modern concept is based on certain principles which have grown out of the findings of science and the viewpoints of such educators as Dewey and Kilpatrick. Recently, Sheviakov and Redl [143: 9–16] listed some democratic principles which guide practices in a modern conception of education:

1. Teachers use positive ways of guidance which communicate this belief in the value of each personality, rather than negative ways which undermine self-confidence and self-esteem.
2. Teachers consider each incident when discipline or order has broken down in relation to the particular persons involved, their needs and their life histories.
3. Our schools provide a climate in which mutual respect and trust are possible.
4. Teachers build understanding and communication between individuals and groups.
5. Teachers help children to understand the reasons for standards and rules, and to foresee the consequences of their own behavior.
6. Schools provide for children's growth in self-government through which they share increasingly in planning their own activities.
7. Teachers study children's behavior scientifically, searching for causes and formulating hunches and hypotheses about how changes may be made.
8. Teachers help young people to understand the reasons for their own and others' behavior and to develop more effective ways of meeting common conflicts.

These principles suggest self-discipline, the internalized behavior that Kilpatrick talked about—control from within rather than total outside control. The teacher assumes vastly different duties in carrying out this concept of discipline. Instead of the authoritarian, dictatorial role, the teacher takes the part of guide and director of learning experiences which will provide opportunities to develop self-discipline. A great deal of planning with the students and evaluation of these plans becomes an important teaching technique. Children help to build their own rules and regulations within which they will operate. Prevention of behavior problems is given keen consideration by both teachers and students. Teachers help children to channel their energies and initiative into socially acceptable behavior.

Children learn the democratic way of life by living it. Since self-discipline is a cornerstone of a democratic way of life, the learning experiences which the school provides must foster law and order from within each individual.

SOME CRITICS OF MODERN EDUCATION

As you read various newspapers, magazines and books, you will find individuals who do not agree with some of our modern educational concepts. Some of them feel that concepts expressed earlier in this chapter should characterize the teaching-learning process. Others feel that school practices should be greatly modified and improved.

Naturally, parents and other community members become quite confused about what to believe as they read these conflicting points of view. They will expect you to help clarify their thinking. For this reason, know who some of the critics are as well as what they believe. As you progress in your preparation for teaching, formulate a clearly reasoned position in regard to these so that you can deal adequately with the concerns of nonprofessional and, to some extent, professional educators. Only five will be mentioned here.

William C. Bagley (1874–1946). Although Bagley is now deceased, the position he took in opposition to modern concepts of education is representative of a number of contemporary critics. He attempted to build a conservative educational position on an organized basis. As an essentialist, he believed that the school should teach only certain tried and tested aspects of our cultural heritage.

Bagley maintained that the school, in contrast to an experimental insituation that may foster change, should help pupils adjust to an existing, fixed society. He did not favor elective programs of study. For him, education was the hard process of imparting the facts, involving a relatively narrow range of studies that were considered to be essential to effective living.

Vice Admiral H. G. Rickover, U.S.N. (1900–   ). In an article entitled "The World of the Uneducated" that appeared in *The Saturday Evening Post* [129:8] Rickover synthesized some of his ideas concerning what is "wrong" with education today. He said that there are two processes by which children are guided into adulthood: education and training. One of our basic troubles is that we do not clearly differentiate between the two. He believes that the traditionalist sees the distinction clearly but the "progressive" does not. The progressive philosophy of education equates education with training. The Russians adopted this American phenomenon for a short period of time, but they dropped it some twenty-five years ago when they found that such an equation does not really educate. As Admiral Rickover sees it, education is the process of developing the individual's comprehension of the world beyond his personal experience and observation. Training is the process of developing the accepted social customs and character traits necessary to good personal appearance. "Training does not stretch the mind." He would have us throw out modern concepts of education and return to a traditional task of the school and the process of teaching.

Arthur Bestor (1908–   ). In *Philosophies of Education*, edited by Philip Phoenix [109:35–45], Bestor contributed an article entitled "Education for Intellectual Discipline" in which he gives a statement of his viewpoint. In this article he endorsed education that will produce a disciplined mind. He further explained that discipline is not equated with punishment, but is a matter of effective training. He would like to see our youth educated in such a way that they can intellectually deal with complex problems in the rapidly changing world.

Bestor stated that there are certain subject areas that can best equip the student, and these include the sciences and humanities—history, language, and literature. It should be every citizen's concern that everyone is carried as far along the line of intellectual discipline as his abilities enable him to go. Bestor encourages the public to insist that our schools engage in serious intellectual discipline and not stress trivial workmanship skills.

James B. Conant (1893–   ). Conant is one of the most widely known critics of American education today. One of his reports, titled *The American High School Today* [32], clearly indicates how he reacts to our American schools, especially the secondary school. Early in this report he set up three things that are necessary in order to have a good high school: first, a school board that is composed of intelligent citizens who can make the distinction between policy making and administration; second, a first-rate superintendent; and third, a good principal.

Conant does not endorse the grouped "tracks" system that categorizes the "vocational," "commercial," and other curriculum plans. Rather, he feels that each pupil should have an individualized program that is carefully supervised and guided. He stresses the importance of such basic subjects as English, social studies, American problems or government, mathematics, and science. An individualized program automatically gives special consideration to gifted and exceptional boys and girls. He feels that, above all, the schools must provide top-quality programs that utilize our manpower and brainpower.

Paul Woodring (1907–   ). In *A Fourth of a Nation* [187] Woodring
set forth a rather complete program of education. He states that any
system of education must be grounded in philosophical assumptions. The
trouble with many American teachers is that they have evolved their own
educational philosophy, a philosophy which is closely related to the folkways and mores of the American people. With this in mind, Woodring
suggests that the schools should assist children in acquiring information
upon which decisions may be based. The process of selecting this information is one that solicits the help of all the people. These decisions are for
all people—not for educators alone. In planning educational activities, the
schools should consider the needs and rights of children, parents, teachers, and all citizens. They should not consider the needs of the child
society exclusively. He urges that good potential teachers be found, that
they be educated better, and paid adequately.

These five individuals are not necessarily representative of all the modern critics and their views. They indicate only some views that exist
today—views with which you must be familiar. Strive to acquaint yourself further with these views as well as others, possibly using the bibli-
ography in the Resource Section for Part IV as a springboard.

SUMMARY

The influences of outstanding men and the various contributions of science briefly discussed in preceding paragraphs have had a profound
effect on the concepts and practices of education in the United States.
Two different concepts of education, the conventional and the modern,
have been noted in the development of educational theory.

The conventional concept of education centers upon formalism and
routine procedure. It views the education process as that of "keeping
school." According to this view, the materials of the curriculum have been
selected, classified, graded, and organized into a program of subject matter and classes. The business of the school is to see to it that boys and
girls acquire the content of this predetermined curriculum to train the
mind, gain knowledge, and prepare for adult life. The master teacher is
the one who can encourage, cajole, and drive the inherited content of
the course into the minds of the pupils.

The modern concept has grown out of attempts to free the school of its
formalism, tradition, and selectivity. It centers its attention on the student
rather than on subject matter—on stimulating and organizing the pupil's
experiences so that his interests and needs may be used to facilitate learning. Units, projects, and activities are made a framework for learning,
and the readiness of the pupil for a new kind of educational experience
is carefully studied. A variety of teaching techniques and materials provides for individual differences. Internalized behavior is promoted
through experiences in self-discipline and self-responsibility. Critical and
diligent study of the most desirable forms of social life are undertaken
to determine which skills, attitudes, and abilities should be built in the

lines of the young. According to this concept, subject matter and the development of skills become means to an end rather than ends in themselves.

QUESTIONS FOR YOUR CONSIDERATION

1. In what ways have early concepts of education influenced modern educational practices?

2. What different concepts of discipline exist in homes and in schools today? What is your concept of discipline?

3. What contributions are the various fields of science making to education today?

4. What do educators mean when they talk about the "whole child" attending school? What are the implications of this concept for you as a teacher?

5. What competencies should children have at the end of the sixth grade in school? Which of the two dominant concepts of education discussed in this chapter is most likely to develop these competencies? Why?

6. What differences exist between training a dog and educating a child?

7. What is meant by the term "progressive education"?

8. What is your concept of authority, freedom, and guidance?

ACTIVITIES FOR YOU TO PURSUE

1. Construct a historical calendar of outstanding thinkers and indicate their contributions to education.

2. Contrast the concept of (1) man, (2) learning, and (3) subject matter held by the early thinkers as opposed to educators today.

3. Visit psychological laboratories, testing bureaus, and any similar facilities in order to see what contributions they make toward improving educational practices.

4. List some of the ways educational practice has lagged behind educational thinking today.

5. Visit a number of classrooms, especially in the elementary school, to see how children are grouped for effective learning.

6. Make a list of modern critics of education and indicate the points of criticism of each.

7. Visit several classes and discover the purposes which lie behind the kinds of learning experiences the pupils are having.

8. Examine a number of standardized tests to ascertain the types of achievements they are trying to measure.

RESOURCE SECTION FOR PART IV

- Calendar of Some Important Events in Education
- Suggested Films, Filmstrips, and Recordings
- Suggested Readings
- Figure Credits

• CALENDAR OF SOME IMPORTANT EVENTS IN EDUCATION

As you can sense from this chapter, a number of important events have occurred in the development of education in America. It may prove helpful to organize several in chronological order, so that you may get a bird's-eye view of them. For this reason the following calendar of events is presented.

1635	Founding of the Boston Latin School, first college-preparatory school
1636	Founding of Harvard, first permanent college in English North America
1647	Massachusetts Act ("Old Deluder Act," which followed the 1642 law ordering that children be taught to read)—first general school law in America
1693	Founding of College of William and Mary, first permanent college in the South
1753	Chartering of Benjamin Franklin's Academy, representing the transition between Latin schools and a more practical curriculum
1785, 1787	Northwest Ordinances, the beginnings of national aid for education
1819	Famous Dartmouth College Decision of the U.S. Supreme Court, which established the inviolability of a college's charter
1821	First high school in the United States, in Boston
1839	Founding of the first state normal school, Massachusetts
1852	Enactment of the first compulsory school law, Massachusetts
1857	Founding of the National Teachers' Association, now the National Education Association
1862	Passage by Congress of Morrill Bill, which became the basis of land-grant colleges
1867	Federal agency now known as the U.S. Office of Education, created by Congress
1873	First public kindergarten in the United States in St. Louis
1874	Kalamazoo Decision by Michigan Supreme Court, which established a state's legal right to public funds for high schools
1890	Passage of the second Morrill Act which provided for money grants to institutions of higher education
1893	Significant report of NEA Committee of Ten, first of a series of NEA reports with far-reaching effects on curriculum and standards
1897	Founding of the organization now known as National Congress of Parents and Teachers
1902	First junior college in the United States, in Joliet, Illinois
1909	First junior high schools established at Berkeley, California, and Columbus, Ohio
1914	Smith-Lever Act providing for extension work in agriculture and home economics
1917	Smith-Hughes Act providing Federal assistance for vocation education in public schools
1918	Publication of the Report on Reorganization of Secondary Education—"Cardinal Principles of Secondary Education"
1919	First public nursery school established in the nation
1920	Compulsory education became effective in all states
1923	Formation of World Federation of Education Associations, forerunner of the present World Confederation of Organizations of the Teaching Profession
1933	Federal government began aid to schools operating nonprofit school lunch programs

1937	Enactment of the George-Dean Act which provided Federal aid for vocational education and distributive education
1941	Publication of the Eight-Year Study by the Progressive Education Association
1944, 1952	Enactment of GI Bill of Rights for World War II and Korean veterans
1945	Creation of United Nations Education, Scientific and Cultural Organization (UNESCO)
1949	Organization of National Citizens' Commission for the Public Schools—a nonprofit organization designed to improve education.
1952	Ruling of the U.S. Supreme Court on released time for religious instruction
1954	Ruling of U.S. Supreme Court on nonsegregation in the public schools
1955	White House Conference on problems of school housing, finance, personnel, and organization
1958	Enactment by Congress of the National Education Defense Act providing Federal funds for the improvement of instruction in various subject areas, and for guidance, audio-visual aids, and student loans and fellowships
1959	Publication of Conant's study: *The American High School Today*
1960	Golden Anniversary White House Conference on Children and Youth called by the President
1962	Controversy developed in congress over Kennedy's proposals for Federal aid for public school buildings construction and teachers' salaries
	Ruling of the U.S. Supreme Court on prescribed prayers being required of pupils.

● **SUGGESTED FILMS, FILMSTRIPS, AND READINGS**

The number in parentheses following each suggestion denotes the chapter for which it is best suited.

Films (16 mm)

American Teacher   (March of Time, 15 min). Presents some pros and cons of the progressive-education movement, and points out the citizen's responsibility toward the schools; also gives a brief history of education in the United States, including the present emphasis upon psychology. (12)

Better Tomorrow   (Overseas Branch of Office of War Information, 20 min). Shows progressive-education systems in three New York schools, demonstrating how learning is connected with everyday experiences in children's lives on the preschool, junior high, and senior high school levels. (12)

Broader Concept of Method: Part I, Developing Pupil Interest   (McGraw-Hill, 13 min). Presents typical student attitudes and responses to the conventional, teacher-dominated, lesson-hearing type of high school class recitation. Contrasts the effects of the informal, group-discussion type of class in which students are permitted to share in the planning of the work and are thereby stimulated toward worthwhile and meaningful learning experiences. (12)

Education in America: The Nineteenth Century   (Coronet, 16 min, color). Describes significant historical developments and the changing character of American education in the nineteenth century. Points out contributing factors of change, such as the establishment of the first high school, problems growing out of the Civil War, the teachings of Horace Mann, compulsory laws, the trend toward uniformity under state regulations, and the beginnings of teacher-training schools. (11)

Education in America: The Seventeenth and Eighteenth Centuries (Coronet, 16 min, color). Gives historical background to the early developments in American education—in New England, the South, and the Middle Colonies. Relates the character of the different schools—dame, Latin grammar, private, parochial, pauper, academy, and college—to prevailing social, economic, and cultural conditions. (11)

Education in America: Twentieth-Century Developments (Coronet, 16 min, color). Reviews significant developments in American education in the twentieth century and relates these developments to the social, economic, and cultural life of the nation. Considers the influences of outstanding educators, educational theories and movements, and major trends and problems. (11)

Experimental Studies in the Social Climates of Groups (Kurt Lewin, Iowa State University, 32 min). Presents a study of the effects of types of social organizations upon the attitudes and learning of junior high school children. The social climates developed in the experimental situations are democratic, laissez-faire, and autocratic. (12)

Horace Mann (Emerson Film, 19 min). Portrays important episodes in the life of Horace Mann, "the father of the common schools"; reviews his activities as teacher, lawyer, state senator, board of education member, and college president; emphasizes his work in pointing up the need for well-built schools, good textbooks, democratic methods of learning, schools for teachers, and universal education in the United States. (11)

The School (Two Thousand Years Ago) (Gaumont-British, 15 min). Portrays the educational methods used by the Jewish people of Palestine at the time of Christ. Shows the techniques practiced in the instruction of boys in the formal temple schools, and the girls in their informal learning at home, where their mothers were primarily responsible for the instruction. Stresses that most learning was based on reading, memorizing and discussing the laws and the writings of the prophets. (11)

Section Sixteen (Westinghouse Broadcasting Company, 14 min). Describes the historical development of free, compulsory public education in the United States. Uses realistic settings and costumes to portray the character and spirit of the changing public school. Points out important legislation contributing to educational progress and observes other influences upon education of major historical events. Focuses attention upon the problems confronting public education today. (11)

Willie and the Mouse (Teaching Film Custodians, 11 min). Contrasts Willie's father's education, in which facts were learned by repetition, with Willie's education, in which life situations are dramatized in the classroom. Various experiments with white mice demonstrate that some mice learn by sight, others by ear, and still others by touch. Shows how such experiments as these have caused individual differences to be recognized in the classroom. (12)

Wilson Dam School (Tennessee Valley Authority Film Services, 22 min). Depicts daily activities at the Wilson Dam School in Alabama. From the time the elementary pupils arrive in school buses until they leave, they are seen engaging in functional learning experiences, including such activities as caring for pets and chickens, group singing, gardening, and playing games which require coordination and imagination. A medical examination given at the beginning of each year and parent cooperation and visiting are also shown. (12)

Filmstrips
Bulwarks of Democracy (McGraw-Hill, 50 fr., color). Presents an historical sketch of the development of the American educational system, showing the early colonial private classes, the founding of the first American university, the growth of the pub-

lic education system, the establishment of the first Negro college, and the growth of library facilities. (11)

Comenius (UNESCO, 50 fr.). Describes the teachings of John Amos Comenius, apostle of modern education and world understanding. (11)

Education in America (Museum Extension Service, 43 fr., color). Presents the story of the growth of education in America. (11)

Growth of American Education   (Yale University Press, 40 fr.). A documentary on the first schools in America and the struggle for a free public school system. The influence of Horace Mann, Emma Willard, and other leaders. Graded schools and their effect. Private and parochial schools. Higher education, education for women, and the land-grant colleges. Educational opportunity as an expression of true democracy. (11)

Horace Mann   (Encyclopaedia Britannica Films, 51 fr.). Portrays important episodes in the life of the "father of the common schools in the United States." Reviews the activities of a distinguished educator who helped to arouse the people's interest in raising their standards of education. (11)

Schools   (International Visual Education Services Inc., 33 fr., color). Points out that instead of lunchrooms and libraries and gymnasiums, the early settlers' children had to sit on benches and write on birchbark with goosefeather pens and homemade ink. Today's school children learn about the world, they learn to think, and they have teachers who help them to work alone and with others. (12)

School at Four Corners   (Curriculum Films, 38 fr., color). A typical school day 100 years ago, reenacted in the school constructed at Farmers Museum. (12)

Your Educational Philosophy: Does It Matter?   (Wayne University, 40 fr.). Presents a number of views of the classrooms of two teachers. Compares similar situations in these two classrooms to indicate how the teachers' educational philosophy affects the types of classroom activities planned for pupils. (12)

Recordings

Concept of Discipline   (National Tape Recording Project, 60 min). Dr. Hymes lectures on the problem of discipline and the measures by which we can take to correct this. This program is on two tapes, 30 minutes each. (12)

Developing Good Classroom Discipline   (Educational Recording Service, 33⅓ rpm). Myron S. Olson, professor of education, University of Southern California, presents new concepts of classroom discipline. (12)

Heredity and Environment   (National Tape Recording Project, 15 min). How these factors work together in human development; limits imposed by heredity; setting up a stimulating environment. (12)

Lift a Mountain   (University of Illinois, 15 min). A dramatized event in the life of Horace Mann, the father of American Education. (11)

● **SUGGESTED READINGS**

The number in parentheses following each suggestion denotes the chapter for which it is best suited.

Bestor, Arthur: *The Restoration of Learning,* Alfred A. Knopf, Inc., New York, 1955. Describes the kind of education the author believes to be essential for democratic America in the mid-twentieth century. (12)

Bruner, Jerome S.: *The Process of Education,* Harvard University Press, Cambridge, Mass., 1961. Presents some very interesting and challenging views on education resulting from a conference attended by leading scholars and educators. (12)

Butts, R. Freeman: "Search for Freedom—the Story of American Education," *National Education Association Journal,* vol. 49, no. 3, pp. 33–48, National Education Association, Washington, March, 1960. Describes how schools throughout the years have contributed to the freedom of our nation. (11)

Callahan, Raymond E.: *An Introduction to Education in American Society,* 2d ed., Alfred A. Knopf, Inc., New York, 1960. Chapter 6 emphasizes the social and economic factors that have affected the development of education in America. Chapter 7 discusses ideological characteristics of American society and education. (11) and (12)

Conant, James Bryant: *The American High School Today,* McGraw-Hill Book Company, Inc., New York, 1959. Contains a number of recommendations based upon an extensive study for improving the high schools. (12)

Good, Hany G.: *A History of American Education,* 2d ed., The Macmillan Company, New York, 1962. Traces the history of American public schools and stresses the value of education for the undecided citizen. (11)

Hechinger, Fred M.: *The Big Red Schoolhouse,* Doubleday & Company, Inc., New York, 1959. Presents a clear and vivid description of Russia's schools, a critical analysis of our own education, and an interpretation of the similarities and differences. (12)

Massey, Harold W., and Edwin E. Vineyard: *The Profession of Teaching,* The Odyssey Press, Inc. New York, 1961. Chapter 2 presents a good review of the development of education in America. Chapter 3 describes conflicting philosophies of education and indicates some educational implications of each. (11) and (12)

Mayer, Frederick: "Education and the Crisis of Our Time," *Phi Delta Kappan,* vol. 43, no. 7, pp. 300–302, April, 1962. Indicates that the teacher may be our most negative and destructive critic. Discusses the role teacher must play if schools are to be an important instrument of survival. (12)

Mayer, Frederick: *A History of Educational Thought,* Charles E. Merrill Books, Inc., Columbus, Ohio, 1960. Explores the religious as well as the philosophical foundations of educational thought. (11)

Pounds, Ralph L., and James R. Bryner: *The School in American Society,* The Macmillan Company, New York, 1959. Chapter 3 indicates how schools historically have been related to the societies in which they developed. (11)

Rickover, H. G.: *Education and Freedom,* E. P. Dutton & Co., Inc., New York, 1959. Stresses the fact that we must train better scientists and technicians, as well as more responsible citizens. (12)

Shayon, Robert Lewis: "Let the Debate be Honest," *National Education Association Journal,* vol. 48, no. 2, pp. 16–18, National Education Association, Washington, February, 1959. Reacts to Admiral Rickover's book *Education and Freedom* and points out weaknesses in criticisms of the public school. (12)

Thayer, V. T.: *The Role of the School in American Society,* Dodd, Mead & Company, Inc., New York, 1960. Part III discusses conceptions of learning in their American setting. (12)

Van Til, William: "Is Progressive Education Obsolete?" *Saturday Review,* Feb. 17, 1962, pp. 56–57, 82–84. Indicates that the questions raised by the progressive movement are not obsolete, have not been solved, and cannot be escaped. (12)

Washburne, Carleton: *What Is Progressive Education?* The John Day Company, Inc., New York, 1952. Presents a brief, practical analysis of the progressive education movement and the meaning of the term progressive education. (12)

Wiggin, Gladys A.: *Education and Nationalism,* McGraw-Hill Book Company, Inc., New York, 1962. Deals with the relationship of American education to nationalism from both an historical and contemporary standpoint. (11)

Willis, Margaret: *The Guinea Pig After Twenty Years,* Ohio State University Press, Columbus, Ohio, 1961. Consists of a detached follow-up study of students who graduated in 1938 from the experimental laboratory high school at Ohio State University. (12)

Wilds, Elmer H., and Kenneth V. Lottich: *The Foundations of Modern Education,*

Holt, Rinehart and Winston, Inc., New York, 1961. Traces the development of education from primitive times to the contemporary scene. Outlines the aims, organizations, agencies, content, and methods in each period of educational development. (11)
Woodring, Paul: *A Fourth of a Nation,* McGraw-Hill Company, Inc., New York, 1957. Presents a program of education that would upgrade American education. Considers the aims, building problems, and reorganization of American schools. (12)

● FIGURE CREDITS

Figure 45. (*Source:* Calvin Grieder and Stephen Romine, *American Public Education: An Introduction,* The Ronald Press Company, New York, 1955, p. 97.)
Figure 46. (*Source:* Data adapted from *Statistical Abstract of the United States,* U.S. Department of Commerce, Bureau of the Census, 1961, p. 123.)

BROADER CONCEPTS OF EDUCATION

The rapidity and complexity of change in the social, economic, political, and technological aspects of life present major problems in designing educational programs in keeping with the needs of youth—most of whom will be alive in the year A.D. 2000. These needs differ very significantly with the needs of youth 50 years ago. To what extent has the function of the school changed, and to what extent is it geared to these rapidly changing conditions? How can schools do an even better job of educating youth when they are faced with learning so much in so short a period of time?

Part V is designed to help you view the broad aspects of education and the professional challenge with which teachers today are faced. In Chapter 13, attention is given to the changing nature of community living, to various community educative forces, and to the implications of these conditions for teaching. Chapter 14 indicates, for your consideration, some principles basic to our schools and some educational objectives that seem desirable. A number of controversial issues and problems which you will face are explored in Chapter 15. As you plan for teaching, weigh carefully the ways in which you can contribute effectively to the fuller realization of the schools' function and to the solution of these issues and problems.

13
COMMUNITY EDUCATIVE FORCES AND THEIR IMPLICATIONS

As you reflect upon your life, you doubtless can identify many experiences outside the classroom that have shaped your beliefs, attitudes, opinions, and ways of behaving. Actually you have been under the influence of the school only a very limited portion of your life. For the first five or six years of your life you had no direct exposure to the school. Thereafter, you spent only about seven hours a day for 180 days a year in a formal school setting. Hence, the vast portion of your learnings have been derived from your out-of-school experiences.

In planning a career in teaching, consider how the profession appears when it is conditioned by the various educational forces within the community. Without an understanding of these forces and a conscious concern for them as you deal with each boy and girl in the classroom, you cannot successfully and effectively fulfill your function as a teacher.

Before considering some of these forces and their educational implications, certain abstract terms should be defined. The term "community" refers to a group of people living together in a region where common ways of thinking and acting make the inhabitants somewhat aware of themselves as a group. Thus a community involves more than a geographic district, although certain factors limit its scope and others extend it outward until the boundaries are indeterminate.

The term "education" refers to the broad function of preserving and improving the life of the group through bringing new members into its shared concerns. Education is thus a far broader process than that which occurs in schools. It is an essential social activity by which communities continue to exist. In complex communities this function is specialized and institutionalized in formal education, but there is always the education outside the school with which the formal process is related. What is said here about the function of the schools relates to education in its broader sense.

UNDERSTANDING THE CHANGING NATURE OF COMMUNITY LIVING TODAY

Thoughtful students of American community life today are increasingly concerned with the profound social changes which have been occurring and will continue to occur in the years that lie ahead. You become more and more aware of these changes as world-jarring events draw attention to the new conditions under which you live. Two world wars, a worldwide depression, the use of atomic submarines and ships, the launching of satellites, the orbiting of men in space, the planning of trips to the moon, and a host of other sensational developments have been experienced within the life span of many Americans. These have focused attention upon the rapid, pervasive, and fundamental changes in our cultural scene. You can appreciate and plan for the proper role of the school in today's affairs only when you understand the consequences of these basic changes in living conditions. You will therefore want to study the characteristics of our contemporary culture, not for the sake of agreeing with a list of facts but because today's altered living conditions set the stage for the serious student of education. The ramifications and implications of these conditions should be considered in order to guide the growth of the young; factors that shape our world today should be elaborated upon. The statements here are only the beginning of a continuous and enduring concern of all thoughtful teachers.

1. *Community life today is increasingly affected by industrial and technological processes rather than by agrarian conditions and simple processes of production.* People today have great industrial know-how. Inventions and new ways of making the basic commodities of life have moved from hand manufacture to a machine process which is largely automatic and highly technical in nature. Through mass production, enormous factories turn out great quantities of products. The simple agrarian life and modes of production of our forefathers (and in many other parts of the world today) are in sharp contrast with this industrial and technological proficiency.

The increasing size and complexity of industry, business, and professional organizations result in growing needs for educational services. A study of employment trends [90:10–11] reveals that, during the past decade, professional office and sales workers as a group have exceeded for the first time in our history the number of persons employed in occupations which include skilled, semiskilled, and unskilled workers. It is believed that in the coming decade this trend will continue. The most rapid growth will occur among professional and technical occupations, especially engineers, scientists, and technicians. The need for skilled

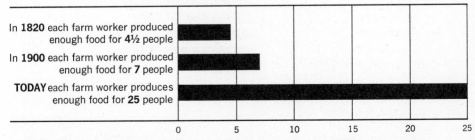

Figure 47. Despite the decline in farm population, farmers still have been able to supply the nation with ever-growing quantities of food and other products by means of improved methods and equipment. (*Source: American Observer.*)

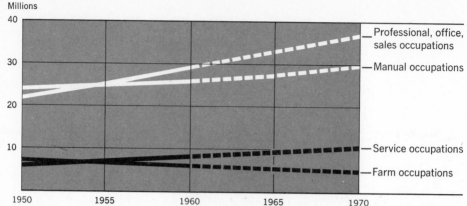

Figure 48. Employment trends by occupations, 1950–1970. During the 1960s, the employment needs of business and industry will change considerably. (*Source:* U.S. Department of Labor.)

craftsmen among the manual occupations will increase, but the number of unskilled jobs will stay about the same, which means, actually, that they will decrease in proportion to the others. A study of the occupational change in employment during the 1960s (see Figure 49) clearly indicates that the largest increases in employment will occur in occupations requiring the most education and training.

2. *Extreme ease of production has led to a high standard of living for many of our people and a potentially higher standard of living for all our people.* In spite of the range of differences existing within our society, we enjoy the highest standard of living in the world. The results of our scientific and industrial knowledge have provided us with more of the material things than ever before. Not only is this high standard available for our population but it is being extended to people beyond our shores.

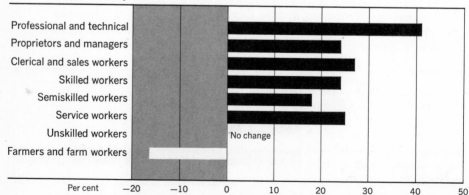

Figure 49. Per cent change in employment, 1960–1970. The largest increases will occur in occupations requiring the most education and training. (*Source:* U.S. Department of Labor.)

In the United States our manpower potential is great enough, with continued technological improvements, to increase the production of goods and services by approximately 50 per cent from 1960 to 1970. We began the 1960s with a gross national product of $500 billion. It is anticipated that we can reach a level of 750 billion dollars by 1970 [90:2–3]. This would mean that we should provide our expanding population with an increase of approximately 25 per cent in its standard of living. The uses to which our production potential will be put is today a problem of top priority. How should a potentially stable economy of abundance be managed?

3. *Human energy is being used less and less to provide the energy of production.* Today mineral forms of energy—coal, petroleum, natural gas —are used to turn the wheels of industry. There are vast new sources of energy to use, control, and divert for purposes which must be determined. Unquestionably, in the near future atomic forms of energy will be used on an increasingly greater scale. Men and animals contribute less than six per cent of our energy output. On the other hand, it is anticipated that more than 100 million persons will be working at some time during the year in 1970—a number equal to the total population of the United States around 1920 [90:13]. How can we deal with an increasing labor force and technological progress in which the man hours required for the production of goods is decreasing?

4. *Modern living is increasingly urban.* Our forefathers lived close to the land and knew and used the soil for their livelihood, but today our

In the future, increasing numbers of women will fill many skilled and semi-skilled positions outside of the home. What will be the educational implications of this change in home and community living? (*Photograph by Carl Purcell, National Education Association.*)

people live in cities and are far removed from this. In 1940 only 2.9 per cent of our population lived on farms; 56.5 per cent lived in cities; and 20.6 per cent lived in rural nonfarm locations. Figure 49 shows the percentage anticipated decline in farm employment from 1960 to 1970. There will be decided increases in such occupational groups as professional and technical workers, proprietors and managers, clerical and sales workers, skilled and semiskilled workers, and service workers during the 1960s. For the most part, these occupations are located in urban areas. What further changes in the character of living and the education needs of youth will result from this further increase in urbanization?

5. *Today production and consumption are far apart.* In the days of our fathers and grandfathers, goods were produced and consumed at home. Today the production of one industrial worker is geared to the production of many others, and the product is distributed to consumers thousands of miles away. Between producers and consumers are many intermediary occupations of handling, shipping, advertising, billing, and financing. Certain problems arise concerning the relationships between them. How can the production and consumption of goods be managed in so complex a culture?

6. *Today we can communicate readily, so that the other side of the globe is immediately in touch with local events here.* Communication advances have shrunk distances, making each local community a neighbor of every other and bringing people into close contact with the events, customs, and concerns of other cultures. How can people get along together in this smaller world in whi. all are neighbors?

7. *Productivity, new markets, new economic and distributive occupations, communication, and urbanization have been influenced by new patterns of ownership.* Today's society is corporate. Yesterday's society was characterized mainly by individual ownership and direct proprietary control over the means of production. Today the ownership of industry is diffused. The stockholder or bondholder rarely understands or manages to any appreciable degree the enterprises in which his money is invested. Furthermore, many industries are now organized into large corporations. Labor groups are similarly highly organized and are corporate in character. The forces which direct our economic and productive affairs are corporate groups that are increasingly directed by professional managerial experts. Today you find your functions more and more in terms of the groups with which you come in contact. What is good citizenship, and how can you educate for it in the modern economic world?

8. *These conditions of modern living mean that money and the media of exchange occupy a far more important position in people's lives today than they did formerly.* The processes of exchange were more simple and more direct in the agrarian society. Today people are called upon to make decisions about matters which have far-reaching consequences in other aspects of our economy. The problems of regulating an industrial, money-based society call for different skills and for skills that are more complicated than those needed in earlier days. How can you determine, acquire, and lead others to achieve economic literacy?

A research group of United States business executives, called the Committee for Economic Development, was so concerned with the economic illiteracy of high school graduates that it created the National Task Force on Economic Education, which, in turn, has formulated a description of

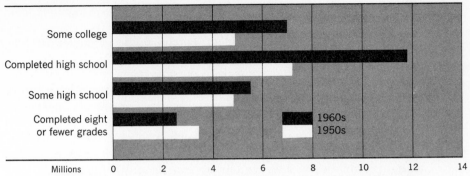

Figure 50. Amount of schooling of new young workers in the 1950s and 1960s. New young workers in the 1960s will have more education than those in the 1950s. Seventy per cent of the new young entrants to the labor force in the 1960s will be high school graduates or better.
(*Source:* U.S. Department of Labor.)

the minimum understanding of economics essential for good citizenship and attainable by high school students. The Task Force stresses the kind of economic teaching that will lead students to examine and think through major economic problems such as actions of labor unions, the farm problem, and the social security problem.

During the 1960s approximately 70 per cent of the new young entrants to the labor force will be high school graduates or better, as compared with 60 per cent in the 1950s [90:15]. Approximately 2,500,000 of the 7,500,000 non–high school graduates who will enter the labor force during the 1960s will not have completed a grade school education [90:16]. How can we encourage more boys and girls to further their education? What kinds of education will best suit those pupils who will be leaving

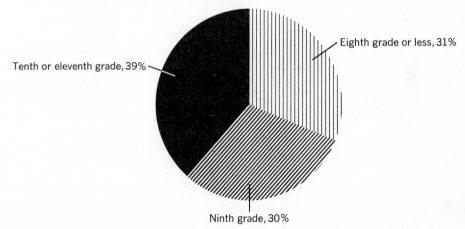

Figure 51. School grades of youth leaving before high school graduation. Probably 30 per cent of all young workers entering the labor force during the 1960s will lack a high school education. What should the school attempt to do for these boys and girls? (*Source:* U.S. Department of Labor.)

school early? How can we do a better job of counseling and guiding these boys and girls?

9. *Today our population is highly mobile.* Both our modern technological advances and the general high standard of living in an economy which is extremely productive make it possible for people to move about with great ease. A rising birth rate leads to a larger eventual labor supply with a corresponding increase in mobility. This means that people no longer may be educated to fit the requirement of only one restricted community. They are much more in touch with each other and consequently know more about how others live. Personal aspirations are altered as the possibilities of a better life are experienced firsthand.

Every year millions of workers change jobs. The U.S. Department of Labor has found that in one year more that 8 million different workers made 11,500,000 job changes [90:12]. About two-thirds of these job changes involved completely different industries, and one-half of them involved completely different occupational groups. More than 3,500,000 workers moved to a different state during a period of one year. How can we educate in an age which feels the consequences of easy transportation for an increasing population?

10. *We are living in a highly interdependent world community.* A dislocation in one major industry affects the industrial actions, health, and economic well-being of large numbers of people in distant areas. War

Based on 1959 data

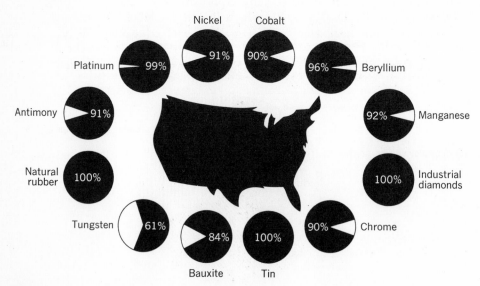

Figure 52.   Strategic materials from other free nations are essential to United States industry. What are the implications of this situation for schools and for our society? (*Source:* Bureau of Public Affairs.)

today is a total warfare of all the people; depression is global in proportions. Having all people produce and control the energies now at their disposal seems imperative. What are the skills and knowledges necessary to enable people to live together in this complex, interdependent society?

11. *In the agrarian society of the past, producers of goods planned for their continued production, and the goods produced were disposed of in the market place according to the supply and the demand.* Today people are increasingly aware that planning involves much more extensive control over the making and distributing of goods. The government tries to exert some control over the modern industrial economy, which does not seem to regulate itself. Does this condition call for a new attitude and a readiness to experiment with the enlarged function of government?

12. *The older controls in our social life no longer operate as they did in our earlier agrarian period.* The family, for instance, was at one time an institution around which centered the production and marketing of goods, personal services such as laundering and tailoring, recreation of all members, and a large part of the group's education and worship. Today practically all these activities are performed through some other community institution or organization. The parent used to supervise the chores of the young, but today, if work is available, children are generally without the supervision of parent or teacher. What is the place of the school in providing for learnings previously guided by parents at home and now largely unsupervised?

13. *Today's community life seems to many to be highly impersonal compared with small-town agrarian life in the past.* In the contemporary metropolitan area the individual is often unknown to his neighbor; personal identity becomes lost in the confusion of urban life. Here one is less accountable for his actions, less subject to the pressures of a society in which every individual is well known by his neighbors. The problems of finding an adequate sense of belonging and competency seem to become more difficult under such conditions. How can the school promote physical and mental health under modern conditions?

14. *Technological advancements will provide increasingly greater amounts of leisure time.* In 1859, a little more than a hundred years ago, the average worker in our society had only 12 hours of leisure time each week. It is predicted that by 1975 the average amount of leisure time for the workers will be 52 hours a week. Some economists forecast that by 2050, a man will work only one day each week, spending the other six at leisure. According to Jackson M. Anderson, assistant executive secretary of the American Association of Health, Physical Education, and Recreation, the average workers since 1929 have gained one full day of leisure a week, and nearly one additional week a year for extended vacations.[1] Each year Americans now spend more income for leisure-time pursuits than for all public elementary and secondary schools.

---

[1] From an address delivered at the Department of Elementary School Principals Association Annual Meeting, St. Louis, March 27, 1960.

According to Anderson, approximately 16 million Americans bowl, 8 million play softball, 7 million pitch horseshoes, 6 million water ski, 5 million play golf, and millions more participate in tennis, badminton, and various other sports. Approximately 37 million Americans participate in boating, 30 million go fishing each year, 20 million enjoy shooting and hunting, and 5 million participate in archery. Most of us engage in some type of social activity, such as attending club meetings, square dancing, visiting with friends, playing some form of cards, and the like. Millions of people spend time on such hobbies as stamp collecting, gardening, photography, and music. Many people spend part of their leisure time conscientiously trying to improve their lives as well as the lives of others. They contribute their time and talents to church work, charitable agencies, boy and girl scouts, school activities, and a host of other activities designed to improve life in their communities.

In spite of the constructive benefits that have been derived from the increased amount of leisure time available to the average individual, some questions having educational significance may be raised. How can we account for the low state of physical fitness of children, youth, and adults throughout America? Why, according to J. Edgar Hoover, has serious crime reached the highest point in history, and why is it increasing four times as fast as the population? How constructively do those over 65 years of age spend their time? Why have so many homes, the basic unit in our society, disintegrated because of the high divorce rate?

Our future generations will be faced increasingly with problems concerning the wise use of vast amounts of leisure time that will be theirs. Toynbee, the great historian, finds that never in the history of man has any nation been able to accumulate a vast amount of leisure time for its people and survive. Is it possible for us to avoid disintegration as a result of mass leisure?

15. *While the forces suggested so far have been molding the world today, people's lives and thinking have also been influenced by the growth of science.* Many events which used to be explained by magic or supernatural intervention are now being explained through objective investigation into their causes and conditions. People are becoming scientifically minded, but at the same time they are faced with many problems which they do not solve in conformity with the requirements of modern science. They are scientific in making automobiles but unscientific in using them. They are scientific in measuring intelligence but find it difficult to determine the use to which intelligence should be applied. Science will doubtlessly continue to affect our lives more and more. What kinds of minds must be developed to deal with the new worlds which science offers?

16. *Today's society demands the conditions of peace and peaceful settlement of competing international interests.* Though the need of cooperative endeavor is recognized, the threat of war continues, even after the most destructive total conflict that man has experienced. With new forms and forces of destruction loose in the world, society is in critical

need of some form of international sovereignty. In the time of Alexander the Great, the soldier with one spear killed one enemy. Napoleon's cannon with one firing killed 12; the Big Bertha of World War I killed 88; Hitler's V-2 rocket killed 168. An American B-29 dropped one atomic bomb and killed almost 1 million people [104]. The testing of multimegaton bombs, as well as the talk of astroidal bombs, dramatically displays man's increasing ability to destroy his fellows and the imperative necessity for determining the causes of war and for arriving at a program for implementing the conditions of peace. How are wars begun in the minds of men, and by what processess may the defenses of peace be constructed?

17. *Today's society is one in which an understanding of totalitarianism and an ability to meet its challenge are imperative.* With the current trend toward dictatorship, an enlightened citizen should study the significance of the suppression of the individual's thoughts and actions, not only in the international scene but also in our domestic affairs, and be prepared to oppose tyrannies over free men's self-government. This ability to lay bare the basis of totalitarianism is of crucial importance today; in our technological society the bigotry of the demagogue may immediately reach a whole people rather than be merely disseminated by word of mouth from one speaker to a handful of others. The forces which make for tyranny over the minds of men may use the devices of modern science for their own purposes. To find ways of disclosing the purposes and evaluating the efforts of totalitarianism of all kinds is an imperative need in modern society.

18. *The citizen today needs to make finer and more subtle discriminations in what he says and hears than did his ancestors.* Through radio, movies, television, and the press, modern citizens receive opinions and attitudes which tend to be uncritical expressions of emotion and exhortation rather than critically examined statements of conviction. We are asked to distinguish between groups, interests, and pressures whose purposes are not always explicit and whose avowals may be different from the intentions which underlie them. To avoid a feeling of hopelessness, anxiety, and frustration, it is necessary to have the techniques and skills by which a thoughtful evaluation may penetrate to the real significance of what goes on in contemporary society. What is the difference between liberal and subversive activities, indoctrination and education, freedom and license, control and dictatorship?

These characteristics of modern living are of course not exhaustive of the changes that have occurred in our culture, but they are representative. They reveal some of the modern conditions with which you as teachers are faced. They set the stage on which you are to act. They define the requirements of the context in which you must develop professional proficiencies. If schools are to keep pace with the conditions of modern life, they should consider how well they are meeting the demands of the contemporary social scene. To what extent has education been aware of the pervasive changes of modern living, and to what extent has it defined the content and methods of formal education in terms of these conditions?

COMMUNITY EDUCATIVE FORCES

According to the broader meaning of education, all the activities of a community which influence the growing individual are educative. These activities vary widely from simple to extremely complex community influences. The way in which people rear their children, the manner they employ in greeting each other, the way in which they choose and wear their clothes, the methods through which they use their natural resources, the ways in which they compete or cooperate, and the way in which they carry on a number of other activities are fundamental community characteristics which enter the experiences of a child and constitute part of his education.

Almost no child can escape his community. He may not like his parents, or the neighbors, or the ways of the world. He may groan under the processes of living, and wish he were dead. But he goes on living, and he goes on living in the community. The life of the community flows about him, foul or pure; he swims in it, drinks it, goes to sleep in it, and wakes to the new day to find it still about him. He belongs to it; it nourishes him, or starves him, or poisons him; it gives him the substance of his life. And in the long run it takes its toll on him, and all he is [10:7].

Examples of Community Educative Forces.   An exhaustive analysis of the community forces that enter into the education of young people is beyond the scope of this book. Since you probably will devote considerable attention to these forces in subsequent courses, only a very few will be discussed at this time.

The family.   Undoubtedly the family is the most basic educational agency in the lives of boys and girls. It is here that foundational attitudes and habits are formed. In satisfying the child's basic needs for food, shelter, and the other requirements of growth, the mother builds into the infant the attitudes and understandings of which that particular society approves.

As a result of the work of Margaret Mead and other cultural anthropologists, it is now known that some communities encourage attitudes of withdrawal from reality; other societies encourage patterns of affection and cooperation; still other communities encourage feelings of conflict and competition by a severe pattern of child development [93]. This process of encouraging fundamental dispositions which may operate through the lifetime of the individual is a basic aspect of community influence upon the individual. Although it is most evident in simple societies that lie some distance away, the same educational process is occurring continuously in our own immediate families. Those skills and abilities approved of and valued by a community are encouraged in the early family interactions. The fundamental habits which are recognized as normal by the community are built into the lives of the young by the parents. The parents endeavor to eliminate those habits which seem un-

While part of each child's day may be spent in the classroom, teachers must recognize the constant influence of the home and family associations upon the lives of their pupils. (*Photograph from the National Education Association.*)

desirable and abnormal. In so doing, the basic motivations of the young are channeled and directed.

Community pressures may be so reflected through the actions of father and mother that the youngster feels that he belongs and has genuine affection in the home. On the other hand, the community tensions and problems may have such an effect upon the family relation that the youngster feels a lack of acceptance and intimate belongingness within this primary social group. These basic social-psychological habits of adjustment are learned to a large extent in the formative years of early childhood through the interpretations which the father, mother, sister, and brother extend to each individual. Feelings of inadequacy in performance and in status and privilege in regard to other people begin in the early years in the home and are continuously developed as the child matures in his family group. From these early experiences the individual's value structure—that which is deemed worthy and worthwhile—is molded. The wishes and aspirations as well as the frustrations and disturbances which more mature people find basic in their experiences may frequently be traced back to the early educational patterns of the home. How has the educational pattern of your home affected your life? Identify two radically different home environments and study the extent to which specific behavorial patterns of children in these homes are being affected. If you were the teacher of these children, what adjustments would you make in your work?

Peer and adult groups. As the child develops, his maturing interests and abilities bring him into intimate contact with playmates. Here he learns habits and dispositions of behavior appropriate for his peers. He comes to find out that some of his wishes may run counter to those of his peers and that his own desires and urges must be controlled and modified in the light of their habits and attitudes. In brief, he learns that his skills, habits, and attitudes have to be related to what other group members may choose and be able to do.

Teachers in drawing upon the out-of-school experiences and informal learnings, of their students can enrich their formal learning in the classroom.
(*Photograph from Marie Fraser.*)

Gradually the growing youngster reaches out from his early intimate contacts with parents, siblings, and playmates and becomes aware of various adult members of the social world around him. He learns that some of the community functions are performed by certain adults and not by others. He obtains an early view of the various occupations which a community contains, the specialized skills and abilities which mark off one member from another. These occupational influences are reflected in his early childhood games; he plays at being the milkman, the doctor, the schoolteachers, the nurse, the policeman.

In many instances the growing child finds himself in conflict with the attitudes and behavior patterns of his broadening adult world and finds that he must make some kind of adjustment to a community which does not afford him the satisfactions which he seeks. For example, consider the following case and the related educational implications [10:48]:

Isabel is unhappy and sensitive because her family is one of the Spanish-speaking families in the community with many of the home ways of the Spanish-American culture. Isabel feels that she is rejected and her family is rejected by the other children because their ways are 'different.' It is the problem of the school to help Isabel appreciate her parents' culture in order that she may not have her security in her home threatened. At the same time she needs to learn

American ways in order that she may be accepted by the other children. In the curriculum activities connected with home improvement Isabel may find help in her difficulties.

The life of the gang may also be so influenced by the community attitudes toward the young that the members of the gang find no room for performances which are to them important. As a result, boys and girls may form social groups which endeavor to provide satisfactions for the members which are not available elsewhere. For example, the delinquency gang is to be understood primarily as a manifestation of the inadequacy of the contemporary American community to satisfy the growing demands of young people in that community. The gang itself is an educative agency which develops from the community patterns and which seeks to satisfy the fundamental needs of its members.

Special-purpose agencies. There are social influences, in addition to those characterized by face-to-face intimate relationships with other people, which develop from special purposes within community life. They attempt to fulfill some specific need of the members. For example, a Sunday school or a scout troop or a group in school is a community agency which seeks to fulfill a special function such as providing religious training, experiences in out-of-door living, or training in becoming a mature member of the society. Can you identify all of these organized secondary groups in your home community that are influencing growing children by building into them a knowledge of the approved ways of behaving? How have they affected your life?

The many secondary groups in which boys and girls receive their education may be dichotomous in emphasis, scope, and purpose. What is learned within our group as normal and desired behavior may be regarded in another group as fundamentally undesirable and subject to penalty. For example, a scout troop may value trustworthiness and honesty highly, whereas a boys' gang may reward its members for such practices as stealing and lying. The various community influences may thus be inharmonious and contradictory, and the youngster may have considerable difficulty in relating what he learns in one social situation to his activities in another. Can you identify any such influences in your home community, and to what extent were you affected by them?

In one sense growing up in the community means encountering conflicting roles, statuses, and values in various situations, and learning to compromise and amalgamate them into a relatively consistent and harmonious way of behaving.

Consider the college student who, in planning his career in teaching, wrote as follows:

I became a combination bell hop and odd job boy for a hotel. As I look back now, I can see that this experience taught and filled a void in my makeup that school and home had been unable to touch. I earned my own money, managed my time, and saved that money through planning. The responsibilities and the self-confidence that I received were compensation enough for that job. Above all,

I think it was the contact with the adult world of people that left the greatest and most lasting impression on me. I met older people; I learned discernment in judging people and caution in accepting them. I heard men talking in the lobbies; I knew of their actions. I saw and heard things that were not according to the moral code that I, my family, and the school had established. I wondered at it. I thought that perhaps moral rules and living principles were things that you implicitly believe until you reach an age when you see into them. I became skeptical. I saw that the ideals my elders had taught me were lightly regarded by themselves. I wonder even yet that I survived this critical period.

You can sense that this student experienced considerable learning from his work experience. With what conflicting values was he confronted? How did he seem to resolve them? What effect did his home life apparently have upon the manner in which he resolved these conflicts? To what extent did his formal school experiences apparently help him in facing such problems? Should teachers feel a responsibility for preparing students to face such problems? What values did this student gain from his work experience?

Reflect upon your own life and attempt to identify some of the many experiences outside the classroom that have shaped your thinking and behavior. Consider how these experiences affected your school experiences. To what extent did your teachers take into account, or fail to take into account, these community learnings as they planned your school experiences?

Communication facilities. The rapid expansion of the many forms of communication has increased the number of community groups to which the developing child is exposed. In the United States alone there are more than 3,515 radio stations, 571 television stations, 1,761 daily newspapers, 8,408 weekly newspapers, 2,850 magazines [11:3–6], and a host of comic books and movies. All of these media bear upon the way youngsters feel and think. As you analyze some of the programs on television, for example, you recognize that some of them are in direct contradiction to the values we hope children will develop. Advertisements in print and on the air influence the needs and desires of people. Various organizations and institutions of the community can reach large numbers easily, rapidly, and vividly. They serve to influence the members of the community to do things in a particular way, to spend their money for certain products, to think about other people according to certain stereotypes, and to project themselves into the ways in which other people behave or would like to behave. How will you as a teacher attempt to deal with these kinds of community learnings of youth?

Recreational facilities. The recreational facilities of a community are particularly important educational influences today. They do not center in the activity of the family, as was the case a generation or so ago. In this modern period of rapid transportation and communication our pastimes tend to be outside the family. Movies, dance halls, taverns, bowling alleys, pool halls, swimming pools, beaches, club rooms, skating rinks, amusement parks, carnivals, race tracks, and recreation centers are aspects of the modern community which satisfy our desire for new experiences, for excitement, for escape from the monotony of the work world, and for doing what other people do. The high degree of mobility of youth creates situations in which an increasing number of their activities are unsupervised by adults concerned with the character and moral development of the young. These community influences channel and divert the ways in which young people grow. They lead youth to expect to

(Photograph from the film Mike Makes His Mark *by the National Education Association.)*

(Photograph by Carl Purcell, National Education Association.)

The facilities of a community for recreation have significance for teenagers. What lack of proper facilities do these pictures suggest?

participate in the activities which they see and hear about. How many recreational facilities and what kinds of facilities are available in your community? Are these recreational facilities supervised in such a manner that they promote or hinder the character and moral development of the young? In what ways did these facilities help or hinder your development?

Other forces.   Such community forces are only a few of the many that tend to mold the developing behavior patterns of boys and girls. A more exhaustive listing certainly would include the influences of geographic and ecological conditions; organized religious, economic, and political institutions (church, bank, store, police department, court); the formal educational agencies in addition to the school (library, museum, art gallery); the service clubs, labor unions, and farm groups; the work experiences of youth, which provide direct contact with the life of the community; the socioeconomic levels, through which youth learns the discriminations of the established social order and takes on the stereotypes, prejudices, and discriminatory attitudes of a particular socioeconomic class. Gain a thorough understanding of these and many other forces as you consider them in subsequent college courses.

Generalizations Regarding Community Educative Forces. Concerning the many educative forces at work in the community, the following significant generalizations may be drawn:

1. The school operates as a formal educational agency within the context of other formal and informal educational influences. The school itself appears as only one of the assets of the community. Some of the informal educational influences, such as radio, movies, and the press, seem to be more influential than the school in determining the ways in which boys and girls develop.

2. Community influences are extremely varied in their effect upon youth. They range from the formative influence of the family to the conversations at the corner drugstore; from the Sunday school class to the gang; from the community library to the crystal-gazer of the carnival. Apparently some appraisal, selection, and control over these educational influences are necessary if a young person is to be able to discriminate and profit from his exposure to them.

3. The child is molded in skills, attitudes, habits, concepts, motives, and values by the forces in the community that bear effectively upon his development. In some communities, for example, the skills of weaving may be given such an emphasis that they become much more important than the skills of reading and writing. The community also educates boys and girls to take certain attitudes toward people who are different—in skin color, for instance. By the time the youngster is of school age the community has already established within his behavior pattern the readiness to respond in a particular way. The community may also dictate that some things are not to be discussed in an open fashion; for example, matters pertaining to sex. The habits of the community expressed in its folkways and institutions are basic in determining the types of responses which the boy or girl may make.

Concepts, beliefs, and ideas are also directed by community influences. In our country the concepts of free enterprise, private property, and unrestrained competition are built into the individual through many aspects of group living. In another nation, beliefs in government control over enterprise, state ownership of property, and direction by a central authority of prices and wages make for other concepts regulating social organization.

The motives that drive people vary as well. Some appear to reach throughout all the levels of the community. Boys and girls are taught, for example, to strive to rise in social position, to value material rewards of success, to base many of their habits on the profit motive. At the same time the habits of one socioeconomic class may cause its young to be motivated by goals which do not influence members of another class. Some children may be taught to value formal education very highly; others may place a low value upon it. The level of aspiration of the individual may be determined in very fundamental fashion by his socioeconomic position.

Judgments are also affected. Youngsters who have found that they are discriminated against, or that other members of the society exploit them or their kind, may have an evaluation of democracy which differs from that of children brought up under conditions which protect them from exploitation and discrimination. Young people are likely to deem worthwhile those things which their community perpetuates to satisfy their basic needs.

4. Community influences change as the individual develops. In the early years of a child's growth the family seems to be the primary source of his education. But as he matures, other community agencies take on a much more important educational role. The child learns to conform to and depend upon his family for the satisfactions of most of his needs. In later childhood and adolescence he learns to grow out from the family, to identify himself with other institutions, and to seek his satisfaction independent from the family patterns.

In planning to teach, make a study of the various conflicting and contradictory influences which bear upon children and their development. There is a profusion of community educational influences. The individual may be pushed in one direction by one force and in an opposite direction by another. The contradictory nature of many of these community influences should lead you to consider carefully what the function of the teacher is in such a context. This problem seems particularly important today when the modern American community is being subjected to many novel influences and many forces which extend the school experiences beyond the local boundaries of a particular restricted region.

IMPLICATIONS FOR TEACHERS

The previous discussion leads to the conclusion that it is hazardous for the school to ignore the wider educational influences of the community. If teachers continue to separate the learnings of the classroom from the learnings of the broader community, as they have in the past, the school will experience decreasing influence in the lives of boys and girls. As you prepare for teaching, formulate plans for making the school a more realistic agency in the lives of youth.

In making a decision as to how you will function as a teacher, consider the following implications of the educational forces in community life. Not all these implications are of equal importance, nor are they separate in their meaning and importance.

Knowing the Community's Development.   Whenever a teacher enters a community, he finds it to be already structured in terms of its educational patterns. These patterns have been in operation for a long time and have acquired status and prestige. They have become the way they are by a process of growth. Study the history of the community's educative processes in order to gain a thorough understanding of them. This does not mean that you must learn in a routinized fashion the dates and occasions that mark a community's history. Nor does it mean a formal acquisition of the facts of the history of education. It does mean that you function effectively in terms of the social forces that have made the community and its school what they are today. You then can understand present trends and future probabilities. In brief, gain a functional history of education in the local community, as it will serve you in decisions on how to make your influence felt in the educational patterns of community life.

Participating in Selected Community Activities.   Your task in the community is always to promote certain tendencies and to minimize others. In noticing all the educational influences of the group, recognize that you cannot support them all; you must choose those which you prefer to encourage and which will promote growth among community members. Evaluate the various educational agencies and have some basis for judging the ones most worthy of your participation.

There are some community groups whose purpose is to foster the total life of the community and to equalize the opportunities for a better life for all. In many communities, however, there are social groups or organizations that are interested in obtaining prestige or privileges for their members at the expense of other members of the total society. More specifically, a parent-teacher association will, by and large, aim at the elevation of the life of all the members of the community, while other groups, like most high school fraternities and sororities, will have as their objective the improvement of the status of their own members and the exclusion of others in the student group.

Your function in the community is that of selecting, balancing, harmonizing, and purifying the community influences on the child. You will be concerned, then, with encouraging those commercial movies which are most desirable, emphasizing those radio programs which have more

Through participation in community groups teachers help improve community living and the influences to which young people are subjected. (*Photograph by Carl Purcell, National Education Association.*)

positive educational value, balancing the claims of one advertisement against another, and seeing that the interests of a larger number of people are being cared for in the total educational process. Thus you will be concerned with helping boys and girls to discriminate between the various competing claims made upon them by the groups in their society. You will be interested in the consumer's needs and interests as well as in those of the producers and sellers of goods. You will help youngsters to distinguish between the agencies that educate and those that indoctrinate. Become an expert in revealing the varied community endeavors and in leading the young to distinguish between the forces playing upon them.

Appraising the Community's Educational Influences. The teacher today appraises the informal educational influences of the community in an effort to relate them to the formal classroom learnings. Modern teachers realize that a formal education will not succeed if it runs counter to the other learnings in a community. Pupils learn the correct forms of expression in school, only to have these learnings negated by experiences in poor forms of communication in the home, market place, and recreation center. They learn to be good citizens within the school setting; at the same time they learn through their informal community influences the common prejudices and easy ways of getting along in the practical world. Boys and girls may learn to think, talk, and act in a democratic way in school, while they learn undemocratic habits in their community life. The modern educator has been more and more concerned with problems created by the isolation of the school from its community context.

As a teacher, you have a responsibility in helping the growing youngster assimilate his informal community learnings and relate them to the education he is obtaining within the walls of the school. For example, a child may need guidance in harmonizing what he has learned about democratic living with his view of people who are inferior in the eyes of his older family members. The teacher has a real and pressing interest in dealing with the totality of a child's experiences; the child should be led to deal with human beings of all kinds in terms of the respect due them simply as fellow humans. The teacher needs to accept and appraise these total educational experiences and, appropriate to the developmental level of the child, to help him see the significance of his informal learnings and the extent to which he should or should not be incorporated into his responses to future situations.

Be a careful student of these community learnings so that you will be able to make the classroom education as effective as the informal learnings of the family, playground, or gang. Consider how readily a child learns the rules of a game, or adopts an attitude of teamwork, when he is playing with his agemates on the corner lot. Consider again how slow and difficult are his learnings in a spelling class. Be interested in finding ways to make the academic learnings as effective and permanent as those attained in the informal play situation.

Using Community Resources in Curriculum Planning. The teacher in the modern school uses the community to create a more realistic, lifelike, and vital school curriculum. It is important to survey the community's needs in order to gear instruction to the demands on the child and to determine what assets the community contains for promoting the classroom program. Seek to promote a curriculum which will supply children with the experiences which the community demands, and use local industries, institutions, documents, and key personnel to produce a dynamic and true-to-life school program.

Olsen and his colleagues point out the following ways in which the school may effectively relate to the life of the community [103:146–345]:

1. Documentary materials such as magazines, newspapers, records, and deeds
2. Audio-visual aids such as records, transcriptions, maps, posters, charts, films, slides, models, and television
3. Resource visitors and people with specialized abilities or accomplishments who can present to a school group an experience of unique value
4. Interviews with authorities who can enrich the content of the course of study
5. Field trips or excursions with instructional objectives
6. Surveys or the determination of a selected existing state of affairs in a community
7. Extended field studies to some distant locale
8. Camping or an informal but organized rural-living experience
9. Service projects in which boys and girls contribute to civic welfare under educational guidance
10. Work experiences directed toward eventual success in some occupational field

Every community has resources that may be used in making learning more meaningful. In this photograph a local resident is sharing his specialized hobby with a group of high school students. (*Photograph by Carl Purcell, National Education Association.*)

Students need a chance to discuss, to think through, and to arrive at realistic conclusions regarding their role in life and how the lives of others may be enhanced. (*Photograph from the Department of Instructional Materials, Oregon Public Schools.*)

A thorough study of the means of relating the school program to the life of the community is basic in preparation for teaching today. As you sense the importance of a community-centered school you see the impelling need for teachers who have imagination and enthusiasm to create the newer, more functional course of studies. Only through the work of such teachers will the schools be able to retain boys and girls during their formative years and give them an education which will prepare them for life in the modern community.

Leading Students to Realistic Appraisals of Their Community. In making use of community resources, the modern teacher in today's school helps young people make an accurate and true-to-life appraisal of their community. Such an appraisal is necessary if pupils are to find in their school experience a vital and valid introduction to modern American life. The teacher, then, guides them in their analysis of modern social conditions and stimulates activities of significance in the life of the community.

As you plan for teaching, consider the importance of knowing and studying each pupil's work experiences in his community. Often these experiences are not recognized as educational in nature. Since job learnings are seldom integrally related to a student's school learnings, the teacher does not make the program of formal education vital and real to him. Study and guide a pupil's work experiences so that they may become more profitable and so that the curriculum can be related to his job concerns.

Teachers of modern youth have a major function to perform in helping boys and girls realistically appraise their vocational abilities and interests in the light of the existing distribution of employed persons and probable changes in this distribution. Because of advancing technology and the increased level of education, the degree of skill required of the working force is increasing. Table 8, compiled by the Research Division of the National Education Association [153:8], reveals striking changes in the occupational distribution of workers between 1900 and 1975. Forty-one per cent of the workers in 1900 were employed in professional (technical and kindred), managerial, clerical, sales, crafts, and operative occupations. This percentage rose to 62 per cent in 1940 and will probably increase to 76 per cent in 1965 and to 78 per cent in 1975. On the other hand, 49 per cent of the workers in 1900 consisted of unskilled laborers, service workers, and farmers. This percentage decreased to 38 per cent in 1940 and will probably decrease to 24 per cent in 1965 and to 22 per cent in 1975. In 1975 the per cent of unskilled laborers probably will be only one-half of that in 1940. Likewise, the per cent of those engaged in farm occupations will probably be only one-third as great in 1975 as in 1940. These changes in the distribution of employed persons have significant implication for the manner in which young people should prepare themselves to earn a living.

TABLE 8   OCCUPATIONAL DISTRIBUTION OF WORKERS, 1900–1975
(In per cent)

Occupation	1900	1920	1940	1950	1965	1975
Professional, technical, and kindred	4.3	5.4	7.5	8.6	11.3	14.0
Managerial	5.8	6.6	7.3	8.7	10.3	10.8
Clerical	3.0	8.0	9.6	12.3	14.4	14.4
Sales	4.5	4.9	6.7	7.0	6.5	7.4
Craftsmen	10.5	13.0	12.0	14.1	13.5	13.7
Operatives	12.8	15.6	18.4	20.4	19.6	17.5
Laborers	12.5	11.6	9.4	6.6	5.0	4.4
Service	9.0	7.8	11.7	10.5	11.8	12.4
Farm	37.5	27.0	17.4	11.8	7.6	5.3
Total, in millions	29.0	42.2	51.7	59.0	73.5	86.9

Source: Adapted from "Status and Trends: Vital Statistics, Education, and Public Finance," *Research Report 1959–R13*, National Education Association, Research Division, Washington, 1959, p. 8.

Helping the Community Find a Real Place for Its Youth. In your attempt to understand the tasks of the teacher today, note the tendency of the school to foster the real participation of the young in the affairs of the community. In the days of our ancestors, boys and girls were responsible members of their communities at an early age. But nowadays local affairs are in the hands of older people, and group life tends to be dominated by adult interests. The average age of our population is increasing. According to the 1960 census, our population between 1950 and 1960 grew both older and younger. During this period of time the number of children and youth under 18 years rose by 36.7 per cent. The number of retirement-age people, 65 and over, made a 34.7 per cent increase in the 1950–1960 period. The middle group, ages 18 through 64, gained only 7.2 per cent and in 1960 comprised only 55 per cent of our total population as compared with 61 per cent in 1950.

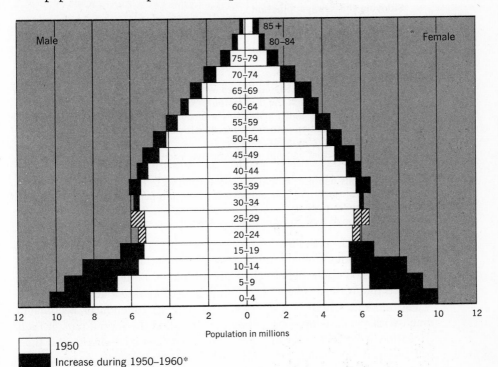

Population in millions

1950
Increase during 1950–1960*
Decrease during 1950–1960*

Alaska and Hawaii included in both years

Figure 53.   Population of the United States by age and sex in 1950 and in 1960. What important changes in population took place and what effect will they have upon opportunities in education? (*Source:* U.S. Bureau of the Census.)

There is greater need today for an agency to bring the interests and activities of youth into the life of the adult community. Not only would boys and girls have a fuller sense of belonging and participation in civic affairs, but also the adult group would benefit from the fresh vitality and idealism of youth.

Schools have a function to perform in helping the community find a real place for its youth. Young people may work at helping a group solve its traffic, sanitation, and public health problems, its needs for planning and coordinating local agencies and services, its demands for more adequate recreation and leisure-time resources. Consider how the health program in an elementary school in Petersburg, West Virginia, extended into the community. Here are some of the things the boys and the girls did that were adapted especially to their resources and ways of living [10:17]:

Seventh- and eighth-grade groups initiated the program.

All groups had a part in the work.

Thirteen committees had responsibility for school and community experiences which the school could do something about. These included:

Improving garbage disposal methods

Studying the sewage situation

Street cleanliness

Studying the water supply

Surveying city-dump situation

Getting rid of mice and rats

Making a study of school health

Reducing colds and other diseases which interfere with school attendance

Studying ways in which the city restaurants handled food

Getting rid of flies and mosquitoes and conditions which breed such pests

Studying the situation with regard to livestock within city limits

Getting more recreation for the town

Studying the situation with regard to rest rooms and making recommendations

Most of the pupils had part in making questionnaires to fit the study.

Learning how to make and use maps of parts of the community was of practical help to the younger pupils.

Older pupils learned how to represent the school in community organizations.

Through such activities young people gain further respect for the worth of individuals, enjoy the sharing of common interests and concerns, and strengthen their beliefs that the problems of modern life can be solved through the application of intelligent cooperative action.

The modern school is also concerned with its function of keeping in touch with young people after they have finished the formal part of their education. Teachers today are not so sure that they have discharged their full responsibility when boys and girls have graduated from or left the school. Follow-up studies on the nature and extent of the youth's adjustment in the adult world are an integral part of the educational task. Such guidance services are not yet common practice in our schools, but they seem clearly indicated.

Becoming a Better Adult Educator.   Contemporary studies of educational needs in our society indicate that the age group most in need of educational facilities and guidance are the adults. These findings are not startling when we consider the rapid advancement and changes being made in our times. Social and economic changes resulting from scientific and technological advancements demand new knowledge, skills, understandings, and attitudes on the part of everyone. The adult can no longer depend solely on the education provided him in his childhood and youth. According to the U.S. Office of Education, "Adult education is becoming the 'fourth arm' of education and a coequal in importance with elementary, secondary, and higher education. In many communities more adults than children and youth are already participating in educational programs, because there are more adults to educate" [46:106].

It has been estimated that about 9 million adults are benefiting from formal instruction and at least another 40 million are engaged each year

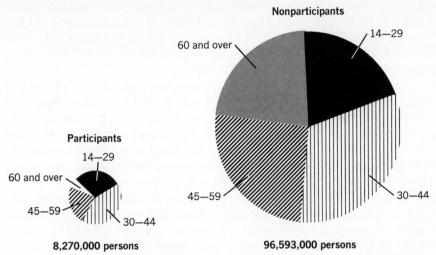

Nonparticipants

60 and over

14—29

45—59

30—44

Participants

14—29

60 and over

45—59

30—44

8,270,000 persons

96,593,000 persons

Figure 54. Number and age of participants in adult education and the number and age of nonparticipants, October 1957. How should society attempt to meet the imperative need for more adult education? (*Source:* U.S. Office of Education.)

in informal learning activities [1:6]. They participate voluntarily, on a part-time basis, in these activities. Over three-fourths of these participants are between the ages of 20 and 60, with the greatest concentration being in the 30–45 age group. The participants are divided almost equally between men and women. The programs attract larger numbers from professional, managerial, and skilled occupations than from laborers, operatives, service workers, and persons engaged in agriculture. Types of educational programs which attract large numbers of participants include civic and public affairs, general academic, home- and family-living, trade, and industrial and vocational courses [1].

Reports on the first comprehensive statistical survey in the field of adult education, issued by the U.S. Office of Education, state that an estimated 2.9 million adults are participating in adult-education programs offered by local public school systems [119:52]. The vast majority of the various adult programs are under the sponsorship of health and welfare agencies, labor unions, local and national church organizations, business and industry, and various government agencies.

Members of the Adult Education Division of the National Education Association estimate that there are over a hundred million adults in our nation who should be considered. Grave concern has been expressed for the individuals below the age of 25 who are out of school and out of work. Too often they are a loss to themselves and a liability to their communities. The number, of course, fluctuates, depending in part on economic conditions.

An increasing number of school systems throughout the nation are visualizing their function in terms of this wider conception of education.

Many teachers who have concentrated in elementary or secondary teaching will be needed to assume responsibilities in adult education. As has been said of the Emily Griffith Opportunity School in Denver, the modern school endeavors to "offer everything the school has to anyone who wants it and can absorb it."

Although most teachers think of themselves as specialists in the education of children, actually every teacher is involved in the education of adults. You will find that you cannot educate Johnny, aged eleven, unless you also have an effective understanding of Johnny's family life, and that you cannot guide the development of the group in the elementary school without many fruitful contacts with the home. Parent-teacher-association meetings are only one way of providing these contacts.

In many of the informal conversations between teacher and citizen you will find an opportunity to serve as a friend and counselor in an informal adult-education setting. Parents will present you with educational problems and questions about how to guide Sally's development or how to encourage Henry in his arithmetic. You must be prepared to serve the parents' needs in these cases. You must visit the home and spend some time with the neighborhood activities of boys and girls in order to be well acquainted with your group and with the family relationships of each child. To be a teacher today means to have considerable expertness in the role of an adult educator.

Attaining Expertness in Human Relationships.   A teacher today is interested in studying the ways in which the community influences its young, not merely by the geographic location of industries, stores, and churches but more fundamentally by the qualities of human relationships which it inculcates through informal learning. The community does not influence all its youth in the same way. Environment is not identical for all boys and girls, and each child is molded by his particular set of environmental conditions. It is your responsibility to study how these various influences bear upon each youngster for whose education you are responsible.

Boys and girls growing up in different socioeconomic classes have quite different concepts of human relationships as a result of their class position. Think of the learnings which Priscilla indicates in the following passage when talking to her father [180:90–93]:

"I'm in the doghouse again, and this time it's an awful big doghouse. I can't stand it any longer. I'm going to quit that terrible high school. I want to get a job and go to work. . . .

"Everyone up there hates me. No one likes me. The teachers hate me, and the kids won't have anything to do with me. . . .

"I got caught playing hookey again. That old Swenson caught us. He's always snooping. He thought we were going down by the river to meet some boys, but honest we weren't. Florence, Ruth, Carol, and I just wanted to have a little fun. Just wanted to get away from those snooty kids. And ·I'm not going back. . . .

"The way a lot of us girls are treated at school no one can blame us for the way we feel. There's nothing there for a lot of us but just coming to classes,

How may the attitudes, beliefs, and behavior of these children be affected as a result of low socioeconomic conditions? (*Photograph by Carl Purcell, National Education Association.*)

listening to the teacher, reciting our lessons and studying, and going home again. We're just pushed out of things.

"There are a group of girls there who think they're higher than us. They're a group of girls from the wealthier families. They look down on us. They have a club that's supposed to be outside the school, but it's really in the school. They can do things we can't afford, and they just go from one club to another and hog all the offices, and are in all the activities. They just talk about what they're doing and what they're going to do, and they ignore us. They won't pay any attention to us. . . .

"I don't want the kids in high school to know that Mother takes in washing to get a little extra money to get some of the things that she needs. . . . They'd look down on me if they knew it. And we can't do the things they do. We have a large family, and I know, Dad, you're only a working man, and we can't afford to do a lot of things. . . ."

While Priscilla spoke, Mr. Sellers looked at the floor. He said nothing. He knew what she said was true. His two older children had told him the same thing when they quit. He and the Missus had gone up to school and raised hell, but it didn't do any good. Now it was Priscilla's turn.

Now by way of contrast notice the quality of human relationships which Kenneth experiences [69:100–101]:

Everybody likes Kenneth, even Sally, and Kenneth does not tease Sally the way some of the others do. Kenneth knows that everybody likes him. The teachers like him, they say, because he learns so fast and has such a nice disposition. The other children like him because he "plays nice," he doesn't try to boss everything, and he doesn't try to have his way all the time, and he invites a lot of children to his parties and he lets other children play with his things. Kenneth doesn't like to have to take a bath as often as his mother says he must. Sometimes he wishes he had more brothers and sisters so that his mother wouldn't have as much time to work on him and try to make him cleaner and better dressed than everybody else.

Kenneth has an individual personality that makes everybody like him. Probably most people would like him even if his father was not the owner of the lumber company and even if his mother was not the president of the Women's Club. But Kenneth also has a cultural personality. He has learned certain manners of speech and of dress. He has learned certain attitudes about the school and the teacher. These manners and attitudes form his cultural personality and since he lives in a community which rates his particular cultural personality as most desirable, he is continually rewarded for being what his family has made him.

It is clear that community influences of very different kinds are molding the characters of these two youngsters.

As a teacher today, you must be a student of community influences on human relationships and must attempt to foster democratic forms of living for all youth. Seek to understand these influences so that you may help pupils control their responses to the social norms which are molding their personalities. Help the community provide for a higher level of respect for each of its members and help young people understand why their social opportunities are not yet of a truly democratic nature. Try to construct a school program which will provide for the needs of all. Develop expertness in human relationships, in teaching, and in guiding others to a life of fuller democratic participation.

Becoming a Better Student of Intercultural Processes.   The world is no longer one in which groups are isolated. Consequently, the problems of intercultural and international education become problems of every modern teacher. In performing the immediate tasks of the classroom, the teacher should have in mind the major requirements of world citizenship. How can a teacher lead boys and girls to accept without prejudice people of other races, creeds, and economic and political persuasions? What processes may be used in helping youngsters locate their prejudices and stereotypes? What units of instruction may be devised to lead boys and girls to more adequate concepts of people who differ from themselves? What experiences should all children have to develop a democratic tolerance of others and a respect for personality regardless of surface differences? How should a teacher study and understand the local community in its patterns of discrimination, and to what extent and by what processes should he make his weight felt in leading the community to change its restrictive mores? Such questions are the immediate and practical problems of an ever-increasing number of teachers today.

The resources for obtaining aid in these endeavors are very extensive and include such things as bureaus and agencies for promoting intercultural education, extensive bibliographies covering the field, films of outstanding instructional merit, and the experiences of communities in establishing councils charged with planning for a fuller realization of the brotherhood of man. The modern teacher knows of these resources because in his training he has taken time to prepare himself thoroughly for the demands of the community in which he is to serve.

Interpreting the Traditions of the American Way of Life.   The most basic task of the teacher who is concerned with the community backgrounds of education is that of interpreting to the community the traditions of the democratic way of life. At no other period of our history has there been such a compelling demand for teachers who are alive to their role as leaders.

SUMMARY

Thoughtful students of education are increasingly concerned with the profound social, economic, political, and technological changes which have been occurring and will continue to occur. A number of these changes have been identified in this chapter. Attention also has been given to some of the powerful community forces which influence the educational growth of the individual.

Many of the tasks of the teacher are strongly influenced and determined by the forces in community life today. Obviously, the particular responses of each teacher will be determined only as local conditions are studied and defined. Consideration has been given only to problems which are common to most present-day communities and which suggest preparations that ought to be part of the living resources of any new teacher. These problems range from understanding the causes of delinquency and planning a curriculum to avoid them, to the high level of abstract thinking needed to discriminate between conflicting values in the community today.

As you proceed with your preparation for teaching, continue to probe more deeply into the educational implications of such community forces as have been mentioned in this chapter. Your efforts should help you in formulating a clearly reasoned and functional concept of the role of the school and of the teacher in effectively guiding the total educational growth of pupils. Herein lies a tremendous challenge for you. The check list in the Resource Section of Part V should help guide you in your preparation to meet this challenge.

QUESTIONS FOR YOUR CONSIDERATION

1. Eighteen major changes in community living were noted in the first part of this chapter. How do you feel in regard to the questions raised in the discussion of each of these changes? What implications do you see for educating boys and girls?

2. Reflect upon the agencies within your home community which exert an educational effect upon the young people. In your opinion, are the agencies other than the school doing all that they can to exert positive effects? What improvements might be made?

3. From what sources do you feel you obtained the values you hold—those things which you judge to be of most worth and which determine your choices, sacrifices, and ambitions?

4. In what ways are mass media affecting the developing behavior patterns of boys and girls today? What are some of the educational implications for you as a prospective teacher?

5. In what ways does a school have the opportunity to contribute to the improvement of its community?

6. To what extent should the community dictate the curriculum of the school? The methods to be used in teaching the pupils?

7. Why will it be important for you as a teacher to know the development of the school's community?

8. How do teachers influence the attitudes of the public toward schools?

9. In what ways can a teacher take an active role in the up-grading of community forces?

ACTIVITIES FOR YOU TO PURSUE

1. What have been the outstanding sources of learning in your life? Begin with school, home, church, and other organized agencies of education, and proceed to the more incidental and unorganized sources such as movies, comics, gangs, television, and radio. Then attempt to evaluate the various agencies by rating them as exceedingly effective, very effective, moderately effective, slightly effective, or of no effect.

2. Make a list of what a teacher should know about the nature and extent of the recreational activities of a community? What factors influence the nature of community recreation?

3. In your home community try to find out where the pupils go after school. Do they engage in constructive activities?

4. Visit and study the kind of education obtained in a typical adolescent "hangout" in a community.

5. Study how young people in a typical community obtain their spending money? What education do they obtain in the process?

6. Visit a slum area in a large city. Observe especially the behavior of boys and girls. Study the kinds of educative forces to which they are being subjected.

7. Spend some time, if possible, as an assistant in a settlement house. Become well acquainted with some of the boys and girls. You may wish to do case studies on one or more of the children. Study especially the forces that have shaped and are shaping their behavior patterns. List all the meanings that these experiences have for you as a prospective teacher and as a potential parent.

8. Reflect upon your own public school experiences. To what extent were community forces considered by your teachers and used to help you develop to your maximum capacity for democratic living? In what ways do you plan to be different from your former teachers?

9. Attempt to determine the extent to which you have developed the social and civic competence required for relating the school closely to the life of its community. The check list in the Resource Section for Part V should help you in this regard.

10. Consult your local recreation department, civic clubs, and other such organizations to find out how they are coordinating their programs with the school. Are all of them pursuing common aims or are they operating independently?

11. Ask a juvenile court official to indicate causes of juvenile delinquency and what a teacher might do in order to lessen these causes.

14
PURPOSES OF EDUCATION IN AMERICAN DEMOCRACY

What do they mean by fads and frills in education? Upon what bases should you select educational experiences for your pupils? What methods can you use in guiding learning? How will you handle the behavior of boys and girls? What kind of relationships should exist with parents and citizens? The way you answer these and many other questions which teachers face is determined, in the last analysis, by the way you view the function of present-day education. Teachers today, more than ever before, need to be very clear in their thinking in this regard.

Modern educators tend to view the school within the context of the modern social scene. They believe that a school program which is unrelated to the conditions of the place in which it originates and which it is to serve is dead and inert. They feel that organized knowledge is man's greatest resource for individual and community growth; but also that this knowledge must be functionally related to meeting life's problems rather than mastered for its own sake. Thus the curriculum of the modern school is seen as the study of community life in all its aspects. The aim of this study is to produce citizens who can take over the management of their own participation in the life of the group and their contribution to that life.

This view of the purpose of the school is based on the idea that teachers will be guided by continuous and careful study of the child—his abilities, maturation rates, and unique assets and liabilities—but that such study, useful as it is in guiding school practices, is not sufficient to define the aims of the educative process. Only by critical and diligent study of the most desirable forms of social life can you determine which skills, attitudes, and abilities should be built into the lives of the young.

RELATING THE SCHOOL TO DEMOCRATIC LIVING

In the period of the rise of the common school in America, the chief concern of the teacher was to provide a standard curriculum which would make possible the task of teaching the large numbers of pupils who came into the public school. In this era of school expansion it was altogether natural that specific subjects should be established as the content of education. With large classes, many poorly prepared teachers, and a highly complex and confused social scene, the schools needed a curriculum that could be taught formally. The school was also influenced to be selective and to prepare for college those who had the academic, social, and economic advantages necessary for higher education.

The changing conditions in the American scene necessitated that schools be free of the rigid formalism, tradition, and selectivity of pupils. Youth were graduating or withdrawing from school and meeting community conditions to which the school program had not been geared. A new, positive educational program was needed.

Considering the Schools Today.   Although the schools have made considerable progress in developing programs that are responsive to the needs of youth as well as to the requirements of modern society, much yet remains to be done. Criticisms of the nature of the programs in one school suggest that some basic assumptions are being uncritically followed. Too frequently we assume (1) that the child goes to school for the sole purpose of acquiring mastery of *prescribed bodies* of knowledge and that the mastery of this knowledge will ensure effective citizenship, (2) that education is preparation for life and has no particular significance for living while it is being acquired, (3) that children feel the same needs for acquiring subject matter as adults feel, (4) that learning primarily is a passive rather than an active process, (5) that obtaining the correct answer to a problem is more important than the process of solving the problem, (6) that all boys and girls in a grade or class must meet the same grade standards in order to be promoted, (7) that learning devoid of purpose or interest provides good discipline, (8) that it is more important to measure what has been learned than it is to learn, (9) that youth has no part to play in conceiving, planning, and appraising the educative processes, and (10) that the school's curriculum consists of a rigid predetermined content to be mastered by the pupils.

These beliefs are of such long standing and are so thoroughly built into our thinking by tradition that they frequently are not recognized. Carefully analyze the teachers you have had to determine the extent to which they operated in terms of these assumptions. Perhaps you can identify other assumptions that should be added to the list.

Thoughtful educators today are more and more concerned with the discrepancy between the conditions of modern life and the assumptions upon which the schools have, in general, been operating. As you plan to teach, recognize the extent to which many educational practices are continuing to lag behind the salient characteristics of our modern culture. Develop the habit of thinking critically about how you will see the proper business of the school today and how you will make your weight felt in leading the community toward a wider concept of the function of the schools.

A "call to teaching" places heavy responsibilities upon those who join the profession. You are called upon to be students of the current social context in which formal education occurs. Ferret out information concerning (1) what is done in schools, (2) the common assumptions upon which these actions rest, (3) the state of the current culture which the school is to serve, (4) the ways in which the educational process should change in order to better fulfill its function in the group. Studying these problems puts a vital and serious content into the business of teaching. Without this content the schools will be out of step with the conditions of modern life.

Formulating Some Principles Basic to Our Schools. What, then, are the principles or new assumptions which should underlie any move to bring the program of the schools up to date and to vitalize their function? To answer this question is to embark upon an activity that will consume your time and energies throughout your career as an educator. Yet it is most important that you begin to study your profession in this way if you are to sense the challenge facing all teachers. Consider the following 10 statements of educational principles to see whether or not they are more adequate than the usual assumptions underlying educational practices:

1. *The child goes to school in order to acquire behavior patterns which will enable him to meet the problems of his time and to grow in ability to handle them successfully.* In this basic principle it is maintained that the function of the school is far more than the acquisition of existing bodies of academic subject matter; it is to guide youngsters in their

The speed and ease of mass communication has made the entire world, with its varied conflicting opinions, beliefs, ideologies, and problems, the community and the concern of modern youth. (*Photograph from the National Broadcasting Company, Inc.*)

ability to behave in certain ways. As such, everything that goes on in a school is an active part of the curriculum. The basic business of the teacher is to channel this behavior which is built into the character of the pupil.

If the primary task of the school is to lead the youngster to acquire habits, abilities, and skills which will be his behavior resources, then it is your responsibility as the teacher to distinguish between those actions which are appropriate to the problems which boys and girls face and those which are not helpful or which are hindrances to their abilities to meet problems. Be continuously inquiring into the problems which youngsters are facing, and attempt to gear new behavior modes to the content of their experiences.

Not only should school experiences be provided in terms of the problems of the contemporary community, but they should also be provided in terms of individual behavior patterns—patterns which encourage the youngster's abilities to handle the problems he faces. It is the business of the teacher to study the behavior patterns that are being built, in an attempt to encourage those which are more fruitful and to remove those which are less likely to lead to successful problem solving.

2. *The growth of youth toward constructive citizenship is a continuous process with which the school is primarily concerned.* You should be constantly concerned with behavior that promotes good citizenship and behavior which may detract from it. In seeking ways of building the former into the range and experience level of the pupils, find situations in which children can learn, appropriate to their developmental level, the characteristics of desirable citizenship. The future calls for citizens with broad perspective, who have a critical and constructive approach to life and standards of value by which they can live effectively and constructively. We desperately need citizens who have ability to think, to communicate, to make valid judgments, and to evaluate moral situations. We need citizens who have a deep sense of responsibility for their fellow men, who are concerned with moral and spiritual values, and who do not shape their philosophy of life entirely in terms of materialistic considerations. We need citizens who realize that the democratic way of life not only cherishes freedom but entails obligations and sacrifices for its preservation. We need citizens who are capable of making creative, constructive adaptations to the inevitable changes that will take place in our technological and social world.

Thoughtful teachers are concerned with describing in common language the characteristics involved in citizenship so that the educational process may be directed with them in mind. At every level of guidance we must be concerned with seeing to it that these characteristics are encouraged and that the techniques of acquiring them are freely available to all youngsters. We must see to it that behavior which embodies these characteristics is rewarded and made more satisfactory to the learner than less constructive ways of behaving. Thus a thoughtful and critical understanding of the meaning of citizenship may be built into the methods and techniques with which you guide the learning experiences.

3. *The democratic way of life which has been wrought by our ancestors is sufficiently valid and vital today to provide continuous direction for educational activities.* As a teacher, you are charged with building and employing a clear conception of the democratic process. We must see to it that boys and girls learn to distinguish at all points between behavior

patterns which have the quality of democracy and those which are fundamentally autocratic, totalitarian, and anarchistic. This means that we
must become increasingly more competent students of the democratic
way of life and must interpret democracy in more than its superficial and
partial aspects. Specifically, we must help boys and girls to develop depth
of understanding of, and deep-seated convictions to, such basic aspects
of democratic life as respect for the dignity and worth of the human
being, the principle of human equality and brotherhood, the freedom of
speech and of group discussion, the ideals of honesty and fair-minded-
ness, the supremacy of the common good, the obligation and right to
work, and the need to be informed and concerned about the affairs of
our society.

In all the activities of the school, the characteristics of the democratic
way of life should be at work giving youth educational direction and
guidance. As a teacher, see to it that full and free participation is provided in all learning experiences. Help boys and girls to solve problems
on the basis of democratic action and the free play of intelligence as
opposed to methods of coercion and dogmatic acceptance of belief. Encourage the members of a group to accept each individual as a contributing member. Welcome a large variation between students as an
opportunity for teaching a basic democratic value, that of the precious
worth of an individual, whose own way of saying, thinking, and doing
contributes to the welfare of all. Show pupils how to distinguish between
bigotry and intolerance, on the one hand, and between freedom of inquiry and the use of minority dissent on the other, in planning and work-

**Faced with conflicting world ideologies, today's youth needs to appreciate
democratic principles such as respect for the dignity and worth of the
individual, equality, and brotherhood.** (*Photograph by Carl Purcell,
National Education Association.*)

ing together. It is your business to be a persistent student of the ways in which democratic character may be built into behavior patterns of boys and girls.

4. *Through careful study of modern society and ideal concepts of democratic living, teachers may become leaders in building a democratic society which can meet the test of our troubled times.* Not only will you be constantly concerned with building democratic behavior in youth, but you will always be attentive to the community's needs for democratic leadership in meeting its problems. Because you are a careful and thorough student of the conditions of the modern community as well as an interpreter of the meaning of democracy today, you will be able to interpret crucial problems to the group and to provide democratic processes for solving them. In the long run, then, you are a key figure in leading the culture toward a fulfillment of its democratic values.

This does not mean that you become a militant authority, striking out blindly for what you may deem desirable from your point of view. Nor does it mean that teachers working together should establish a cut-and-dried program for community living and seek to impose it upon others. It does mean that you carefully and critically study current economic, social, and political problems, appraise existing conditions in terms of the democratic values, and seek to help the community to appraise their effects upon the youth. This calls for an expertness in social action which teachers in general have still to achieve. It is one of the challenges to the educational profession in modern times, the response to which will determine whether teachers become a fully professional group or remain merely "keepers of schools."

Whether they have recognized it or not, teachers have had this role of interpreting and inculcating in political statesmanship. Wherever totalitarianism has gained power in countries, one of the first acts of the dictators has been that of capturing the educational process for indoctrination of their form of tyranny. In today's society it is more imperative than ever before that teachers be able to foster the democratic life, not only within the school program but also within the total life of the community. Only as you perform your function in social leadership will you be able to help the learning within the school to become effective in the real life of the neighborhood and the nation. This means that you should encourage those forces within the local and national scene which are productive of the democratic process, and should seek to identify and minimize those agencies which violate it. In this way you will contribute to making the ideals of democracy operate more effectively in the lives of the next generation.

5. *The modern concept of educational leadership affords you the best opportunity to study human development in all its aspects.* It is an outstanding responsibility of the teacher to provide learning experiences appropriate to the maturity level of the learner. However, you need a fundamental concept of your role in the social process in order to determine what *direction* the content of education ought to take. As has been

indicated, direction may be suggested by a careful study of the democratic way of life.

One of the aspects of democracy is the right—and the implied ability—of the individual to think for himself. Try to encourage individual thinking in your students, but in so doing decide what kinds of problems they should deal with and the degree to which they will be successful. Adapt the problems to the level of their abilities. See that youngsters follow through the problems they select for study and make as complete and thorough an investigation as they can. Give youngsters the opportunity to figure out and experience the consequences of their study. And make it possible for boys and girls to carry their learning activities beyond the confines of the school into the community, where the real test of their education will be made.

The modern concept of educational leadership, then, means that there is no real opposition between education geared to the needs and requirements of the young and education devoted to the study and leadership of society. A child-centered school and a community-centered school are not in conflict. Only as both these aspects of the teacher's business become related can any adequate sense be made out of either.

6. *Youth, adults, and teachers have a part to play in conceiving, planning, and appraising the educative processes.* As you have noted in the preceding sections, the function of the school is not one that is discharged wholly within the walls of an academic building. The real business of the school goes on within the total life of a community. This means that teachers operating by themselves, without including pupils and the lay members of the community, may not hope to fulfill the functions of social leadership and guidance of human growth.

There are many instances today in which schools which have failed to establish adequate working relationships with their communities have been unable to carry on programs designed to meet the current needs of young people. The school which fails to interpret its endeavors to the public finds itself out of step with the thinking and activities of the community. For this reason it is particularly important that teachers include the layman in their educational planning. As a modern teacher, you need skill in interpreting your position to the adults of the community, and ability to recognize in your community the resources which may be drawn upon to fulfill the educational purposes better.

But there are reasons other than this practical one for the participation of the lay community in the educational process. Only as parents and adults understand the function of the modern teacher can they help achieve his purposes by providing out-of-school experiences and learnings which will support the school program. If the learning within the school program is rendered ineffective by the informal educational process, it can hardly be expected to succeed in producing a democratic life for all. Thoughtful adults, when they have an opportunity to study what is involved in an education for democracy today, are anxious to help provide a more effective context for the learning that the school is fostering.

The teacher in today's school should not overlook the fact that in almost every community there are quite able people who can serve as good resource persons if they are properly approached. It is important to recognize and utilize these people in planning and in providing quality educational programs. It is impossible for the teacher to possess all of the skills and knowledge that are demanded in meeting the intellectual needs of youth today. It is shortsighted of any teacher if he fails to utilize these talents. Furthermore, the frank and happy use of the abilities and qualifications of community members may do more to establish the teacher and enhance the school in the community than any amount of social propagandizing about the values and dignity of the profession.

7. *An education for democratic citizenship includes disciplined effort*

Education for democratic citizenship includes disciplined effort for mastery of subject matter. (*Photograph by Carl Purcell, National Education Association.*)

for mastery of subject matter. If you are genuinely interested in an education to meet modern social conditions, you will recognize that this education is not achieved by letting boys and girls follow their own immediate whims and fancies to the exclusion of discipline and persistent work to achieve desired objectives. To meet the conditions of contemporary society, a more rigorous and a more disciplined system is necessary; but this does not mean that the pupils will not know what they are doing or will have no part in determining what they shall learn. Nor does it mean merely the development of a disciplined mind by sharpening it on a whetstone of formal subject matter. Rather, the disciplined effort needed to meet modern requirements is one in which boys and girls organize their efforts carefully over a period of time and persist in their endeavors in the face of difficulties and discouragements. This disciplined effort is fundamentally social in quality. It results from working together on common concerns in which each individual finds his appropriate place. It means the ability of an individual to subordinate his immediate and personal liking for an eventual outcome that will benefit everybody.

In such a disciplined education there is much subject matter, but not subject matter established by an exterior authority and imposed upon an unwilling learner. Instead, subject matter becomes the accumulated experience of other people who have worked at similar problems; who have acquired comprehension of the difficulties and necessities in solving these problems; and who make their information available to others working toward their objectives. The subject matter in modern education is related to the needs and demands of the citizen in the modern world; it does not exist for its own sake.

8. *Human relations and the ways that people work together are matters as worthy of study as subject matter.* As has been repeatedly emphasized, learning for democratic citizenship is essentially a social process. In this process, youth must work together in groups, large and small, and must feed their own individual efforts into the work of the group. Such a process demands skills and abilities which are learned primarily from experience with other people rather than from books. The meaning of participation with others should be studied, evaluated, and recreated in the democratic tradition. The skills and techniques of group participation are vital learnings which may be achieved only through a disciplined effort equal to that normally applied to the formalized subject matters. This means that you, as a teacher, should become expert in guiding human relationships and developing the skills of participation in social undertakings. At the same time, provision must be made for self-realization upon the part of each.

9. *Your professional abilities are inadequate if you fail to relate your*

The development of good human relationships among pupils should be a major concern of all teachers. (*Photograph by Carl Purcell, National Education Association.*)

teaching skills to the broader functions of the school in a democratic society. Be proficient in the uses of all the techniques and devices by which the readiness and abilities of students can be applied. Be expert at learning how to control the classroom situation so that desirable learning can be achieved and aimless disorder avoided. Know the methods which have most commonly succeeded in instructing youth. Be an expert at the professional business of the classroom.

It is urgently required that your professional skill be related to the basic aims and purposes of the learning process. Do not let the techniques of your trade become ends in themselves. Continuously adapt them to the basic objectives of your function as social leader in a democratic society. Be careful not to use your skills so that they negate your broader educational duties. Cultivate a wide concept of method, in which your role in guidance of individual growth and social processes indicates the skills you are to use.

Thus teaching becomes more than a matter of studying the techniques of other teachers and adopting them. It is not primarily a matter of employing what works in one situation as a technique in another. Rather, your function is to study the particular educational situation and, with a broad background of skills, to devise and use those methods which will most effectively bring about a desirable outcome.

10. *The ability to think for oneself and the willingness to inquire critically into all problems are as important as the acquisition of special knowledge.* If our democratic way of life is to meet today's critical social situation, an effort must be made to create more effectively than ever before the citizen who knows how to think for himself; who is willing to do so; who is committed to the results of his thinking. You must be increasingly effective at showing boys and girls how they may work creatively at the solutions of problems and how they may test the results of their thinking. It is particularly important in our complex and interrelated society to build behavior patterns into each individual that will make him able to isolate problems, to determine the facts which are pertinent to them, to create with imagination possible solutions, and to test the consequences of these solutions. As a teacher today, be particularly concerned with seeing that the pattern of critical thinking becomes useful in *all* the areas with which boys and girls are concerned.

When it is maintained that youth should be able to apply the method of critical intelligence to all problems, it means that they should learn to think critically about what should be done as well as about finding the existing facts. Recognize the responsibility of increasing the amount of critical intelligence in the areas of value choices and factual judgments. In modern society, with all its insecurity, conflict, and confusion, to be able to think well about the purposes or objectives of our actions is particularly important. An education to meet modern social conditions should be one in which youth learn to apply their best intelligence to the question of the ends for which they live. You will always be concerned with the basic question as to what experiences are of most worth. In modern

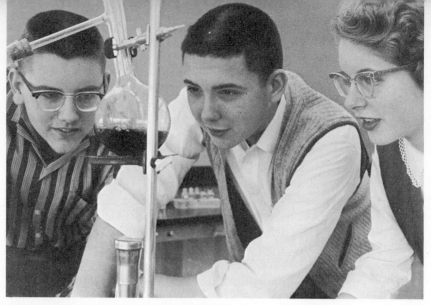

The development of skill in working together is as worthy as the study of formalized subject matter. (*Photograph by Carl Purcell, National Education Association.*)

times a critical and free intelligence working toward the tentative solutions to these important questions is a basic responsibility.

Perhaps most central in your thinking about the basic function of the school is your belief about the place of the school within a changing society. Some believe that the school does not influence the nature of society to any appreciable extent. "Education does not, strictly speaking, have an effect upon culture at all; *it is a part of it. . . .* It is not people who control their culture through education; it is rather the other way around; *education is what culture is doing to people . . .* determining how they shall think, feel, and behave" [183:241].

On the other hand, one may believe that "education is the fundamental method of social progress and reform" and that "it is the business of every one interested in education to insist upon the school as the primary and most effective instrument of social progress and reform . . ." [39:15–16].

OBJECTIVES OF EDUCATION

Clearly defined objectives are essential to provide direction to educators in planning experiences for boys and girls. Unless a teacher has a clear understanding of the particular changes he is responsible for developing in students, he proceeds aimlessly in his work. The effective teacher plans educational experiences in terms of both immediate and ultimate objectives. The latter provide the broad framework within which the former derive meaning and purpose. A study of the numerous attempts made during recent years to state objectives reveals the desire of educators to modify the school's program in response to changing conditions.

Origin of Educational Objectives. Education has been defined as (1) the aggregate of all the processes by means of which a person develops abilities, attitudes, and other forms of behavior of positive value in the society in which he lives; (2) the social process by which people are subjected to the influence of a selected and controlled environment (especially that of the school) so that they may obtain social competence and optimum individual development [60:191].

In light of this definition it may be concluded that educational objectives have as their origin the fundamental values, ideals, and aspirations that our society accepts as desirable. This fact is very well stated in the following quotation [2:132–133]:

The purpose of the school cannot be determined apart from the purposes of the society which maintains the school. The purposes of any society are determined by the life values which the people prize. As a nation we have been striving always for those values which constitute the American way of life. Our people prize individual human personality above everything else. We are convinced that the form of social organization called democracy promotes, better than any other, the development of worth and dignity in men and women. It follows, therefore, that *the chief purpose of education in the United States should be to preserve, promote, and refine the way of life in which we as a people believe.*

Since educational objectives are determined by the nature of our society rather than by the particular value pattern held by a teacher or a school system, it becomes the responsibility of each teacher to be a diligent student of our democratic society.

It would be a rather simple procedure to formulate the objectives of education if all people in our society were in agreement regarding desirable values in life. Because of the differences that exist, it is rather difficult to gain much agreement upon any statement of objectives.

General Objectives of Education.   One of the most significant statements of educational objectives was formulated in 1938 by the Educational Policies Commission of the National Education Association. Over a thousand educators collaborated in the development of these objectives. The members of the commission identified four major objectives (each related to the others) and analyzed each in terms of the specific behavior patterns that should characterize an educated person. Because of the wide acceptance of these objectives, they are indicated below in outline form.[1]

The Objectives of Self-realization

The inquiring mind. The educated person has an appetite for learning.
Speech. The educated person can speak the mother tongue clearly.
Reading. The educated person reads the mother tongue efficiently.
Writing. The educated person writes the mother tongue effectively.
Number. The educated person solves his problems of counting and calculating.
Sight and hearing. The educated person is skilled in listening and observing.
Health knowledge. The educated person understands·the basic facts concerning health and disease.
Health habits. The educated person protects his own health and that of his dependents.

[1] For a more thorough study of these objectives, read the publication of the Educational Policies Commission in which they appeared and were interpreted [120: 50, 72, 90, 108].

Public health. The educated person works to improve the health of the community.
Recreation. The educated person is participant and spectator in many sports and other pastimes.
Intellectual interests. The educated person has mental resources for the use of leisure time.
Esthetic interest. The educated person appreciates beauty.
Character. The educated person gives responsible directions to his own life.

The Objectives of Human Relationship

Respect for humanity. The educated person puts human relationships first.
Friendships. The educated person enjoys a rich, sincere, and varied social life.
Cooperation. The educated person can work and play with others.
Courtesy. The educated person observes the amenities of social behavior.
Appreciation of the home. The educated person appreciates the family as a social institution.
Conservation of the home. The educated person conserves family ideals.
Homemaking. The educated person is skilled in homemaking.
Democracy in the home. The educated person maintains democratic family relationships.

The Objectives of Economic Efficiency

Work. The educated producer knows the satisfaction of good workmanship.
Occupational information. The educated producer understands the requirements and opportunities for various jobs.
Occupational choice. The educated producer has *selected* his occupation.
Occupational efficiency. The educated producer succeeds in his chosen vocation.
Occupational adjustment. The educated producer maintains and improves his efficiency.
Occupational appreciation. The educated producer appreciates the social value of his work.
Personal economics. The educated consumer plans the economics of his own life.
Consumer judgment. The educated consumer develops standards for guiding his expenditures.
Efficiency in buying. The educated consumer is an informed and skillful buyer.
Consumer protection. The educated consumer takes appropriate measures to safeguard his interests.

The Objectives of Civic Responsibility

Social justice. The educated citizen is sensitive to the disparities of human circumstance.
Social activity. The educated citizen acts to correct unsatisfactory conditions.
Social understanding. The educated citizen seeks to understand social structures and social processes.
Critical judgment. The educated citizen has defenses against propaganda.
Tolerance. The educated citizen respects honest differences of opinion.
Conservation. The educated citizen has a regard for the nation's resources.
Social applications of science. The educated citizen measures scientific advance by its contribution to the general welfare.
World citizenship. The educated citizen is a cooperating member of the world community.
Law observance. The educated citizen respects the law.
Economic literacy. The educated citizen is economically literate.
Political citizenship. The educated citizen accepts his civic duties.
Devotion to democracy. The educated citizen acts upon an unswerving loyalty to democratic ideals.

These objectives provide a framework for educational activities on all school levels. They describe the kind of person which the school should seek to develop for our society. They constitute guideposts in terms of which you may decide the kinds of learning experiences desired for boys and girls. Although you should give attention to the development of each behavorial factor, you will be able to contribute more to the development of some than of others. For example, such factors as homemaking and occupational choice receive more attention on the secondary school level than on the preschool level. Furthermore, the subject area in which you teach will affect the behavorial factors to which major emphases will be given. If you plan to teach social studies, or music, or chemistry, or some other area, which behavioral characteristics will you seek most to develop? How will you attempt to develop them? Keep such questions as these in mind as you take subsequent academic and professional courses.

In 1961, a committee under the auspices of the Educational Policies Commission issued a statement regarding the central purpose of American education [25:1–21]. The committee recognized that the American school must be concerned with all of the objectives indicated in the 1938 statement of the Educational Policies Commission if it is to fulfill its function. On the other hand, these objectives place upon the school an immense, if not impossible, task. Neither the schools nor the pupils have sufficient time or energy to engage in activities that will enable pupils to achieve fully all of these goals by the time these pupils graduate from high school. Furthermore, education does not cease when pupils graduate. As a result, the committee expressed the feeling that a guiding principle was needed so that the school would be able to identify its necessary and appropriate contributions to individual development and the needs of society.

The members of the committee maintained that the development of the individual's ability to think should undergird the statement of objectives published by the Educational Policies Commission in 1938. For example, each of the school's traditional objectives, such as teaching the so-called "fundamental processes," can be better achieved as pupils develop the ability to think and as they learn to apply reflective thinking to all the problems that face them. Developing the rational powers of the human mind, therefore, constitutes the central purpose of the school.

The rational powers of the human mind have always been basic in establishing and preserving freedom. In furthering personal and social effectiveness they are becoming more important than ever. They are central to individual dignity, human progress, and national survival.

The individual with developed rational powers can share deeply in the freedoms his society offers and can contribute most to the preservation of those freedoms. At the same time, he will have the best chance of understanding and contributing to the great events of his time. And the society which best develops the rational potentials of its people, along with their intuitive and aesthetic capabilities, will have the best chance of flourishing in the future. To help every person develop those powers is therefore a profoundly important objective and one which increases in importance with the passage of time. By pursuing this objective, the school can enhance spiritual and aesthetic values and other cardinal purposes which it has traditionally served and must continue to serve.

The purpose which runs through and strengthens all other educational purposes—the common thread of education—is the development of the ability to think. This is the central purpose to which the school must be oriented if it is to accomplish either its traditional tasks or those newly accentuated by recent changes in the world. To say that it is central is not to say that it is the sole purpose or in all circumstances the most important purpose, but that it must be a pervasive concern in the work of the school. Many agencies contribute to achieving educational objectives, but this particular objective will not be generally attained unless the school focuses on it. In this context, therefore, the development of every student's rational powers must be recognized as centrally important [25:11–12].

The members of the committee expressed the feeling that "man has before him the possibility of a new level of greatness, a new realization of human dignity and effectiveness. The instrument which will realize this possibility is that kind of education which frees the mind and enables it to contribute to a full and worthy life. To achieve this goal is the high hope of the nation and the central challenge to its schools" [25:21].

Need for Educational Objectives according to School Levels. As the child seeks to develop in his environment and under the conditions provided for him, there are certain developmental tasks that he must perform in order to move to more difficult and complex tasks. Havighurst, who is chairman of the Committee on Human Development at the University of Chicago, has formulated a list of tasks with which an individual is confronted during certain periods of his life. Since his list has had considerable impact upon the formulation of educational objectives at various school levels, it is outlined below [68: Chaps. 2, 4, 9, 10, 16, 17, and 18].

Developmental Tasks of Early Childhood

Learning to walk
Learning to take solid foods
Learning to talk
Learning to control the elimination of body wastes
Learning sex differences and sexual modesty
Learning physiological stability
Forming simple concepts of social and physical reality
Learning to relate oneself emotionally to parents, siblings, and other people
Learning to distinguish right from wrong and developing a conscience

Developmental Tasks of Middle Childhood

Learning physical skills necessary for ordinary games
Building wholesome attitudes toward oneself as a growing organism
Learning to get along with agemates
Learning an appropriate masculine or feminine social role
Developing fundamental skills in reading, writing, and calculating
Developing concepts necessary for everyday living

Developing conscience, morality, and a scale of values
Achieving personal independence
Developing attitudes toward social groups and institutions

Developmental Tasks of Adolescence

Achieving new and more mature relations with agemates of both sexes
Achieving a masculine or feminine social role
Accepting one's physique and using the body effectively
Achieving emotional independence of parents and other adults
Achieving assurance of economic independence
Selecting and preparing for an occupation
Preparing for marriage and family life
Developing intellectual skills and concepts necessary for civic competence
Desiring and achieving socially responsible behavior
Acquiring a set of values and an ethical system as a guide to behavior

Developmental Tasks of Early Adulthood

Selecting a mate
Learning to live with a marriage partner
Starting a family
Rearing children
Managing a home
Getting started in an occupation
Taking on civic responsibility
Finding a congenial social group

Developmental Tasks of Middle Age

Achieving adult civic and social responsibility
Establishing and maintaining an economic standard of living
Assisting teen-age children to become responsible and happy adults
Developing adult leisure-time activities
Relating oneself to one's spouse as a person
Accepting and adjusting to the physiological changes of middle age
Adjusting to aging parents

Developmental Tasks of Later Maturity

Adjusting to decreasing physical strength and health
Adjusting to retirement and reduced income
Adjusting to death of spouse
Establishing an explicit affiliation with one's age group
Meeting social and civic obligations
Establishing satisfactory physical living arrangements

Since individuals at different maturity levels are confronted with somewhat different tasks, each segment of our school system has its particular
contribution to make in the sequential development of a person. While
the objectives of education that have been presented provide the broad
framework within which this contribution is made, teachers and administrators need objectives appropriate for the particular school level in
which they work. It may prove valuable to examine selected statements
of objectives for these levels.

Pre-elementary Education. As has been noted, increasing attention is being given to the educational growth of very young children. It is recognized that the early years of a child's life have a very significant bearing upon his later development. There is evidence to indicate that some juvenile delinquency, many nervous breakdowns, and certain adult psychoses may be traced to maladjustments which could have been prevented or corrected in early childhood.

Parents frequently feel that the home training of their young children needs to be supplemented by nursery and kindergarten experiences. Many factors contribute to this feeling. Some parents believe that they are unable to provide the best kind of guidance to their children at this age. Also, an increasing number of mothers find it necessary to work outside the home, and their children need to be placed in a healthy, happy, and constructive learning environment for at least part of the day.

Nursery Schools. The most common forms of organized educational activities for very young children consist of the day nursery and the nursery school. The day nursery, frequently called a "child-care center," is concerned mainly with the physical well-being of the child. With approximately one third of the married women employed, the day nursery constitutes an important agency. The nursery school, on the other hand, has the characteristics of both a nursery and a school. In a sense, it is a downward extension of the kindergarten, and is designed to provide valuable educational and social experiences for children.

Moustakas and Berson of the famous Merrill-Palmer School indicate the objectives of a good nursery school in the following statement [95:17–18]:

> We see the nursery school as an educational center that furthers the full development of the young child and the successful functioning of a group of young children. Its goal is to maintain a balance between spontaneous behavior and conformity to society's standards. It is concerned with the feelings and attitudes of young children and their developmental skills. It seeks to help children realize their potential and at the same time aids them to accept the limits of life in a democratic society.
>
> The nursery school recognizes how important it is for young children to learn routine health habits. Activities are planned to strengthen and facilitate the use of their large and small muscles, build coordination, and develop sound, strong bodies.
>
> The nursery school guides the child in experiencing the stimulation and enjoyment that come from the association with persons both younger and older than himself, as well as with those of the same age. It offers many opportunities for sharing and cooperating and helps children learn when and how to share.
>
> The encouragement of rational thinking, fair play, self-reliance, and individual freedom and responsibility are all part of the nursery school's value. . . .
>
> The nursery school must be concerned with the enhancement of the child's individuality, and the development of attitudes, interests, understandings, and beliefs which will enable the child to be a happy, secure, contributing member of society. To reach these goals the nursery school must have an emotionally warm, friendly, relaxed atmosphere.

Kindergarten. The kindergarten experiences of children are somewhat similar to those of the nursery school except that they are adapted to the maturity level of five-year-olds. The kindergarten provides a transition between home and school or between nursery school and formal school. Provision is made for rich experiences that will help prepare children for further schooling, although such formal training as instruction in actual reading is withheld.

In Florida, where kindergartens are financed as a part of the public school program, provision is made for each boy and girl who attends kindergarten to have experiences and to develop in the following [65:9]:

1. Live, work, and play with others in a program of learning activities that provide daily practice in sharing possessions, assuming responsibility for his own acts, acting as a leader and follower, and adjusting individual wishes or plans to the good of the group.

2. Develop a sense of security and well-being in a school situation.

3. Have experiences with books, stories, music, dramatic play, science and art materials. These activities not only will enrich the life of the child, but will provide experiences which increase vocabulary and will arouse an interest in reading.

4. Use materials freely and constructively which may result in increasing initiative, creative power, independence and motor coordination.

5. Develop motor skills and coordination through play with appropriate apparatus. This improved motor control is reflected by better handling of classroom equipment—blocks, pencils, scissors, crayons, as well as other equipment.

6. Express himself freely within a group situation and be stimulated to independent thinking in organizing and communicating his ideas.

7. Establish desirable health habits such as proper eating practices, relaxation during rest period, toilet routine and hand washing.

Elementary School. An outstanding formulation of objectives for the elementary school was prepared by the Mid-century Committee on Outcomes in Elementary Education [80:35–40]. The committee, consisting of outstanding educators throughout the United States, was sponsored by the Russell Sage Foundation, Educational Testing Service, U.S. Office of Education, and NEA Department of Elementary School Principals. It assumed that the elementary school should attempt to bring about behavior changes that are desirable in a democratic society. It also attempted to identify the objectives in such a manner that they might be susceptible to measurement, evaluation, and critical philosophical analysis.

The committee identified nine broad areas of elementary school learning: (1) physical development, health, and body care; (2) individual social and emotional development; (3) ethical behavior, standards, values; (4) social relations; (5) the social world; (6) the physical world; (7) esthetic development; (8) communication; (9) quantitative relationships. As a child learns in these areas, changes should take place in his knowledge and understanding, his skill and competence, his attitudes and interests, and his action patterns (broad generalized ways of behaving, such as response to problems through the use of intelligence, good work habits, and scientific methods of thinking).

As may be noted in the graphic presentation of elementary school objectives (Figure 55), the committee felt that a fifth column, titled "Determining conditions," should be added to account for the many forces, in addition to the school, that mold or limit the young learner. These conditions, more than anything else, represent the biological and sociological context in which children and schools carry on together.

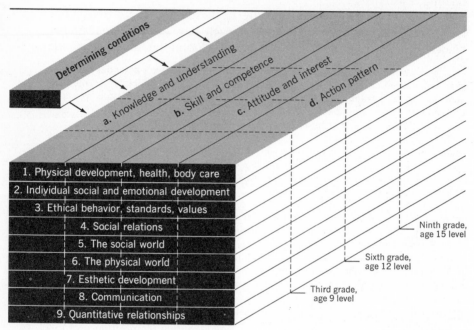

Figure 55.   Elementary school objectives. The behavior continuum—broad curriculum areas intersecting major behavior categories.
(*Source:* Russell Sage Foundation.)

The committee chose to visualize the objectives by means of a grid arrangement to convey the idea that growth, development, maturation, and learning are continuous in all of the subdivisions. Similarly, they chose to consider outcomes in terms of the range of abilities within a group of children or of the traits in one child at each of three levels.

Secondary Education.   Since the founding of the Boston Latin School in 1635, designed to prepare the intellectually elite boys for college, the objectives of secondary education have undergone many changes.

In response to considerable criticism of secondary schools, the National Education Association appointed the Commission on Reorganization of Secondary Education in 1912 for the purpose of studying desirable objectives for secondary schools. The report of this commission in 1918 was instrumental in expanding greatly the objectives of secondary education. The following, which have become known as the "seven cardinal principles," were recommended: (1) health, (2) command of fundamental processes, (3) worthy home membership, (4) vocation, (5) civic education, (6) worthy use of leisure time, and (7) ethical character.

For many years these objectives exerted considerable influence upon educators in the development of the secondary school curriculum. A number of educators, however, became increasingly concerned over the extent to which the secondary school curriculum was dominated by college entrance requirements. They felt that a good high school should serve the needs of both college-bound pupils and those who would not go to college. In response to this feeling, the Progressive Education Association conducted an experimental study during the period of 1933–1941, in which 30 school systems were freed from the traditional college entrance requirements. These schools were asked to provide the best total educational programs possible for all of their pupils, so that the progress of those who would attend college could be studied. Upon entrance into college, the graduates of the experimental schools did substantially better academically and in student leadership positions than did the graduates from the other schools [2]. As a result of this study, objectives of secondary education were designed more in terms of meeting the life needs of all youth attending the secondary school.

In 1944, the Educational Policies Commission of the National Education Association issued a statement concerning the most imperative educational needs of youth in America which the school should seek to satisfy. These 10 needs are indicated below [111:9]:

The Ten Imperative Needs of Youth

All youth have certain educational needs in common.
All parents can agree that the school should meet these needs, which become the
modern goals of education.

1. All youth need to develop salable skills and those understandings and attitudes that make the worker an intelligent and productive participant in economic life. To this end, most youth need supervised work experience as well as education in the skills and knowledge of their occupations.

2. All youth need to develop and maintain good health, physical fitness, and mental health.

3. All youth need to understand the rights and duties of the citizen of a democratic society, to be diligent and competent in the performance of their obligations as members of the community and citizens of the state and nation, and to have an understanding of the nations and peoples of the world.

4. All youth need to understand the significance of the family for the individual and society and the conditions conducive to successful family life.

5. All youth need to know how to purchase and use goods and services intelligently, understanding both the values received by the consumer and the economic consequences of their acts.

6. All youth need to understand the methods of science, the influence of science on human life, and the main scientific facts concerning the nature of the world and of man.

7. All youth need opportunities to develop their capacities to appreciate beauty —in literature, art, music, and nature.

8. All youth need to be able to use their leisure time well and to budget it wisely, balancing activities that yield satisfactions to the individual with those that are socially useful.

9. All youth need to develop respect for other persons, to grow in their insight into ethical values and principles, to be able to live and work cooperatively with others, and to grow in the moral and spiritual values of life.

10. All youth need to grow in their ability to think rationally, to express their thoughts clearly, and to read and listen with understanding [111:9].

In the light of these needs, members of the Educational Policies Commission feel that every youth in these United States—regardless of sex, economic status, geographic location, or race—should obtain a broad and balanced education that will be of value to him in the following respects [44:216]:

1. Equip him to enter an occupation suitable to his abilities and offering reasonable opportunity for personal growth and social usefulness.
2. Prepare him to assume the full responsibilities of American citizenship.
3. Give him a fair chance to exercise his right to the pursuit of happiness through the attainment and preservation of mental and physical health.
4. Stimulate intellectual curiosity, engender satisfaction in intellectual achievement, and cultivate the ability to think rationally.
5. Help him to develop an appreciation of the ethical values which should undergird all life in a democratic society.

It should be pointed out that these major objectives of secondary education apply to both the junior and the senior high school. Because of differences in the maturity levels of the pupils, the more specific objectives for the junior high school differ in some respects from those for the senior high school. Actually, the goals of junior high schools tend to be somewhat similar to those of both elementary and senior high schools. This is to be expected since, from an organizational standpoint, the junior high school provides for the transition of pupils from the elementary to the senior high school.

Junior College.   As indicated previously, there is considerable debate as to whether the junior college belongs to secondary or to higher education. Traditionally, it has been defined as a higher-education institution which gives two years of work equivalent to the first two years in a college or university. The feeling has developed, especially in California, where the greatest number of junior colleges has been established, that it should be considered as an extension of the secondary school. Three types of junior colleges can be rather definitely identified: (1) the community junior college, which attempts to serve any local community needs which are not being served by other institutions of the community; (2) the special junior college, which attempts to excel in a few areas of instruction and admittedly neglects certain other community needs; (3) the junior college that attempts to offer the first two years of a senior college curriculum.

The community junior college which establishes its function in terms of the needs of the geographic area in which it is located has the following major objectives:

1. To provide for the extension of education designed to meet the added requirements of life and work.
2. To provide preparation for further college study to students who will be transferring to a senior college.
3. To provide opportunities for individuals to continue, on a part-time basis, their education as the need and interest arises.
4. To relieve the pressure of enrollments increasingly experienced by regular colleges and universities.
5. To provide a center for adult education activities.

In his book, *The Open Door College: A Case Study,* Clark [28:168–176] indicates a number of problems concerning the character and role of junior colleges. Undoubtedly, increasing clarification will be gained in the future with regard to such factors as (1) the unique function of the junior college, (2) the quality of instruction that may be provided, (3) financial support, (4) local or state control, and (5) accreditation. Regardless of these problems, the junior college seems destined to play an increasingly significant role in the extension of educational opportunities for youth as well as for adults.

Higher Education.   Institutions of higher education have four interlocking types of programs to offer: liberal or general education, professional or vocational education, graduate study and research, and public services. Colleges and universities differ greatly throughout the United States in the extent to which they emphasize each of these four offerings.

According to the American Council on Education, general education should enable the student [87:14–15]:

1. To improve and maintain his own health and take his share of responsibility for protecting the health of others.
2. To communicate through his own language in writing and speaking at the level of expression adequate to the needs of educated people.
3. To attain a sound emotional and social adjustment through the enjoyment of a wide range of social relationships and the experience of working co-operatively with others.
4. To think through the problems and to gain the basic orientation that will better enable him to make a satisfactory family and marital adjustment.
5. To do his part as an active and intelligent citizen in dealing with the interrelated social, economic, and political problems of American life and in solving the problems of postwar international reconstruction.
6. To act in the light of an understanding of the natural phenomena in his environment in its implications for human society and human welfare, to use scientific methods in the solution of his problems, and to employ useful non-verbal methods of thought and communication.
7. To find self-expression in literature and to share through literature man's experience and his motivating ideas and ideals.
8. To find a means of self-expression in music and in the various visual arts and crafts, and to understand and appreciate art and music as reflections both of individual experience and of social patterns and movements.

9. To practice clear and integrated thinking about the meaning and value of life.

10. To choose a vocation that will make optimum use of his talents and enable him to make an appropriate contribution to the needs of society.

The modern world requires that highly skilled technicians be prepared to perform the necessary services to society in such areas as education, medicine, law, business, engineering, communication, and transportation. For this reason a large percentage of the students attending college are preparing for a profession. In addition to the vocational competencies required for their respective vocations, these students also need to acquire a general educational background that will assist them in being effective citizens.

In addition to instructional obligations, higher-education institutions have the responsibility to society of contributing new knowledge through research. For this reason the larger institutions, especially those having good financial resources, often have graduate schools and research facilities to provide for training above the baccalaureate level in almost all fields of learning. Although various independent research agencies have been developed in such fields as science, business, and agriculture, institutions of higher education continue to contribute a very substantial amount of the findings.

Colleges and universities have become centers of information and trained ability to which society can bring its problems. Increasing demands for assistance in almost every area of human endeavor are being made upon college and university staff members. Through such activities institutions of higher education assume a leadership role.

Adult Education.   Frequent mention has been made of the growing importance of adult education. Since adulthood involves a large part of life, "adult education includes the larger portion of life-long learning. It involves experiences which cause persons to evaluate and adjust their ideas and opinions, and to broaden their range of learning into new fields" [151:5].

Adult education is broad and diverse in its nature. Too frequently it seems to consist merely of courses of instruction taught in a school building, but more than 90 per cent of all the education of adults carried on in America is done outside the school building. Other types of adult education take place through such media as newspapers, group discussions, magazines, radio, television, books, forums, speeches, advertisements, movies, and pictures and cartoons.

Three important objectives of adult education are:

1. To assist all persons to know more about themselves.

2. To help people to understand their relationships with their fellow men.

3. To help persons learn more about their jobs as workers and citizens of a free society.

It is important to remember that adults must be convinced of the need to learn. They generally want the type of learning that is both useful and down to earth. Most adults find little meaning in abstract goals, regardless of how essential they are to the advancement of civilization, unless they can see the specific relationships between these goals and ideas that are already familiar to them. However, as mature people have the opportunity to participate in the development of concrete ideas, even the more abstract goals become meaningful and acceptable to them. As a result, adults are stimulated to expand their intellectual horizons and their competencies as useful citizens in a democratic society.

Members of the Adult Education Association of the United States maintain that our concept of adult education must change from an optional to an imperative activity in our society. They feel that, if adult education is to fulfill its new mission as "an imperative of our times," the following conditions must be met [1:14–15]:

1. There must be a *national perception,* especially on the part of those who control educational policy, of the essential role of continuing education in preventing human obsolescence and in preserving and further developing the American society.

2. The education of children and youth must be reoriented to a *conception of learning as a lifelong process.* Teachers in schools and colleges must learn to teach youth so that they leave formal schooling (*a*) with an insatiable curiosity, (*b*) with a mastery of the tools of learning, and (*c*) with a commitment to continue learning through the rest of their life span.

3. *The agencies of adult education must clarify their respective tasks* of establishing between themselves orderly working arrangements and interrelated planning and to ensure that the resources of adult education are used effectively in meeting the adult educational needs of individuals, institutions, and communities.

4. A *coherent curriculum* of adult education must be developed that provides for the sequential development of the knowledge, understanding, skills, attitudes, and values required to maintain one's effectiveness in a changing social order.

5. The *corps of leaders and teachers* of adults must be enlarged and provided with the knowledge and skills required for them to help adults learn efficiently.

6. A special responsibility is placed on the universities of the country to expand the resources available for *research and advanced professional training* in adult education.

7. Community agencies of adult education, especially schools and colleges, must upgrade the *standards of professional competence* required of those guiding adult learning, and employ personnel with these competencies.

8. There must be a *national commitment* to provide the resources and moral support necessary for the development of lifelong learning as an integral element of the American way of life.

SUMMARY

In the first part of this chapter, attention was given to several basic assumptions which operate in some schools today. The validity of these assumptions in fulfilling the school's function for today's youth was questioned. Ten statements of educational principles and their implications for educational practice were submitted on the assumption that the school provides the primary means of social progress. Governed by these principles, teaching becomes a most challenging and adventuresome profession.

Teachers are responsible for providing a most vital function—directing the experiences of the young in such a manner that the welfare of the group may be raised. The future of democracy depends upon the resources, insight, and courage with which teachers accept this basic social responsibility.

In the second part of the chapter, attention was focused upon the objectives of education as they pertain to education in general and to the various levels ranging from pre-elementary to adult education. Educational objectives grow out of the life values which people prize. They are essential in order to provide direction to the planning and appraisal of educational activities.

The general objectives prepared by the Educational Policies Commission in 1938, as well as the statement of central purpose of American education issued in 1961, provide a broad frame of reference within which each level of our educational system makes its particular contribution in terms of the maturity of the learner. A clear understanding of the general objectives of education as well as of the objectives for the particular level upon which you plan to teach will give direction to your professional preparation and to your work as a teacher.

QUESTIONS FOR YOUR CONSIDERATION

1. What are the so-called "broader" functions of the school?

2. What values in our society should the school seek to preserve, promote, and refine?

3. In what ways do the objectives of education in our American democracy specifically differ from those in a totalitarian country?

4. If you assume that pupils go to school in order to acquire desirable behavior patterns, how will you attempt to evaluate the progress made by your pupils? What instruments and techniques will you use?

5. What is meant by the statement that a more rigorous and a more disciplined kind of education is necessary in order to meet the conditions of contemporary society? What are the implications of this statement for you as a teacher?

6. To what extent do the four objectives developed by the Educational Policies Commission adequately describe the kind of person schools should seek to develop for our society?

7. How do the objectives of nursery and kindergarten differ from elementary education?

8. How have the objectives of the secondary school changed during the past 50 years?

9. How does the statement on "The Ten Imperative Needs of Youth" differ from the statement of objectives published by the Edu-

cational Policies Commission in 1938? What does the 1961 statement on "the central purpose of education" add to the previous statements of objectives?

10. Do the objectives of education in a rural community differ from those in a large metropolitan community?

11. What is meant by a community-centered school or college?

12. In what ways may you as a teacher serve as a key figure in leading the community toward a fulfillment of its democratic values?

13. What can the public school do in meeting adult-education needs?

ACTIVITIES FOR YOU TO PURSUE

1. Appraise the public school experiences you had in light of the function of the school as presented in this chapter. In other words, how adequately were the schools you attended fulfilling their purpose as herein defined?

2. Make a list of the competencies for teaching which the content of this chapter suggests.

3. Review the 10 assumptions which seem to characterize the way some of our schools operate. Discuss with your colleagues the extent to which these assumptions seem to be sound.

4. Match the "Developmental Tasks of Early Childhood" with the objectives of education for each school level. Do they seem to be compatible?

5. List ways in which you will attempt to help your pupils achieve the objective of human relationship, as formulated by the Educational Policies Commission. Repeat the process in connection with the other three objectives.

6. Perhaps you have heard people express the feeling that certain school subjects were good for disciplining the mind. Discuss this point of view with your colleagues and explore its educational implications. As you engage in this activity, attempt to describe the behavior characteristics of a well-disciplined democratic citizen.

7. School superintendents frequently question candidates for teaching positions regarding their views toward education. Write on two or three sheets of paper what you consider the school's function to be. Compare what you write with the opinions of your colleagues.

8. Many school systems distribute bulletins to teachers and parents containing statements of the school's function. Collect one or more of these bulletins and critically appraise the statements made.

9. Select a school system that seems to be fulfilling the function of the school as described in this chapter. Plan with the superintendent, or some other school official, to make several classroom observations. Discuss these observations with your colleagues, your college instructor, and, if possible, the classroom teachers whom you observe.

10. Have some of your public school teacher friends show you examples of the day-to-day as well as the more ultimate objectives which they use in planning suitable classroom activities. What relationship do these objectives have with the general objectives of education discussed in this chapter?

15
CONTROVERSIAL ISSUES AND PROBLEMS

Do you know of any major improvement that has taken place in society without attendant problems? Difficulties are certain to be present whenever changes in the thinking and behavior of people are involved. This is true in the field of education as well as in any other major field of endeavor.

As you move into education you are faced with the challenge of aiding in the solution of major problems that emerge because schools strive increasingly to fulfill their function in a democratic society. You have a professional obligation to become familiar with these problems and to plan ways in which you may aid in their creative and effective solution.

A number of educational problems have already been discussed in this book. The purpose of the present chapter is to bring into focus other controversial problems, some of which have been previously indicated but not probed extensively. All these problems are interrelated and are separated only for the purpose of discussion. The order of discussion in no way indicates their relative importance.

In the brief discussion that follows, an attempt is made to indicate some of your responsibilities in regard to certain problems rather than to formulate any solutions to them. As you continue your preparation for teaching, and throughout your professional career, plan to give these problems the thoughtful consideration that each deserves. The ways in which you work toward their effective solution will need to be modified as conditions change and new information emerges.

What Should Be the Relationship between Religion and the Public Schools? One of the outstanding community problems which face us today is that of relating the functions of the public schools to the programs of organized religions. The efforts to obtain Federal aid for education have been entangled, as you know, with several other problems in American life. One has been the nature and extent of Federal control over educational endeavors. This has still to be worked out. An aspect of control that is much feared is the effect of Federal legislation on religious instruction in the schools and the purposes of religious institutions in education. Here is a matter of great concern to all those who plan to teach as well as to all enlightened citizens. Every teacher needs to be well informed about the history of the relationships between church and state in America and to understand the significance of our American tradition of separation.

A teacher should be well versed on the purposes of the Founding Fathers in their creation of the First Amendment ("Congress shall make no law respecting an establishment of religion, or prohibiting the free exercise thereof."), the history of the Supreme Court's interpretation of the Fourteenth Amendment, the efforts of various religious organizations   419 to obtain a measure of support for their educational endeavors from the public funds, the history and desirability of programs of released time in the school day, and other aspects of our country's attempts to maintain and build a public education that is not connected with the problems of conflicting religious beliefs.

In 1948 the United States Supreme Court, in connection with the Mc-Collum case, ruled against sectarian religion being taught in the Champaign, Illinois, public schools, hence in any public schools. In connection with the Zorach case in New York City in 1956, the Court ruled that public schools may accommodate their schedules to a program of sectarian religious instruction, provided such instruction is not coerced, conducted on public school property, or supported by tax money.

A teacher should be very clear in his understanding of the term "teaching religion." To some people it means the teaching of doctrines, dogmas, or creeds of a religious denomination or sect in an attempt to influence a pupil to accept these teachings as truths. To other people the term refers to a study of religion as an empirical fact. They maintain that, without involving a discussion *about* religion, it is impossible for a pupil to gain a thorough understanding of the history of the Middle Ages, or the conflict between Eastern and Western cultures, or any other topics in which the culture of people are involved.

In the preceding chapter you noted that the school is concerned with promoting the moral growth and character of pupils. Some have held that morality may not be promoted without its counterpart in religious beliefs. Others have held that spiritual values may be developed in the public school and actually are in all good education, without the support of particular religious creeds. For example, the Educational Policies Commission feels that moral and spiritual values can be promoted in the public schools by [94:80]:

1. Defining as goals the accepted moral and spiritual values in our society.
2. Encouraging and helping the individual teacher.
3. Giving attention to moral and spiritual values in teacher education.
4. Teaching these moral and spiritual values at every opportunity.
5. Utilizing all of the school's resources.
6. Devoting sufficient time and staff to wholesome personal relationships.
7. Assuming an attitude of friendly sympathy toward the religious beliefs and practices of students.
8. Promoting religious tolerance activity.
9. Teaching about religion as an important fact in our culture.

A number of arguments are advanced by those who feel that our public schools should be concerned with religious education. A few of their arguments are as follows:

1. Many boys and girls do not go to church and therefore do not receive any significant amount of religious instruction. The school should provide for the needs of these pupils.
2. It is necessary to teach religion if boys and girls are to gain desirable moral values.

3. The teaching of religion in the public schools would promote greater under-standing and tolerance of the various religions.

4. The teaching of religion is as important in the lives of boys and girls as other subjects that are taught in the schools. Therefore, the school should provide time for such instruction.

5. Teachers are better trained to teach religion than are parents.

6. If the teaching of religion is forbidden in public schools, pupils are encour-aged to feel that religion is not important in their lives. Therefore, our schools are atheistic.

Those opposed to the teaching of religion in public schools argue that:

1. The teaching of religion is a responsibility of the home and of the church.

2. It is impossible to teach religion objectively.

3. Teachers are not prepared adequately to teach religion.

4. The Supreme Court has ruled that the teaching of religion in public schools is unconstitutional.

5. With so many different religions represented, it would be impossible for pub-lic schools to meet the religious needs of all pupils.

6. The curriculum of the school already is crowded.

In summarizing legislation regarding the separation of church and state in public schools, Burt came to the following conclusions [adapted 20: 14–15]:

1. The use of school facilities for religious instruction is illegal throughout the United States.

2. "Released-time" programs for religious instruction on the school grounds is not presently in violation of the United States Constitution. Courts in some states, however, have disapproved promotion of attendance at such religious classes by public school authorities.

3. The question of the legality of Bible reading in the public schools is not settled in most states.

4. The courts are divided on the legality of prayer in the public schools. The United States Supreme Court is studying this question.

5. The United States Supreme Court has upheld public expenditures for trans-portation of and the purchase of textbooks for parochial school pupils upon the grounds that such expenditures are for the benefit of the child, as contrasted with benefit to religion.

6. The use of school facilities by churches on a short-term basis generally is upheld by the courts.

Since Burt drew the conclusions indicated above, the United States Supreme Court, on June 25, 1962, ruled that it is unconstitutional for prescribed prayers to be required of pupils. The particular case upon which the ruling was made involved a 22-word nonsectarian prayer, known as "The Regents-Prayer," which had been officially prescribed for use in New York state schools. In speaking for the majority of the court, Justice Hugo L. Black stated that "Government in this country, be it state or federal, is without power to prescribe by law any particular form of prayer which is to be used as an official prayer in carrying on any pro-gram of governmentally-sponsored religious activity."

Regardless of the level and area in which you teach, it will be impossi-ble for you to escape questions about religion being asked by the pupils. At this point, you will want to keep in mind the distinction between teaching religion and teaching *about* religion. You also will want to be well informed in regard to the issue involved but to remain as objective as possible in dealing with it.

How Should the Schools Be Defended against Unwarranted Attacks?

Probably more attacks are being made upon the work of the public schools today than have ever been made in the history of mankind. As a prospective educator and as a citizen you will want to have a clear understanding of these attacks and be able to discuss with school patrons their nature, probable causes, and justification.

What are the reasons for these attacks? Are they due in part to the increased amount of education which each succeeding generation has gained. As people become more educated, they tend to place a higher value upon schooling and to become increasingly critical of educational practices. Have the two major opposing ideologies in the world today contributed to an outburst of concern for the education of the young? Are these attacks due to an increasing awareness upon the part of the general public of the importance of education as a means of preserving and promoting democratic living? Are these attacks sincere efforts designed to improve the education of the young, or are they motivated by desires to weaken our schools, curtail educational costs, or spread seeds of suspicion? To what extent do these attacks represent differences in opinion or confusion in regard to the school's function in a democratic society? To what extent are the attackers misinformed or unaware of valid research findings in terms of which modifications have been made in educational practices? These are only a few of the questions which you should keep in mind as you appraise the criticism that has been made, is being made, and will be made in the future.

The public has a right, in fact an obligation, to prescribe policies by which the public schools shall abide and to appraise the extent to which these policies have been fulfilled. Furthermore, the public for many years has exercised the right to criticize educational endeavors. Aristotle in 384 B.C. wrote the following: "There are doubts concerning the business of education, since all people do not agree in those things they would have a child taught." Some of the people at that time, and even earlier, complained that the children preferred sitting around chatting to participating in athletic activities, had bad manners, were disrespectful of their elders, and ruled the household. Confucius approximately twenty-five hundred years ago, noted: "The teachers of today just go on repeating things in a rigmarole fashion, annoy the students with constant questions, and repeat the same things over and over again. They do not try to find out what the students' natural inclinations are so that the students are forced to pretend to like their studies, nor do they try to bring out the best in their talents" [106:1].

John Erskine, in *My Life as a Teacher*, said, regarding his teaching at Amherst in 1903, "A large proportion of my first Amherst freshmen were unable to spell."

Horace Mann, in his report of 1838, stated:

I have devoted special pains to learn, with some degree of numerical accuracy, how far the reading, in our schools, is an exercise of the mind in thinking and feeling, and how far it is a barren action of the organs of speech upon the atmosphere. . . . The result is, that more than eleven-twelfths of all the children in the reading classes, in our schools, do not understand the meaning of the words they read; that they do not master the sense of the reading lessons, and that the ideas and feelings intended by the author to be conveyed to, and excited in, the reader's mind, still rest in the author's intention, never having yet reached the place of their destination.

In 1845 the Grammar School Committee of Boston, after having administered various tests to the pupils, reported that:

They (tests administered) show beyond all doubt that a large proportion of the scholars in our first classes, boys and girls of 14 and 15 years of age, when called on to write simple sentences, to express their thoughts on common subjects, without the aid of a dictionary or a master, cannot write, without such errors in grammar, in spelling, and in punctuation, as we should blush to see in a letter from a son or daughter of their age.

Do these statements have a familiar ring to you—even though some of them were made over two thousand years ago?

You undoubtedly have heard older people appraise present conditions and practices in terms of "the good old days." There seems to be a human tendency to glamorize and "haloize" days past, which in reality were not half so good as they are today. Furthermore, there is a tendency to resist change and to impose an element of rightness to our own past experience. These tendencies may operate as older people appraise the products of today's schools.

How do boys and girls in present-day schools compare with the products of an earlier system? The *Kiplinger Magazine* for June, 1954, in an article titled "The Truth about Our Schools," reports a number of experiments in which pupils were given subject-matter tests that had been administered to pupils of the same age as much as a century earlier. From the results, the following conclusion was drawn: "The truth is that your youngster, unless he's the victim of some unfortunate exception, probably is getting a better education today than he ever could have got in the public school before. That means in both grade school and high school. Modern schools and modern methods are, by and large, turning out a superior product despite enormously increased enrollments." Furthermore, in comparing college freshmen with those of yesteryear, the investigation conducted by the *Kiplinger Magazine* reported that "today's students, taken as a whole, have been found to have an amazingly vaster fund of information on national and world problems, human relations, self-government, and similar topics, and sharper and better-reasoned opinions."

Shane, in an article titled "We Can Be Proud of the Facts" [140:44–47], made an extensive study of research findings in regard to the following questions: Are elementary schools "too easy" on children? What has happened to history and geography? Are we "brain wasting" gifted children? Are Europe's elementary schools better than ours? Have our high school programs deteriorated? Are languages being ignored? How competent are our teachers? Does public education cost too much? What do report cards report? Does education lack purpose? As a part of your preparation for teaching, read Shane's stimulating and very informative article as well as other good magazine articles and books that contain sound evidence which may be used to counteract the rash of off-the-cuff statements made by various individuals and the irresponsible reporting being done on school conditions and accomplishments.

It is to be recognized, however, that very valid criticisms have and can be made of educational practices in specific situations. Conditions differ from school to school and from classroom to classroom. Perhaps you can recall various teachers in your school experiences who failed to use good educational practices. You may know of schools that are falling far short of fulfilling their functions in our society. Such teachers and school situations may justly deserve all of the criticisms made of them. Education of the young is serious business, and the public has a moral responsibility for safeguarding the welfare of youth.

On the other hand, some of the attacks may result from a lack of understanding between the general public and the school. Perhaps teachers far too often have expected parents and other community members to place blind faith and implicit trust in them. Some teachers may even resent any questioning upon the part of parents. If effective changes and improvements are to be made in our educational practices, parents and other community members must be involved in the process.

School people in the past have not paid sufficient attention to the importance of thinking *with* parents and other community members on such matters as the changing function of the school, newer practices and procedures, ways of improving the effectiveness of the school, and the responsibilities of parents in the education of children. Actually the classroom teacher holds a key position in the development of mutual understanding and cooperative efforts of home and school. How creative and effective will you be in this regard?

How Can Freedom to Teach and to Learn Be Provided?   Freedom to think, speak, and write as reason and conscience dictate is basic to the survival of a democratic society. Our forefathers recognized this fact as they formulated the First Amendment to the Constitution of the United States. It would seem, therefore, that the development of skill in thinking and expression constitutes one of the very important tasks to which the school should give attention. The development of this skill takes place most effectively in an environment where individuals feel free and are encouraged to think and express themselves; one which offers opportunities for young people to come to grips with problems of real concern to them. Many such problems will be of a controversial nature.

Academic freedom refers to the freedom of teachers to seek and to present the truth on problems and issues without fear of interference from school boards, governmental authorities, or pressure groups. From a learner's standpoint it refers to the opportunity to study all points of view in regard to a problem or an issue and to arrive at reasoned conclusions. The teacher does not have a right to tell pupils what to think, nor does he have the right to advocate one theory only. The teacher's concern is the development of skill in thinking, expression, and problem solving on the part of his pupils. Unless both teachers and pupils feel free to examine, discuss, think, and arrive at reasoned conclusions on issues affecting their daily lives the school is handicapped greatly in fulfilling its function in a democratic society.

Do teachers and pupils feel free to teach and to learn? They frequently do not. Teachers in some communities feel that they would run considerable risk of losing their jobs if they permitted students to examine all sides of issues concerning trade unions. In some sections of the country it would be extremely hazardous to encourage free inquiry and discussion of the racial problem. The discussion of sex education is forbidden in some school systems. You already have noted in this chapter certain difficulties regarding moral and spiritual instruction. Certain textbooks in some communities have been censored. A number of teachers

Teachers must feel free to help pupils contrast realistically democratic and communistic principles. (*Photograph from the film* Freedom to Learn *by the National Education Association.*)

have been accused of being Communists if they permit pupils to learn *about* communism. These and many other instances which may be cited indicate that teachers and pupils are not entirely free to teach and to learn.

In order to assure promotion of democratic ideals, many public schools, colleges, and universities require teachers to sign loyalty oaths in which teachers swear that they do not believe in, advocate, or teach the overthrow of the United States government. Many teachers feel that such a requirement casts a cloud of suspicion upon the integrity and loyalty of the teaching profession. They point out that such people as ministers, journalists, and broadcasters, who also mold public opinion, are not required to make this kind of public declaration. They maintain that loyalty oaths have little or no value, since schools and colleges already have adequate authority to remove teachers who are using their positions to propagandize and promote subversion. They feel that this procedure would be ineffective in screening out a disloyal person, because such an individual would have no hesitation in signing the oath. They also believe that this type of requirement might lead to other requirements that would foster feelings of submissiveness, conformity, and timidity upon the part of teachers. How do you feel about loyalty oaths being required of teachers?

Another issue closely related to the one indicated above pertains to the employment or dismissal of a teacher who is known to be a Communist. The National Education Association officially takes the position that Communists should not be permitted to teach, since such membership involves adherence to doctrines and discipline completely inconsistent with the principles of freedom on which American education depends. Such membership, and the accompanying surrender of intellectual integrity, render an individual unfit to discharge the duties of a teacher in this country.

Those who argue against permitting Communists to teach generally maintain that: (1) a Communist relinquishes his right to think and act as a free individual; (2) he is unable to teach in such a manner that his students are encouraged to think open-mindedly, to explore, and to seek the truth; (3) Communists are unable to assume the role of public servants, since their basic motive is conspiracy against the government of the United States; and (4) there is no violation of civil rights in barring them from teaching, since these rights do not include such a thing as freedom to be employed as a teacher.

Those who would permit Communists to teach generally maintain that: (1) it is undemocratic to forbid anyone, upon the basis of his political views, to pursue an academic career; (2) students are denied the intellectual stimulation that could come from having a Communist as a teacher; (3) a commitment to the communistic point of view may have no bearing at all upon a teacher's classroom activities.

Even those who favor the employment of Communists as teachers generally agree that it should be limited to the college level. Children in the elementary schools, for example, have not developed the maturity that would enable them to exercise the free play of intelligence in considering the different ideologies of the world.

You can sense from the preceding discussion that herein lie matters of concern not only to educators but also to the American public. The issues are rather clear. How to resolve them presents difficult problems. It is important for teachers to remember that academic freedom should never be used as a protective device in terms of which society suffers. Teachers in our democratic society have a basic responsibility to their pupils and to their communities to promote freedom of thought, freedom of expression, and the pursuit of truth. Society, in turn, has an obligation to provide and to promote these conditions.

How Can Educational Opportunity Be Equalized? A fundamental ideal in the American school system is equal educational opportunity for all children. Since early colonial days, considerable progress has been made toward this, but much yet remains to be done. The problem of providing equal opportunity exist within the particular community as well as on a national scale. As a teacher, you will have the opportunity to guide the thinking of others on the extent and nature of educational inequalities between sections of our country today.

(*Photograph by Russ Metz.*)

One evidence of existing inequalities in educational opportunities throughout the United States may be found in school buildings. In what ways could the quality of education of pupils attending these two schools differ?

(*Photograph from the Battle Creek Public Schools, Battle Creek, Mich.*)

Evidence of inequalities can be found in the fact, already noted, that teachers' salaries vary widely among states (Figure 40). Teachers in Mississippi, for example, receive approximately half as much salary as teachers in California. Educational opportunity in rural areas, also, is not comparable with that in urban centers. As compared with country schools, city schools have a longer yearly school session, a higher expense per pupil in average daily attendance, and a higher valuation of school property per pupil enrolled.

On the other hand, remember that community learning experiences in urban areas are quite different from those in rural areas. One student of these matters states [83:352]:

Rural and urban life represent still, in spite of their approaching similarity, vast differences in value systems and life goals. These patterns of life each create their unique problems of adjustment for youth.

Three basic values predominate in the farm community: work, land ownership, and family. For many classes in urban society, life is pleasure-motivated rather than being work-motivated and production-minded. Work is but a means to an end. The labor union has tended in many instances not only to reduce hours and raise wages but to reduce production. Rather than having the family as its goal, marriage is considered a means to personal happiness rather than to the begetting of children. Land and property ownership as major goals are much less important than the lavish consumption of goods. To use Veblen's famous phrase, conspicuous consumption rather than the acquisition of real property seems to be the objective of urban life.

There are good reasons for these differences. The farm person takes pride in the output of his land, his manual accomplishments; his land and crops are there for all neighbors to see. They know they are his. This sort of pride is not possible in an urban culture. A person's neighbor cannot see the fruits of his labor. In his desire for group approval and to gain the attention of others, he resorts to "conspicuous consumption," that is, spending for show.

These values reflect rather directly in the experience and motivation of youth. The urban youth, instead of expecting to get ahead by work and faithful diligence in the performance of tasks as does the rural youth, is more likely to feel that pull, contacts, knowing the right people, dress, putting the best foot foremost, and other such traits are more likely to get one ahead than ability to accomplish a particular task.

As a prospective teacher, study the background of our present status in equal educational opportunities and see the relevance of current attempts to remedy inequities. Be prepared to interpret to the members of a community the significance of Federal aid to education. To do this study carefully and critically the current legislation and the agencies and forces which are at work to promote or defeat this imperative need in our time.

Various arguments have been advanced both for and against Federal aid to public schools. Some of the arguments for and against Federal aid to education are summarized in Chapter 17.

In the face of the great differences that exist in educational opportunities, be prepared to help young and old alike maintain their faith in democracy despite its limitations in American life. You, as a teacher, will have to teach youngsters and adults the actual state of affairs today, at the same time fostering a belief in the great American dream of equality for all and a democratic respect for the uniqueness of the individual. This is a task of a political nature, a task of statesmanship, and one of the most important aspects of the role of the teacher today.

How Can Problems of Discrimination and Segregation Be Lessened?   In addition to the financial inequalities that have existed within the American school system, educators have long been confronted with problems arising from racial discrimination and segregation. These problems are precipitated when attempts are made to provide equal educational opportunities for boys and girls regardless of race, color, and religion. Although much progress has been made during the past century in lessening the amount of discrimination and segregation, problems still remain. Teachers are confronted with the task of helping the profession in further resolving these very complex problems.

On the surface, the problems appear to be primarily racial in which Negro versus white and North versus South are involved. Perhaps, as a result of the Civil War, attention has been focused upon this aspect of discrimination and segregation. But the problems are much broader in scope and more complex in nature.

From your study of social problems you have found varying degrees of prejudice and discrimination existing throughout the United States wherever minority groups are involved. You have noted that race, color, and religion affect to some degree job opportunities, housing, churches, labor unions, clubs, and political groups. In various parts of the country definite discriminatory practices exist with respect to such minority groups as Jews, Orientals, Latin Americans, and Negroes. As an example, the large influx of Puerto Ricans in New York City presents a major problem of integration. In order to gain a grasp of the nature and magnitude of this problem you may wish to read Yinger and Simpson's article, "The Integration of Americans of Mexican, Puerto Rican, and Oriental Descent" [188]; and for the various state laws affecting the use of parks, playgrounds, bathing and fishing facilities, amusement parks, race tracks, theaters, public halls, telephone booths, wash rooms, and hospitals [170: 473–501]. James B. Conant's book *Slums and Suburbs* [34:7–32] vividly indicates problems of integration involved in metropolitan school areas. Conant makes some very interesting and practical suggestions for dealing with these problems.

As Thayer indicates [170:479–480], court decisions affecting the education of Negroes, oddly enough, date back to a decision of a Massachusetts court in 1849 (*Roberts v. the City of Boston*, 5 Cush. 198, 206). In this particular case a Negro child claimed the right to attend the school nearest her home rather than the one to which she had been assigned, since the Massachusetts constitution stated that all persons are equal before the law or without distinction of age or sex, birth or color, origin or condition. In denying this right, the court maintained that, "when the great principle (of equality) comes to be applied to the actual and various conditions of persons in society, it will not warrant the assertion, that men are legally clothed with the same civil and political powers, and that children and adults are legally to have the same functions and be subject to the same treatment; but only that the rights of all, as they are settled and regulated by law, are equally entitled to the paternal consideration and protection of the law, and their maintenance."

Following the termination of the Civil War, Congress took steps to ensure the equality of Negroes and whites. As a result, the thirteenth, fourteenth, and fifteenth amendments were added to the Constitution.

Furthermore, states applying for statehood were required to include in their constitutions provisions for the establishment and maintenance of free public schools [170:479].

In meeting their educational obligations, the southern states segregated Negroes upon grounds that they would be provided with equal facilities. This action was upheld in various courts, using as a precedence the "separate but equal" decision that had been pronounced by the Massachusetts court in 1849. In 1896 the United States Supreme Court, in the famous case *Plessy v. Ferguson* (163 U.S. 537), validated the "separate but equal" practice of dealing with Negroes. Although the actual case involved segregation on a railroad engaged in interstate commerce, in a number of states the policy was subsequently applied to public facilities, such as parks, beaches, and golf courses, and eventually to public schools.

After the turn of the century, a number of decisions rendered by Federal courts began to weaken the rigid tradition and state laws regarding segregation. In 1915 the court declared that the grandfather clause was a violation of the Fifteenth Amendment (*Guinn v. United States*, 238 U.S. 347). Subsequent cases, involving such matters as housing and seating on buses, further weakened the legality of segregation practices: In 1950, a Negro student sought admission to the Law School at the University of Texas. The Court (*Sweatt v. Painter*, 339 v.629) ruled that he must be admitted. In May, 1954, the Supreme Court (*Brown v. Board of Education of Topeka*, 347 U.S. 483) interpreted the Constitution to mean that compulsory segregation is unconstitutional. In the words of Chief Justice Warren, the decision was as follows:

Today, education is perhaps the most important function of state and local governments. Compulsory attendance laws and the great expenditures for education both demonstrate our recognition of the importance of education to our democratic society. It is required in the performance of our most basic public responsibilities, even service in the armed forces. It is the very foundation of good citizenship. Today it is a principal instrument in awakening the child to cultural values, in preparing him for later professional training, and in helping him to adjust normally to his environment. In these days, it is doubtful that any child may reasonably be expected to succeed in life if he is denied the opportunity of an education. Such an opportunity, where the state has undertaken to provide it, is a right which must be made available to all on equal terms.

We come then to the question presented: Does segregation of children in public schools solely on basis of race, even though the physical facilities and other "tangible" factors may be equal, deprive the children of the minority group of equal education opportunities? We believe that it does. . . .

We conclude that in the field of public education the doctrine of "separate but equal" has no place. Separate educational facilities are inherently unequal. Therefore, we hold that the plaintiffs and others similarly situated for whom the actions have been brought are, by reason of the segregation complained of, deprived of the equal protection of the laws guaranteed by the Fourteenth Amendment.

Undoubtedly, you are fairly familiar with some of the problems encountered in the implementation of this decision. In a great many cases the integration of the races in the public schools has been without difficulty. In some cases, however, the ruling has met with defiance and subterfuge. Obviously, it takes time to implement such a ruling, since in a number of cases it strikes deep into the heart of tradition, feelings, and emotions. Legislation does not quickly change such factors.

From an educational standpoint, we are responsible for understanding the problems of discrimination and segregation in evidence in all aspects of life, and for relating these problems to the basic tenets of a democratic society. As a teacher you have the opportunity to help pupils as well as adults to identify these inconsistencies in our society and to formulate ways for effectively resolving them.

Without doubt, teachers have played a very significant role in the progress that has been made over the years. Teachers work primarily with younger people who tend to be more tolerant than their elders. Furthermore, research indicates that people tend to become more tolerant as they become better educated.

A careful examination of countries throughout the world will reveal that problems of segregation and discrimination are not unique to the United States. They exist in every society. In many countries they are of much greater magnitude than they are here. Furthermore, in some countries the problems are becoming decidedly more acute. As teachers, you have a responsibility for understanding these problems as they exist on a world-wide basis and for aiding in the resolution of them. Most of all, you must do everything possible to foster progress in the solution of these problems in the United States, so that our country may be increasingly effective in demonstrating to the world a better way of life.

How Can Enough Good Teachers Be Recruited and Kept?   In Chapter 5 you noted that the demand for good teachers on all levels far exceeds the supply. The future strength of the American school system depends upon the extent to which good teachers are recruited for and remain in the profession.

The recruitment and retention of good teachers is a responsibility that must be shared by members of the profession as well as the public in general. Although there has been a burst of concern for good teachers on the part of the general public, relatively little has been done, in a systematic manner, to interest more outstanding students in preparing for teaching. This is a point at which members of the teaching profession may exercise leadership in their communities.

In one of the White House Conferences [125] much attention was given to the recruitment and retention of good teachers. In order to increase the supply of good teachers, the groups agreed that the following three basic considerations should be kept in mind:

1. The prestige and status of teaching must be comparable with those of other professions within the community.
2. The salary structure must be high enough and flexible enough to compete effectively with other fields bidding for quality manpower.
3. The teacher's job must be so defined as to challenge and attract the interest of talented people.

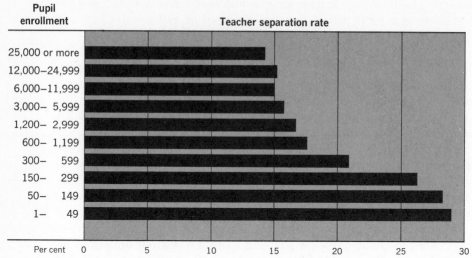

Pupil enrollment

Teacher separation rate

25,000 or more	
12,000–24,999	
6,000–11,999	
3,000– 5,999	
1,200– 2,999	
600– 1,199	
300– 599	
150– 299	
50– 149	
1– 49	

Per cent   0   5   10   15   20   25   30

Figure 56. Teacher turnover in schools of various sizes. The turnover of teachers in small schools is much larger than in large schools. What are the reasons for this great difference and how might the difference be lessened? (*Source:* U.S. Office of Education.)

The groups were also of the opinion that the supply of good teachers can be increased through several avenues—the recruitment of high school youth, stimulated by the example of dedicated and inspired teachers; the formation of Future Teacher Clubs; participation in Career Days and other guidance activities focused upon teaching; the extension of public and private grants to qualified teacher candidates; the enlistment of all community agencies in the recruitment of teacher candidates; and the evidence of teachers expressing enthusiastic pride in their profession.

Another avenue of approach suggested was that of providing excellent programs of teacher preparation. This includes strong general education and a professional program keyed to educational problems and responsibilities as well as motivation for continued study after appointment. Institutions of higher education should accept greater responsibility for the recruitment and preparation of teachers. There should be a review and evaluation of teacher-training programs for the purpose of making them as challenging, effective, and attractive as possible. There is ample evidence that lowering standards of preparation and certification will not assist teacher recruitment. It is important, also, that teacher-training institutions have a competent, well-qualified professional staff provided with adequate funds.

Recruitment of well-trained former teachers can be facilitated by the use of state surveys of potential teachers, the provision of practical and dynamic retraining programs, providing scholarships for in-service and preservice training programs, and changes in restrictive laws governing tenure and employment. Improved working conditions and salaries, relaxation of compulsory retirement provisions, part-time employment, and the establishment of more teacher reciprocity agreements between states also can help alleviate the problem.

If teachers are to be retained, then every school system is obligated to provide personnel services which have been recognized as necessary for an individual to achieve job satisfaction. These are:

1. Selection of teachers capable of providing educational leadership to children, parents, and the community.
2. Good personnel relationships.
3. More attractive living and working conditions.
4. A continuous orientation program that will enable the teacher to become a functioning member of the community and the teaching staff.
5. A program of communications adequate to keep the teacher informed and able to participate in the operation of the school.
6. A cooperative evaluation program to assist each teacher in identifying teachers' strengths and weaknesses.
7. A salary schedule that will enable the classroom teacher to secure rewards commensurate with those of other professions.
8. An in-service training program that will enable teachers to develop to the maximum of their potential.
9. The strengthening of policies related to tenure, retirement, group insurance, sabbatical and emergency leaves, and released time for professional meetings and courses.
10. The encouragement of parental emphasis on the good conduct of their children.
11. Adequate personal and professional guidance for beginning teachers.
12. Service awards in recognition of outstanding teaching accomplishment.

How Can the Public Become Better Informed in Regard to Educational Needs and Practices?   Many of the unwarranted attacks upon public schools, mentioned previously, are caused by a lack of understanding and facts. Members of the teaching profession are confronted with the especially difficult task of informing and interpreting educational theory and practices to the layman. Effective teaching is one of the most difficult tasks with which mankind is confronted. In the complex of human relations, it is easy for misunderstandings to arise. Furthermore, teachers deal with the most precious possessions of mankind—their children.

Teachers have not been inclined to give much attention to the inescapable public relations aspect of teaching. They have been hard working individuals who have centered their attention upon getting the pupils taught as effectively as possible. If there were shortages of materials, equipment, etc., they have been inclined to accept the situation and do the best they can under the circumstances. Seldom have forceful attempts been made to share with the public the problems encountered through lack of adequate facilities and conditions, and to point out the resultant losses in the education of their boys and girls. There are no people in the world more generous of their talents and money than Americans who are thoroughly aware of needed improvements in the welfare of people and various public enterprises.

In general, it is difficult to convey to the general public the economic value of education to the individual and to society. It is not possible to translate into dollars and cents the exact capital gains that accrue from having studied American literature for one year or music in the third grade. When asked to pay more taxes for schools, however, the American public tends to ask such questions as "Will we get our money's worth?" or "Can we afford better schools?"

In a later chapter of this book you will note the staggering costs of education with which the public will be confronted if future generations are to be at least as well educated as children are today. Actually, the quality of education must be improved if future generations are to be prepared to deal adequately with the increasing complex social, economic, and technological problems. Somehow the general public must remember an old saying that may be paraphrased as follows: "We cannot use yesterday's tools for educating youth to do the job today and expect to be in business tomorrow."

There are a number of activities at the community level that are being used, and perhaps could be used even more effectively, to acquaint the general public with the activities, purposes, and outcomes of schools. These include such activities as participation in parent-teacher groups and various educational associations; the observance of special days and weeks devoted to education; wide use of television, radio, and newspapers; the formation of study groups, local conferences, board-appointed lay advisory committees, counsel groups, and scheduled individual parent-teacher conferences; work on school newspapers; community use of school buildings; extracurricular activities; preparation of illustrated annual reports by school boards; class reunions; student participation in community activities; teacher participation in community affairs.

Many of the activities heretofore mentioned have proved helpful at the state level as well. Additional activities found valuable include participation in:

1. Research and dissemination of information on educational matters by agencies broadly representative of all facets of society
2. Organized programs of state-wide associations of teachers, school boards, and PTAs
3. State citizen committees
4. State fairs exhibiting the work of students
5. State-wide teacher-recognition days
6. Legislation interim commissions, including both laymen and legislators
7. Educational programs of civic services, business, labor, agriculture, etc.

Many of the activities listed above may be applied on a national level. Additional ways of creating nationwide understanding of schools include:

1. Compilation and distribution of pertinent information concerning education by government agencies such as the U.S. Office of Education, national organizations representative of the professional, business, and citizen groups, and private foundations
2. Observance of National Education Week
3. Holding of White House Conferences

Recommendations which may prove helpful in encouraging greater understanding of schools at local, state, and national levels are as follows:

1. Additional channels for educational television should be set aside and more effective use should be made of them.

2. School-board meetings in all communities should be open to the public, and citizens encouraged to attend them.

3. All citizens should be encouraged to participate more in school campaigns and to go well informed to the polls at school elections.

4. There should be greater emphasis on instruction of students in the organization, financing, and purposes of public and nonpublic schools.

5. Boards of education should initiate programs that relate to educational matters.

6. A cooperative relationship between the school and public libraries should be encouraged.

7. Local and national publications should be distributed to publicize the names and accomplishments of outstanding students in the community, state, and nation in the same manner as they do the achievements of outstanding athletes.

8. Public relations should be an organized and planned part of every school program.

SUMMARY

Attention has been given in this chapter to various problems with which educators have been and will be confronted for some time. As you move into the profession you will be confronted with the challenge of aiding in their solution.

As a prospective teacher, study the function of the school in promoting moral growth and character without giving instruction in particular religious faiths and doctrines. Gain a clear understanding of the nature and causes of the attacks being made against the school and be able to discuss the reasons for and the validity of these attacks. A considerable portion of them may be caused by a lack of understanding on the part of parents and other community members. You as a teacher will hold a key position in which you will be able to develop harmonious relationships between the home and school.

Freedom to think, to speak, and to write as reason and conscience dictate is basic to the survival of a democratic society. The development of skill in this regard constitutes one of the very important tasks to which you and the school need to give attention. Be ever mindful that academic freedom is coupled with the grave responsibility of guiding the growth of boys and girls toward higher levels of effective democratic living.

Great differences exist throughout the United States in the educational opportunities afforded boys and girls. Various attempts are being made to remedy these inequalities through improved financial programs, and through the resolution of problems concerning discrimination and segregation.

The recruitment and retention of good teachers is a responsibility that rests with the profession as well as with all community members. Every effort possible should be made to interest our most able young people in a teaching career. Furthermore, we face a problem in keeping the public well informed in regard to current education needs and practices. Such information is necessary if the public is to gain increasingly greater confidence in what we are doing, and to provide the staggering amount of financial support for education that will be needed in the future.

QUESTIONS FOR YOUR CONSIDERATION

1. What will you consider to be your responsibility for promoting moral and spiritual values in your pupils? How will you attempt to fulfill this responsibility?

2. A number of people feel that an amendment should be written into the Constitution proclaiming the United States to be a "Christian nation and giving full legal sanction to religious expressions in public schools and other governmental activities." What would your reaction be to such a proposal? Why?

3. What, in your opinion, are the reasons for attacks being made upon the work of the public schools today? How do you plan to deal with these attacks when you become a teacher?

4. How might teachers misuse academic freedom?

5. Are there any controversial issues that should not be discussed in public schools? Explain.

6. What are some pros and cons regarding teachers signing loyalty oaths?

7. What will you do if you had positive proof that a teacher in your school system is a Communist?

8. How will you attempt to promote greater equalization of educational opportunities for all American youth?

9. How will you attempt to lessen discrimination and segregation as they relate to race, color, and religion?

10. What evidence can you present to indicate that the problems of segregation and discrimination are not unique to the United States?

11. How will you attempt to interest outstanding pupils in preparing for teaching?

12. When you become a teacher, how will you attempt to promote a high level of support for schools in your community?

ACTIVITIES FOR YOU TO PURSUE

1. Organize a panel discussion on ways of equalizing educational opportunities throughout the United States.

2. Have a group of students collect data on the extent to which

boys and girls in your state have equal educational opportunities. Discuss how any differences that exist may be corrected.

3. Conduct a survey of the opinions of community members regarding Federal aid for schools. Attempt to discover the reasons for their opinions. Compile lists of the reasons for and against Federal aid to schools, and compare these reasons with those listed in this chapter.

4. Arrange for a public school official, such as a superintendent of schools, to discuss with your class the ways in which his school develops moral and spiritual values in boys and girls. You may wish to discuss this matter with several teachers.

5. Read the Educational Policies Commission publication titled *Moral and Spiritual Values in the Public Schools* and review the book for your colleagues.

6. Review for your colleagues an article such as "We Can Be Proud of the Facts," by Shane. Discuss the reasons why people frequently feel that the three R's were so much better taught in "the good old days."

7. Have a group of your colleagues visit one or more of the modern schools and one or more of the very traditional schools. Compare and contrast the learnings gained by the pupils. Which type of school is helping pupils the most in terms of effective democratic living?

8. Have a group of students talk with their former public school teachers regarding the extent to which the latter feel they have academic freedom. Compile a list of any restrictions which they note.

9. View the film *Freedom to Learn*, which was produced by the National Education Association, and discuss the educational issues involved in the film.

RESOURCE SECTION FOR PART V

- Appraising My Fitness for Work in a Community-centered Program of Education

- Suggested Films, Filmstrips, and Recordings

- Suggested Readings

- Figure Credits

- **APPRAISING MY FITNESS FOR WORK IN A COMMUNITY-CENTERED PROGRAM OF EDUCATION**

Directions to the teacher: How well are you fitted for work in a school which is closely related to the life of its community? The following check list will help you determine the extent to which you have developed the social and civic competence which such teaching requires of you. Indicate the degree of growth you think you have achieved by placing an X in the appropriate column opposite each item. Remember that you should evaluate yourself in terms of your *actual behavior in life situations*, not merely in terms of your present ideals.

Viewing myself objectively, I think I have achieved

This degree of learning—   In this area of learning—

Much	Some	Little	None	
				I. *A Realistic Approach to the Study of Human Relations*
				1.1. Understanding the community-school movement and its significance for democratic education and the conscious improvement of human living
				1.2. Comprehending life in various types of communities with regard to such fundamental factors as:
				a. The land and its resources
				b. The people
				c. Utilizing natural environment
				d. Appreciating the past
				e. Adjusting to people
				f. Exchanging ideas
				g. Making a living
				h. Sharing in citizenship
				i. Maintaining health and safety
				j. Improving family living
				k. Securing education
				l. Meeting religious needs
				m. Enjoying beauty
				n. Engaging in recreation
				1.3. Understanding social forces at work in the community:
				a. Caste and class
				b. In-group and out-group relationships
				c. Pressure groups and propaganda
				d. Democratic leadership and cooperation
				1.4. Applying effective methods of community analysis and inventory in relation to basic social processes as they are carried on in everyday life
				1.5. Understanding some of the more persistent problems of our modern social and economic society
				1.6. Comprehending the socioeconomic and cul-

Source: Reprinted by permission of Prentice-Hall, Inc., from Edward G. Olsen (ed.). *School and Community*. Copyright 1954, by Prentice-Hall, Inc., Englewood Cliffs, N.J., pp. 399–401.

APPRAISING MY FITNESS (*continued*)

Viewing myself objectively, I think I have achieved

This degree of learning—   In this area of learning—

Much	Some	Little	None	
				tural position of my community in its regional, national, and international setting

1.7. Understanding methods of community organization, coordination, and planning
1.8. Seeing possibilities for improvement of group life through a knowledge of what some communities and people are doing to enrich and advance life

II. *Effective Thinking and Research in the Social Area*

2.1. Awareness of community conditions which give rise to important problems and conflicts
2.2. Ability to see what might be done to solve or adjust to these problems
2.3. Ability to define an area for study and to formulate a plan of work
2.4. Ability to gather significant and pertinent data, using field and library research techniques:
  a. Observation
  b. Participation
  c. Interview
  d. Questionnaire
  e. Mapping
  f. Documentary materials
  g. Background reading
2.5. Ability to differentiate between data that are significant, valid, and relevant and those that are unimportant, invalid, and irrelevant, and to interpret findings
2.6. Habit of suspending judgment until sufficient facts are available for drawing a legitimate conclusion
2.7. Ability to summarize the results of an investigation and to present findings in vital written, oral, or graphic form
2.8. Practice of making decisions and of acting on the basis of these decisions where such action is desirable and possible
2.9. Habit of testing actions in the light of consequences and in terms of the principle: "Has this action promoted the personal development of the people affected by it?"

III. *Social Participation and Social Action*

3.1. Knowing the people of the community as parents, neighbors, workers, worshipers,

APPRAISING MY FITNESS (*continued*)

Viewing myself objectively, I think I have achieved

This degree of learning—   In this area of learning—

Much	Some	Little	None	
				consumers, citizens, and formulators of community customs, standards, and beliefs

3.2. Participating constructively in the life of the community by:
  a. Contributing to some community activities such as boys' and girls' clubs, church groups, community councils, armed services, etc.
  b. Helping direct some community activity such as Boy Scouts, League of Women Voters, Red Cross, etc.
  c. Working in the community at jobs other than teaching
  d. Meeting effectively problems of personal relationships incidental to participation in community life

3.3. Exercising responsible leadership in significant movements designed for intelligent community betterment

3.4. Participating effectively in district, state, national, and international group life:
  a. Functioning as a member of state and national organizations
  b. Using techniques of communication characteristic of larger group participation, such as petitions and letter writing

3.5. Creating in students social sensitivity and the inclination and habit of participating constructively in community affairs

3.6. Utilizing community resources in personal living and professional work

IV. *Cooperative Living*

4.1. Understanding democracy as the opportunity for development of maximum capacity of all individuals

4.2. Expressing democratic values through behavior, attitudes, and beliefs in all the areas and relations of life

4.3. Recognizing free interaction, cooperation, and sharing as the methods of democratic group life

4.4. Utilizing effectively in school and community those techniques essential to cooperative living:
  a. Free and fruitful discussion
  b. Democratic planning

APPRAISING MY FITNESS (*continued*)

Viewing myself objectively, I think I have achieved

This degree of learning—   **In this area of learning—**

Much	Some	Little	None	
				c. Sharing responsibility for group undertakings d. Evaluating the effectiveness of group action 4.5. Realizing the sterility of much academic procedure and developing in its place effective methods of group work in the classroom

● SUGGESTED FILMS, FILMSTRIPS, AND RECORDINGS

The number in parentheses following each suggestion denotes the chapter for which it is best suited.

Films (16 mm)

And So They Live   (New York University Film Library, 26 min). Documents the tragic poverty of families living in the southern mountains, the land, the lack of proper diet, inadequate housing, absence of sanitation, and the complete lack of adaptation of the school program to the local situation. (13)

Broader Concepts of Curriculum   (McGraw-Hill, 19 min). Points out the great increase which is taking place in enrollments in secondary schools and some of the causes for this growth. Presents four main needs of youth-civic competence, vocational orientation, preparation for family living, and health and physical fitness. Shows class activities and other responsibilities of the school relating to the development of each of these needs. (14)

Children Growing Up with Other People   (British Information Service, 23 min). Describes the child's emergence from involuntary dependence to a world of individualism and cooperation. Presents the problem of the child's increasing awareness of other people and the restraint of his aggressive individualism. (13)

Children in Trouble   (New York State Youth Commission, 11 min). Discusses the causes of juvenile delinquency, what happens to the juvenile delinquent; the role of the home, the church, the school, the police, and community clubs in preventing and controlling juvenile delinquency. (13)

Defining Democracy (Democracy and Despotism)   (Encyclopaedia Britannica Films, 18 min). Contrasts democracy and despotism and explains four conditions in a community essential to democracy. Points out that respect for one another and power in the government must be shared by all the people. Asserts that shared power and shared respect in turn depend on balanced economic distribution and enlightenment through an uncontrolled, socially responsible information system. (14)

Design of American Public Education   (McGraw-Hill, 15 min). Through animation, compares and contrasts the assembly-line kind of educational process with one that is tailored to meet young people's needs. Shows how in the former little or no consideration is given to individual needs, whereas in the latter a decentralized educational system can fit the curriculum to local community setups. (14)

A Desk for Billie   (National Education Association, 57 min). Presents portions from the life story of Billie Davis, "The Hobo Kid." Through dramatization and narration, shows how Billie's family, consisting of her parents, two brothers, and a sister, travel from place to place looking for a ready market to sell homemade baskets of flowers. Discloses Billie's quest for becoming like "real" people and attending church and school. Shows her achieving this upon graduation from high school. (13)

Effective Learning in Elementary Schools   (McGraw-Hill, 20 min). Shows a fifth-grade teacher and her class as they plan their daily work for the study of a unit on pioneer life. Pictures class activities as the teacher gathers material and the pupils work individually and in committees; construct a mural; make models and maps; practice folk songs and dances, and study reading with a play being given by the pupils for parents and teachers. (14)

Freedom to Learn   (National Education Association, 27 min). Shows how a teacher, charged with teaching Communism in her classroom by well-meaning parents, explains that the purpose of teaching is to help children learn to think rather than to tell them *what* to think. Pictures Mrs. Orin's classroom activities and shows her students seeking facts and exchanging ideas. Points out that freedom to learn facts as they are is essential to a democratic way of life and that this freedom must be extended to children in the schools. (15)

Getting the Facts   (Encyclopaedia Britannica Films, 12 min). Shows how a group of adults gain greater understanding of a school problem after gathering the facts concerning the case. Warns against deciding on plans of action in favor of prejudices and gathering only the facts which support preconceived opinions. Suggests a number of sources—magazines, newspapers, experts, and newscasts. (15)

Importance of Goals   (McGraw-Hill, 18 min). Shows, through the story of Tommy, the importance of goals in learning. His natural curiosity thwarted in school, he seems bored. By contrast, he readily learns to gain recognition, to overcome jealousy, and to keep his small newspaper business flourishing because there are definite goals involved. His teacher finally realizes what has been missing in the classroom. (14)

The Junior High School Story   (National Education Association, 28 min, color). Interesting examples of programs and activities in 50 junior high schools in California. Shows well the relationships between the curricular and cocurricular. (14)

Learning Democracy through School Community Projects   (Educational Film Service, 21 min, color). Depicts experiences in democratic learning which are provided in Michigan schools. Includes student councils, student elections, Junior Red Cross, youth centers, a community council meeting, a cleanup campaign, a vocational-guidance conference, a school safety patrol, an audio-visual service club, and a rural field day. (13)

Preface to a Life   (National Institute of Mental Health, 29 min). Portrays the critical formative years of a child's life when his personality is being affected by the attitudes and actions of his family and associates. Pictures Michael as an ill-adjusted man because of a too-demanding father and too-protective mother. Contrasts with this sequence, using frequent flashbacks, Michael's developing into well-adjusted adulthood as a result of wiser parental guidance. (13)

Principles of Development   (McGraw-Hill, 17 min). Compares children's likenesses and differences in development at various ages. Explains that development follows a correlated pattern, that development proceeds from general to specific responses, and that there is a right time for learning everything. (14)

Problem Method: Part I, Defining the Problem and Gathering Information   (McGraw-Hill, 19 min). Shows how a high school class and the teacher define a problem and seek out resources that provide information relevant to it. The class selects the problem of "What should be done about pressure groups," lists a number of sub-questions, collects information from a variety of sources, and discusses the different viewpoints that are discovered. A local situation in the city provides a concrete example of the action of pressure groups to affect the mayor's decision on a particular question. (14)

Problem Method: Part II, Using Information to Solve the Problem   (McGraw-Hill, 16 min). Shows a high school class proceeding through the final steps to solve a sociopolitical problem. A report to the class reveals that definite influence by a pressure group was used to affect the mayor's decision as to the passage of a highway through the main street of the town. Acting on information already gathered as to what should be done about pressure groups, the class lists four suggestions, decides on ways of testing each one, and proceeds to test them to arrive at one acceptable conclusion. The steps in the whole process of problem solving are reviewed, and the class then considers the highway bill according to the procedure already discussed. (14)

The Quiet One   (Athena Films, 66 min). Donald Peters is a mentally disturbed Negro boy, an only child, and the victim of a disrupted home in Harlem. At the age of ten he is sent to the Wiltwyck School at Esopus, N.Y., a correction school for delinquent boys which was founded by the Protestant Episcopal Church. With the aid of the psychiatrist and counselors he receives the training and emotional comfort which help him rehabilitate his personality. (13)

School and the Community   (McGraw-Hill, 13 min). Through animation, shows a school which is isolated from the community, neither benefiting its community nor being benefited by it. Then describes the advantages to be derived from cooperation between school and community. Points out that the school can be used for adult activities, the teachers can be leaders in community groups, and the pupils can be taught more about community life. (13)

School in Centreville   (National Education Association, 20 min). Shows children, the staff in a multiteacher rural school, and parents planning together the procedures that best relate the curriculum to the children's needs. Emphasizes the need for taking into account individual differences in interests and aptitudes. Tells how children learn to practice scientific thinking in problem solving. (14)

The Sixth Chair   (National School Service Institute, 18 min). Highlights such problems in education as building construction and modernization, class size, more teachers, and up-to-date educational tools; and portrays the dangers of the public's complacency towards education. A picture that will help to put the public squarely behind a better financial program of action. (14)

Which Way for Human Rights?   (Teachers College, 8 min). Uses drawings and still pictures to portray the background developments leading to the Universal Declaration of Human Rights. Points out that human rights are still violated throughout the world and describes what the UN and various countries are doing to achieve greater recognition of the human-rights concept. Raises several pertinent questions for discussion regarding the clarification of the concept and various programmatic and procedural problems. (14)

Who's Delinquent   (RKO, 17 min). Describes the action of a newspaper in inciting a community to remedy a wave of juvenile delinquency. Shows two youths who with a stolen car have run down a policeman, and pictures some other characteristic delinquents. Follows the action of the paper in research, study, publicity, and action; and pictures the community factors contributing to the problem. (13)

Filmstrips

Crises in Education   (Wayne University, 34 fr.). Reviews the significant causes of the critical problems facing educators in the public schools in the United States. (15)

Education for All American Children: Summary—Teach Them All   (National Education Association, 50 fr.). Presents plans for improving the education of children in the light of the major conclusions and recommendations of the Educational Policies Commission. (14)

Every Teacher . . . An Active Political Citizen   (National Education Association, 13 fr., color). Suggests ways for teachers to participate in community affairs. (13)

Guidelines for Decision   (Department of Elementary School Principals, NEA, 134 fr., color). Deals with the realities of society and of learning which serve as guidelines for decisions about contemporary issues in elementary education. (15)

Objectives of Education   (Erle Press, 43 fr.). Explains the four areas of development and living which serve as objectives of education as stated by the Educational Policies Commission of the National Education Association. (14)

School Looks at the Community   (Wayne University, 36 fr.). Visualizes the experiences of a representative school system, to illustrate what can be done to make the school aware of the community's needs and make-up, in order to improve school-community relations. (13)

Tommy Goes to Kindergarten   (Eye Gate House, Inc., 38 fr., color). Tommy is invited to visit the school for a day. Here he observes the children's many activities. At home, he asks his mother how soon kindergarten will start. (14)

Toward Better Schools for All Children through Federal Aid   (National Education Association, 54 fr.). Makes a simple presentation of statistics which show the need for better public education. After emphasizing the varying ability of different states to support their schools, the filmstrip presents the case for Federal aid. (15)

What Has the Nursery School to Offer?   (Association for Childhood Education International, 69 fr.). Designed to help teachers and others to understand the program of the nursery school. (14)

Your School and Community Relations   (Museum Extension Service, 50 fr., color). Shows that the community should understand what the schools are doing, their needs and why. School people must understand the community desires and needs. (13)

Recordings

Are the Criticisms of the Schools Justified?   (National Tape Recording Project, 15 min). A Minneapolis January town meeting in which Leo J. Brueckner, Malcolm B. Keck, Mrs. Agnes Sommer, and Edward Haynes discuss criticisms of the school. (15)

The Community College and Its Functions   (Educational Recording Service, 33⅓ rpm). Jesse P. Bogue, executive secretary, American Association of Junior Colleges, discusses the functions of a junior college. (14)

Critical Issues in Education: Are the Schools Neglecting the Fundamentals?   (National Tape Recording Project, 40 min). Albert Lynd and Professor Roma Gans present opposing points of view. Each is allowed 20 minutes to make his presentation. (15)

Critical Issues in Education: What Should Be the Relation of Religion and Public Education?   (National Tape Recording Project, 40 min). Dr. Henry P. Van Dunsen and Professor John K. Norton present opposing points of view. Each being allowed 20 minutes to make his presentation. (15)

Doorway to the Future: Challenge to Academic Freedom   (National Tape Recording Project, 30 min). Dramatization of school problems with suggestions for solutions through constructive participation of citizens. (15)

Doorway to the Future: The Negro and the Public Schools   (National Tape Recording Project, 30 min). Discusses the problems of integration with possible solutions. (15)

Education for Living   (University of Illinois, 15 min). Describes the aims of vocational and terminal education. (14)

How Can the American Educational System Best Meet the Needs of Our Society?   (National Tape Recording Project, 30 min). The needs of youth to be fulfilled by the American school system are seen through the needs of society. (14)

Improving the Services of Extra Class Activities   (Educational Recording Services, 20 min, 33⅓ rpm). Dr. J. Lloyd Trump discusses ways and reasons for improving extraclass activities. (14)

The Meaning of Education   (Academic Recording Institute, 33⅓ rpm). Ashley Montagu, interviewed by Virgila Peterson, discusses the function of education in terms of skills development, the communication of a body of knowledge, the growth of human relations practices, and the expansion of the individual. (14)

Our Schools—Educational Waste Lands or Fertile Fields   (National Tape Recording Project, 90 min). A debate between Alan Griffin, professor of Education at Ohio State University, and Arthur Bestor, historian, University of Illinois. Settles into the question of intellectual training versus life-adjustment education. Disagreement centers on methods and techniques for arriving at educational goals. (15)

Some National and International Problems (Educational Recording Service, 33⅓ rpm). Karl J. McGrath, former U.S. Commissioner of Education, discusses various national and international problems. (15)

A Reply to the Attacks on Our Schools (Educational Recording Service, 33⅓ rpm). Louis Kaplan of the University of Southern California defends the public schools against various attacks made against them. (15)

Socioeconomic Influences upon Children's Learning (Tape Recording Project, 15 min). Shows the effects of different cultural levels on the learning process. (13)

A Superintendent Speaks · (University of Illinois, 30 min). Describes the joint obligations of teachers and school administrators in carrying forward a sound school program. (14)

● **SUGGESTED READINGS**

The number in parentheses following each suggestion denotes the chapter for which it is best suited.

Alcorn, Marvin D., and James M. Linley: *Issues in Curriculum Development,* Harcourt, Brace & World, Inc., New York, 1959. Contains a number of readings on issues on curriculum. (15)

Association for Supervision and Curriculum Development: *What Shall the High Schools Teach?* Yearbook, National Education Association, Washington, 1956. Stresses the point that the school brings together in a common endeavor all of the children of all of the people and helps each to take his place as a contributing member of our democratic enterprise. (14)

Bailey, Thomas D.: "The School Administrator's Responsibility for Providing an Adequate Program of Adult Education," *School Life,* vol. 42, no. 6, U.S. Office of Education, February, 1960. Presents an excellent treatment of the school's responsibility for meeting adult education needs in our rapidly changing society. (13)

Bent, Rudyard K., and Henry H. Kronenberg: *Principles of Secondary Education,* McGraw-Hill Book Company, Inc., New York, 1961. Gives a comprehensive orientation to the secondary school. (14)

Chandler, B. J.: *Education and the Teacher,* Dodd, Mead & Company, Inc., New York, 1961. Chapter 3 presents an excellent discussion of the impact of controversial issues on public education. (15)

Callahan, Raymond E.: *An Introduction to Education in American Society,* 2d ed., Alfred A. Knopf, Inc., New York, 1960. Chapter 8 discusses the social and economic characteristics of American society and education. (13)

Christianson, Helen M., Mary M. Rogers, and Blanche A. Ludlum: *The Nursery School,* Houghton Mifflin Company, Boston, 1961. Presents an excellent overview of the function, organization, and program for nursery schools. (14)

Clark, Burton R.: *The Open Door College: A Case Study,* McGraw-Hill Book Company, Inc., New York, 1960. Discusses the junior college as a part of the enterprise of higher education. (14)

Commission of the Professors of Adult Education: *Adult Education: A New Imperative for Our Times,* The Adult Education Association, Washington, 1961. Indicates eight conditions that must be met if adult education is to fulfill its new mission as "an imperative of our times." (14)

Conant, James B.: "Another Look at the Comprehensive High School," *National Education Association Journal,* vol. 51, no. 5, pp. 29–30, National Education Association, Washington, May, 1962. Reviews progress being made in terms of recommendations he previously made for the improvement of secondary schools. (14)

Conant, James Bryant: *Slums and Suburbs,* McGraw-Hill Book Company, Inc., New York, 1961. Presents the findings of an extensive study of schools in metropolitan areas, and makes recommendations for improving especially schools in the slum and suburban areas. (13), (14), and (15)

Cook, Lloyd Allen, and Elaine Forsyth Cook: *A Sociological Approach to Education,* 3d ed., McGraw-Hill Book Company, Inc., New York, 1960. Ties together communities, children, and the schools in a logical, coherent view of what public education in a time of change and confusion should be and do. (13)

Dale, Edgar: "The Educative Environment," *The News Letter,* vol. 26, no. 8, pp. 1–4, Bureau of Educational Research and Services, Ohio State University, Columbus, Ohio, May, 1961. Indicates various community forces that affect the behavioral development of the child and suggests ways in which the school program may be related to the community. (13)

Educational Policies Commission: *The Central Purpose of American Education,* National Education Association, Washington, 1961. Indicates that the development of the rational powers of man constitutes the central purpose of education. (14)

Educational Policies Commission: *The Contemporary Challenge to American Education,* National Education Association, Washington, 1958. Presents an excellent statement of short, intermediate, and long-range needs of youth. (14)

Educational Policies Commission: *Contemporary Issues in Elementary Education,* National Education Association, Washington, 1960. Presents an excellent statement of some issues with which our elementary schools are confronted. (15)

Educational Policies Commission: *Education and the Disadvantaged American,* National Education Association, Washington, 1962. Indicates that one of the major problems confronting the nation's schools today is how adequately to help millions of culturally deprived children to realize their full potential as individuals and members of society. (15)

Ehlers, Henry, and Gorden C. Lee (eds.): *Crucial Issues in Education,* Holt, Rinehart and Winston, Inc., New York, 1959. Presents various viewpoints on such issues as freedom in education, loyalty oaths, religion and education, moral and spiritual values, racial segregation, Federal support, aims and ends in modern education. (15)

Fletcher, C. Scott, (ed): *Education: the Challenge Ahead,* W. W. Norton and Company, Inc., New York, 1962. Contains an excellent discussion of new goals for education. (14)

Grambs, Jean D., Clarence G. Noyce, Franklin Patterson, and John Robertson: *The Junior High School We Need,* National Education Association, Association for Supervision and Curriculum Development, Washington, 1961. Presents an excellent discussion of the type of junior high school needed today. (14)

Havighurst, Robert J., and Bernice L. Neugarten: *Society and Education,* 2d ed., Allyn and Bacon, Inc., Englewood Cliffs, N.J., 1962. Analyzes certain major educational topics and problems from a sociological point of view. The material presented should help the teacher understand how the individual becomes a cooperating member of a complex society. (13)

Heffernan, Helen, and Vivian Edmiston Todd: *The Kindergarten Teacher,* D. C. Heath and Company, Boston, 1960. Describes the nature of kindergarten children and effective ways of working with them. (14)

Hollinshead, Byron S.: "American and European Education—Why the Differences?" *National Education Association Journal,* vol. 48, no. 2, pp. 56–59, National Education Association, Washington, February, 1959. Contrasts European and American education and appraises the advantages of each. (15)

Kauper, Paul G.: "The Constitutionality of Aid to Parochial Schools," *Phi Delta Kappan,* vol. 43, no. 8, pp. 331–337, May, 1962. Discusses questions regarding the legality of providing Federal aid to parochial schools. (15)

Kelley, Earl C.: *In Defense of Youth,* Prentice-Hall, Inc., Englewood Cliffs, N.J., 1962. Analyzes the problems of juvenile delinquency and makes some specific suggestions for solving them. (13)

Lowell, C. Stanley: "Federal Aid to Church Schools: Questions of Constitutionality and Social Desirability," *Phi Delta Kappan*, vol. 43, no. 8, pp. 338–343, May, 1962. Maintains that, if aid to church schools were given now, it would upset the entire American tradition of church-state separation. (15)

Mallery, David: *High School Students Speak Out,* Harper & Row, Publishers, New York, 1962. Explores the values and frustrations of high school students and the faculty concern about them. Attempts to draw together the relationship between youth and adults. (14)

Manpower: Challenge of the 1960's, U.S. Department of Labor, 1961. Presents an excellent picture of the manpower needs during the 1960s and indicates some educational implications. (13)

Pounds, Ralph L., and James R. Bryner: *The School in American Society,* The Macmillan Company, New York, 1959. Part III discusses problems as they relate to the American economy, family life, social change, crime and delinquency, population growth, intergroup relations, and world interdependence. Chapter 15 presents contrasting viewpoints as to the role of the schools. (13) and (14)

Scott, C. Winfield, Clyde M. Hill, and Hobert W. Burns (eds.): *The Great Debate: Our Schools in Crisis,* Prentice-Hall, Inc., Englewood Cliffs, N.J., 1959. Contains a collection of writings that bear upon a number of issues in education. (15)

Shane, Harold G.: "We Can Be Proud of the Facts," *The Nation's Schools,* vol. 60, pp. 44–47, September, 1957. Presents factual evidence that refutes the charges that school achievement is decreasing, and that European schools are better than American schools. (15)

Thayer, V. T.: *The Role of the School in American Society,* Dodd, Mead & Company, Inc., New York, 1960. Part II discusses changes in the economic and social status of youth. Part IV contains excellent discussions on such critical issues as public education under fire, religion and morality in public education, freedom to teach and to learn, segregation in American education, and Federal aid to education. (13) and (15)

Wiles, Kimball: *Teaching for Better Schools,* 2d ed., Prentice-Hall, Inc., Englewood Cliffs, N.J., 1959. Chapter 14 indicates how a teacher may exert leadership in a community. (13)

Wiles, Kimball, and Franklin Patterson: *The High School We Need,* National Education Association, Association for Supervision and Curriculum Development, Washington, 1959. Discusses such questions as: What curriculum should be offered in the secondary school? What type of school organization will enable the student to secure the most desirable education? (14)

● **FIGURE CREDITS**

Figure 47. (*Source: American Observer,* Feb. 26, 1962, p. 3.)
Figure 48. (*Source: Manpower: Challenge of the 1960's,* U.S. Department of Labor, 1961, p. 10.)
Figure 49. (*Source: Manpower: Challenge of the 1960's,* U.S. Department of Labor, 1961, p. 11.)
Figure 50. (*Source: Manpower: Challenge of the 1960's,* U.S. Department of Labor, 1961, p. 15.)
Figure 51. (*Source: Manpower: Challenge of the 1960's,* U.S. Department of Labor, 1961, p. 16.)
Figure 52. (*Source: An Act for International Development: A Program for the Decade of Development,* Department of State Publication 7205, General Foreign Policy Series 169, Office of Public Services, Bureau of Public Affairs, Washington, 1961, p. 166.)

Figure 53. (*Source:* U.S. Bureau of the Census, *U.S. Census of Population: General Population Characteristics, United States Summary,* Final Report PC(1)-1B, U.S. Government Printing Office, 1961, p. xiii.)

Figure 54. (*Source:* Marie D. Wann and Marthine V. Woodward, *Participation in Adult Education,* U.S. Office of Education Circular 539, 1959, p. 6.)

Figure 55. (*Source:* Nolan C. Kearney, *Elementary School Objectives,* Russell Sage Foundation, New York, 1953, p. 38.)

Figure 56. (*Source:* "Teacher Turnover," *School Life,* vol. 43, no. 2, p. 19, U.S. Office of Education, October, 1960.)

VI

NATURE OF OUR SCHOOL SYSTEM

The structure of school organization is extremely complex. Teachers work under conditions that are highly organized, where policies and procedures are already well established. Your success and happiness in teaching will be greatly influenced by the adequacy with which you understand the different patterns of organization, adjust to these patterns, and work effectively toward the full realization of the school's function in our society.

The financial support of education, too, can hardly escape your concern. What it costs to operate public schools, where the money comes from, how it is distributed and used, how adequately the real needs of children and youth in school are provided for financially—these and other monetary matters have much to do with teachers and the kind of work they can do in school.

From an understanding of how schools are organized and financed, you will be in a better position to make critical analyses of present conditions, exert more positive influence in gaining community support of school, and aid in the improvement of learning conditions. Every alert teacher brings such concerns to his professional work. Part VI should aid you in regard to these matters.

16
ORGANIZATION AND ADMINSTRATION OF SCHOOLS

How are schools organized both geographically and locally in order to accomplish the task of educating millions of boys and girls? How will you fit into this organizational structure? To whom will you be responsible? What changes in the organization and administration of schools may be expected in the future? What opportunities and responsibilities will you have in determining changes that will take place?

The answers to the above questions have a bearing upon the way you plan your career, and the happiness and success you have as an educator. It is important, therefore, that you take a rather careful look at the total organizational and administrative structure for education in our nation.

Since schools are organized and administered in order to implement the educational program, school administrators increasingly seek the advice and use the creative thinking of teachers. You may expect, therefore, to be involved in the development of school policies. How will you answer such questions as the following: How should pupils be grouped for instruction? Upon what bases should pupils be promoted? How large should classes be, and should all of them be of the same size? Should foreign languages be taught throughout the elementary school? What bases should be used for admitting children to the first grade? Should there be departmentalization in the elementary school? What special provisions should be made for the gifted, the physically handicapped, the mentally retarded and the emotionally disturbed? What extracurricular activities should the school sponsor? What courses should be required of all pupils, and what elective courses should be offered? Should the school district build a junior high school that would involve grades 7, 8, and 9, or should it involve some other combination of grades? With all of the emphasis upon establishing community colleges, should your school system add grades 13 and 14 to its educational structure?

In order to assist you in answering the many questions with which you will be confronted, this chapter has been organized into two parts: public school administration according to geographic units, and organization for instruction in basic local school districts. An understanding of the legal basis of public education, first of all, will help you gain a perspective for a consideration of these two parts.

Legal Basis of Public Education. Unlike many other countries, the United States does not have a national system of public education in which power over schools is concentrated at the national level of government. Since the United States Constitution does not mention education, there is no legal basis for such a system.

The constitutions of all the states, on the other hand, provide either
directly or indirectly that a system of public schools be maintained. Court

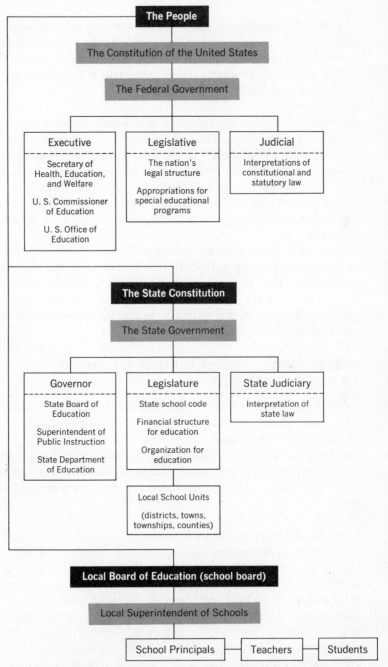

Figure 57. Structure of the organization of education in the United States. (*Source:* McGraw-Hill Book Company, Inc.) 453

decisions throughout the history of the United States have consistently upheld the state's responsibility for maintaining free public schools. In reality we have a collection of 50 state systems of education which may be spoken of as the American systems of education rather than a national system.

Although education is legally a state function in the United States, you will find that each state relies upon both the local school district and the Federal government to play a role in the operation and development of public education. In effect, public education is a shared responsibility of local, state, and Federal governments.

Structure of School Organization and Administration.   An educational program demands a plan and an organization for implementing the plan. Organization is the means of effectively concentrating the efforts of a group of people on the attainment of a common goal. A school organization does not exist as an end in itself, but rather as a means to an end. In the case of public education, the organization is structured to provide instruction, and the role of school administration is to facilitate this instruction.

Each state legislature has complete power in providing a school administrative structure, subject to the limitations of the state and Federal constitution. The state may create or abolish school districts at will, either with or without the consent of the people living within the districts. It may vest the educational authority in any local body it chooses or it may operate the schools itself.

PUBLIC SCHOOL ADMINISTRATION ACCORDING TO GEOGRAPHIC UNITS

In most states you will find three units of school administrative structure: (1) local districts, (2) intermediate units, and (3) the state department of education. Some states, known as "county unit states," have merged the local and the intermediate units. In addition to these units, national and international governmental education offices are playing increasingly important roles in the development and implementation of educational policy.

Local School Administrative Districts.   You will recall from Chapter 11 that education in America has been mainly a matter of local concern. The charge to educate the young has fallen upon families and groups of families in neighborhoods and towns. Local districts establish schools, raise money, erect buildings, provide materials and supplies, control the employment of professional personnel, and supervise pupil admission and attendance. They also regulate in essential detail such matters of curriculum and teaching which actually determine the kind of school experiences youngsters will have. In most school affairs, the local community is almost completely independent. In fact, this tenacious regard for local autonomy among smaller and sparsely settled communities is one of the main hinderances to school-district reorganization designed to provide better educational opportunities for the youngsters in those areas.

The local school administrative district consists of an area in which a single board or officer has the immediate responsibility for the direct administration of all schools located therein. It is a subordinate unit of the state, performing the duties of the state in the conduct and maintenance of the public schools.

Throughout the United States, there are over 50 different names used in referring to this basic unit. These names refer to program scope, to population, to sociological structure, or to local civil governmental subdivision. For example, in terms of program scope, districts may be called elementary school districts; in terms of sociological structure, community school districts; and in terms of a local civil-governmental subdivision, township school districts, town school districts, or city school districts. Other common classifications are common school districts, independent school districts, and country unit districts. As you will recall from your studies of government, local civil governments are responsible for the general government of a community, whereas the local school government is responsible only for the operation of schools.

The number of school districts in the United States reached a peak of about 125,000 in 1933. By 1962, through reorganization and consolidation, the number had been reduced to 35,330, with the number per state varying from 17 in Nevada to over 3,500 in Nebraska [137:4]. The President's Commission on National Goals recommended that states pass laws making reorganization mandatory under direction of each state depart-

Basic administrative units, thousands

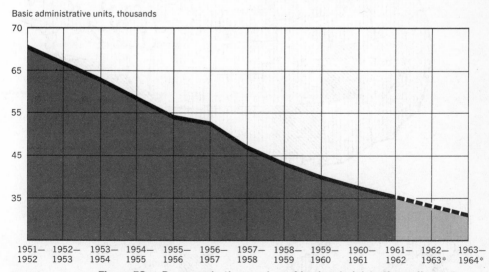

*Estimates.   **Figure 58.**   Decrease in the number of basic administrative units since 1951–1952. What are the reasons for this decided trend?
(*Source:* National Education Association.)

ment of education and that the number of local school districts be reduced to 10,000 by 1970 [114:95].

This reorganization will further eliminate many of the small high schools, especially those enrolling fewer than 100 pupils. Educators feel that extremely small schools are undesirable, and modern transportation facilities, except in sparsely settled and mountainous areas, make it possible to consolidate these small schools into larger ones. Pupils in small schools without question, suffer educationally for the following reasons [63:219]:

1. A very limited curriculum is usually offered.

2. It is not possible to provide adequate libraries, laboratories, auditoriums, lunchrooms, and gymnasiums, except at exorbitant expense.

3. It is difficult to get good teachers to live in small communities, and this disadvantage is exaggerated by the small salaries usually paid in the smaller communities.

4. The opportunities for extracurricular activities are lessened by reason of the smaller number of students interested in different activities, and the small number of staff members available to sponsor extracurricular activities.

5. The teaching load is greater in small schools, and more daily preparation is required for different subject fields, often fields in which the teacher is poorly trained.

6. Since the teaching and administrative staffs are almost always paid smaller salaries, they are less experienced, less well trained, and very likely not to remain long enough to come to know well the community and its people, problems, and educational resources.

7. Supervision is usually lacking in both quality and quantity.

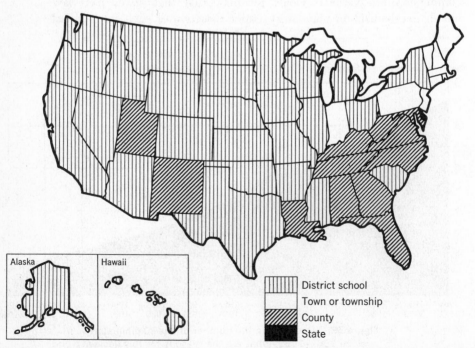

Figure 59. Prevailing types of local school organization in the United States.

8. There is less opportunity to provide good guidance and other services, such as those related to health, especially for physically and otherwise handicapped children.

9. There is limited opportunity for youngsters in the way of desirable social education, since there are so few of similar age and sex in each grade.

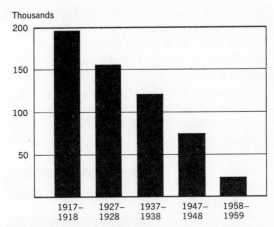

Thousands

Figure 60. Trend in the number of one-teacher schools. What factors have contributed to the decided decrease in the number of one-teacher schools? (*Source:* National Education Association.)

An examination of Figure 58 would indicate that your chances of working in a school district of respectable size are very good.

Local School Officers. Each district or unit has its own board of education, which is responsible for policy making and supervision of the schools. They may also be called trustees, directors, or committeemen. In 1961 there were approximately 200,000 local board of education members in the United States [97:6].

State laws specify whether school-board members shall be elected or appointed. Some of the laws prescribe certain qualifications of board members, such as age and residence location. Most school-board members are elected by popular vote in nonpartisan elections. When members are appointed rather than elected, they are usually appointed by city or town councils.

School-board members, who usually serve without salary, play a very important role in the community. They are responsible for levying taxes, maintaining buildings, contracting for the construction of school buildings, purchasing supplies and equipment, employing the local administrative head of the school, approving salary schedules, and establishing policies in regard to the employment of school personnel and the content of the curriculum. In fulfilling their responsibilities, boards of education comply with the regulations established by the legislature and the educational agencies of the state in which the district is located. Each state generally sets the minimum standards which all local schools districts are required to meet.

It is not the function of the board of education to administer the schools. The board selects a competent administrator who, as superintendent, serves as chief executive officer of the board and is responsible for administering policies formulated by the board. A board has the power to make and to enforce reasonable policies, rules, and regulations. When you consider signing a contract, note the rules and regulations with which you will be expected to comply.

Remember that board action, in order to be valid, must be taken in an official meeting of the board. Individual board members have no official authority in school matters, since the laws vest power to act in the board as a body. Also, as a general rule, officers and members of a board of education are not personally liable for loss or injury resulting from acts within the line of their duty unless the acts are performed willfully, wantonly, or with malice or a corrupt motive.

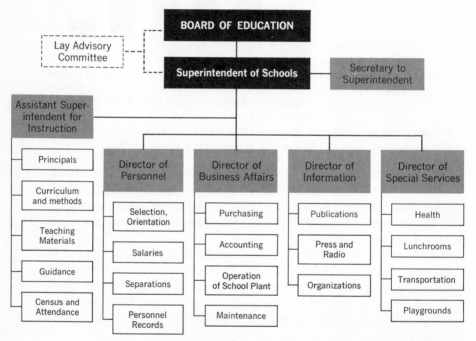

Figure 61.   Organization of the superintendency in a middle-sized school system. A position assigned to a director in this figure might be filled in a smaller system on a part-time basis by a classroom teacher or principal who is relieved of other duties for part of each day. In a larger system such a position might be assigned to an assistant superintendent.
(*Source:* National Education Association.)

Intermediate School Administrative Unit.   An intermediate school district is "an area comprising the territory of two or more basic administrative units and having a board or officer, or both responsible for performing stipulated services for the basic administrative units or for supervising their fiscal, administrative, or educational functions" [96:52].

Historically, the unit has served as an intermediary between the local school district or unit and the state educational agency.

When states were first organized in the United States, the country was established as a local unit of government and was regarded as an appropriate area for the general promotion and supervision of public education as well as for other governmental services. Thus, the origin of the intermediate unit was on a county basis and its primary concern was with county rural and village schools. As the villages became cities and experienced a rapid growth of population, they were eventually empowered to operate schools that were independent from the rural schools and from the intermediate district. As a result, the intermediate district offered leadership predominantly to rural schools [89:3].

Today, an intermediate school administration unit generally serves the following functions [89:97]: "(a) to aid the state central office in exercising general supervision over schools; (b) to provide an organization whereby special supplementary services can be made available on a pooled basis to local districts which, because of small population or other reasons, cannot administer them alone economically; (c) to have responsibility for special phases of the educational program, such as certain vocational training, classes for handicapped children, and so on; and (d) to provide a program of education for post-high school youth who do not attend college."

Trends in Administration of Intermediate Units. A number of intermediate units provide excellent services to basic school units, particularly in the State of California. However, there seems to be no apparent national trend in extending the authority or services of the intermediary unit. McLure [adapted 89:152–153] sees the need for an intermediate administrative unit in two types of areas: (1) the sparsely settled rural areas, where the problem is one of consolidating schools and defining conditions of local administrative units for appropriate intermediate districts; and (2) the big cities and adjacent suburban areas, where the problem is one of decentralization and the establishment of semi-autonomous intermediate units to work with the centralized organization.

State Department of Education. Each state has a state department or a state education agency. The department or agency usually consists of a state board of education, a chief state school officer, and his professional, technical, and clerical staff. During your professional career you will likely have contact with state-department officials who work in your subject area.

The state department serves a number of functions. Attempts are made to provide comprehensive plans for the total state program of education and to coordinate all educational efforts within the state for the purpose of promoting unity and encouraging proper balance in education. It suggests educational measures for the consideration of the state legislature and executes those laws which have been enacted. It distributes state moneys for the support of local school units, usually on the basis of the attendance of pupils in the separate schools. The state department also establishes certain minimum standards and regulations relating to such matters as certification of teachers, building construction, health and safety factors, and programs of instruction. In most cases, courses of study or units or syllabuses or other instructional materials issued by the state department are meant to be suggestive rather than prescriptive. The minimum requirements are seldom more than the mediocre teacher with an ordinary class would accomplish.

The state department also serves certain supervisory purposes. It checks to see that the laws are carried out and that at least the minimum prescribed educational opportunities are available in every community. This alone is no small task where local districts are large in size and sparsely settled, and particularly where resources are meager. Together with its supervisory function, the state department often provides significant professional leadership and services; for example, research and experimentation designated to aid all communities in the state. New York, California, Michigan, Wisconsin, Illinois, Virginia, and Florida have been conspicuous in such matters. Research reports as well as other professional information and suggestions appear in the many journals, bulletins, and other publications of the state department. In-service education programs are encouraged for the continuing growth of teachers and administrators. Efforts are made to inform the public of educational needs and progress, and encouragement is given to the public to participate in the formulation of educational policy. Consultant service and advice, essential to the continuing improvement of education, are provided to schools. As mentioned in a previous chapter, many state departments maintain placement bureaus for educational personnel.

State Board of Education.   The chief function of the state board of education is to interpret educational needs, practices, and trends to the people of the state, and to develop the policies of education which people seem to desire. These policies are usually carried out by executive officers and other professional staff members. All of the states have state boards of education with the exception of Illinois, Michigan, North Dakota, and Wisconsin. In these four states the chief state school officer determines the policy for education and administers the state educational program.

State boards of education vary in many ways. In four states (Florida, Idaho, Montana, and New York) the state board of education has general supervision of institutions of higher education as well as of the public schools. In size, they range from 3 to 102 members, with seven out of eight boards having a membership ranging from 5 to 15. The usual term of office is six years, although the range is from two years to life. In seven states, state board members are elected by popular vote, and there are some indications that the number of states electing board members in this way may increase. In the other states the board members usually are appointed by a high-ranking government official, such as the governor of the state.

Beach and Will of the U.S. Office of Education point out a number of advantages in having a board of education, whether it be a state board or a local school board, instead of having an elected or appointed policy-making individual. These advantages, briefly stated, are as follows [13:4]:

1. A board of education is more representative of the total population it serves than an individual policy-making agent is.
2. A board of education can make wiser and sounder policy decisions than an individual can.
3. A board of education serves as a safeguard against the abuses of discretionary powers.
4. A board of education acts as a safeguard against the involvement of education in partisan politics and the spoils system.
5. A board of education is a safeguard against needless disruption in the continuity of an educational program.
6. A board of education provides an economical means for management and control of the educational program.
7. A board of education provides a safeguard against fraud and malfeasance.

Chief State School Officer. The chief school officers in the various states are known by different titles, such as superintendent, commissioner, or director. There is a definite trend toward having the state board of education appoint the chief school officer rather than having him appointed by the governor or elected by the people. Between 1945 and 1961 the number of state boards following this procedure increased from 8 to 23. The officers' terms are typically four years, though in a few states they are indefinite as long as the work of the officers is acceptable to the board. The duties of a state school officer normally should include the following [148:112–113]:

1. General supervision of the public schools.
2. Acting as the executive officer of the state board of education, and, also, if there is one, of the separate board for vocational education.
3. Nominating required members of his professional and clerical staff and recommending the removal of any employee whose services are so unsatisfactory as to warrant such action.
4. Organization of the state department of education, subject to the approval of the state board.
5. Preparation of an outline for each state course of study and approval of courses of study for use in local school districts.
6. Preparation for submission to the state board of education, or, if there is no state board, to the governor, of a budget for the current expenses of the state department of education; also a budget setting forth the amount of state funds that should be appropriated to the school districts of the state and to each of the institutions of the state under the control of the state board of education or under the state school officer's supervision.
7. Interpreting the school laws and deciding such controversies as may be appealed to him by teachers and others from the decisions of local school boards.
8. Preparation of forms for reports from local school districts and from state educational institutions to the state department of education.

9. Evaluation of credentials and issuance of certificates to teachers, principals, and supervisors.

10. Approval of school sites and school-building plans.

11. Withholding state funds from school districts that fail to comply with state laws.

12. Review of proposals for the consolidation of schools or of school districts and submission of his recommendations to the state board.

13. Reporting to the state board of education and to the governor regarding the status and needs of the schools in the state and making recommendations for their improvement.

14. Approval of curriculums for teacher-preparing institutions.

15. Distribution of state school funds in accordance with state law.

Other State Department of Education Personnel.   There has been a phenomenal increase in the number of professional and nonprofessional personnel in state departments of education. For example, there were only 177 persons serving with state departments in all states during 1900, while there were 15,375 in 1955 [172:117].

Increase in personnel is accounted for both by additional services offered by the state education agency and by the change in nature of the services. Additional services include those in areas such as guidance, instruction, audio-visual and library, school lunch, transportation, and vocational education. These areas and others require professional specialists, whereas at the turn of the century, the chief state school officers and a few clerical officers were capable of handling the routine statistical and inspectional duties performed by the state agency.

Trends in State School Administration.   Chief state school officers and their staffs and the Council of Chief State School Officers have been engaged in a series of intensive studies on state departments of education. Every state has made fundamental changes in either the structure or internal organization of its state education agency, primarily to provide greater leadership to the public educational system. You have already noted the trends toward the popular election of state school-board members, and the appointment of the chief state school officer by the state board of education [13:29–30].

Education and the Federal Government.   The Federal government, throughout its history, has shown a considerable amount of interest in the educational welfare of the nation. In Chapter 1 you read various statements of Presidents of the United States in which they expressed great concern for the education of our citizenry. As you read Chapter 17 you will learn of the extensive financial support which the Federal government has given to education.

The government has shown its concern for education in another very important manner. Upon the recommendation of the National Association of State and City School Superintendents, which is now called the American Association of School Administrators, Congress enacted into law in 1867 the establishment of a department of education, to be directed by a commissioner appointed by the President. The department was to be responsible for "collecting such statistics and facts as shall show the condition and progress of education in the several states and territories, and of diffusing such information respecting the organization and management of schools and school systems, and methods of teaching, as shall aid the people of the United States in the establishment and maintenance of efficient school systems, and otherwise promote the cause of education throughout the country." Henry Barnard, an outstanding educator of his day, was appointed the first Commissioner of Education.

The U.S. Department of Education operated as an independent agency until 1869, when it became an office attached to the Department of Interior. In 1870 the title was changed from Office of Education to Bureau of Education, but its former title was restored in 1929. In 1939 the Federal Security Agency was created and the Office of Education was placed under its jurisdiction, and in 1953 the Office of Education became one of the units in the Department of Health, Education and Welfare, which replaced the Federal Security Agency.

The major functions of the U.S. Office of Education today are very similar to those prescribed in 1867: educational research, educational services, and the administration of the various educational grants. In order to carry out the first function, the Office of Education employs a staff of research specialists who collect and distribute a wide variety of information. Copies of the publications, which deal with almost every aspect of education, may be secured at cost through the Superintendent of Documents, Government Printing Office, Washington, D.C. Every two years the Office of Education publishes the Biennial Survey of Education in the United States, which provides valuable information to educators on educational trends and conditions throughout the nation. The Office of Education also conducts educational conferences, by means of which information is disseminated and problems are discussed.

The official journal of the Office of Education is the monthly publication titled *School Life*. This journal, for which the yearly subscription is only $1.75, contains valuable information regarding current research, problems, and events in the field of education.

The Office of Education employs specialists in such areas as elementary, secondary, and higher education, international education, vocational education, and library education, health and visual education, and school administration including school finance, housing, business administration, and allied fields. These specialists provide consultive services and general leadership in their respective areas in addition to conducting research.

In April, 1962, the U.S. Office of Education was reorganized in order to provide greater service and leadership to schools throughout the nation. The new table of organization may be noted in Figure 62.

Office of the U.S. Commissioner of Education. The U.S. Commissioner of Education is the chief education officer of the Federal government, and is responsible for formulating educational policy and coordinating

Program Direction and Services

Special Advisory Committees

COMMISSIONER
Deputy Commissioner

National Panel of Consultants to the Commissioner

Office of Information
- Publication Branch
- Educational Information Branch

Office of Administration
- Personnel Management Branch
- Financial Management Branch
- Management Analysis Branch
- Administrative Services Branch

Office of Legislative and Program Planning
- Legislative Services Branch
- Program Planning Branch
- Federal Education Programs Branch

Office of Field Services

Program Operations

Associate Commissioner
Bureau of Educational Research and Development

Associate Commissioner
Bureau of International Education

Associate Commissioner
Bureau of Educational Assistance Programs

Division of Educational Statistics
- Surveys and Studies Branch
- Technical Operations Branch
- Field Programs Branch

Division of Educational Research
- Cooperative Research Branch
- Educational Media Branch

Division of Higher Education
- Academic Affairs Branch
- Administrative Affairs Branch

Division of Elementary and Secondary Education
- Education for Exceptional Children Branch
- Instructional Programs Branch
- Administration Branch

Division of Continuing Education and Cultural Affairs
- Adult Education Branch
- Library Services Branch
- Cultural Affairs Branch

Division of International Education Studies
- Comparative Education Branch
- Educational Materials Branch

Division of Technical Assistance and Exchange Programs
- Technical Assistance Branch
- Educational Exchange and Training Branch

Division of Vocational and Technical Education
- Area Vocational Education Branch
- Agricultural Education Branch
- Distributive Education Branch
- Home Economics Education Branch
- Trade and Industrial Education Branch

Division of School Assistance in Federally Affected Areas
- Technical Operations Branch
- Field Operations Branch

Division of State Grants
- Instructional Equipment Branch
- Counseling and Guidance Branch
- State Plans and Reports Branch

Division of Institutional Grants
- Student Assistance Branch
- Institute Programs Branch
- Graduate Fellowships Branch
- Language Development Branch

Figure 62. Organizational chart for the United States Office of Education. The Office of Education was reorganized, effective April 1, 1962, in order to more effectively provide for new developments in education and increased responsibilities. (*Source:* U.S. Office of Education.)

educational activities at the national level. The commissioner is appointed by the President, by and with the advice and consent of the Senate. He is responsible for the operation of the Office of Education, for the administration of educational legislation, and for the performance of other functions assigned by Congress and the Executive Office of the President.

Among the major functions which the Commissioner of Education performs are the following [66:14]:

To determine policy and program objectives; to provide executive leadership for the operations; to render consultive services to educational agencies; to co-ordinate Office of Education work with related programs within the Department of Health, Education and Welfare; to establish liaison with the executive, legislative, and judicial branches of the Government; and to advise with National, State, and local officials and international bodies on educational problems.

Trends in the Relationship of the Federal Government to Education. There are some discernible trends in the relationship of the Federal government to education which include (1) increased Federal aid without any extension of Federal control, and (2) development of a coordinated policy for education at the Federal level.

Federal Government and Education at the International Level. Since the welfare of our nation is affected by the welfare of all other nations, you face the problem of being concerned with the education of people throughout the world. Increasing amounts of attention are being given to education at the international level. The Act for International Development also provides for direct assistance, upon the part of the United States, to developing countries in the field of education. In Chapter 8 you became acquainted with the purposes and work of the United National Educational, Scientific, and Cultural Organization, to which the United States lends great support, and of the World Confederation of Organizations of the Teaching Profession. Through such organizations as these we are in contact, on a far greater scale than ever before, with the educational policies and practices in other nations all over the world.

Provisions are made for the exchange of students and teachers and the sharing of various instructional materials and procedures with other nations. Educational contacts throughout the world will undoubtedly broaden and deepen mutual understanding and appreciation among the various peoples participating, and will eventually affect teaching and learning in all public schools.

In its report on *A Federal Education Agency for the Future*, members of the Committee on the Mission and Organization of the Office of Education recognized the educational challenge of the world community as follows [54:40]:

No aspect of the educational task of the 1960's surpasses in significance the fact that education is basic to the effort to bring about an enduringly peaceful world.

The developing nations of the world are seeking desperately to raise their standards of living and improve their economic and social conditions. They recognize that education is the key to this advancement and they will continue to look increasingly to the United States for aid.

The next decade will bring closer and multiple relationships with Ministries of Education abroad and international organizations, much as UNESCO, The Organization of American States, International Bureau of Education, and others working in the field of education, as problems in education are attacked bilaterally and multilaterally on a worldwide basis.

At home, greater attention to the study of comparative education, history, languages, geography, economics, and comparative government must be given in order to prepare students to understand the world of tomorrow. Likewise, teacher preparation, textbooks and the curriculum in these subject fields must be improved in the decade ahead.

ORGANIZATION FOR INSTRUCTION IN BASIC LOCAL SCHOOL DISTRICTS

As indicated previously, give careful thought to the age of pupils with whom you can work most effectively. The organizational patterns and practices which you find at the various levels within a public school district may influence your choice.

You have a wide range of levels from which to choose. With the necessary qualifications, you may step into your teaching job at any rung in the educational ladder. These divisions are normally described as follows:

Nursery: Prekindergarten experiences for youngsters from two to four years old and sometimes for those as young as eighteen months.

Kindergarten: Preprimary experiences for youngsters, usually five years old.

Primary grades: The work of the first, second, and third grades for children approximately six to eight years old.

Intermediate grades: The work of the fourth, fifth, and sixth grades for the nine- to eleven-year-olds.

Junior high school: The work of the seventh, eighth, and ninth grades for pre-adolescents or about twelve- to fourteen-year-olds.

Senior high school: The work of the tenth, eleventh, and twelfth grades for adolescents who are fifteen to seventeen years old.

Junior college: The thirteenth and fourteenth years of work, usually for eighteen- and nineteen-year-olds, though at this point the age range is not so predictable as at the earlier stages.

College or university: For age groups that usually range from eighteen to twenty-one years, though the actual range is often far greater; usually includes what is called junior college, together with programs leading to the bachelor's, master's, and doctor's degrees, and postdoctoral studies.

Adult education: Designed for mature persons of all ages, to keep them intellectually alive and help them gain new knowledges, skills, and understandings relating to work, hobbies, household arts, child care, literature, social issues, citizenship, health and safety, and other areas in which people show need or interest. The distinguishing features of adult education are that entrance requirements are liberal—unlike typical colleges, active participating in group work is emphasized, and the organization of instruction is extremely flexible.

Each of these divisions may be found in our public school system and each is controlled and supported, at least in part, by the people, but some divisions are more prominent than others—that is, they are older, or are more numerous, or include a far higher percentage of their respective age groups, or are more completely supported by public funds. For example, our public elementary schools and secondary schools number in the thousands; but our public junior colleges have not yet reached the 700 mark in number.

The same range of opportunity that is more or less available to Americans in public education from the nursery school through the college level is also offered in private schools. Actually private nursery schools far outnumber public nurseries, and private colleges and universities outnumber their public counterparts by about two to one.

Patterns of Organization.   Local school districts in the United States are customarily organized in one of the four basic patterns, the so-called 6-3-3, 6-2-4, 6-6, or 8-4 pattern. Generally, a 6-3-3 district has an instructional pattern of six elementary grades, three junior high school grades (grades 7, 8, and 9), and three high school grades (grades 10, 11, and 12). An 8-4 pattern means that a school district has one or more elementary schools consisting of grades 1 to 8 and a high school program of grades 9 to 12.

It is very apparent from an examination of Figure 63 that no single plan of organization has received unanimous acceptance in the United States.

Years of schooling

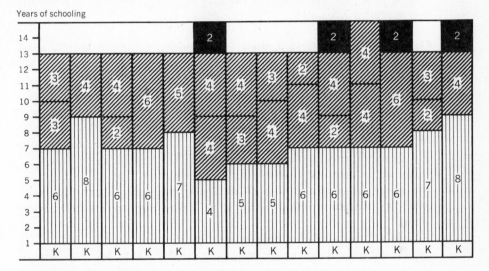

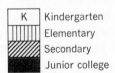

| K | Kindergarten |
| Elementary |
| Secondary |
| Junior college |

Figure 63.   Prevailing types of school organization in the United States. The numerals signify the number of grades at each level.

Local conditions still largely determine the organization of schools. Certain advantages and disadvantages are claimed for the many different plans. Large cities use the 6-3-3 plan far more widely than do smaller cities, while the smaller urban communities use the 6-2-4 and 8-4 plan to a greater degree. Factors which tend to influence the organization of a particular school or school system include the following: established practices, available buildings, financial support, educational leadership, equipment, and transportation [105:1].

One-third of the local districts in the United States are organized on a 6-3-3 plan, about one-fourth are on the 8-4 plan, and about one-sixth are on the 6-2-4 plan. These plans account for over three-fourths of the nation's districts. Following these in order of popularity are the 6-6 and the 7-5 plans. Other combinations may be noted in Figure 63.

You will find considerable confusion in the use of the terms "elementary schools" and "secondary schools." There has never been a clear-cut official distinction between elementary and secondary programs, since grades 7 and 8 may be a part of the elementary school, or may be included with grade 9 to form a junior high school, or be prefixed to the final four years of high school to form a six-year secondary school. However, you will be safe in assuming that grades 1 to 6 are included in an elementary school and that grades 10, 11, and 12 are included in a secondary school. During your professional career you may help in giving definite identification to grades 7, 8, and 9.

Elementary School Organization.   The results of a careful study made by the U.S. Office of Education, in cooperation with all of the state departments of education, may prove helpful to you in understanding the organization of elementary schools. This study involved a survey of practices in 343 new elementary schools and 25 laboratory schools throughout the United States which had been cited as having good educational programs. Most of them were located in urban areas (areas of 2,500 population or over) and in suburban areas of 25,000 population or over.

The study revealed that the K-6 (kindergarten through sixth grade) and 1-6 organizations were most frequently used [159:14]. In rural areas (with populations of less than 2,500) the 1-6 pattern was most frequently found.

Most of the schools reporting had enrollments of from 300 to 750 pupils, with the largest number being in the 300-to-400 pupil range. Many principals and teachers expressed the viewpoint that schools with enrollments of 150 to 300 provided better opportunities for young children than those with enrollments of 600 to 1,000. It was found that there are some elementary schools which enroll over 1,000 children, while others in remote areas may have as few as five.

In another U.S. Office of Education study pertaining to classroom organization, it was found that for grades 1 to 6, more than three-quarters of the elementary schools throughout the nation were using the one-teacher-per-classroom type of organization [36:30]. Slightly less than 10 per cent of the schools were using partial departmentalization. Complete departmentalization was found to be negligible. If you plan to teach on the elementary level, you may expect, therefore, to be responsible for guiding all of the experiences of your pupils.

In this same study it was found that approximately one-third of the urban schools include grades 7 and 8 in the elementary schools. Approximately 39 per cent of the districts indicated complete departmentalization in grade 7, while 33 per cent reported partial departmentalization.

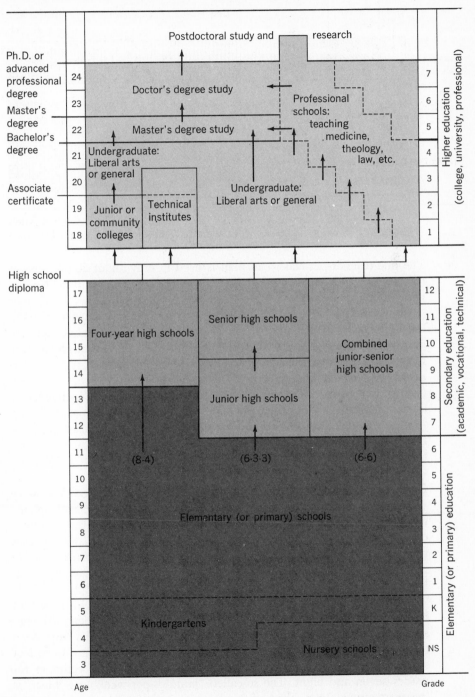

Figure 64. The structure of education in the United States.
(*Source:* U.S. Office of Education.)

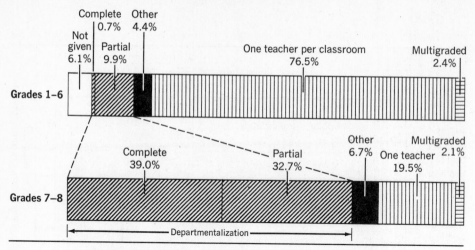

Figure 65. Percentage distribution of types of instructional organization in grades 1 through 6, and in grades 7 and 8. (*Source:* U.S. Office of Education.)

The one-teacher-per-classroom plan is used in only about 20 per cent of the seventh and eighth grades when these grades are considered to be a part of the elementary schools.

The typical length of the elementary school day (exclusive of noon lunch periods but inclusive of recess and play periods) is between five and six hours in grades 1 to 6. When grades 7 and 8 are in the elementary school organization, the school day for these youngsters is typically between 5½ and 6 hours.

Most of the urban places in the United States maintain elementary school programs of between 175 and 180 days during the school year. Among the geographical regions of the nation, the Northeast tends to have more than 180 school days per year; while the North Central states, the South, and the West tend to have fewer than 180 days.

Elementary School Curriculum. The curriculum of the elementary school has evolved into a pattern of seven broad subject fields: language arts, arithmetic, science, social studies, art, music, and health and physical education. The main curriculum problem at the local district level is to organize a balanced educational program, with provision for a proper proportion of subject-matter offerings in the seven broad academic areas listed above.

You will find that the amount of time allocated for teaching each of the subject-matter fields is decided by the local school districts, although state departments generally suggest desirable allocations. The "suggested time" approach policy is generally used in guiding teachers in the first six grades, whereas the "prescribed-time" policy is most common for grades seven and eight. The so-called "minutes-per-week-per-subject" is the most prevalent method of implementing the policy throughout all grade levels of the public elementary school.

In many elementary schools the subject-matter fields are organized into broad units, so that many subjects are learned at the same time. For example, science and social studies are often taught together, especially in connection with such topics as transportation, communication, or conservation. Other combinations may include literature and social studies, mathematics and science, and health and physical education.

Increased emphasis is being given to providing more than just a textbook education. For example, teachers in good elementary schools are providing children with more opportunities for reflective thinking. Modern schools include experiences that are [46:20]:

More like these

1. Many pupils asking questions, teacher paying attention to them and helping pupils to find answers in a number of sources
2. In relation to a topic or problem, many pupils participating in a discussion about purposes, helping to make plans, and accepting responsibility for carrying them out
3. Books, pamphlets, and other sources of information on reading levels of at least four or five grades available and used by pupils

Less like these

1. Teacher asking questions, pupils reciting information from a single textbook
2. Teacher making assignments, requesting pupils to read a certain chapter in the textbook and to find answers there
3. All pupils in the class using the same textbook apparently trying to find answers to the questions in one source

The textbook continues to be a primary source for organized information, but films, pictures, posters, charts and library books, maps, globes, and science experimental equipment are used in connection with the varied subjects.

Promotional Policies in the Elementary School. There is a tendency for schools to take into consideration a number of factors in deciding upon the promotion or retention of pupils. Factors usually considered besides academic achievement include the child's intellectual, personal, social, physical, and emotional capabilities and development. However, a majority of districts promote primarily on the basis of the academic achievement of pupils and parents generally approve of this policy [36:58–59]. The so-called "social promotion" as a sole basis of judgment is practically nonexistent.

Grouping of Elementary School Pupils. Increased interest is being expressed again in the desirability of assigning children to work in groups upon the basis of ability. Since Sputnik I, a number of reports have called attention to the fact that our brightest youngsters may not be challenged according to their abilities, and that, as a result of this waste of human excellence, our nation's defense and future are being weakened.

Diverse grouping plans have been suggested, initiated, discarded, revised, and in some cases used again. Some of the plans are described as follows:

Chronological age grouping. Children of a specific age are placed in a grade group and one teacher works with them. For example, six-year-old children are placed in a first grade group, and seven-year-old children are in a second grade group.

Heterogeneous grouping. Children in a grade group are taught by one teacher irrespective of their intelligence and achievement.

Homogeneous grouping. This is known as "ability grouping." Determinants of classroom placement include intelligence, readiness, and achievement test data.

Winnetka Plan grouping. This is a form of heterogeneous grouping, but provision is made for use of self-instructional materials. Individual goal cards encourage optimum academic growth by each child.

Other grouping plans have been termed XYZ grouping, Dalton plan grouping, platoon grouping, organismic age grouping, intra-classroom grouping, interclassroom grouping, opportunity room, self-realization room, and ungraded primary or intermediate [139:1–11].

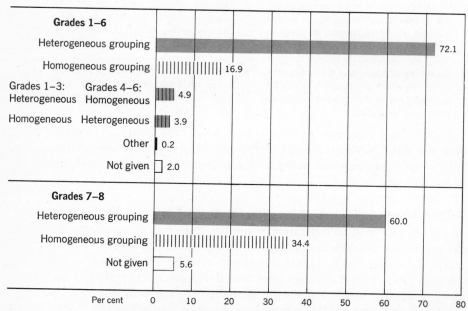

Figure 66.   Percentage distribution of basic grouping policies for public elementary schools in urban places with populations above 2,500. What advantages and disadvantages do you see in each type of grouping? (*Source:* U.S. Office of Education.)

As is indicated by Figure 66, approximately 72 per cent of the urban schools in the United States use heterogeneous grouping in grades 1 to 6, and 17 per cent group children homogeneously [36:68–71]. Forty-six per cent of these schools predicted that there would be an increase in homogeneous grouping; approximately four per cent predicted an increase in heterogeneous grouping, and forty-seven per cent felt that there would be no change in policies pertaining to grouping.

As you read educational literature you will note that considerable attention is especially being given to the primary unit of the elementary school. You may find such terms as the following being used: the ungraded school, the ungraded primary, the nongraded elementary school, the primary department, a continuous growth plan and the primary group. In general, it involves various plans by means of which children are grouped to permit continuous progress during a period of two or more consecutive years. In some instances the teacher may remain with the same group for more than one year. A few schools are experimenting with this type of organization in the intermediate years, but ordinarily it is linked with the primary years, sometimes including the kindergarten [108:166].

Representative systems with some type of nongraded pattern of organization include: Corona and Torrance, California; Pocatello, Idaho; Moline and Park Forest, Illinois; Baltimore and Germantown, Maryland; Marblehead, Massachusetts; Dearborn, Michigan; Reno, Nevada; Dayton and Youngstown, Ohio; Savannah, Georgia; and Milwaukee, Wisconsin.

The most frequently mentioned reasons for having nongraded groups are [108:167]:

(a) Learning should be continuous; (b) children grow and learn at different rates and each should have the opportunity to achieve at his own rate; (c) school programs should be flexible so as to meet varying developmental needs and growth patterns of individual children; and (d) greater achievement will result when children experience success in school.

Probable Developments in Elementary Schools.   Because of the unique decentralization characteristic of schools in the United States, it is extremely difficult to generalize in regard to future developments in education. However, it is highly probable that the following trends in elementary schools will continue [45:21–22]:

1. To evaluate growth in terms of the personality of the child as well as subject matter.
2. To individualize teachings as much as possible.
3. To utilize the findings of child development research in the construction of curriculum and in guidance of children.
4. To relate the curriculum to the needs of children in the community where they live.
5. To select and organize the work of the school around the interests of children and around problems which children can comprehend.
6. To make the school an integral part of the community and the community an integral part of the school in every way possible. . . .
7. To extend public school services (1) to children below 6, (2) after-school hours and (3) to months when school is not formally in session.

An increasing number of elementary schools are experimenting with TV teaching, programmed learning, instruction in modern foreign languages and in modern mathematics, and learning by discovery or by problem-solving methods. Special provisions are being made for teaching exceptional children, including those with special education needs and those with exceptional talent.

Downward Extension of Elementary Schools. If you are planning to become a kindergarten or nursery school teacher, you will be interested in the extent to which state laws provide for the education of children three, four, and five years of age. Public nursery schools are authorized, either directly or by implication, in 17 states. There are no reliable statistics available to show the number of three- and four-year-olds who go to a nursery school. The total number may be greater than one might expect. One study indicated that 4.5 per cent of the total urban places in the United States are offering a public program of nursery school education [36:14]. Almost one-half of the existing programs are supported by a combination of public and private funds, one-third solely by private funds, and less than one-fifth by public funds alone. Only in the South is there any appreciable use of public funds for nursery schools.

All states except one have laws permitting kindergartens to be operated in public schools, and state aid for this purpose is provided in nearly half of our states. Approximately 70 per cent of the urban places in the United States maintain public elementary school kindergartens. Nationally, more than 80 per cent of these kindergartens are supported solely by public tax funds [36:16].

Secondary School Organization. You probably were unconcerned with the organization of secondary schools when you were a high school student. As a prospective secondary school teacher, however, organizational patterns have definite meaning for you since they definitely will have an effect upon your future work.

Secondary schools may be classified into the following five major categories [adapted, 57:10–12]:

Traditional high school: a 4-year school preceded by an 8-year elementary school.

Combined junior-senior high school (predominantly 6-6 system and 7-5 system): a reorganized school in which the junior and senior high schools are combined under one principal.

Junior high school (predominantly 6-3-3 system and 6-2-4 system): a reorganized school in which the junior high grades are grouped separately under one principal.

Senior high school (6-3-3 system): a reorganized school in which the last three years are grouped separately under one principal.

Four-year high school (6-2-4 system): a 4-year school similar to the traditional high school in organization but with important differences. The system has been reorganized, often in our larger cities, to include 2-year junior high schools.

In 1959 [57:11] 42 per cent of the nation's 24,000 secondary schools were the combination junior-senior high school type, while the traditional high school (8-4) prevailed in 24 per cent of the schools. The strong upsurge of junior high schools since 1952, both in number of schools and in size of enrollment, appears to be a dominant trend in organization. Eighty-two per cent of our total secondary school population now attends a school having a junior high school.

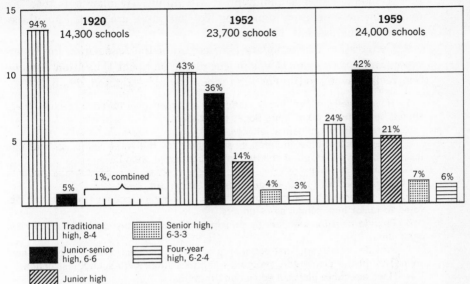

Figure 67. Types of organization of public secondary schools. For what reasons have changes been made in the types of organization of our public secondary schools? (*Source:* U.S. Office of Education.)

Junior High School. The junior high school is the intermediate unit in a program of general education, its purposes being separate and distinct from those of both the elementary school and the senior high school. Principles upon which it was founded were included in Chapter 14. The junior high school has evolved as an institution to meet the unique physical, social, emotional, and intellectual needs of the late preadolescent and early adolescent. Emphasis is upon exploratory experiences. Some of these experiences are included as part of a core program, or they may be offered as required exploratory courses. Exploratory experiences include [78:59]:

Art	General business	Music appreciation
Choral music	General language	Photography
Choral speaking	Hobbies	Poetry writing
Crafts	Homemaking	Public speaking
Creative dramatics	Journalism	Science
Creative writing	Literature	Typing
Folk dancing	Manual arts	

The Southern Association of Colleges and Secondary Schools recommends that the size of a three-year junior high school should range from a minimum of four sections per grade to a maximum of eight sections per grade. If you assume that each section is to have a maximum size of 30 pupils, the range in enrollment for the school would be from 360 to 720 [78:74]. Conant, who completed an extensive study of junior high school programs, recommends that a separate three-year junior high school should enroll a minimum of 375 pupils. He maintains that "for really efficient operation, something like 750 pupils are needed in a three-year junior high school" [33:39].

A Commission on Secondary Curriculum of the Association for Supervision and Curriculum Development of the National Education Association feels that a good junior high school should [adapted, 29:35]:

1. Have a well-stocked library staffed by a professional librarian-teacher. There should be a ratio of 10 or more books per student.

2. Provide ample guidance services.

3. Offer block-of-time instruction each year for the three years, so that one teacher will have a group of children for a substantial period.

4. Maintain flexibility of scheduling. For example, some seventh-grade students are better placed with ninth-grade students for certain classes.

5. Be staffed with teachers prepared for junior high school teaching and devoted to junior high school age students.

6. Provide help for teachers by principals, by supervisory staff, and by clerical personnel.

7. Provide a modern instructional program in subject areas. Changes now under way in the elementary program will affect junior high school instruction.

8. Have adequate physical education programs.

9. Have ample laboratory and workshop facilities.

10. Have an established reasonable teacher load.

Senior High School.   One of the unique aspects of the American public education system is the comprehensive high school which provides educational opportunities for all of the boys and girls in a community, regardless of their economic status, sex, family background, education, and vocational ambitions. Many educators from other countries visit the United States in order to observe this type of high school with the hope that they may make adaptations of it in their countries.

The programs in the comprehensive high school are flexible enough to meet the changing needs of pupils and desires of parents. A senior high school pupil may change from a course in agriculture to one in music, or he may change from an industrial arts program to a college-preparatory program. Such change in course selection may come about as a result of a pupil's changing interests and needs. Late-blooming talents of a high school pupil may become evident in his sophomore, junior, or senior years, and the comprehensive high school provides the flexibility to enable him to make the changes easily.

Offerings in the comprehensive high school most frequently include the general, the college preparation, the business education, and the vocational curricula. Students majoring in each curriculum are scheduled to take both required courses and restricted electives. They generally are permitted to elect one or more subjects not included in the required curriculum sequence.

From your experiences, you know that high school pupils are required to study English, social studies, mathematics, science, health, and physi-

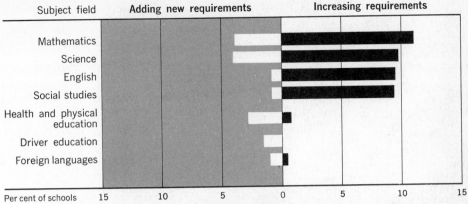

Figure 68. Per cent of change occurring in a period of five years in requirements for high school graduation. Why must the school continue to change its requirements? (*Source:* National Education Association.)

cal education. They may elect to take courses in industrial arts, home economics, foreign language, music, art, business, and vocational education.

State departments of public instruction and the local school districts establish standards and requirements for the subjects to be taught, the number of years they are to be studied, the number of years of required pupil attendance, the minimum graduation requirements, and the requirement of textbooks and other instructional materials. As a secondary school teacher, you will undoubtedly have opportunities to participate in reviewing standards and requirements that apply to the school in which you teach and in recommending changes that should be made.

The diversified offerings and the flexibility of the comprehensive high school in meeting the changing needs of pupils account in part for the increased enrollments and holding power of the schools. The American high schools enroll over 90 per cent of the boys and girls who are 14 to 17 years of age [152:105], while in 1890 the number of pupils attending high schools was approximately 7 per cent of the 14 to 17 age group. More than 62 of every 100 youths of this age group are now graduating from high school; approximately 40 per cent of these graduates are entering college on a full-time basis, and an additional 9 per cent enter college on a part-time basis.

An example of the increased holding power of the American high schools is indicated by the fact that from 1930 to 1958 there was an increase of 13.5 per cent in the population of those 14 to 17 years of age, while during the same period of time the percentage of high school graduates increased at a rate of 128.2 per cent [153:24–25]. Educators and others are concerned with the current drop-out problem, but the figures cited are encouraging and indicate that comprehensive high schools have increased their holding power through provision not only for those who

In the comprehensive high school, better facilities, diversified offerings, and the flexibility of programs which meet the changing needs of pupils, account in part for increased enrollments and holding power of the schools. (*Photographs by Carl Purcell, National Education Association.*)

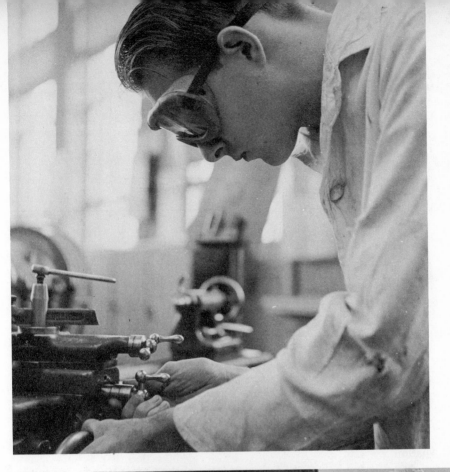

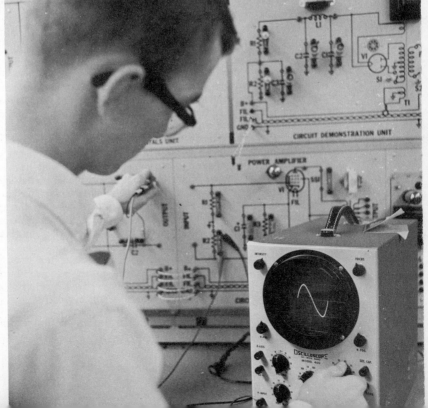

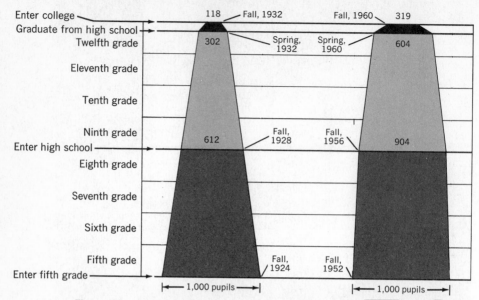

Figure 69. Survival rates of groups of 1,000 pupils entering the fifth grade in 1924 and in 1952. What factors have contributed to the fact that the drop-out rate has continued to decrease? (*Source:* U.S. Office of Education.)

are going to attend colleges or universities after high school graduation but also for those who are going to enter the world of work upon graduation.

At a hearing before the Subcommittee of the Committee on Appropriations in the House of Representatives during the Eighty-sixth Congress, Dr. Lawrence G. Derthick, who was then U.S. Commissioner of Education, presented a dramatic contrast to the comprehensive high school in the following manner [127:11]:

> What would it be like to have the traditional European system? At approximately age 11, your child would take a series of national achievement tests, and his performance on these tests would largely determine his future track or specialized secondary school, if any. His whole future might well depend on these tests. Think of your own experience back in the fifth grade of elementary school. What marks were on your report card? Would you have been placed in the classical high school for collegebound professionals or would you have been placed in another school where your education might have ended at the age of 14? Would you have been happy to have somebody else determine what your future would be by deciding what type of education you should have after the age of 11 or 12?

> Let us ask, too, why have the rigid class barriers of many Western European nations been maintained? Why have most class barriers in this country been removed?

> More than 50 years ago American parents decided that they would not give any person the right to close any doors to the future for their 11-year-old children. They made this decision with a full knowledge of the system of education used in Europe—and of the social consequences of this system.

The report of the President's Commission on National Goals states that "it is essential that the tradition of the comprehensive high school be preserved and strengthened."[1] This report emphasized that youngsters should never be handled in such a way that some appear to belong to an elite group while others are classified at a lower level. Do you feel that any improvements in our school can be made along this line?

Conant and his staff studied the educational programs of 103 high schools in 26 states and personally visited 55 of the schools. In his report concerning the study, Conant stated:

I can sum up my conclusions in a few sentences. The number of small high schools must be drastically reduced through district reorganization. Aside from this important change, I believe no radical alteration in the basic pattern of American education is necessary in order to improve our public high schools. If all the high schools were functioning as well as some I have visited, the education of all American youth would be satisfactory, except for the study of foreign languages and the guidance of the more able girls. Most of the schools which I found unsatisfactory in one or more respects could become satisfactory by relatively minor changes, though I have no doubt that there are schools even of sufficient size where major improvements in organization and instruction would be in order [32:40].

Conant proposed that a high school must have a graduating class of 100 in order to offer adequate curricula and to provide enough class sections to accommodate pupils of varied abilities. He estimated that only 4,000 of over 20,000 high schools in the United States have graduating classes of over 100.

In his report, Conant made 21 other recommendations for improving the American high school. Since these recommendations may have a significant impact upon the public schools, become quite familiar with them. You may find them in the Resource Section for Part VI of this book. Discuss their implications with your instructors and colleagues. If all of these recommendations were to be implemented, how would your work as a teacher be effected?

Trends in Secondary Education.   Several trends in secondary education are in evidence as attempts are made to meet the needs of increasingly greater numbers of boys and girls. These trends may be summarized in the following manner:

1. Emphasis is being placed upon quality of the education program.
2. New approaches utilizing television, teaching machines, and team teaching are utilized increasingly.
3. Curriculum changes in the fields of mathematics, science, and foreign language are notable; and teaching in these areas is being emphasized. More courses are being offered in these subject fields, and the academically talented students are engaging in more advanced study of the courses.
4. The total guidance program is being extended and increased.
5. Remedial classes in English and arithmetic for pupils who are deficient in the basic skills of reading, writing, computation, and arithmetic are being provided.

[1] The President's Commission on National Goals, *Goals for Americans*, © 1960 by The American Assembly, Columbia University, New York. Reprinted by permission of Prentice-Hall, Inc., Englewood Cliffs, N.J., p. 85.

6. The holding power of the secondary school is increasing.

7. Emphasis is being given to the problem-solving method of teaching.

8. The school day organization is becoming more flexible as it becomes more apparent that all courses do not require the same length of class period.

9. Principals and/or directors of instruction are playing a more active role in the improvement of instruction.

Associations of Secondary Schools and Colleges. Many of the secondary schools throughout the United States belong to associations of secondary schools and colleges. These are quasi-legal, voluntary associations. There are six such regional associations, four of which were founded before the turn of the twentieth century:

Association	Date founded
New England Association of Colleges and Secondary Schools	1885
Middle States Association of Colleges and Secondary Schools	1892
Southern Association of Secondary Schools and Colleges	1895
North Central Association of Colleges and Secondary Schools	1895
Northwest Association of Secondary and Higher Schools	1918
Western Association of Secondary Schools and Colleges	1930

The states included in each of the respective associations are indicated in Figure 70.

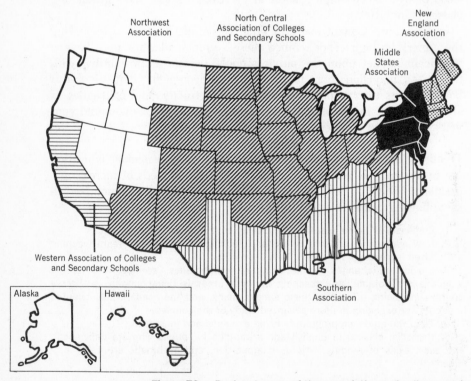

Figure 70. Regional areas of the associations of colleges and secondary schools in the United States. To which association does your college and your secondary school belong?

The primary purposes of these associations include the improvement of instruction at each level, closer articulation between levels, and the accrediting of schools. The New England and the Western Associations are exceptions in that they do not accredit schools. The North Central Association has been the most conspicuous of the group in size, activity, and influence. The Southern Association has engaged in noteworthy experimentation and exploration in education.

Accreditation by a regional association means that the school concerned meets, in general, the pattern of standards set by the association. In that case, pupils in accredited schools are assured of more adequate educational opportunities; they have easier access to other institutions at the same or at a higher level. Both pupils and institutions gain some measure of prestige. Very careful surveys of local educational situations are made by the regional associations, and significant improvements are often affected as a result of their work.

Accrediting classifications include such categories as the following: accredited, accredited-advised, accredited-warned, withdrawn or discontinued, and dropped. An advisement is, in effect, a conditional approval and may be continued beyond one year if the school makes satisfactory progress toward correcting the deficiency. If satisfactory progress is not made, the school is warned that the cause of warning must be removed within a year if membership is to be continued.

Specialized Schools.   Besides those divisions which are ordinarily considered in our present educational system, there are many other schools, the majority of which are privately supported. Religion-affiliated schools will be discussed in the next chapter. In addition to these, there are schools organized as military academies, boarding schools, college preparatory schools, finishing schools, and the like. A great number of specialized schools are almost purely vocational in character, such as the large technical schools, the very specialized High School of Fashion Industries, the Juilliard and Eastmond Schools of Music, or various schools of nursing, commerce, business, electronics, or flying. Such schools as the Bronx High School of Science in New York and the Boston Latin School cater to students with special abilities, and may even require rigid entrance examinations. Other kinds of specialized schools include those for the physically handicapped in sight, hearing, or muscular coordination. Many of these schools are state supported. Special schools also are available for the mentally retarded and the emotionally disturbed. If you have interest in teaching in any of these types of schools, the opportunities are great.

Higher Education.   Higher education includes those educational programs which require approximately 12 years of previous schooling or its equivalent for admission. There are more than 2,000 higher-education institutions in the country, all except 475 of which are coeducational. Approximately 59 per cent of the colleges and universities are public supported. It is anticipated that these figures will reach 65 per cent by 1970. Students have differing needs and are served by a host of diverse institutions and programs.

Enrollments in institutions of higher education increased 229.1 per cent in the period from 1930 to 1959 [153:25], and institutions of higher education are being urged to handle up to a 50 per cent increase in the present college-age population by 1970 [114:90]. Figure 71 indicates how the students who comprised approximately one-third of the population in the age group 18 to 20 were distributed in 1960 in the various types of institutions.

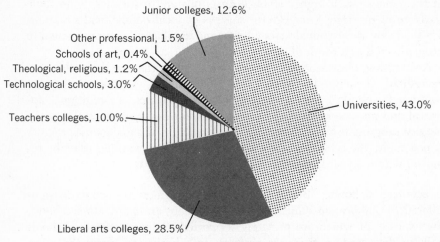

Figure 71. Percentage distribution of degree-credit students enrolled in the various types of institutions of higher education in the United States, fall, 1960. (*Source:* U.S. Office of Education.)

A college may be a separate institution or a unit within a university. The term "university" stands for an organization consisting of a liberal arts (or arts and sciences) college as its foundation, as well as a number of professional schools such as schools of education, law, engineering, and business.

Many of the teachers colleges and technological schools are currently placing more emphasis upon provision for liberal arts programs. As indicated previously, the names of many teachers colleges are being changed to state colleges. In addition, land-grant colleges or universities, so named from the fact that they were originally set up by the states on the basis of endowments of land granted by the Federal government, offer a wide range of programs in the humanities in addition to the programs in agriculture, mechanic arts, home economics, and military tactics as mandated by the Morrill Act of 1862 and subsequent acts.

Junior College.   Approximately two-thirds of 678 junior colleges existing in 1960 were publicly supported [81:28]. The junior colleges normally offer higher education free or at nominal cost to student within commuting distance. Most offer a two-year program of general education and courses that prepare for occupations requiring less preparation than a four-year degree program.

The President's Commission on National Goals has recommended that "there should be roughly within commuting distance of every high school graduate (except in sparsely settled regions) an institution that performs the following functions:[2]

a. Offers two-year terminal programs for students not going on to a four-year college career
b. Offers transfer programs for students who do wish to complete a four-year program
c. Serves as a technical institute for the community, serving local needs for vocational and subprofessional education
d. Offers continuing education to adults

Adding more public junior colleges to the present educational set-up would provide the following gains [115:10]:

1. Pressures of increased post–high school enrollment would be lessened.
2. Higher education would become more democratic.
3. Vocational and technical training would expand.
4. Human resources would be conserved.
5. Junior colleges would become community-service centers.
6. Local high schools would be upgraded.
7. Community colleges would serve as a screen device for four-year colleges.

Graduate Schools.   The graduate schools have the responsibility of providing advanced training for college graduates of high ability. It is evident that the maintenance and development of the more highly complex society of the future will depend a great deal upon the success of the graduate schools in recruiting and training our most capable people.

As indicated in Chapter 5, there will be a great demand for teachers to meet the needs of the great numbers who will be in higher education and to meet the increasing demands of industry and government for educated talent.

Adult Education.   A number of educators feel that there should be greater coordination of efforts in adult education at the local, state, regional, national, and international levels. In nearly every state there is an adult-education specialist within the department of public instruction; and at the Federal level, leadership is provided by the Adult Education Section in the U.S. Office of Education.

There are now 15 colleges and universities offering doctoral training programs in adult education, and approximately 140 other institutions of higher education offering some specified training in adult education. Some of the special programs emerging include education for aging,

[2] The President's Commission on National Goals, *Goals for Americans,* © 1960 by The American Assembly, Columbia University, New York. Reprinted by permission of Prentice-Hall, Inc., Englewood Cliffs, N.J., p. 91.

fundamental and literacy education, civic and public-affairs education, elementary and high school level education for adults, and community education about school needs and leadership training [46:110].

Informal Education.   In addition to the systematically organized approaches to education, there are many informal educational opportunities ranging from activities in a home to activities provided by social clubs, women's groups, labor unions, and industrial concerns. The President's Commission on National Goals recognized this informal structure and proposed that during the 1960s all organizations in our society should "seek to discover how they may help their members to continue personal growth. Each organization should find the specific ways in which it may be of help in (*a*) arranging for courses to be given by neighboring schools or universities; (*b*) assisting members to arrange group study programs; (*c*) building the philosophy of individual fulfillment into its organizational practices, so that every member has the opportunity to grow."[3]

The commission suggested that a more flexible system of credit by examination be devised so that assessment and certification of accomplishment within the informal structure would be recognized. The commission also suggested that by 1970 many leading universities or state boards of education should be offering credit by examination in the standard academic subjects.

SUMMARY

The patterns of school organization have been many and varied, depending upon the needs of different communities. With the passing decades, conditions have changed so markedly that these elements of organization have undergone considerable change.

Sincere efforts are being made to improve the organization of our schools. Very impressive strides are being made to consolidate certain districts in order to provide better school facilities, better teachers, and better education programs. School programs are being reorganized to provide greater continuity and educational effectiveness.

Traditionally and constitutionally, education in the United States is a state responsibility. Each state delegates such responsibilities to its local communities and encourages them to use a large measure of initiative, support, and control. However, in order to bring about greater equality of educational opportunity and to spread knowledge, understanding, and fellowship abroad in the world, the Federal government and even international organizations have assumed increasingly greater roles of leadership.

Attention has been given to the various organizational levels of educa-

---

[3] The President's Commission on National Goals, *Goals for Americans,* © 1960 by The American Assembly, Columbia University, New York. Reprinted by permission of Prentice-Hall, Inc., Englewood Cliffs, N.J., p. 94.

tion. Present practices, trends, and recommendations for improvements have been noted. Throughout the chapter it is evident that the organization and administration of our school are changing. Undoubtedly you can look forward to many more changes being made as educators and others work together in order to provide the best setting possible for the education of future generations. You have an opportunity to provide leadership in this great endeavor.

QUESTIONS FOR YOUR CONSIDERATION

1. What authority does your home state have for establishing a uniform public educational system?

2. What advantages and disadvantages do you see in having local communities responsible for providing educational facilities for their children?

3. What role does the board of education play in your home community? What are the occupational backgrounds of the board members? How representative are they of the entire community?

4. What qualifications should a school-board member have?

5. Many countries have ministries of education that exercise great control over the educational systems in their respective countries. Should the U.S. Office of Education exert a greater role of leadership?

6. What are the advantages of having a state superintendent of schools appointed by a state board of education rather than having him elected by popular vote? What are the disadvantages?

7. How do you account for the tremendous decrease in the number of school districts in the United States?

8. What advantages and disadvantages do you see in the self-contained classroom in the elementary school?

9. What behavior patterns are characteristic of junior high school pupils and what special provisions should be made in the school's program?

10. What do you consider to be the unique characteristics of the comprehensive high school?

11. What are your reactions to the recommendations of Conant in regard to the high school (see Resource Section for Part VI)?

12. How can the holding power of the secondary school be further increased?

13. What advantages do you see in regional associations of secondary schools and colleges?

14. Why have junior colleges developed more rapidly in the west than in the east?

ACTIVITIES FOR YOU TO PURSUE

1. Investigate and share with your colleagues specific details relating to the organization and support of the high school from which you were graduated.

2. Outline the boundary of your own school district. Ascertain the pupil population and the educational facilities available in the district. What do your findings suggest concerning the adequacy of your school-district organization?

3. Collect data upon the extent to which the number of one-teacher schools has been reduced in your state during the past 20 years.

4. List the criteria you would use to determine whether or not a school district should be consolidated with another?

5. Invite a school superintendent to discuss with your class the financial and organizational problems of his school.

6. Discuss with various school officials methods they use in grouping pupils. What are the advantages and disadvantages of each method?

7. How does your community provide for the education of youngsters who are deaf or blind or paralyzed to some extent? How does it provide for those who are extremely slow to learn or those who are unusually gifted? Describe the specialized school situations available for such persons.

8. Observe in a good junior high school to determine how provision is made for the efficient transition of pupils from elementary to senior high school. In what ways might this transition be improved still further?

9. Prepare a display of publications issued by the U.S. Office of Education and share the display with your colleagues.

17
FINANCING OUR SCHOOLS

What is your reaction to the fact that education is the largest single non-defense governmental business in the United States and that $18 billion was spent for public elementary and secondary education alone during the 1961–1962 school year? Perhaps you feel that such information is no concern of the teacher but rather of the statistician, the politician, or the public school administrator.

How do you react to the fact that, between the years of 1948 and 1960, Americans spent $78 billion for public elementary and secondary schools; while during this same period of time they spent $150 billion for tobacco, alcoholic beverages, and cosmetics; $127 billion for recreation; and $73 billion for highways? Perhaps these figures cause you to ask: "Don't Americans know the value of education?" By now it should be apparent that you have a responsibility as a teacher to be informed about matters of school finance so that you can inform adult and young citizens about the problems and possible solutions of school finance.

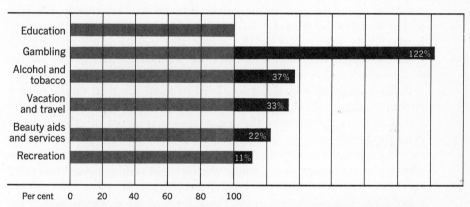

Figure 72. Comparison of the cost of education with other expenditures. How much can we afford to pay for education? (*Source:* McGraw-Hill Book Company, Inc.)

What happens in the future so far as school finance is concerned will affect your teaching salary, your personal and teaching welfare, and the facilities and equipment which you and your pupils will have in the important process of teaching and learning. Can our nation afford to educate an additional 1 million pupils a year during the decade 1960–1970? Can our nation afford to train and to hire an additional 437,000 instructional personnel and to construct 600,000 new classrooms during this period of time? In this chapter you will note the mounting costs of public education. Unless the American public is willing to absorb these mounting costs, how can we expect the quality of education and the welfare of teachers to improve?

In your many contacts with members of the community you will have the opportunity to acquaint them with the financial needs of schools in the future. (*Photograph from the film,* The Big Classroom *by the National Education Association.*)

Obviously, every teacher should feel a vital responsibility for understanding school finance to the extent that he will be able to interpret school costs to lay citizens. In fact, teachers should feel an increasing responsibility for convincing the public that even greater expenditures than those predicted should be made for schools in order to provide the quality of education which the future demands.

In your study of school finance, keep in mind the total public finance structure, since school finance is a branch of public finance. In other words, keep in perspective the importance and needs of other government-supported services and the relationship between factors such as public expenditures, population growth, and economic growth. For example, it is important to remember the fact that public expenditures and tax loads have increased in greater proportion than has the nation's population. The population in 1962 was less than 2.5 times the population of our nation in the early 1900s, but public expenditures were approximately 90 times that level. The nation's tax bill at all levels, including local, state, and Federal, was $100 billion in 1959 as compared with $1.4 billion in 1902 [56:25]. Knowledge of these trends provides you with a sufficiently broad public finance background to place local, state, and Federal financial support for education in the proper perspective.

Another important factor to remember is that expenditures for national defense in the future will undoubtedly have first priority. The increase or decrease in defense outlay will mean a more favorable or less favorable financial promise for nondefense projects, including education. Priority for national defense and international relations in the past is evident by the fact that expenditures for these functions combined were 293 times greater in 1959 than in 1902, while those for education were only 70 times greater [4:12].

These concepts, and others to follow in this chapter, should help you understand the basic principles of school finance. Emphasis, however, will be placed upon the modes of providing local, state, and Federal financial support for public elementary and secondary schools.

BASES OF CURRENT SCHOOL FINANCE PROBLEMS

The state's responsibility for maintaining and operating the American public school systems necessarily includes the obligation of each state to make provisions for financing its school system. Generally, the states have relied chiefly upon local financial support for public schools. At the turn of the twentieth century only 17 per cent of school funds were provided by the states. Since the economic depression in the 1930s, however, the amount of state funds to aid local school-district support has increased significantly. For the 1961–1962 school year, it was estimated that 40.2 per cent of the total school revenue in the United States was derived from state sources, 56.1 per cent from local sources, and 3.7 per cent from Federal sources.

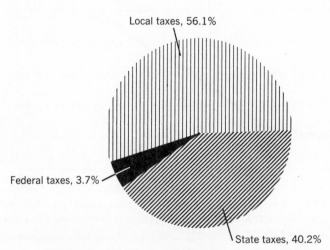

Local taxes, 56.1%

Federal taxes, 3.7%

State taxes, 40.2%

Figure 73.   Percentage distribution of school support in the United States. To what extent does your state deviate from this percentage distribution and how do you account for this deviation? (*Source:* National Education Association.)

As you read this chapter, keep in mind that the development of the public schools during the twentieth century has not been the same in all states, partly because each state has had different goals at different times. Other reasons for the variations in the development of public school programs among states include differences in tax systems, economic conditions, centralization of local school districts, political beliefs, fear of change, and willingness to provide funds for education [8:93–94].

As our nation has moved through the industrial revolution and into a scientific revolution, the educational system in each state has had to undergo varying adaptations to the changing economic and social conditions in order to best serve the educational needs of individuals and of society. Basic and intermediate school administrative units have not always been able to cope adequately with financial problems, partially because of constitutional and organizational limitations. Constitutional limitations have included debt limits and tax limits as well as provision for earmarked taxes. While earmarked taxes have assured districts of a definite source of income, educational services have been generally limited because local educational revenues have been tied to a yield from a tax whose rate has been difficult to increase. Small administrative units have often lacked an adequate tax base and sufficient pupil population to provide a quality educational program.

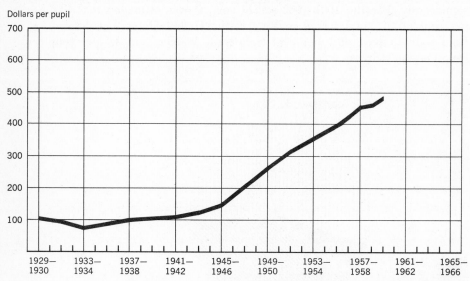

Dollars per pupil

Figure 74.   Total expenditure per pupil in average daily attendance 1929–1930 to 1959–1960. Has the upward trend in expenditure continued? (*Source:* U.S. Office of Education.)

In addition to the above factors, school finance problems are the result of five major forces: (1) record increases in school enrollment, (2) demand for greater quality in education, (3) rise in educational costs due to inflation, (4) extension of educational services, and (5) war-time backlog of school construction. Each of these forces will be discussed.

School Enrollment Increases.   The extent of increase in public school enrollments is indicated by the fact that in the decade of 1950–1960, there was an increase of 4 million children of preschool age, over 13.5 million in the 5–19 age group, and of over 15 million pupils in public and private elementary and secondary schools and colleges. In addition, more pupils were staying in school, as is evidenced by the fact that the average adult in 1961 had 11 years of education as compared with 8.4 years in 1940 [24:3].

The increase in public elementary and secondary school enrollment between 1950 and 1960 averaged 44.3 per cent in the United States. Four states had enrollment increases of over 100 per cent (Nevada—177.9 per cent; Alaska—165.0 per cent; Florida—128.0 per cent; and Arizona—127.6 per cent). California's school enrollment increased 95.1 per cent during this period of time.

Quality of Education. Our system of government, our economy, our position of world leadership, and the race for space have combined to bring education into national focus with emphasis upon the goal of quality education. Educational research is greatly concerned with the problem of relating the cost of education and with educational quality. One of the most ambitious research projects of this type has been the Quality Measurement Project of the New York State Education Department in which 70,000 youngsters have participated in a mass testing program over a three-year period as they moved from grade to grade. In this project it has been found that there is a partial correlation of .31 between expenditure levels and composite achievement-test scores for pupils in grade 7. The powerful effects of socioeconomic factors are indicated by the fact that there is a correlation of .32 between expenditure and the achievement of pupils of high socioeconomic status. For pupils of average socioeconomic status this correlation is only .04, and for pupils of low socioeconomic status the correlation is −.18 [56:76].

Another comprehensive research project, being conducted by Professor Kreitlow of Wisconsin, concerns the effects of school-district organization upon the quality of education. This longitudinal study was begun in 1949 with a study of youngsters who were in the first grade in five newly reorganized school districts and in five matched control communities. The effects of reorganization in terms of educational opportunities, achievement, cost, and social impact were measured at first, sixth, ninth, and twelfth grades, with follow-ups to be made for a five-year period after pupils had graduated from high school. Initial results indicated that both boys and girls in reorganized districts were ahead in 21 of 22 measures of achievement. In the ninth grade the results again favored those in reorganized districts [82:384–386].

It is important for you to follow the progress of these projects and become thoroughly conversant with the results since they may have a significant impact upon the future of education. They provide objective data with which you may be able to justify higher costs of education and reorganization of schools.

A number of curriculum revisions have been accomplished in numerous school districts since Sputnik No. 1 and the resultant cry for quality in the schools. Our affluent society has been taking stock of its values, and quality education is emerging as a vital want and need. As is true of almost everything else in life, quality products and programs cost more money.

Inflation.   According to the 1959 report of the Committee on Tax Education and School Finance of the National Education Association, the prices that state and local governments pay for their goods and services have risen faster since 1947 than those in any other major segment of the economy [116:26]. The economy as a whole experienced about a 30 per cent rise in prices from 1947 to 1957, while the price of state and local government services rose over 50 per cent during the same period. This is regarded as an adverse price development by economists as far as the state and local segment of the economy is concerned.

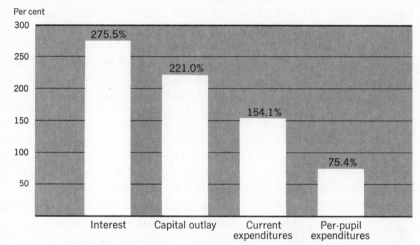

Figure 75.   Increases in school costs, 1949–1950 to 1959–1960. (*Source:* National Education Association.)

Extension of Educational Services.   In the previous chapter, attention was given to the tendency to extend formal education to 3-, 4-, and 5-year-old youngsters, and to increase higher-education opportunities. In addition, state legislatures have been placing more and more demands upon the public schools to provide greater amounts for guidance services, adult education, special education, and vocational education. Frequently the demands for these additional educational programs and services have been made without providing the necessary means to finance them.

School Construction.   Comparatively few new school buildings were erected during the years from 1930 through 1950 because of the national depression and war emergencies. By 1950 a backlog of needed construction, plus needed remodeling, faced many school communities. The problem was intensified by the postwar inflation which materially increased the cost of construction. Evidence of the school construction boom of the 1950s is offered by the fact that 44 per cent of the nation's classrooms available in 1961 were built during the 1950–1960 decade.

The nation's 35,330 school districts are generally faced with financial problems created by one or more of the forces described above. Solutions of the problem are not easy, but progress is being made through effective planning and through coordination of local and Federal government efforts.

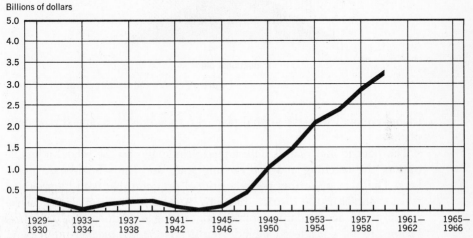

Billions of dollars

Figure 76. Trend in capital outlay expenditures for public schools, 1929–1930 to 1959–1960. Has the upward trend continued? (*Source:* U.S. Office of Education.)

THE SCHOOL BUDGET

In order to cope intelligently with financial problems created by forces such as those cited above, local school districts prepare long-term and annual school budgets. Effective school administrators and boards of education are planning educational programs and anticipating revenue needs for 10 to 20 years in the future. Long-term projections of pupil enrollments are made on the basis of each annual school census; long-term financing is exemplified by cumulative building levies which provide funds so that educational facilities can be partially paid for on an installment plan in advance of the actual construction of the facilities.

The Annual Budget. You will be personally interested in the annual budget presented in your school district each spring since it will reflect teacher-salary increases and other rewards for your professional efforts. You may have an opportunity to work with a committee of teachers, administrators, and school-board members on salary problems.

The annual fiscal budget, generally prepared for a calendar year, is a financial plan consisting of three aspects as exemplified in the budget

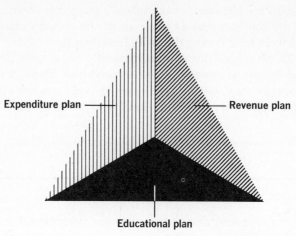

Expenditure plan ————

Revenue plan

Educational plan

Figure 77. Annual fiscal budget for schools.

triangle above: the educational plan, the spending plan, and the revenue plan.

The educational plan is determined principally by the school administration, the teaching and nonteaching staff, and the school-board members. The plan prescribes the educational program that is to be provided for the pupils in the district. Lay-citizen groups often participate in expressing and accumulating opinion concerning the educational program. Factors to be considered include pupil population, teacher-pupil ratio, curriculum, the program scope (i.e., kindergarten through junior college), state department directives, parental aspirations, the impact of technological changes upon teaching methods, and teacher quality.

In the spending plan, expenditures are determined by translating the accepted educational plan into costs. Expenditures are ordinarily classified to show the amount which will be spent for each educational function. Classifications generally include instruction; administration; fixed charges (rent and insurance); operation and maintenance of physical plant; services such as health, transportation and school lunch; summer school; community college; capital outlay; and debt service. Typical percentages of expenditures for the various functions are shown in Figure 78.

The revenue plan involves a listing of the sources of funds, other than those to be raised by local taxation, and the estimated amount of revenue to be received from each source. For example, state school authorities ordinarily let the local school administrators know how much money they can expect to receive from the state government. In addition, the local school administrator anticipates receipts from the Federal government as well as from tuition fees or other charges. Local property and/or nonproperty tax rates necessary to raise the balance of funds needed are then computed.

After the budget has been approved by the school board, the chief school administrator and the board ordinarily defend the budget at pub-

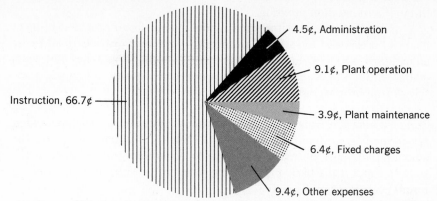

Figure 78. How the current school dollar is spent. (*Source:* American Book Company.)

lic hearings conducted by local and state tax commissioners. Such a system of checks and balances forces the school administration to review the allocation of resources for varied phases of the educational program at least once annually. Funds are then committed for expenditure, as defined by the spending plan, for the ensuing budget year.

STATE SCHOOL FINANCE PROGRAMS

The Rockefeller Brothers Fund publication indicates that: "all the problems of the schools lead us back sooner or later to one basic problem—financing" [121:33]. Likewise, solution of local school-district financial problems leads us back to the provision of the state for financing its schools. Local school districts have only the taxing authority delegated to them by the state government, and needed funds, other than those raised at the local level, must be provided by the state.

Since there are 50 state systems of education in the United States, there are 50 different systems of state school finance. The amount of state support, for example, ranges from 6 per cent in Nebraska and New Hampshire to 81 per cent in Delaware. A few states, such as Delaware and North Carolina, provide most of their school funds from state tax sources. The majority of states have favored a partnership plan of state and local support, with minor support from the Federal government.

State funds have been used in our nation's history to (1) help communities establish the operation of a school system; (2) afford relief to those districts unable to provide sufficient local funds; (3) encourage new programs (such as special education, audio-visual communications, and transportation) and support services (such as new buildings, salaries, textbooks, and pupil transportation); (4) provide emergency aid, such as in the 1930s, by relieving the tax burden on the property holder; (5) provide payments in lieu of taxes through property lost by local districts to new state parks or to new industry which received tax exemptions for a period of years; and (6) provide general support for schools through a foundation program.

As is evident, much of the state school aid has been provided to meet financial crises and to serve as an incentive for local districts to add new educational services. Such aid has been piecemeal and has not been made within the framework of a comprehensive and systematic state school-support program.

State Foundation Programs.   More than 40 states have developed what are termed "state foundation programs." Such a program designates the amount that must be made available to all administrative units in the state to support the basic instructional program considered to be essential for all youngsters in the state.

The steps in the development of a state foundation program include the following:

1. Definition of the educational program.
2. Translation of the educational program into costs necessary to provide the essential educational services.
3. Determination of the local district's share of cost according to measures of fiscal capacity. The tendency is for programs to require that wealthier districts pay a greater local share than districts of less wealth and conversely, that they receive less state aid than the poorer districts. This equalization concept is typical of many foundation programs.
4. Determination of the total state share to each district.

A state foundation program normally includes expenditures for current operation, school facilities, transportation, and special education. The scope of the program in some states includes nursery school through the junior college. Most of the existing programs provide funds for elementary and secondary schools enrolling grades 1 through 12.

State foundation programs attempt to guarantee all children in a state a respectable education. Funds are disbursed generally from general funds appropriated by the state legislature rather than from restricted earmarked funds. Local leeway is advisable, so that a local school district has power to tax itself to support a better program than is provided through the foundation support.

Effectiveness of a foundation program is geared to the adequacy of a state's tax system to finance the program. A state's tax system provides the means for both state and local governments to obtain needed revenue.

State Tax Systems.   Each state has its own system of taxes with different types of taxes, different items included in the tax base, and different rates of taxation. In addition, each state gives local units within its boundaries certain taxing privileges which often differ from those enjoyed by similar local units in adjoining states.

The reason for these great differences is that our present tax system has developed a little at a time. As changes occur in our economy and in the distribution and form of sources available for taxation, the old taxes become less effective and new ones must be added to the old to provide the necessary funds for governmental activities. The history of taxation indicates that a tax, once it is imposed, is rarely repealed.

Most, but not all, payments made to the government are taxes, and these payments are termed "revenues." Nonrevenue receipts by governments include such payments as fees and charges for services received, money obtained by borrowing through sale of bonds or otherwise, and income from sale of governmental property. In general, the primary purpose of a tax is to produce revenue for a unit of government. A secondary purpose in some cases is to regulate an activity.

The yield of a tax is of paramount importance. As you discuss problems of taxation with community members, use the following criteria for deciding what taxes are to be imposed in any unit of government, including school districts:

1. Stability. Does the tax provide sufficient funds in spite of economic conditions?
2. Flexibility. Is the tax able to meet changing conditions?
3. Equity. Does the tax treat alike all those in similar circumstances?
4. Economic effect. Does it interfere with desirable business activity in the state?
5. Convenience and enforceability. Is it convenient for the taxpayer and for the tax collector?
6. Directness. Is the tax directly and readily seen by the taxpayer as a contribution to the cost of government?
7. Economy of collection. Does it take a disproportionate percentage of the yield to assess and collect the tax in question?

Most states are relying upon sales and income taxes to finance state obligations. In 1960, the sales tax was employed by 34 states and was the main source of state tax revenue. In that year it yielded 24 per cent of the total state tax revenue in the nation, and between 35 and 50 per cent in a few states, such as Georgia, Hawaii, Illinois, Michigan, Missouri, and Washington [56:52]. In addition, municipal sales taxes have developed in 11 states, and these have lessened property tax rates for city functions and released more funds for school operation.

You probably will find that sales taxes will increase in importance over the years in state-local finance. Increasing the number of items to be taxed, rather than increasing sales tax rates on items currently taxed, will provide greater equity of taxation.

Thirty-one states have personal income taxes and thirty-five states have corporation taxes. The greatest problem encountered with personal income tax is enforcement. There is a need in most states for additional auditors to check accounts and returns on income taxes.

The advantage of the individual income and the general sales tax is that they have a broad tax base and have a capacity for producing a large amount of revenue at a relatively low rate. It is apparent that the use of many state taxes creates less taxpayer resistance than is encountered when a single source of tax revenue is used.

As noted earlier, state taxes, such as sales, income, and inheritance taxes, provide approximately 40 per cent spent for public elementary and secondary schools in the United States. Local school districts, on the average, provide the greater portion of school funds.

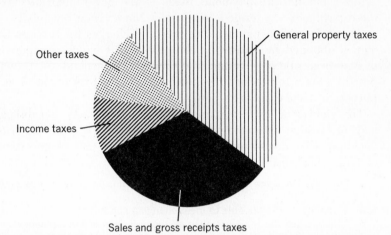

Figure 79.   Sources of state-local tax income in the United States, 1959. To what extent does the diagram represent sources of tax income in your state and local community? (*Source:* National Education Association.)

Local School District Taxes.   You can expect considerable comment about property taxes in your school district. For this reason, you will want to know for what purposes revenue from property taxes are used. Property taxes account for 98.6 per cent of all taxes collected from local sources by school districts. Property taxes originally developed as "ability to pay" taxes. It was assumed that the ability to pay taxes was evidenced by wealth, which in turn was evidenced by the amount of property an individual owned. However, in the early days of our nation, real property constituted 75 per cent of our wealth. It is estimated that today real property constitutes only 25 per cent of our wealth.

Since the advent of the industrial revolution in the United States and the resultant change in economic and social conditions, financial experts have been seeking new taxes to replace the property tax. This trend was accelerated particularly during the depression years of the 1930s, when many property owners were unable to pay their taxes. It is becoming more evident today that local school districts and other local governmental agencies in most states will continue to rely on the property tax, and emphasis will be on improvement rather than on replacement of the tax.

You will find school districts in the United States which must subject their budgets to the approval of taxpayers before a tax levy for school purposes is certified. You hear of school budgets being vetoed in many districts. Some claim that unreasonably high property tax rates are the cause of such a vote. On the other hand, it may be caused by opposition upon the part of voters to the total local, state, and Federal tax load rather than opposition to taxes for schools. Bear in mind that a school election operates at the "grass-roots" level. At a school election it is much easier for an individual to express his feelings toward the total tax burden than for him to be heard in the halls of the state legislature or in the halls of the United States Congress.

One advantage of the property tax is that it provides residual tax support for local services. Other taxes are established at a fixed rate, such as 3 per cent, whereas the property-tax rate is adjusted to each budget to provide that part of expenditures not covered by other receipts. Thus, a property-tax rate might be $3.65 per $100 of assessed valuation one year and $3.95 the following year in order to provide the balance of funds needed in each case.

Local school-district property-tax rates are usually expressed in terms of dollars per $100 of assessed valuation, or in terms of mills per dollar of assessed valuation. If your home, for example, is assessed at a valuation of $3,000 and the local school tax rate is $3.65 per $100, your school tax would equal 30 × 3.65, or a total of $109.50.

Since property taxes play such an important role in the support of schools, you may be interested in how this method of taxation may be improved. Suggestions for improving the administration of the property tax include the following: (1) assessment districts in most states should be enlarged, and assessors should be trained to effect uniform assessments; (2) the personal property tax, which has been a negotiated tax should be replaced, or personal property should be assessed according to a state classification of "book values"; (3) property-tax exemptions should be reviewed, since such exemptions result in higher tax rates to offset the exemption or to shift tax responsibility, sometimes unfairly; (4) the law pertaining to assessments should either be applied to all taxpayers or be changed.

Local Nonproperty Taxes.   States may give permission for local governments to levy nonproperty taxes. Some states have allowed their local units considerably more tax leeway than others. Local governments in 44 states levy a nonproperty tax; for example, cities in Alabama place a tax on admissions and amusements, alcoholic beverages, business gross receipts, cigarette and tobacco, gasoline, hotel occupancy, income, insurance, motor vehicle sales, public-utility gross receipts, sales, and soft drinks.

Local school districts in the United States have not generally been given authority to levy nonproperty taxes. In fact, most of the nonproperty taxes collected by school districts in the nation are collected in one state—Pennsylvania. Pennsylvania school districts may impose taxes on income, deed transfers, polls, mercantile licenses, trailers, business privileges, occupations, and amusements.

Combined State and Local Financial Effort.   Support of public education is becoming more and more a cooperative state-local enterprise in
the United States. For this reason you should examine state and local
taxes combined in order to better understand the great range of tax effort
within the United States.

You will find that in 1959, state and local tax revenue was highest in
California, amounting to $265 per capita, followed by New York, with a
per capita amount of $253, and Nevada, with a per capita amount of
$245. Combined state and local tax revenue exceeded $200 per capita in
13 states [24:20]. South Carolina, on the other hand, had a low per capita
state and local collection of $109.06. Other states with low per capita
collections were Kentucky, $110.40; Alabama, $111.31; and West Virginia,
$121.63.

A measure of financial effort is to be found in the relation between the
combined state-local tax collection and personal income. The tax load
was heaviest in Utah in 1959, when state and local taxes amounted to
$4.90 per $100 of personal income. The tax load was lightest in Connecticut (excepting the District of Columbia), where state and local taxes
amounted to $2.18 per $100 of personal income [107:32].

The combined state and local financial effort provided 96.3 per cent

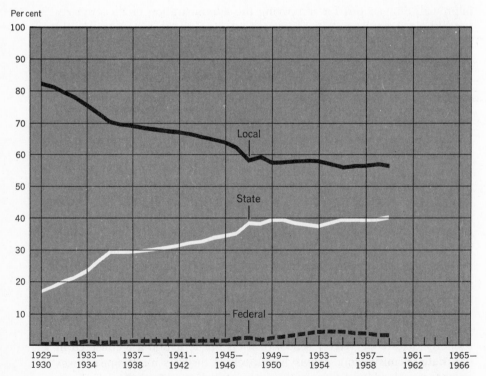

Figure 80.   Trends in school support represented by the percentage
of revenue for education derived from Federal, state, and local sources.
(*Source:* U.S. Office of Education.)

of the public elementary and secondary revenue in 1961–1962. Remaining funds were provided by the Federal government.

FEDERAL SUPPORT FOR EDUCATION

Although education in the United States is a state function, national interest in education has always been evident. An average of only 3.7 per cent of school revenue, however, came from Federal sources in 1961–1962. The number and variety of Federal aids, on the other hand, indicate a national interest and concern for public schools.

The Federal government has been aiding education for over 175 years. During this period of time, more than 150 Federal laws regarding support for education have been passed. Several specific programs for which Federal appropriations are being made regularly are listed below [74:1–2]:

Atomic Energy Commission Grants to Colleges
Books for the Blind
Civil Defense Education
College Housing
College Student Loans
Education for the Blind
Education in Fishery Trades
Education of Military Personnel
Education of Public Health Personnel
Education of the Indians
Educational Exchange Programs
National Library of Medicine
Office of Education
Police Training Schools
Practical Nurse Training
Public Assistance Consultation and Training
Public Health Research
Research
Scholarships
School Lunch Program

School Milk Program
Schools at Military Installations
FBI National Academy
Fellowships
Guidance, Counseling and Testing
Improvement of Educational Statistics
International Education
Kings Point Merchant Marine Academy
Land-Grant Colleges
Language Development
Library Services
Meteorological Education and Training
Science, Mathematics and Foreign Language Institutes
Support for Federally Affected Areas
Traineeships for Health Personnel
Training of Personnel in Public Welfare
Vocational Education
Vocational Training for Indians
Veterans Education
War Orphans Education

The statement given in Section 101 of Public Law 85–864, commonly known as the National Defense Education Act (NDEA) of 1958, represents a typical Congressional statement of interest in education:

The Congress hereby finds and declares that the security of the Nation requires the fullest development of the mental resources and technical skills of its young men and women. The present emergency demands that additional and more adequate educational opportunities be made available. The defense of this Nation depends upon the mastery of modern techniques developed from complex scientific principles. It depends as well upon the discovery and development of new principles, new techniques, and new knowledge. . . .

We must increase our efforts to identify and educate more of the talent of our Nation. . . .

The Congress reaffirms the principle and declares that the States and local communities have and must retain control over and primary responsibility for public education. The national interest requires, however, that the Federal Government give assistance to education for programs which are important to our defense.

Types of Federal Interest in Education.   Federal interest in public education may be classified under four categories: (1) unconditional land grants; (2) conditional grants for advanced education; (3) conditional grants for secondary education; and (4) emergency grants.

As you will recall, beginning with the Ohio Act of 1802, the Federal government *unconditionally* granted one section or more of land to new states for the use of schools. Money from the sale of these lands totalled approximately a half billion dollars. The Federal government never officially questioned the states concerning school-land policies, and there was no Federal control over expenditures.

Conditional grants of land for advanced education began under terms of the Morrill Act in 1862. Beginning with the second Morrill Act, passed in 1890, and continuing with supplemental acts, land-grant colleges or universities have received Federal appropriations. In 1960 these appropriations provided each land-grant institution with $70,000 in flat grants. In addition, a total of $1,501,500 was allocated to the states in proportion to population.

The Morrill Act and the supplemental acts, which are examples of conditional grants for advanced education, introduced the following changes in Federal educational policy: (1) some control by specifying programs (land-grant institutions were to include agriculture and mechanical arts in their curriculum as well as military science and tactics); (2) annual appropriations for programs in addition to the original land grants; (3) reimbursement of the state after Federal authorities were reassured that money had been spent for the purposes designated by law.

Conditional Federal grants for secondary schools is illustrated by the Smith-Hughes Act in 1917, followed by supplemental acts, which provides appropriations annually for vocational education at the secondary school level. Federal funds allocated for vocational education of less-than-college level totalled nearly $48 million in 1959–1960. Under the Smith-Hughes Act, the Federal appropriations are matched dollar for dollar by the states.

A fourth type of Federal support was in operation during the depression years of the 1930s when the Federal government provided several hundred million dollars annually during the emergency period to aid distressed school districts. This aid also included assistance for needy secondary, college, and university students so that they might continue their education during the depression, as well as provisions for nursery schools, literacy classes, correspondence instruction on both secondary and college levels, vocational education, parent education, work for unemployed teachers, and funds for school buildings.

Recent legislation of the emergency type includes provision for Federal assistance where both increases in school enrollments and reductions in taxable valuations due to the Federal purchase of property have continued to burden certain communities in financing school services. Public Laws 874 and 815 are known as SAFA ("School Assistance to Local Educational Agencies in Federally Affected Areas"). During the 1950–1960 decade these two laws provided nearly $2 billion to over 5,250 school districts.

Public Law 874 approved contributions, beginning in 1950, toward the "maintenance and operation" of school districts which suffered a financial burden due to the provision of educational services for children whose parents are employed on Federal property or to sudden substantial increases in enrollments because of Federal activities. In 1960, applications for Public Law 874 funds were received from 3,963 local educational agencies in the 50 states, Guam, and the Virgin Islands; and all but 142 of these applications were declared eligible. A total of $177.6 million was appropriated for the eligible districts which involved more than 1½ million federally connected children [178:17].

During the 1950s, Congress appropriated, under Public Law 815, approximately $926.6 million for assistance in the construction of minimum school facilities for federally connected children. Minimum facilities include instructional and auxiliary rooms and initial equipment, but do not include auditoriums and gymnasiums.

Another recent program of federal support for education is exemplified by the National Defense Education Act (NDEA) of 1958. This act contains 10 titles that authorize funds to the extent of more than $1 billion for grants and loans over a period of a few years. Use of the funds is specified by the Act, and states are required to match the Federal funds. Funds have been provided for: loans and fellowships to students; strengthening instruction in mathematics, science, and foreign language; guidance counseling and testing; area vocational education; research in uses of television, radio, and movies; science information service; and improving statistical service. This act touches levels of education from the elementary schools through the graduate schools, both public and private.

The NDEA represents an expression of the Federal government's concern over the fact that the long struggle of the free world against Communism could be won or lost in the classrooms. Particular interest was shown in improving mathematics, science, and foreign-language instruction. Thus, the Federal government encouraged improvement in these and other educational areas by offering financial incentives to the states.

U.S. Office of Education Grants to States.   In 1960, approximately $350 million in support of education was disbursed by the U.S. Office of Education. The largest expenditure was for Public Law 874. This figure does not include expenditures for education by the other cabinet departments, such as the $300 million expended for school lunch programs by the Department of Agriculture and the $45 million expended for the education of Indians by the Department of the Interior.

The Issue of Federal Aid to Education.   The question of the role of the Federal government in school finance has been heatedly debated, particularly in the postwar years, by such varied groups as PTA organizations, informal social groups, labor and management representatives, state legislators, and, of course, members of the Congress. Virtually all of these people are sincerely devoted to public education and to the improvement of public education.

Although most of the Federal aid for education in the past was geared to support a specific educational program, interest in the general support of education by the Federal government is increasing. Some proponents of general support are advocating that funds be made available to states for educational purposes and that the states be allowed to spend the money for any educational expense they choose. Other proponents of general support suggest some Federal control by proposing that the funds be used for school construction and/or for teachers' salaries.

Justification for general support by the Federal government is based primarily upon the need to equalize educational opportunity in the

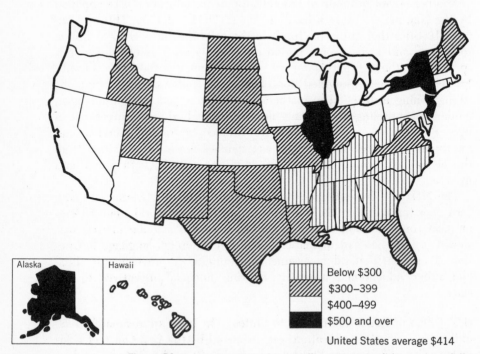

Below $300
$300–399
$400–499
$500 and over

United States average $414

Figure 81.   Average current expenditures per pupil in average daily attendance for public elementary and secondary schools 1961–1962.
(*Source:* National Education Association.)

United States, a need evidenced by the great range in the amount spent per pupil and the capabilities of the 50 states to support an adequate educational program (see Figure 81). Although a high expenditure of money does not guarantee a better quality of education, it is reasonable to assume that the educational opportunities of boys and girls in New York are greater than those in Mississippi.

Differences in the amounts spent per pupil in average daily attendance by the various states do not necessarily indicate differences in the willingness of the states to support education. In many cases they represent differences in the resources available. Some of the states actually spend more, in proportion to their personal incomes, to support their schools than do states having high personal incomes (see Figure 82). Since these states seem to have little prospect of increasing expenditures through state and local funds, a number of educators advocate the need for additional Federal assistance to these states.

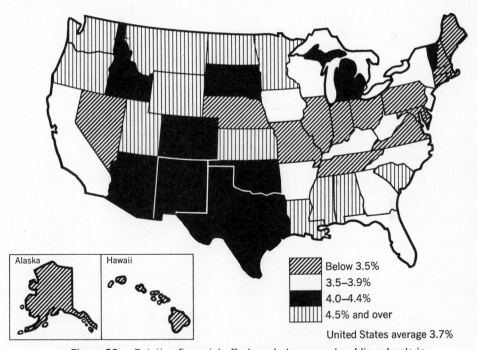

Below 3.5%
3.5–3.9%
4.0–4.4%
4.5% and over
United States average 3.7%

Figure 82. Relative financial effort made to support public schools in 1960–1961, expressed as a per cent of personal income for 1960. Compare the relative effort of various states with the amount of expenditure indicated in Figure 81. What do these differences mean and what are the implications for the future financing of public education?
(*Source:* National Education Association.)

Undoubtedly you are forming or have formed your viewpoint concerning Federal aid for schools. Do you have any arguments in addition to those listed on the next page [adapted, 30:15–16]:

TYPICAL PRO AND CON ARGUMENTS ON FEDERAL AID TO EDUCATION

Pro	Con

1. Education is a Federal problem

Federal assistance has been an accepted part of our tradition from the Land Ordinance of 1785 through the National Defense Education Act.

Local governments can best determine the needs of their schools, and the several states are responsible for education. Federal control would likely follow Federal aid.

2. Classroom shortage is critical

Survey in the fall of 1960 showed the shortage had climbed to 142,000 classrooms, as compared with a 135,000 shortage in fall of 1959. There are nearly 2 million pupils in excess of normal classroom capacity.

State and local agencies have done much to meet the needs for new school construction. The rate of increase of enrollment is expected to taper off, so that new construction can eliminate the backlog soon.

3. Teachers' salaries are very inadequate

Many teachers who leave the profession for other occupations cite their low pay as a principal reason. By the fall of 1960, there were 91,000 persons teaching with substandard credentials.

From 1953 to 1961, the average teacher's salary went up 52 per cent as compared with a 32 per cent rise in per capita income generally. Higher salaries will not guarantee better teachers. Federal money for teachers' salaries on an emergency basis would be dangerous and difficult to discontinue.

4. More money for public education is essential

The most pressing problems of public education can be traced to lack of money. State and local sources cannot keep up even with present needs.

The real problem of the schools is not more money but inadequate use of manpower and facilities.

5. Federal taxation is best source of additional funds for education

The Federal government already collects nearly three-fourths of all tax moneys and can most effectively tax personal and corporate income. The Federal government can put the money in areas where the needs are greatest.

The Federal government has only the tax resources of the 50 states, and if it takes a larger tax bite this leaves even less for state and local governments. Most states are not as debt-ridden as the Federal government and are not asking for Federal aid to education.

6. Federal control of public education is not a real danger

The Federal government has been aiding education for almost two centuries without any real evidence of Federal control.

The Federal government imposes policies on state and local school authorities and can exercise indirect control by threatening to withhold funds.

PUBLIC FUNDS AND THE NONPUBLIC SCHOOLS

Nonpublic or private schools are not part of the state school systems but are under the immediate operational control of a private individual or organization. The state, under its police power (i.e., the state's power to safeguard the health, morals, and safety of its citizens), may regulate and supervise nonpublic schools for the purpose of ensuring each child an education equivalent to the education offered in public schools.

It is the established right of parents and guardians in the United States to send their children to nonpublic schools. Approximately 14 per cent of the total number of elementary and secondary pupils were enrolled in nonpublic schools in 1960. Nonpublic school enrollments have steadily increased since the turn of the twentieth century when they accounted for 8 per cent of the total elementary and secondary enrollment.

Nonpublic schools may be sectarian schools, which are operated under religious auspices, or they may be nonsectarian. They may be profit or nonprofit organizations and are generally supported by private funds.

An issue since the establishment of the American public school systems, currently being debated in 1962, is whether or not public financial aid, particularly Federal aid, can be provided for the support of sectarian schools—schools which account for over 90 per cent of the nonpublic education institutions. The constitutional provisions separating church and state prevent direct aid to sectarian schools. However, the main point of the issue is whether or not indirect public financial aid can be provided.

Courts of the several states differ with regard to indirect aid—the crux being what is or what is not indirect aid. For example, as has been indicated previously, textbooks have been given to parochial school pupils in Louisiana and Mississippi under a child-benefit theory, which is based upon the premise that a child rather than an institution receives the benefit of a service. The child-benefit theory has been approved by the Supreme Court of the United States but has not been approved by the majority of state courts.

Proponents of general Federal aid to sectarian elementary and secondary schools argue that public funds are used to finance fire, police, and other governmental services to people of all religious sects, and that aid to sectarian schools is analogous. Opponents of general Federal aid to sectarian schools are fearful that such assistance would lead to the eventual destruction of the public school system.

It seems likely that during the 1960s the United States Supreme Court will be faced with the problem of clarifying the legality of the use of public funds in financing nonpublic school services.

SCHOOL FINANCE IN THE 1960s

It is generally accepted in the United States that it is the obligation of the free public school to provide for every person the educational opportunity which will enable him to be an intelligent and responsible citizen. Such an objective requires a quality program of education. The quality program which Americans seem to be accepting for the 1960s will generally consist of provision for a student's education, typically from kindergarten through junior college; competent teachers in each classroom plus adequate auxiliary services such as counseling and health; functional, healthful, and safe school buildings; and programs appropriate for exceptional children, including both the gifted and retarded.

School finance needs in the 1960s will depend principally upon the quality program demanded by citizens, upon pupil enrollments, and upon teachers' salaries. A brief summary of apparent financial needs for public elementary and secondary schools and for higher education follows. Probable school finance trends are listed in conclusion.

Public Elementary and Secondary Schools.   In Table 4 you noted the anticipated increase in public school enrollments during the 1960–1970 decade. This will mean an increase of nearly 1 million pupils a year as noted previously. This increase in enrollment will require that at least 400,000 additional teachers be hired, and at least 600,000 new classrooms be constructed during this period of time.

It is probable that teachers' salaries will need to increase at a rate greater than that of the annual increase in the gross national product if school districts are to compete favorably for trained personnel. Forecasts of economists indicate that the GNP will increase at a rate of 3 per cent or more each year until 1970. If teachers' salaries increase even at the 3 per cent rate a year, salaries will be 30 per cent higher in 1970 than in 1960.

Figure 83 indicates various predictions of school costs in 1970. One of

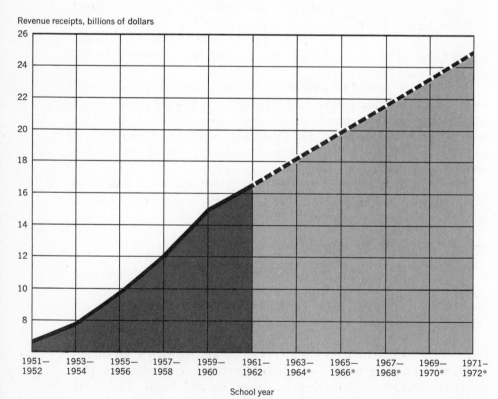

Revenue receipts, billions of dollars

*Estimates.

Figure 83.   Past and projected increase in public school revenue receipts.
(*Source:* National Education Association and American Book Company.)

the highest projections of expenditures for public elementary and secondary schools for the 1969–1970 school year is $30 million [121:34]. Obviously, the 1960s will call for new sources of revenue to supplement existing revenue sources. The amount of revenue available will also depend on the responsiveness of present tax sources. These factors will be influenced by the amount of economic growth which our nation experiences during this period of time.

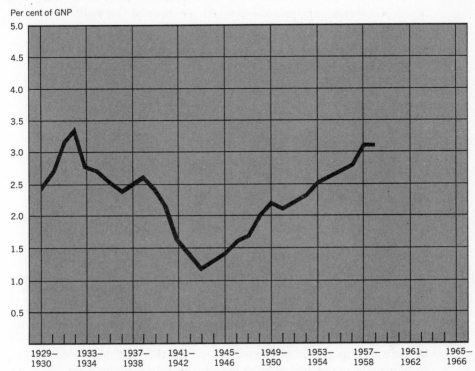

Figure 84. Total expenditures for public schools as a per cent of the gross national product of the United States, 1929–1930 to 1958–1959. Will we be able to afford the increased cost of schools reflected in Figure 83? (*Source:* U.S. Office of Education.)

Higher Education. The 2,000 public and private institutions of higher education in the United States expended approximately $4 billion for programs of instruction in 1960 besides approximately $1 billion for buildings, equipment, and land [132:8]. It is expected that colleges will add students at the average rate of 200,000 a year and that enrollments will double between 1960 and 1975 [17:10].

Doubling the enrollment between 1960 and 1975 will require at least a doubling of total current education and general expenditures for higher education [132:8]. By 1965, according to a conservative estimate [132:9], an annual capital outlay between $2 billion and $2.25 billion will be required. This amount would be three times the amount spent for capital outlay in 1955–1956.

Russell [132:9] feels that between 1970 and 1975 the above factors, plus the added factors of a possible doubling of faculty salaries and of continued inflation, will mean that requirements for financial support of higher education will increase five or six times over the total amount expended in 1960.

Four sources of financial support for institutions of higher learning are of major importance: endowments, gifts and grants, student fees, and appropriations from governments. Appropriations from local, state, and Federal governments provide over 60 per cent of the funds for public higher education.

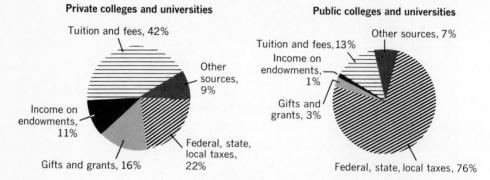

Private colleges and universities

Tuition and fees, 42%

Other sources, 9%

Income on endowments, 11%

Gifts and grants, 16%

Federal, state, local taxes, 22%

Public colleges and universities

Other sources, 7%

Tuition and fees, 13%

Income on endowments, 1%

Gifts and grants, 3%

Federal, state, local taxes, 76%

Figure 85.   Approximate percentage distribution, according to sources, of the educational dollar for higher education in the United States. Philanthropy and taxes share college costs with the student.
(*Source:* U.S. Office of Education.)

It is expected that all sources of support for higher education will increase in the 1960s. The big question is whether there will be a new form of state tax for public higher education. In the past, higher education, in general, has not had the benefit of any new taxes or earmarked tax sources for its support. It is likely that Federal aid for public and private higher education will increase at a faster rate than increases in aid from other sources.

Trends in School Finance.   During the 1960s it is highly probable that you will see the following trends in public school finance:

1. Elimination from school finance programs of features that help perpetuate poorly organized school districts.
2. Continuation of the property tax as a primary local school-district tax source.
3. Improvement of equalization of property assessments by state authorities.
4. Tendency for states to finance an increasing share of public education, primarily through state foundation programs. Foundation programs will gradually include provision for operation, capital outlay, and debt service.
5. Increase of Federal support through general grants administered through state departments of education and without additional Federal control.

SUMMARY

Education is the largest single nondefense government enterprise. Approximately 40 per cent of public school revenue in the United States is derived from state sources, 56 per cent from local sources, and 4 per cent from Federal sources.

Since each state has its own school financial system, it is to be expected that there is considerable variation among the states in the manner of financing education. However, each state delegates a large measure of responsibility for education to its local communities and encourages them to use a large amount of initiative, support, and control. In order to provide a greater amount of equality of educational opportunities, state governments have had to provide increasing amounts of support. The Federal government, since the Ordinance of 1787, has continued to exercise a definite interest in education.

Increasing enrollments and demands for more and better education will necessitate tremendous increases to be made in the amount of money spent for education on all levels. The extent to which the general public will be willing to absorb these mounting costs will depend, in part, upon each citizen having a clear understanding of the need for more school revenue, being convinced of the economic value of education, and being willing to provide greater support for the education of all the children of all the people. As a teacher, you will have a responsibility for fostering increasingly greater amounts of support for education. Your success and happiness in the profession are integrally related to the problems of school finance.

QUESTIONS FOR YOUR CONSIDERATION

1. Why has the amount of state funds to aid local school districts increased significantly since the depression in the 1930s? Will this trend continue?

2. How does your home state compare with other states and with the national average in the amount of money it spends on education and in the effort it makes to support public education? What is the average cost per classroom unit?

3. What are the sources of school revenue in your home community? Do these seem to be the best sources?

4. To what extent are Federal moneys used for education in your home town? What percentage of total school costs are met by Federal support? What specific school affairs does the Federal program support?

5. Is your home community able to support a quality program of public education or do you believe that more financial assistance should be provided by the state?

6. Of what significance are the Quality Measurement Project of the New York State Education Department and the comprehensive research project being conducted by Professor Kreitlow?

7. Do you agree with the statement in the Rockefeller Brothers Fund publication that "all the problems of the schools lead us back sooner or later to one basic problem—financing"? Explain.

8. As you see it, what are the arguments for and against the use of public tax money to support nonpublic schools?

9. What major differences in principles of school finance might be found in democratic and totalitarian nations?

10. What solutions can you propose for financing higher education within the next decade?

ACTIVITIES FOR YOU TO PURSUE

1. Analyze the amount of money your home state spends for education in one year. If possible, compare this amount to expenditures made for tobacco and liquor products.

2. Organize a panel to discuss the advantages and disadvantages of having local communities primarily responsible for providing educational facilities for their children.

3. Analyze a local school-district budget and prepare a bar graph indicating the percentage of the budget devoted to each educational function, such as administration, instruction, maintenance, etc.

4. Invite a school superintendent to discuss with your class the financial problems of his school.

5. Organize a panel to debate the advantages and disadvantages of Federal aid to education.

6. Make a study of the various grants for research in education being made by the U.S. Office of Education. In what ways may these grants improve educational practices?

7. Write a skit to portray the personalities who are striving to cut taxes in your home community. Analyze the values these people seem to hold.

8. Study the various countries in the world for the purpose of determining any relationship that may exist in regard to good education and national wealth.

RESOURCE SECTION FOR PART VI

- Recommendations of Conant

- Sample Application Form for a Teaching Position

- Suggested Films, Filmstrips, and Recordings

- Suggested Readings

- Figure Credits

• RECOMMENDATIONS OF CONANT[1]

The following recommendations were submitted by Conant for the improvement of public secondary education in the United States:

1. *The counseling system.* In a satisfactory school system the counseling should start in the elementary school, and there should be good articulation between the counseling in the junior and senior high schools if the pattern is 6-3-3 or between the counseling in the elementary school and the high school if the system is organized on an 8-4 basis. There should be one full-time counselor (or guidance officer) for every two hundred fifty to three hundred pupils in the high school. The counselors should have had experience as teachers but should be devoting virtually full time to the counseling work; they should be familiar with the use of tests and measurements of the aptitudes and achievement of pupils. The function of the counselor is not to supplant the parents but to supplement parental advice to a youngster. To this end, the counselor should be in close touch with the parent as well as the pupil. Through consultation, an attempt should be made each year to work out an elective program for the student which corresponds to the student's interest and ability as determined by tests of scholastic aptitude, the recorded achievement as measured by grades in courses, and by teachers' estimates. The counselors should be sympathetic to the elective programs which develop marketable skills; they should also understand the program for the slow readers and be ready to cooperate with the teachers of this group of students.

2. *Individualized programs.* It should be the policy of the school that every student has an individualized program; there would be no classification of students according to clearly defined and labeled programs or tracks such as "college-preparatory," "vocational," "commercial." In advising the student as to his elective program, the counselor will be guided by the minimum program recommended as a matter of school policy for the academically talented or by recommended sequences leading to the development of skills marketable on graduation. It will turn out that many students of similar ability and vocational interests will have almost identical programs, but a student who has elected an academic sequence may shift to a vocational sequence and vice versa. Furthermore, with individualized programs, the students themselves do not feel that they are labeled according to the program they have chosen in the ninth or tenth grade. If flexibility is combined with a declaration of policy in regard to the programs for the academically talented and if a good guidance service is available, the academic inventory should show results as satisfactory as the results in a school which has a clear-cut academic or college-preparatory track.

3. *Required programs for all.* The requirements for graduation for all students should be as follows: four years of English, three or four years of social studies—including two years of history (one of which should be American history) and a senior course in American problems or American government—one year of mathematics in the ninth grade (algebra or general mathematics), and at least one year of science in the ninth or tenth grade, which might well be biology or general physical science. By a year, I mean that a course is given five periods a week throughout the academic year or an equivalent amount of time. This academic program of general education involves nine or ten courses with homework to be taken in four years and occupies more than half the time of most students, whatever their elective programs.

4. *Ability grouping.* In the required subjects and those elected by students with a wide range of ability, the students should be grouped according to ability, subject by subject. For example, in English, American history, ninth-grade algebra, biology, and physical science, there should be at least three types of classes—one for the more able in the subject, another for the large group whose ability is about average, and another for the very slow readers who should be handled by special teachers. The middle group might be divided into two or three sections according to the students' abilities in the subject in question. This type of grouping is not to be confused with

---

[1] James Bryant Conant, *The American High School Today*, McGraw-Hill Book Company, Inc., New York, 1959, pp. 44–76. Material used by permission of the publisher.

across-the-board grouping according to which a given student is placed in a particular section in *all* courses. Under the scheme here recommended, for example, a student may be in the top section in English but the middle section in history or ninth-grade algebra.

5. *A supplement to a high school diploma.* The awarding of a diploma is evidence only that a student has (1) completed the required work in general education to the best of his ability, and (2) has finished satisfactorily a certain sequence of elective courses. In addition to the diploma, each student should be given a durable record of the courses studied in four years and the grades obtained. The existence of such a record should be well publicized so that employers ask for it rather than merely relying on a diploma when questioning an applicant for a job about his education. The record might be a card that could be carried in a wallet.

6. *English composition.* The time devoted to English composition during the four years should occupy about half the total time devoted to the study of English. Each student should be required to write an average of one theme a week. Themes should be corrected by the teacher. In order that teachers of English have adequate time for handling these themes, no English teacher should be responsible for more than one hundred pupils.

To test the ability of each student in English composition, a schoolwide composition test should be given in every grade; in the ninth and eleventh grades, these composition tests should be graded not only by the teacher but by a committee of the entire school. Those students who do not obtain a grade on the eleventh-grade composition test commensurate with their ability as measured by an aptitude test should be required to take a special course in English composition in the twelfth grade.

7. *Diversified programs for the development of marketable skills.* Programs should be available for girls interested in developing skills in typing, stenography, the use of clerical machines, home economics, or a specialized branch of home economics which through further work in college might lead to the profession of dietitian. Distributive education should be available if the retail shops in the community can be persuaded to provide suitable openings. If the community is rural, vocational agriculture should be included. For boys, depending on the community, trade and industrial programs should be available. Half a day is required in the eleventh and twelfth grades for this vocational work. In each specialized trade, there should be an advisory committee composed of representatives of management and labor. Federal money is available for these programs.

The school administration should constantly assess the employment situation in those trades included in the vocational programs. When opportunities for employment in a given trade no longer exist within the community, the training program in that field should be dropped. The administration should be ready to introduce new vocational programs as opportunities open in the community or area. In some communities, advanced programs of a technical nature should be developed; these programs often involve more mathematics than is usually required for the building trades or auto mechanics programs.

As stated in Recommendation 3, the students enrolled in programs which develop marketable skills should also be enrolled in English, social studies, and other courses required for graduation. Furthermore, efforts should be made to prevent isolation from the other students. Homerooms may be effective means to this end (see Recommendation 20).

8. *Special consideration for the very slow readers.* Those in the ninth grade of the school who read at a level of the sixth grade or below should be given special consideration. These pupils should be instructed in English and the required social studies by special teachers who are interested in working with such students and who are sympathetic to their problems. Remedial reading should be part of the work, and special types of textbooks should be provided. The elective programs of these pupils should be directed toward simple vocational work, and they should be kept out of the regular vocational programs for boys, the distributive education program, and the

regular commercial program for girls. These students should not be confused with mentally retarded students. The education of the mentally retarded is a special problem which in some states is also handled in the regular high school through special instruction and the use of special state funds.

9. *The programs of the academically talented.* A policy in regard to the elective programs of academically talented boys and girls should be adopted by the school to serve as a guide to the counselors. In the type of school I am discussing the following program should be strongly recommended as a minimum:

Four years of mathematics, four years of one foreign language, three years of science, in addition to the required four years of English and three years of social studies; a total of eighteen courses with homework to be taken in four years. This program will require at least fifteen hours of homework each week.

Many academically talented pupils may wish to study a second foreign language or an additional course in social studies. Since such students are capable of handling twenty or more courses with homework, these additional academic courses may be added to the recommended minimum program. If the school is organized on a seven- or eight-period day (Recommendation 12), at least one additional course without homework (for example, art or music) may also be scheduled each year.

If as school policy a minimum academic program including both mathematics and a foreign language is recommended to the academically talented pupils and their parents, the counselors will have the problem of identifying as early as possible the members of the group. It may well be that, in the next lower 10 or 20 per cent of the boys and girls in terms of scholastic aptitude on a national basis, there are a number who ought to be guided into similar but less rigorous programs.

10. *Highly gifted pupils.* For the highly gifted pupils some type of special arrangement should be made. These pupils of high ability, who constitute on a national basis about 3 per cent of the student population, may well be too few in number in some schools to warrant giving them instruction in a special class. In this case, a special guidance officer should be assigned to the group as a tutor and should keep in close touch with these students throughout their four years of senior high schoolwork. The tutor should see to it that these students are challenged not only by course work but by the development of their special interests as well. The identification of the highly gifted might well start in the seventh or eighth grade or earlier.

If enough students are available to provide a special class, these students should take in the twelfth grade one or more courses which are part of the Advanced Placement Program. This program has been developed in recent years by schools and colleges working cooperatively under the aegis of the College Entrance Examination Board. Under the program a student in the twelfth grade may take such courses as college mathematics, college English, or college history and, after passing suitable examinations, may be given college credit for the courses and also sophomore standing in these subjects. This program should be adopted not only because of the benefits which accrue to the students involved, but because it may well have a good influence on students of somewhat less ability by raising the tone of the whole academic program. Information about this program may be obtained by writing to the Director of the Advanced Placement Program, College Entrance Examination Board, 425 117th Street, New York 27, New York.

11. *The academic inventory.* In order to provide meaningful statistics about the education of the academically talented, a school board through the superintendent should ask the principal each year to provide an academic inventory. As explained earlier, the academic inventory summarizes the programs of the academically talented students in the senior class without giving their names. In a school in which the range of intellectual ability corresponds to the national norm, 15 per cent of the students would be included in this inventory. In other schools the percentage may vary. The academic inventory should include information as to what per cent of the academically talented boys and girls went on to a two-year college, a four-year college, or a university. This academic inventory of the graduating class might well be published each year.

12. *Organization of the school day.* The school day should be so organized that there are at least six periods in addition to the required physical education and driver education which in many states occupy at least a period each day. A seven- or eight-period day may be organized with periods as short as forty-five minutes. Under such an organization, laboratory periods as well as industrial arts courses should involve double periods.

The flexibility provided by such an arrangement is to be contrasted with the rigidity of that of the six-period day. With a six-period day, one period of which is taken up by physical education, the academically talented student cannot elect the wide academic program recommended above and at the same time elect art, music, and practical courses. The importance of this recommendation can hardly be over-emphasized in connection with the education of the academically talented students.

13. *Prerequisites for advanced academic courses.* Standards in advanced courses should be such that those who enroll in each successive course of a sequence have demonstrated the ability required to handle that course. To this end, admission to eleventh-grade mathematics should depend upon the student's receiving at least a C in tenth-grade mathematics, and for admission to twelfth-grade mathematics at least a C should be required in the eleventh-grade course. Similarly, if the physics course is given in the twelfth grade, it should be open only to those students who have studied three years of mathematics and obtained a grade of at least C in each course. Also, in the foreign language sequence, a grade of C should be required for entry into the second-year course.

14. *Students should not be given a rank in class according to their grades in all subjects.* In many schools, it is customary to designate a rank in class on graduation as determined by the marks received; the position of valedictorian is usually held by the student whose rank is number one. The ranking is calculated by averaging the grades in all subjects taken during the four years. I have found that in many schools the desire to rank high has led bright students to elect easy courses in order to obtain high grades. This fact emerges clearly from an examination of many programs sent to us by schools as part of their academic inventories. The use by some colleges and universities of rank in class as the basis of their admission policies has increased this tendency of bright boys and girls to avoid stiff programs. Following the practice in at least one school visited, I strongly recommend that the graduating class not be ranked on the basis of grades obtained in all subjects and that a valedictorian not be named on this basis. Admission officers in colleges and universities should be urged to examine the transcript of a student's entire record rather than to rely on the misleading rank in class. The main purpose of studying a foreign language is to obtain something approaching a mastery of that language. And by a mastery is surely meant the ability to read the literature published in the language and, in the case of a modern language, to converse with considerable fluency and accuracy with an inhabitant of the country in question.

15. *Academic honors list.* At the end of each marking period, a list should be published of the students who had elected courses recommended for the academically talented and had made an average grade of B. On graduation a notation might be made on the diploma if the student had placed on the academic honors list in all four years.

In order to provide an incentive for the election of a meaningful nonacademic sequence, those students whose achievement was outstanding in the courses that are usually labeled "commercial" or "vocational" should receive some special recognition. By such devices I believe the ambitions of students in various elective programs can be stimulated as much as by the granting of separate types of diploma.

16. *Developmental reading program.* A school should have the equipment for a developmental reading program. The program should be available on a voluntary basis for all the pupils in the school. The counselors and teachers of English should be asked to view this program sympathetically and to urge students to take advantage of the opportunity to increase reading speed and comprehension.

17. *Summer school.* The school board should operate a tuition-free summer school

in which courses are available not only for students who have to repeat a subject, but also for the bright and ambitious students who wish to use the summer to broaden the scope of their elective programs.

18. *Foreign languages.* The school board should be ready to offer a third and fourth year of a foreign language, no matter how few students enroll. The guidance officers should urge the completion of a four-year sequence of one foreign language if the student demonstrates ability in handling foreign languages. On the other hand, students who have real difficulty handling the first year of a language should be advised against continuing with the subject (Recommendation 13).

19. *Science courses.* All students should obtain some understanding of the nature of science and the scientific approach by a required course in physical science or biology. This course should be given in at least three sections grouped by ability (Recommendation 4).

To accommodate students who are interested in science but do not have the required mathematical ability, two types of chemistry courses should be offered. For entry into one, at least a C in algebra and tenth-grade mathematics should be required. The other course should be designed for pupils with less mathematical ability. The standards even in this second course, however, should be such that those with less than average ability (assuming a distribution of ability according to the national norm) will have difficulty passing the course.

In addition to the physics course given in the twelfth grade with mathematics as a prerequisite (Recommendation 13) another course in physics should be offered with some such designation as "practical physics." The standards in this second course should be such that students with less than average ability have difficulty passing the course.

20. *Homerooms.* For the purpose of developing an understanding between students of different levels of academic ability and vocational goals, homerooms should be organized in such a way as to make them significant social units in the school. To this end, students should be kept together in one homeroom for the entire senior high school course (three or four years), and care should be taken to have each homeroom a cross section of the school in terms of ability and vocational interest. The teachers in charge of the homerooms should be persuaded by the administration that their work as homeroom teachers is important. Sufficient time should be allotted to the homeroom so that students may use this period to develop a sense of community interest and to have practice in a small way in representative government. The homerooms should elect one or two representatives to the student council, and these representatives should report back after each meeting of the council. They should listen to the opinions of their constituents and be guided by their opinions in voting on matters before the student council. To be effective, the student council should be treated sympathetically by the school administrators so that there will be some important questions each year with which the student council can be concerned and which, in turn, can be presented to the homerooms by the representatives.

21. *Twelfth-grade social studies.* In the twelfth grade a course on American problems or American government should be required. This course should include as much material on economics as the students can effectively handle at this point in their development. Each class in this course should be a cross section of the school: the class should be heterogeneously grouped. Teachers should encourage all students to participate in discussions. This course should develop not only an understanding of the American form of government and of the economic basis of our free society, but also mutual respect and understanding between different types of students. Current topics should be included; free discussion of controversial issues should be encouraged. This approach is one significant way in which our schools distinguish themselves from those in totalitarian nations. This course, as well as well-organized homerooms and certain student activities, can contribute a great deal to the development of future citizens of our democracy who will be intelligent voters, stand firm under trying national conditions, and not be beguiled by the oratory of those who appeal to special interests.

● **SAMPLE APPLICATION FORM FOR A TEACHING POSITION***

APPLICATION BLANK

I. Name in full _____

Present Address _____ Telephone _____

Permanent Address _____ Telephone _____

Date of Birth _____ Place of Birth _____

Height _____ Weight _____ General Health _____

Estimate of occupational time lost due to illness during the last 5 years _____

List any Physical defects _____ Do you wear glasses? _____

Is your hearing normal? _____ Marital Status: Single _____ Married _____ Widow (er) _____

Separated _____ Divorced _____ Number and ages of children _____

Are you a citizen of the United States of America? _____

If a war veteran or defense worker, give length of service _____ (months)

Branch of service or activity _____

Theatre of operation _____

Rank _____ Type of work you did _____

What foreign languages do you speak? _____

II. Present Position _____
               Grade   Subject
       _____
               School   Place

Present Salary _____ When can you accept a position? _____

List Position for which you are applying: _____

List in order of preference the subjects you like to teach:

(a) _____ (b) _____ (c) _____ (d) _____

Are you certified to teach in the State of New Jersey? _____

Kind of certificate held _____ Major _____ Minor _____

Are you willing to come to this school for an interview at your own expense? _____

III. EDUCATIONAL PREPARATION PRIOR TO BEGINNING TEACHING

School	Name	Location	Dates Attended	Course Major & Minor	Degree or Diploma	Date Graduated
Elementary						
High School						
College						

---

* From Hanover Park Regional High School District, Hanover, N. J.

Scholastic Honors_____

High School and College_____

IV   EDUCATIONAL TRAINING RECEIVED AFTER BEGINNING TEACHING

Institution	Dates Attended	Course Major and Minor	Degree or Diploma	Date Graduated

Scholastic Honors_____

_____

At present matriculated for_____ degree, to be conferred about _____

by_____University or College.

   List and give extent of any special training you have had that is not mentioned above:
e.g., music, art, industrial training, military courses while in military service, etc.

_____

_____

_____

V. TEACHING EXPERIENCE (Do not include practice teaching)
                 List in order beginning with present position

Period (years and dates)	School and Location	Grade or Subject Taught

A. Student or Practice Teaching:_____

_____

B. College, Part-Time, Substitute, Night or Summer, Etc.,_____

_____

_____

List the experiences you have had with children (other than the above):

Camp _____

Scouting _____

Home _____

Community _____

Church _____

Recreation _____

Other _____

What type of work experience as an adult have you had other than teaching?
(Business, trades, summer occupations, church work, social services, etc)

Dates From____To____	Employer and Location	Type of work and/or Position	Years

Were you trained for another profession or occupation before entering teaching?

_____ If so, what? _____

Indicate the approximate number of credits taken in each of the following areas in your
undergraduate college courses:

_____ a. The humanities (other than literature: i.e., music, art, foreign literature,
                     philosophy, etc.)

_____ b. The physical sciences (Chemistry, physics, astronomy, etc.)

_____ c. Mathematics

_____ d. Social Sciences (History, sociology, economics, anthropology)

List participation within the last two years in any professional activity for the improvement of the school
or schools where you have been employed. (e.g., Curriculum Revision, Pupil Progress Report, etc.):

_____

_____

(If not employed in a school system within the last two years, write "not so employed")

List any professional organizations of which you are a member (mention any offices or positions of responsibility you have held in these organizations):

_____

_____

_____

_____

_____

List the non-educational societies, organizations or clubs to which you belong (mention any offices or positions of responsibility you have held in these organizations):

_____

_____

_____

_____

_____

VI. INTERESTS AND HOBBIES
Indicate below any interests or hobbies you may have outside the professional field.

_____

_____

_____

_____

_____

Indicate briefly what professional and general magazine and book reading you have done in the past six months.

_____

_____

_____

_____

_____

VII. List student activities, clubs, or athletic programs you would be competent to teach or sponsor.

_____

_____

_____

_____

_____

VIII. TRAVEL
List below your most outstanding or interesting travels. (Include foreign countries)

Year	To	Reason for Trip	Why Outstanding to You

IX. REFERENCES
These should be persons qualified and willing to give an honest appraisal of your fitness for the position you seek. Please include superintendents and principals with whom you have worked.

Name	Address	Position or Occupation

A. Professional References:

1. _____

2. _____

3. _____

4. _____

B. Personal References:

1. _____

2. _____

3. _____

• SUGGESTED FILMS, FILMSTRIPS, AND RECORDINGS

The number in parentheses following each suggestion denotes the chapter for which it is best suited.

Films (16 mm)

And No Bells Ring (Sterling Movies, 56 min). Presents a review of the "Trump Report" on reorganization of secondary school staff utilization. Figures are given to explain how this program will better utilize teachers in teams of large group presentation personnel, small group teachers, and teacher assistants. Large lecture groups are observed along with pupils in smaller discussion groups and in individual study. (16)

Better Schools for Rural Wisconsin (University of Wisconsin, 29 min, color). Discusses the question of centralizing the rural schools in Wisconsin, using New York rural school organization as an example. Shows a typical one-room school, and then pictures the advantage of the central school, including diversified and specialized education, health services, adult education, night school, and community activities. (16)

Design for Learning (Photo and Sound, and Franklin and Kump Architects, 18 min, color). Shows the building of a modern school and explains new methods of planning construction. The completed building is shown in detail with emphasis given to reasons for using new departures in architecture. (16)

The Dropout (Mental Health Film Board, Inc., 28 min). Presents one of the millions of youngsters who leave high school without graduating. Shows how a community, through remedial reading programs, work experience programs, and other educational activities may tackle the problem of underachievement. (16)

Fight for Better Schools (March of Time, 21 min). Dramatizes the story of how the citizens of Arlington County, Virginia, fought to reorganize their school system. Also describes the efforts of other communities and organizations, such as the National Citizens Commission for the Public Schools. (16)

How Good Are Our Schools? Dr. Conant Report (National Education Association, 29 min). Uses two comprehensive high schools—one in Oakland, California, and the other in Labette County, Kansas—to show what every secondary school should be equipped to do. Shows various classroom situations illustrating how the schools provide for the varied interests of all the students in their communities. (16)

Investment in Youth (Hollywood Film Enterprises, Inc., 22 min). Develops the theme that youth is Canada's most natural resource, and that public expenditure for their development is a sound investment. (17)

"Pop Rings the Bell" (National School Service Institute, 23 min). Develops the part the well-equipped school will play in maturing the leaders of tomorrow. Principal Forsythe succeeds in convincing all the businessmen who attend a school party, except Fred Bates, that education is a good investment. Pop, the custodian, "rings the bell" with him. (17)

School Board in Action (National School Board Association, 26 min, color). Shows how a school board meets community problems in education through democratic action. Depicts, in a series of school board meetings with citizens, the manner in which the community and the board deal with such problems as censorship of textbooks, teachers' salary increases, selection of new school-board members, and the floating of a bond issue to build a new school. (16)

Schoolhouse in the Red (Encyclopaedia Britannica Films, 42 min, color). Describes a typical rural community debating whether to change from a system of individual small rural schools to a larger school-district system. Discusses the sociological and psychological factors involved and pictures the facial expressions, actions, and opinions of the local citizens. Shows how the little school district has become outmoded and emphasizes the considerations involved in the change of an educational system. (16)

Schools for Tomorrow (Wayne University, 22 min). Deals with the planning of school buildings and shows how one community used citizen's advisory committees, school personnel, an architect, and a school building consultant to help plan their schools. (16)

A Way of Life   (International Harvester Co., 25 min, color). Presents the story of school at Beaverton, Michigan, and how the problem of finance for educational purposes was solved, providing broader educational opportunities for the young and new ideas and better living for the whole community. (16)

Filmstrips

Cooperative School Plant Planning   (Indiana University, 100 fr., color). Presents a functional approach to dynamic group action as applied to the community planning of school buildings. Many details of administration are covered, as well as ways in which cooperating groups and individuals can benefit. (16)

Day in the Kindergarten   (Herbert M. Elkins Co., 40 fr.). Shows the typical activities of a kindergarten class at a well-organized and well-equipped school. (16)

Design of American Public Education   (McGraw-Hill, 41 fr.). Describes the effectiveness of the decentralized system of education in the United States with each state determining how its schools are organized and administered. (16)

Learning Goes On   (American Council on Education, 48 fr.). Suggests the importance of one aspect of adult education in the United States—participation in group learning activities to satisfy individually recognized needs. Deals with noncredit courses offered by a community evening school. (16)

School Building and Equipment   (American Council on Education, Part I—55 fr., Part II—58 fr.). Shows current trends in school building and equipment, and indicates how these support the educational programs of the modern elementary and secondary schools. Part I deals with the elementary school and Part II deals with the comprehensive high school. (16)

School Buildings   (National Education Association). A series of three filmstrips of varying number of frames showing external and interior views of school buildings which represent the best in school planning. (16)

School Days   (Eye Gate House, Inc., 28 fr., color). Shows school activities that encourage the formation of good character: student court, school safety patrol, election of officers, etc. (16)

Toward Better Schools for All Children through Federal Aid   (National Education Association, 54 fr.). Makes a simple presentation of statistics which show the need for better public education. After emphasizing the varying ability of different states to support their schools, the filmstrip presents the case for Federal aid. (17)

Recordings

Doorway to the Future: Bond Issue for Cross River   (National Tape Recording Project, 30 min). Dramatizes a school problem and suggests solutions through constructive citizen participation. (17)

Doorway to the Future: School Finance   (National Tape Recording Project, 30 min). Discusses the problems of school finances with possible solutions given. (17)

The People Act: In Arlington, Virginia   (National Tape Recording Project, 30 min). Suburban commuters win new schools for their children—and their area by cooperating to defeat a political machine. (16)

The People Take the Lead: They Can't Wait   (National Tape Recording Project, 25 min, 46 sec.). How we can get the best education for our children; the problem which faces public education. (16)

● **SUGGESTED READINGS**

The number in parentheses following each suggestion denotes the chapter for which it is best suited.

Babbidge, Homer D., and Robert M. Rosenzweig: *The Federal Interest in Higher Education,* McGraw-Hill Book Company, Inc., New York, 1962. Contains an excellent discussion of the interest of the government in higher education. (17)

Barr, W. Monfort: *American Public School Finance*, American Book Company, New York, 1960. Discusses the problems of school finance throughout the nation, analyzes current developments, and suggests direction for the next decade in financing our schools. (17)

Bent, Rudyard K., and Lloyd E. McCann: *Administration of Secondary Schools*, McGraw-Hill Book Company, Inc., New York, 1960. Presents a comprehensive discussion of the organization and administration of secondary schools. (16)

Callahan, Raymond E.: *An Introduction to Education in American Society*, 2d ed., Alfred A. Knopf, Inc., New York, 1960. Chapters 9 and 10 discuss the legal foundations, and the organization and administration of American schools. Chapter 11 discusses financial support of American education. (16) and (17)

The Case for Adult Education, National Education Association, National Association of Public School Adult Educators, Washington, 1959. Points out the need for adult education, the public school's responsibility and how adult education can be strengthened. (16)

The Case for Federal Support of Education, 1961, National Education Association, Washington, March, 1961. Presents factual information on the need for Federal support of public elementary and secondary schools. (17)

Committee on Educational Finance: *Financing Education for Our Changing Population*, National Education Association, Washington, 1961. Indicates the implications for school finance of our changing population. (17)

Conant, James B.: *The American High School Today*, McGraw-Hill Book Company, Inc., New York, 1959. Presents a number of recommendations based upon the results of an intensive study for improving American high schools. (16)

Conant, James B.: *Education in the Junior High School Years*, Educational Testing Service, Princeton, N.J., 1960. Presents a number of suggestions for improving education in the junior high school. (16)

DeYoung, Chris A., and Richard Wynn: *American Education*, 4th ed., McGraw-Hill Book Company, Inc., 1960. Part I presents a comprehensive discussion of the organization and administration of public education in America. (16)

Does Better Education Cost More? National Education Association, Committee on Tax Education and School Finance, Washington, 1959. Indicates the relationship of educational equality to the level of expenditure of a school system. (17)

Education in the United States, U.S. Office of Education, 1960. Presents a broad view of education in the United States. Especially written for a person who is not acquainted with educational programs and their organization in this country. (16)

Educational Policies Commission: *National Policy and the Financing of Public Schools*, National Education Association, Washington, 1959. Reviews the importance of education to the national life, assesses the financial base upon which American schools are presently operated, and discusses the implication of these matters to national policy. (17)

"Elementary School Organization," *The National Elementary Principal*, vol. 41, no. 3, National Education Association, Department of Elementary School Principals, December, 1961. Presents an excellent discussion of the purposes and patterns of elementary school organization. (16)

A Federal Education Agency for the Future, U.S. Office of Education, 1961. Reflects the thinking of a committee in regard to the function and leadership role that the Office of Education should play in the future. (16)

Financing the Public Schools, 1960–1970, National Education Association, Special Project on School Finance, Washington, 1962. Contains an excellent treatment of problems to be faced in financing public schools during the current decade. (17)

Fuller, Elizabeth Mechem: *About the Kindergarten*, National Education Association, Department of Classroom Teachers and the American Educational Research Association, Washington, February, 1961. Presents research findings on a number of items which promise to be helpful to the kindergarten teacher. (16)

Hutchins, Clayton D., and Dolores A. Steinhilber: *Trends in Financing Public Education,* U.S. Office of Education Circular 666, 1961. Presents numerous charts indicating trends in the financing of public education. (17)

Johnson, Mauritz, Jr.: "School in the Middle-Junior High: Education's Problem Child," *Saturday Review,* July 21, 1962, pp. 40–43. Presents some of the problems involved in educating junior high school pupils and emphasizes the need for competent teachers. (16)

Klausmeier, Herbert J., and Katherine Dresden: *Teaching in the Elementary School,* 2d ed., Harper & Row, Publishers, New York, 1962. Chapters 4 and 5 discuss curriculum organization and planning for classroom instruction in the elementary school. (16)

Knoll, Erwin: "The Maturing of the Junior College," *National Education Association Journal,* vol. 50, no. 2, pp. 27–29, National Education Association, Washington, February, 1961. Presents a brief history, the present situation, and the possible future of the junior college on the American educational scene. (16)

Kreitlow, Burton W.: "Reorganization Makes a Difference," *National Education Association Journal,* vol. 50, no. 3, p. 55, National Education Association, Washington, March, 1961. Research data indicate that reorganization of school districts does make a difference in the quality of education offered. (16)

Morse, Arthur D.: *Schools of Tomorrow,* Doubleday & Company, Inc., Garden City, N.Y., 1960. Chapters 2, 3, and 6 describe experiments in nongrading practices and in developing excellence in pupils. (16)

Progress of Public Education in the United States of America, 1961–1962, O.E.–10005-62-A, U.S. Office of Education, 1962. Contains an excellent description of education in the United States, especially areas in which considerable adjustment to new economic and social conditions has taken place. (16)

Read, Katherine H.: *The Nursery School: A Human Relationships Laboratory,* W. B. Saunders Company, Philadelphia, 1960. Contains an excellent description of the nursery school, its equipment and curriculum. (16)

Russell, John Dale: "Financing Higher Education in the Sixties," *Phi Delta Kappan,* vol. 42, no. 1, pp. 5–11, October, 1960. Indicates the startling financial needs of colleges and universities as more students attend college. (17)

"School Dropouts," *National Education Association Journal,* vol. 51, no. 5, pp. 51–59, National Education Association, Washington, May, 1962. Indicates the problem and what some school systems are doing about the problem of school dropouts. (16)

Thayer, V. T.: *The Role of the School in American Society,* Dodd, Mead & Company, Inc., New York, 1960. Chapter 4 presents an historical analysis of local antonomy in education. Chapter 5 discusses the problem of providing equality of educational opportunity in the United States. (16) and (17)

Trump, J. Lloyd: *Images of the Future: A New Approach to the Secondary School,* National Education Association, Commission on the Experimental Study of the Utilization of the Staff in the Secondary School, National Association of Secondary-School Principals, Washington, 1959. Presents some new approaches to educating pupils in the secondary school. (16)

What Everyone Should Know about Financing Our Schools, National Education Association, Washington, 1960. Outlines the basic elements for understanding present conditions and methods of public school finance. Contains many excellent charts and graphs. (17)

Wright, Grace S.: *Block-Time Classes and the Core Program in the Junior High School,* U.S. Office of Education Bulletin 1958, no. 6, 1958. Presents the results of an extensive survey of core programs in junior high schools. (16)

Wrightstone, J. Wayne: *Class Organization of Instruction,* What Research Says Series, no. 13, National Education Association, Department of Classroom Teachers, American Educational Research Association, Washington, May, 1957. Contains an excellent compilation of research findings that have significance for elementary and secondary school organization. (16)

● **FIGURE CREDITS**

Figure 57. (*Source:* Edward J. Powers, *Education for American Democracy,* McGraw-Hill Book Company, Inc., New York, 1958, p. 80.)

Figure 58. (*Source:* Data from "Estimates of School Statistics, 1961–62," *Research Report* 1961-R22, p. 6, National Education Association, Research Division, Washington, December, 1961.)

Figure 60. (*Source:* "One-Teacher Schools Today," *Research Monograph* 1960-M1, p. 9, National Education Association, Research Division, Washington, June, 1960.)

Figure 61. (*Source: The American School Superintendency,* Thirteenth Yearbook, National Education Association, American Association of School Administrators, Washington, 1952, p. 88.)

Figure 62. (*Source:* Adapted from a news release of the U.S. Office of Education, Feb. 28, 1962, p. 6.)

Figure 64. (*Source: Education in the United States of America,* U.S. Office of Education, Washington, 1960, p. 5.)

Figure 65. (*Source:* Stuart E. Dean, *Elementary School Administration and Organization,* Bulletin 1960, no. 11, p. 30, U.S. Office of Education, 1960.)

Figure 66. (*Source:* Stuart E. Dean, *Elementary School Administration and Organization,* Bulletin 1960, no. 11, p. 68, U.S. Office of Education, 1960.)

Figure 67. (*Source:* Edmund A. Ford, "Organizational Patterns of the Nation's Public Secondary Schools," *School Life,* vol. 42, no. 9, p. 11, U.S. Office of Education, May, 1960.)

Figure 68. (*Source:* "High-School Graduation Requirements," *Research Bulletin,* vol. 37, no. 4, p. 126, National Education, Research Division, Washington, December, 1959.)

Figure 69. (*Source: Progress of Public Education in the United States of America, 1960–61,* p. 19, U.S. Office of Education, 1961.)

Figure 71. (*Source: Progress of Public Education in the United States of America, 1960–61,* U.S. Office of Education, 1961, p. 28.)

Figure 72. (*Source:* Richard Wynn, *Careers in Education,* McGraw-Hill Book Company, Inc., New York, 1960, p. 77.)

Figure 73. (*Source:* Data from "Estimates of School Statistics, 1961–62," *Research Report* 1961-R22, p. 14, National Education Association, Research Division, Washington, December, 1961.)

Figure 74. (*Source:* Clayton D. Hutchins and Dolores A. Steinhilber, *Trends in Financing Public Education, 1929–30 to 1959–60,* U.S. Office of Education, Circular 666, 1961, p. 88.)

Figure 75. (*Source:* "Spotlighting Public Education in 1960," *Research Bulletin,* vol. 38, no. 1, p. 21, National Education Association, Research Division, Washington, February, 1960.)

Figure 76. (*Source:* Clayton D. Hutchins and Dolores A. Steinhilber, *Trends in Financing Public Education, 1929–30 to 1959–60,* U.S. Office of Education Circular 666, 1961, p. 106.)

Figure 78. (*Source:* Montfort W. Barr, *American Public School Finance,* American Book Company, 1960, p. 230.)

Figure 79. (*Source:* "State-Local Taxes and You," *Research Bulletin,* vol. 38, no. 4, p. 113, National Education Association, Research Division, Washington, December, 1960.)

Figure 80. (*Source:* Clayton D. Hutchins and Dolores A. Steinhilber, *Trends in Financing Public Education, 1929–30 to 1959–60,* U.S. Office of Education Circular 666, 1961, p. 39.)

Figure 81. (*Source:* "Where Does Your State Stand?" *Research Bulletin,* vol. 40, no. 1, p. 10, National Education Association, Research Division, Washington, February, 1962.)

Figure 82.   (*Source:* "Where Does Your State Stand?" *Research Bulletin,* vol. 40, no. 1, p. 11, National Education Association, Research Division, Washington, February, 1962.)

Figure 83.   (*Source:* "Estimates of School Statistics, 1961–62," *Research Report,* 1961-R22 p. 14, National Education Association, Research Division, Washington, December 1961, and Montfort W. Barr, *American Public School Finance,* American Book Company, New York, 1960, p. 377.)

Figure 84.   (*Source:* Clayton D. Hutchins and Dolores A. Steinhilber, *Trends in Financing Public Education, 1929–30 to 1959–60,* U.S. Office of Education Circular 666, 1961, p. 86.)

Figure 85.   (*Source:* Data secured from the U.S. Office of Education, 1962.)

18

MOVING AHEAD: YOUR PLANS AND YOUR FUTURE

In ancient times the Romans had a famous god by the name of Janus, after whom the month of January was named. He was the god of gates and doorways. He was pictured with two faces, one looking forward and the other backward. People declared that he could look both ways at the same time. Perhaps you, too, have wished that you had the ability to look both forward and backward so that you could clearly see the future and the past as you faced many of life's problems.

YOUR STATUS IN PLANNING FOR TEACHING

In this book you have spent considerable time and energy examining various aspects of teaching as a career. Your attention has been focused primarily upon how to plan a career in education, how to gain the competencies required for teaching, and how to help perform the function of education in our democratic society. Often the process of stocktaking enables you to gain perspective and direction in your thinking and planning. What then, in brief, are some of the gains that should have resulted from your efforts?

Progress in Your Planning. You sense very clearly the nature and importance of planning in an increasingly complex and interdependent society, not only as it relates to you personally but also as it pertains to the educational needs of the boys and girls whom you may teach. Planning is an inescapable aspect of life which extends to all phases of living and continues throughout one's life. Furthermore, plans for the future are always tentative and are changed whenever developing situations seem to warrant it.

Career planning is only one aspect of life planning. It necessitates that you first identify the things that really seem important to you—that you clarify the values around which you wish to rotate your life. You further test a career in education to make certain that it is in harmony with the values you hold. Like all other professions, a career in education dictates certain requirements you must meet in order to be really successful and happy. You appraise yourself critically and comprehensively in terms of these requirements. You then develop long-range as well as immediate plans in as much detail as possible for moving from where you are to where you want to go—with the idea constantly in mind that modifications in the details of your master plan, or blueprint, are to be made as unforeseen situations develop.

Clarification of Values and Nature of Your Task. By now you should be quite clear in your thinking regarding the values you hold in life, how you happened to acquire them, the internal consistency that exists within them, and the extent to which they agree with the general pattern of values held by the society in which you live.

In Chapter 1 and in other parts of the book you tested whether values generally associated with a career in teaching were compatible with your personal values. In Chapters 6, 7, 8, and 16, you considered such matters as the nature of your work, some professional obligations you will meet, and the type of organization in which you will work. Chapters 13, 14, and 15 stressed the philosophical foundations of education today. Chapters 9, 10, and 17 provided you with information regarding the economic and financial aspects of teaching.

Chapters 11 and 12 considered why educational practices and school organizations became what they are today. Chapters 1 and 5 attempted to point out the critical importance of education today and the wide variety of opportunities which you have as you assist the schools in meeting the tremendous challenge with which they are faced. From your consideration of these chapters you should see how, with dignity, pride, and satisfaction, you can become a part of our schools today and can contribute effectively to the fuller realization of the school's function in our society.

Analysis of Requirements for Teaching. Much of your attention has been devoted to a consideration of the personal and professional requirements for successful teaching. Chapter 3 specifically indicated those competencies generally associated with successful teachers, and the requirements for graduation from teacher-education institutions. Chapter 4 outlined the requirements for teaching as they are affected by such matters as certification requirements specified by the various state departments of education and by in-service education requirements essential for continued personal and professional growth.

Appraising Your Prospects for Teaching. Throughout the book you have been encouraged to appraise yourself critically in light of the requirements for and demands made upon teachers. From your efforts you should have a relatively clear picture of your strengths and weaknesses for the profession, and of how you can build up your good points and overcome your weaknesses.

If you have come to the conclusion that you are not suited to become a teacher, do not despair and feel that your efforts have been wasted. In the first place you have saved yourself considerable time and money by not fully preparing for an occupation which probably would prove unsuitable for you. Also, you have spared yourself the unhappiness and   533 frustration that would result from choosing the wrong occupation and having to readjust to another kind of work. Furthermore, the understandings you have gained regarding a career in education planning should help you to locate a more suitable occupation and to plan effectively in terms of the new field. In addition, you have gained further appreciation of the teacher's work and the function of education in our society. In the years that lie ahead, this should prove valuable to you for a number of reasons. You will be a taxpayer, and public schools are supported by taxation. You will be a member of some community in which school problems will be of general concern. You probably will be a member of some service group which holds more than casual interest in the education of boys and girls. It is highly probable that you will become a parent, in which case the education of your child will become of vital concern to you. In the final analysis, you should feel that you have gained much from your efforts.

PLANS FOR THE FUTURE

In planning to teach, there are many things to which you will want to direct your attention as you move ahead. By all means, plan in terms of the three major periods in your life which were discussed in Chapter 2. Keep in mind that when you are attending college you are living in an environment that differs appreciably from the one in which you will find yourself later; i.e., your objectives, the nature of your work, your resources, and your opportunities will be altered. After graduation you will have such problems as becoming established in a position, building up financial resources, and starting your married life and family.

After this period of major adjustment, which may vary greatly in length for different individuals, you enter a later period in which your problems become somewhat different. Regardless of how far distant and nebulous this period in life may seem to you at the moment, you face the problem of making tentative plans for it. To "grow old gracefully" you must build certain interests and plan a definite old-age program. Pleasures derived from a grown family necessitate that children be raised. Retirement on a comfortable allowance necessitates deliberate sacrifices during a number of years in life.

Many suggestions have been made throughout this book, either directly or indirectly, that should help you in planning for the three major periods of life suggested above. However, plans necessarily are highly personal in nature and must be worked out only by you. As you move ahead in this, keep in mind the few practical hints that follow, along with the many suggestions that have been indicated previously.

Developing toward Student Teaching.   The course work you take should be thoughtfully and carefully planned. First of all, make certain that you meet the requirements for graduation and for the type of teacher certification you desire. Second, use your elective courses for strengthening certain weaknesses that you may have in your ability to teach, for broadening your general background, for increasing the number of areas for which you may be certified, and for pursuing special interests.

Your attitude toward course work is of major importance in determining the value you will gain from it. For example, if you earn only a passing grade in a history course, just sufficient enough to be counted toward graduation and certification requirements, you probably will have little to enrich your life or the lives of the pupils whom you will teach. On the other hand, if you could seek to gain from the history course a deep understanding of the social, economic, and political forces that have shaped society into the form in which you find it today, you certainly should be a better student of current problems, more capable in interpreting them to your pupils, and better able to predict and shape future societal happenings. In the final analysis, what you gain from your course work is a matter that rests largely with you.

Seek out every opportunity possible to broaden and deepen your understanding of the behavior growth of boys and girls and to gain skill in effectively guiding this growth. A number of suggestions already have been given to help you plan such experiences. Regardless of the amount of encouragement provided by your teacher-education institution, try to participate in situations with students which will contribute significantly to your professional understandings, insights, and skills.

Your student teaching will probably prove to be the most important single course you take during your preparation for the profession. For this reason, plan to make it of maximum benefit. Within limits you should be able to exercise some control over the semester, the grade level, and the subject area. Since many colleges and universities now have off-campus student-teaching programs, you may have considerable latitude in the location of your course. If this be the case, ask to be assigned to a situation comparable to that in which you hope to begin teaching.

There are many sources of help in planning for your student teaching. Do not hesitate to discuss your ideas with your instructors and with students who have completed or are engaged in student teaching. You can also find some excellent books and films concerning the topic. Furthermore, all of the professional laboratory experiences which you have prior to student teaching will prove valuable as you formulate your plans.

Exercise independent and wise use of the many resources for personal growth to be found on your college campus and in its surrounding community. The library, the museum, the art gallery, the musical recitals, the various kinds of clinics, the entertainment and lecture series, the outstanding visitors, the conferences—these and many other resources normally are at your disposal. The extent to which you avail yourself of them will depend upon the amount of individual initiative you wish to exercise.

College life provides abundant opportunities for social growth, and teachers need a high degree of social competence. Everyone, regardless of his past experiences, can improve in his ability to work effectively with others. Therefore, make efforts to increase your understanding of other students and to work with them on common problems that require thought and planning.

Your opportunities for growth normally are so great that you are faced with the problem of using your time and energy most effectively. There are, however, many things that you *must* do to meet the demands of college life. Establish the most efficient work habits possible so that you can fulfill these responsibilities with the minimum time and effort. For example, everyone can improve his reading skills and his efficiency in getting things done; in so doing he has more time for other things.

In planning your college life you do not want to overlook the need for establishing a healthy balance between work and recreational activities. Each individual requires some recreational activities in order to maintain a healthy attitude toward his life and work. Furthermore, many recreational activities are rich sources of learning for prospective teachers. The teacher of today needs to be skilled in the wise use of leisure time, not only for his own personal benefit but also for guiding others in that direction.

Locating a Position.   As you continue your preparation for teaching you should attend to certain things that may have a decided effect upon the position you secure. Become well acquainted with several of your college instructors so that they will be able to write letters of recommendation regarding your promise as a teacher. College instructors hesitate to recommend highly those students with whom they are vaguely acquainted.

During the later stages of your preparation for teaching, you probably

Registering with your teacher-placement office is a vital step in securing a good teaching position. (*Photograph from the Audio-visual Center, Indiana University.*)

will register with your college teacher-placement office. This usually necessitates providing letters of recommendation and various personal and academic data on your training and background. The placement office uses this material in referring you to employing officials who have vacancies along the lines for which you are qualified. The school officials then normally invite for an interview one or more of the most promising candidates recommended for the position. Obviously you will want to plan your college career so as to have as strong a set of teacher-placement credentials as possible. In addition to the letters of recommendation, academic achievement, participation in extracurricular activities, success in professional experiences—especially student teaching—enter as significant factors in your placement. Throughout your preparation for teaching, you are, in a sense, building the credentials upon which you will be recommended for various teaching positions. The need for careful planning in this regard should be self-evident to you.

Your teacher-placement office will be concerned with the type and the general location of the teaching position you desire. Some important questions arise in regard to those matters. Do you prefer to teach in your home school system or in one located some distance away, possibly in another state? Do you prefer to teach in a strictly rural district, a town, a small city, or a large city school system? The answers to these questions may have a significant bearing upon the nature of your plans

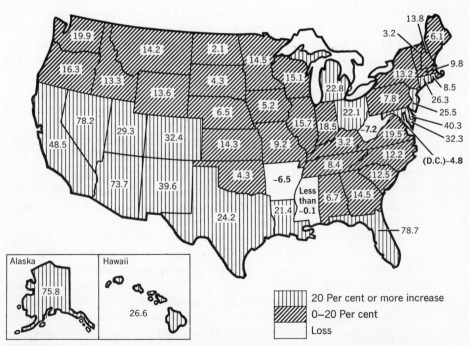

Figure 86. Percentage change in population according to states, 1950–1960. Job opportunities are affected by changes in population. (*Source: American Observer.*)

for teaching. Questions such as these, therefore, warrant your early attention. The answers to them may necessitate considerable thought and effort upon your part.

At least 18 state departments of education and 18 state education associations provide placement services [6:142–143]. There also are a number of commercial placement bureaus that offer services to teachers on either a national or a regional scale. The U.S. Office of Education can supply you with a list of these commercial agencies. Since there is considerable difference in the reliability and effectiveness of commercial agencies, secure some reliable advice before you apply to one of them. Usually you have to pay a registration fee. If you secure a position through the efforts of a commercial agency, you normally pay a commission of approximately five per cent of your first year's salary.

You may be able to secure a position by requesting that your name be placed on file in the school system in which you may wish to be located. So long as you do not apply for a specific position known to be filled by another teacher, you would not be violating the Code of Ethics presented in Chapter 8. You would want to avoid indiscriminate distribution of applications. If you make such a request of a superintendent, also indicate where he may secure your placement credentials and any other information that might be helpful to him in determining your qualifications and capabilities.

Regardless of any influential friends or relatives that you may have on the school board or in the community, scrupulously respect the official professional head of the school. Conduct all of your employment negotiations through him. Expect him to request much information about you such as your academic record, areas in which you are qualified to teach, extracurricular activities, previous jobs, and the reasons why you wish a position in that particular school system. Although it may appear to be absurd, many written applications for positions are not favorably considered because of poorly written letters, misspelled words, incorrect grammar, and tactless statements.

If you should be called for an interview, the superintendent or his delegated employing official will be especially interested in your personal appearance, skill in communication, mannerisms, prejudices, professional outlook, aspirations, technical competence, and plans for the future. During the interview, attempt to be relaxed, natural, professional, mature, and enthusiastic.

If you seem to be a promising candidate for a position, the superintendent may invite you to visit in the school system. During this visit you will have an opportunity to meet some of the teachers and other administrators, study the school plant and other facilities, gain additional information regarding teaching assignments, extracurricular duties, administrative policies, community expectations, living accommodations, and the nature of the community. If you and the superintendent are in agreement, he will recommend your appointment to the board of education.

Entering into Teaching.   Success and happiness in teaching require continuous planning, even though you have received your certificate and have secured an excellent position. In fact, the effort that you put forth and the wisdom reflected in your planning will determine largely the extent to which you will realize the values inherent in a teaching career. You should find the following suggestions helpful:

1. *Become an integral part of your working situation.* In order to be very successful in your work and in improving conditions within your school, you must first be accepted and respected by other members in the school and community. Unfortunately some beginning teachers feel an obligation to bring "up to date" all the other teachers and administrators in their schools. They may try immediately to change things. Obviously, such techniques do not contribute greatly to a program of genuine progress in which a group moves forward together.

2. *Avoid the feeling that theory is one thing and that practice is another.* Actually, theory provides direction in terms of which improvements in practice may take place. Practice, then, may be evaluated in terms of the degree to which it is consistent with theory; therefore, do not be discouraged if you find theory to be relatively far in advance of practice in your school. Such a condition should challenge you to become effective in improving practice. In your attempts to improve it, however, keep in mind that progress within a school takes place rather slowly. During your first years of teaching, therefore, feel very successful if you are able to improve only a few of the general practices.

3. *Concentrate upon the positive aspects of your situation rather than upon the weaknesses only.* It will be difficult for you to maintain good mental health if you are able to see only the difficulties, problems, and shortcomings in your situation. There are always some good things to be found.

4. *Approach your work with enthusiasm.* Enthusiasm is a contagious sort of thing which tends to facilitate learning and to improve working conditions. It generally reflects a healthy attitude toward life, a happy disposition, and a feeling of pride in your work. It tends to release energies through which greater accomplishments are made possible.

5. *Assume an experimental attitude toward your work.* Each day you should seek to develop your competence as a teacher. Whenever you feel that you have no more room for improvement, you should consider yourself professionally dead. Plan that each year will be a year of new experience rather than a mere repetition of the preceding year, and that it will bring forth new understandings, insights, and ways of doing things. You will need to be realistic as you appraise your work, avoiding pretense, and other factors that tend to warp your thinking.

6. *Expect changes to take place within the field of education.* Professional education of teachers will continue to advance. Educational research will continue to bring forth new understandings of human growth, new techniques, and new materials to be used. The nature of our society will also change as scientific, economic, political, and social advance-

Through careful planning, teachers find their work extremely challenging and rewarding throughout their professional careers. (*Photograph from the* Planning for Teaching *series of motion pictures.*)

ments are made. These changes will bring forth new values, functions, and purposes in education. You may therefore assume that the future will be different. You will need to adopt a positive, intelligent attitude toward change as it affects your personal life and your responsibilities as a teacher.

7. *Learn to differentiate the important from the unimportant tasks.* Some teachers lose perspective with respect to their primary function. As a result they tend to become lost in details which may or may not have real educational significance. For example, grading papers or various clerical duties may become more important than planning learning experiences of the pupils. Arrange your work so that you will be able to devote your time to the tasks that will bring the greatest educational returns to boys and girls.

8. *Establish habits of orderliness, accuracy, and promptness.* If your daily routine is systematic and well arranged, you will spare yourself much confusion and irritation. Establish the habit of routinizing as many daily activities as possible, of anticipating problems, and of developing well-organized, yet flexible, plans for solving them promptly and accurately. By so doing you gain an added sense of accomplishment and free yourself for engaging in other kinds of activities.

9. *Seek assistance on professional problems whenever you need it.* There is little if any merit in keeping your problems to yourself with the hope that you finally will be able to solve them. The sources of help are many—your school administrator, supervisor, colleagues, books, and periodical literature. As you share problems with others you may gain insight into them, clarify your thinking, receive helpful suggestions, build

self-confidence, and develop common interests and wholesome working relationships with others.

10. *Maintain a good sense of humor.* Look for the humorous side of life as well as the serious aspects. Laugh with others and be able to laugh at yourself. A sense of humor may keep you from taking yourself too seriously. The ability to laugh often provides an excellent counterbalance for the many fears, anxieties, and disappointments normally encountered in life.

11. *Cultivate adequate, realistic self-concepts.* With all of the stresses and strains involved in teaching, you have the problem of coping with the inner self. Strive to face realistically feelings of anger, hostility, and anxiety. Recognize that these are normal feelings which all human beings experience. Search out the causes of these feelings and gain further skill in controlling and in resolving them to the extent that you are able to maintain a healthy positive outlook upon life and effective working relationships with others. Gain feelings of real success through identifying purposes which seem genuinely worthwhile, and through attempting to make a realistic amount of progress in achieving them. Think of yourself as a person with areas of ability as well as areas of inadequacy. Emphasize your areas of ability and realize that you are contributing something worthwhile to the lives of your pupils and to the over-all program.

12. *Continue to improve your perception of others.* Good teaching depends upon your sensitivity to and understanding of the pupils with whom you work as well as the interpretations you make of their behavior. Strive to gain increasing skill in making accurate judgments regarding the behavior of your pupils as well as of your colleagues.

13. *Continue to strengthen your academic background.* New knowledge is being gained so fast that a teacher's academic background quickly becomes obsolete unless he continues to be a scholar, especially in his area of specialization. Continued growth in your academic background will give you added feelings of security and adequacy for meeting the growing interests and concerns of youth.

14. *Know when to quit your work for the day.* Conscientiousness and attention to duty are indeed admirable traits. However, you do not want these traits to overtax your energies to the extent that the quality of your work suffers. Some teachers work far into the night grading papers and performing similar school duties, thus exhausting their energies for the next day and warping their perspectives. Fatigue reflects itself in the mental attitude of the teacher and the emotional tone of the classroom, and this affects the education of pupils. You therefore will want to establish a desirable balance between work and the activities that will restore your physical and mental health.

15. *Cultivate adult friends outside of the teaching profession.* Through day-to-day contacts with your colleagues you normally will develop a number of friends within the profession. Since you share with them so many common interests, and since it is so easy to "talk shop," you may

have a tendency to limit your contacts to teachers. You owe to yourself as well as to your profession, however, a fairly wide circle of friendships —people with varied interests and occupations. Through the cultivation of these friendships you have the opportunity to widen your background of information, improve your human relationships, gain a broad and wholesome outlook upon life, and extend your influence in the community.

16. *Maintain interests outside your school work.* You have basic civic responsibilities as a member of society. Furthermore, you owe it to yourself and to your family to have a normal, happy home life. All these extra-school factors operate together in such a manner that your effectiveness as a teacher is actually broadened and strengthened.

17. *Prepare for the type of school work in which you are most interested and for which you are best qualified.* If you think you will be happiest as a classroom teacher, prepare yourself through additional training and activities so that you may be the best teacher possible. If you feel that you have definite interest and ability in other types of school work, such as administration, you should prepare yourself well academically and secure types of professional experiences that will lead you in the direction in which you wish to move.

18. *Build a satisfactory functional philosophy of life.* Your life will be governed according to certain fundamental ideas and beliefs which you hold in regard to the nature of the universe, your place within it, and your relationships with others. In view of this rapidly changing world, it is difficult indeed to develop a consistent and harmonious way of looking at life. It calls for searching thought and effort on your part if you are to gain direction and peace of mind.

19. *Never lose sight of the great challenge that is yours.* There may be times when you will feel discouraged. It may help you to remember that other good teachers have sometimes felt discouraged too—Jim Baker, for example. There were many times when Jim's smoothly functioning group of pupils seemed almost adult—and then again everything would seem to go wrong. He was not a philosopher, but every once in a while he remembered what a professor had said to him when he was trying to make up his mind about becoming a teacher:

Jim, teaching's not an ordinary job. It's a real adventure, filled with all the danger and excitement a spirited person could ask for. The teacher stands entrusted with the welfare and security of our country's greatest treasure—its youth. The people say to the teacher, "Here are our boys and girls; teach them what they must know to live in a world of varied races and cultures, in a world of uncertainty and change." From all the heritage of the race the teacher must select that which is to be passed on. From all the influences that surround his young charges he must choose those to encourage, those to ignore, those to fight. From all the possible and distant goals for which peoples may strive, he must choose the most worthy and magnify them for children's eyes. In the midst of conflicts and confusions, he must hold aloft democracy's lamp; he must keep it bright and help his pupils to walk in its light. Teaching is not for the immature or the timid. It is for those who care about what happens to the world and its children and who are prepared to do something about it. There's your job, Jim. Will you be a teacher?

SUMMARY

Throughout this book an earnest attempt has been made to help you in your orientation to the field of education and in planning your life work. The book has been written to encourage you to appraise critically and honestly both the profession and yourself. It is hoped that you feel rewarded for your efforts in reading it and that you like what you see in yourself and in the field of education.

QUESTIONS FOR YOUR CONSIDERATION

1. What changes have you made, as a result of this course, in your plans for teaching?

2. During this course, how have your views toward the function of the school changed?

3. What are some illustrations of the concept that effective planning extends to all phases of living and continues throughout one's life?

4. How can you gain from your college environment the greatest amount of growth toward teaching? To what extent are you using the resources available to you?

5. Why do a number of teachers fail to assume an experimental attitude toward their work? How can you avoid such pitfalls?

6. Why do some teachers feel that theory is one thing and that practice is another? What is the relationship of the two?

7. What would be some advantages and disadvantages of teaching in your home community?

8. Why should you file your application for a position with the superintendent of schools rather than with the president of the board of education?

ACTIVITIES FOR YOU TO PURSUE

1. Talk with some of your teachers who you feel have a wholesome outlook upon life and who have gained much enjoyment and satisfaction from teaching as a career. Try to determine the factors, conditions, and practices that have contributed to their success and happiness.

2. Talk with some teachers who seem to regard teaching as a burdensome job from which they gain little or no satisfaction. In what ways do they differ from teachers who seem to derive much happiness from teaching? List any pitfalls which you will want to avoid.

3. Consult with school administrators, college instructors, and placement officials regarding problems common to beginning teachers. You may be able to find research studies that have been made along this line. Plan ways in which you may be able to avoid many of these problems.

4. Suggest to your instructor that some student teachers be invited to your class to discuss the kinds of pre-student teaching experiences that proved to be of most help to them. Incorporate into your plans any good ideas which you gain from the discussion.

5. Suggest to your instructor that arrangements be made, if possible, for your class to view and discuss some good films concerned with student teaching.

6. List or describe in detail the conditions which you hope will characterize your later life. What plans must you follow in order to achieve these conditions?

7. Examine a number of blanks used in applying for a teaching position, including the one in the Resource Section for Part VI. What kinds of information are requested?

8. Now that you have completed this book, review critically any written plans you had made previously regarding your future. What changes must you make in order that they be inclusive, adequate, realistic, and suitable for you?

OTHER SOURCES OF IDEAS AND INFORMATION FOR CHAPTER 18

● SUGGESTED READINGS

Armstrong, W. Earl and T. M. Stinnett: *A Manual on Certification Requirements for School Personnel in the United States*, pp. 141–147, National Education Association, National Commission on Teacher Education and Professional Standards, Washington, 1961. Contains suggestions and aids for obtaining a teaching job in the United States and overseas.

Bernard, Harold W.: *Mental Hygiene for Classroom Teachers*, 2d ed., McGraw-Hill Book Company, Inc., 1961. Chapter 19 is concerned with the teacher developing and maintaining a positive view toward the profession. Chapter 20 stresses the importance of the teachers' philosophy.

Massey, Harold W., and Edwin E. Vineyard: *The Profession of Teaching*, The Odyssey Press, Inc., New York, 1961. Chapter 15 discusses procedures to use in obtaining a position. Chapter 16 deals with a number of topics concerning the professional growth of teachers.

Shull, Martha: "My Paths to Personal Growth," *National Education Association Journal*, vol. 48, no. 5, pp. 27–28, National Education Association, Washington, May, 1959. Discusses the importance of personal growth for teachers.

Wiggins, Sam P.: *Successful High School Teaching*, Houghton Mifflin Company, Boston, 1958, pp. 46–62. Stresses the point that the teacher's picture of himself guides his teaching.

Wingo, G. Max, and Raleigh Schorling: *Elementary School Student Teaching*, 3d ed., McGraw-Hill Book Company, Inc., New York, 1961. Contains a comprehensive discussion of problems faced by student teachers.

Zirbes, Laura: *Spurs to Creative Teaching*, G. P. Putnam's Sons, New York, 1959. Chapters 14 and 15 deal with creativity in student teaching and in in-service education.

● SUGGESTED FILMS, FILMSTRIPS, AND RECORDINGS

Films (16 mm)
Elementary Teacher: Beginning Student Teaching (Indiana University, 10 min). Discusses both the training and functions of the teacher in a world of rapid change. Shows prospective teachers in study and training situations, and follows Janet, a student teacher, as she acquaints herself with a classroom, the school, and its program, and does practice teaching. Uses flashbacks to emphasize the points being discussed by the teaching supervisor and Janet during an evaluation of the latter's progress.

Planning for Personal and Professional Growth (McGraw-Hill, 17 min). Shows four schoolteachers who have made adjustments and achieved success, to various degrees, in their teaching. A middle-aged woman found teaching dull with many frustrations. She was not aware of her problems and found it difficult to adjust. A science teacher made long-range plans for his growth through graduate study, but found that he had to reevaluate his ambitious plans. A foreign-language teacher found conflict between family life and teaching, but by relating her teaching to life she made an adjustment. An elderly woman was enthusiastic about teaching, loved children, and found teaching a rich, rewarding experience.

Secure the Blessings   (National Education Association, 25 min). Discusses the role of education in the United States as it prepares people to use the democratic method of solving problems. Shows five adults who are trying to solve their various problems in human relations objectively and points out that it was in school where these individuals learned to make decisions.

Filmstrips

Focus on the Future   (National Education Association, 78 fr., color). Concerns the future teachers of America and the quest for quality teachers.

Your Educational Philosophy: Does It Matter?   (Wayne University, 40 fr.). Presents a number of views of the classrooms of two teachers. Compares similar situations in these two classrooms to indicate how the teacher's educational philosophy affects the types of classroom activities planned for pupils.

Recordings

A Forward Look for the Teaching Profession   (Education Recording Service, 33⅓ rpm). W. S. Elsbree, professor of education, Columbia University, presents a challenge to anyone planning to teach.

● **FIGURE CREDIT**

Figure 86.   (*Source:* "U.S. Population Drama of 20th Century," *American Observer,* vol. 30, no. 30, p. 1, Washington, April 24, 1961.)

GLOSSARY

The reader may find some of the terminology that is used in this book and in the field of education to be confusing. For this reason a few of the terms and phrases are defined according to meanings generally assigned to them by educators.[1]

Ability grouping. Classifying pupils into homogeneous sections with reference to intelligence for purposes of instruction.

Academic. Pertaining to the fields of English, foreign languages, history, economics, mathematics, and science; (higher education) pertaining to the liberal arts fields.

Academic freedom. The opportunity for the teacher to teach, and for the teacher and the student to study, without coercion, censorship, or other forms of restrictive interference.

Academy. An independent secondary school not under public control.

Accelerated program. The more rapid advancement of superior children through the school grades by means of extra promotions.

Accessory material. Workbooks, charts, cards, and other devices that are used to supplement the basic textbook in reading.

Accredit. To designate an educational institution as meeting required standards or accepted criteria of quality established by a competent agency. (Use of the word is frequently accompanied by an indication of the agency that does the accrediting.)

Accreditation. The type of recognition held by an education institution that has met accepted standards applied to it by a competent agency or official association.

Accrediting agency. An organization that sets up criteria for judging the quality of educational institutions, determines the extent to which institutions meet these criteria, and issues some sort of public announcement concerning the quality of the institutions.

Activity concept. The generalization that activities, whether physical or intellectual, are necessary if learning is to occur.

Activity curriculum. A curriculum design in which the interests and purposes of children determine the educative program; selection and planning of activities are cooperatively done by teacher and pupils; problem solving is the dominant method.

Adjustment. The process of finding and adopting modes of behavior suitable to the environment or to changes in the environment.

Adjustment to individual differences. The provision, not only of adapted materials and methods, but also of personal attention necessary for the individual's wholesome development as an integrated personality; implies and includes adaptation of schools to individual differences.

Administrative policy. A statement adopted by a board of education or an administrative agency outlining principles to be followed with respect to specific matters.

Adult education. Organized activities with an educational purpose carried on by mature persons on a part-time basis.

Adult education center. Any local unit, agency, or school promoting formal or informal education primarily for adults; a branch of a school, college, or university stressing service to adults, usually emphasizing nonacademic and noncredit instruction.

Affiliated school. An off-campus school whose facilities are used for student teaching in the program of teacher education.

Aim. A foreseen end that gives direction to an activity and motivates behavior.

Airborne television. Telecasting instruction to schools from an airplane flying at high altitude.

Anecdotal records. A series of notes containing exactly what a child said or did in concrete situations; as observations are accumulated, a variety and continuity of in-

---

[1] Most of these definitions are either taken directly or adapted from Carter V. Good (ed.), *Dictionary of Education,* McGraw-Hill Book Company, Inc., New York, 1959. Used by permission of publisher.

formation yielding a picture of the child's behavior patterns, development in various directions, interests, attitudes, strengths, and problems can be seen.

Apprenticeship. The period during which a young person works under the direction of an experienced, well-qualified adult to acquire increased skill and knowledge needed for competent performance in a given occupation.

Aptitude. A group of characteristics, native or acquired, deemed to be symptomatic of an individual's ability to acquire proficiency in a given area; examples might be of a particular art, school subject, or vocational area.

Articulation. The relationship and interdependence existing among the different elements of the educational program; may designate the degree of relationship among the different curricular offerings, between the curriculum and the institutional regimen, student activities, and provisions for pupil guidance, or between the school's program and out-of-school educational institutions and activities (for example, home, church, scouts, welfare agencies, etc.) or the degree to which the interlocking and interrelation of the successive levels of the educational system facilitate continuous and efficient educational progress of pupils.

Asocial. (1) Indifferent to existing social customs, moral codes, or usual social relationships; (2) devoid of social values or meanings.

Assistant teacher. A teacher who is an aid to one or more regularly employed teachers; engaged especially when large classes are necessary because of overcrowding.

Attitude. A readiness to react toward or against some situation, person or thing, in a particular manner, for example, with love or hate or fear or resentment, to a particular degree of intensity.

Audio-visual aids. Any device by means of which the learning process may be encouraged or carried on through the sense of hearing and/or the sense of sight.

Basic needs. Those needs which everyone has regardless of age, sex, or station in life, such as a sense of personal worth, status, recognition, love, a sense of belonging, and attainment of some measure of success in one's efforts, as well as physical requirements.

Centralized administration. An administrative system in which authority for direction, control, and management is located at one point.

Child-centered curriculum. A curriculum design in which the interests and purposes of children determine the educative program; selection and planning of activities are cooperatively done by teacher and pupils; problem solving is the dominant method.

Child-centered education. Education wherein the child is engaged in reconstructing his own real and concrete experience rather than in learning exclusively from books and subject fields; emphasis is placed upon guidance of growth, everyday life and activity, self-direction and self-discipline by the child, cooperation among the pupils, initiative, originality, leadership in lifelike situations, and flexibility in planning and programming.

Class grouping. The act or procedure of dividing the pupils of a class into two or more groups on the basis of interest or ability, for the purpose of adapting instruction.

Community-centered curriculum. An educational program based on and adjusted to the life, culture, resources, needs, activities, and interests of the community in which it is offered.

Community-centered school. A school attempting to serve not only persons of school age, but all ages and groups of a community, in the evening as well as during the day; its workshop, library, swimming pool, gymnasium, assembly hall, and other rooms are open for use by the people of the community; sometimes used synonymously with "community school."

Community resources. Anything in the community outside the schools that has educative value and is within the scope of school use, for example, museums, theaters, courts, libraries, industries, parks, playgrounds, etc., including outstanding individuals and other human resources.

Consumer education. A study of intelligent and effective methods of buying and using goods and services, competent money management, and the relationship of the consumer to our economic system.

Conventional school. A school that is the outgrowth of custom or common practice.

Cooperative supervision. A plan for improvement of instruction according to which teachers and supervisors are regarded as coworkers, the teachers participating in analyzing and determining such aspects of instruction as objectives, materials, and methods.

Coordinator. A person employed in connection with vocational courses to adjust the work of the school to the needs of business and industry; may also supervise the part-time work experiences of cooperative pupils.

Core curriculum. A curriculum design in which one subject or group of subjects becomes a center or core to which all the other subjects are subordinated and upon which they depend for sequence since they have no independent principle to determine their status in the program.

Core program. (1) The part of the whole educational program that presents those areas in which learning is essential for balanced living on the part of the majority of individuals; (2) the portion of a school program that is required of all pupils (frequently used as a synonym for "core curriculum").

Course of study. A guide prepared by administrators, supervisors, and teachers of a particular school or school system as an aid to teaching a given subject or area of study for a given grade or other instruction group.

Critical thinking. Thinking that proceeds on the basis of careful evaluation of premises and evidence and comes to conclusions as objectively as possible through the consideration of all pertinent factors and the use of valid procedures from logic.

Cumulative record. An individual record that is kept up to date by a member of the counseling staff and which includes educational, social, vocational, and health data.

Curriculum. A body of prescribed educative experiences under school supervision.

Decentralized administration. Any plan for the operation of schools according to which provision is made for scope for local initiative in adapting programs to local educational needs.

Developmental task. A task that arises at or about a certain time in the life of an individual, successful achievement of which leads to his happiness and success with later tasks, while failure leads to unhappiness in the individual, disapproval by his society, and difficulty with later tasks.

Directed activity. Experience with information and materials that are guided or controlled by the teacher.

Education. The aggregate of all the processes by means of which a person develops abilities, attitudes, and other forms of behavior of positive value in the society in which he lives.

Elective system. The practice of permitting a student to make certain choices in planning his school program.

Emotional maturity. The emotional pattern of an adult who has progressed through the emotional stages characteristic of infancy, childhood, and adolescence and is able to deal successfully with reality and to participate in adult concerns without undue emotional strain.

Evaluation. The process of ascertaining or judging the value or amount of something by careful appraisal.

Exceptional child. A loose term used to cover children who have abnormal physical, mental, or social differences. The term may include gifted children.

Experience. The acquisition of knowledge, attitudes, or skills through one's own perception and participation.

Extraclass activities. Activities in which pupils participate outside of the regular class routine, under the supervision of the school.

Extracurricular program. A program of out-of-class pursuits, usually supervised or financed by the school, in which pupils enjoy some degree of freedom in selection, planning, and control (for example, athletics, dramatics, orchestra, school publications, student government, civic-social-moral clubs, etc.)

Faculty adviser. A member of the faculty to whom a student is assigned for advice and assistance with academic, vocational, extracurricular, and personal problems.

Faculty psychology. A term that derives from an attempt by Wolff (1912) to analyze conscious experiences in terms of a mind (soul) endowed with certain faculties or "potencies of action"; Wolff sought to establish a relationship between the location in the soul of a faculty and its ability to re-present specific elements of the universe.

Field laboratory experience. Actual practice away from the college campus, within schools or their environment, in dealing with educational problems; part of the program offered by a teacher education institution, usually conducted in schools that are not formally under the direct control of or affiliated with the teacher education institution; usually more limited and incidental and less formal and concentrated than the extended "internship"; sometimes refers to practice in supervision, administration, or guidance.

General education. A broad type of education aimed at developing attitudes, abilities, perceptions and behavior considered desirable by society. Does not necessarily include preparing the learner for a specific type of vocation.

Grammar school. (1) Historically, a shortened popular designation of the English grammar school of colonial times; (2) popularly and loosely, a term used to designate an elementary school.

Group action. Discussion or work that produces results not likely to have been achieved by the same people acting separately.

Group process. The interaction occurring at a given moment within a group.

Higher education. Includes all education above the level of the secondary school that is provided by an educational institution.

Homogeneous grouping. The classification of pupils for the purpose of forming instructional groups having a relatively high degree of similarity in regard to certain factors that affect learning.

Increment. When applied to salary schedules, it refers to the annual increase.

Indefinite tenure. A system of school employment in which the teacher or other employee, having served a probationary period of a certain number of years, retains his position indefinitely and is protected in his position either by statute or by rule of the school board.

Instructional unit. Any part or division of a course that can be considered as complete in itself and can be taught as a whole.

Intelligence quotient (IQ). The most commonly used device for expressing level of mental development in relation to chronological age; obtained by dividing the mental age (as measured by a general intelligence test) by the chronological age and multiplying by 100. (The chronological age is often fixed as a certain maximum, most commonly 16 years, when growth of intelligence due to maturation has been assumed to cease. Thus, if 16 years were the maximum chronological age used, a testee whose actual age was greater than this would still be assigned an age of 16 years for purposes of calculating the IQ. The maximum chronological age for different tests varies from about 14 to 18 years.)

Job analysis. The basic method used to obtain salient facts about a job, involving observation of workers and conversations with those who know the job, in order to describe in detail the work involved, the conditions under which it must be performed, and the qualifications necessary for the worker who must perform it.

Laboratory school. A school that is under the direct control of or closely associated with a teacher-preparing institution, whose facilities may be used for demonstration, participation, experimentation, and practice teaching.

Laissez-faire system. Any regime in which the policy of noninterference prevails.

Learning ability. The inherent or developed capacity to acquire behavioral patterns, attitudes, and methods of responding to stimuli through exercise of the mental and physical processes (memory, reasoning, neuromuscular activity, etc.) which are relevant to stimulation of new responses.

Liberal education.   A broad academic education, as opposed to a strictly vocational education.

Life-adjustment education.   Educational opportunities designed to equip all American youth to live democratically with satisfaction to themselves and profit to society as home members, workers, and citizens.

Maturation.   (1) Changes in the characteristics of an organism resulting from intrinsic (anatomic, physiological, and neurological) development, with or without the aid of autogenous development; to be distinguished from changes due to special experience or learning; (2) the process of cellular, organic, and functional development of an organism.

Median.   The point on the scale of a frequency distribution above which and below which 50 per cent of the cases fall.

Merit rating.   An evaluation of the effectiveness of teaching, supervision, or administration, based on a definite scale or collection of items accepted as legitimate measures for such purposes.

Motivation.   Broadly considered, the process of arousing, sustaining, and regulating activity.

Nondirective teaching.   A technique whereby the instructor, as resource person, creates for the student an atmosphere of self-directed learning in order to encourage independent judgment, intellectual curiosity, strong motivation, and both subjective and objective evaluation.

Percentile.   An expression of value in terms of per cent. For example, if a person has a percentile rank of 75 on a test, it means that 25 per cent of the student scores are higher than, and 75 per cent below, his score.

Philosophy of education.   A careful, critical, and systematic intellectual endeavor to see education as a whole and as an integral part of man's culture.

Pressure group.   A group of persons with common interests that attempts, by the use of propaganda and mildly coercive measures, to influence officials and groups to adopt its program or purposes.

Primary unit.   A division of elementary education, usually comprising grades 1 to 3, devoted primarily to instruction in fundamental skills and the development of social attitudes necessary for democratic living.

Problem-solving method.   A manner of dealing with that which is problematic; a method involving clear definition of the problem confronted, formation of a hypothetical solution (hunch or suggestion), deliberate test of a hypothesis until evidence warrants its acceptance.

Professional laboratory experiences.   Any experiences, outside the teacher-education classroom, designed to increase the experience background, understandings, and insights of a prospective or experienced teacher.

Programmed instruction.   Used especially in connection with teaching machines in which information is presented in small, logical steps, problems or questions are posed for solution, results of pupils solution are given immediately, and provisions for remedial steps are given if the pupil is in error.

Progressive education.   The designation of an educational movement that protested against formalism; associated with the philosophy of John Dewey, it emphasizes commitment to the democratic idea, the importance of creative and purposeful activity and the real life needs of students, and closer relations between school and community.

Purposeful activity.   (1) Action motivated and directed by reference to an anticipated result and involving (*a*) the projection of a desired goal, (*b*) the construction of a plan of action toward its attainment, and (*c*) persistence and reflective action in carrying out the plan; (2) any persistent goal-oriented behavior whether or not there is awareness of the goal.

Reciprocity in teacher certification. Recognition by certifying authorities of a certificate or license issued by some other certifying authority.

Release period. That part of the school day during which public school children are permitted to attend religious-instruction classes conducted under the auspices of their particular denomination (syn. release time).

Reliability. The degree of consistency obtained between repeated measurements of individuals, with the same device.

School trustee. A person, selected under legal provision, usually chosen by popular election from the district at large for a term of three to five years, to direct, with other members of a board of trustees, the program of education within the territorial limits of the school district.

Secondary school. A more recent term than high school, which refers to the school following the elementary school, usually comprising grades 9 to 12 or grades 7 to 12.

Selective admission. Admission of applicants to an educational institution by selection on the basis of legal residence or of predictive measures or other criteria of scholastic aptitude, personal fitness, and probable future success.

Self-image. The perceptual component of self; the image one has of the appearance of his body; the picture one has of the impressions he makes on others.

Single-salary schedule. A plan by which the same salary is paid to all teachers in a school system who have the same amount of professional experience and preparation and who are given comparable teaching responsibilities.

Social adjustment. The process whereby the individual attempts to maintain or further his security, comfort, status, or creative inclinations in the face of the ever-changing conditions and pressures of his social environment, or the state or condition attained through such efforts.

Social maturity. A state of development in which the attitudes, understandings, feelings, and skills of the individual, with respect to human relationships, social tools, and social institutions, are those which are typical of the adult.

Sociogram. A device for revealing group structure and various types of group members such as isolates, well-liked people, leaders.

Stereotype. A fixed standardized conception of the attributes of a class of persons or social values that is not readily modified by evidence of its falsity.

Student teaching. Observation, participation, and actual teaching done by a student preparing for teaching under the direction of a supervising teacher or general supervisor.

Teacher contract. A formal agreement, usually in writing, entered into by a teacher and the employing authority, stating the salary to be paid and the length of the term of the contract, and setting forth the general duties to be performed by the teacher.

Teacher aids. An individual, usually noncertified for teaching, who assists a certified teacher in caring for various clerical and other routine duties in the classroom so that the teacher may concentrate on instructional activities.

Teacher education. The program of activities and experiences developed by an institution responsible for the preparation and growth of persons preparing themselves for educational work or engaging in the work of the educational profession.

Teaching machine. A mechanical device by means of which a program is presented to a learner. It usually presents one item (frame) at a time, provides some method for the pupil to indicate an overt response, shows whether or not the response is correct, maintains a record of the pupil's responses, provides for relearning if the response is not correct.

Team teaching. When two or more teachers work together in teaching a group of children.

Three-track course of study. A course of study providing for instruction in a particular area on three distinct levels; affords greater individualization of instruction by offering modified curriculum content for the superior, average, and inferior pupils in each class group.

Two-teacher school. An individual school for which two teachers are employed;

may include either the elementary grades alone or both the elementary and some or all of the high school grades; often used as a synonym for two-room school.

Two-track course of study.   A course of study designed to provide instruction in the same general area on two distinct levels, superior and average; affords greater individualization of instruction.

Unit instruction.   An organization of various activities, experiences, and types of learning around a central problem or purpose, developed cooperatively by a group of pupils under the guidance of a teacher. Involves planning, execution of plans, and evaluation of results.

Validity.   The extent to which a test or other measuring device measures what it purports to measure.

Workshop.   A group of educators working cooperatively and intensively on educational problems of concern to the group.

REFERENCES

1. *Adult Education, a New Imperative for Our Times,* Adult Education Association, Washington, 1961.
2. Aiken, Wilford M.: *The Story of the Eight-year Study,* Harper & Row, Publishers, New York, 1942.
3. Alexander, William M.: *Are You a Good Teacher?* Holt, Rinehart and Winston, Inc., New York, 1959.
4. Alford, Albert L.: "School Finance as a Part of Public Finance," *School Life,* vol. 43, no. 7, pp. 12–14, U.S. Office of Education, April, 1961.
5. *Analysis of Teacher Tenure Provisions: State and Local,* National Education Association, Committee on Tenure and Academic Freedom, Washington, June, 1954, pp. 6–7.
6. Armstrong, W. Earl, and T. M. Stinnett: *A Manual on Certification Requirements for School Personnel in the United States, 1961,* National Education Association, National Commission on Teacher Education and Professional Standards, Washington, 1961.
7. Ayres, Leonard P.: "Making Education Definite," *Indiana University Bulletin,* vol. 13, no. 11, Indiana University, Bloomington, Ind., 1915.
8. Barr, W. Montfort: *American Public School Finance,* American Book Company, New York, 1960.
9. Baruch, Bernard: "A Real Teacher," *National Education Association Journal,* vol. 39, no. 6, p. 415, National Education Association, Washington, 1950.
10. Bathurst, Effie G.: "Where Children Live Affects Curriculum," U.S. Office of Education Bulletin 1950, no. 7, 1960.
11. Baumer, Edward F.: "Public Relations: Tool of Effective Communications," *The Toastmaster,* vol. 24, no. 11, pp. 3–6, November, 1958.
12. Baxter, Bernice: *Teacher-Pupil Relationships,* The Macmillan Company, New York, 1941.
13. Beach, Fred F., and Robert F. Will: *The State and Education,* U.S. Office of Education Misc. 23, 1960.
14. Bernard, Harold W.: *Mental Hygiene for Classroom Teachers,* McGraw-Hill Book Company, Inc., New York, 1961.
15. Bestor, Arthur: "How Should America's Teachers Be Educated?" *Teachers College Record,* vol. 56, no. 1, pp. 16–19, Teachers College, New York, October, 1954.
16. Bigelow, Karl: "How Should America's Teachers Be Educated?" *Teachers College Record,* vol. 56, no. 1, pp. 20–24, Teachers College, New York, October, 1954.
17. Bowen, Howard R.: "Where Are the Dollars for Higher Education Coming From?" *Current Issues in Higher Education,* National Education Association, Washington, 1960, pp. 9–16.
18. Bowers, Harold J.: "Reciprocity in Teacher Certification," *National Education Association Journal,* vol. 39, no. 1, p. 14, National Education Association, Washington, January, 1950.

19. Bruner, Jerome S.: *The Process of Education,* Harvard University Press, Cambridge, Mass., 1961.

20. Burt, Lorin A.: "The Separation of Church and State in the Public Schools of Indiana: The Legal Aspects," *Research Bulletin,* Indiana School Boards Association, Indiana University, Bloomington, Ind., February, 1962.

21. Butts, Freeman: "Search for Freedom," *National Education Association Journal,* vol. 49, no. 3, pp. 33–48, National Education Association, Washington, March, 1960.

22. Callahan, Raymond C.: *An Introduction To Education in American Society,* Alfred A. Knopf, Inc., New York, 1960.

23. Carr, William G.: "World-Wide Cooperation among Teachers," *National Education Association Journal,* vol. 50, no. 5, pp. 24–25, National Education Association, Washington, May, 1961.

24. *The Case for Federal Support of Education, 1961,* National Education Association, Washington, March, 1961.

25. *The Central Purpose of American Education,* National Education Association, Educational Policies Commission, Washington, 1961.

26. Chandler, B. J.: *Education and the Teacher,* Dodd, Mead & Company, Inc., New York, 1961.

27. Charters, W. W., and Douglas Waples: *The Commonwealth Teacher-training Study,* University of Chicago Press, Chicago, 1929.

28. Clark, Burton R.: *The Open Door College: A Case Study,* McGraw-Hill Book Company, Inc., New York, 1960.

29. Commission on Secondary Curriculum, *The Junior High School We Need,* National Education Association, Association for Supervision and Curriculum Development, Washington, 1961.

30. Committee on Education and Labor: *Federal Interest in Education,* House of Representatives, 87th Congress, 1st Session, Washington, September, 1961.

31. Committee on the University and World Affairs: *The University and World Affairs,* The Ford Foundation, New York, 1960.

32. Conant, James Bryant: *The American High School Today,* McGraw-Hill Book Company, Inc., New York, 1959.

33. Conant, James Bryant: *Education in the Junior High School Years,* Educational Testing Service, Princeton, N.J., 1960.

34. Conant, James Bryant: *Slums and Suburbs,* McGraw-Hill Book Company, Inc., New York, 1961.

35. *Credit Unions for Teachers,* National Education Association, Research Division and Department of Classroom Teachers, Discussion Pamphlet 6, Washington, August, 1960.

36. Dean, Stuart E.: *Elementary School Administration and Organization,* U.S. Office of Education Bulletin 1960, no. 11, 1960.

37. "Degrees in Education," *National Education Association Journal,* vol. 50, no. 8, p. 4, National Education Association, Washington, November, 1961.

38. Dewey, John: *Democracy and Education,* The Macmillan Company, New York, 1916.

39. Dewey, John: *Education Today,* G. P. Putnam's Sons, New York, 1940.

40. DeYoung, Chris A., and Richard Wynn: *American Education,* McGraw-Hill Book Co., Inc., New York, 1960. Material used by permission.

41. "Do You Know That . . .," *National Education Association Journal,* vol. 50, no. 4, p. 6, National Education Association, Washington, April, 1961.

42. "Economic Status of Teachers in 1961–62," *Research Report 1962-R7,* National Education Association, Research Division, Washington, May, 1962.

43. "Education and Economic Growth," *National Education Association Journal,* vol. 51, no. 2, pp. 46–47, National Education Association, Washington, February, 1962.

44. *Education for All American Youth: A Further Look,* National Education Association, Educational Policies Commission, Washington, 1952.

45. *Education in the United States of America,* Special Series 3, U.S. Office of Education, 1955.

46. *Education in the United States of America,* U.S. Office of Education, 1960.

47. "Educational Growth and Change," *National Education Association Journal,* vol. 49, no. 9, pp. 45–47, National Education Association, Washington, December, 1960.

48. "Enrollment is Rising—How Fast Is the Question," *College and University Bulletin,* vol. 14, no. 3, pp. 1–3, National Education Association, Association of Higher Education, Washington, November 1, 1961.

49. "Estimates of School Statistics," *Research Report, 1961-R22,* National Education Association, Research Division, Washington, December, 1961.

50. Eurich, Alvin C.: "America is Opportunity: Effective Education for the Sixties," an address at the 49th Annual Meeting, Chamber of Commerce of the United States, Washington, May, 1961.

51. *The Evaluation of Student Teaching,* Twenty-eighth Annual Yearbook of the Association for Student Teaching, State Teachers College, Lock Haven, Pa., 1949.

52. "Extra-pay Provisions in 1959–60 Salary Schedules," *Educational Research Service,* Circular 4, National Education Association, Research Division, Washington, May, 1960.

53. "Facts on New College Teachers," *National Education Association Journal,* vol. 50, no. 6, p. 62, National Education Association, Washington, September, 1961.

54. *A Federal Education Agency for the Future,* U.S. Office of Education, 1961.

55. "The Financial Rewards of Teaching," *Research Bulletin,* vol. 38, no. 2, pp. 49–55, National Education Association, Research Division, Washington, May, 1960.

56. *Financing Education for Our Changing Population,* National Education Association, Committee on Educational Finance, Washington, 1961.

57. Ford, Edmund A.: "Organizational Patterns of the Nation's Public Secondary Schools," *School Life,* vol. 42, no. 9, pp. 10–12, U.S. Office of Education, May, 1960.

58. *Fostering Mental Health in Our Schools,* National Education Association, 1950 Yearbook of the Association for Supervision and Curriculum Development, Washington, 1950.

59. Gardner, John W.: *Excellence,* Harper & Row, Publishers, New York, 1961.

60. Good, Carter V. (ed.): *Dictionary of Education,* McGraw-Hill Book Company, Inc., New York, 1959.

61. Good, Harry G.: *A History of Western Education,* The Macmillan Company, New York, 1960.

62. *A Good Start in School,* Department of Public Instruction Bulletin 226, Indianapolis, Ind., 1958.

63. Grieder, Calvin, and Stephen Romine: *American Public Education,* The Ronald Press Company, New York, 1955.

64. "Group Insurance Programs for Teachers," *Research Bulletin,* vol. 39, no. 3, pp. 92–93, National Education Association, Research Division, Washington, October, 1961.

65. *A Guide for Organizing and Developing a Kindergarten Program in Florida,* Revised, State Department of Education Bulletin 53A, Tallahassee, Fla., January, 1955.

66. *Handbook Office of Education,* U.S. Office of Education, 1960.

67. Harap, Henry: "Teacher Preparation: 5-Year Programs," *School Life,* vol. 44, no. 2, pp. 18–21, U.S. Office of Education, October, 1961.

68. Havighurst, Robert J.: *Human Development and Education,* Longmans, Green & Co., Inc., New York, 1953.

69. Havighurst, Robert J.: 'Knowledge of Class Status Can Make a Difference," *Progressive Education,* vol. 27, pp. 100–101, February, 1950.

70. Heil, Louis, Marion Powell, and Irwin Feifer: *Characteristics of Teacher Behavior Related to the Achievement of Children in Several Elementary Grades,* Brooklyn College, Brooklyn, N.Y., 1960.

71. Heller, Walter W.: "Education and Economic Growth," *National Education Association Journal,* vol. 50, no. 7, p. 9, National Education Association, Washington, October, 1961.

72. "How Long Is a School Day?" *Research Bulletin,* vol. 39, no. 1, pp. 8–10, National Education Association, Research Division, Washington, February, 1961.

73. Hughes, James Monroe: *Education in America,* Harper & Row, Publishers, New York, 1960.

74. Hutchins, Clayton D., Albert R. Munse, and Edna D. Booher: *Federal Funds for Education,* U.S. Office of Education Bulletin 1961, no. 14, 1961.

75. "Index Salary Schedules for Teachers," *Research Bulletin,* vol. 39, no. 4, pp. 108–112, National Education Association, Research Division, Washington, December, 1961.

76. *An Introduction to Phi Delta Kappa,* Phi Delta Kappa, Bloomington, Ind., (brochure).

77. Jersild, Arthur T., and Associates: *Education for Self Understanding: The Role of Psychology in the High School Program,* Bureau of Publications, Teachers College, Columbia University, New York, 1953.

78. "The Junior High School Program," *Bulletin of the Southern Association of Colleges and Secondary Schools,* Atlanta, Ga., 1958.

79. Kauffman, Grace I.: "How Professional Am I? *National Education Association Journal,* vol. 39, no. 4, p. 286, National Education Association, Washington, April, 1950.

80. Kearney, Nolan C.: *Elementary School Objectives,* Russell Sage Foundation, New York, 1953.

81. Knoll, Erwin: "The Maturing Junior College," *National Education Association Journal,* vol. 50, no. 2, pp. 28–29, National Education Association, Washington, February, 1961.

82. Kreitlow, Burton W.: "Organizational Patterns: Local School Districts," *Review of Educational Research,* vol. 31, no. 4, pp. 380–392, National Education Association, American Educational Research Association, Washington, October, 1961.

83. Landis, Paul H.: *Adolescence and Youth,* McGraw-Hill Book Company, Inc., New York, 1952.

84. Landon, Margaret D.: *Anna and the King of Siam,* The John Day Company, New York, 1944.

85. Leonard, George M.: "The Truth about the Teacher Crisis," *Look Magazine,* Feb. 21, 1956, pp. 40–48.

86. Lindsey, Margaret (ed.): *New Horizons for the Teaching Profession,* National Education Association, National Commission on Teacher Education and Professional Standards, Washington, 1961.

87. McConnell, T. R.: *A Design for General Education,* American Council on Education Studies, ser. 1, no. 18, pp. 14–15, Washington, 1944.

88. McDonald, Ralph: "Professional Salaries for Teachers," *National Education Association Journal,* vol. 38, no. 9, p. 662, National Education Association, Washington, December, 1949.

89. McLure, William P.: *The Intermediate Administrative School District in the United States,* Bureau of Educational Research, College of Education, University of Illinois, Urbana, Ill., February, 1956.

90. *Manpower: Challenge of the 1960's,* U.S. Department of Labor, 1961.

91. Martz, Velorus, and Henry Lester Smith: *An Introduction to Education,* Charles Scribner's Sons, New York, 1941.

92.   "Maximum Salaries for School Administrators," *Research Bulletin*, vol. 38, no. 4, pp. 121–123, National Education Association, Research Division, Washington, December, 1960.

93.   Mead, Margaret: *From the South Seas: Studies of Adolescence and Sex in Primitive Societies*, William Morrow and Company, Inc., New York, 1948.

94.   *Moral and Spiritual Values in the Public Schools*, National Education Association, Educational Policies Commission, Washington, 1951.

95.   Moustakas, Clark E., and Minnie P. Berson: *The Nursery School and Child Care Center*, Whiteside, Inc., New York, 1955.

96.   National Commission on School District Reorganization: *Your School District*, National Education Association, Department of Rural Education, Washington, 1948.

97.   National School Boards Association: *Delegate Assembly Workshop Record*, Philadelphia, Pa., May 2–3, 1961.

98.   *NEA Handbook for Local, State and National Associations, 1961–62*, National Education Association, Washington, 1961.

99.   *New England's First Fruits, in Collections of the Massachusetts Historical Society for the Year 1792*, vol. 1, p. 242, T. R. Marvin, Printer, Boston, 1859.

100. "New Horizons in Teacher Education and Professional Standards," *National Education Association Journal*, vol. 50, no. 1, pp. 55–68, National Education Association, Washington, January, 1961.

101. Noar, Gertrude: *The Junior High School—Today and Tomorrow*, Prentice-Hall, Inc., Englewood Cliffs, N.J., 1961.

102. "Objects of the National Congress of Parents and Teachers, *The PTA Magazine*, vol. 55, no. 10, p. ii, Washington, June, 1961.

103. Olsen, Edward G. (ed.): *School and Community*, Prentice-Hall, Inc., Englewood Cliffs, N.J., 1954.

104. *One World or None*, Film Publishers, Inc., New York, 1946, 16mm, black and white, sound, 8 minutes.

105. "Organization Plans in the Elementary School," *Research Memo 1961–17*, National Education Association, Research Division, Washington, April, 1961.

106. "Our Schools Aren't Good Enough," *The News Letter*, vol. 20, Bureau of Educational Research, Ohio State University, Columbus, Ohio, November, 1954.

107. *Paying for Better Public Schools*, Committee for Economic Development, New York, September, 1961.

108. Perkins, Hugh V.: "Nongraded Programs: What Progress?" *Educational Leadership*, vol. 19, no. 3, pp. 166–169 and 194, National Education Association, Association of Supervision and Curriculum Development, Washington, December, 1961.

109. Phoenix, Philip H.: *Philosophies of Education*, John Wiley & Sons, Inc., New York, 1961.

110. Pi Lambda Theta: *Booklet of Information*, Pi Lambda Theta, Washington, 1960.

111. *Planning for American Youth*, National Education Association, National Association of Secondary School Principals and the Educational Policies Commission, Washington, 1951.

112. *Policies and Criteria for the Approval of Secondary Schools.* North Central Association of Colleges and Secondary Schools, Chicago, Ill., 1960.

113. Powers, Edward J.: *Education for American Democracy*, McGraw-Hill Book Company, Inc., New York, 1958. Material used by permission.

114. The President's Commission on National Goals: *Goals for Americans* copyright 1960 by the American Assembly, Columbia University, New York. Reprinted by permission of Prentice-Hall, Inc.

115. Price, Hugh G.: "There's an Increasing Need for Public Schools Through

Grade 14," *National Education Association Journal*, vol. 48, no. 9, p. 10, National Education Association, Washington, December, 1959.

116. "Problems and Opportunities in Financing Education," *Proceedings of the Second National Conference on School Finance Problems*, April 30–May 1, 1959, National Education Association, Washington, 1959.

117. *Professional Organizations in American Education*, National Education Association, Educational Policies Commission, Washington, 1957.

118. *Professional Salaries for Professional Teachers*, National Education Association, Committee on Educational Finance, Washington, 1961.

119. *Progress of Public Education in the United States of America 1960–61*, U.S. Office of Education, 1961.

120. *The Purposes of Education in American Democracy*, National Education Association, Educational Policies Commission, Washington, 1938.

121. *The Pursuit of Excellence: Education and the Future of America*, copyright 1958 by Rockefeller Brothers Fund, Inc. Reprinted with permission of Doubleday & Company, Inc.

122. Ragan, William B.: *Teaching America's Children*, Holt, Rinehart and Winston, Inc., New York, 1961.

123. "Reduced Progress in Urban Teacher's Salaries," *Research Bulletin*, vol. 39, no. 3, pp. 67–74, National Education Association, Research Division, Washington, October, 1961.

124. Reeder, Ward G.: *A First Course in Education*, The Macmillan Company, New York, 1946, pp. 495–499. (Quoted from Samuel Hall.)

125. *The Report of the White House Conference on Education*, Washington, November 28–December 1, 1955.

126. "Reporting to Parents," *Research Bulletin*, vol. 39, no. 1, pp. 24–25, National Education Association, Research Division, Washington, February, 1961.

127. "Review of the American Educational System," *Hearing before the Subcommittee of the Committee on Appropriations*, 86th Congressional Session, House of Representatives, Washington, 1960.

128. Richey, Robert W., and William H. Fox: "A Study of Some Opinions of High School Students with Regard to Teachers and Teaching," *Bulletin of the School of Education*, vol. 27, no. 4, pp. 45, Indiana University, Bloomington, Ind., July, 1951.

129. Rickover, H. G.: "The World of the Uneducated," *The Saturday Evening Post*, Nov. 28, 1959, p. 8.

130. Roper, Elmo: "What U.S. Thinks about Its Schools," *Life Magazine*, New York, October 16, 1950, pp. 11–18.

131. Rothney, John W. M.: "Evaluating and Reporting Pupil Progress," *What Research Says to the Teacher*, no. 7, National Education Association, Department of Classroom Teachers, American Educational Research Association, Washington, 1960.

132. Russell, John Dale: "Financing Higher Education in the Sixties," *Phi Delta Kappan*, vol. 42, no. 1, pp. 8–11, Bloomington, Ind., October, 1960.

133. Ryans, David G.: *Characteristics of Teachers*, American Council on Education, Washington, 1960. (Used by permission.)

134. "Salaries and Salary Schedules of Urban School Employees, 1958–59," *Research Report*, 1959-R-16, National Education Association, Research Division, Washington, October, 1959.

135. "Salaries Paid and Salary Practices in Universities, Colleges, and Junior Colleges, 1961–62," *Research Report 1962-R2*, National Education Association, Research Division, Washington, February, 1962.

136. "The Scheduling of Principals' Salaries," *Research Bulletin*, vol. 39, no. 4, pp. 99–103, National Education Association, Research Division, Washington, December, 1961.

137. "School Statistics, 1961–62," *Research Bulletin,* vol. 40, no. 1, pp. 3–6, National Education Association, Research Division, Washington, February, 1962.

138. Shane, Harold G., and E. T. McSwain: *Evaluation and the Elementary Curriculum,* Holt, Rinehart and Winston, Inc., New York, 1958.

139. ———: *Resume of Grouping in the Elementary School,* Indiana Association of Supervision and Curriculum Development, 1960. (Mimeographed.)

140. ———: "We Can Be Proud of the Facts," *The Nation's Schools,* vol. 60, pp. 44–47, September, 1957.

141. Shannon, Harold D.: "Credit Union Lesson for Teachers," *National Education Association Journal,* vol. 50, no. 5, p. 14, National Education Association, Washington, May, 1961.

142. Sharp, D. Louise (ed.): *Why Teach?* Holt, Rinehart and Winston, Inc., New York, 1957.

143. Sheviakov, George V., and Fritz Redl: *Discipline for Today's Children and Youth,* National Education Association, Association for Supervision and Curriculum Development, Washington, 1956.

144. Silberman, Charles E.: "The Remaking of American Education," *Fortune,* New York, April, 1961, pp. 125–130 and 197, 198, 201.

145. Skinner, B. F.: "Teaching Machines," *Scientific American,* vol. 205, no. 5, November, 1961, pp. 90–102.

146. Smith, Louis M.: "Group Processes in Elementary and Secondary Schools," *What Research Says to the Teacher,* no. 19, National Education Association, Department of Classroom Teachers, American Educational Research Association, Washington, 1959.

147. "Social Security Amendments, 1961," *Research Bulletin,* vol. 39, no. 4, p. 113, National Education Association, Research Division, Washington, December, 1961.

148. *State Boards of Education and Chief State School Officers,* Bulletin 12, U.S. Office of Education, 1950.

149. "State Minimum Salary Laws and Goals for Teachers, 1960–61," *Research Report 1960-R13,* National Education Association, Research Division, Washington, November, 1960.

150. "State Sick Leave Provisions," *Research Bulletin,* vol. 39, no. 3, pp. 94–95, National Education Association, Research Division, Washington, October, 1961.

151. *A Statement for Growing Adults,* Community Services in Adult Education, Indiana University, Bloomington, Ind., 1953.

152. *Statistical Abstract of the United States, 1961,* U.S. Department of Commerce, Bureau of the Census, 1961.

153. "Status and Trends: Vital Statistics, Education, and Public Finance," *Research Report, 1959-R13,* National Education Association, Washington, August, 1959.

154. "The Status of the American Public-School Teacher," *Research Bulletin,* vol. 35, no. 1, National Education Association, Research Division, Washington, February, 1957.

155. "The Status of the Teaching Profession," *Research Bulletin,* vol. 28, no. 2, National Education Association, Research Division, Washington, March, 1940.

156. Stinnett, T. M.: *The Teacher and Professional Organizations,* National Education Association, Washington, 1956.

157. *Student NEA Handbook,* National Education Association, National Commission on Teacher Education and Professional Standards, Washington, 1961.

158. "Summer Schools—Opportunity," *Research Bulletin,* vol. 38, no. 1, pp. 23–24, National Education Association, Research Division, Washington, February, 1960.

159. Taylor, James L., Lillian L. Gore, and Hazel F. Gabbard: *Functional Schools for Young Children,* Special Publication 8, U.S. Office of Education, 1961.

160. *Teacher Leaves of Absence,* National Education Association, Research Division and Department of Classroom Teachers, Discussion Pamphlet 7, Washington, May, 1961.

161. "Teacher-opinion Poll," *National Education Association Journal*, vol. 49, no. 7, p. 64, National Education Association, Washington, October, 1960.

162. "Teacher-opinion Poll," *National Education Association Journal*, vol. 50, no. 2, p. 32, National Education Association, Washington, February, 1961.

163. *Teacher Retirement*, National Education Association, Department of Classroom Teachers and Research Division, Discussion Pamphlet 2, Washington, November, 1957, pp. 21–22.

164. "Teacher Supply and Demand in Public Schools, 1961," *Research Report, 1961-R9*, National Education Association, Research Division, Washington, April, 1961.

165. "Teacher Supply and Demand in Public Schools, 1962," *Research Report, 1962-R8*, National Education Association, Research Division, Washington, April, 1962.

166. *Teacher Tenure*, National Education Association, Department of Classroom Teachers and Research Division, Discussion Pamphlet 1, Washington, July, 1954.

167. "Teacher Tenure Laws Benefit Teachers in 37 States," *Research Bulletin*, vol. 38, no. 3, pp. 81–85, National Education Association, Research Division, Washington, October, 1960.

168. "Teachers and Principals Agree on Best Class Size," *Research Bulletin*, vol. 39, no. 4, p. 107, National Education Association, Research Division, Washington, December, 1961.

169. "Ten Years of Change in Teacher's Salary Schedules," *Research Bulletin*, vol. 39, no. 2, pp. 52–53, National Education Association, Research Division, Washington, May, 1961.

170. Thayer, V. T.: *The Role of the School in American Society*, Dodd, Mead and Company, New York, 1960.

171. *The Three R's of the Profession as Expressed in the Code of Ethics, Bill of Rights, Code of Competence*, Pennsylvania State Education Association, Harrisburg, Pa., 1956.

172. Thurston, Lee M., and William H. Roe: *State School Administration*, Harper & Row, Publishers, New York, 1957.

173. Toynbee, Arnold J.: "Our Massive Heritage," *National Education Association Journal*, vol. 50, no. 2, p. 9, National Education Association, Washington, February, 1961.

174. Trump, J. Lloyd: *Images of the Future: A New Approach to the Secondary School*, National Education Association, Commission on the Experimental Study of the Utilization of the Staff in the Secondary School, National Association of Secondary-School Principals, Washington, 1959.

175. Trump, J. Lloyd, and Dorsey Baynham: *Guide to Better Schools: Focus on Change*, Rand McNally and Company, Chicago, 1961.

176. Turner, Richard L., and Nicholas A. Fattu: "Skill in Teaching, Assessed on the Criterian of Problem Solving," *Bulletin of the School of Education*, vol. 37, no. 3, Indiana University, Bloomington, Ind., May, 1961.

177. "TV Research and Findings to Date," *Phi Delta Kappan*, vol. 43, no. 8, p. 329, Bloomington, Ind., May, 1962.

178. "Two Billion Dollars in a Decade: Public Laws 815 and 874," *School Life*, vol. 43, no. 7, pp. 16–17, U.S. Office of Education, April, 1961.

179. Visher, Stephen S.: "Civilization's Most Valuable Resources," *Social Education*, vol. 17, no. 1, p. 23, January, 1953.

180. Warner, W. Lloyd: *Democracy in Jonesville*, Harper & Row, Publishers, New York, 1949.

181. "What Do You Know about Today's Schools?" *Research Bulletin*, vol. 39,

no. 1, pp. 26–31, National Education Association, Research Division, Washington, February, 1961.

182. "What Happened to Any 100 Teachers between Spring and Fall, 1959," *School Life,* vol. 42, no. 9, p. 17, U.S. Office of Education, May, 1960.

183. White, Leslie A.: "Man's Control over Civilization," *The Scientific Monthly,* vol. 66, March, 1948, p. 241.

184. "Why Few School Systems Use Merit Ratings," *Research Bulletin,* vol. 39, no. 2, pp. 61–63, National Education Association, Research Division, Washington, May, 1961.

185. Witty, Paul A.: *Mental Hygiene in Modern Education,* Fifty-fourth Yearbook of the National Society for the Study of Education, Part II, University of Chicago Press, Chicago, 1955.

186. Witty, Paul A.: "The Teacher Who Has Helped Me Most," *National Education Association Journal,* vol. 36, no. 5, p. 386, National Education Association, Washington, May, 1947.

187. Woodring, Paul: *A Fourth of a Nation,* McGraw-Hill Book Company, Inc., New York, 1957.

188. Yinger, J. Milton, and George E. Simpson: "The Integration of Americans of Mexican, Puerto Rican, and Oriental Descent," *The Annals,* March, 1956.

INDEX